Gloria Glickstein Brame graduated magna cum laude with a degree in English Literature from York College in 1977, received a diploma in language from the Alliance Francaise in Paris in 1977 and a MA in English from Columbia University in 1978. Since then she has worked as a junior financial analyst and as a writer, and has been published in numerous literary magazines. In 1987, Gloria founded an on-line Dominance and Submission support group, and since 1989 has worked privately as a peer counsellor, pyschodramatist, and lay therapist. A native New Yorker, she lives in Atlanta.

William D. Brame received a BA with honours in anthropology from Southeast Missouri State University and has worked as an archaeologist, writer and editor. In 1989, Will led an on-line support group in the Human Sexuality Forum of CompuServe Information Services where he met his wife Gloria. A native of the Missouri Ozarks, he lives in Atlanta.

Jon Jacobs began his career as a journalist in the late 1960s after working in the Southern civil-rights and antiwar movements. He has worked as an assistant editor and has written for several publications. A native of Pittsburgh, he lives with his wife in Atlanta.

'The definitive guide to sexual styles of those who walk on the wild side' – *Kirkus Reviews*

DIFFERENT
LOVING

THE WORLD OF SEXUAL DOMINANCE
AND SUBMISSION

Gloria G. Brame, William D. Brame,
Jon Jacobs

C

CENTURY · LONDON

Published in the United Kingdom in 1997 by
Century

1 3 5 7 9 10 8 6 4 2

Copyright © 1996 Gloria G. Brame, William D. Brame and Jon Jacobs

The right of Gloria G. Brame, William D. Brame and Jon Jacobs to be identified as the
authors of this work has been asserted by them in accordance with the Copyright, Designs
and Patents Act, 1988

First published in the United Kingdom in 1997 by Century
Random House UK Ltd
20 Vauxhall Bridge Road, London, SW1V 2SA

Random House Australia (Pty) Limited
16 Dalmore Drive, Scoresby, Victoria, 3179

Random House New Zealand Limited
18 Poland Road, Glenfield
Auckland 10, New Zealand

Random House South Africa (Pty) Limited
PO Box 2263, Rosebank 2121, South Africa

Random House UK Limited Reg. No. 954009

A CIP catalogue record for this book is available from the British Library

Papers used by Random House UK Limited are natural, recyclable products made from wood
grown in sustainable forests. The manufacturing processes conform to the environmental
regulations of the country of origin

Printed and bound in Great Britain by
Mackays of Chatham PLC, Chatham, Kent

ISBN 0 71 267792 5

ACKNOWLEDGMENTS AND DEDICATIONS

We dedicate this book to the precious memory of poet Judson Jerome, whose commitment to candor inspired and first guided us.

We were blessed to have Russell Galen as our mentor, literary agent, critic, and friend. We are grateful to our editor, Peter Gethers, for his vision, commitment, and courage. Also to Sharyn Rosenblum for her loyal support.

We owe special thanks to NP, whose hard work and innumerable contributions to this project only the authors can know; and to Garison Kaufman, whose insights enhanced the quality of the final text. Dr. Robert H. Nightingale's medical expertise and friendship were indispensible. Miguel Garcia provided valuable assistance.

This book is the result of a collaboration among three good friends and, since inception, has been enthusiastically supported by the large network of friends who comprise our extended family. We cannot list everyone, but must single out John Gallant, Bruce Bawer, Chris Davenport, Jay Riggs, Helen Jacobs, Berné Poliakoff, and Berl Boykin, all of whom sustained us with their loyalty and love.

Although we cannot thank them individually, scores of helping professionals and activists lent support to this project. We would especially like to thank William Henkin, Howard and Martha Lewis, the late Roger Peo, Fakir Musafar, Robin Young, Thomas Gramstad, and Marie-Constance.

A NOTE ON INTERVIEWS AND NAMES

Different Loving includes extensive quotes and personal profiles drawn from in-depth interviews with well over 100 participants in and experts on dominance and submission. They were conducted between the spring of 1991 and the spring of 1992. Our interviewees were uniformly open and forthcoming, and, naturally, many of the interviews tended to wander, often far afield of the main theme of this book. We have edited and compacted the interviews so as to allow each person to speak for him- or herself while keeping this book at a readable length.

Each of our interviewees was given the option to appear under his or her true name or under a pseudonym. Most chose, for obvious reasons, to appear under pseudonyms; some, who are already publicly known, appear under their real names; and some others who appear under their real names do so here for the first time in terms of their interests in D&S: They have chosen to use *Different Loving* as an opportunity to come out.

CONTENTS

SECTION FOUR:
INDIVIDUALIZING THE BODY

SECTION FIVE:
TRANSLOCATIONS OF DESIRE

SECTION SIX:
MASCULINE AND FEMININE

SECTION SEVEN:
FLUID MYSTERIES

DISCLAIMER

This book explores highly controversial and risky sexual activities. **Readers should not attempt any of the activities described in these pages.** Neither the authors of this book, nor its interviewees, nor its publishers assume any responsibility for the exercise or misuse of the practices described herein.

As the statements of our interviewees make clear, D&Sers are exquisitely aware of the hazards inherent in what they do and take care to anticipate them, to understand them, and—most important—to avoid them. The authors provide only basic and incomplete health warnings in the appropriate chapters to remind readers of the serious hazards involved.

D&Sers make a real and absolute distinction between explicitly consensual acts between adult partners for their mutual pleasure and all acts of violence against unconsenting partners. Imposing any sexual activity on a reluctant partner is morally offensive; imposing it on an unwilling partner (or upon anyone who cannot give legal consent) is a criminal offense. Further, state laws vary: Some of these activities, even between consenting partners, are illegal in certain jurisdictions.

SECTION ONE

DIFFERENT LOVING

One

INTRODUCTION

In order to understand unusual sexualities such as dominance and submission (D&S), one first has to consider the question, "What is normal?" If the unique function of sex is reproductive—and the only reason men and women should engage in sex is for the purpose of creating new life—then only heterosexual intercourse is normal. Masturbation, oral sex, and even contraception must be considered aberrant. Reproductive relevance was the Victorian standard of normalcy, and even today many of the laws defining criminal sexual behaviors in the United States still abide by that model. In reality, however, people have always pursued sex for reproduction *as well as* for pleasure and well-being.

> *The term* normal *is meaningless in terms of sexuality. It is commonly used as the opposite of* abnormal *and therefore as a euphemism for "good" versus "bad." The consensus among sex therapists is that anything that occurs between consenting adults that harms no one is acceptable.* —HOWARD AND MARTHA LEWIS

We start from the premise that sex for pleasure is a normal human drive and is acceptable when it brings pleasure to both partners. From this perspective, D&S is simply a "different" kind of loving.

This book is biased toward heterosexuals quite simply because there are more heterosexuals than homosexuals in the general population as well as in the world of D&S. Gays and lesbians are nonetheless a vital and vocal component of the D&S communities and a pioneering force for the dissemination of reliable information and safety guidelines.

We use the term D&S to describe erotic activities more commonly known as sadomasochism (S/M) or bondage and discipline (B&D). Since many of our interviewees make careful distinctions among these three categories, we honor their choice of terminology in interviews and citations. In fact, defining a universally accepted label for sadomasochistic behaviors is controversial. (See Chapter 3, "The ABCs of D&S," for detailed discussion.)

Few mutually consensual sexual activities are regarded with as much censure as D&S. The dearth of sensible, candid information about D&S has fostered exaggerated, negatively charged stereotypes. Dominatrices are, for example, typically portrayed as destroyers of men—a combination of the mythical enchantress Circe and the voluptuous Marlene Dietrich in *The Blue Angel,* hell-bent on emasculation. Female submissives are depicted as neurotic, self-destructive victims. And the very word *sadist* conjures the image of a criminal inflicting violent torture on helpless victims. When serial killers, such as Ted Bundy, announce that they were influenced by sadomasochistic pornography, the educated and uneducated alike accept the idea that a sociopath is an exemplar of a sexual behavior. Do some sadomasochists commit felonious assault? Undoubtedly. So do some devout Christians. Sadomasochists are prey to the same failings as regular people, because they *are* regular people.

WHAT IS SADOMASOCHISM . . . REALLY?

For active D&Sers sadomasochism is a thoughtful and controlled expression of adult sexuality that holds the promise of intense intimacy and sharing. The people interviewed for this book repeatedly describe the profound gratification their sexuality affords them. They explain why an erotic piercing effects a visceral change, how pain can feel like pleasure, why bondage is psychologically liberating. And, although our interviewees' private lives may seem unusual, these men and women are not one-dimensional sexual anomalies: Their personal aspirations and public lives will be familiar to all Americans.

The Victorian scientist, Richard von Krafft-Ebing, identified the erotic interest in inflicting pain as "sadism," after the Marquis de Sade, and condemned sexual acts that did not result in procreation as perverse. One of the great ironies is that de Sade, who by his own admission had scant experience of sadomasochism, has come to represent sexual behaviors that violate his own philosophical precepts. De Sade's novels advocate the ultimate philosophical liberty: freedom to violate and destroy.

The kind of sexuality [de Sade] has in mind runs counter to the desires of other people . . . they are to be victims, not partners . . . the partners are denied any rights at all: this is the key to his system. —GEORGE BATAILLE[1]

The practices and attitudes of contemporary sexual dominants and submissives, in contrast, largely abide by the credo of "Safe, Sane, and Consensual." Partners emphasize equal and honest communication, negotiation, and consent; mutual trust is fundamental. A partner's limits and preferences are respected. De Sade would be disgusted.

The lonely pornographer of the Bastille is not the only writer whose sadomasochistic fiction has been mistaken for reality. The novels of Leopold von Sacher-Masoch (the namesake of masochism), Pauline Réage, and Anne Rice—a modern writer of sadomasochistic erotica—are typically misconstrued as models for real relationships. Similarly, most pornography dealing with bondage and sadomasochism depicts severely dehumanized portraits that are as relevant to the actual practice of D&S as a sleazy porno movie is to romantic love. The masturbatory spectacle is all: The emotional content nonexistent.

Allusions to spanking, bondage, transvestism, and other so-called perversions permeate popular culture, so that sadomasochists have become both the butt of lewd jokes and delectably dark figures of forbidden sensuality.

Whether it's talk-show host Arsenio Hall asking his female guests if they enjoy spankings or filmmaker Mel Brooks's satires of whip-wielding sadomasochists in *High Anxiety*, coy references to aspects of dominance and submission provoke sexual innuendo and titillated snickers. How many times in just the last few years has "kinky" sex captivated readers and viewers? Tabloids delightedly jumped on rumors that actors such as Cary Grant, Nick Nolte, and Jack Nicholson enjoy spanking women. Madonna's book *Sex* contains sadomasochistic images, which, on the whole, are now a stock-in-trade of pop music videos.

For over a century we have lived with a cultural paradox: Descriptions of these sexual behaviors are so compelling that the media can always bank on their depictions to stir interest and increase profits. At the same time, we condemn these behaviors, which we do not understand, and regard people who make D&S a regular part of their lives as intrinsically different, frightening, wrong.

In this book we place each of the controversial sexual practices we discuss in its larger, real-life context. Most of all, we present sexual dominants, submissives, and fetishists as *they* see themselves: loving and compassionate individuals who care about their partners' enjoyment and welfare and who engage in D&S for the pleasure and mutual satisfaction that it affords. These are contributing and respected members of society: our next-door neighbors, our parents, our brothers and sisters, our teachers and our doctors, Hollywood's brightest stars and the grocery store's nicest cashiers, our politicians and our clergy.

This chapter opens the candid discussion of D&S. In addition to in-depth interviews, in this chapter and throughout the book, we will also quote interviewees whose profiles appear in other chapters. Our first interviewees are:

- Dr. Ronald Moglia is the director of the Human Sexuality graduate program of New York University's Department of Health Education. He received his Ed.D. from Temple University. Dr. Moglia joined the NYU graduate program in 1979 and has chaired it since 1988.
- Howard and Martha Lewis are a husband-and-wife team and the authors of numerous texts on human sexuality. They edit the *Journal of Sex Education and Therapy, Medical Aspects of Human Sexuality, Sexuality and Disability,* and other medical journals. They are also the chief administrators of the Human Sexuality Forums of CompuServe Information Service, the nation's largest on-line sexuality data base.

DEFINING D&SERS

Very generally speaking, two groups of people engage in D&S. First are those who fantasize about D&S and may periodically and casually experiment with it. These individuals add spice to a sexually conventional relationship by engaging in some form of D&S eroticism, such as spanking or roleplaying. The second group comprises those who are primarily and unequivocally aroused by D&S and who actively seek out sympathetic partners and, usually, support as well as education. The anecdotal information in this book is largely derived from this second group. We located most of our interviewees through D&S support groups, publications, and word of mouth. Our research, however, suggests that the majority of people who engage in D&S belong to the first group.

According to estimates by the Kinsey Institute and others, 5 percent to 10 percent of the adult American population regularly engages in some form of D&S. Numerous sexuality studies report that conquest and captivity scenarios are the most popular fantasies among all adults.

> *The range of the erotic imagination is almost limitless. . . . One person fantasizes about animals, another about movie stars, another about enemas, diapers, or South Sea islands. . . . The stylistic variations of sexual fantasies reflect the richness of the human mind . . . [and] most sex therapists feel that any sexual activity between willing adults that does not result in physical harm is normal and acceptable.* —MASTERS AND JOHNSON[2]

The husband and wife who privately roleplay as conqueror and captured maiden are expressing the basic impulse of D&S, just as those who hold a partner's wrists down or bite their lovers during lovemaking understand that rough stimuli may enhance sexual response. Many couples who enjoy extended D&S roleplaying do not know that there is a term for this aspect of their sexuality, nor that their erotic lives might be perceived by others as outside of the mainstream.

The two important distinctions between those who playfully incorporate aspects of D&S into sexual intimacy and those who define themselves as D&Sers are consciousness and degree of erotic need.

CONSCIOUSLY
COMING TO GRIPS WITH D&S

D&S-like fantasies are apparently common to all children and are dramatized in such games as cowboys and Indians or cops and robbers. While most people may outgrow a predilection for captivity games, the control aspects of such scenarios are the foundation of the D&Ser's erotic hierarchy.

> *I have given a lot of thought to my sexuality. [I think] the stuff was always there, and my guess is that it probably is for almost everybody. I remember when my nursery-school class went to see a musical production of* Daniel Boone *in Central Park. At one point Daniel Boone is tied to a tree. For weeks after that, the nursery-school personnel were very hard-pressed to keep the clotheslines at home. The four-year-olds kept bringing them in and tying each other up with an intensity that was quite beyond tree climbing or playing with jigsaw puzzles, and then the interest passed.*   —MITCH KESSLER

A typical pattern for a D&Ser is to be keenly interested in a particular fetish or activity in early childhood; to experiment with this vaguely, at least during masturbation in puberty or teen years; and to repress the desire once dating begins. Knowledge of being erotically different becomes increasingly clear over time, sometimes painfully so.

> *I'm from the Midwest and the suburbs. [Sex was] the things you would find out in the popular press, or what your friends would talk about—but certainly never something as unusual as D&S. After I realized that I had this interest, the next thing was, "What's wrong with me?"*   —JOHN H.

> *I was raised as a Mormon. It wasn't until I was in my early 20s that I thought maybe there was even one other person in the world like me. So it was not only a closely guarded secret, it was a guilty secret. I went through a lot of mental anguish and turmoil. I considered it to be very,* very *perverted. Over the years, however, I've had a chance to leave a lot of that behind, and overall when I look at myself I see a pretty valuable, capable, kind, responsible person.*   —GENE

By adulthood most D&Sers discover that the need can no longer be repressed. Although some of our interviewees found sympathetic partners while young or discovered that their mates were willing to experiment with

D&S, D&Sers often marry unsympathetic (and unsuspecting) partners and later develop significant marital problems. Many D&Sers maintain a lonely and secret sexual identity.

I've thought about why am I interested in this for a long time. It obviously rules a lot of people out of relationships. It's not a subject you bring up on a first date: "By the way, let's go home, and you can tie me up." [But once] I discovered that I had these desires, I knew that I did not want to go through life suppressing them. One of the things that I find saddening [is that] there are a fair number of people who are married—usually men—and whose wives have no interest in D&S. They seem to be very unhappy. I don't want to go through life like that. —JOHN H.

D&S support groups are proliferating as more Americans become aware that the companionship and sympathy of people like themselves are available.

I first discovered S/M pornography in my 20s. I eventually figured out that if they were making this stuff, it wasn't just for me. Even then, most of it is pretty sleazy. From what I saw I didn't want to be one of "them." What really made me start to feel okay about this part of my sexuality were some of the people I talked to in an S/M support group. These were mostly ordinary people in the good sense. They weren't weirdos. They had jobs like me, and wives that didn't understand them, and stuff like that. —JOHN M.

THE NEED THAT DOESN'T QUIT

For the majority of adults who enjoy periodic D&S fantasies, roleplaying is one color on the sexual palette, in line with Alex Comfort's supposition in *The Joy of Sex* that D&S can be an embellishment of erotic play. Though D&Sers typically enjoy orgasmic sex as an integral part of their encounters, they generally agree that sexual submission or dominance is *the* essential component of a satisfying erotic encounter.

Sexuality and sensual pleasures have always been important to me, so D&S is just a logical extension . . . what Alex Comfort called "gourmet sex." If [I'm] with a partner who's not into it, it can often be almost totally ignored. On the other hand, a certain amount of energy or exchange of power takes place even in the most vanilla of my love interests, either as top or bottom. For example, [to be] tied and held down, or to hold someone down, or to be a little rougher than might be necessary—I find it exciting. —LEONARD

Although D&S is most often used as foreplay to conventional sex, some D&Sers would sooner forego intercourse than D&S activity, and some individuals, particularly fetishists, may not be aroused by conventional sex.

WHO REALLY DOES IT?

I'm a very clean-cut, educated person with a good job. The references to B&D, S/M, spanking, [and] bondage in mainstream media usually portray [D&Sers] as drug-crazed killers or prostitutes or deviants. I think, because of that, a lot of D&Sers have to keep a very low profile. You can just imagine if your doctor was an openly professed sadist who had a masochistic female whom he led around on a leash. —BIFF

While no accurate single profile can be drawn of the average D&Ser, a majority of our interviewees—whom we believe to be a reliably representative sampling of self-acknowledged D&Sers—are in long-term or permanent relationships. Many of them are parents, and most described themselves as monogamous. But D&S monogamy is iconoclastic. It often means that the person will have conventional sex only with a life-partner but that he or she may engage in D&S activities with others.

[Our relationship] is monogamous in the sense of the term that I came up with—I'm proud of it!: We're "body-fluid monogamous." Think of the flexibility if you adhere to that one constraint! —MR. HAPPY

Our interviewees tended to be fairly religious. In addition to Christians (Catholic and a spectrum of Protestant sects, from Episcopalian and Methodist to Mormon and Christian fundamentalist) and Jews, many were New Agers, pagans, Buddhists, and members of other minority religions. Many perceive a direct connection between spirituality and sexuality.

I see my sexuality as a gift from God . . . My interest in my sexuality has a spiritual base. I feel very much in touch with myself through my sexuality. If I were an artist, maybe I would be painting and expressing my spirituality that way. But for me, I feel that my "art form," if you want to call it that, is my sexuality. —VICTORIA

We interviewed people in 23 states, from every region of the country. We also interviewed a few Canadians and one European. The vast majority of our interviewees are college educated, with a preponderance of white-collar workers, small-business owners, and postgraduate-educated professionals. The most likely explanations for this demographic quirk are, first, that social involvement in D&S and fetishism generally requires leisure time and disposable income. Second, while sexual dominance or submission indubitably occurs in all economic classes, the organized D&S Scene's emphasis on education and networking probably appeals most to the middle class.

Sexuality theorists traditionally have held that men are more likely than women to have sadistic sexual fantasies, that fetishism is a uniquely masculine phenomenon, and that women are more likely than men to have masochistic fantasies. No evidence, anecdotal or otherwise, supports these conjectures. Indeed, submissive men are the single largest component of the D&S communities, and widespread male interest in sexual submission is an observable phenomenon.

> *Why did I in fact receive far more fantasies from men that express masochistic desires than the other way around? The ratio was four to one.*
> —NANCY FRIDAY[3]

As a group men are certainly more visible than women in the D&S subcultures. This, however, is in keeping with the overall social phenomenon that men more readily, confidently, and aggressively pursue sexual encounters than do women. Among our interviewees the numbers of men and women who prefer the dominant role is roughly equal. The majority of all interviewees enjoy both dominant and submissive roles.

Finally, while many interviewees pleaded for greater acceptance of all sexual minorities, D&Sers are not necessarily more tolerant than are most Americans of those D&S interests they do not share. Some spanking fetishists openly deplore "whips and chains," many foot fetishists are appalled by pain scenarios, enema enthusiasts may express distaste for infantilists, and so on. D&Sers are as likely as anyone else to condone what they do in bed with the person they love and to criticize what somebody else does in bed with his or her partner.

Also, despite the current "pansexual" trend, which stresses unity among gay, lesbian, and heterosexual D&Sers (pansexuality is particularly popular in the burgeoning radical sexual communities of Northern California and the Pacific Northwest), there is as yet only an uneasy alliance between some heterosexual and homosexual segments of the D&S community.

WHERE'S THE STUFF I LIKE?

We limit discussion in this book to those activities that may involve a power exchange and that meet the D&S communities' standards of "Safe, Sane, and Consensual." We therefore refrain from investigating such activities as pedophilia, zoophilia, and necrophilia. Since children, animals, and corpses cannot give informed or legal consent to sexual activity, such encounters cannot be consensual. Our choice was facilitated by the fact that we did not encounter any D&Sers who expressed interest in these activities. Many other unusual sexual practices (such as voyeurism or swinging) are omitted because they are not typically associated with power exchange, the essential, defining element of all D&S activity. But we recognize that we may have also bypassed people who could provide a different perspective on certain activities or who may have described D&S activities with which we remain unfamiliar.

WHY WE WRITE

This book is not an apologia for sadomasochism. Our approach is humanistic journalism, and our goal is to explain what people do, why they do it, and what they get out of it, and to do so candidly and sympathetically. We are not scientists, psychologists, or sociologists. We do not take a quantitative approach, nor do we claim scientific accuracy. We do, however, take issue with some of the theorists who have presented theories as fact.

Over 200 people volunteered to speak with us; an edited selection of hundreds of hours of interviews appears on these pages. Our interviewees are exceptional in their frankness, but perhaps even more significant, they are productive, private citizens who are contented with their choices. They do not commit sensational crimes. They are not the malcontents who appear in clinical studies.

> . . . when people are comfortable with what they do, it doesn't come to the attention of therapists. And as long as it doesn't tread into the area of assault—e.g., nonconsensual or pedophilia or cases which end up in the emergency room—there are no records.
> —HOWARD AND MARTHA LEWIS

We provide a record. So impoverished is the world's present knowledge of and education in human sexuality that most of us can only stand by helplessly as political activists fight to become the self-appointed moral guardians of our sexual freedoms, assigning values that predate our grandparents to acts of love which predate recorded history.

With this book we hope to demystify a topic which has long suffered under a vast and oppressive cloud of antiquated mores and pseudo-scientific rhetoric. Until now honest information on alternative sexuality rarely has been available outside of scholarly magazines and partisan publications.

We also hope to add to the greater body of knowledge about what people *really* do behind closed doors with the people they most love and trust. Perhaps *Different Loving* will help open the door for further research into the mystery, beauty, and complexity of human life and its diverse expressions.

INTERVIEWS

DR. RONALD MOGLIA

I am director of the Human Sexuality graduate program in the Department of Health Education [at] New York University. We look at sadomasochism from many perspectives: clinically, socially, legally, personally, and culturally. My students are going to be professionals in the sexuality field. They're looking at everything with a scientific eye.

We have everybody from medical doctors to undergraduates and social workers and psychologists coming through the program we run for a graduate degree specifically in human sexuality. Part of it is studying groups of people who have nontraditional lifestyles. People who practice S/M and B&D are [in] that group of people, and we try to look at how society labels these behaviors. We [also try to see] how the individual in the behavior labels and understands the behaviors. Of course, there's often very great conflict.

It's the classic kind of anthropological dilemma: An American goes to Sri Lanka, studies the sexual behaviors of the culture, writes it up, and sends back a report. That's different than talking to a Sri Lankan and saying, "Tell me why these behaviors exist." One of the things that we do in the study of S/M and B&D is [that] we look [at them] from outside. That is okay, but you also have to combine it with the experience and knowledge and the definitions of the person inside. [We do this] by having people who live that lifestyle come and talk to us [and] by going to organizational meetings like [the] Eulenspiegel [Society] [Author's note: a New York City S/M support group] and having cross-cultural experiences. We've been going to Scandinavia every other year now for the last five years and comparing Eulenspiegel [members] with people who belong to an S/M organization in Denmark. It's phenomenally different. Eulenspiegel has to be subdued and quiet, whereas the [Danish group is] considered a social organization and gets funding from the government, as does every other social organization. It's got to create a difference [in] self-esteem [for its members].

One of the problems with these types of behaviors—and I don't mean purely S/M [but] all kinds of behaviors that are not perceived as standard behaviors among the general population—is that we tend to look at them and try to categorize them. In reality, if you look at heterosexual intercourse, you don't ask, "Is heterosexual intercourse an appropriate manner of behavior?" Sometimes it is, sometimes it isn't. When it's done by consenting adults, who are over 21, using safe sex practices, in a committed, monogamous relationship, it certainly is healthy. When it's used by the rapist to rape an individual, it's not healthy. [Yet] they're both heterosexual intercourse.

There is a range of behaviors [in S/M]. There are people who are using it in an adult manner, between consenting adults, within the parameters of our legal society, and they're living a healthy life and contributing to society. There are people who may not even be in the S/M–B&D social structure but [who] are using those kinds of behaviors and are unhealthy. You certainly wouldn't [include] a rapist in what you'd call the mainstream, heterosexual-intercourse population. [Similarly], there are people using B&D behaviors that are not the mainstream of the healthy S/M society. [Jeffrey Dahmer is] a classic example of somebody who's at the one end of the spectrum. For general society to group him with people who belong to the Eulenspiegel Society is ignorance. I would say tying and spanking behavior between consenting adults is no more intrinsically unhealthy than wanting to have coital sex or engaging in any kind of precoital behavior that occurs between consenting adults. [But as a society] we don't recognize fringe behaviors that are done in an acceptable, healthy way.

From my limited knowledge [from] field experiences, [sadomasochists] seem to have healthy relationships—if we know what that means. In the old days—[meaning] my parents' and your parents'—a healthy relationship was one that didn't end in divorce. [Nowadays] I don't know what a healthy relationship is. I guess it's when two people are satisfied with the relationship, [and] certainly I've met a number of people [in S/M] who feel that way.

I don't use the theoretical approach [that sadomasochism represents arrested sexual development]. I think it's an unknown, and I certainly think social learning is a great influence. There's so much we don't know about how our sexual ideas are formed. People often perceive sexual behaviors in a political manner. A lot of our behaviors are as a result of our social-cultural learning and influences, and certainly, in women, that's a great force. But to then take that and apply it to people who behave in a masochistic way—or in any other particular kind of way—makes me question how scientific the observations are, how politically biased the observations are, and what [such people] would say about the sadistic female that's appropriate and the masochistic female that's inappropriate.

Such theories are political and have no realm in trying to understand the phenomenon. That's another question: Do we need to understand S/M and B&D, or do we need just to accept it? When you look at the history of fetishes, three or four fetishistic behaviors were discovered between 1870 and 1900—they weren't [actually] discovered; they were just named by a medical source. All of a sudden we are compelled to understand and interpret them. Perhaps what social scientists should be doing is trying to understand the people who can't accept the behaviors.

I want to tell one story about Sri Lanka. When I was there, we had to take a ride; it was only [about] 30 or 40 miles, but it was across country. In Sri Lanka that takes about seven hours by car. We didn't know that, so we kept asking the driver, "What time will we get there?" He kept saying, "Oh, soon, fine, pretty soon, just a little while now." The next day I told a medical colleague who's Sri Lankan, "I'm amazed at how people don't care about time here," and I related the story. He started to laugh and said, "You don't understand. Time is in God's hands. If that driver said, 'We'll be there in six hours,' he's taking God's right to determine how long it's going to take to make that trip."

How stupid of me, to take my values and my cultural learnings and throw it on this person's shoulders. I think that's what we tend to do all the time with behaviors like S/M and B&D. We take our learnings and our understandings, being outside of that subculture, and try [to] understand and explain it . . . or [we] just reject it.

HOWARD AND MARTHA LEWIS

We have written [many] books about medicine, health, psychology, and human sexuality. When CompuServe [Aus.: a million-member, international electronic network] opened their service to a variety of subjects, we proposed to do a human sexuality information service [HSX]. In 1983 we began the HSX Information Advisory Service [as] an electronic magazine with a hotline. There were special features, interviews with experts, letters to the editor, and questions and answers. That turned out to be the most important part of the service: People could read thousands of questions and answers stored there. [CompuServe] is a perfect match of medium and message. A lot of people are concerned about their sexuality. They have large areas of ignorance. Here they can anonymously ask questions of a very intimate nature. Over our hotline we get hundreds of messages a week, questions that people can't ask anywhere else. We've established a direct line between [them] and the foremost authorities in the country from various areas of sexual medicine.

[In 1984] we realized that support groups were needed: The same value served by the text service could be served by an interactive forum. We were familiar with heading support groups and encounter groups.

We started [with] one forum; now we have two. One is the HSX Open Forum [HSX100]; the other is the HSX Adult Forum, (or) HSX200. [HSX100] is open to everybody. [HSX]200 is closed, except to people who qualify for membership. Many of its sections deal with sensitive issues. We feel that people are more likely to acknowledge a variation of sexuality in this medium than they might in conversation with family and friends. Participation in [HSX]200 far exceeds the participation in [HSX]100. It's logical, because these people are getting support from each other and acknowledgment and important information. HSX200 probably [has] about 15,000 active members.

We've gotten a glimpse into human sexuality that's much broader than what people see in the movies or magazines or [in] a standard sex-education class. Our consultants tell us—and it is verifiable in our experience—that everybody's wired differently. The narrow picture of what is sexually acceptable doesn't describe the great range of human sexual expression. Somehow people have assumed a stance of morality connected with what they think is [sexually] normal.

We feel strongly that everyone is entitled to privacy: You don't have to answer to anybody about your root personality. It's who you are, and your sexual expressions—to the extent that they don't hurt anybody else—fall within that. Everybody has different personas. You have a business persona, you have a friend persona, a family persona; you also have a sexual persona. If you look at any group of people in a business setting, you don't have any idea what they are like in their bedrooms or in their bathrooms or anywhere else. It's as irrelevant to their business persona as what they're like in church or what they're like with their parents. That's important to realize. People feel guilty [when] they find themselves relating sexually in a way that they don't relate in any other part of their life. But that's true if they were to analyze any other personas they've adopted. The enlightened view of sexuality is that conventional heterosexuality is one of many expressions of sexuality.

[In HSX200] we have a section called *Variations I* [and] another called *Variations II*. *Variations I* is devoted to fetishes [and] things that people ordinarily consider nonmainstream. Conversations might deal with various forms of pleasure giving [and] sexual enhancement practices. *Variations II* is devoted to bondage and discipline, domination and submission, sadism and masochism, [and] power-exchange relationships. We also have *Adult Babies* for infantilists; *GenderLine* for transvestites, transsexuals, and transgenderists; *Biways* for bisexuals; *Gay Adults;* and *Watersports* for klismaphiliacs, urolagniacs, and people into douching. *Variations I* and *Variations II* have [the most] access requests. An area that seems to have taken off lately is *GenderLine*. It may have to do with outside publicity. There was a recent [*CompuServe Magazine*] essay contest. A transsexual was one of the winners and wrote about how his/her transition was made easier by the support gained on *GenderLine*. There were letters—some objecting strongly, some saying this was a great thing.

We handle these subjects in a medical [and] psychological context. We're careful not to use slang language. It's treated seriously. [We would] love to be all things to all people, but we are not there for salacious entertainment. We encourage the widest possible exchange of ideas, experiences, and emotions. We're not an all-purpose sexual utility: We're a support group.

We're part of a global village. We have somebody in England who is leading conferences. We are developing a conference series with someone in Australia and [another person] in Singapore. The fellow in Singapore is 23 years old. He [says] that he really knew nothing about sex; nobody talks about it. Teenagers are kept ignorant. He'd found HSX educational and supportive. A lot of people have [said this]. For example, we started *Gay Young Adults*. Gays are born evenly distributed throughout the population, but when gays graduate from high school, classically they tend to cluster into regions. If a gay is in New York or San Francisco, [it's] all right, because there's a whole community. But if a gay remains in a small town, he or she is isolated—and the most isolated of the isolated are gay kids, who really have a lot of questions, not always about sex but about relationships and their own identity. We created a special, closed section restricted to people 21 or under. We've gotten two unsolicited letters from people who said, "You saved me from suicide." There are people walking around this country who we have reason to believe are alive because of something we provided. That's a nice feeling.

Two

VICTORIAN GENESIS
AND THE
MODERN SCENE

*The prize offered by Helio-gabalus for a new and original deviation is
still unclaimed after two millennia.*

—ALEX COMFORT[1]

The practices and desires we will examine are as old as eros. Yet we are so
accustomed to accepting the idea that unusual or unfamiliar sexual practices
are "perverse" that we rarely ask how these behaviors came to be so classified.
What forces or individuals asserted what constitutes a sexual norm? How have
these beliefs been assimilated into popular consciousness?

In this chapter we trace the rise of S/M as an observed phenomenon,
beginning with the first attempts to scientifically unravel the mysteries of
human sexuality until now. We also trace the roots of the organized S/M

communities, an expanding network of educational resources, support groups, and social organizations for sexual minorities.

At chapter's end we feature three interviews:

- William A. Henkin is a certified sex therapist and licensed marriage, family, and child counselor. He is past president of the San Francisco Bay Area chapter of the Society for the Scientific Study of Sex, a member of the Harry Benjamin International Gender Dysphoria Association, and a Ph.D. candidate at the Institute for Advanced Study of Human Sexuality.
- Hilton is 38 years old and was raised in Europe. He lives in New York, where he works in a high-technology industry. He is on the board of directors of the Eulenspiegel Society, America's oldest S/M support group.
- Carter Stevens is 46 years old and lives in New Jersey. He owns and operates fetish video companies and publishes *The S&M News*.

IN THE BEGINNING . . .

In 1844 the first *Psychopathia Sexualis* was published in Leipzig by a Ukrainian physician, Heinrick Kaan. Forty-two years later Richard von Krafft-Ebing chose the same title for the first edition of his massive *Psychopathia Sexualis: A Medico-Forensic Study*. Between the first *Psychopathia* and the second lay the gropings toward the first scientific study of sex. Obviously influenced by Kaan's work and publishing the more graphic details in Latin, to—as it has been suggested—"protect the imperfectly educated,"[2] Krafft-Ebing's tome was at the pinnacle of Victorian scientific inquiry into human sexuality.

In other cultures—notably the Hindu culture of India—*ars erotica*, which treat sexuality as an art form or a discipline to be mastered, were long established. *The Kama Sutra* and its imitators are essentially how-to manuals for the upper classes, as much concerned with proper sex etiquette for the well-born as with the varieties of sexual play. Erotic arts were not only deemed worthy of respect but were thought to be divinely revealed. This may partly explain why the how-to of sex was explored while the how-come? was largely ignored: A gift of the gods is not open to scrutiny.

Between the *ars erotica* of the East and the *studium erotica* of the West lies a gulf that is still only beginning to be bridged. Although sexual repression was hardly invented in the 19th Century—Michael Foucault, for example, suggests that the 17th Century was a watershed in censure of sexual pleasure;[3] and taboos against masturbation and sodomy were recorded in the

Old and New Testaments—it is ironic that the first attempts to demystify sexuality were born of one of the most sexually repressive cultures in history.

THE VICTORIANS

The Victorian period is the point of departure for sexual research. A convergence of factors made it possible: Science, philosophy, and social sciences were growing emancipated from religion; an age of curiosity flowered within an age of hypocrisy.

> *Perhaps the peculiar prudishness and sexual repression associated with the Victorian period helped escalate serious thinking on the subject: The discrepancy between the ideal and the real was too great to go unnoticed. But there was also the emergence of empirical science, the growth of medicine and psychology, a weakening of belief in traditional religions and moral codes in general.*
>
> —EDGAR GREGERSEN[4]

Victorian society was prudish to an extent that seems unimaginable today. Piano legs were discreetly hidden beneath fabric skirts in the interest of modesty, and the Bible was capable of wounding refined sensibilities because it contains such words as *whore* and *fornication*. Victorians were so nervously and negatively obsessed with sex that almost anything held the danger of titillation.

> *It became indelicate to offer a lady a* leg *of chicken—hence the still surviving tradition that she is offered the breast; but even this was called the "bosom" in the nineteenth century.*
>
> —G. RATTRAY TAYLOR[5]

Whereas earlier Christians may have perceived sex for pleasure as sinful, the Victorians viewed it as disgusting, animalistic, and depraved. It was even supposed that sex endangered the health; discharging semen was seriously believed to shorten one's life. Parents went to extraordinary lengths to safeguard their male children from masturbation or nocturnal emissions, in some cases fitting them with locked penis cages, spiked rings to render erections too painful to endure, and even alarm devices that caused a bell to ring in the parents' room should the penis become erect.

In medieval times the evils of temptation and carnality were blamed upon women who, like Eve, led men to ruin. By the Victorian Age, it was believed that lust was a masculine phenomenon and that women were sexually lifeless.

A writer in The Westminster Review *said that women's sexual urges were dormant or nonexistent. "Nature has laid so many burdens on the delicate shoulders of the weaker sex: let us rejoice that this, at least, is spared them." If they realized how great their sexual potential was, "sexual irregularities would reach a height of which, at present, we have happily no conception." This was unlikely as long as a frail, unsensual constitution invalided them out of the bestial sexual fray. The distinguished writer on sex, Dr. William Acton, said that to claim women were capable of sexual impulses was a "vile aspersion." William Hammond, U.S. Surgeon General, said that nine tenths of the time decent women had no pleasure from intercourse, and the famous Swiss gynecologist, Dr. Fehling, called sexual desire in young women pathological.* —ARNO KARLEN[6]

While the surface of Victorian society was shrouded in respectability, contemporary novels such as *Dr. Jekyll and Mr. Hyde* or *The Portrait of Dorian Gray* are allegories on the duality of Victorian life. In London as many as 40,000 prostitutes plied their trade. Brothels proliferated at a rate never seen before or since, catering to every imaginable taste. "Molly houses" (male brothels), child brothels, and flagellation brothels flourished.

Economic and religious influences are key elements in the spectacle of Victorian prudery. What we have come to call Victorianism was initially a phenomenon of the middle classes. As the economic power of the middle classes grew, their moralistic attitudes increasingly influenced the upper classes, and their effect on the lower classes was decisive. The experience of the Industrial Revolution and the concomitant stresses caused by the shift from an agrarian rural culture to a mechanized urban society were directly responsible for the development of sprawling slums whose squalor has never been rivaled. Victorian slums were the breeding ground of prostitution, crime, and violence; their misery was virtually inescapable. Only by adopting middle-class mores could the slum dweller aspire to that class.

The religious ideals of Methodism—the most powerful of the middle-class denominations—complemented Victorian social ideals. Modesty and restraint were unquestioned virtues. Proper gentlemen and ladies of the period eschewed strong emotion: Excessive laughter or grief were as objectionable as sexual excess. The appearance of respectability was paramount. To appear otherwise was to be common, and to be common was to be spiritually flawed, economically hopeless, and socially repugnant.

That anyone saw fit to study and publish work on sex—much less unusual sex—in this atmosphere may seem surprising. But the Victorian Age embraced paradoxes: Romantic extravagance in art and literature existed beside the grim sobriety of daily life; fervent humanitarianism beside the institutionalized racism of colonialism; hyper-prudishness beside profligacy. Moreover, this was a golden age for science, which seemed to promise the salvation from human misery that only Christianity had previously offered.

THE SCIENTISTS

Victorians appreciated science so long as it supported and confirmed their social ideals, which, by no coincidence, it generally did. The work of Charles Darwin, for example, had a profound impact on Victorian thought. While the possibility that man had evolved from a simian ancestor outraged many, Victorians nonetheless eagerly extended his theories of evolution to society. They saw themselves as occupying the uppermost rung of a tall ladder of social evolution. Just as Calvinism and its diluted form, Methodism, held that God demonstrated divine pleasure in the elect by rewarding their worthiness with wealth and comfort, so Social Darwinism held that Nature had rewarded the most worthy—i.e., the Victorians—with advanced civilization and technology. Social Darwinism was a direct transposition of religious belief into secular science. It provided a philosophical framework to account for such phenomena as urban slums and colonization. Those who did not prosper were unfit to prosper. Those who were colonized were unfit to rule themselves. That they be ruled by those whom evolution had blessed to be fit was only natural and right.

Darwinism also had a profound impact on contemporary psychiatry, itself a new discipline. The term *psychiatry* had first been employed in 1808; by the time of Darwin's publication of *On the Origin of the Species* in 1859, psychiatry was primarily a system of classification braced by a body of unsupported theory. Only 50 years earlier insanity was commonly believed to result from the disposition of humors (bodily fluids) or sorcery. Psychiatry held that insanity was organic, the result of disease or injury, but this failed to account for a large number of remarkably physically fit lunatics. Natural selection and inherited traits provided plausible explanations: Insanity could be hereditary, and the insane biologically cursed with a weak nervous system. Further, if the etiology could be established, a cure ultimately might be discovered. Science could then fulfill its promise of delivering humanity from psychological woe.

The latter half of the 19th Century saw doctors and theorists hunting busily for the hereditary factors of insanity and psychosexual deviance. Many believed that congenital conditions were manifest in anatomy and physiognomy. Physicians asserted they could diagnose, at a glance, a neuropath afflicted with "masturbatory insanity." He would be, if not raving, at least identifiable by his pallid complexion, downcast eyes, and air of brooding melancholy. Similar fallacies (some of which will be familiar to contemporary readers) spread as gospel: Lesbians were all mannish; homosexual men couldn't whistle.

Neuropaths aside, however, there was a larger question that nagged at Victorian scientists: If modesty, reserve, and sexual continence were the imperatives of human goodness, why were these qualities absent in so many Victorians?

PSYCHOPATHIA SEXUALIS

He was not the first to devote himself to the study of sexuality, but no one had a greater impact on the future course of sexology than Richard von Krafft-Ebing. He popularized the terms *sadism* and *homosexual,* invented the terms *masochism* and *paranoia,* and his classification system of sexual deviance remains the foundation of modern psychiatric diagnostics. But science and its theories do not develop in isolation: Krafft-Ebing's assumptions mirror many of the prejudices of his age. His biases remain a matter of debate.

> *By drawing on over 200 cases collected from his own patients, other doctors, earlier medical literature, and defendants in criminal courts, Krafft-Ebing provides testimony for his view that unbridled sex can undermine the health and honor of individuals as well as the very foundations of society. By mixing extreme cases (e.g., murder and cannibalism) with seemingly innocuous deviations, he gives the overall impression that* all *sex is dangerous.*
> —SUZANNE G. FRAYSER[7]

> *Prior to Krafft-Ebing, S/M was neither a sickness nor a sin.*
> —CHARLES MOSER[8]

Like Freud after him, Krafft-Ebing considered reproductive relevance the benchmark of sexual normality. Psychiatry was the heir of moral theology: Sex was a biological mechanism devised by God or Nature to ensure the production of offspring. Sex for pleasure and intimacy which did not induce pregnancy was a perversion of biology as much as of God's will. In this system "missionary," man-on-top intercourse—a position believed to aid man's seed in reaching its goal—was the only acceptable position; it also spared women from too active a role in their disagreeable but obligatory reproductive duties. Given this narrow definition of acceptable sexual activity, it is not surprising that Krafft-Ebing found an abundance of deviance.

We are still living with the Victorian notion that sex itself is bad. Western society has not always believed that, but it believed it with a kind of a vengeance after Krafft-Ebing—a man who as far as anybody can tell had intercourse with his wife enough times to produce a couple of children and may not have done anything else sexually thereafter—wrote Psychopathia Sexualis. *He held as the worst possible sexual practices homosexuality, transgenderism (he was particularly addressing transvestism), sadomasochism, and masturbation.* —WILLIAM A. HENKIN

Three things are remarkable about *Psychopathia Sexualis.* The first is its breadth of inquiry; then and now, psychological theory often rests on an extremely limited statistical base. Second is his compassion toward those who practiced acts that personally disgusted him; he advocated leniency, tolerance, and legal reform, arguing that one should not be punished for a condition for which there was little hope of a cure, as in the case of homosexuals. But most remarkable of all was the enormous distribution of his book: Krafft-Ebing, a medico-forensics expert who was specifically interested in the legal ramifications of sexual deviance, never intended *Psychopathia Sexualis* to be popular.

He did not want the public to read his book, so he gave it a scientific title, employed technical terms, and inscribed the most exciting parts in Latin. Despite these handicaps, the author proved to be a magnificent reporter: the public swooped down on his book.
—VICTOR ROBINSON[9]

It was sensational, shocking, and irresistible. As a medical book it escaped the taint of deliberate salaciousness; its stringent moral tone reinforced social ideals. Genteel readers entered a dizzying vortex of vampires, ghouls, lust murderers, shoe fetishists, groveling masochists, heartless sadists, pederasts, and bestialists—many of whom apparently drank tea in the cozy drawing rooms of bourgeois Europe.

Actually, Krafft-Ebing's behavioral "discoveries" had been known for centuries, if not millennia. Yet some readers found in *Psychopathia Sexualis* the first inklings that their sexual desires were not unique.

HAVELOCK ELLIS
AND THE OBSERVER EFFECT

For the first time there was an exhaustive, accessible work that dealt not only with sex but with the types of sex that people seldom discussed. But even as *Psychopathia Sexualis* was going to press in Stuttgart, in England Havelock Ellis had begun the research that would culminate in his massive—and virtually unmatched—*Studies in the Psychology of Sex*.

Contemporaries in time and discipline, these two scholars had dissimilar motivations. Ellis had a vested interest in demystifying sexuality: He had a lifelong titillation with urination that he credited to his mother having urinated openly in front of him when he was 12. His vocation as sexuality educator resulted from a religious experience he had as a young man. While reading a work by Dr. James Hinton that attempted to reconcile Christianity with science, Ellis was struck by a sense of utter harmony and euphoria. He decided then to become a doctor and to devote himself to the study of sexual behavior so that future generations might be spared the shame that ignorance and repression had caused him.

Ellis ultimately produced the seven volumes of *Studies in the Psychology of Sex* (1897 to 1928), but his greatest goal was never achieved. His works had limited success in combatting condemnation of unusual sexual behaviors. Freudianism was already growing apace, and its emphasis on psychoanalysis and intuitive theory was at odds with Ellis's cross-cultural studies and scholarship. Still, Ellis's sympathetic point of view helped popularize his work among members of the sexual minorities he wrote about, some of whom seemed to receive his conclusions as gospel. After reading in Ellis's *Sexual Inversion* (1897) that turn-of-the-century American gay male prostitutes wore red ties, for example, countless gays began wearing them as a recognition device.

> *Bullough notes that the Chicago Vice Commission in 1909 found that the numerous male homosexuals there (estimated at 10,000 or more) also made use of the red tie convention to identify each other. Bullough comments: "This leads to a question of whether homosexuals had adopted red as a color in Chicago or whether they wore red because Havelock Ellis told them it was the thing to do."*
> —EDGAR GREGERSEN[10]

The possibility that gay men, after reading Ellis, wore red ties illustrates *the observer effect*. Simply stated, the observer effect involves learning of a behavior (whether by direct observation, reading, or word of mouth), finding the behavior personally appealing, and then emulating that behavior. This is not an unthinking imitation of the "monkey-see, monkey-do" variety. The observation elicits feelings of identification in the observer. By emulating the behavior, one gains an affiliation with one's fellows which leads to increased self-esteem and social power. The gay men who learned that red ties could discreetly communicate their orientation to other gay men adopted the code as a standard, much like the contemporary gay man who wears a colored hankie in a rear pocket to "flag" his sexual interests.

This process of observation-identification-emulation-affiliation must be distinguished from fallacious assertions (such as those made by the Meese Commission in its study of pornography in the 1980s) that exposure to unusual sexuality (paraphilia) contaminates individuals who are otherwise uninterested.

> *Paraphilias are not socially contagious. They are not caught by association with paraphiles or reading about them, or by looking at movies or videos of them engaged in paraphilic activity. The myth of social contagion, especially from exposure to visual depiction of paraphilias, underlies officialdom's current panicky fascination with pornography and with driving it underground. The truth is that paraphilic pornography does not defile normophilic lovemaps. It simply does not appeal to anyone except those whose lovemap already mirrors it.* —JOHN MONEY[11]

A heterosexual cannot be transformed by reading Ellis—or anyone else—into a homosexual, any more than this book will transform a sexually conventional reader into a sadomasochist. The person whose sadomasochistic desires were previously limited to fantasy or occasional furtive encounters is the one whose behavior may be affected by discovering that a community of shared interest and sympathetic understanding exists.

THE 20TH CENTURY

The life sciences still battle for the ground that was scorched and denuded before the 19th Century's end. Science has failed to adequately explain the origins of sexual proclivities. Instead, today's popular media, bolstered by rafts of self-appointed experts, seize on idiosyncratic theories, such as sexual addiction, as if they represent progress in thought and knowledge. But the "diagnosis" (that too much sex is always bad) is warmed-over Victorianism, and the "treatment" is unchanged: strive to overcome, sublimate, repress.

Indeed, the scientific study of sexuality languishes. Scientific methodology demands, among other things, that when an experiment is repeated under all the same conditions, the results must be identical. A truly scientific study of sexuality is perhaps an impossible task, since we do not have the ability to replicate genetic structure or behavioral conditions in different human beings. Further, scientific study requires long and painstaking research and, most important, funding.

Sexual research has invariably incited storms of hostility and outrage. In Britain Havelock Ellis's publisher faced criminal prosecution for issuing *Sexual Inversion*. The Institute for the Study of Human Sexuality (1919–1933), founded by eminent German scholar Magnus Hirschfeld, was sacked and its priceless documents and library burned by the Nazis, who shipped some of its staff members to concentration camps.

In the United States *Sexual Behavior in the Human Male* (1948) was a pioneering work that gained Alfred Kinsey the title "The Columbus of Sex" from *Time* magazine. Kinsey examined sexual behavior as practiced, not as idealized. Among many other findings, he reported that 20 percent of the men and 12 percent of the women who participated in his original surveys expressed some degree of arousal in response to sadomasochistic stories. By 1954 Kinsey was under attack from the American Medical Association and Congress for the depravity his works allegedly engendered. The House Committee to Investigate Tax-Exempt Foundations pressured the Rockefeller Foundation to withdraw financial support from Kinsey's Institute for Sex Research. The U.S. Customs Service seized materials addressed to the Institute. Kinsey died of a heart attack in 1956, his research incomplete, and colleagues allege that the "scrutiny, criticism, and harassment took an emotional and physical toll."[12]

A decade later William E. Masters and Virginia Johnson published *Human Sexual Response*, based on 12 years of direct laboratory observation of sexual activity. Laymen and clergy attacked their work for, among other things, the use of sexual surrogates in studying orgasm and for their conclusion that almost all sexual dysfunction originates in religious orthodoxy. Conservative psychoanalysts ignored or dismissed some of Masters and Johnson's more controversial findings.

Between 1988 and 1991 three federally funded studies of potentially invaluable worth (particularly at a time when transmission of the HIV virus that causes AIDS is epidemic) were proposed to examine patterns of sexual behavior. The two that were approved were ultimately canceled under pressure from Senator Jesse Helms and Congressman William Dannemeyer. The third was dismissed as political suicide despite the high regard with which it was received in peer review.[13]

Although over 100 years have passed since Krafft-Ebing first identified sadomasochism and classified it as a pathology, his theories remain the foundation for current perceptions and clinical diagnoses. Official changes in the classification of unusual sexuality—when they occur—seem to be driven by changing social attitudes rather than new data.

> *If you look at the first edition (1952) of the* Diagnostic and Statistical Manual *of mental disorders, fellatio, cunnilingus, and masturbation are all mental illnesses. By 1980, with the third edition of the DSM, you find as mental illnesses reduced desire, incapacity, and so forth. And that's changing again. Psychology, in this sense, is very much a sociological creature. We follow the scripts of the society. When the society says it's good to have sex then it's psychologically sick not to, and when the society says it's bad to have sex then it's psychologically sick* to [have sex]. —WILLIAM A. HENKIN

In discussing the American Psychiatric Association's decision to reclassify homosexuality in 1973, Dr. John Money points out that politics and pocketbooks inform scientific bias.

> *A major political struggle of gay activists to have homosexuality upgraded from an illness to a social status required having it declassified from the* Diagnostic and Statistical Manual *of the APA. . . . Inevitably, the old guard fought back. They were loath to relinquish their conviction that homosexuality is always a disease for the cure of which they provided a treatment (and earned an income).* —JOHN MONEY[14]

Although attitudes are changing about what constitutes acceptable sexuality, the view that paraphilia is an illness requiring treatment prevails.

> *Most of the psychological literature is bent on demonstrating that alternate (which I prefer to "deviant") sexual practices or lifestyles are in some ways sick. This is a consequence of the medicalization of psychology. I'm not very happy that psychology is seen as a medical process. It seems to be far more a philosophical inquiry, if you will. Nobody knows why people become anything.* —WILLIAM A. HENKIN

In the last few decades knowledge about D&S behaviors and customs in the D&S subculture has largely been disseminated not by scientists, but by sexual practitioners themselves. Increasingly sophisticated modes of communication (beginning with the explosion in the publishing industry, and extending to television talk shows and, especially significant, to computer bulletin boards) have provided individuals with a wealth of information about sexuality. And the observer effect has played a significant role in the growth of minority sexuality communities. Open communication about D&S has attracted thousands of fetishists and sadomasochists to D&S support networks. There is no more instructive example of the observer effect than the transformation of the Old Guard of sadomasochistic homosexuals into contemporary D&S culture.

THE LEATHER EVOLUTION

I think S/M is changing now because the opportunity for communication exists in a fashion that it has not had ever before. Kinky sexuality is talked about more on television and radio talk shows. The purpose of the people producing all of this media [may be] to sensationalize in many cases, but the effect is that people are not living in dark, separate corners, as I was when I was young, believing that no one does any of this stuff. They are [informed] by general media that [such] fantasies are acted upon. —JOSEPH BEAN

The gay leather scene traces its ancestry to two sources: the barracks of World War II and the motorcycle outlaws of the 1950s and 1960s. As the origin mythology describes it, leathermen derived their complex authoritarianism from the first source while from the second they acquired an abiding fascination with black leather and bike clubs.

The massive American military mobilization of World War II uprooted millions of men who might otherwise have found scant opportunity even to travel from their hometowns and placed them within a huge, exclusively male society under pressure of a cataclysmic drama. Men whose homosexuality might have remained repressed or hidden were given an extraordinary opportunity to explore and gratify their desires. For gay men of a sadomasochistic bent the military offered a further thrill: power and discipline within an authoritarian framework. Gay leather sex then and now is a celebration of Greco-Roman ideals of masculinity—a hypermale society that embraces classical male values and rituals such as honor, service, initiation, mentoring, and paying one's dues.

Upon their return to the States about 1946, many of the gay vets wanted to retain the most satisfying elements of their military experience and, at the same time, hang out socially and sexually with other masculine gay men. They found that only in the swashbuckling motorcycle culture did such opportunities exist and so the gay bike clubs were born. —GUY BALDWIN[15]

By the early 1960s the existence of this subculture had reached the attention of the avant-garde. The film *Scorpio Rising* (1963)—described by author Hunter S. Thompson as "a bizarre little comment on twentieth-century America, using motorcycles, swastikas and aggressive homosexuality as a new culture trilogy"[16]—depicts men slowly and sensuously dressing in leather jackets and Levis, and contains a few sadomasochistic vignettes.

Leathermen did not generally welcome public attention. Entering their society was intentionally made difficult. Each newcomer had to prove his worth in a controlled social environment where experienced people guided him through a lengthy training period. Failure to abide by the complex unwritten rules governing dress and demeanor meant at least a lessening of social status and at worst ostracization. This social milieu has since come to be known as the Old Guard, and networking was among its key social regulators.

> *One of the mechanisms that keeps the S/M community relatively safe is networking: People know people within the community who know new people within the community, and so on. I'm talking specifically about the male subculture, which is what I know best.*
> —Joseph Bean

Although Old Guard conventions continue to influence gay and straight leather and D&S communities, its rigorous etiquette has been considerably diluted. This is largely attributable to a sizable influx of men (and women) who seek sexual acceptance among peers. The very things that made the Old Guard strong—a highly evolved social structure and a sense of community—attracted new members and, ultimately, contributed to its demise.

> *[When] Tom of Finland became widely known—his art primarily dealt with gay male leather imagery—suddenly there were a couple of years when leathermen were the living icons of gay sexuality. The result is that the network breaks down. There is an influx of endless numbers of curious people; there are more people showing up at play parties and the bars than could possibly be assimilated. In my view, for the S/M community to remain somewhat underground and somewhat unaccepted, so that people have to approach warily and have to prove themselves as trustworthy individuals, is in fact a very high value for the community.*
> —Joseph Bean

The leather community met a previously unfulfilled social need. And as novices flooded in, activists became keenly aware of the vital importance of educating those who would not have the opportunity for individual mentorship.

THE MODERN SCENE

In the second edition of *The Leatherman's Handbook,* author Larry Townsend writes:

> *A little over ten years ago I signed a contract to write* The Leatherman's Handbook. . . . *It was a virgin field, wide open, and, except for my disagreements with a few shrinks here and there, the ideas I was suggesting were fresh and new. This time, however, I am faced with a mountain of written material expressing the opinions of a great many people. . . . Making the present task far more difficult . . . is the enormous increase of people participating in a very wide area of activities.* [17]

The blank slate upon which Larry Townsend wrote in the early 1970s had rapidly filled by the 1980s. Until the 1960s the main sources for information on D&S were clinical studies; by the mid-1980s a wide array of nonfiction and fiction about D&S (much of it produced by gays and lesbians) became available. For a time it seemed that the 1960s' relaxation of sexual mores had opened the door to free discussion—and exploration—of unconventional sex.

Increasing numbers of individuals began to form D&S alliances. Leather had begun as a uniquely gay, subterranean culture centered around motorcycle clubs and bars; in the 1970s heterosexuals—influenced by the early and exhilarating victories of gay liberation as well as the formation of consciousness-raising groups by feminists—seized on the idea of forming S/M support groups. The Eulenspiegel Society, the first such group in the United States, was founded in 1971. Two decades later the National Leather Association—an umbrella organization for S/M support groups and social clubs—reported "an international network of well over 400 Leather/SM/Fetish organizations." [18]

A backlash in the gay and lesbian communities against S/M, however, temporarily inhibited the burgeoning subculture. Three events—all occurring in 1980—helped excite anti-S/M sentiment. The film *Cruising* portrayed the leather scene as inherently sordid and violent. That same year CBS Television aired *Gay Power, Gay Politics,* a documentary that erroneously stated that S/M is a mostly gay male practice and that 10 percent of all gay deaths in San Francisco were S/M-related. Neither claim could be substan-

tiated, and the producers were later censured by the National M
but the documentary had already conveyed its message about le
ity. That same year the National Organization for Women (NO
resolution advocating homosexual rights and condemning S/ ... These
events and the 1982 publication of *Against Sadomasochism,* a collection of
feminist essays that harshly condemn S/M, have cast an enduring pall over
relations between non-leather and leather gays and lesbians. The same year
also saw the publication of *Coming to Power: Writings and Graphics on
Lesbian S/M,* a collection of essays and fiction by lesbian feminist sadomasochists, which provides an intellectual framework for reconciling sadomasochism, lesbianism, and feminism.

Krafft-Ebing's legacy lives on in popular opinion. Although contemporary Americans are certainly more likely to perceive sex for pleasure as an
acceptable activity than did the Victorians, deliberately nonreproductive
sex—and particularly any form of sex which does not have heterosexual
intercourse as its main ingredient—is generally regarded as perverse.

The last two decades have witnessed a social phenomenon. The diverse
leather communities—prolific in their writing and sophisticated in their
organization—have attracted thousands of D&Sers in search of community,
support, and the opportunity to socialize and meet like-minded partners.

Unification, however, remains problematic. Many organizations limit
membership according to same-sex or opposite-sex preferences. Many
heterosexuals are uncomfortable socializing with gays, and homosexuals perceive straight sadomasochists as swinging thrill seekers, uniquely interested in
D&S as an episodic erotic event rather than as a committed lifestyle.

> *The heterosexuals into radical sexuality have never felt the need to
> build specialized communities in the same way as their homosexual
> counterparts. In the Gay/Lesbian sub-cultures, garments and even
> toys become symbols carried well beyond the area of play into the open
> light of public spaces. They speak of a tribal affiliation that is as
> strongly social as it is sexual. . . . For most straights, radical sexual
> practice begins and ends in the bedroom or the playroom.*
>
> —GEOFF MAINS[19]

As the organizational network expands, however, leather traditions—
particularly the adoption of leather dress codes, respect for seniority, and a
tribal spirit—are more widely emulated. Heterosexuals who once largely
looked to pornographic novels for role models—and who typically discovered that the fiction provided no advice on the daily problems of real
people—are turning to the D&S communities for advice and support.

This evolution has led to "pansexualism": Gays, straights, bisexuals, and transgenderists fraternize and attend parties together. The National Leather Association has taken a leadership role in unifying all D&Sers, regardless of partner preference, into a cohesive political and social force.

> *There is a lot of separation between the straight, gay, and lesbian S/M communities. But there is also pan-S/M consciousness. As one wise woman who has been doing this for many years has said, "Leather is thicker than blood."* —GAYLE RUBIN[20]

Finally, one of the most significant developments in heterosexual D&S has been the rise of the electronic samizdat. Hundreds of D&S-oriented electronic bulletin boards have formed since the late 1980s. For many people still laboring under the Victorian ideas of acceptable sexual behaviors and living in sexually and politically conservative regions, the anonymity and accessibility of these on-line networks has permitted a free interchange of ideas on topics formerly too distressing to discuss even with relatives or friends.

As of this writing, international electronic networks have become a primary medium of communication and socialization for millions of people interested in D&S-related sex. The on-line environments offer everything from peer support and discussion groups to sites dedicated to personal ads, erotica, and graphic images. On the Internet, news groups prefixed by "alt.sex" treat individual topic areas (female dominants, water sports, fetishism, spanking, inter alia). The most heavily-trafficked area is "alt.sex.bondage," which features lively, sometimes acrimonious, debates on D&S issues and technical "how-to" discussions. On the World Wide Web, new D&S sites are constantly emerging, hosted by enthusiasts and vendors from Hoboken to Hong Kong. On Compuserve, the Human Sexuality Forum's Variations II (founded in 1987 by Gloria Glickstein Brame), is the nation's oldest on-line D&S support and education group.

The observer effect has held powerful sway in cyberspace, where large numbers of newcomers emulate the behavior of loquacious veterans and eagerly adopt the prevailing mores, etiquette, and slang. The net effect seems to be a growing emphasis on the technical elements of D&S and on its enormous potential as casual, safe-sex play. One of the more intriguing phenomena has been the proliferation of "play parties" and "munches," regional social events organized by and for D&S cybernauts who meet for "3-D" interfacing.

INTERVIEWS

WILLIAM A. HENKIN

Every society has taboos. Most of them have sexual taboos. Those societies that do not have sexual taboos have mouth taboos, either on eating or on talking. What the connection is between the beginning of the alimentary canal and the end of it, or between the tongue and the genitals, I will only leave for speculation.

There are two reasons, as far as I can tell, why S/M is taboo in our culture. The first has to do with control. As a society, we are as frightened of control issues as we are of anger issues. They are related. To express anger seems like losing control. So it's taboo to look at those things that frighten us. Second, if you control people's sexuality, you control their lives. If you tell them what they may or may not do sexually, you have in a very real and a very deep way told them who they may be, who they may not be, what they may be, what they may not be. The organization of any society needs—or feels that it needs—to control its citizens.

As far as I can see, there is no engagement between two mammals that does not include a power relationship, a jockeying to determine who is the alpha animal. In my observation, most relationships between two people do not include any awareness of this need to resolve the power dynamic. People attempt to determine their power relationships implicitly, not explicitly, and consequently human interactions are generally fraught with arguing and bickering to see who gets to control things. This complex process may result in a lot of manipulative behavior, with people who are physically or psychologically weaker trying to gain control from underneath, covertly, and people who are clearly stronger physically or psychologically feeling that they're being manipulated, but not quite knowing how, getting frustrated, and hitting their partners. I'm speaking hypothetically, but it's been my observation that that's part of what goes on in a lot of spousal abuse, partner abuse, battering relationships.

I'm perfectly willing to be wrong about this, but I don't know of a battering situation, for instance, where [either] the batterer, the batteree, or both have not come from situations where power was dealt with unconsciously. I have worked in situations where I had to deal with many people who had been battered, either as adults—spouses or partners—or children. I don't recall a single one of those situations where consensual S/M or D&S

was a component. I'm not sure that such erotic games would have been acceptable to most of those people.

If one is being unconsciously and nonconsensually domineering, one will behave brutally [physically or psychologically]. If you're unconsciously submissive, then I think there's potential for a great deal of self-deprecation. If you don't really want to give in to your partner's demands, but you do it continually, and feel resentful, I think it's very psychologically self-destructive. It leads to considerable anxiety and suppressed rage. Similarly, you can be brutal [by] demanding things that could be asked for. When you start to make the dynamics of these interactions conscious, you begin to have some choice in the matter. Some people may become conscious of being domineering or brutal—or submissive or self-demeaning—and may decide that they don't like these configurations in themselves and want to stop. Then they encounter a new process: learning how not to behave in their old patterns and to behave in new ways. Others [may] find something valuable in dominant or submissive behaviors under certain circumstances. For some people, not only do D&S and S/M provide a safe and consensual arena for these activities, but, because they eroticize them, they make pleasurable experiences that are less pleasurable in noneotic contexts. So if you're accustomed to being domineering and you find that you can get into a sexual situation where you can be dominant and have what you want, you may find that when you go back to the office, you don't have to bully everybody.

There are theorists who will say the cause is genetic; there are theorists who will say the cause is psychodynamic: Something happens in childhood that plays itself out later on in life. The theory I am most comfortable with is a combination of nature and nurture, some kind of biological or genetic or psychological predisposition which gets activated somewhere along the line. I am happiest so far with John Money's theory of lovemaps. He posits that whether or not there is some kind of biochemical predisposition, each person has a kind of mental map delineating what he or she will find erotic.

For example, a child listens to his or her parents in an ongoing, though unconscious, dominant-submissive relationship. Dad is very aggressive, very loud, very forceful about how he wants things to be done. Mom, though she may be as intelligent [and] competent, is meeker. Hearing his parents argue or fight or debate, the little child feels some fear. The fear sets up nervous reactions and, because there are a lot of nerve endings in the genital region, the child [is] stimulated. Children are all sexual. There are videos of children just a few months old masturbating. There are photographs of little boys *in utero* with erections. So there's some connection for the little child. If this happens traumatically, or if it happens repeatedly over a period of many years, a lovemap is activated so that when the child later encounters situations in which control—expressed as D&S—are prominent, he or she may [be] erotically stimulated. If the child begins to masturbate around fantasies connected with this, or starts to engage in other sexual activities, the lovemap already established is set firmly in place.

People don't get involved with sexuality that is concerned with control, power, and intense sensation without having control, power, and intense sensation as issues in their personal lives. I can't say whether there's a higher percentage of people involved in D&S and S/M activities who were abused as children than otherwise, partly because the people I see as a therapist are coming to me because they have problems. They're not coming to me because they feel great. I'm seeing a skewed population. This is the problem with interviewing psychotherapists under *any* circumstances: We see people who are in trouble, so we cannot extrapolate from our clientele to the real world. Also, we are in a period right now when the notion of child abuse is extremely prominent. It's part of the popular culture to talk about abuse and it's easy to see childhood itself as a nonconsensual situation. We are all socialized and we need to be socialized. But to be socialized means that we are dominated, without our consent, by people who have power over us. If we then are unhappy as adults, it's easy to look back and say, "I was abused." We were all abused. But we need to start talking about degrees of abuse and what constitutes the differences between trauma and abuse.

We can call anything arrested sexuality or arrested development. When I'm driving in rush-hour traffic and I see intelligent, successful adults screaming at each other, cutting off other cars, risking their lives and dozens of other lives in order to grab 20 feet of space, I see infants functioning in adult bodies. The same can be true in some people's sexuality, whatever the nature of their sexual behavior might be. It may be that some people in [S/M–D&S] communities had unusually difficult childhoods, but then so did a lot of people outside them. You probably could find a similar profile among professional politicians or policemen or the military or physicians or lawyers—anybody who finds satisfaction in controlling other people or the circumstances of their lives. One of the things I find conspicuous about the people I have seen in these [S/M or D&S] communities is the relatively high level of consciousness they exhibit about what they're doing and their willingness to investigate it farther.

It is plausible that the usual notion of normative heterosexuality is what people are mostly supposed to become, but we'll never know as long as we make sex so dirty for children. John Money suggested that if we really wanted children to grow up to be sexually healthy adults, we would treat them the same way we treat young athletes. We'd say, "Go out and practice as much as you can, and when you do well, we'll reward you." Instead, we hide sexuality. It should come as no surprise to those of us who think there's a model of sexuality that people are supposed to follow that lots of people don't. I know that there are some people who are involved with S/M or D&S activities who really cannot get off in any other way, but the same thing is true of missionary position, male-female heterosexuality. I look to maximize options. If people can get off with ordinary missionary-position sex and also with D&S and also with this, that, and the other, then they have many more opportunities for pleasure.

Certainly there are people who engage in D&S and S/M activities for whom it is a problem or the expression of a problem—but so also there are people who cannot engage in anything but ordinary penis-vagina intercourse for whom sex is a problem or the expression of a problem. If someone is really the sort of person who is likely to become a serial killer, he probably won't be talking about it and he probably won't be in so relatively conscious a relationship as S/M. He'll much more likely be repressed or out there doing mayhem.

The fight for sexual freedom that we see waged in the streets and in the courts in our country—and which is not even allowed as a fight in many other countries—is not an irrelevant fight. It is essential to our freedoms and our identities as individuals and as a society. If you control people's sexuality, you control people. The people I have worked with who were involved in conscious S/M or D&S relationships have not seemed to me to have been destroyed, damaged, or abused by those relationships. If people are not damaging themselves or others, it really is nobody's business what they are doing.

HILTON

I'm heterosexual [and] switchable. I consider myself to be not so much dominant as sadistic and masochistic. I need S/M to have a good sex life—something I found out when I was about 22. I was never shy with women. I remember my friends, after sex, would always say how wonderful it was. I'd have sex and it was okay, but it was nothing special. I could take it or leave it. I knew that whenever I saw a woman dressed in leather, rubber, latex, anything tight and shiny, I would get turned on, but I never related it sexually. But at 22 I was traveling in Denmark [and met] a woman who was about 35—an "older woman"—and I complimented her on her beautiful clothing. She invited me to her apartment and, lo and behold, she happened to have a dungeon. I didn't know anything about S/M: All I knew is that she was beautiful and an older woman, which turned me on at the time. She began tying me up, playing with me, spanking me, and to make a long story short, I had an orgasm. [That's when] I realized that my sexuality was tied into a lot of the fantasy things. That basically started me on my career of S/M.

I was fortunate that at an early age I found people and places to go to. I didn't have damaging emotional relationships. Once I knew that I was really into it, I wouldn't have a lover unless she was interested in S/M, because it's very frustrating to be in a relationship where you're not sexually satisfied. I think it's deceitful to be with someone and have to go secretly outside of the relationship to get satisfied. I see a lot of people coming to the group who are married: Their spouses are either not into it or know nothing about it. I think it's very sad that people do things like that, because the whole purpose is to share and explore our sexuality together.

Many people don't like the word *sadomasochism* [because of its connotations]. I know people who would never give or receive pain but think of themselves as into S/M—transvestites, foot fetishists, clothing fetishists. What's D&S to one person is S/M to another. You can spend days, weeks, and months trying to define things. [Some] people are into the Scene and hate to use the word S/M; some get hung up on the terminology. I'm not worried about it. Whatever makes someone feel comfortable is really what's important.

For me, S/M is a very important part of a relationship. I enjoy dominating or submitting to someone that I really like. It doesn't have to end in intercourse. However, for me, when I'm in a relationship, and I currently am, the S/M is foreplay and it ends up in what I call S/M intercourse.

I went out with a woman for five years; we were madly in love. I met her at an S/M club. We had everything in common—the same music, same eating habits, same everything—except our sexuality. At first we would play a lot with each other, [but] she stopped playing and grew to resent the Scene. It's amazing, because everything was together except our sexuality. I started suppressing my S/M fantasies. I found that it's like a bubble in water: You suppress it, the bubble pops up; you push the bubble down, it stays down a little longer, [then] comes up about twice as fast. I suppressed for six months, and then I had to have S/M. Even today we're still the best of friends. However, sexually, we're just not compatible.

I'm an optimist. I've never been depressed or thought I'm the only one in the world. I've always been comfortable with what I'm into because it's always been consensual and something I've enjoyed. I've never felt guilty. I don't feel I can or even want to change. It's like going to someone who's gay and saying, "You're going to be straight tomorrow." It doesn't happen.

I like fetish clothing. I love wearing it and want my lover or friends to wear it. I have a lot of clothing which probably could be construed as feminine—latex panties and things like that—but I've never thought of myself as a cross-dresser. Secondly, I like converting pain into pleasure. I really get into spanking [and] a lot of caning. I went to an English school: We used to get caned and spanked [there]. I used to hate that until I was about 14. Then we had female teachers who were in their 30s and they used to spank us. When I was spanked by them, it never really hurt and I suddenly started enjoying it. But I never saw a sexual connection, although from age 14 I started having spanking fantasies. As regards wearing tight clothing, that goes back to when I was seven or eight years old.

[My S/M fantasies really] grew once I started understanding them in a positive manner. I have certain fantasies which I really enjoy playing out, [such as] worshiping a goddess. I [also] like wrestling with a woman. My girlfriend's really into that—that's a lot of fun and very physical. You can do it in a very sensual and erotic way.

I like groups that have workshops. [One can] learn about the dangers of doing bondage, which a lot of people are unaware of. There are do's and don'ts for everything. We have a few doctors in the Scene who are very good, and once in a while they'll give a talk on the health and safety aspects.

I have been a member of Eulenspiegel since 1980 and on their board since 1982. The Eulenspiegel Society [TES] was founded in 1971 in New York by Pat Bond for masochists only. They met in his apartment. After a few months [they] decided to open it up to everyone in S/M. TES is a nonprofit group. It's purely voluntary, and [its] main purpose is educational. Eulenspiegel comes from German mythology. When the group was formed, a woman attended who loved the name Till Eulenspiegel, based on a mythological German masochist. He used to run up and down a mountain carrying a pail of water. He hated running down the mountain, because then he thought of carrying the pail up; but he enjoyed carrying the pail up, because he then thought about carrying it down.

We have two meetings a week. The first is open to everybody. We have a talk [or] demo [which] lasts an hour. The second [hour], we have a circle where people listen or talk. Everyone introduces himself by name or pseudonym. You're free to sit and listen. People talk about their interests or S/M-related topics and issues. People find it very therapeutic and informative. The second night of the week we have special-interest groups. We have a dominant-men–submissive-women's group and a dominant-women submissive-men's group. Occasionally we have a switchables groups. We have a transvestites group. Another important group is [our] novices group. New people are usually very shy. Often they want to know where you can find toys and how to use them. We may talk about how we got into the Scene, how we play. How to meet people who have similar interests is a very common question. We tell people it can be at a local movie house, a local art gallery—

anywhere you meet the person of your dreams. You're not always going to find someone at an S/M club.

We open the meeting with 10 minutes of announcements about membership or our quarterly newsletter. We tell people about major events in the future—like parties or fund-raisers or the Gay Pride Parade. Then the guest speaker talks. They end the lecture with a question-and-answer period. Then we put all the chairs in a big circle. The rules for the circle are that you [must] raise your hand, because cross-conversation [is] disruptive. Every week different people run the circle to keep it interesting. Afterwards, we usually go to a restaurant [with] a big room in the back and socialize and get to know people on a different level.

The Eulenspiegel Society has a mailing list of about 500 ex-members, so between past and present members our membership is close to 1000. We average between 30 to 70 people at a meeting. There are many more who've [visited but] who never [joined]. We also get between five and 10 human sexuality classes from the local universities every year. We've had a few students who've been hostile about S/M, but usually when they find out that we're regular folk, they don't have too much to say. The bottom line is [that] it's consenting, caring adults. We're not blatant at the meetings; we don't play. It's a forum to talk. However, we do play at parties.

We look at [our goals] as sexual liberation for all. We don't discriminate against any segment of the population. We feel everyone should have the same protection. We've always been politically active with the gay leather community, and we've always helped and participated in local fund-raisers. We're probably going to get more politically active. The leather community has to be strong and stick together if we're going to withstand harassment. Personally I think we have to get involved if we're going to survive. Otherwise people will walk all over our civil liberties. I would like to see more networking and shared resources within our community. There [are] a lot of lawyers, doctors, and professional people [in the Scene]. If we were all aware of each other, and our strengths, we could have a strong business bloc. I think there are a lot of very good political activists out there, especially in the National Leather Association [who] are doing outreach programs [to] the "straight" community to spread the word in a positive way.

I've always felt this from the bottom of my heart, and it's a very simple thing: Everyone is different. If you can learn to live and love and accept each other's differences, the world would be a better place.

CARTER STEVENS

My mother, God rest her soul, was a phenomenal woman whose basic attitude toward sex is that when sex is good, it's great, and when it's lousy, it's not too bad. She and my father brought me up without the guilt so often associated with sex, so I have been able to enjoy my sex life. I do [have] a lot of recreational sex, but I realize and appreciate the difference between that and a warm, loving relationship. I've been married twice; at one point in my life I was living with five women at a time; at other points in my life I've had single, monogamous relationships. I've run the gamut. The relationships are what stick out in my mind more than the scenes.

I'm very much a hedonist. Any kind of D&S scenes that I get into are strictly a form of fantasy foreplay. The point of the entire scene is still sex [not] as a substitute for sex. I have many nonfetish-oriented relationships which I enjoy entirely. I'm strictly dominant, but I've had long-lasting relationships with dominant women [in which we] hung our whips on the door outside the bedroom.

D&S is a part of my life, but I can walk away from it tomorrow . . . at least for a week. It's the old saw: Nobody wants to eat steak every night of the week. I tend to be attracted to women who are independent outside of the bedroom, so sometimes that can cause a lot of sparks; but I've had relationships that [were] totally slave-master 100 percent in every detail.

When I was young, there was only one thing on my mind: getting laid. I can't [say] exactly when my D&S interest began. It would have to be after I got into the sex business. [As] a professional photographer and cinematographer specializing in the adult field, I started getting hired to shoot this stuff. It interested me, and [if] something interests me, I will experiment with it. I found that I enjoyed it. I'm much more into B&D or D&S rather than S&M. It is part of my personality—the same part that makes me want to be a film director. I like to control emotions. When I make a film, I am, by definition, controlling an entire audience's emotions, and I carry that same feeling into the bedroom. Controlling a woman's emotions gives me the same kind of thrill, and pushes the same buttons in my psyche. I'm [also] very pushy, and tend to be opinionated, loud, and forceful outside of the bedroom, so it tends to carry over.

I enjoy bondage, leather, spanking, straight sex. I can get into a lot of different things, depending on the partner I'm with. I'm not into pain, but I have gone into heavy scenes with partners who, because they were so turned on by it, brought me past the point I would normally stop.

The real nature of S&M was driven home to me about 15 years ago. I was doing a movie called *House of Sin*. There was an S&M scene [with] a mistress and her slave, who were, in real life, living together. She had him on the floor, with his hands tied behind him. She had a dog chain wrapped around his cock and balls and was lifting him off the floor by his cock and balls and smacking him across the nuts, hard enough so that every guy in the room had his legs crossed. Two things stuck in my mind: First, that while this was happening, this guy had an incredible erection, and two, as soon as I yelled, "Cut!" he immediately started to bitch and moan about the fact that he was lying on a hardwood floor and didn't have a pillow behind his head. At that moment I realized that what she was doing to his genitals was not painful; the little bit of pressure on the back of his head, that's what his brain was interpreting as pain. But the hard pressure of her hand coming in contact with his nuts was erotically stimulating. I realized that in S&M, if it's painful, you're doing it wrong.

The body feels stimulation; the mind interprets [it]. The way that the mind interprets it determines whether it's pleasure or pain. Who knows what determines that—probably a combination of what determines everything in this life: heredity, education, and environment. Someone much brighter than me once said that there is only one erogenous zone in the human body, and that's the space between the ears. If your brain interprets [something] as erotic, you will not feel it as pain. What makes someone aroused by the smell of three-day-old sweat socks? Damned if I know. But I know it happens, and more power to them. They're not harming anybody. If that's what gets them through the night, God bless them.

There is a misconception about the people involved in the Scene—what we term "Ted Bundy-itis." When you discuss S&M, the first thing people think about is a Ted Bundy type preying on unsuspecting women and getting sexual kicks by maiming and killing. It's as far away from the Scene as it is from mainstream society.

The people in this Scene are, by and large, older, more intelligent, and probably better off economically than the average person. Maybe they need more mental stimulation to be erotically aroused. Maybe as you get older, you need more to keep your interest. I've been involved in the Scene in Europe, and I find that the people who are seriously involved can buy and sell me three times over, whereas, I guess, the poor garage mechanic is willing to hump whatever he can grab on a Friday night. I don't know if that's an elitist attitude; it's certainly self-serving, since I'm into the Scene. But it's a personal observation. That's one of the reasons I started *The S&M News.* It is a newspaper aimed strictly at adults. We're trying to cover every aspect of the fetish scene. [It's] strictly informational, not erotic. I am gratified to say that the response has been nothing short of phenomenal.

My personal beliefs are basically [that] whatever people want to do without causing permanent harm to another is [okay]. Personally, I do not like any kind of a scene that causes injury. I would never draw blood. I believe that the skin of the body is there to protect what's in your body from outside forces, be it germs, or whatever. Scatological play, to me, once again, is on the edge of being unhealthy. [It] turns me off. I have gone as far as I want to go. I would not go any further. I do not get off sexually [from] inflicting pain.

My [college] degree is in photographic science. After graduating from the Rochester Institute of Technology, I went to work for a large motion picture processing laboratory, and ran that for a while, then worked for an English corporation building an emulsion coating plant in the United States. I'm a former class-A photographer with the film union and shot original footage for the film *Taxi Driver*. That's basically how I got into this business.

I have three different companies. One is Carter Stevens Presents, where I produce and direct adult videos. I specialize in fetish-oriented material because the market for "straight" adult material is glutted. Most of my stuff is released by Chain of Command here in the States, and under Amsterdam in Europe. I also shoot and provide production services for many other fetish companies. About a year ago I started *The S&M News*. Our press run at the moment is about 10,000. I [also] have a partner in Europe, and the two of us sell American product to Europe and try to sell European product to America, although that's not as easy. Americans have this thing about foreign films: They don't like them. [Also], the adult material in Europe is much more adult. The stuff that they're making, especially in the fetish field, is too hard for current American standards.

[Generally], you have people who want to turn out a decent product, you have people who are turning product just for the bucks, you have people who are exploiting a market, and there are people who are trying to cater to a market. Everybody's taste is different, too. There are people who don't want the real stuff. They want pretty girls who look like they tied themselves up and could just as easily untie themselves. There's another market that wants to know that this girl is truly well bound and helpless. And by the same token, there are people who get turned on if [the actress] looks like she is not enjoying it, and there are other people who will get turned on if she looks like she's enjoying it tremendously. But it's Sturgeon's Law: 99 percent of everything is crap.

The first, probably the most important [problem] in this day and age is legal constraints. It's not that the laws have changed; it's the way personal freedoms are interpreted. [For example], I could never film a golden shower in one of my videos today. It is not more illegal, but it is economically unfeasible. The average prosecutor wants to go after pornography. Say it's getting close to an election: The prosecutor will pick an easy target. Pornography is one of the easiest targets. But to the average audience, straight, good old-fashioned humping is no longer as taboo as it used to be. He knows that if he goes after run-of-the-mill porno, he is going to have a harder time getting a conviction. Golden showers, fist fucking, enemas, things that the average person is going to interpret as perverse: Since I'm very allergic to jail cells, I leave [these things] out of my films because [then] I am less likely to get picked off the shelf in Podunk, Iowa, and face a court battle which would make it economically unfeasible for me to do business.

I do not have any sex in my fetish films. I do a lot of shooting in Europe [and] I make two versions because the Europeans are strange: They like sex in their sex films. So I shoot two versions of everything that I do in Europe. Hard core [is] for release in Europe only. Every time I go to Europe, I'm less excited about coming back here. There have been increased prosecutions all over the country. [But] I'm here and I'm in the fight. I don't like to be, but my only other choice is getting out of the business I've been in for 22 years. I'm [definitely] *not* a champion of pornography. I don't think we're doing any great social work. These are fuck films. They're entertainment, not brain surgery. On the other hand, I don't think we're doing any harm. We make these for adults with adults, and what adults want to do in their own damn home is their own damn business, as long as nobody is harmed. I am a champion of personal freedom. The right to have fun is not in the Constitution [and] not protected. So I vote Liberal and pray for the Supreme Court justices to see the light.

Three

THE ABCs OF D&S

The things that seem beautiful, inspiring, and life-affirming to me seem ugly, hateful, and ludicrous to most other people. This may be the most painful part of being a sadomasochist: this experience of radical difference, separation at the root of perception. Our culture insists on sexual uniformity and does not acknowledge any neutral differences—only crimes, sins, diseases, and mistakes.

—PAT CALIFIA[1]

This chapter is a primer of the principal issues and concepts that are familiar to members of the D&S communities. The D&S subculture has a highly sophisticated ethos to guide erotic play, which comprises ethical codes, safety rules, and communication tools. The intention of this mostly unwritten *ars erotica* is to help ensure that a maximum number of people experience D&S as a positive and loving expression of sexuality. Also, as the subculture has expanded, it has developed its own philosophies and jargon.

We feature four interviews:

- Victoria is 29 years old and a high-school English teacher. She lives with Leonard.
- Leonard is 50 years old and the owner of a private business.
- Biff is 37 years old and married. An armed-forces veteran, he now works as a paramedic.
- Genevieve Reynolds is 29 years old and works as a computer professional. She lives in California.

WHAT'S IN A WORD?

Redefining sadomasochism has become an important task for many D&Sers. The English language does not make the distinction between the criminal sadist who enjoys causing desperate agony in a victim and the sexual sadist who seeks romantic fulfillment with an eager and consenting partner. Thus, some D&Sers wish to change the negative connotations of *sadomasochist* and use the word as a proudly political statement. Others prefer to use the slightly less controversial terms *dominance and submission* (D&S) or *bondage and discipline* (B&D).

> *The connotations of S/M are loaded. Every notorious person in history has been called a sadist, and every [human] doormat has been known as a masochist. I think that as a community we'd be better off abandoning those terms. I don't choose to use those words myself. I think that people should know that the Scene is made up of people like themselves: ministers, accountants, shipping clerks, psychologists, dentists, attorneys, sculptors, anything.*   —LANCE

The war over words is regularly fought and seldom won. The linguistic dilemma has no easy solution. Support and educational groups and private collectives continually debate D&S terminology and its practical meaning. For example, if the sexual sadist's pleasure derives in great part (as most D&Sers claim) from the pleasure of the submissive, is it really sadism? And if a dominant's first priority is to give pleasure to a submissive, is this really dominance?

> *In essence, the dominant is pleasing her submissive. In that sense, she is submissive to the will of the other.*   —MARIE-CONSTANCE

Similar debate rages over the terms *submissive, masochist,* and *slave.*

> *To me a slave is someone who is controlled out of fear, who has no other place to go because all the other options have been chopped off.*

I can't understand how a woman could allow herself to be referred to as a slave. It turns my stomach. I don't [think] that most white people are educated enough about slavery to understand the implications of the term. To me it's not a term you play with. The moment I become a slave [is] the moment I give up my will. And the moment I give up my will, I shouldn't expect anyone to respect me at all. And I demand respect from everyone, including my lover.

—VICTORIA

Debate notwithstanding, D&S jargon is familiar to most people in the Scene. Below is a brief glossary; other terms are explored in greater depth throughout this chapter.

B&Der: one who includes aspects of bondage and discipline in erotic life.

Bedroom D&S: D&S confined to a purely erotic encounter.

D&Ser: a person who enjoys sensual dominance or submission.

Dominant, or Top: a person who exerts sensual control. *Top* may also be used as a verb (e.g., "She likes to top macho men").

Flagging: traditional gay-male practice of displaying a colored bandanna in a rear pocket to identify one's erotic interest.

Leatherman, or Leatherwoman: usually a gay or lesbian D&Ser, but any member of the leather communities.

Leathersexuality: originally, gay leather subculture.

Left-Right Codes: bandannas, keys, or leather items worn on the left signify dominance; worn on the right, they signify submission.

Lifestyle: refers to people who view D&S as central to their erotic lives.

Masochist: one who is aroused by receiving pain.

Master: a male dominant.

Mistress, Dominatrix, or Fem Dom: a female dominant.

Play: D&S erotic encounters.

Play Parties: social gatherings where D&S play may occur.

Power Exchange: the willing surrender of sensual control by a submissive to a dominant.

Professional Dominant, or Pro Dom: a dominant who is paid to engage in D&S activity. (Professional submissives exist, but are considerably rarer.)

S/Mer (also S&Mer), or Sadomasochist: generally, a person for whom the giving or receiving of pain is erotic.

Sadist: one who is aroused by giving pain.

Scene: the organized or social aspects of D&S. To be "in the Scene" may mean that one openly participates in support groups, attends clubs, or joins in other social activities. "A scene" may also refer to a particular interest (e.g., "His scene is bondage"), or, more narrowly, to a specific erotic episode (e.g., "She did a scene with her submissive last night").

Session: an erotic D&S episode (e.g., "We had a hot session the other day"). Usually refers to professional dominance.

Slave: usually refers to submissive who—in fantasy or in reality—participates in ownership scenarios.

Submissive, or Bottom: a person who is sensually controlled. *Bottom* may also be used as a verb (e.g., "She bottoms to him").

Switch: a person who enjoys both the dominant (or sadistic) and submissive (or masochistic) role and "switches" roles.

Vanilla: conventional relations, or any intimate relations that do not include D&S or S/M sexuality.

THE CREDO:
"SAFE, SANE, AND CONSENSUAL"

[A D&S relationship] . . . takes place in a context of awareness. Its purpose may be emotional bonding, a way of achieving new levels of intimacy; it may be spiritual, seeking to transcend ego states. In the S/M and D&S communities there is a rubric that goes "Safe, Sane, and Consensual." In my observation, the people who are engaged consciously and volitionally in S/M and D&S relationships by and large adhere to this phrase. —WILLIAM A. HENKIN

"Safe, Sane, and Consensual" is the universally accepted credo and philosophical core of the D&S subculture. The phrase—formulated by gay men in and around the Gay Male S/M Activists [GMSMA]—articulates basic moral guidelines for contemporary D&S relationships. While the ramifications of "Safe, Sane, and Consensual" are subject to debate, we summarize below the basic ideas underlying the credo.

SAFE

This refers to physical safety, which is a cherished priority of "serious players" (i.e., those who are sincerely committed to D&S sexuality), who recognize the potential risk of inflicting extreme stimulus upon even a willing partner. The limits of genuinely safe play are constantly debated in the D&S community. Nonetheless, certain tenets are universal.

- Safe Sex: AIDS awareness and adherence to safer sex guidelines.
- Protection of Vital Organs: no activity which injures vital organs.
- No Meaningful Damage: no irreversible damage of any kind, nor any kind or degree of pain that the submissive did not request or knowledgeably consent to.

To ensure physical safety, most couples use a *safe word* (also known as a *safety word,* a *stop word,* or a *code word*). The submissive may use the safe word to signal distress. Dominants either cease all activity when the submissive pronounces the safe word or declare a temporary time-out, during which they may discuss the submissive's feelings or reassure or cuddle the submissive. Safe words are selected before any D&S activity begins. They may be negotiated between partners or assigned by the dominant. The word(s) chosen is intentionally inappropriate to an erotic context, so that there can be no mistaking a "no" which means "yes" for an unequivocal "stop!" If a submissive is gagged or otherwise muted, a *safe gesture* or other signal is substituted.

A safe word allows the submissive to retain some control over how far things will go and permits the dominant to feel secure that he or she isn't genuinely harming the submissive, but a safe word is *not* a substitute for communication, nor for responsibility on the part of the dominant. Experienced D&Sers advise novices to question a dominant carefully before beginning an encounter or to obtain word-of-mouth recommendations from mutual friends.

Some D&Sers fear that safe words encourage complacency. Safe words do not guarantee a safe encounter if the dominant is irresponsible or untrustworthy or if the submissive is extremely naive or self-destructive. Some also believe that safe words allow submissives to *run the scene,* or *run it from the bottom* (in other words, the submissive determines the limits of any given activity) and that this conflicts with the notion of a genuine consensual surrender of power. Nonetheless, safe words are a preferred communications tool and are particularly important early in a relationship. Over time, they may become unnecessary.

Another key communications and safety tool is a *contract* (also known as a *slave contract*), which bears a vague resemblance to a prenuptial agreement. D&Sers often prepare formal written agreements that specify the nature of the prospective D&S relationship and delineate the guidelines partners will observe. These agreements are meticulously negotiated by both partners in a nonerotic context, so that power roles do not bias judgment. Contracts typically stipulate limits and give concrete expression to each partner's expectations and commitments.

SANE

Everything within an SM exchange is done with the intent of producing physical or emotional pleasure. This is the basis for the whole scene and, simplistic as the statement may seem, it is the universal key. —LARRY TOWNSEND[2]

We will not take it upon ourselves to define sanity. "Sane," in this context, however, generally means, first, that any given D&S activity is done for the pleasure of everyone involved. Erotic play should not cause emotional anguish; it should not abuse the submissive's vulnerability or subject a submissive to unreasonable risk. And a submissive should not have to worry that the dominant will exceed his or her personal limits.

The concept of limits is crucial to an understanding of both "safe" and "sane" D&S. To *respect limits* means that a dominant will honor a submissive's personal boundaries—in terms both of physical limits (degree or type of stimulus) and of psychological limits (degree or type of roleplaying). Limits are, of course, entirely individual: One person's paradise is another person's purgatory. For example, Jane might find very light bondage to be the height of ecstasy, whereas Jack is aroused only by stringent bondage. If you put Jack in light bondage, he may be frustrated, but if you put Jane in rigid restraints, she may be traumatized. If Jack and Jane submitted to an experienced dominant, their individual limits would be carefully discussed before any bondage occurred.

Respecting a partner's limits is the foundation for trust.

In all S/M play both parties—top and bottom—agree to what they're doing, respect the other person for trusting enough to allow the play to happen, and revel in the fact that trust has been established. One of the main things I get out of topping someone is a fantastic thrill that the person has faith in me and enough trust to put her body in my hands. A very deep sense of love and closeness comes out of that. —ROBIN YOUNG

Dominants also have personal limits. Novice dominants may stumble upon this surprising intelligence when they are urged by an aggressive submissive (also known as a *smart-ass masochist,* a *sam,* or just *greedy sub*) to do something they later regret.

Pushing limits, or *stretching limits,* describes erotic encounters in which a dominant presses the submissive to accept a greater level of stimulation than the submissive originally expected. This delicate and risky process is primarily the purview of long-term partners who have discussed *expanding limits* in hopes of enhancing a given activity's erotic potential. In order to push a limit, one must first be certain where the limit lies; one must also be confident that the submissive will not be harmed by heightened intensity.

CONSENSUAL

Consensuality is really the first law of the D&S communities—and with good reason. Our interviewees incessantly emphasized the consensual nature of D&S, no doubt because of extreme sensitivity over the popular perceptions of sadomasochists. Dominants, and especially novice dominants, are often confused or distressed by comparisons with violent criminals.

> *Those people who practice [D&S] behaviors [between] consenting adults and then fear whether they're mass murderers—I think that's probably a function of society's lack of teaching that there's a range of allowable sexual behaviors in the human experience and between consenting adults. Within the parameters of law there's even a larger range of behaviors. I think those people are, unfortunately, wallowing in a pool of ignorance because society doesn't teach about those kinds of things.* —DR. RONALD MOGLIA

Submissives, meanwhile, struggle against comparisons with battered spouses or pathological victims.

> *One of the things which distresses me immensely, as a high-school teacher in an inner-city school, are the number of young women who allow men to hit them, beat them up, get them pregnant, and leave them. It's not D&S: It's something far more horrifying than anything I would ever put up with. And yet if I came out in my classroom and said, "Yes, I do this," they would think I was sick. To me, those girls are slaves, because they allow men to do these things and don't question why. You have to be able to question why somebody is doing something, even if you're submissive. If your lover or your master or your mistress is doing something to you that you feel is wrong, you question [it].* —VICTORIA

Clear, informed, and verbalized consent is the moral dividing line between brutality and D&S: Partners must voluntarily and knowingly give full consent to D&S activity before it begins. D&Sers typically avoid any relations with minors, for example, because it is generally accepted that minors cannot give informed consent. Some D&Sers are even reluctant to enter into relationships with novices, often preferring people with D&S

experience. The D&S community also promotes open discussion and debate about safety issues. Abuses are rarely tolerated: Dominants who mistreat submissives will be openly criticized or ostracized.

> *I have seen dominants who misuse their authority. We have a term for that here in San Francisco: "top's disease."* —M. CYBELE

THE IDEA OF COMMUNITY

> *It's hard to be in a community that has no real name for itself. The only names that we have to call ourselves are names that others call us: perverts, or kinky people. We are human beings with a sexuality that simply happens to be different.* —ROBIN YOUNG

Throughout the following chapters our interviewees frequently refer to the Scene as "the community." A distinct communal spirit has marked the leather scene since its inception; at first self-protective, the idea of community has become an important source of group esteem and identity.

Specific support groups and social clubs are actually independent communities, but the vast majority of them actively network; D&Sers coast-to-coast exchange information and cooperate on educational outreach. National community events and symposia bring together D&Sers from across the nation and the world.

The trend toward broadening and strengthening the D&S community seems to be growing; it is a significant phenomenon at a time when nuclear families are suffering turmoil and dissolution. For some the D&S subculture is a kind of tribal organization whose advocates, spokespersons, and senior members are leaders and spiritual guides. For others support groups are a contemporary version of the extended family.

> *I view our group as a sort of anarchist convention. Somehow we find community with all these diverse interests, diverse backgrounds, and diverse careers and get together and have a wonderful time. Perhaps that diversity is what makes the chemistry. It's like an extended family. I feel proud to say that they're some of the most wonderful people I've ever met in my life, [who] have wonderful relationship[s] with each other. It's a terrific thing. You find this quite an amazing community. They're the kind of people that I would be drawn to even if I wasn't in S/M. They're wonderful folks.* —LANCE

WOMEN, POLITICAL CORRECTNESS, AND SEXUAL FREEDOM

D&Sers are, by nature, politically incorrect, *if* by political correctness one means adherence to the puritanical notions of sexuality espoused by some feminist apologists. Although the fact may at first seem paradoxical, most D&Sers of both genders actually support feminism on principle and in practice. Our female interviewees perceived a direct connection between their sexuality and their goals as feminists.

> *S/M gave me tools to be a feminist. Feminism gave me lots of ideals to strive for. Feminism said to me, "You must be a strong woman, you must have control in your own life," but it never gave me any tools to attain that strength. It just said, "Do this. If you don't do it, you're a bad feminist—you're not liberated, you're not strong enough." In fact, if you are taught to be insecure in childhood, you can't just be told—you have to be taught how to [be strong].*
> —GENEVIEVE REYNOLDS

Our female interviewees agreed that real sexual freedom implies freedom of choice: One should be free to decide for oneself what kind of sexual activity affords the maximum of sensual pleasure.

> *For me, feminism is extremely important, but the word that we use most in feminism is* choice. *I'm choosing to submit to a man because I want to. When I stop wanting to, I can walk out the door. I can tell him to go sit on it and rotate if I want to.* —VICTORIA

The submissive in a consensual relationship does not relinquish social or professional power, nor is she likely to accept authority from anyone but her dominant. Many submissives told us that the ability to surrender sexual power privately and to fulfill taboo fantasies is a profoundly empowering experience.

While submissive women often bitterly resent stereotyping as passive victims, dominant women are in a double bind: Even if they overcome the anxiety that sexual assertiveness is "unfeminine," they may then grapple with feminist theory which mitigates against any overt expression of power in intimate relationships.

> *More than a few lesbian feminists have formulated theories which are dependent on targeting S/M. We are told S/M is responsible for practically every ill and inequity . . . . including rape, racism,*

classism, spouse abuse, difficult interpersonal relationships. . . .
Sadomasochism . . . is tacked onto just about anything hated or
feared. As S/M lesbians, we say that our experience contradicts
many of those closely held theories, and that this examination of our
experience is a feminist inquiry. —KATHERINE DAVIS[2]

Some feminist rhetoric suggests that the desire for power is a uniquely
masculine impulse and that sadomasochism is an outgrowth of male oppres-
sion of women. Not only is this view historically groundless and intellectually
hollow, but it has helped to sanitize and dismiss the diversity of female
sexuality as thoroughly as did the Victorians. It is little wonder that the
parochial view of female sexuality espoused by some feminists has garnered
political support from the reactionary Right.

While women increasingly believe that they have a right to demand
power in the boardroom, as a group, they have yet to demand sexual
satisfaction in the bedroom, much less to seize (or even to accept) consensual
power. Female dominance may be a final frontier in the empowerment of
women.

INTERVIEWS

VICTORIA

Sometimes I scratch my head and wonder what I'm doing here. And then I look over at my honey and realize exactly why. For some women I think there would be a conflict. For me there isn't. [But] I can't really picture myself submitting to anybody else but Leonard. I think that if I did walk out of this relationship tomorrow morning, if I were in another D&S relationship with a man, I'd probably be dominant. But certain things in my personality and his gel a certain way so that we're happy. As long as it is a matter of choice and I know he really does not think that he owns me, I feel secure in doing what I'm doing.

I have never been subservient. I am submissive. To me there is a difference. If I was subservient, when I came home and he said, "Hey, babe! Go in the kitchen and get me a beer and fix dinner and get right to it!" I would do it because I would be a brainless little booboo-head [who] wouldn't know what [she wants]. I know what I want. If he tells me to go get a beer and I have something to do, then he's going to have to get the beer for himself. I have a choice. He wouldn't order me around like that in the first place. He understands. A lot of women do not have choices, which is why they're forced to be subservient.

I grew up in a household where I saw what subservience is like. My mother gave my father the best part of the chicken all the time, because he was a man and was supposed to have it. She just accepted it. I asked her one time, "Why do you always give it to him when you like that part too?" She said, "Because he is a man," and she gave me this helpless look. I swore to myself at that moment that I would never get that helpless look in my eyes. I have a choice [as to] what kind of relationship I want. There are certain emotional and physical needs that I have—if I could satisfy them another way, maybe I would, but at this point in my life I choose to be with this man in this way.

There is a definite difference between abuse and dominance. My father was verbally dominant and even somewhat abusive. I remember one time my mother and I were very upset. My father had a big argument with her and got physical. He put bruises on me, and we left and went to a women's shelter. There were women who had horror stories that would make someone completely ill. There was one woman [whose] husband had tied her up with rope over a Christmas vacation and brought in prostitutes and had sex with them in front of her and told her that if she told anybody in her family, he'd kill her and their children. That wasn't D&S, although some newspaper writer would probably make it sound like an S/M relationship because he tied her up. She was not a willing participant, and he was obviously doing this as a form of deep humiliation and showing her that he was a man and he could do whatever in the world he wanted to.

When I first started getting into D&S, I wondered, Is this some kind of desire for abuse? But then I realized that there was a great deal of difference. Leonard constantly asked me, "Do I have permission to do this?" I was enjoying it. When I got to the point where I didn't enjoy it anymore, he would stop. In abuse, the abuser doesn't care whether you're enjoying it or not. In fact, he doesn't want your enjoyment! He wants you to be miserable, because that way he can feel really powerful. When I say "he," I'm not saying that there aren't men who are abused—I know that there are.

As far as I know, I am one of the few black female submissives. I've had more problems dealing with that emotionally than dealing with being a feminist and submissive. Here in New York there aren't a lot of black people who are into [D&S], at least not openly. I'd say that there probably are a lot of black people who are into it, but they either don't call it that, they're [only] doing it in their bedrooms, [or] it's part of their everyday relationship and how they relate to each other. I think that the reason why you see so few people of color in the [S/M] clubs is because a lot of them, quite frankly, don't have the money to spend on the clubs. Also, I think that among black people S/M [and] even things as mild as oral or anal sex are seen as a white peoples' thing—one of those sick, kinky things that white people do. "*We* would never do that." The same attitude exists about homosexuality. Even though some of the greatest activists and writers among African-Americans have been gay, lesbian, and bisexual, most black people will not acknowledge this because they see that as a white person's thing. "If you do that, it must be because some white person seduced you and made you do it." There's a lot of denial.

Sex and sexuality [are] just not something you talk about. Therefore, if you're some little black girl or little black boy who's having naughty fantasies about being tied up, you figure you're sick in the head, and you keep quiet. You never do anything about it. I happen to be an extremely nervy person so I try all kinds of crazy things. But I'm unusual. I find it hysterically funny that the stereotype among whites [is that] blacks have wild and crazy sex. In fact, most black people are horrified at the things that white people do. My students who think that they're wild and crazy [will] say, "Yeah, I like getting busy [having sex]," but they'll tell you all the things that they would never do, like, it's disgusting to have oral sex of any kind. And they would never have anal sex—oh my God! That's something homos do. They can't even picture heterosexuals doing that. There's a whole laundry list of things that they either haven't heard of or, if they've heard of them, they just know that they're wrong. It's kind of amusing.

Why am I bisexual? To me, that's like "Why are my eyes brown?" I don't know! I think that God made certain people so that they can understand both the masculine and the feminine a lot better than others. As far as D&S: I think it's a way for me of exploring power. I like to be in control of myself. I've never been interested in drugs, and I've never been interested in some of the other ways that people use to get outside of themselves. This is the way that I do it. I find that spiritually, if I'm in the middle of a really good scene—and just about every scene that I've ever had with my lover has been absolutely wonderful—[it's] almost [an] out-of-body experience. The closest that I've ever come to doing that in a nonsexual context would be through meditation, because I've been doing meditation work for quite a few years now. So to me, it's part of a larger continuum.

I've expressed some of my dominant feelings with my lover, but it's not a major fantasy of mine. I've had occasional fantasies where I'd have him tied up to a chair and torture him by playing with myself and not allowing him to touch me, or playing with him and then telling him that he can't come, because if he does, I'm going to give him a spanking. I sometimes keep those fantasies in the back of my head as an extra special turn-on.

As far as my work life, it's a totally different thing. I'm a schoolteacher, so I'm very aggressive and dominant in that situation. I think that's why I like being submissive at home: I'm dominant all day long at work. Our roles do carry outside of the bedroom. Not all the time, but, for instance, when we go out to eat, I'll tell him what I want, and he'll order for me. Lately we've done things like shop for clothing, and he goes with me and helps me pick out things that he really likes.

That's not much different from the way a lot of women live their lives, but they wouldn't call it a D&S situation. They would call it a typical marriage. The difference is that, first, I'm aware of what I'm doing. Second, to a certain extent, I would say that it's a fantasy life—we don't have to live this way; it's not like if we stopped doing it, our lives would end. I've always considered myself a feminist, and I know that I am equal to my lover. That's different than a lot of women who are in traditional relationships where they fool themselves into believing that the man is supposed to have his way because he's a man. I don't believe that.

I realized since about the age of about five or six that I liked both boys and girls. When I got a bit older, I found myself drawn to strong women, because we have a lot of strong women in my family. And I liked that feeling of power, both within myself and with other people. When I got into high school, a woman friend was into Victorian pornography, which has a lot of S/M and D&S, whipping scenes. I would read it and go, "Oooh, that's disgusting! That's awful! That's horrible! What's on the next page?" I found it disturbing because the women were objects. I never found out what they were feeling, why they were enjoying it. I thought, That's not me, because, if I were having sex, I'd enjoy it, and these women aren't enjoying it. I'm not a pervert like that.

When I got into college, it was a tradition for graduating seniors to give things to freshmen and sophomores. One woman gave me a copy of *Story of O*. I read [it] and thought, This is absolutely ghastly, this woman gives up her personality, but for years my favorite bedtime reading was the first few scenes of *Story of O*, when she's shown all the instruments of torture and told what's going to happen to her. I thought that was really nasty and dirty and wonderful.

I started reading magazines like *On Our Backs*, a lesbian porn magazine [with] a lot of D&S. I thought that was really hot, so I couldn't understand why I was having fantasies about *men*. I was tempted a couple of times to find someone, but I didn't know where to go. I felt guilty. Maybe these people were awful: I could end up in a body bag. I had horrible fantasies about what could happen to me. What changed was that I heard about a women-only group which met at a D&S club. I went, but I didn't see any really interesting action, because of what I'm into. [Then] I read *Outweek* and answered an ad from a woman who said that she did some D&S. So I went on a blind date with her. She was nothing like what I expected. She was not a terribly interesting person, but she was going to a party and invited me along, and [that's when] I met the man I'm with right now. We hit it off immediately. There was just something about him . . . I wanted to know more about him as a person. There was an aura about him that seemed to show that he was rather experienced. I figured [that] if worse comes to worse, we'll have a couple of dates, and I'll learn why I want to do this stuff.

On our first date we went to see this absolutely beastly movie, and he kept touching my thigh and murmuring subtle threats in my ear. I said, "Oh, my God! I'm going out with a maniac!" But I wanted to go out with him again. Somehow he seemed very gentle. It was really confusing. He told me that he thought that I was really beautiful, that I'd look even more beautiful if I had a collar on, and that he'd really like to put his hands on my breasts and caress them. I was just looking at him like, "I don't believe that you're saying this!" And he said, "You know you don't want to [leave]." That really scared me, because he was right. It was like he could . . . read me. My mouth was saying, "This is horrible; why are you saying this to me?" But I could feel myself getting all warm and excited. So I had to keep on going out with him to figure him out.

A couple of dates later we went to a museum, and while we were walking around, he started whispering things in my ear about how he'd like to tie me up and how he'd like to spank me right there in the museum and let everybody see me with my skirt pulled up and how much I'd probably enjoy exposing myself because I was a naughty little slut. I almost ran out of the museum. But I wanted to hear more, even though I was horrified. Now that I look back, I realize that I was horrified because he was saying exactly what I wanted to hear. I didn't want to believe that a nice girl—whatever "nice" means—could want to do things like that. Before I knew it, I kept going out with him, because I really liked him as a person. And he was great in bed. He was teaching me things that I had only fantasized about before. Some of them I hadn't even fantasized about. I didn't know you could do things like that to the human body. He's very loving and gentle and has a very delicate touch. It feels really wonderful. One feels very trusting—at least one should. To me, it's actually lovemaking.

What I found out from going out with him for a while was that he was interesting, that he was really fun, that he was the kind of person with whom I would like to spend time outside of [a D&S] situation. And I started falling in love with him. I hadn't expected that at all. What I found from talking to him and talking to other people who were in the Scene was that I was not a weirdo. There are plenty of other people who grew up in nice little suburban areas doing the same thing. They didn't die. God didn't hit them with a thunderbolt. It didn't ruin your life. Which surprised me. I thought I was on the highway to hell.

If I could do anything in D&S, I'd really like to help educate people. It's hard, because with my job I'm not exactly going to come out and say, "Hi! I'm in D&S, and I'm happy!" Because people are going to say, "Uh huh! And you also don't have a job!" But I think that, on an individual basis, I could talk to people who are upset by the fantasies that they have and reassure them that there are normal people doing this. I'm healthy and happy. This is not something for everybody, but if you want to do it, you won't drop dead. [Just] be careful about choosing who you do it with.

LEONARD

I'm somewhere between heterosexual and bisexual, switchable, but predominantly dominant. I haven't the foggiest idea how my D&S interests developed. Corporal punishment and discipline had no part in my upbringing, so none of that ever had a charge for me. I do vaguely remember a kind of excitement to tying people up or being tied up in [playing] cowboys and

Indians when I was around nine years old. They probably reoccurred at 11 or 12 with mixed-gender play. "Hey, maybe we can get some girls and we can make them be Indians!" But it was not a childhood obsession. And even as a late adolescent I wasn't really conscious of it, although I suspect it was there.

I was always a sensualist, so it was a place to explore. The trouble was I really couldn't at the time envision my lover surrendering and enduring humiliation and pain. So it grew in little steps. When I was in my mid-20s, in graduate school, I was involved with a woman who was about 10 years older than me who had grown up in Germany and was a business executive. We spent several nights a week at her home. I deferred to her. She would get very impatient with me and say, "Be a man. Tell me what to do. I'll do anything you want as long as I don't have to make the decision! I do that all day long; I get tired of bossing men around." I discovered she would do anything I wanted and enjoy it. Where we went to dinner, what movie, and also sexually, I could give her orders. And she would beg to be taken, and so I said, "Well, you know, somebody I love and respect *can* play this role, maybe not like [in] the fantasy fiction, but there are elements of reality [to it]."

Victoria will ask occasionally to take her collar off and for me to just make love to her rather than have her serve me. I do, and I really wonder whether an observer could tell the difference in our lovemaking. But for her, it is symbolic, and I can appreciate that. Obviously the observer could tell the difference from the times when she's bound, when spanking is involved, when she's covered in clothespins, or [when] nipple clamps are being screwed down as I make love to her. On the other hand, words have the [erotic] power of possession and control. So even while making physically very gentle love, [we] have given it a D&S spin by the labels we attach.

We playfully try to extend our D&S relationship out of the bedroom and into our lives a little bit. She will often address me as "sir." I come from a very liberal background where even grandparents were called by their first names, so it's not a matter of a strict household. "Sir" to my ears means "I love you." So each time she addresses me that way, it's a loving expression. Similarly, I like clothing or jewelry which are symbolic: a chain around her neck or a ring, preferably with a difficult clasp on it.

My favorite activities involve control of my submissive lover. This control can involve just touching her in a certain way at a movie theater and talking to her in a certain way. Or tying her up and making love to her and prohibiting her from coming, so it's a matter of control of sexuality. Control of an almost uncontrollable turns me on. Victoria [and I have done] scenes where she is bound and I place vast quantities of clothespins on her [body]—

50, 60 clothespins in rows on her body. It's pain [and a] sort of tension. I may then also drip candle wax and then use massage and vibrators to build up to the explosive release. I'm dripping sweat but get really turned on by the control I have over her, the power. Now it's not turned on in the literal sense—I may not have a roaring erection—but it's psychologically satisfying.

One part of our relationship is this kind of erotic control. Other parts I also enjoy [are] discipline, inflicting punishment, and Victoria's surrender to it. There are times when it's just a matter of punishment. We've agreed upon a certain number of strokes with a cane or a riding crop or something like that. Sometimes it's her job to begin: She knows she's done something wrong. She tells me, "I've done something wrong," and I say, "You'll have to be punished for that. What do you feel is appropriate?" She'll say, "20 strokes." Sometimes I will agree, and sometimes I'll say, "It was more serious; it will take 30." She will say, "Yes, sir." I'll decide whether to do it now or some later time, at which point I may ask her to bend over, lift her skirt. Or I may wait and take her to bed where she can be tied down, and then we'll start, often asking her to tell me when she's ready, and [to] ask for it. And I'll keep whipping till I feel she's real close to her limits. If she can't take much more, I will go one more and then stop. [With] the combination of whippings and caresses and the talking, she is often about ready to come when I finish.

Victoria likes to please me. But she's not a literal masochist in the sense of liking the pain. On the other hand, we recently visited some friends and were looking at their toys, and there was a very nice cane. Victoria was looking at it in that way that I knew. I lifted her skirt and tried it out. And she came. Victoria comes very easily. So she usually [has] an orgasm. Whereas I don't come easily anymore and don't have to.

Victoria has moved in with me. We are negotiating together how much a part of our life is D&S [and] what [to] label it. We're also negotiating a six-month contract—to see if it works and how far we can go. It will lay out the basic parameters. Her inclination was for a year. I, being older and wiser, shortened it. I feel there will be flack, of course, and I'm really a feminist by nature. An egalitarian. I'd only take a strong, confident person as a submissive, because then it meant it's a very valuable gift and one that I respect.

I [find] Victoria very beautiful and sweet and demure and open and trusting. We established a rapport with very few words. It became a strong relationship in a short time. I love her very much. She's really cute and charming. I have a lot of respect for her: She's a very bright woman. I take immense pride [knowing] that she's mine. I think that summarizes it: a mixture of love and pride.

BIFF

I'm heterosexual. I've had a couple of bisexual fantasies but never tried it. I have tried submissive, but I've been dominant for several years now. I'm not really sure why. I think it's like some people are homosexual; one day they discover that they are. I just discovered that I had this tremendous interest in S/M. It took me a while to discover my orientation, but I really enjoy it. I've had some very gratifying scenes. Something I've explained to my submissives is that I don't get any satisfaction out of it unless I know that the submissive is enjoying it. It is more of a foreplay. And it invariably ends in some type of sexual release.

There was a book I read and it primarily dealt with dominant females, but I think it carried over to dominant males, too. They said that there are some people who are dominant in their regular life and dominant in their D&S life, and they call them natural dominants, and then there were balancers who were rather submissive in their regular life and dominant in their sexual life. I think I'm more of a balancer. In my job I'm not really in charge of anything, but when I play a D&S scene I get to be in charge, and that gives me a very satisfying feeling.

People go to assertiveness training to be more assertive in their lives. I think I learned that from D&S. I [put] that in practice in my job and in my life. I feel surer of myself; I feel better about myself. I get more accomplished now [by] being more forceful and more assertive. In emergency medicine you have to be very diplomatic but very firm. I deal with the public all the time. One of the big problems in my life is that my job really doesn't have a whole lot of chance for promotion, so you don't get any satisfaction that way. It's often a thankless job. When you're out, you don't [usually] have a lot of control over what you're doing. I think that's why it's been so satisfying in my life to be a dominant. I can be in control of something; I can get a lot of satisfaction out of making things happen.

Right after I got out of the service, I started collecting a lot of literature on [D&S]. I realized that most of the literature was in adult bookstores and was kept real hush-hush and that a lot of the mainstream magazines considered it almost a dangerous fetish. It was very difficult for me to talk to my wife about it. I changed by talking to people. I met a couple that were very heavily into it. He was dominant, she was submissive, and they used to invite people over and just sit [and] talk with them. They knew a lot of other people. I started meeting people and seeing magazines that were devoted to it. I started realizing that there were a lot of people out there.

[At the time], we were having a lot of personal problems in our marriage. I think there was a lot of emotional and sexual tension in our relationship because I hadn't come to grips with [D&S] yet. We had a lot of problems until I started mentioning it to my wife. We talked it out. My wife was very understanding. She wasn't into it, [though] she tried it a little bit. She didn't like it, so she allowed me to go out and find partners for it. It took quite a while, but once I found partners and started to practice, I calmed down a lot. I think it's helped our relationship. There had been a lot of sexual tension, some anger and confrontation.

The only person I've ever done a submissive thing with was my wife. She's not a born dominant and it didn't go over very well, but the biggest thing I remember was that I kept imagining being the dominant while I was being submissive, and [I imagined] controlling the whole thing. I think that before a person becomes a full-fledged dominant, they should try a submissive scene. They have to try it first to know what it feels like.

I began to practice [D&S], and began to accumulate toys and video-tapes. I took my wife along to a couple of parties, where she was more or less a spectator. When she realized that I wasn't the only person out there—that I wasn't a serial killer, that it was just something sexual—she loosened up [and said], "Let me try a few things." She's gotten to like a few things. Light bondage and spanking have become a part of our relationship. We use a few toys—vibrators and dildos, a couple of restraints—but not too much. I think my wife still has a little apprehension. She had a very strict Catholic upbringing; [so] I think she thinks it's weird and a little sick. But she's beginning to enjoy it more. She makes a lot more suggestions and mentions it more frequently. In fact, she's asked for it on a few occasions, where she never used to before.

I've had two especially memorable experiences. One, when I first met this couple that I talked about before, it was so tremendously exciting to find attractive, intelligent people who were into the same things I was. I could talk freely with them about all this. They weren't afraid of it [and] didn't bear animosity towards me because of my feelings. Later in our relationship, they played a scene that they thought up, where she was delivered to my home and given to me. All she was wearing was a raincoat, a pair of handcuffs, fishnet nylons, and high heels. I was told that I could do anything I wanted with her. In the course of the next couple of hours, I tied her up to the ceiling, whipped her lightly; I took her down and put a dildo in her and brought her to orgasm a couple of times, played with nipple clips and stuff, and then had her do oral sex on me. Then her boyfriend arrived, and he said, "Now I get my payment," and he took my toys and went into my bedroom and played with her for about an hour. Afterwards, we all sat and had a drink, and it was very enjoyable for everybody. [It] was one of my ultimate fantasies to have a slave delivered to my door and just given to me. It was just fantastic.

The other scene that really sticks out was just recently. I [had] brought this girl along for several months, starting out very slowly. She was very apprehensive but very interested. It isn't a tremendous, overpowering part of her life, like it is for me, but she's still very turned on. We went to this group, and I guess she finally graduated. I never pushed her, [but] she finally said, "Maybe it's time for us to play." She stripped down to just high heels and cuffs and a collar, and I chained her up to a big cross and started whipping her and put nipple clips on her, and she started to moan. As I was playing with her, I asked, "Do you want me to stop?" And she said, "God, no!" I just kept playing with her vagina and clitoris and whipping her, and she came to three or four really powerful orgasms. It was a memorable scene, because she had been so apprehensive and so shy [before], and here she was, and we had maybe 20 people looking on. A couple of people actually clapped. It was quite a performance.

I would like my wife to come along and help me dominate my submissive. Maybe it's just because I want her to be a part of my life. I have expressed this fantasy to my wife. At first she said no, and in the last few months she's said maybe. I have this very attractive female submissive in Chicago. I've been visiting her, and my wife has gotten a little jealous over it. I think she realizes that we have a solid relationship, and it's going to stay that way, [but] S/M has to be part of my life. If she put her foot down and said, "You're not going to do that ever again. Give away all your toys, your movies," I think I would have to seriously consider ending our relationship.

The best advice I could give to somebody would be just write, write, write, write, write. Write ads; write letters; go to a club or an organization that deals with D&S. It took me years to get where I am, especially in a sleepy little Midwestern town. It takes forever to find somebody, but there are people out there. Don't get discouraged.

GENEVIEVE REYNOLDS
S/M, especially when I first was learning about it, was very explicit, very step-by-step. It made me aware of the process of taking control. S/M said, "You have the power to make choices for what happens in your life, and here's how you do it: say, 'This is what I need.' You have the power to make choices, and this is how you do it: negotiate." So, while feminism told me to act in certain ways, S/M actually showed me how.

For a long time when people would ask me, "Are you a top, bottom, switch?" I would say, "I'm a switch but mostly bottom; I get out my top energy dealing with the real world by being in charge of my own life." I've been able to take the ideas outside of my sex life into, say, dealing with bureaucracy. I learned early on that I could go into a situation and say, "I need you to do this for me." I try not to do it meanly, but people aren't used to women being in charge in their own lives—it takes them aback.

Sadomasochist is the most fully inclusive and descriptive word for me. I experimented actively with it in some of my earliest sexual relationships. S/M isn't what I do all the time, but it's the single thing that always has my attention. That's why I choose to say that I'm a sadomasochist rather than a bisexual woman or a lesbian sadomasochist or any of those other ways that I can describe myself.

As long back as I can remember, I've been fascinated by women's bodies. I had a hard time seeing where it fit into my everyday life. I was also interested in boys and in men, but that was more of a given, it was easier to do. Physically, a woman's body will always have my attention. A man has to be pretty darn special for me to pay much attention to him. Far too many men have accepted what the mainstream tells them they should be like; they just don't have enough humanity in them.

I was always very sexually curious, very precocious, always read well above my grade level, and was looking for information about all aspects of sex: reproductive information, sexual-variations information. I was intensely curious.

By age 14 or so, I [was reading] about bondage and anal sex. Those two had the biggest kicks for me then. I first read a publication by Samois [Author's note: a lesbian feminist S/M collective] when I was 18 or 19, and that was my first exposure not only to people doing this on purpose—I had been exposed to that before—but people doing it on purpose and thinking hard about it and applying analyses to it.

I never worried why I had these interests. My first boyfriend and I had been going out for a while before something reminded me there was this other stuff, too. I wanted him to top me in a very mild way. I really wanted to struggle a little and have him hold me down. But I didn't tell him. I couldn't bring myself to say a word. So while we were kissing and rolling around in the bed and kind of necking and doing foreplay things, I pushed him away just a little bit, not trying to really push him away. He was confused. He pulled back and gave me a funny look and tried to kiss me again. I tried it again, and after two or three times, he got up and walked to the other side of the room, all grumpy and *very* confused. He didn't have a clue about what I was trying to do! So we sat there unhappy for a few minutes, and I said, "What's wrong?" And he said, "What's going *on*? I'm confused!" That was probably the hardest moment of my life! I had to get the words out to say, "I want you to hold me down; I want you to push a little bit." Then he said, "If that's what you want, sure, we can give that a try." So we gave it a try, and we talked about it afterwards. He'd be happy to do it for me if I wanted him to, but he didn't really get it! We did it a few more times. I suspect we didn't do it more because it didn't do anything for him, and so a lot of the thrill wasn't there for me, either.

I've always been a switch, but I'm in a transition. I always got a great deal of pleasure from bottoming—direct visceral pleasure. The pleasure I got from topping was not as direct; I am not a natural top. I enjoy [it], but topping wasn't something that I automatically wanted to do: It was specific to a person who wanted me to do that. Just recently I have found women I was attracted to who were interested in S/M. My attraction was so intense that I just thought, I want to do S/M with this person; I don't care how it has to happen. I have a girlfriend of several months now. We didn't intend to get serious, but it's gotten very serious. She is a bottom, and I've been doing all the topping. We've both been enjoying it a great deal.

As a bottom I like things that make me the center of attention. A few times I've been in scenes where I was ignored for long periods. I got very bored. I like a lot of physical attention, both painful and nonpainful. I like sexual play, and sometimes I like play where nothing sexual happens at all. I haven't done formal meditation, but it seems to me that [pain] does something similar to what meditation [or] yoga can do, because you're focusing your body, and your mind can be free to drift and not think analytically at all.

S/M is the only time that I'm only paying attention to one thing. Even in the middle of sex, I find myself being distracted [by] work or the dishes! S/M gets me completely focused. There have been a few times when everything has been just right, and it got to where I could take anything. I don't know where the energy goes. It's like a balloon breaking! I'm getting closer and closer to something, [it's] swelling up in me, all the energy from the beating is going inside and staying there, and as I get to that stage, it's broken. The energy is flowing real freely through my body and out of my body and, God, yes, anything can happen at that point.

Unfortunately, the first time I lived away from my parents' house, I was young and uncertain. I lived with a dominant who was a couple of years older than me. He had a lot more experience. I deferred to his life experience and stopped trusting my own intuition. There was emotional domination that wasn't Scene domination. I got into S/M for good reasons, but the relationship itself got twisted because we were both young. We did lots of play where I was submissive in ways that more than anything else looked like a traditional heterosexual relationship.

If you've ever talked to women who are in battered relationships, you'll hear a lot of what I'm saying here. I'd gotten very confused; I lost my sense of who I was. I lost the ability to objectively and independently judge what was going on around me. I was trying to figure out why this stuff that had been so exciting and wonderful at the beginning had gotten so scary. I puzzled it through and realized that there was an emotional dynamic that was happening which wasn't S/M. Coming to the realization—that the S/M was great, but that the things that were going on that I didn't like were not the same as the S/M—was very powerful for me. [This] allowed me to get out of the relationship and not blame the sex. To be able to separate those things is very valuable. I've read writings by women who were "saved" from a life of perversion; they didn't separate those things. I read sadness in their words.

[In order for a] full-time D&S relationship to work, you have to be much more aware and negotiate more thoroughly and be able to talk about stuff and say, "When you did this, I felt that way." S/M is not a matter of activity nor of degree: It's a matter of intention.

IMAGINATION AND DESIRE

Four

POWER

To lie at the feet of an imperious mistress, to obey her commands, to ask her forgiveness—this was for me a sweet enjoyment.
                                                                —JEAN-JACQUES ROUSSEAU[1]

Power—its uses and abuses—makes the world go 'round. To most people, power is a political, economic, or social phenomenon which often entails the assertion of superiority over others for personal or group gain. But to the D&Ser, the power exchange between lovers is a fundamental source of erotic excitement, shared by equals, and often an intellectually enlightening experience.

A lot of people think S/M is about conquest: about domineering rather than domination. For me, that's not what it's about at all.

When we begin to play there [may] be some resistance, because we're not trained to gracefully surrender personal power. Submission is an alternate way of dealing with power, a way of exploring the nature of your own power, how to access it and choosing to turn it over or not. Choice is the key. S/M is a tool for surrender.

—M. CYBELE

In this chapter, we explore the erotic potency of power. We profile six people for whom the power exchange is a critical aspect of their sexual play:

- M. Cybele is 42 years old. She is a professional dominant, sex educator, and transformation counselor to the transgender community. Her life partner is James W.
- James W. is 47 years old. He is a writer and a teacher.
- Sri Shivaynanda is 48 years old. He is a former Air Force pilot and now works in the film industry in California. He is a spokesperson for the Service of Mankind Church (SMC).
- Morgan Lewis is in her 50s and is on the board of directors of the Eulenspiegel Society. She is an entertainer and a professional massage therapist. She has children.
- Ralph R. is 32 years old and married. He works in biomedical research.
- Rising Star is in her mid-30s. She is a computer programmer and lives with her husband and children.

WHY DOES THE SUBMISSIVE YIELD POWER?

Submission, as it is popularly defined, is an act of resignation or defeat, a bowing against one's will to a superior, frequently impersonal authority. While some D&S roleplaying may emulate such dismal realities, for most D&Sers submission is often, paradoxically, an act of liberation and also the realization of a private and profound need.

My soul yearns to be able to let somebody else take control, to be able to not have to make the decisions, to not be concerned about what errors I'm going to make. —SLAVE V.

Desire precedes action: Submissives consciously seek out opportunities to enact pleasurable fantasies of being sexually controlled. Historically, psychologists have attributed the desire to submit sexually as a craving for expiation of sexual guilt. This generalization appears to hold true for some submissives, for whom the psychodrama of coercion—in which the dominant, albeit consensually, "forces" them to accept erotic activity—relieves their individual responsibility for sexual desire. When lust is viewed as a shameful moral flaw, erotic coercion helps the submissive to surrender to sexual pleasure.

> *I think some of this goes back to 12 years of Catholic school: It's dirty to have sex. The Virgin Mary was the mother of Christ, and she's the one we're supposed to look up to. [Having been] taught that sex is bad, I've wondered if perhaps the only way I can enjoy it is if I'm completely tied down and helpless. Because, if I'm helpless, I can't stop the person from doing that terrible sexual scene to me; I can't help it if I came, because I'm tied down, and he made me come.*
> —SLAVE V.

Other classic and condemnatory explanations for sexual submission include low self-esteem, weakness, passivity, and regressed sexuality. Theorists who have suggested these causes have relied primarily on anecdotal information from a limited base of troubled clients. The resulting theories seem to reflect the theorists' individual biases against sexual variations.

> *The outside world thinks that submission is a place of low or no esteem and no personal power: that [submissives] are wimps. In fact it is an exchange, an alternate way of looking at power. It's also a way of exploring what your power is. You know, the more power you give away, the more power you must have! You can't give away what you don't have.*
> —M. CYBELE

Theories that submission is inherently a behavior of victims may account for the neo-Freudian (and pseudo-Darwinian) eagerness to classify submissiveness as a predominantly female phenomenon. Such theories fail to consider that consenting submissives are unlikely to exhibit these characteristics in other areas of their lives. Furthermore, submissive men comprise the single largest component of D&S culture. What clinicians have not explored is the main source of pleasure for the sexual submissive: a transcendent delight in surrender.

> *[I want] to surrender as a way to give up my need to control my universe. To trust that my top, Cybele, will take care of it and take care of me, to trust that I can let go and have whatever experience I'm going to have. In my life this experience tends to be transcendental and cosmic because I'm that kind of guy. For somebody else it may be something else.*
> —JAMES W.

The predominant truism in D&S culture is that the sexual submissive is usually someone who, in daily life, has weighty responsibilities. Which comes first is unknown: the submissive impulse, which may lead one to overcompensate in adulthood by pursuing high-power careers, or stressful careers, which lead individuals to seek an outlet in submission. The archetypal submissive is said to be a top executive who longs to yield all responsibility to another person during erotic play.

> *The people who are submissive are generally the most dominant in life: They're heads of corporations, they're people who are in a decision-making process all the time. What they're saying is, "I'm tired of making decisions; I'm tired of having control all the time. I want to relax. Do me! Take the control away from me. Let me have some time."* —MARIE-CONSTANCE

This need to escape responsibility is hardly limited to high-powered executives; it extends to others encumbered by the tensions and responsibilities of daily life, including dominants.

> *I'm predominantly a top, but I [occasionally] bottom: I'm so in charge in most of my life that it is a relief for me to turn my vulnerability and power over to someone I respect and trust. It is a great joy for me not to have to be in charge for a certain amount of time. I do not want to abdicate responsibility in life. I love life and what I do. But it's a breather, and different [from] a massage or a hot tub. I'm involved with someone who will take me beyond where I could go alone, someone who will respect the gift of my submission.* —M. CYBELE

The period of submission is, in effect, a time when worldly obligations are cast aside; a time of surrender and receptivity to the stimulus that the dominant bestows. No decisions must be made, and no distractions reduce the intensity of perception.

> *I characterize [my submissiveness] mostly as a chance to let loose. After a day of making decisions, [it] is a chance to not be in control and to not always have to worry about [everything]: letting somebody else take over.* —PHIL T.

Submission is a turning away from the social and a penetration into a sacrosanct internal space. This may be why many submissives compare their erotic experience to a religious or spiritual surrender. The surrender is a means of achieving a kind of freedom from ego, a condition where one is completely trusting and undefensive.

Since adolescence I have loved to sit in churches, temples, mosques, synagogues, it really doesn't matter: Sacred space is sacred space. I don't see any value in separating eroticism and spirituality. I see them as deeply allied. The process of S&M spirituality, of going into role as into a prayer space and maintaining that for days, for weeks even, makes me serene and beneficent. I try to borrow from that space when I teach, because it is a space of absolute service. By learning to surrender that way, I learned to top. —JAMES W.

For many, submission is a supreme form of nakedness—a desirable exposure. It permits one to explore absolute powerlessness in a safe context, knowing that no actual harm will occur and that one will not be condemned or ridiculed. The sexually timid or socially introverted person may find in submission a place where outrageous exhibitionism is not only permissible but profoundly exciting to the partner. Submission is, in some ways, a topsy-turvy world where the submissive is precisely what he is not (and would not choose to be) in daily or social life: Macho men are petticoated trollops; feminists are love slaves; the fastidious are soiled; hedonists accept extreme pain; and the liberated enter stringent bondage only to find, paradoxically, that they feel even freer.

Breaching taboo is an important element in many submissives' pleasures. In this respect, submission is deliberately antisocial. Behaviors normally circumscribed or prohibited in conventional sexual relations are explicitly supported and investigated. These explorations delve into everything from taboo mental games to extreme invasions of physical privacy or experimentation with forbidden stimuli. Some individuals feel exhilarated precisely because of the thrill of defying sexual conventions. They are "playing at the edge" of sexuality and taboo.

Another key element of submission is a warm combination of trust and consolation.

When I submit, I have to trust somebody a lot more than I would ordinarily think of trusting someone and I show a lot more of myself. That's very satisfying. It's a sense of belonging, being at home, being comfortable. —RISING STAR

Emotional gratification is as important to most submissives as are individual acts. Unlike masochism, submission is not primarily physical. Within the context of a power exchange, a deeper emotional drama of acceptance is played out. Again, it's worth noting the fundamental paradox of D&S: People who are unlikely to be trusting in their social lives may, sexually, place a complete trust in the dominant partner. When this trust is well placed, submissives often experience a shock of delight. The same things that might be perceived by the sexually conventional as flaws or failures (such as a raging libido or sexual fetishes) are acceptable and appreciated in a D&S context.

Submissive activities cover a broad range. Some people (and this seems more true of men than of women) enjoy being ordered to do simple things, such as cleaning the dominant's house. Elaborate conquest fantasies in which the submissive is forced to accept punishment are also popular. The variety is endless (which is why we devote individual chapters to some of the most popular forms of erotic play). Suffice it to say that submission in a D&S context is one of the rare times when the revelation of one's deepest and most forbidden sexual desires is not merely tolerated but is lovingly encouraged and rewarded. This acceptance often makes submissives feel very grateful toward the understanding and concerned dominant.

Because the conscious submissive makes a clear choice—alert to the implications of submitting, aware of the risks, and intent on maximizing personal pleasure—the D&S dynamic is often described as a power exchange. Many see this as a therapeutic transaction between equally powerful individuals.

> For me, submission is not about being passive or giving up because you're weak. It's about voluntarily turning over your own power to somebody else. When I bottom I do [it] from the point of view that I have great power ana give it as a gift with full trust that the top will respect and appreciate the gift of my vulnerability. As a top, I'm interested in people giving me their power. I don't need to rip it from them. I don't elevate myself by putting them down.
>
> —M. CYBELE

Finally, intellectualizing aside, our interviewees agreed on one point: For them, submission is a path to sexual ecstasy.

> I tried submitting, but nobody ever found that mental key [to reach] inside me. And then one time I submitted, and there was a great deal of teasing combined with some whipping. It built into incredible arousal. What made an impression on me was that I was begging to come! I was finally given permission to come, and one hand was untied, but I was only allowed to come if I masturbated with the handle of the whip. I didn't care what would have happened, who could have walked in then; I couldn't have stopped. This was something I had to do!
>
> —RISING STAR

> One of the things I discovered through S&M was that Wilhelm Reich was right: It is possible to have a whole body orgasm. I can still

*have an ordinary genital orgasm—that's fine, I like it—but I've
also discovered an orgasm that starts at the base of the spine; rides
up my spine; convulses my body; snaps my head back and forth;
explodes out the crown of my head; makes my feet go shake, shake,
shake, and twitter; twitter, twitter, and just keeps going on and on
and on and on and on and on, and when it finally stops, I can do
it again. And again and again. It's more intense, more compelling,
more complete than a genital orgasm and doesn't stop me from
having the genital orgasm, too. That, for me, is the physical pleasure
of erotic surrender.*   —JAMES W.

Such testimony may partly explain why the majority of D&Sers switch
roles. A number of our interviewees stated that after acting out dominant
fantasies and observing the exaltation of submissives, they were eager to
discover whether they could enjoy a similar pleasure.

WHY DOES THE
DOMINANT SEIZE POWER?

Dominance is the yang to submission's yin: It is the desire to exert control
over a consenting partner for the purpose of mutual gratification. If submission is an escape from ego, dominance is the ultimate ego trip, a time when
one exerts absolute control over another's reality and holds the key to his or
her partner's pleasure. The exhilaration of dominance begins with a psychological and intellectual satisfaction, a satisfaction that extends to the erotic.

*The personal enjoyment I [derive] is, first, intellectual: I can figure
out what the person needs. Then there's aesthetic enjoyment: knowing
how to do it. And there's knowing the level of trust that's given to
me: It's a tremendous trust.*   —CLÉO DUBOIS

Perhaps the single most important element in the power exchange is the
solid emotional bond that develops between dominant and submissive, a
bond born of the submissive's trusting compliance in the moment of submission.

*An S/M whipping is an act of love. It's using a tool, the whip, to
create a bond between two people, to take the bottom out of herself
and to let the top take the trust and the energy and build it higher
and higher until it becomes magic. I actually like the term S/M
better than S&M, because S/M to me means "Sexual Magic."*
                                 —ROBIN YOUNG

Most dominants seem specifically aroused by their partners' pleasure.

When I top somebody, I know I have them in control, and I get an erotic rush out of their erotic rushes. Knowing my partner is getting off on it [is] wonderful for me. —JEAN L.

Generally, the dominant is aroused by his ability to control circumstances, to award or withhold pleasure.

I often feel ineffectual, that the world goes on, and no matter what I do, I cannot influence it. So when I see clearly that there's even one person who I can exert an influence on and to whom my every action is very important, it's satisfying. It's a feeling of affirmation.
—LEONARD

Dominants, too, may enjoy the submissive's dependency and emotional nakedness—at least for the term of play. Most of the dominants we spoke with stressed that they seek equals as partners, people who are in control of their daily lives, but taking such an individual and reducing him to a condition of erotic helplessness is electrifying for the dominant, reaffirming the dominant's sense of personal power.

While some dominants are turned on by fairly stringent codes of etiquette (for example, that all submissives must address them as "Master" or "Mistress"), overall, dominants are likely to be flexible about what activities actually occur in a D&S encounter. A majority of dominants whom we interviewed indicated that they experiment with a broad range of fantasies and activities.

Members of the D&S communities frequently debate exactly how much power a dominant genuinely possesses. Many of our interviewees, for example, felt that in the final analysis, the submissive runs a D&S relationship.

Dominants are generally submissive to the will of submissives. They are good at what they do. I'm talking about good dominants, people who really understand what the Scene is about. I'm not talking about masochists and sadists, but about submissives and dominants at this moment. —MARIE-CONSTANCE

A submissive can control a scene. Actually, ultimately, the submissive controls the scene totally, unless she's with a nut.
—CARTER STEVENS

Although dominants may not be mere facilitators of the submissive's fantasy, many certainly place a priority on pleasing the submissive by acting according to his or her demands.

A lovely phrase that someone [used during] a lecture on the subject was, "Try not pleasing your submissive one time, and find out who's actually in control. They won't be around very long!" [D&S] acts are always discussed ahead of time, especially until you know new people and where they're headed and what their likes and dislikes are. —GYPSY

This point of view is not shared by all dominants. Many dominants avoid and disdain submissives who set too many conditions and firmly believe that a good dominant retains absolute rights over exactly what will take place. Lifestylers, particularly, may adhere to the principle that once the submissive has consented to the relationship, the dominant then establishes and controls all limits.

Styles of dominance are often extensions of closely held religious or social philosophies. A small percentage of dominants, for example, believes that the opposite gender is inherently inferior. Others seem to equate dominance with nobility, which may account for the proliferation of Scene names such as "Lord" or "Lady," "Duchess" or "Duke," and even "Empress." A large number of our interviewees were influenced by cult books, such as *Story of O,* and strive to replicate the fiction in reality. Others experiment with their partners to see what type of activities are most rewarding for both and do not bother with labels. Those active in the Scene often avoid playing the role of omniscient dictator and prefer unaffected behavior.

I don't tell people I'm perfect. I'm real. I think that if I couldn't be myself, if I [could] only be the mistress on a pedestal, I could not keep doing this work. —CLÉO DUBOIS

In traditional leather culture dominants undergo a period of apprenticeship to an experienced dominant during which they learn responsible dominance. Some dominants experiment with submission to gain insight into the submissive experience. This is called *starting from the bottom.*

I think you've got to get into somebody's shoes to know how it is for that person. So I like to submit from time to time. —MASTER CHRIS

The willingness or ability to switch does not, however, apply to all D&Sers.

Dominants particularly enjoy cultivating their imaginative abilities and inventing new ways to play.

If I start a relationship with a submissive woman, I have a lot of work to do because I've got to come up with something new and

different every time. I think that if we were to do the same scene over and over again, after two or three times it wouldn't be interesting.
—MASTER CHRIS

Some dominants use the metaphor of playing a musical instrument to describe the process of arousing their partners to an intense pitch of excitement. They prod the submissive to accept increased input and intensity of stimulus. This is called *pushing limits* or *stretching limits*.

I enjoy pushing people to their limits, no matter what that means. I enjoy bringing people to that place where they are not sure if they can go just a little bit more and [then] taking them there, stretching [their] limits. That's where I get the rush of the S&M.
—CLÉO DUBOIS

A final but important component is the aesthetic of D&S: Whether it is pride in one's skilled bondage techniques or selection of outfits that accentuate the submissive's sex appeal, dominants frequently enjoy complex and lengthy rituals of altering the visual and the physical to create an unusual and deeply satisfying image.

EROTIC COERCION

Force is not a part of the province of sadism and masochism, not part of the territory of leather and latex, bondage and discipline. It is normal. Coercion is an accepted part of daily life for most people.
—PAT CALIFIA[2]

A complex and apparently self-contradictory aspect of D&S roleplaying, erotic "coercion" refers to the submissive being compelled to do something which he protests and which may be fundamentally humiliating. At the same time, this sense of coercion is precisely what makes the experience so arousing.

Erotic coercion is based on mutual consent; the activity is often planned in detail beforehand. For example, a male-to-female transvestite might fantasize about meeting a woman who will unexpectedly compel him to dress, walk, talk, and act like a girl. That any given woman, no matter how charitable, will spontaneously attempt to transform a man into a woman is highly unlikely. Further, that a sensible submissive would yield power to someone he doesn't know or trust is even less likely. The transvestite must find someone who is amenable—and discuss his fantasy in detail. Consequently, how believable is it that the female is *forcing* someone who has so assiduously sought out and meticulously delineated a scenario?

Suspension of disbelief is a requirement in coercion scenarios. The competent dominant is charged with the responsibility of making the scenario believable. To the outsider, there is no external logic. How is it that a petite woman can force a man twice her size to his knees in shivering, whimpering helplessness with nothing more than a few soft words? But the internal logic is indisputable, if one assumes that the mind is a person's most powerful erotic tool. Coercion scenarios depend on the submissive's ability to enter into the fantasy and to feel that he is being forced to accept something, even if that something is precisely what the submissive craves. The dominant, correspondingly, is aroused by the fantasy of forcing someone to bend to her will.

> *I am into intellectual games. I like control. I like to find out what my submissive partner most enjoys. It might mean that my male partner is drawn to the idea of dressing in women's clothes. A man in women's clothes does not turn me on [in] itself. But [if] my partner [is] struggling with the desire to do it versus feeling uncomfortable or guilty about it—now that turns me on. I have the power to do that to him. The ideal submissive, from my point of view, is someone with a lot of imagination, who isn't totally comfortable with everything that he's doing or has room to learn something.*
>
> —RISING STAR

If the dominant is convincingly stern, or if other elements—such as pain or bondage—are involved, the submissive believes, within the moment (and often long after the moment has passed), in the dominant's absolute authority.

Coercion scenarios take so many forms that any catalogue would be incomplete. Naughty schoolboys are compelled to accept spankings from indignant governesses; feisty submissives are forced to wear the collars of strict masters; foot worshipers are imperiously commanded to kiss a lover's toes; captive maidens must submit to ravishment by conquering lords. Literally thousands of scenes are played out in which the submissive is "forced" to do essentially what the submissive really wants to do. Regularly, thousands of submissives are forced to achieve multiple orgasms.

Coercion can, of course, have a darker side, even when the relationship in which it is practiced is negotiated. This darker side arises when dominants push submissives to accept activities that the submissives may genuinely dread. A dominant may, for example, compel her partner to accept increasing levels of intensity of stimulation. And some dominants punish submissives who willfully disobey; the intent is not to harm the submissive, but it may cause the submissive discomfort or sadness. Some D&Sers do not believe in punishment but it is a real phenomenon, particularly in lifestyle relationships, where discipline may form a critical aspect of the dynamic. In fact, lifestyle submissives often desire both the risk and the reality of punishment, because it reinforces the reality of the power relationship. Sometimes a submissive will purposely misbehave—usually in playful ways—to incite the dominant to punish him or her.

THE WORSHIP OF POWER

D&Sers are intrigued by power. In some respects they are as responsible as mainstream individuals for perpetuating the myths about dominants as ruthless or imperious. Nowhere is this truer than among people who have evolved their fantasies and understandings about power relationships from cult books (such as the novels of de Sade, Pauline Réage, John Norman, and Anne Rice) and the seemingly limitless supply of fetish and S/M pornography. The literature that kindles so many fiery fantasies depicts characters who are almost always one-dimensional, no doubt because the purpose of most S/M-oriented literature is specifically licentious and not concerned with reality.

Novice D&Sers may believe that dominants are singularly appointed, semimystical creatures endowed with the power to reduce submissives to craven supplicants. This charming fantasy often succumbs to the reality of humanity among those who seek full-fledged relationships. Many who confine their experiences to episodic encounters, however, prefer to cling to the fantasy of the dominant as *ubermensch* (or *uberfrau*).

The dominant, for some, is the embodiment of a childish nightmare of the cruel or monstrous parent. Thus, even though all dominants are not cruel (some are), some submissives need them to be cruel—at least for the sake of erotic stimulation. But not all power is ruthless. A favorite activity among many D&Sers is the worship of a benign (albeit inherently quixotic) figure. In D&S culture this is usually a dominant woman who is perceived either to be a goddess herself or to embody the spirit of a goddess.

One of the better-known groups associated with the D&S Scene is the Service of Mankind Church (SMC), a California-based religious group whose theology is founded on goddess worship. The focus of a sociological study (*Erotic Power*),[3] the SMC's philosophy specifically stresses spiritualism, but its rituals have been a magnet for secular submissive men and dominant women as well. The church holds that women who pursue a certain spiritual path may embody the spirit of goddesses worshiped in other (usually Eastern) cultures. In this hierarchy men are inherently submissive to women who manifest divine qualities.

> *The female of our species has the capacity to be a goddess when [she] believes in the religious path that we follow. We [sometimes] have a problem with dominant women because potentially they are goddesses, but they have to recognize that [the] goddess spirit is being worshiped itself. There are some really hot dominant females out there who'd love to sit on a throne, but we have pointed out that when you sit on the throne [and] men grovel in front of you, you must enter into a meditational space [and] focus that goddesslike energy. A lot of women just can't do that.* —SRI SHIVAYNANDA

Goddess worship may take any of several forms. It may be a natural outgrowth of the spiritual aspects of sexual submission.

> *For me, submission is a spiritual practice. I look to surrender in a kind of transpersonal way. Cybele's mistress persona is very closely allied with a goddess persona. I don't want to say that she thinks of herself as the goddess—I'm sure she would say that everybody is a god or goddess. She is willing to acknowledge that and to work with that energy. There is a persona for me who is a priest. The priest likes to be naked on his knees and to worship. We're not very interested in washing windows, though we do that service, you know.*
> —JAMES W.

The worship may involve practical service, such as caring for the dominant's possessions (e.g., boots, clothing, equipment). These services become symbolically loaded.

> *The thing that [my friend] likes most is doing everything that I want. That seems to be his main thing: to surrender to me and do things to make me happy. He's more or less worshiping me as a goddess. I like that. I believe this sincerely: I've always felt like I was a queen. Some men [including him] have this idea that women are superior and that all men should bow down to [them]. He believes this in his whole karma.*
> —MORGAN LEWIS

Although goddess worship seems to be the domain of straight submissive men, nontheological body worship is practiced by both male and female submissives. In a D&S context the submissive honors and adores the dominant by ecstatically kissing or caressing body parts—usually legs and feet, but also hands and arms and, of course, erogenous zones—often in a kneeling or prone position.

> *[Some men] just want to worship my body, my body odors, whatever my body's doing. One guy wanted to stick his nose into my armpit.*
> —MORGAN LEWIS

Body worship is a supreme romantic surrender by the submissive to her dominant, and, for the dominant, an exciting display of the submissive's humility and devotion.

INTERVIEWS

M. CYBELE

[S/M has] affected and expanded my life in a very positive manner. I'm a convert to D&S and S/M from being a bisexual, multiorgasmic, fun-loving gal who thought S/M was sick. In the late '70s I had a successful career as a burlesque artist. The idea was to entertain—not to get people off, but to tease. Men brought their wives. It was quite erotic and fun. I was sexually sophisticated but misinformed about S/M: All I knew about it came from bad pornography. But then in 1979 a new roommate moved in with me. I found her extremely domineering and bossy, and when she told me she was getting into S/M, I thought, No wonder she's so aggressive—she's into that sick stuff of abusing and humiliating people!

Then my roommate joined the Society of Janus. After only two meetings she said, "I'm sorry for being nonconsensually dominant. I only want to do power games in the bedroom, and then with people who want to do them with me. S/M is not what you think it is." I was amazed by the change in her and became intrigued because if something was happening sexually that was good that I didn't know about, well . . . where do I sign up? I went to a Janus orientation and was astonished: People were committed to talking about the forbidden and about safety. They were working on communicating, on negotiating. I'm an est graduate, and I've been in a lot of groups, [but] I had never seen *this* level of conversation. Most people don't even talk about straight sex!

The people at Janus were talking about what worked and what didn't and *why*, and how to negotiate what you want and don't want when you do S/M. I was fascinated by the level of honesty. Janus has a rule, which is that if you don't have an interest in S/M, you're not allowed to join. This keeps out the people who are just curious, journalists, and therapists who want to study us like bugs under a microscope. I wanted to join so I was very frank. I said, "This is all new to me, and my erotic interests are mainly costume, sexual theater, and masturbation. I enjoy sex with people, and I'm very multiorgasmic when I masturbate. I don't know if I qualify, but I'm seriously interested in joining." They decided that my interest in costume and sexual theater could be considered a fetish, and they felt I would be a good addition. I appreciated that. I attended almost every program they had because I quickly realized that I didn't know *anything*. I went to programs on piercing, bondage, sensory deprivation, gender, fetishes, whipping, you name it. I didn't know where I fit in, but it was erotic, informative, and fun. I don't fantasize when I have sex [or] when I masturbate. I never have. I'm very much in what I see and hear and smell and feel and taste. So when a young man approached me at a Janus meeting and said, "I'd like to be at your service, anything you want," I wasn't able to tell him a thing. I didn't know how to get the dynamic [started]. But I kept going to meetings, I kept talking to people, and I kept listening and asking questions.

I couldn't seem to find my niche, yet I knew that there was a higher drama than what I was experiencing. One reason I was into masturbation is that no matter how much I loved somebody, after a while the sex was predictable. My mind would wander. I thought, Why can't I stay focused? Am I afraid of intimacy? The truth is that I need high drama, or intensity. After the first flush of infatuation wears off, the drama's gone. In S/M this drama can be very intimate and very personal; it's not phony drama. It's also difficult to let the mind wander if you're truly involved in a D&S or S/M scene. More than just the genitals are involved. When the purpose of the interaction is not just orgasm but another kind of release as well, one moves to a deeper level of relationship that is more sophisticated and requires more thought and communication.

In 1983 I went to work for a phone sex company. Within two weeks my dominant persona emerged. Boom! I think I had been afraid to take power. I [remember] that when I was nine—my parents were separated when I was four—my mother and I [had] a big argument. I won and she was reduced to a helpless, hysterical quivering pile of tears. I had this *enormous* rush of power like, "TA DA!! I'm in charge!" followed by hysteria, because, if at nine years old I was in charge, we were in big trouble! Later in life it was hard for me to start scenes because I was scared about what was going to happen next. But on the phone, it's so distant; and most of the people I was dealing with didn't really want to submit. They wanted somebody to play out [a] fantasy. The fantasy [aspect] made it safe for me to act the role and ease my way into true dominance. Eventually *pretending* to be dominant became boring and a little frustrating. I began to ask the client if he would be willing to try genuinely being dominated over the phone. Some agreed and I started to explore the actual world of D&S. This has *never* been boring, professionally or personally. I've found it to be challenging, rewarding and a true path of self-awareness. Once I started playing with power in an erotic context I became aware of its uses and abuses in the rest of the world. I became a better communicator and negotiator—not only did I know about power games, I had played them out in a safe, fun, erotic way.

I went to work as a mistress-in-training for a professional mistress in late

1983. I was submissive to her and—under her instruction—dominant over the clients. I learned how to start a scene, what to do in the middle, and how to wrap it up. I found a framework upon which to hang my own interests. After about a month or two, I put an ad in the paper. In 1985 my roommate moved out so that we could turn her bedroom into a dungeon, and we began working together. I opened my own place and I did it mostly by slave labor. I got a phone call from a young man who was a painter and plasterer interested in D&S. We had a satisfying relationship on both sides, and he replastered and repainted my entire apartment.

I'm very involved in the S/M community in San Francisco now. I teach in it, I play in it, most of my friends are S/M people: not all, but most. I can be all of who I am in that world. When I go into a community that is not S/M-positive, sometimes I tell them that I'm a sex educator. I can be who I am, but not completely, because there's a part of me that may not [be] fully respected and accepted in that world. In my community I feel loved and accepted. When I got sick and was hospitalized with a herniated disc, all [my] money went towards paying bills. But the community raised money for me, did my shopping, cleaned my house; people came and bathed me at the hospital. Six months later people still called, asking, "What can I do?" I have an experience of being part of a tribe that appreciates its elders—I mean, I'm not that old, but I'm appreciated for what I know, what I give, and how I learn and teach.

[Professionally] I specialize in gender play, infantilism, and slave training with a pleasure-pain dynamic. Each [situation] has different emotional, physical, psychological, sexual, and spiritual intents. My erotic interests are extensive and varied both privately and professionally. This is important professionally because unless you're remarkably skilled it's difficult to make a living with only one interest, such as bondage or S/M. So I do a wide range of activities, including fetishism, such as shoe/boot/foot worship, or various psychodrama scenarios.

I don't do anything illegal. I don't do degradation scenes. That's a limit *I* have. I have a hard time both privately and professionally doing something that I believe could encourage or reinforce low self-esteem. For me humiliation and degradation are two very different activities on a large continuum, starting with mild embarrassment and ending with extreme self-abasement and degradation. In the middle could fall teasing, mockery, humiliation, and the stripping away of *false* pride. I believe it's possible to do degradation scenes safely but that it's very tricky and requires follow-up aftercare by the top. I don't do anything unsafe in terms of S/M or health. There's no oral sex, anal sex, intercourse, or masturbation by me for legal reasons. The second reason I don't do anything directly sexual is that I like keeping something for my life partner. As a sex worker, I feel it's very important to have activities that are only for my personal relationships.

One group of clients I see are people who are interested in giving up power in a manner that is not competitive or rebellious. I do a lot of slave training and mental control. Usually such a person is someone who is in control a great deal in his life. He is looking for a place to relax and safely put all his power. Mental control alone is not always sufficient. Pain can be an aphrodisiac, but it also can be a very powerful reminder to someone that he is right here right now and not in charge. It's difficult to let your mind wander when your body is experiencing a very intense [physical] sensation. I use some bondage so that people have the experience of being unable to get away, or so that their bodies are altered in some manner. It's an experience that is separate from the rest of their lives. It's an experiential process, not an analytical one.

Being told how to stand, sit, kneel, lie, where to look, how to address me, how to serve me food or drink, how to be there just for me, can be very freeing. To put someone else's desires ahead of one's own, to receive pleasure solely from pleasing someone else can be very good for the soul. I've heard slaves say that they feel most free inside when they're enslaved. When you affect the body—whether with ropes, diapers, clothes, sensation, or other control—you affect the mind.

There are many games and many different styles. What's a turn-on for me may be a turn-off for another dominant and vice versa. One of the most exciting experiences for me, both professionally and in my private life, is to be with someone who wants to please, serve, and submit. Resistance games are fun, but I don't find it erotic to have my power repeatedly challenged. My friend does; she works perfectly with this dynamic and so I refer those clients to her. I like to lead someone down an intense road of submission, service, and S/M. I'm strict and sadistic, yet gentle and compassionate. I want a person to get outside himself. Pain and bondage are means to this end. I love to look at complicated bondage, but it seems to me that the person usually goes on an inner journey. This is a profound journey, but I'm not this type of guide.

I'm a neopagan, goddess worshiper. I believe that in every human being there is a spiritual source. Some people call it a higher power; for me it's the higher power within *and* without. I like to be worshiped and adored, but I'm clear that it's not the ego-inflated human but a greater power within that's being adored.

JAMES W.

I think of every day as an adventure in my life, and every day as an adventure in my relationship. I love to find out where my limits are and go beyond them. For me, what goes on in all of these experiences is the exchange of what I call "psychic energy." When Freud used the term *libido,* he meant sexual energy. When Jung used the term, he meant life-force energy, which is much closer to what the Hindus mean by kundalini, the energy that's supposed to lie coiled at the base of the spine until experience wakes it. In my experience, when S&M does not work, the result is simply two egos or bodies getting together. When it does work, it involves a different level of interaction and being. For some people, this level is activated by intense sensation. For others—and this is more true for me than not—that level is reached through mind games. It's not that somebody else controls my mind but that I voluntarily give up the power to make certain kinds of choices. What I give up is negotiated in a specific situation at a specific time. This to me [is] the universe of D&S.

Although I have been in a specifically S&M or D&S relationship for only several years, it looks to me as if the exchange of erotic power has been present throughout my life, in all my relationships. And as I look at the way most people interact, it seems to me that it is present in most people's relationships most of the time. There is a little dance in which one person becomes the seeker and one person becomes the sought; one person becomes the dominant and one person the submissive. It's not necessarily erotic. But there's an organization of energy, so that we can continue with our lives. The problem in most relationships is that this process is unconscious.

If you're an ordinary person having ordinary intercourse, there are a lot of questions you never have to address about who you are, who your partner is, what issues of control [exist]. When you leave the world of vanilla sex—particularly the heterosexual vanilla world—you have to start asking [such] questions of yourself. Doing so opens up the opportunity, or presents the problem, of consciousness, of growing in self-knowledge. I'm not saying that just because you get conscious [about D&S], there aren't other unconscious things going on. But this consciousness seems to me one of the greatest values, though not necessarily one of the greatest pleasures, in this mini-universe. Actually this is a great pleasure for *me.* I'm a process junkie; I like to work things to death. But I know some extremely intelligent, experienced players who want no truck with that attitude. They do S&M for fun. Period.

[As for the] physical reality, well, in the sexually vanilla world, people are forever fucking each other while the person on top is pinning the wrists of the person on the bottom, or lightly slapping or tickling him or her. Since I'm a boy in this culture, and since more of my partners have been girls than boys, mostly those were situations in which I was on top, holding her wrists or slapping her butt, and sometimes the results were very gratifying. I [once] grabbed one girlfriend when she walked past me, threw her over my lap, hiked up her skirt, pulled down her panties, and spanked her, and she turned and gasped at me over her shoulder, "Oh, James, how did you know?" That was nice, but knowing what I do now, I see it was also nonconsensual. She could have taken what I did as abuse instead of as a sexual delight.

In 1987 I was divorced. Ours looked for all the world like a straight-on vanilla relationship, and in some regards I guess it was. But she had run through a string of abusive partners—guys who threw her down the stairs, broke her nose, broke her ribs, blackened her eyes—a real horror show. I have a white-knight complex, so I was going to save her. We had a great sexual relationship and a little vanilla slap and tickle, and that was fine. But we also had a lot of manipulative disagreements, and somewhere in the midst of this marriage, I discovered one night that I really wanted to deck her. Even though I never did anything of the sort, I *felt* like an abuser. I didn't like this about me at all. I had never felt that way; I had never been in an abusive relationship. Nobody was hitting anybody, but it felt lousy, and with whatever discussion we were able to have, it didn't look as if there was any way we were going to resolve it. It [was] untenable for me. This was not where I was going to spend the rest of my life. So I ended the relationship.

[My D&S sexuality] was very difficult for me to acknowledge. Cybele has never been in the closet about anything; I've been in the closet about everything: Awareness is a constant process of coming out for me. Like many vanilla folks, I had a certain number of S&M experiences that I did not call S&M. And though my fantasies were elaborate, one thing that was clear to me was that I didn't know what I was doing. I didn't quite know how to find out.

Since I didn't know anybody who knew anything about the subject—it turns out I [did] know people who were involved, but they weren't talking, and I wasn't asking—I started visiting professionals. Some of my fantasies were submissive, but they were vague, because I didn't know what *submissive* meant or what a submissive did. Most of my fantasies involved substantial dominance, with me as top, just as they had when I was younger. I wanted to top helpless women who would swoon and love me. I searched for a submissive who was very experienced, to teach me to top. She was not easy to find, so I visited a number of professional dominants, trying to figure out what to do. None of those dominatrices was very good. Now that I am in this community, where there are several excellent professionals, I see none of those others around, so I conclude that they are people who simply do S&M professionally. Unlike the professionals in the community, the activity is not meaningful to them; it's just a way to earn a living.

[But then] I spent several hours one evening with a man who advertises as a professional dominant. He was intelligent, educated, informed, and articulate and able to explain to me what was going on in a language I could grasp. He was also a very adept leather top. On the one hand, I learned something about how to top; on the other, I discovered that I had a genuine submissive side that I had not seen before.

[With his approach in mind], I answered an ad that turned out to be Cybele's. I got her answering machine, and her message was grammatically correct. I'm a writer with a graduate degree in English and experience teaching college English, so it was important to me to have a grammatically correct partner. We traded messages and talked a number of times before we met. She was anticipating somebody much straighter than I, as she tells the story; a voice went off in the back of her head when I opened her door, saying, "Oh, it's you." But since she's a good professional, she ignored the voice, and we had our little introduction and the session. However, this session, which was supposed to last an hour, went several hours. A woman who works with her listened at the door at one point, afraid that some harm had come to Cybele.

One of the things that is most engaging right now—I mean that in all senses—is that Cybele has a persona who really wants to bottom to me. [And] her baby persona—Baby Pixie—is very happy to have a submissive daddy. However, the context of our erotic relationship has been very different from that, and it is hard for me to come out as a top with her. Mistress and slave really undergird our relationship.

SRI SHIVAYNANDA
SMC is a church dealing with goddess worship—the dark-side goddess. It got its origin about 10 or 11 years ago when a group of people were fantasy playing with S&M energy and female-domination energy. At the same time, goddess worship was being discussed at an academic forum on the other side of town [among] sociologists at U.C. Berkeley. To make a long story short, there was a convergence of people acting out some old mythologies of dominant goddesses and sacrifices to them. It was merely speculative at first, but a few people decided to organize this energy under a religious corporation. This group ultimately became the Service of Mankind Church, which is a funny, yuppie name, but they wanted to come up with a nonthreatening

name [so] the church could function without attracting attention. People didn't want it connected with [the] other strange things coming out of Berkeley.

The articles of incorporation define the church as based around worship of a dominant goddess. SMC's religious practices are varied. One of the things that we would like to get people into doing—especially since so many people are attracted to us because of an erotic interest—is a search within. We have a woman who leads a group in basic guided visualization. She talks for several minutes and then asks people to sit quietly and imagine themselves in [a] particular scene. We'll also chant the names of goddesses, because that helps center the mind and gets individuals out of individualism and into the group. The religious part is merely the acknowledgment of that goddess [and] surrendering, making an offering to that goddess.

We've done a lot of rituals. We find some interesting little mythology [about] some goddess, and [a] woman will play the role of that particular goddess. We're not worshiping that particular goddess or that particular woman: It's an acknowledgment of the feminine aspect of divinity. [For example], there is a ritual practiced principally in Nepal. A young virgin girl is seated on a throne; she incorporates the spirit of a goddess. The village people will come in and lay down fruit and gifts and flowers. They're not worshiping that little girl; they're worshiping the feminine aspect of divinity. It's symbolic. We're not Kali worshipers; we invoke different goddesses [symbolically].

Perhaps [it was] my Catholic school background and dealing with the Blessed Virgin that influenced me. Through grade school and high school I saw the Blessed Virgin as a surviving form of goddess worship. I think that drew me to [goddess worship] as a young person. [But] the Judeo-Christian point of view is that good and evil are located in two different deities: All good is in God and Jesus, and all evil is in another god, called Satan. In the Hindu pantheon and in other [Eastern religions], good and bad are combined in one deity. In monotheism we separate these [aspects]. The dark-side goddess—[from] the Eastern point of view—is not evil; it implies that we have to recognize within ourselves the potential for the maximum of good as well as the maximum of evil. To believe in the dark-side goddess is to acknowledge within ourselves just this potential. We worship the dark-side goddess because she is the one who can take these energies and do mass destruction. If we're aware of what she is [and] give her acknowledgment, she could be quite benign. Keeping her benign [is] why you worship the dark-side goddess.

From a Jungian point of view, there is not evil but a dark or hidden side of our psyche [containing] various taboos [and] things we try to hide from ourselves. And if, from the Jungian point of view, you have a support situation in which to open these doors and face these things directly, it is like looking at the dark or hidden side. Certain alternative sexual persuasions run parallel to what we call Shakti. Shakti's a form of goddess worship, goddess power.

Going through Tantric books, books on other Indian practices, there was this recurring theme of a male figure on the ground [and a] goddess figure standing on his prone body. There's one particular rite where one male is selected who becomes the human-assailant symbol of the god Siva. He is usually put down flat on the ground, and he's usually bound. He crawls forward toward a female sitting on a chair, who is emanating the focus of this goddess energy. [She is] the Kali figure. He makes a long slow crawl—because he's bound, it's very laborious. When he finally gets there, he becomes the basis upon which she stands: A triumphant standing on the male god. Such images go back quite some time. And [then] you go through pictures of beautiful women you find in S&M magazines. There are men down on the floor with a woman's feet on their heads. I found out that this is a sex picture; [it's] there to turn some guys on.

Tantra recognizes that the way to thinking about the oneness of the universe can be achieved by traveling an erotic path. When an erotic path is established, it's not sexuality. [In] Tantra you hold that energy, and as long as it's being held rather than released, there is an altered state of consciousness. When a man [has] an erection, he'll do anything that the woman wants, because he wants some realization of that. During that time he's in an altered state of consciousness. The same goes for the female. We try to get that kind of a state going so that during that period one can have this inner trip. For example, the priestess playing the part of the spirit who sits on the throne [is] usually dressed erotically [to] get that male energy going. We use the iconography of this dominant goddess. That's when the ritual [and] the chanting occur. We have icons of Kali standing barefoot on the chest of Siva. The mythology is that Siva lies dormant as dead until Kali steps on him, and at that point her power, her sexuality, her Shakti is so strong that she's able to raise an erection in this corpse. From the Western viewpoint, this is a bit crude and weird, but this is the Hindu point of view: First comes the erection, and then comes life. She brings him back to life. As the legend goes on, they eventually copulate, and when they do, that sustains life in the universe. In other words, this union makes life go on.

We never [have] an orgy or anything like that. In order to give up all of his symbols of power and ego, a man may strip himself naked and lie prostrate at the feet of the goddess. Only certain individuals are selected to perform that symbolic surrender of the male to the feminine aspect. In some cases he's bound, in some he's scourged—to show that he's making his ultimate surrender. To straight people, that's not sexuality; that's just plain weirdness. But to others, like dominant women who're watching, that's very hot, very erotic, and they're sure it's explicit sexuality.

The Service of Mankind Church is our official name, but our subname is Sanctuary of the Goddess. And in the Sanctuary of the Goddess we wanted to establish a sacred place. [Our] mission is to make a reaffirmation of [our] theology, [to] define a group of people—men and women—who can learn more about the spiritual trip and actually become a part of it. We want priestesses and monks to carry on the ritual as well as to teach others. We call it the Inner Circle. We are doing this as a means of separating ourselves from the army of hedonistic men and a few women who see the Church as a place to expand their sexual and social lives, a place where they can meet a woman who is into S&M and female dominance. We're being drowned by these people.

MORGAN LEWIS

I became a dominant because, since I was three years old in the playground, [I was] a take-charge person. I don't like to follow directions; I usually pick people's directions apart. If I could have worked in camouflage for the military, I would have. I always see how things could be made better. I'm an innovator. I like dealing my own deal. I'm used to leading groups of people. I've been the head of organizations, on the national board of [the massage] organization I belong to. This is me: I walk in, and I take over. I do what needs to be done.

I got into S&M because I had a sexual partner, and we had been together for eight years. We were trying to find something new to do, and I played with cross-dressing and he became completely submissive. And that's how I got into it. I didn't know what to do at that point. So I went to the Eulenspiegel Society and learned what S&M was. I [would] go every Monday night, come home, and tell him what I saw. We played the games at home. Then it became a part of my life.

I'll tell you what S&M has done for me: It's made me a better business-person, a better mother. I get along better with people. I've been able to be more real with myself. I was an entertainer all my life: I'm even better [now], because I'm not afraid of people anymore. It's made a complete person of me, because I have this power and this control.

People who dig black women will come to me. There's no doubt that's what they want. One thing about people in the Scene: They won't come to you if that's not what they want. If I advertise anywhere, I always say I'm a big, black, buxom woman; a lot of men have been attracted to me because

I am big and black, and prominent. I don't think of myself in any ethnic form. The mere fact of being a woman never affected me until I realized I could flaunt it. But I've always used my body to get what I want; I've always conned men into doing what I want. Being a woman, being black—these things aren't deterrents for me. They've been very advantageous for me. I don't think that black people really know where they're coming from, so I'm not coming from anywhere but my consciousness as a woman; and it so happens that I am black.

I particularly [enjoy making] a dominant man submissive: That's really a big kick of mine. [And] I like meeting new slaves and watching them submit. I love walking into a room and watching guys just scramble to get me a seat, to make sure that everything's okay for me, and coming up to me to see if there's anything they can do for me. I love the idea of being paid attention to, being paid homage to. Usually someone will come up to me after I've led a meeting at the Eulenspiegel Society, and we'll go out for coffee and talk. I'll know if I want to be with them by the body movement they have and by the way they look. [Many] men respond to me, but a lot of times I just slough them off. I have to be visually, physically, [and] mentally turned on to them. If I decide that I want to see him again, I'll give him my card: If he calls and I really like him, we'll set up a time [to] meet and talk [again]. I'll ask them things about their life and what they want to do and how they want to do it. And if a man sees I'm receptive, there's such relief; if I've just met them and I say, "Give me a call," the response is "Wow, you really want me to call?" And if I like the guy, if we have any chemistry between us, I'll know. I may touch them; I may let them kiss my feet, kiss my hand. It all depends on how I feel.

I recently met someone who I think is an absolute dream. He answered my [personal] ad, [which] said that I wanted him to write me a 500-word essay concerning himself and how he would worship me. My ad said I was a brown goddess. On the telephone he said that we met [once] at the Eulenspiegel Society. I didn't remember it; that's how nondescript he was. Before inviting him over, I sent him on a treasure hunt. I wear Opium perfume, and [Bloomingdale's was] having a sale, so I had him go pick that up. He brought that with him, and he came, and we sat here, and we just talked. We like the same things. He's in music, so we spent three hours talking about music and the people in the business that we knew in common. [When] he got ready to leave, he [was] still nondescript to me. At the door, I turned to him and gave him a kiss on the lips. His lips were so soft, I said, "Hmmm." I was holding his hand, and his hand was soft, and I said, "Hmmm." [After that] we talked almost every day, and we made a date. Over dinner he told me that he had a breast piercing. [I asked], "Why did you do that?" He said, "Because I knew that one day I was going to meet a queen, and they would already be done for her. That's you." So at home I helped take off his shirt. I [had also] told him to buy a pair of red lace bikini panties, and [to] be wearing them. He took off his clothes, and he was wearing them. There was [his] gorgeous chest, this beautiful tan, and these things in his nipples. It just looked so hot.

I had always wanted to attach someone to my massage table and do things to them. I put him on the table and shackled him to [it]. I started tickling him all over and playing with his breasts. I took my cat-o'-nine-tails [and] whacked him on his feet. He didn't like the pain: Some people are turned on by that, but he wasn't. I realized he didn't like what I was doing to his feet; he didn't like the pain; he liked the loving touch. I unhooked him and invited him to follow me to my bedroom. He came in, and I was lying on my bed. I looked at him and said, "You may kiss me now." And he surrendered on the side of my bed on his knees and reached up and kissed me. It was a very romantic evening. This was something I'd never done before; his lips were so soft! It was a very romantic, beautiful thing we had, and we've had some wonderful times together since. We see each other a lot.

I have another person who's been in my life for about a year now, and he believes he was born to be submissive. I know another who believes that he was born to come to this country—he's from Greece—and find me and be submissive to me. These two don't really worship me, [but] I'm the most superior [and] most wonderful thing in their lives, plus I can be a sexual person with them. [With] most of the people who are submissive to me, there's nothing sexual at all about it. The experience [of domination] is great. I enjoy it, but I [also] enjoy afterwards [when] they're not around. I enjoy masturbating, thinking about it. It's not something I want to do in front of them. I feel that if I become very sexual with them, I'm losing my power. Once you get into a sexual situation with another person, you kind of surrender. If I'm going to stay in power, I can't surrender.

It's unbelievable that these guys enjoy worshiping me and being with me. The one I just met does not want to have an orgasm, because he always wants to have an erection, so that I can use his body in any way that I want to. My girlfriends and I have been laughing, because I said, "I've got to tie him to the bed. He always has such a firm erection—I could just ride up and down on him!" My girlfriends said, "You're terrible!" [But] I'm going to one day; I just haven't had a chance.

I'm sometimes very sadistic. I like suspending people and whipping them very much. I like to torture their feet. I particularly like to tie cocks and balls up with rawhide. I like pinching nipples. Another thing I like is to slap their faces. I think that's the most humiliating thing you can do to a man. My most exciting experience began at a club, playing with someone I had been seeing a couple of years. I had him suspended, and I was beating him and playing with him and kissing him. Things got so hot that we [had to] go home. We had a real romantic, unbelievably sexual thing going, but I didn't know how submissive he really was [until then]. He really succumbed to my pain. [With] every blow I gave him, he became more sexually aroused. When I would kiss him, it was this hungering, lingering kiss. I would squeeze his nipples, and he would squirm and scream, and his dreamy blue eyes would just go crazy. It was like he was reaching out for me but couldn't because I had his hands bound.

I've lived all my fantasies. If someone's going to be with me, he's going to do the things I want. So I've done everything I want to do. I'm living the lifestyle. It's not something I just do on Saturday. I like men who are in the Scene, [and] a lot of my friends are in the Scene, though I have straight friends, too. I find it's the most comfortable thing for me. The people in it are the people that I want to be with. I want men and women around me who I don't have to explain myself to, who can understand and be relaxed with it. It's good for me.

RALPH R.

My wife and I have some D&S aspect in probably 50 percent of our sexual encounters, but it's not that big an issue. When someone who doesn't do it looks on it, it's somewhat frightening, it's somewhat strange. But the actual effect it has on our lives is probably less than the effect that the kind of literature we read has on our lives.

I could cope without D&S in the same sense as I could cope without ice cream. I like ice cream a lot; it would take a lot of pleasure out of my life if I didn't have it. So it probably wouldn't cause me to do poorly in my job or break up my marriage, but it would take a lot of pleasure out of life.

I'm a straight monogamous male. And, parenthetically, both my wife and I are very active in our church and consider ourselves Christians. I've been married for nine and a half years, with a moderately satisfactory sex life, which I guess is a reasonable way of putting it. In terms of D&S, I would be switchable if my wife were, but she really does not enjoy being submissive at all, so I'm primarily submissive, by exclusion. On the whole I'm fulfilled, trying to separate fantasy from its fulfillment—which are not always the same, as we've discovered in some of our experimentation. I'd like to have a more switchable relationship. I'd like to take the dominant role. My wife has submitted to me a number of times. She just gets angry. It's really interesting, because she's not an angry person—she's a sweet person. But she doesn't get excited at all. These things are done for mutual pleasure. If the pleasure isn't mutual, you can't do that.

[D&S] is kept in the metaphorical bedroom, except in the context of verbal play: My wife likes to harass me about enjoying pain—not in public, but not necessarily in a sexual context either. For us, D&S is foreplay. I don't think that [it] would be satisfying as anything [else]. It's used as a condiment, as it were, to sex, rather than as an end in itself. I think [that] as an end in itself, for me, it would be like eating black pepper: pointless. Whereas black pepper makes steak, instead of boring, much, much more interesting.

As far as realizing when I was interested, [that was] probably during the pre- and early sexual phase of my relationship with my wife. When we were exploring our sexual relationship, it came out as something that I was interested in, and we started experimenting. [What] was most instrumental in enabling us to pursue that in the further psychological sense was finding a couple of chapters in *The Joy of Sex* about it. That book told me that this existed and people did it, and [there were] names [for it]. [I did] not really [have trouble coming to terms with my desires]. How do I put this? Lots of thoughts come to mind, but I never take them very seriously. I know I'm not sick.

[My wife] likes to tie me down. We have some clothesline, and we have a couple of leather straps that she whips me with. She uses a vibrator to stimulate me anally. We have used wax in the past, but that's just too messy and not enough fun. That is pretty much the extent of it.

I expect I fall into the category of the greedy sub. One time my wife got satisfied early and was still a little interested, so [she] felt like spending the time to work me over a couple hours. That was probably the best we've ever had. Usually there's a tension between her patience and what she'd like to do and the fact that I could go on for a long time, in just the D&S part, before ever getting to sex. [That time, it was] more prolonged. And that made it more intense and one of the most exciting experiences.

I've had dominant fantasies that I don't particularly get a chance to act out. These are related to my wife or to particularly attractive women I know. Beyond the sort of stripping-and-whipping kind of thing, the most interesting would be—and I have no idea how this would be implemented—having a woman really want to be made love to and begging. [Another fantasy] that's really interesting to me is of my wife making love to another man while dominating me. I've got a pretty good idea why that's attractive to me. She's very attractive, and anything involving her sexually is exciting. I'm sure that's also interesting because of the dominant symbolism in it—the notion of men competing for mates and losing in that competition.

I haven't thought about how D&S may or may not have affected my life. I think the only areas that it would be likely to have affected is my marriage, and I would be hard-pressed to say [how]. I think that honesty was there before and would exist without the D&S. I think that the D&S was enabled by that, but I would be skeptical if that's a significant effect. It's a fair statement that it enriches my life.

RISING STAR

I am both dominant and submissive [but] more often dominant in the outside world. I draw on what I've learned from dominant play. Being submissive is a very important side of me but one I protect very closely—I don't show [it] to the outside world.

I didn't set out to be dominant. I did not know that I was doing anything special. The first sexual and emotional relationship that I got involved in, I was the dominant partner. But saying that it just happened because of the first couple of relationships is far too passive a way of looking at it. I think they happened because my personality is very dominant. I had fantasies of being the warrior queen as a young child, of having my choice among the captives.

I'm married to someone who does not participate. It was hard to make a decision to marry someone outside of the lifestyle. I was involved with someone in a long-distance relationship, a mostly submissive gentleman, also switchable, who I cared a great deal for. But he was a politician in a state where I would not be happy living. Our career objectives, where we wanted to live, even religious differences all came into play.

I began as a dominant, and I switched some. I played the other role for a very simple reason: I don't feel comfortable using the technique unless I know how it feels. But then I had an eye-opening experience which started me toward self-discovery. I looked back on when I had submitted in the past, and I found that there were a lot of things that I had enjoyed about submitting beyond the feel of the whip or the sexual attention.

In the past, if I had to pick one side, there would have been no question: I would have been dominant. Now if I had to pick one side, I'd have to ask an additional question: Are we talking about a lot of people or just one person? If I was talking about a single relationship, I would prefer to be submissive. I think I needed the power more before. Perhaps by being secure that I have the power if I want to use it, I'm not worried about using it, so I'm free to explore other parts of my sexuality. There's a parallel with my work. At some points in my career I've had a great deal of responsibility; at other times it's been primarily performing a technical task someone told me to do. If I have a lot of responsibilities in my life, my need to submit becomes stronger—my pleasure in letting somebody else take charge of the situation increases. Conversely, when I don't have a lot of control over my work, the dominant side becomes stronger.

As a submissive, what excites me is being given no choice in what's going to happen and having to satisfy my partner in whatever way he wishes—I should say "or she." I've dominated women; I think it would be interesting to submit to one. I submitted to a gentleman who'd tell me to be naked under my clothes "for my master." Going out wearing only a dress and garter belt and stockings was not particularly exciting to me until he put it in those terms; then the sense of giving up control made it exciting. When we would go out he might choose to unbutton several buttons, or we might be in the car and he would pull my skirt up to my waist. That's exciting! When we were driving around in the car and my skirt was pulled up and I was exposed, I could see the reaction of truck drivers around.

As a dominant, I use other people's fetishes, but that's not what interests me. The most exciting fantasy—and I have done this a little bit—is the ability to bring my partners to orgasm without touching them or allowing them to touch themselves. I'll just tell someone about something that they should imagine happening. And I watch the response. Instead of doing those things to them, I'm just talking—but if I understand what excites them well enough, that should be all I need.

Five

HEAD TRIPS AND ROLEPLAYING

That god forbid that made me first your slave
I should in thought control your times of pleasure,
Or at your hand th'account of hours to crave,
Being your vassal bound to stay your leisure.
O, let me suffer, being at your beck,
Th' imprisoned absence of your liberty . . .
—SHAKESPEARE[1]

No one who has ever loved is unaware of the power of a lover's words, the infinite meanings a lover's gestures can convey, the intoxicating ardor a lover's glances can incite, or the cruel yet often compelling power of a lover's rejection. All who have loved passionately have quivered at least a little, at least once, when the object of desire has cast a stormy look your way; if you haven't, you haven't loved.

D&Sers have found that playing on the essential dichotomy of love, that fusion of anxiety and delight that is the soul of passion, vastly enhances their pleasure. They consciously orchestrate language and behavior so as to increase the erotic tension between dominant and submissive.

At chapter's end we profile:

- Master Chris, who is 33 years old and is married with children. He owns a software company and operates an electronic bulletin board.
- Anne is 40 and married with children. She has worked in medical and behavioral research and has taught emotionally disturbed children.
- Lance is in his late 40s and works in the fine arts business. He is married to Trudi.
- Trudi is 47 years old. She is a sculptor.

WHAT IS IT?

A head trip is a mental game in which a dominant upsets—or audaciously fulfills—the expectations of a submissive. The express purpose is to make a submissive feel little or no control over events or even over emotions in the moment. Erotic head trips are phenomena separate and distinct from the tales of dreary psychological cruelty that fill talk-shows. Instead of sparking alienation, a D&S head trip creates a bond; instead of shaking a person's emotional foundation, erotic head trips provide a safe outlet for fantasies.

Seen from the outside, a head trip can baffle—even outrage—the uninformed observer. When one witnesses, for example, a grown man being scolded like a child, chastised for disobedience, or threatened with a bizarre humiliation—such as being forced to wear a dog collar—it is easy enough to believe that some lunacy is afoot, and either that the submissive is being involuntarily abused or, even worse, so downtrodden as to crave mistreatment.

From the inside, however, a head trip is, first of all, a mutually consensual act, a private conspiracy between partners who establish clear rules and limits. Head trips may include unpredictability and anticipation with a goal of mutually erotic gratification. In this consensual context, emotions that would normally be distressing or hurtful—such as embarrassment, confusion, and anxiety—are instead electrifying. Head trips may, at times, permit submissives to face insecurities and fears with a safety net; for dominants, the ability to control a partner psychologically can be intensely exciting.

Many D&Sers say that a well-crafted intuitive head trip can be as exciting as any physical act. This may be the reason that psychological domination tends to be particularly popular among imaginative D&Sers.

WHAT IT ISN'T

A bad—or ineptly handled—head trip is one in which a partner may feel degraded, confused, insulted, or frightened. A bad head trip causes emotional anguish, if only by stirring memories of genuine insults and taunts. Because such activity may cross the line separating D&S and abuse, most practitioners are extremely conscientious.

All of the activities described in this chapter carry significant psychological dangers and require the most extreme caution and clear, informed consent by both partners.

> *There's a difference between abuse and sexuality. There's a difference in intent. It would not give [my husband] pleasure to cause me emotional pain or make me cry. He does things because they give him pleasure but also because he wants to give me pleasure. I trust him to know how far to push me, but not to hurt me. I would never stay with somebody who was disposed to abuse me.* —ANNE

To understand this difference better, we'll look at two typical types of interactions that have an inner, understood reality quite different from their external, observed reality.

1) Master A tells Submissive B that for the rest of the day B may not look him directly in the eyes and may not speak unless spoken to; if B does not abide by these restrictions, A will severely discipline B.

To the outsider this scenario may seem to imply that A is demeaning B's humanity or rights as an equal and that B is oppressed or is somehow degraded and is not being treated fairly.

To the insider this scenario may be an explicit expression of a fantasy or may be a power exchange the couple has discussed and negotiated, in which B has made it clear that being obliged to act as an inferior is an exciting fantasy or a compelling sexual need. By issuing the orders, A is fulfilling B's fantasy in a safe context. While the foreground may be the couple's erotic excitement, the psychological background is that A's understanding of B's need makes B feel comforted, cared for, and loved. A, meanwhile, enjoys the power of enforcing the scenario.

2) Mistress C chastises Submissive D at length for being naughty or lascivious, chiding D as one would a disobedient or willful child.

To the outsider this scolding may seem absurd or downright insulting, since in our culture it is considered shameful to be treated as—or to be perceived as—a child.

To the insider the scolding is a reinforcement of an agreed power dynamic. The scolding itself may produce in D feelings of childlike embarrassment which themselves are highly erotic. D may also feel grateful that C cares enough to take an aggressive interest in correcting and supervising D's behavior. C derives pleasure from her power over D and his emotions.

Responsible dominants make every effort to distinguish between mental games that arouse the partner and ones that cause upset, making certain to avoid the latter. There are no set scenarios that will work on all submissives.

WHO INITIATES HEAD TRIPS?

Head trips can be initiated by the dominant or the submissive, wholly depending on the couple's style of interaction. Few dominants expect the submissive to be passive (in fact, most dominants prefer highly spirited partners). Many submissives therefore consistently strive to offer creative scenarios for both partners to pursue. A submissive may write down ideas for her fantasy evening and respectfully present them to the dominant; or the submissive may offer to perform some service (giving the dominant a massage, or inventing some amusing naughtiness which requires punishment).

Interestingly, in some couples the submissive will intentionally break the rules of the game in order to intensify the play and to give the dominant an excuse to fulfill the threat of punishment. Submissives who genuinely challenge authority for the sake of provoking an unpleasant encounter, however, are rarely considered desirable partners, and dominants who do not respect the submissive's needs or limits before engaging in head trips are viewed as dangerous.

UNPREDICTABILITY
AND ANTICIPATION

Unpredictability and anticipation are among the most popular elements in the structuring of a head trip. While the mainstream person may find that a kiss hastily snatched in a doorway is erotic, for D&Sers the doorway might instead be used for a tug on restraints hidden under the submissive's clothes.

The dominant is likely to do or say something (usually erotic in nature) when the submissive least expects it. The variations are boundless; for example, a dominant may suddenly order the submissive to remove his clothing and to submit to erotic fondling while the couple is engaged in some nonerotic activity, like watching television together. The submissive will suddenly and powerfully experience both vulnerability and a consciousness that his sexual excitement can be aroused at his partner's whim.

> *He's capable of anything if the mood strikes him! He could call me at work and tell me to do something. I never say no. I'm vulnerable to verbal stimulation, so he'll say cute words that will get me excited and embarrassed, even though I might be alone in my office. It's the chance that somebody knows what I'm doing. I have no way of explaining to anyone at work that my husband calls me up to say things that aren't even dirty words. It's the risk of exposure [that's so arousing]; we're both real fond of that.* —ANNE

Our interviewees reported many extraordinary occasions when a playful dominant surprised an unsuspecting submissive. Anne says that her husband of 22 years has played many physical and verbal games in elevators, friends' homes, and even during church services.

> *In church he'll sit next to me and wiggle his hand up my skirt, into my underpants, and I'm sitting there squirming. So there's this church full of little old Swedish ladies, and here's this crazy woman wiggling and squirming and giggling like a maniac. And he'll just look at me and say, "Shhh!" very quietly. He doesn't care what anyone thinks. He's having a hell of a fine time. If I really didn't like it, he wouldn't do it, of course.* —ANNE

Unpredictability also serves another function: It helps D&S couples to maintain highly charged erotic relationships. Couples who've spent a long time together often say that the abilities of their partners to surprise them continually with new games or new angles on old ones keeps the romance alive.

While unpredictability throws a person off balance by prompting an erotic response during what is, until that moment, a sexually neutral experience, anticipation builds erotic tension. The dominant may hint at some inevitability or may keep the submissive impatiently guessing. For many the anticipation is as exciting as the consummation.

> *If there's a hunger for anything in [D&S] for me, it's for that sensation of anticipation or for seeing that sensation within the submissive. It's like, "God, what's gonna happen next . . . oh, my God, it could be anything!"* —MASTER CHRIS

Anticipation scenarios are limited only by the partners' imagination. For example, the dominant partner may tell the submissive to wear some unusual article, such as a restraint, under her clothing in the morning without explaining why he wants her to, only hinting suggestively that something is planned for the evening—a vague proposition that will keep the submissive wondering, and tantalized, all day long. Or the dominant may bind the submissive's wrists and put him in a corner without revealing what will happen next. During that period of not knowing, the mixture of anxiety and expectancy makes the submissive's excitement escalate before any physical acts take place.

The unpredictability is exciting. I like that mysteriousness. I like that darkness.   —ANNE

WHAT IS ROLEPLAYING?

I'm your servant and your concubine! You're my king, my idol!
        —GUSTAVE FLAUBERT, *Madame Bovary*[2]

We all play roles: parent, child, professional, citizen. D&S roleplaying is a mutually agreed upon psychodrama in which the partners assume temporary fantasy roles that express a power dynamic. Many D&S couples believe that the ability to experiment with varied roles sustains erotic novelty for the duration of a marriage or partnership.

An exciting role can have many sources. For example, many interviewees discussed their childhood fascination with movies in which heroic characters wore colorful costumes and savored wild adventures.

I identified very much with the old sailing ship movies of the period: the swashbuckler films with Erroll Flynn. The flogging scenes were exciting for me; I always identified with the victim.   —LANCE

D&S roleplaying is often a means of confronting a taboo—fantasies which, made into reality, would be horrifying. Consensual psychodrama enables D&Sers to experience the erotic thrill of extreme fantasies but with safe limits and, perhaps most importantly, with the knowledge that the play will end and that the partners will revert to their accustomed interactions.

We do our "German soldier and Jewish maiden captive." I'm Jewish and he's German, so we refight World War II every once in a while. It involves a lot of tying and tickling, mostly teasing and embarrassment.   —ANNE

Not everyone enjoys roleplaying: A fair number of D&Sers insist that roleplaying is artificial and that it trivializes the partners' genuine power dynamic. Still, many D&Sers have an unabashed fondness for elaborate roleplaying and particularly for dramatic costume. Leather bars, for example, regularly sponsor parties for which all attenders are required to wear military or police uniforms. Leather garb itself is a kind of uniform, and in the past some leather bars did not allow patrons in street clothes to enter. Leather, unlike a military uniform worn for a specific party, however, has never implied a temporary role among the traditionalists of the leather communities— leather is usually a statement of preference or even social status. But with evolutions in style and sexual expression, for better or worse, many occasional players now do treat leather as decorative and role oriented.

Roleplaying also allows exploration of the potential for expressing different facets of one's personality. Some D&Sers perceive a multiplicity of erotic roles to be a natural extension of the roles that all people play in the social sphere.

> *The relationship that I have with my life partner is extraordinary: He is my slave, I am his mistress. He is my priest, I am his goddess. We work together and we're best friends. He is also my baby boy, and I am his mommy. He is my daddy, and I am his baby girl. And the baby boy and baby girl are childhood sweethearts. When we are babies we don't wear diapers and it's usually not erotic. However, it is sweet, loving, and carefree. We need that kind of balance in our lives.* —M. CYBELE

Roleplaying is another way of stepping outside oneself and into the realm of fantasy and imagination. It can help individuals to experiment with transformation and the perceptions of reality, and it may deepen partners' emotional bond, as they perceive each other in a spectrum of different personae.

HUMILIATION AND EMBARRASSMENT

The term *humiliation* causes confusion even in the D&S communities, although many practitioners do engage in some form of this head trip. Some distinguish between humiliation and embarrassment; others between humiliation and degradation.

> *I've found that [for] most people who use the service of professionals, humiliating means embarrassing. Now, some people mean degrading. "Tell me that I'm a piece of shit." I don't like that. I say, "If you're a piece of shit, I have no interest in you." For some people,*

it's necessary and important, but it doesn't work for me, so I won't do it. —CLÉO DUBOIS

To many submissives, situational embarrassment—where the submissive is teased about his or her actual erotic vulnerability—is sexually arousing. It can reinforce feelings of helplessness and heighten awareness of the bottom's vulnerability.

I find a certain amount of embarrassment extremely arousing. For example, I giggle very easily—so my husband will say something to me very softly in public so only I can hear it. He says it to make me blush and laugh. —ANNE

Situational embarrassment is always distinguished from personal embarrassment, where the individual is criticized for genuine flaws or failures. For situational embarrassment to work, of course, it must involve activities that the submissive perceives as embarrassing.

When people ask for humiliation, I ask: "What do you mean by humiliation? What you might find humiliating might be what somebody else finds erotic or plain old boring." I had a friend who found that a golden shower was completely unhumiliating. It was her fetish. She loved it. There was no humiliation in it whatsoever. [Yet] most people find golden showers humiliating. I try to clarify, since it has to do with the upbringing [and] the psychological makeup of the person. —CLÉO DUBOIS

Similarly, there are those who may find it extremely erotic to shave a partner's pubic hair as an aspect of foreplay, without any suggestion of humiliation. But in a power context, it may be scintillatingly exciting for the dominant to shave a submissive or to require that the submissive remain smooth skinned at all times. Some dominants may shave not only pubic hair but, in the case of male submissives, hair on the torso, legs, or buttocks. The submissive may feel pleasantly embarrassed at having a childlike appearance when naked; or may be embarrassed by the tangible evidence of the dominant's power over even the most intimate types of grooming.

Another aspect of humiliation comes into play when the dominant embarrasses the submissive by accentuating his helplessness. If the submissive really enjoys being helpless, it might seem logical that he shouldn't feel embarrassed about it; but, in fact, here is an area in which cultural conditioning conflicts with sexual desire. We—men particularly—are taught to feel ashamed of helplessness and vulnerability, and although a submissive may well crave to be in a helpless position, he may also feel that he shouldn't have that craving or that experience—thus, he feels humiliated.

D&S head trips can be highly complex mechanisms with subtle grada-
tions. For example, some submissives wish to be scolded or taunted for being
wanton. They may not be wanton (in fact, they may be anything but), yet
they may enjoy being chastised for this putative defect. Both partners understand that the bottom is aroused both by the idea of being slutty and by being
rebuked and corrected. This can be erotic for both partners. But in nearly all
cases, the eroticism would disappear if the dominant scolds the submissive for
a genuine character flaw.

Overall, humiliation and embarrassment scenarios depend on the dominant's ability to accentuate the submissive's feeling of defenselessness and
exposure—with the purpose of enhancing the power dynamic—while avoid-
ing making the submissive feel that he or she is any less worthwhile as a
human being. Exposure and exhibition, in particular, may be an exhilarating
experience for a submissive.

> One time when we were at [an S/M club] they served cake. My lover
> asked for extra icing. He pulled down my top and smeared icing all
> over my nipples and started licking it off in front of everyone. And
> these guys started standing around and just looking like they wanted
> to eat me! I felt a little bit humiliated because it was like, "Please!
> We're in public and you're sucking on my breasts!" At the same
> time, it was rather pleasurable, like "Oooh look! Everybody's looking
> at me and look at the admiration and the lust that's in their eyes!"
> I guess that's where the pleasure comes [from] the humiliation; I'm
> not really sure if it's humiliation [or] sheer exhibitionism. I think
> that for me it's part of being able to be a bad girl for a few minutes.
> It plays with the image that people very often have of me. I'm a
> rather petite woman, in fact I look younger than I am. So people
> always think, "Oh she's such a sweet innocent thing." When I do
> something that's not quite so innocent it's kind of fun seeing the
> surprise.   —VICTORIA

Many D&Sers enjoy acts that fall outside the regular scope of intimacy,
and the more outrageous the better. In this way the partners may both feel
that they have entered a private universe where very different rules apply.

> One of my favorite things is something I've done with virtually every
> woman that's been submissive to me: I'll have her get into a particu-
> lar position that I like. I'll have her get on her knees with the knees
> wide apart, and have her bend forward until her head is touching
> the bedspread, preferably blindfolded. And then I'll have her reach
> back and hold her buttocks open for inspection. From her perspective,

the anticipation of the moment is very high, knowing that she's more exposed in that private area than she ever has been. That kind of thing turns me on. The humiliation or embarrassment of it is the biggest turn-on, not the pain. —MASTER CHRIS

Obviously such scenarios work best when partners know each other and when there is a profound level of trust. All such psychological games can have enormous risks for both partners if an underlying sense of respect and compassion does not prevail.

Among other possibilities, head trips may trigger memories of former abuse, and emotional trauma could result from casual or unthinking experimentation.

DENIAL

Elements of head trips are described throughout this book. The final one worth separate discussion in this chapter, however, is the concept of sexual denial.

As we discuss in Chapter 10, numerous ploys can be used to ensure a submissive's chastity, the most obvious being, of course, the chastity belt. There is a fairly vigorous market for chastity devices in the D&S community. But many D&Sers incorporate psychological play on this theme without the assistance of equipment. Instead of having the submissive wear a belt, some dominants may verbally deny the submissive permission to climax. This order may be given either during an actual encounter or may pertain to an extended period of time when the partners are to be separated.

Usually denial is a means of protracting the submissive's excitement. (In a reverse behavior the submissive is sometimes ordered to climax repeatedly—either autoerotically or with the dominant lending a hand and possibly a vibrator; this activity is sometimes called *milking* when it refers to men, in reference to the obvious similarity in draining a cow's udder.) A submissive may be denied orgasm either as a method of psychological control or, sometimes, as a form of punishment. For some submissives being forced to contain sexual impulses for hours, days, or longer can in itself be a delicious exercise in anticipation; for others, it's simply punishment.

Although we have not spoken with anyone who regularly engages in denial scenarios, some professional dominatrices advertise that they require their submissives to have all their orgasms controlled in this way.

Some control over orgasms is common among D&Sers, though most dominants seem not only to be lenient with permission but may perceive it as a point of pride to be able to excite the submissive to transcendent, earth-shattering orgasms. Still, most dominants do claim the prerogative of determining when and under what circumstances the submissive may climax.

Some couples practice other types of denial. Privileges, for example, may be revoked in the case where a submissive has engaged in willful disobedience, and some dominants, while training a submissive, may keep rewards of all sorts—including pain or bondage—to a minimum until the submissive seems appropriately humble.

Denial, like all other D&S scenarios, demands clear communication and a certainty that both partners agree that they are getting what they want out of the experience. One submissive whom we interviewed reported that her dominant tried to train her by consistently denying her permission to visit with him, claiming that her reward for remaining passive would ultimately be to earn the privilege of spending more time with him. She had never expressed any interest in this denial scenario and was instead distressed by what she perceived as cat-and-mouse play. Finally, she decided that spending any time with someone so insensitive to her needs would be no privilege.

INTERVIEWS

MASTER CHRIS

I'm both dominant and submissive, but predominantly dominant—that's what I fall back to more often than not. I'm dominant both outside my sex life and certainly in my sex life. I'm not a particularly aggressive personality, but control may be an issue for me. When I'm being dominant, all of the attributes that I need to be successful at being dominant and making the whole thing work enter into play, like listening more intently than you would in a normal relationship and making sure that you're taking care not just of your own needs but of the needs of the submissive. That kind of attitude has carried over into my daily life. For example, when I'm working with an employee of mine, I see not just what I need but what the employee needs. It carries over to the way I behave in other relationships. Not that I have to be aggressive or in control, but I extend myself in much the same way that I do while dominant.

I've had several relationships outside of my marriage which have been strictly D&S in nature. It's something that interests me a lot and something that I enjoyed before my marriage and something that is still very much of interest to me. For the [few] times that I have gone outside of my marriage, it has been uniquely for that kind of relationship. My wife knows which way I lean. She just doesn't know that I've gone outside of our relationship to act out. One or two of these relationships have been long, and a couple were short-term.

From time to time I'll switch-hit and play the submissive, which can be fun. My wife enjoys being submissive from time to time, but we don't have a master-slave relationship. It doesn't play a full-time part in my marriage, although I'm a dominant personality generally. I like being in control. I've been this way since I was a kid. My parents never spanked us, aside from a single smack across the seat to have us wake up or something. Corporal punishment was not part of our family. But you know how when you're prepubescent and start playing doctor around the age of 10 or so? When I started playing doctor, it was all tied up in having someone turned over my knee and getting spanked. Or I'd be the doctor and they'd be the patient.

The thing that turns me on most about this whole experience is the anticipation of the moment. I don't have a particular urge to make someone wear a blindfold or any particular garment. But when a girl puts on a blindfold, or even when I'm being submissive and I put on a blindfold, it's like all of one's senses heighten about 2000 percent. And the tension rises about 100 percent.

One of the things that's a turn-on—and which I've both done a few times and had done to me—is to have a woman bound and unable to remove her blindfold in, say, a hotel room. And then to leave the room for a few minutes. Not a long time, just a few minutes. Then I come back, but I don't say anything. You can imagine the sensation for her. I've done the same in the submissive role, where a woman leaves the room and then comes back to find me like that. You know that it's your partner coming back, but you really don't know for sure. You trust her absolutely, otherwise you would have never let her tie you up in the first place. On the other hand it allows your imagination to wander . . . maybe they came in with a friend? There's that unknown: It's a powerful rush. And then being touched for the first moment or touching a woman . . . watching a woman gasp, or tremble . . . it's more and more exciting. Of course, for some people that's just scary. So with such a person you can't play such a game. For them it's a turn-off, so you wouldn't do it.

I also like giving a woman a hand spanking over my knees. I like the idea of having her stand with her nose in the corner after that, knowing that that's kind of embarrassing, because it's childish to be treated like a naughty girl. And I'm very anally oriented. I'll spend a long time with a girl, giving her an anal exam.

One of the images that gets to me the most is when I had a relationship with a woman and arranged to meet her—both of us were from out of town—at a hotel. She called to say she was on her way over, and I said fine and I gave her a series of instructions. She was instructed to go to the hotel where the room key would be waiting for her. I would not be in the room when she arrived. I told her to take off all her clothes and get into [a] position I described. I remember . . . she had to do that by a particular time, exactly 4:00. I then arrived about 4:10, knowing that she had been waiting in that position for me for those 10 minutes.

I remember opening the door to the room. The first thing I could see as I opened the door to the hotel room was the end of the bed, and I could see her feet sticking just off the end of the bed, and then I could see her ass. And then I walked in, and as I did, it was clear that she was completely naked. Absolutely open . . . and vulnerable. And she had done that not knowing who would really enter the room, because she was blindfolded. So I walked in and you could have cut the tension with a knife. I stroked her and touched her and pinched her ass and touched her pussy, and then I said, "How're you doing," and she just went "Ahhhhhh, it's you!" I hold that moment in my mind. That was probably the biggest turn-on, knowing that she was completely vulnerable and that she was submitting to me while knowing that it might not be me . . . she was submitting to the idea of me.

ANNE

I'm sexually submissive in my personal life with my husband. I can't imagine getting tired of [the power exchange], because everything always changes; the only thing that's not different is that he's the master. Underlying everything is the fact that I would do anything that he tells me to. I'm happy with it. I know I'm very valuable to him. I have a strong sense of self-worth. My husband and I have discussed the difference between our relationship and others'. We look around and think we're happier in our relationship than most. We've never had periods of time where we weren't talking to each other. We've never had any really big fights. I'm not talking about squabbles over priorities for money and stuff that everyone has, but we've never had any serious disagreements in all these years.

I seriously think that our relationship eliminates the struggle for power. We're both very comfortable with our roles with each other. I like myself. I look back on my life, and it's been very happy. I've done a lot of interesting things. I've raised three children. My grown daughter is successful and happy; I have two young boys at home, and they're really nice little kids. My daughter understands the relationship between my husband and myself, but not in detail—it's not her business. My sons say, "Ah, Poppa and Mommy are at it again." It's a very natural thing. Again, it's not that my husband says, "Come here, honey, I'm gonna punish you,"—no, no! But I can be in the kitchen cooking, and he'll come in and start fooling around.

The only time that anything ever happened that caused me to question [this openness] was once when the kids suddenly walked in on us. We thought they were outdoors. I was over my husband's lap, and he was spanking me. But nobody panicked. The boys asked, "What are you doing to Mommy!?" They were 6 and 10 years old. I had my underpants on, but my pants were down around my ankles. It was almost funny. My husband was very natural—to him this is the normal way to live. He said, "I'm spanking Mommy." And they said, "How come you can spank Mommy and we can't?" He said, "'Cause, *I'm* the boss." Then he explained: "When I'm home, I'm the boss; when Mommy's the only one home, Mommy's your boss." They wanted to know, "How come you can spank Mommy if she's the boss?" So he explained, "Because I'm Mommy's boss, and Mommy is your boss."

We [established] a chain of command, and that was all there was to it. No big hysterical fuss, no cover-up. Since then, any time that they've caught any ends of anything, it's always "Oh, this is Mommy and Poppa fooling around, and it's no big deal 'cause obviously all mommies and poppies must fool around." I'd rather see them with that attitude than the attitude that mommies and poppas never kiss or mommies and poppas never fool around. They hear a lot of giggling and laughing; they see a lot of affection. So I don't see anything wrong. They're nice, well adjusted, happy little kids who fight all the time.

I remember when we first became aware of our interests. We watched *Story of O,* and I expressed curiosity in being tied up. He tied me up, blindfolded me, and we had intercourse that way. I found it tremendously exciting, extremely erotic. It was very intense. Understanding [about D&S], understanding the motivations, [has] improved it for us. It made me more willing to let myself be pushed farther. For my husband it was a revelation to understand why he enjoys what he's doing with me and why he didn't enjoy other relationships. Nobody's ever responded to him the way I do.

I like being embarrassed, not humiliated; there's a difference. He'll surreptitiously touch me; he knows nobody else sees it. But I'm sure everybody else is watching us—whether they are or not, it doesn't matter! For example, we have a country home. There's nobody around for miles. We have a huge skylight over our bed, and he'll swing the skylight open and stand up and announce, "Okay, satellites, get your spy beams out now; here she is, lying here naked!" Now, there's nobody for five million miles out there, but I'm still embarrassed. You can just see my whole body turning red.

In my relationships in the past I was always submissive. I had a strange life. I was not a quiet child. I was one of those nasty little girls who used to tie up her dolls and hang them. Possibly someone who has more insight than I would say that I was expressing what I wanted done to myself.

I'm intellectually aggressive. But there's always been this submissiveness in personal relationships with men. I did the regular dating thing. Your typical nice little Jewish girl. I joined Mensa Teens and went out with boys who were in Mensa Teens, but I also had a completely separate life. I started an odd relationship with a man which lasted from the time I was 13 until I turned 18. It was not a sexual relationship. I was a virgin, and we never had sex. There was a very strong element of sexuality in the relationship, possibly even more so because there was never any intercourse. Looking back, it was a very peculiar but definitely [a] D&S relationship. He told me what he wanted me to do, and I did it, and I was very happy.

When I met my husband I was a guest at his roommate's party. I'd come there with a date. When I saw my husband, I remarked to the man I was with, "This is the person I've been looking for." My husband told me later that he said the exact same thing to his roommate about me. A week later I was at their house again; we talked all evening and finally went to bed together. In the morning he said, "You know you're not leaving. You understand you belong to me," and I said, "Yes," and that was it. And now it's 22 years later. It wasn't just exciting—it was that we both knew that we were the right person for each other.

In my professional life I'm not submissive. I figure out what people's problems are and tell them what to do about them. I supervise large businesses where I'm the only woman. But I find being personally submissive works very well in controlling people who I have to work with. I'm quietly assertive as opposed to aggressive. I don't get any satisfaction from forcing my way. I find that if I compromise, I can get things so that they're usually satisfactory. I'll find a way around rather than straight through. I have a horror of confrontational relationships. I'm not a yeller or a screamer.

While I like ritual, [my husband] doesn't, so a spanking is unpredictable: It could be anywhere or any time. I might bend over to change the channel on TV, and he'll grab me and put me over his knee or over a chair, as the mood strikes him. I like being spanked. I find it very exciting. I can come to orgasm just from being spanked. And he likes to use his hand.

He's also got an original approach to elevators. If there are cameras in elevators, we must be on videotapes all over the country, because as soon as an elevator door closes, he goes wild. He'll reach his hands under my clothes, or he'll expose himself to me, so that I'll screech and tell him to cover himself. If it's a long elevator ride and the place is isolated, he'll have me give him a blow job. I know the police and [the] FBI are going to break in at any moment! We've even been caught once or twice! The responses were amusing, too. They were: "I don't believe I saw what I just saw." I've been embarrassed but never upset. I was more concerned that my husband was pleased.

LANCE

[I'm] primarily heterosexual. In terms of S&M, I'm primarily a bottom. I consider it quite important in my life. Your sexuality tends to permeate many parts of your life. But [it can't] dominate your life. [In a marriage], other factors enter into one's life. [There are] business and family relationships where the S&M relationship doesn't have any bearing at all. These are roles that one chooses to play at one's leisure or at times [when] opportunity [permits]. One doesn't volunteer for a spanking during a board meeting.

I think [S&M] had a positive effect on my life. It's been a way to express love for a person that is much deeper [and] allows much more room for development than the typical man-wife sexual relationship. I think it creates a deep bond of trust and understanding and gets into your head a lot more than other types of sex play may bring, certainly to me. It's meant a lot to us in our relationship.

My interests are extremely eclectic. I fly airplanes; I'm a sports nut, but I'm also a concertgoer and a ballet lover. I'm very liberal in my politics, very conservative in economics; I'm [increasingly] for the underdog, because I belong to a community of people who are underdogs. I don't know that all of that is a result of S&M. [But] the involvement in a minority community helps me identify with other minority communities.

I really don't see that big of a connection [between sexual power and daily power], because 99 percent of the S&M that you see or visualize is play. I think you see that more in people who display their power in an awful and an ugly way because they can't express or are unaware that they have [S&M] interests. I think the tyrannical boss in the office place is a misplaced character; the doormat personality is a misplaced bottom. These people have no other outlets, so they live it. Dominance and submission within S&M are chosen and accepted roles. Powerlessness or powerfulness in life are not chosen roles.

My wife and I enjoy power play. Fantasy roleplaying is very important. We like forced scenes where the bottom is forced to do something humiliating. Spanking [may] play a part as a statement of authority; over-the-knee spanking is a big thing. But [the] situation may [also] involve some forced cross-dressing or the use of diapers.

I think S&M [which] doesn't necessarily lead to an orgasm to be an enormously powerful and fulfilling experience. I don't think it's foreplay; I think it's another way to love. I can certainly engage in vanilla sex and enjoy the hell out of it, but I can also enjoy the hell out of S&M. I think it's just another choice. It's rather funny that all the sex-research books in the '60s said you can do anything that you want—as long as it ends in intercourse, then it [is] normal. I think a lot of people still use that as a backup.

I started fantasizing about this sort of thing when I was a little kid. Going to a Catholic school and going through all that ritual also had certain aspects that I found exciting. There was plenty [of corporal punishment] at home, but there wasn't any in the school. The nuns were intimidating enough without it! [I grew] up in the late 1950s and early 1960s. Pornography was not generally available. The first pornographic [S&M] literature I can recall reading was in a magazine called *Bizarre*. That seemed so disconnected from the reality of everyday life, that I didn't connect.

[In my teens] I found myself turned on by the thought of a woman or a girlfriend spanking me. I never had the guts to ask one of them to do it. I was real embarrassed to talk about it with anybody. In fact, they were always asking me to do it to them! Much to my chagrin! I had a couple of girlfriends in high school who absolutely loved to get spanked [at] a drive-in or something. It was exciting, but I wanted to be where they were.

I got married in my early twenties. I found myself more and more interested in these things, and my wife and I started playing early on; we've probably been playing from six months after we got married. [Our] S&M games revolved around some alleged punishment. "Say, wouldn't it be fun to correct each other for this or that?" I always ended up doing more misdeeds than she did. It was kind of childlike play, and she definitely got into that early on.

[My wife] had never had specific [S&M] fantasies. She always liked power of some kind and didn't have a way [to] express power. She grew up in a family that treated women as doormats. [For] people in our generation, women didn't have any power. [S&M] became a way for her to enjoy and express herself.

There's a lot of democracy within S&M. The outside world doesn't understand that. The relationships are never static; they're always in a state of change. I don't think that any more dynamic a relationship can exist. It affects your personality and your outlook and your sense of adventure on a level a lot more than other stimuli. And I think that you're always looking for a higher plane within it. A sense of adventure draws us to it in the first place, indicates that we're never quite going to be satisfied with the status quo—we're always going to look for something a little bit beyond. Our marriage grew considerably stronger through the [S&M] play.

TRUDI

I'm dominant, my husband is submissive. We've been married for 27 years. It's more of a head game than a physical game with us. We also do spankings and bondage and things like that, but it's more of a reversal of roles. My husband is very dominant in business, and in our sexual life we reverse these roles.

[My husband] assumed a [sexually] dominant role in the beginning. I was so new at it, I didn't understand much about it. He was far more versed than I. When I was young it wasn't a fantasy: I did not know what S&M was. I was never exposed to it. I [just] always wanted to be in charge. But I was afraid to express that side of myself.

It's very humorous. My whole family was raised to be doormats; I along with them. All the women were very, very submissive, and the man of the house was the king: Whatever he said went. Even as a child I felt that the women of our family couldn't express themselves openly without male dominance reigning over us. I always wanted something better than what my family had. But I didn't know how to express it.

[My husband] noticed this about me and wanted to bring it out without actually saying so. He wanted me to become more assertive and more aggressive in my own life and felt that if he got me involved in some kind of activity—not S&M—[it] would make me more assertive. I always had an interest in horseback riding, for instance. So he was all for that: He wanted me to take the lessons. I did and I became much more assertive and a lot more aggressive—and my curiosity got the best of me when I had one horse and 56 whips. My husband was buying all these whips! As if I had a very naughty horse! He liked the boots and the spurs and the whole nine yards. So he took a roundabout way to introduce me [to it], which I thought was quite clever on his part. He was always making comments like, "Gee, I've really been naughty. Maybe you ought to use one of those on me!" I picked up from there. I found that I really enjoy S&M, and then I started reading more about it and became a lot more comfortable with it.

I really enjoyed it [from the start]. I didn't have any problem with it [although] I wasn't comfortable talking to other people about it. I was afraid that they wouldn't understand what my husband and I enjoyed so much. A lot of times we [heard], "Oh, that's weird!" So we would drop the subject. But when we moved to Washington we were able to join a group called the Black Rose, which was wonderful. We read an ad in *The Washingtonian* when we were up here looking at real estate. Our vision [of] this group—at the time it was called People Exchanging Power, or PEP—was that it was probably a bunch of motorcycle people in leather jackets. This is what a lot of the magazines portray. We didn't feel like we belonged in that [kind of] group. But when we went, there were doctors, lawyers, accountants, and people from all walks of life.

Actually, I got a discount for everybody in the group at an equestrian shop. [The shop] wanted to know if I belonged to an equine association. I said, "Well . . . PEP." They said, "What's that?" and I said, "People Exchanging Ponies." So I got a 15 percent discount on all the whips I bought.

[Our S&M relationship] evolved. It didn't happen overnight. Sometimes [my husband's] behavior was very naughty. He was still insecure, feeling that I wouldn't understand it if he didn't behave in a certain way. I guess I grew a bit faster than he expected. He would stay out late with the boys or [have] too much to drink, and he expected to be reprimanded for this. So he was always pushing my buttons: "Aren't you going to punish me now?" It got to the point where I said "Look, your behavior is beyond the

S&M issue. This is what you really enjoy, and I enjoy too, [so] we can cut out all this other stuff." He basically woke up and said, "Yeah! What am I doing?" We've been much happier ever since.

The most exciting thing for me is my husband surrendering total power to me, being totally submissive and very vulnerable: total trust. That probably fits into the little-boy scenario. It's very exciting [because] here's a person giving total trust and [who has] faith in me to be able to mold him. It takes both of us away from the outside world. We're in a little cocoon by ourselves. We feel secure with one another.

When we had a vanilla relationship, it felt very much like mutual masturbation. It was a sad state of affairs, and it really wasn't enough. It didn't make us feel secure. There's nothing wrong with vanilla sex; we enjoyed [it], but we felt that we needed something more. The only way that we were able to do this was through S&M, because of the alternate high that we received through power play. Releasing all the power and the energy and honesty strips you of everything else. You face the real person.

My husband and I haven't had experience—sexual experience—with other people. We do play with other people in S&M games but we don't have intercourse with [others]. We save that for each other. A lot of people feel the same way we do, that intercourse is a very intimate act only to be shared by the one you're with.

[Sometimes] when he comes home, I'll have certain implements laid out on the bed, or he'll dress a certain way and he'll have a list to follow of things to do. I tell him to go directly to the bedroom and prepare himself properly, which means that he's to [remove] his clothes and put on ladies' underwear. And then when he comes back into the living room, I'll tell him to kneel before me, and I explain to him what scenario I have in store for him that day. It may be a personal thing like [giving] me a bath and a complete body massage and attend[ing] to all my needs. If he doesn't do everything properly, he's placed across my lap and spanked.

I don't have to reach physical climax of any kind, although a lot of times I do. Sometimes I won't let him come until the next day. The excitement builds up that much more for both of us. The day that I decide we're allowed to climax, we'll have very little [S&M] play and a lot of sexual play. It's very satisfying for us.

S&M has led me to being assertive and aggressive in my work. Before, I could never do this. If somebody said, "That's too much money," or "You're a woman and you're not capable of doing this type of work," I would say, "Okay." Now if they give me this argument, I can come back at them. I could never do that before. So it's made me a much better businessperson.

We're always learning, always doing different scenes, enacting different things. Sometimes they work, sometimes they don't, but it's not the type of thing [where] you say, "That's it, I'm never going to learn anything else, I'm never going to evolve [beyond] this one scene." When you're involved in S&M, it opens up your eyes to a lot of differences. [S&M] makes you a more tolerant person.

Six

AGEPLAY

An inner child may live within us all, but the adult world of D&S is brimming with blatant scamps. Whether it's in the role of a rambunctious teenager, a misbehaving schoolboy, or a terrible two-year-old, ageplay is perhaps the most ubiquitous and most sensitive form of D&S roleplaying.

Under this broad heading we draw together a spectrum of ageplayers and organize their interests into three categories: *adolescentilism,* where the submissive imagines him- or herself to be an adolescent or young adult; *juvenilism,* where the submissive imagines him- or herself to be a child of roughly elementary-school age; and *autonepiophilia* (also known as *infantilism* or *adult babies*), where the submissive wishes to feel like an infant or toddler. Although activities and relationships vary, all ageplay depends on the basic premise that one partner assumes the role of a parentlike authority and that the submissive displays the persona of a youth or child.

We quote interviewees whose profiles appear in other chapters and feature profiles of:

- Jeff Britton is 30 years old and is an active member of GMSMA. He lives in New York City, where he works in a corporate mail room. Mr. Britton is also self-employed as a leather crafter.
- Dyke Daddy is 43 years old. She is an accountant.
- Tommy owns and operates the Diaper Pail Fraternity (DPF), the nation's largest support and informational organization for infantilists.
- George G. is 35 years old. He is a quality-control engineer. He founded *Adult Babies,* an on-line support group on CompuServe.
- Glenn is 29 years old. An ex-serviceman, now disabled, he attends college.

WHAT IS IT?

Because so many couples develop a secret language comprised of childish endearments or phrases, because many adults refer to natural functions or body parts with puerile euphemisms, and because so many grown men and women collect teddy bears and toys, one might easily infer that clinging to some childhood behaviors is common. Ageplayers, however, eroticize childishness or youth. (Ageplay is distinct from pedophilia, where a real child is considered to be sexually desirable. Ageplay occurs uniquely between consenting adults.)

In ageplay one partner (the dominant) assumes the role of a parent and supervises, guides, and—among D&Sers—disciplines the submissive who expresses his or her inner child in real, mutually consensual terms.

Being the child serves [submissives'] need to feel taken care of. I think we all feel at some point that we want to let go and not worry—that somebody's going to be there to take care of us. It [allows] them to play with taboo fantasies that we all have probably thought of at some point. A lot of people like to get into games; so it gives them another arena of play. There's [also] the power of being in a position to teach [and] to care for [someone]. It's a parenting thing.

—DYKE DADDY

Each person who seeks to erotically reinvent his or her childhood brings intensely personal and particular needs to the relationship. These needs often reflect one's individual concept of nurturing or training. Some adolescentilists like to roleplay as lazy schoolboys who require harsh physical discipline (such as caning); for many infantilists, conversely, pain has no province.

But creating an aura of authenticity and sympathy is usually an important ingredient of all ageplay. Infantilists, for example, seek the tender, nurturing parent-baby dynamic.

> *A lot of people want to experience [infantilism] in a very positive way. Many of us have had the experience of being caught by an adult or teased by peers for these practices. [People] want a situation where everything is okay and you're told it's okay to be like this. So just the kind of treatment you might normally give infants—undressing them, changing their diapers, giving them a bottle, encouraging them when they wet themselves—[is important].* —GEORGE G.

To other ageplayers, particularly spanking and caning enthusiasts, concerned discipline by a just authority is a fundamental erotic pleasure. The axiom, "Spare the rod, spoil the child" has apparently been integrated into the psychosexual proclivities of many who crave to give or receive canings.

> *If I were to express one [interest], it's that of the schoolteacher or the mother superior disciplining the naughty schoolboy or schoolgirl with a cane.* —MARIE-CONSTANCE

Activities vary according to the age—and sometimes the gender—one has eroticized.

> *The things you do to daddy's boy aren't the same things you might do to daddy's girl in a sexual context. Daddy's little girl is meeker, shyer, and scared and curious about daddy's genitalia. Daddy introduces a sexual context—you put daddy's girl on your knee or spank her. Whereas with daddy's boy, it's different; daddy-boy relationships have more of a roughness. You're not being gentle all the time.* —DYKE DADDY

Some ageplayers seek to replay one key fantasy. One example would be a person who eroticizes a specific age and fantasizes about a specific scenario, such as being caught masturbating by an authority figure who scolds and disciplines him. The clothing worn, the dialogue spoken, and the punishment implements used may be an indispensable sexual signifier. And no matter how often this fantasy is reenacted, its psychosexual spice never fades.

But many D&Sers experiment with a wide range of scenarios.

I'll put diapers and rubber pants on [my husband] and feed him
out of a bottle. He'll have no privileges. Then we have the naughty-
schoolboy scenario. I'll put him through certain lessons. If he doesn't
write proper letters, he's caned. I'll dress in a schoolmarm outfit, very
Victorian looking. I'll use the hairbrush on him. I have different
implements for different scenes.   —TRUDI

WHO DOES IT?

Ageplay seems equally popular among heterosexuals, homosexuals, and those
whose sexual or gender bias is changeable.

[The background of infantilists] seems to be a total cross-section of
society. We have those who seem to have very little education, those
who have [some] education, and those who seem very bright: business
managers, doctors, lawyers, clergymen.   —TOMMY

Although both women and men enjoy the submissive role, heterosexual men
seem a bit more likely to take an interest in expressing a child's persona, and
their female partners are more likely to play the parent. Interviewees con-
curred that infantilism, at least, is largely a male phenomenon.

Only [a small] percentage of the population is interested in [infan-
tilism]. Most are men. However, I have found that if you introduce
baby seats to women, they like it. Everybody likes to be cuddled, to be
petted. It's a very innocent scene. Not everybody needs to wet their
diapers. But it's fun to be babied.   —M. CYBELE

The women ageplayers we interviewed said that the mother (or father)
role combines romance with maternal instincts.

I never knew I would like infantilism until I played with an adult
baby. Now I enjoy being mommy. I've never really analyzed it, [but]
I'm an extremely maternal person.   JEAN L.

It is commonly believed among ageplayers that because girls and
women have socially acceptable opportunities to express their childish personae, erotic impulses to ageplay are sublimated.

I have a theory as to why our membership is primarily male. One
reason that I'm sure of is that males tend to be more active when it
comes to playing out fantasies. [But] I also believe that one of the
causes [for infantilism] is what I call "not being able to express the

soft side." Women are allowed to express theirs. I'll give you one quick [and] obvious example. Go into a women's department store almost anywhere in the United States during the winter, and you'll see women's pajamas that look like baby sleepers. They even have feet on them. You'll never see that in men's stores. It's one example of how women are allowed to express a more childish part of themselves. No one's going to laugh at them. The husband will say, "Oh, how cute." But if the average husband puts one of those things on it's, "What are you doing!"　　　　　　　　　　　　　—TOMMY

There are notable exceptions. Many D&S women enjoy playing the "naughty girl," and nowhere is this more true than for spanking enthusiasts, among whom disciplinarian-male obedient-female fantasies are common. (This is discussed in depth in Chapter 9.) And lesbians seem to be increasingly exploring ageplay fantasies.

Male-to-female cross-dressers who play mommy or female child also exist, as do female-to-male cross-dressers who play daddy or boy. Interviewees Kelly T. and Dyke Daddy (both biological females), for example, combine gender switch with ageplay.

Being Kelly [the persona of a young, gay male] sexually, and allowing myself to be submissive, has really opened sex up for me.
　　　　　　　　　　　　　—KELLY T.

I've always had masculine feelings. The first opportunity I had to be daddy in a relationship was fun. We could get into it and play for hours. I really loved it.　　　　　　　　　　　　　—DYKE DADDY

WHY AGEPLAY?

The parent-child relationship undoubtedly has the single most profound effect on a child's life. The relationship shapes not only one's self-image but in later life is expressed in one's religious biases, social behaviors, and sexual expressions. It is not surprising that some adult D&S relationships may be patterned on this original power model. Many of our interviewees believed insufficient nurturing caused their need to be babied. They felt precipitously rushed into adult behaviors.

Many of the people that I've played with have been toilet trained too early. They tell me about being out of diapers at age one or [the] mother giving enemas, so that the kid would go when she wanted him to!　　　　　　　　　　　　　—M. CYBELE

It is possible that some early punishments merged with some ageplayers' understandings of physical intimacy.

The type of punishment we received as children . . . is often translated into the SM fantasies we have as adults. These flights of mental fancy are not limited to the experiences we actually had, or which our playmates told us about. Much of the direction these adult fantasies take is caused by the prevailing punishments meted out to kids in our particular culture. For instance, the American fascination with "good old-fashioned woodshed discipline" is as firmly rooted in the frontier mentality of Middle America as the "public school" cane is a part of British tradition.

—LARRY TOWNSEND[1]

Interviewees typically recalled periods of great unhappiness in childhood, particularly times when a parent was physically absent or emotionally remote.

When I was a kid, bed-wetting made me feel really rejected. I had a really bad time with it because my parents completely ignored it, apparently in the hope that it would go away. It always bugged me that they didn't do something about it. They wouldn't do anything aside from changing the sheets. I didn't have a real loving family. We weren't physically demonstrative. We were all aloof. Maybe I missed out on affection.

—GLENN

While early experience certainly marks the child, often profoundly, cause-and-effect patterns are not always straightforward. There is no clear correlation, for example, between trauma and eroticism. Television talk shows teem with presumably sexually conventional people who had dysfunctional families, and most unhappy children seem to develop a passionate hatred of any situation that makes them feel childlike again. For the dominant, it is critical to ascertain how the submissive will respond to ageplay before initiating a scenario.

One thing you have to look for when you start playing with this is [the woman's] experience [with] sex. If they were sexually abused as young children, you don't want to get into this. You have to make sure that you're not going to be bringing up incest issues for them. They may not have liked their father at all, or not [have] grown up with a father, or have no feeling for who daddy might be.

—DYKE DADDY

For the ageplayer, reexperiencing childish vulnerability or helplessness in an emotionally and physically safe context satisfies a profound emotional need.

Infantilists commonly feel that they didn't receive all of the love and attention that they needed or wanted when they were babies, toddlers, small children. I think they're striving to fill that deficit.

—TOMMY

To feel safe and loved when at one's most vulnerable seems to be particularly gratifying to the submissive who may, for this reason, form deep and abiding bonds with the parent figure. In cases where the parent figure assumes a mentoring role in the submissive's daily life, the bond may assume central importance. Dominants, conversely, create or emulate the image of an idealized or worshiped parent.

In some cases ageplayers perceive their roleplaying as a safe and acceptable outlet for incest fantasies.

I work with children. I am not about to have any kind of sexual activity with them! I think their innocence must be protected. But when I play with an adult baby, I act out [incest] fantasies in a safe context.

—JEAN L.

Adult sexual contact is not a typical component of ageplay, because it might detract from the authenticity of a fantasy. But there are certainly many exceptions.

I enjoy taking care of people: That's my thrill. It's sexual for them while it's happening; for me, it's sexual afterwards. When I agreed to take [a friend] to an S/M party, I made [him] the New Year's baby. I had him take off all his outer clothes and leave on his diapers. I wrapped computer paper around his chest as a banner [and] wrote "1992" on it. He loved it! I told him that afterwards I was going to take him home and fuck his brains out. So I [gave] vent to my incest fantasies.

—JEAN L.

Ageplay permits another pleasure: guilt-free narcissism. Just as children may be innocently and delightedly self-centered, the submissive ageplayer often makes little effort to return obvious stimulation to the dominant.

His or her sole responsibility is obedience to authority. The compensations are many: All wrongs are righted by a loving authority, and every child, however naughty or dirty at the outset, is ultimately transformed into someone lovable and good. This thrilling resolution of old psychological wounds or conflicts is probably the single most emotionally satisfying experience of ageplay. The fantasy child receives an unconditional approval that the real child may never have known.

ADOLESCENTILISM

Adolescentilist fantasies among heterosexual D&Sers almost always focus on physical discipline. Scenarios involving an unruly high-school or college-aged student who is subjected to stern discipline—and whose comeuppance is delivered with his pants lowered (or her skirt raised)—are popular, as are misbehaving "nieces" with exasperated "uncles" and "woodshed" fantasies, where the submissive is escorted to an outdoor structure for stringent physical discipline.

The authority figure is unlikely to assume responsibility in nonerotic matters, and the fantasy is likely of only temporary duration. The roles, without exception, are played for the sake of psychosexual gratification (although there may be no directly sexual activity), and partners revert to egalitarian (or, among lifestylers, top-bottom) roles.

The very significant exception to disciplinary-based fantasies occurs in daddy-boy relationships, which are well known and accepted throughout gay society. Daddy-boy is a particularly important romantic variation in gay and lesbian D&S.

> *I like to consider myself—although I sometimes don't like the term with my own children—a "daddy." There are a lot of people out there who consider themselves bottom and are always looking for a daddy. I didn't start out that way; [but] more and more people were looking for daddies, and I said, "What the hell? I'll try anything once." I began to enjoy it more and more. Everyplace I go, people look at me and right away they say, "Ooooh, Daddy!"*
>
> —LOGGER V.

Daddy-boy relationships seem to most completely transcend the bounds of fantasy; they are multidimensional and often carry over into a couple's daily life.

> *Daddy-boy relationships have the special possibility of being lived all the time, even when daddy and boy both go off to work. It's still daddy that the boy is going to come home to.* —JOSEPH BEAN

Leather or not, a daddy plays a transformational role in his partner's life and may help shape and improve his partner's self-esteem. Fatherly counsel may include wardrobe selection and social etiquette; it commonly includes an introduction to gay eroticism (even among equally experienced partners, the fantasy of the boy's naiveté may be acted out). The dynamic of the relationship is that a familiar, trustworthy, mature partner intiates a younger partner into adulthood. Frequently the relationship ends when the boy has matured sufficiently to move on to other relationships; in some cases a boy may become a daddy. Some couples, however, form permanent unions.

The daddy in a leather love affair additionally instructs his boy in submissive service.

> *I think the appeal of daddy-boy relationships probably comes from the familiarity of the words and moods and options. A lot of stuff can be unspoken because everybody grew up knowing who daddy was: Daddy's complete ascendancy is not questionable. Yet you may expect [a] daddy to be somewhat permissive or more accepting; certainly more supporting. A master expects his slave to need training, but he certainly does not expect his slave to need to be supported in his emotional growth. He expects that the creature is already adult, whereas a daddy is expected to make a contribution towards raising the boy: providing him with the support and the encouragement and guidance that he may need.* —JOSEPH BEAN

Daddy-boy also enhances the self-esteem of the daddy who derives considerable pleasure from exerting a positive, loving influence over a trusting partner.

> *Going back to the term daddy or top or master: I have always been in that situation—as a husband, as a father. It was drawn out of me in a sexual sense later in life. Now that I see it for what it really is, I really cannot be without it.* —LOGGER V.

Some couples enjoy thinking of the boy as in his early 20s rather than his teens. And a daddy is not always older than his boy, although an age gap is not unusual.

Although daddies are masters in leather romances, the master may periodically order the boy to dominate him.

> *I am a switch who gets into daddy fantasies when I am either being a very good submissive boy to my daddy or I am being a nice top to my daddy—one of my favorite fantasy trips.* —JEFF BRITTON

In lesbian daddy-boy relationships, both partners interact as psychological males. The dynamic is of a character similar to daddy-boy among biological males.

> *In daddy-boy it's a given that we're both butch . . . I've always felt very supportive of the people I've been involved with—wanting to see*

them succeed. Not telling them exactly what to do, but providing
guidance. I've also bought things for my boys—bought them their
first harness or something that they would wear when they go out
with me. —DYKE DADDY

Partly because lesbian daddy-boy relationships propose a fundamentally man-to-man rather than woman-to-woman approach, some couples find themselves under fierce scrutiny and political attack from non-leather lesbians.

The emotional intimacy and bonding of gay daddy-boy relationships has also influenced heterosexual and bisexual D&Sers. Female-to-male cross-dressers too may seek mentors.

While I'm no longer [Sir Adam's] submissive, I am something
different but equally special to him now: I'm his boy. And in
accordance with my liking of head games, it's a delight to tell
straight people, "No, I'm not his slave. I'm his boy," and walk away.
Then they might see me topping him one night at a club and get
totally confused. —LAURA ANTONIO

Finally, according to anecdotal information from interviewees, some straight dominant women have begun to roleplay as daddies to their male submissives.

INTERVIEW

JEFF BRITTON

I have been involved in the leather lifestyle for seven years. I make no secret of my sexual preference, although I am not very blatant about my leather side. I have a picture of me in full leather on my desk at work. It's a part of me and I'm quite proud of it. It helped me get through a very nasty time when I had a major alcohol problem; my leather friends helped me get out of that hole.

I am a recovering alcoholic. I can discuss the fact that I'm gay in an AA meeting; however, if you bring up the subject of leather sex, a lot of people freak out. My first year, I didn't talk about leather sex. [It] was very disturbing because I was hiding a part of myself. I did not like that. I then had the good fortune to go to National Leather Association's Living in Leather conference and was relieved. I could talk about sex [and] the fact that I am an alcoholic in the same room!

When I was young, and listening to religious [stuff] about sins, [being gay] bothered me. But then I thought, What am I going to do? That's the way I am, and I don't feel like changing for anybody. When the leather interest came into being, the same attitude applied: It's just the way I am, and I have no intention of changing. *I* think my higher power exists, because it makes me *me*. I knew I was gay first; [as for leather], I became friends with someone I'm still very close to. He spotted my tendencies before I did and, in a very loving way, slowly groomed me. It was 8½ years ago. I was a college student and a black preppie.

When I was growing up, I never associated with kids my own age. I was always with people older than me. I don't know if it's that I instinctively go to people older than me because I don't relate with my own age, or whether I have been replacing the daddy that I never had. I *rarely* get involved with anyone my age or younger. There has always been at least a 10-year span between me and my partner.

A daddy-son scene for me has always been [with] a man who has taken a parental role where he is, say, telling me the facts of life—not in terms of the birds and the bees, but in terms of how to please a person, how to get to know someone better, and sharing. We act [this] out. In the courting stage I may play dumb, like a kid who needs a loving, helping hand. Would I continue that 24 hours a day? No way in hell! What happens in the bedroom is the bedroom; outside, we're two people [who] sleep together.

JUVENILISM

In juvenilist fantasies the submissive partner projects the persona of a child—usually between the ages of six and 12. There is a fairly typical pattern to juvenilist scenarios: First, an emotional drama precipitated by the dominant's discovery of the submissive's childish mischief or disobedience. The dominant, a stern but ultimately sympathetic figure, then decides on and inflicts an appropriate punishment. Finally, there is resolution and catharsis when the "naughty child" is forgiven and reassured he or she is loved. Partners rarely continue their roles once the scenario is complete.

> *Daddy-girl is a game that's played on a sexual basis. It could happen spontaneously, but it's not ongoing all the time. At least it hasn't been for me. I know there are other butches [for whom] it has, but when I get involved with women long-term, I want equality [and] balance. I have a lot [of] needs; I don't want to be taking care of somebody all the time.* —DYKE DADDY

Although discipline—particularly spanking—is a component of nearly all juvenilist fantasies, the punishment may take a variety of forms. For example, a "baby-sitter" may tell the submissive to stand in a corner for a period of time, or there may be lengthy scolding. Humiliation is a key component in many juvenilist fantasies, but care is taken not to undermine the submissive's self-esteem. Instead, the dominant is likely to suggest that the submissive was naughty in a playful context and that a particular punishment will restore the rascal to grace.

> *The naughty girl or naughty schoolboy [may] need a strict yet nurturing authority figure who tells them what to do and punishes them, usually in a loving manner. A lot of times they have confused punishment with caring. I'm not interested in reinforcing that stereotype.* —M. CYBELE

The parent figure may ask embarrassing questions about the submissive's personal or sexual habits. By stripping away the submissive's privacy, the dominant exposes not only the submissive's body but also her inner nakedness and vulnerability. In some juvenilist scenarios the dominant role-plays as the erotic guide.

> *In bed, you're coming from a place of knowledge; the other person is coming from a place of innocence. It gives you sexual freedom to say, "Daddy's going to do this to his little girl," or "Daddy's going to show his little boy what you might find [out] when you go to the*

gym." It depends on the individual. I've had people I've introduced
sexual techniques to who had never experienced those things; then it's
innocence. Others may just get into playing the role.

—DYKE DADDY

Each aspect of a juvenilist scenario may be laden with erotic meaning:
the austerity of the dominant's demeanor, the precise orders issued. Punishment implements also possess a singular mystique: In English discipline, for
example, the emotional impact of the cane rivals its physical sensation in
sensuality. Or a submissive may feel blissfully chastened when erotically
coerced to wear a tight petticoat or little girl's attire. Such details may have
a critical place in the erotic hierarchy of the submissive; without them, his
satisfaction is incomplete.

INTERVIEW

DYKE DADDY

[I am a] dominant. I've been butch all my life. [As far back as] I can remember I was cross-dressing and doing boy stuff and hanging out with boys. When I became gay, it was natural for me to fall into the pattern of being butch. I think lesbians tend to get into platonic relationships where one person may [be] more together [or] may even be older. There will be a mother-daughter thing going on, but they don't call it that, [and] they don't play at it. A lot of lesbians tend to get together and be sexual and then [change]. After a couple of years, there is [a] platonic relationship; women may stay together for years and not have much sexual interaction. They may cuddle, they may touch each other, but it's not really get-down-get-dirty sex.

I was in a 12-year, live-in relationship, and there's just too much stuff you have to hash out afterwards [when it ends]. I haven't lived with any of my lovers since then. In my live-in relationship, my partner had a daughter. I went into that relationship when I was 18; I was pretty much a kid myself. Being an only child, I didn't have any siblings [that I had] to share with, so I was a pretty selfish kid, too. My relationship with that child was not maternal. Now I'm more of a mature woman. I know what it is to love and care for a child and [to] feel maternal instincts. [Daddy-girl and daddy-boy] feed into that. I have a lot more worldly experience [which] I can share and teach and be nurturing.

[Although] a daddy's girl is more of a turn-on to me than a boy, the biggest turn-on was teaching and having one boy look to me for support, for information, for love, and thinking of me as sexually knowledgeable. With daddy's boy, it's nurturing. One woman I was involved with was daddy's boy: She would learn the butch stuff; we would go out and cruise women together.

I remember going out with one of my boys. We would go to a bar and cruise the chicks, the babes—whatever you want to call it. I'd show my boy how this is done; daddy takes the lead. I've [also] taught some boys how to use the whip, because a lot of them want to be tops: They're gaining some expertise from you as well. We've also done scenes where we've gone to a party and topped someone else. The two of us would top [an]other woman. This woman would [perhaps] be tied up and watching what's going on, and at some point we might break and start kissing or making out or touching each other. It is a turn-on, because this person is tied up and wanting both of you at the same time and not able to have either of you.

With boys it's been intrinsically short-term, because they seem to need change. They may be happy and then feel they want to go on [to] topping. So they're looking to grow out of it real fast. But daddy's girl is more of an equal relationship.

With daddy's little girl, if I was expecting her for the day, I might make breakfast for the two of us, and we might retreat to the bedroom for sex and play around for a while. [I might ask questions, such as], "What did you do last night? Did you go to that slumber party or did you call up boys and have boys come over? And if those boys came over, were you good or did you play around?" Depending on the person and how they feel, they can play off of it. One woman that I was involved with was very good at this. She would say, "No, I wasn't being good!" "What were you doing?" "I let this boy touch me." So daddy would ask, "How did this boy touch you?" and she would say, "He touched me like this!" and show me, or she wouldn't tell me until I explored [it myself]. It would get into a whole thing of making love around that. And then maybe daddy would take his little girl out to the movies. Daddy would dress in butch stuff; daddy's little girl would be in normal femme clothes. She would not be dressed up as a little girl. If we went to the movies, daddy would buy popcorn and Milk Duds or whatever little girls like to eat at the movies. It could be a Walt Disney flick or something [else] that's childish but [which] also would appeal to an adult. Afterwards, we might go for ice cream, possibly at a shop where, when you order certain ice creams, they come and make all this noise, singing stuff and making fun of you. Or we would go play video games or go to the Santa Cruz boardwalk and ride the Ferris wheel, the merry-go-round, the roller coaster, [and] play the games. Daddy would try to win his little girl a prize, of course. And we might go lingerie shopping. [If so], daddy would buy his little girl something very sexy. Then we might go out to dinner; daddy usually picks up the tab.

Not every relationship I enjoy has to have that element to be appealing to me. It's something that I do, but it's not the only way I relate to people. I think it's another part of my sexuality. I like doing it, [and] if I can get away with it, and the person is into it, I enjoy doing it.

To me a master is someone who owns someone, who is totally into top space, and needs to keep that top space at all times in a scene. When you're in a daddy–daddy's girl [or] daddy-boy scene, this person is not under your control all the time. They're not asking [for permission all the time]. It's more playful. If you had a little girl or little boy, and you took them out for the day, they would have a certain amount of freedom. They wouldn't have to wait for your command.

If people are interested in this type of play, they need to check out the other person's background. A lot of people, especially girls and women, have had incest problems. We are discovering that at least one third of women in this country [were] sexually abused as children. Often the women don't even know. You need to be really sensitive and have a feel for what's happening. If something's not working right, don't push it. Women have told me that they didn't even realize they had been molested as children, but that something suddenly happened and memories started coming back. I haven't had it happen to me. I'm pretty cautious. It's not that I'm not there for someone, or [that] I wouldn't be responsible or supportive if it happened—[but] why get into an area that's going to be trouble for you when there are so many other things you can do?

AUTONEPIOPHILIA, OR INFANTILISM

Perhaps the least understood and most maligned form of ageplay is one in which individuals wish to relive an idealized version of early childhood or infancy. The fantasy age range of infantilism runs from approximately six months old to age three or four. Although infantilists are exclusively adults who roleplay uniquely with other adults, this sexual interest is commonly mistaken for pedophilia. In fact, infantilists who recognize and accept their sexuality—and its possible roots in infantile trauma—tend to be acutely protective of real children.

Beyond this misunderstanding of infantilists' motives, the primal nature of their fantasies arouses profound discomfort among uninvolved observers.

We saw a [Phil] Donahue [show] about infantilism and were amazed at the outrage that some people felt about infantilists, who are engaged in something absolutely innocent. They enjoy being in baby clothes and get a certain amount of satisfaction from re-creating their early childhood. Statistically, nobody knows whether it's normal or not. The psychiatrist on the show was very clear on the fact that these people were doing nothing wrong.

—HOWARD AND MARTHA LEWIS

Many D&Sers express discomfort with infantilism as well, perhaps because it is difficult to understand why someone would wish to be as helpless as an infant. But it is precisely that primal helplessness that so charms the infantilist.

Infantilism is about losing control in a very primitive manner. Usually my client had to grow up too fast [or]—for one reason or another—did not get enough childhood experience.

—M. CYBELE

Most infantilists recall that their interest began in early childhood. In some cases, the arrival of a new baby (and possible sibling rivalry) was a turning point.

A typical story would be: "[When] I was five, I watched my little sister getting changed. I sneaked one of her diapers into my room. I put it on, and it felt sort of nice." —TOMMY

Interest in impersonating a baby may be further affected by health or incontinence problems.

My feeling is that I'm trying to recapture the childhood I feel I was twice denied. I had a very difficult childhood. I was hospitalized at age seven and required brain surgery. I had to rush through growing up. Because of medications, I was a heavy sleeper and a bed-wetter from ages seven to 12. I entered puberty still wetting the bed. You often continue to associate [with] whatever was in your life at that time. —GEORGE G.

Infantilism is primarily a male phenomenon and is practiced by straight and gay men. (It should not, however, be confused with daddy-boy relationships.) Female infantilists are known but scarce. If lesbian infantilists exist, they are as yet entirely private. It seems far more common for women to roleplay as mommies to male babies. A number of professional dominants who specialize in this scene have nursery equipment built to scale for clients. In addition to biologically female mommies, some dominant male-to-female cross-dressers express a maternal persona. And a number of male-to-female cross-dressers wish to be treated like baby girls.

Some incontinent adults may also explore infantilist eroticism.

I think possibly 10 percent of all incontinent people—and that's a huge number—[have] some sort of related infantilistic involvement. I have a small company that sells to incontinent people, and the catalogue states clearly that all of the products were copied after infant wear. They actually sell some diapers with baby prints. Ten or 15 percent of the customers buy those. —TOMMY

Infantilism provides an important erotic outlet for some disabled individuals.

[Infantilism] is my main coping mechanism for the multiple sclerosis. The disease can flare up to the point where I can't take care of myself; that is my way of dealing with it. I'm in diapers all the time anyway because of the MS. Before [being] confined to the wheelchair, I had a vague interest in it—not so much in acting like a baby as in wearing diapers. But I thought [infantilism] was strange and that no one else would ever think anything like that.   —GLENN

Infantilists seem to have the greatest uniformity in desirable scenarios. Their ageplay patterns the basic model of parent-infant relations.

When I start a session with an adult baby, I like to do bonding, like you would with a real baby. I'll get out a bottle and have them put their head in my lap. I'll stroke them and murmur and do little baby things to them. I'll play with toys with them. I'll give them a bubble bath. I will make them do things like memorize little poems and do little dances.   —JEAN L.

Dominants find that assuming a maternal or paternal role is a tender and fulfilling experience.

For a lot of people infantilism brings a feeling of reassurance; for others [it] fulfills the need for nurturing, often without having to worry 24 hours a day about caring for a small child. It makes me feel comforted, relaxed. At times it makes me feel like I'm getting away with something the world doesn't want me to be able to get away with!   —GEORGE G.

For the submissive infantilism permits expression of a vulnerability that would be inappropriate to his adult persona.

It's the old story of the boss at the corporation who pushes everybody around and has all the power; [then] he goes home, puts on his diaper, and his wife gives him a bottle. I think these are people whose fathers told them, "Boys don't cry; boys aren't soft!" whereas I think we know that boys are a combination in varying degrees.

—TOMMY

Yet while infantilism may represent the ultimate surrender of power, adult babies tend to be extremely explicit as to exactly what they expect and enjoy.

Some babies just want to be cuddled, petted, taken care of. They want to be vulnerable, but believe me, babies are not passive. They're also not very submissive. They're quite demanding: "Waahh! Feed me! Waaah! Change me!" Babies are naughty. They're very sweet.

—M. CYBELE

Authenticity is usually an erotic requirement. This includes not only the garments and toys of infants, but also age-appropriate behavior.

The more realistic it is, the more it excites me. To make it more realistic, you have to be more whatever your appropriate age is. Some people like to pretend to be older—three [or] five. When I'm really sick, I can't walk [so] that would be not quite good enough. I generally stick around the area of a 12- or 18-month-old.

—GLENN

While humiliation is a common interest, some adult babies wish to experience infancy without such D&S elements as humiliation, coercion, or punishment. Infantilists usually prefer gentle, teasing, nurturing experiences.

There can be a mix of S/M and nurturance. And the S/M usually takes the form of spanking. It's mainly to give them the experience of not being in charge. They get [spanked] for disobeying.

—M. CYBELE

Diapering scenarios are perhaps the single most common erotic practice. But diaper fetishists—who do not consider themselves adult babies—exist as well.

Unlike adult babies, I consider myself a grown individual. I buy diapers for the feeling, not for the child fantasy that people tend to build [or] the toys and equipment. I don't see myself as a small child, but as an adult who just gets a kick out of wearing them.

—PHIL T.

Infantilists rarely wish to combine their roleplaying with adult sexual encounters: There is little or no direct sexual contact during the roleplaying. However, conventional sexual intimacy may be the culmination of the roleplaying.

[For me] sex is an adjunct, not an end. Some people treat being a baby as foreplay; once they've come, it's over. They get dressed and they say, "Golly, that was fun." When I've come, I want to be cleaned up and given another bottle. I don't want it to end. Sex is a pleasant thing and really fun—but not a goal.　　—GLENN

All the infantilists we spoke with reported at least an intermittent desire to live out the infantile fantasy over extended periods of time. For some, the craving for infantilism moved in inverse proportion to daily stress: the higher the stress in the outside world, the more powerful the craving to retreat into a state of infantile irresponsibility at home. Nonetheless, our interviewees emphasized the importance of maintaining a clear balance between fantasy and reality.

> *I've [devised] systems to avoid obsessing. Putting myself in a situation where it's more frequent in my life and using it as a relief or safety valve has really helped. When I would try and deny myself, I would find myself getting fairly depressed. By being able to do it as much as I need, I find that I'm much more relaxed, not only about the infantilist part of my life but other parts as well.*
>
> —GEORGE G.

INTERVIEWS

TOMMY

Infantilism is a deep-seated psychological need that arises usually at a very early age, possibly for two reasons. One is that [infantilists have] the feeling of not getting loved enough when they're very young; the other is not being able to express the softer sides of themselves. [Infantilism] becomes a very strong drive, so strong that there's no way of getting rid of it. But there's no reason to get rid of it, because it is not harmful. It lets a person fantasize and/or share with other people—lovers, spouses, friends.

There's a psychological theory that if you didn't complete all of the [childhood] stages, there's a deficit [that] you never fully outgrow. You're always trying to fill it. The causes of not being understood for the person you are—basically the definition of a dysfunctional family—has many other results. People become drug addicts or alcoholics; they become very unhappy. I think that infantilism, though it may sound strange or weird to a lot of people, is probably the least harmful way of coping as long as you don't let it dominate your life. If you can put it in a place where you use it to help you feel good about yourself, get some happiness and satisfaction, and [if] it doesn't interfere with your ability to function in your job, with your spouse, with your children, then it's a satisfactory way of meeting a psychological need.

The Diaper Pail Fraternity (DPF) was founded in 1980. Being an infantilist and having made some friends through personal ads, I decided to form a little newsletter. What started out as a newsletter shared by a few friends continued to grow over the years. [Today] it's got over 2000 members. I should qualify: Not all members are current. At any [given] time there are about 1000 actively listed members and 1000 temporarily inactive members. We're about two-thirds straight and one-third gay. [This is] a little heavier than the average on gay, because we were originally a gay organization.

Upwards of 95 percent [of our members] are male. This is gradually changing. We're beginning to attract more and more women. Because of the [limited] number of women we have at the present time, it's hard to be sure why women are attracted to DPF. They appear to be primarily infantilists themselves. A fair percentage of the dominant women that we're getting are professional; a few are the wives of infantilists. One thing I do see is that, because of increasing publicity and education, male and female infantilists are beginning to come out of the closet and to know that there are others. And if they meet, there's a chance of forming a relationship. We have that happen. [Members] get married, find lovers.

Besides the newsletter, DPF tries to distribute, manufacture—or have others manufacture—things of interest to the members, [such as] stories, videotapes, audiotapes, [or] resource directories to locate products. We also have an extensive list of products for infantilists, such as adult-sized diapers, plastic pants, [and] baby clothes.

I have 144 people who I track in a data base. I'm pretty sure this is representative: 13 percent report an interest in S&M; 49 percent gave a general interest in punishment and discipline; 49 people, or 34 percent are interested in enemas; 26 percent like cross-dressing—the cross-dressers are primarily straight people. Spankers make up 48 percent. We also have 29 percent who like a little bondage—being tied to a crib so you can't get out or having a pacifier tied into your mouth.

The great majority of [members] want to take the baby or child role. If they really feel free and start making friends, then they're going to have to be daddies because there aren't that many dominant women in the club. So they will switch and diaper each other at different times. It's a trade-off: Somebody's sacrificing a bit, but [he's] doing it because he knows he will get something in return. The great majority of the heterosexuals—probably 90 percent—want to be the baby. They have a tough time because there are so few mommies. For the homosexuals, it's a little easier, because approximately one third of the homosexual members say that they will be dominant at times. And 15 percent to 20 percent are primarily dominant [and] like being the daddy.

The biggest social challenges infantilists face are, first, that they're hidden. Those still in the closet are very unhappy people; they don't know that there are others out there. They think that they're really crazy. The majority of them aren't so unhappy that they're suicidal, but they're thrilled when they find out that there are other people. A fairly good portion of married men are afraid to tell their wives. Or they've brought the subject up and were rejected. [They] try to tell their wife, and [she] can't deal with it [and] makes comments like, "I married a man, not a baby." Second, they feel that nobody understands them. They are afraid that the general public will think that they want to involve children and are pedophiles. Many people are afraid to use their real names when they list in the roster because they fear that somehow they'll be found out—that coworkers will find out that they wear diapers at home. This would be a terrible, humiliating, or even threatening thing; [they worry] they might lose their job.

GEORGE G.

I've experienced many times the desire to just take everything I have and throw it out and tell myself I'm not going to be involved, very much like you hear from people involved in cross-dressing. The urge doesn't go away, but I've learned to do things in balance so that I don't ever desperately feel like I've been denying myself. I know [that] if I don't do [it] for myself, I'm not going to be happy. So it's a drive. [It's] something I need. It's a fairly constant part of my life.

I come from a family that openly discussed medical and sexual issues. I was the youngest child. My mother would catch evidence of my involvement in [infantilism]. She sat me down when I was 12 years old to explain that she didn't want me to do these things because the only people who did were homosexual perverts.

As a boy, I would steal safety pins or old diapers from the rag pile. When they were no longer available I would use whatever absorbent cloth was practical. I really enjoyed playing with toys that were much too young for me—stuffed animals, rattles, teething rings. I would set up in a corner and regress. By my age [35], you can see [that] this was the era of cloth, not disposable, diapers. There's a split in interest that goes down generational lines. I'm seeing more and more preferences for cloth over disposable or vice versa. Then you have the enthusiasts who are very interested in rubber, because there was a time when baby garments [were changed from] rubber to plastic.

I'm somewhat bisexual. With the right person, gender doesn't matter. We've all been brought up with certain conceptions about gender. They're very difficult to get past. Through my teenage years I was struggling with [that] more than the infantilism. I struggled with my sexual identity, my sexual preference. I had the support of siblings, but there was secrecy and gameplaying. I was already fairly good at trying to hide my practice of infantilism.

One of the things that stuck with me through most of my adolescent years was my mother's voice reminding me that there were others out there. I filed that little piece of information away. I found references to an infantilist organization called the Diaper Pail Fraternity in *Drummer*. Looking through their ads [and] through the *Berkeley Barb,* I discovered that there were people out there, but I didn't contact any for a number of years.

When I was about 28, [I was] doing research for a book on [electronic] bulletin boards. I found references to the interest. The first real positive contact I made was through local BBS's; one regular writer recommended I try CompuServe. I did and found out that DPF was just normal folks. I joined.

I was invited to a party and housewarming at the home of Tommy, who runs DPF. That was the first time I [met] a large number of infantilists all at once. I had never seen these people face to face and wasn't sure if, for all the talk, anyone else actually dared to go so far as to wear diapers or drink from bottles. Maybe they just all talked about it, and I would go wearing a diaper under my clothes and find myself terribly embarrassed that no one else did! First thing I saw when I arrived was someone with a huge wet spot in front being scolded. That relaxed me a little bit. The host of the party was an especially good host. He took me in and changed me and insisted upon using his supplies. A number of people had shed their pants and were walking around in diapers; the conversation was like [that of] any normal party. There was a little [talk] about the interest here and there, but people were drinking beer and eating snacks, and some were in the hot tub. It was a very nice setting.

Through all of this, Tommy kept making sure I always had something to drink. I couldn't quite figure out why. Later I was in the living room, sitting and talking to people, and all of a sudden [I] heard [a] little music— like a watch alarm that plays "Yankee Doodle." I'm looking in the sofa cushions, trying to figure out where the sound is coming from. Everyone else in the room is staring in my direction. Tommy came over and took me by the arm and said, "Aha! I think this baby needs changing." He had thrown [a] musical diaper alarm inside my diaper—a little sensor that plays music when it gets wet. So there I was, amid 30 people [and] turning beet red. It was a pretty good experience.

I get to know the people on-line or through letter writing or phone calls quite a bit before [meeting]. If there aren't [also] noninfantilist and nonsexual common interests, I don't follow through. If we both happen to be interested in computers or in hiking, it gives [the relationship] a chance. Otherwise . . . the word I want to use is "cheapened," but that's not [quite] right. Let's say it has less potential.

One experience that definitely sticks out occurred when I was being parent for one friend for a week. There's a lot of activity in supporting someone; it gets tiring. At one point I said, "Look, I'm just too tired. Take care of yourself and put yourself down for a nap. I need to lay down!" I went and lay down. The next thing I knew, he brought me a blanket and a bottle and started to cradle me in [his] arms. He held me like a six-month-old, gently swayed and rocked me, and said, "It's okay," stroking my head and my hair, cuddling. The next thing I remember is waking up and looking up to see him still staring down at me and smiling. [I felt] very relaxed and very blissful.

There are a lot of people out there, I'm sure, who are happily doing parts of this in their regular relationship [and] who have no need to express it outside their own relationship. I was involved in a relationship with one particularly interesting woman for a couple of years. Ninety percent of the time or more [she] would be the nurturer. One of her favorite scenes was to [catch] me wetting my pants, spank me, put me in diapers, scold me, and tell me I shouldn't be given an opportunity to grow up. Often in the middle of the change she would molest me and take advantage of me and want me to be passive. Which was a lot of fun! Mommy taking advantage of me. Fun! I found it a good experience. [Unfortunately] there were other things in the relationship that were incompatible, so it didn't last.

One of the big issues that comes up is how to do those things yet keep it secret from others. The fear of other people discovering and ridiculing you is strong. I still have a lot of that. My parents and relatives, and friends not involved in this interest, visit quite frequently, and it's difficult. I don't have people casually dropping in. I also find that I'm spending more and more time with friends who are involved in [this] or who are understanding.

There aren't that many support areas for this. That partly accounts for my commitment to running the *Adult Babies* section. The biggest message [that] I hope comes across to readers is what comes up in letters I receive all the time. *You should know you're not alone.*

GLENN

I'm heterosexual and an infantilist: I like to be treated as a baby or small child, and [be] taken care of by my significant other. I prefer a female caretaker, but more important than the traditional sexual issues is the form of the caretaking—that is [my] primary concern. I would never consider dating a man, but I've had male nurse's aides, and although I was uncomfortable at first, I found that if the person is a good caretaker, [the gender] didn't bother me. I have MS, and I'm in a wheelchair. Sometimes people assume [that] if you're in a wheelchair you're stupid. I've had a few instances where people have talked to me like I was a baby or a child—people I didn't know, cashiers at checkout counters.

I'm not interested in S&M, but dominance and submission is built into infantilism. The submissive is a nonresponsible person submitting to the authority of an adult figure. A lot of infantilists—and I have to include myself—are pretty dominant about how they're submissively treated. But within the relationship itself they are told what to do with or without any feedback from them at all.

[When] living at home, I was in a supervised environment. I could hardly go out and [get] diapers. I would be terrified to death that I would be caught and [that] my parents would freak out. Then I was in the service for two years. I lived on the post, and we had periodic inspections. Most of my off-post activities were concerned with fantasy roleplaying games and war simulation, so I was at a friend's house or the recreation center most weekends. I suppose I could have done something, but it wasn't that strong a drive [then]. I wavered, thinking it'd be neat, then, Oh, man, that's silly. When I came back from the Army, I was immediately in college. I had a bit more opportunity but never a reason to do it.

In the summer of 1983 I started getting sick. By the time October rolled around I was in the hospital. The MS was seriously affecting my coordination, strength, and stamina. They performed a number of tests. One [a spinal tap] was real unpleasant. One of the side effects is post-puncture headache. At one point my head hurt like crazy, but with that much codeine in me I didn't care. I had to go and I didn't want to get up, so I wet the bed. I thought it was tremendously funny.

Eventually I was released. I was in a wheelchair; I could use a walker, but I wasn't really great with it. I kept ditching out and falling down, which I didn't like. I was probably home for four months when I started to have a small bed-wetting problem. It was just every couple of days or so, but I started wearing diapers at night. I was [also] rather fond of doing marijuana at the time, which makes my condition worse. It exaggerates some of the neurological symptoms. It got to the point where, if I got really high, I'd start wetting during the day. That happened a couple of times. Even at times when I could have gone without them, I wore diapers. I thought, I've always wanted to do this, so it doesn't bother me that much. It was my way of saying, "It's not that bad."

In 1985 I had a really bad flare-up of the MS. It put me in the hospital and messed me up real good. For a long time I wasn't capable of taking care of myself at all. We started having nurse's aides over because my wife couldn't take care of me all the time. I was in a bad state of depression. I dealt with the wheelchair pretty easily and the diapers didn't bother me, but having no stamina and no coordination at all was a little bit much. That year of my life was not a lot of fun. I had a lot of times where I was really unpleasant to be around.

[It was] when I was totally unable to take care of myself [that] the "being a baby" coping mechanism cropped up. I'd been diapered for a while. I was used to the fact that other people had to diaper me. It turned me on tremendously the first time [an aide] changed me. I thought it was wild. Here was this person I didn't even know changing my diaper. Eventually I got her to give me backrubs, which would turn into her masturbating me. I wanted that kind of contact. There wasn't any babying—it was just the fact of her seeing me in the diaper, putting the diaper on me, checking the diaper to see if it was wet. [That] was exciting and emotionally gratifying.

[The babying] crept up gradually. It started with the bottle. I keep a glass of lemonade in my headboard to drink, and I'd been reaching for it and knocking it off. I told my wife that we should get a nursing bottle for me, half hoping she'd use it. She got some, but we never used them. Another nurse's aide was here when I got back from the hospital. She was a tremendous help to me. I told her there were bottles in the sink so I wouldn't spill, and she got the bottle for me. [Around this time] I [also] ordered a few things from [an adult-baby mail-order house] as an experiment. One was a bodysuit with snaps that go up over the diaper. I started wearing it at night. [My caretaker] thought it was great. She said, "Wow, this makes it so much easier to change you." I said, "That's cool." I was afraid she'd look at them and laugh. Eventually she brought over a pacifier. The first time she did, I stepped over the line from what needed to be done to what I wanted to be done.

I started to accumulate baby toys, and she started referring to herself as my baby-sitter. It went on from there. All the stuff I've got is snap-crotch. All the bottles I have are juvenile-print nursers. When I was really sick I had to order an adult transport chair [which] could be pushed by an attendant. I got the one most like a stroller. I try to get as many babylike things as possible: diaper stackers with little bears on them, juvenile clothing. I have collected a small amount of toys: I have Busy Box. The last year and a half that she visited, there was an assumption on both our parts that I was a completely dependent infant. She dressed me; if I was really sick, she would play with my toys with me.

My wife doesn't care for [infantilism] very much. She will baby me when I'm really sick. It's primarily limited to what needs to be done. She won't take time out and play with me when she changes me. [But] she's gotten more accepting over the years. Most of [my] evolution as a baby came about in periods where the MS was flaring up or I was moderately sick with a cold. There [were] times when I did not need a nurse's aide, I just wanted to be babied. Any time I'm sick, any time that I cannot do everything myself, it's a very important part of my life.

The best day I ever had was around a year ago. [My caretaker] came over on a Friday and left on Sunday. That Saturday, from the moment I got up until I went to sleep, I was the total baby. I spent the entire waking part of my day without saying an intelligible word. Everything I needed was taken care of, often before I really thought I needed it, by somebody I had feelings of trust and affection for. So my idea of a caring, loving relationship is where she spent the entire day babying me, fed me when it was appropriate, changed my diapers, dressed me in baby clothes, played with me with my toys. At the end of the day she bathed me, dried me off, put me in my sleeper, fed me a nighttime bottle, played with me a bit more, sang little lullabies to me, and masturbated me until I fell asleep. It was absolutely the best day I've ever had.

Everybody has different ideas on what constitutes great sex in conjunction with infantilism. For me [it] varies, depending on who's taking care of me. With my aides and baby-sitters, I'm delighted if I can get them to masturbate me. And with one exception, that's as far as it's ever gone. With my wife—somebody I really care about—then I want it to go to the point of intercourse or oral sex. I have a problem maintaining an erection when there isn't any direct stimulation. And because I have slightly reduced sensitivity, I last forever, which my wife does not complain about at all, except when she's giving me what we euphemistically call a "front rub," which I get her to do every now and then. In conjunction with being treated like a baby, that's probably my favorite thing.

The release [aspect], where you actually come, is not as important as you would think. When you think of sexual activity, you think of two people making out or making love. But for me, the more I can be made to feel like an infant or a child, the more turned on I am, the more comfortable I get. When the release itself can come, I prefer that to be like a mother doing it to quiet the baby. I consider being masturbated to be more an adjunct to babying because the person who's doing it to you doesn't get any gratification from it. [She's] just doing it because [she] cares about you; it's part of taking care of a baby. It's possible she's excited by her authority, and if so, I'm tickled pink.

There are some things I fantasize about doing that I wouldn't honestly dare do. If we ever get a house, one of my requirements is for me to have a nursery. I would really love to spend some time—a week or a month—as a dependent infant, full-time, 24 hours a day. There's no question in my mind that I could be babied a lot more and be comfortable with it. On the few occasions [when] I did wear juvenile clothes in a public situation, it did not bother me. If other people had a problem with it, fuck 'em.

Seven

DEPERSONALIZATION

He who makes a beast of himself gets rid of the pain of being a man.
—SAMUEL JOHNSON[1]

Of all the roles that D&Sers may play out with partners, the fantasy of becoming less than a person is among the most controversial. Depersonalization fantasies are about a radical transformation whereby the person becomes a subperson. For the D&Ser who explores depersonalization, the play is often the realization of a deeply held desire to know—or to inflict—almost supernatural powerlessness. It is a fantasy that suggests the workings of some ruthless, often capricious power to which the submissive has no choice but to succumb and, in surrender, to become other.

Under the heading of depersonalization we include, first, behaving and being treated like an animal; second, the fantasy of being an inanimate object, such as a piece of furniture; and third, institutional scenarios in which the submissive is treated like a prisoner, a hospital patient, or a reform-school student—in other words, someone whose rights have been revoked by an omnipotent, impersonal, and usually heartless system. Some element of depersonalization may be present in other types of D&S activity—for example, the master-slave relationship—but for purposes of organization we limit depersonalization to these three general categories.

Our profiles in this chapter include:

- Danny the Wonder Pony, a performance artist who has turned his fetish into his profession. He lives in New Jersey.
- Max is 50 years old. He is an artist and real-estate investor and lives with Lindsay (profiled in Chapter 20).

WHAT IS DEPERSONALIZATION?

That depersonalization finds a place in D&S sexuality is hardly surprising: It is a driving force in the human imagination. One has to look only to the extraordinary popularity of fairy tales about frog princes and beauties with beastly mates; women-behind-bars movies and prison fiction; our cultural fascination with war crimes, political torture, Nazis, and slavery; and the public thirst for the details of lurid crimes. Even so-called ordinary people develop romantic obsessions with serial killers or join crowds when an execution takes place. To enjoy the spectacle of another person being inhumanely subjugated or violated requires that we see him as intrinsically less human than ourselves. The sexual kick that these spectacles may provide is widely known but rarely admitted.

D&S roleplaying rarely explores this darkest side of human psychology. For the most part depersonalization, while certainly bizarre, usually comprises playful acts. The fantasies result from negotiation and achieve the purpose of mutual gratification. Still, depersonalization is an uncomfortable activity for many D&Sers. Those who do explore this area are usually extremely cautious about negotiating the scene and frequently reserve this form of play for long-standing partners. They also recognize the fundamental dichotomy between a safely enacted fantasy and a dangerous reality, but that dichotomy itself may be fundamental to their arousal.

Some D&Sers categorically object to depersonalization. For them, this type of play simply exceeds the bounds of safe play; for others, the passivity of the submissive-as-object is not arousing. Not surprisingly, depersonalization scenarios where the dynamic includes lively interaction between dominant and submissive seem to be the most popular.

Depersonalization seems to be particularly popular among dominants who enjoy exerting stringent psychological control over a partner.

My fantasies basically [revolve around] having women slaves, using women as pets or as objects. —MAX

For the submissive, depersonalization is a means of total surrender. If submissives relish the feeling of abdicating control, the person who enjoys depersonalization fantasies takes this powerlessness further. He experiences the most radical transformation possible: He becomes less than human, even nonhuman.

My master likes to say he imagines me as a tiny person dangling on his keychain. He takes his finger and flicks me! And I spin back and forth. I love being conscious of being someone's puppet, someone's toy. There's nothing like that in the world. It's the most wonderful feeling. —BAMBI BOTTOM

The metaphor of the puppet or toy perhaps best expresses an aspect typical of depersonalization fantasies. The submissive must behave only as the dominant wills and in this sense ceases to exist as an independent entity.

I like to fantasize about going out in public and being led on a leash and thinking about what other people seeing me would think about this person who's less than a person, who's owned by someone else. —BAMBI BOTTOM

Nonetheless, even the animal or the object wields its own power—if only in the sense that it is a source of fascination to the dominant. And some submissives see their roles as antic, purely pleasurable, alternate personae.

[Even at an S&M club, I say], "No spanking the ponyman! The ASPCA gets all upset." I tell them that. They can kick lightly, for effect or signaling, but I'm not into pain. I'm not into humiliation. That's not my thing. I'm there to have a positive response from people. That's why I call myself "the Macho Submissive" at the S&M clubs. I'm not going to be a wimp to please the women—it's a masculine, powerful thing that they can enjoy if they wish. I'm not about to be abused. I wish to give them pleasure, not to give myself displeasure. —DANNY THE WONDER PONY

Depersonalization can also be degradation in its most literal sense: The person is degraded, his status diminished to a level that would be both unthinkable and unacceptable were it real. The submissive revels in helplessness.

> *I don't see degradation as a punishment or something that's done to make people feel bad. It makes me feel wonderfully good. It's part of the whole dynamic of being so absolutely in someone's power that he can do anything with you, including make you [into] an object. I like feeling insignificant. I like feeling little, not big and powerful, and there's nothing like being someone's footstool that'll do that to you.* —BAMBI BOTTOM

Depersonalization fantasies rarely involve direct erotic activity. They are based on head games; any activity that occurs is simply a means of reinforcing the scenario's credibility.

> *[When I'm a footstool], I think of how I'm serving my master. I think of how I'm glad he has something very soft and cushiony to put his feet on. I think of how he's not really paying any attention to me. It's kind of like being put in the corner, another activity that I really enjoy. I love having my face pressed into a corner and my buttocks sticking out and having to stand in the corner like a bad little girl while my master does something else. It's just wonderful to know that I've been put in storage as a piece of furniture—there for his use.* —BAMBI BOTTOM

Because depersonalization fantasies do not always require the submissive or dominant to be active at all (or even most) times, some couples extend the play over long periods of time (hours, or even days), taking breaks only to meet professional or social obligations. Their main thrill is psychological. Depersonalization is seldom foreplay, and sexual release rarely forms a part of these scenarios. Finally, depersonalization is usually only one of many fantasies acted out in a couple's play: We do not know of anyone who consistently remains in these roles.

DOG AND PONY SHOWS—
AND WORMS

When the witch Circe transformed Ulysses's crew into swine, it was an act of cruel degradation. Since Western culture places man at the pinnacle of the animal kingdom, animalistic behavior is, figuratively speaking, beneath us. Yet some submissives covet the opportunity to get feral. Bestial fantasies seem to focus on one of three creatures: dog, pony, and worm (though undoubtedly other beasts lurk in other menageries). The dog's slavish and submissive relationship to humans and its complete lack of privacy in the human domain may well explain the popularity of humiliating canine games.

> *I'm looking forward to doggy training—being treated for a whole day as a puppy and being made to crawl around on all fours and bark and beg like a dog and eat from a doggy dish.*
>
> —BAMBI BOTTOM

The bestial fantasy is a sublime paradox: It is behavior utterly without civilization, since no animal, however tame, can be civilized. Thus, the creature is completely liberated from the rules and restrictions that constrain human behaviors. At the same time, the animal is a slave to the will of its master. The domesticated animal has no privacy and is subject to its owner's whims. Bestialization, therefore, represents simultaneous emancipation (from one's humanity) and subjugation (to a human's will), a curious blend of anarchy and submission.

One of our interviewees suggested that some individuals equate being an animal with being lovable.

> *As a professional, I once had a man in dog training. He was dressed, but when I pushed his face into the dog food, he had an orgasm in his pants. The moment I pushed his face into the dog food, [he had] a revelation. His father was a veterinarian and gave more love to animals than to him. He realized how much he wished his father had paid attention to him and how he wished to be a dog because he wanted his father's attention. Everything just became clear to him, and he never came back.* —AVA TAUREL

Bestial play comprises many of the same behaviors one might observe between real pet owners and their pets, but it does *not* involve any real animals. The submissive-as-dog also has numerous ways of expressing personality without leaving the fantasy role.

> *When I was watching TV and my dog kept running over, putting his face in his bowl, I got him some dog biscuits and got him to do some tricks for them. When my partner becomes my dog, he can bark, but he'll probably be punished for it. When he's a dog, I only use a dog quirt on him; I wouldn't hit him with a whip or flogger. [During that time], he lives on the floor. He isn't allowed on the furniture when he is being a dog.* —JOSEPH BEAN

Second to dogs, ponies are favorite fantasy roles. The D&S community's best-known animal impersonator is Danny the Wonder Pony, a performer in the New York area. Danny is a bit unusual in that he's seized the reins.

> *It took a long time to get the Wonder Pony mystique up. I give myself a lot of credit for having moved this into the regular world and [having] it accepted. No one had ever heard of it in the straight world before I did it. The only people that knew about it were the S&M people.* —DANNY THE WONDER PONY

A famous scandal revealed that the late Alfred Bloomingdale, the clothing mogul, hired women to perform as ponies and rode them, whipping their flanks. Ponygirls are a fixture of D&S pornography, although they seem to be slightly more of a British phenomenon than an American one. It is a rare ponygirl who can support the weight of a man, and this restricts most play to prancing and training. The ponyboy, however—and particularly Danny—can rise to weighty occasions. He reports that the ride is sensual for beast beneath and rider above.

> *There is something very sensual about a pony ride—not only watching it from my point of view, but for the lady the physical sensation is erotic. So I've been told, anyway. The saddle seems to contact parts of their bodies. It also has a mental situation, where it's a big, powerful thing between their legs that they have control over.* —DANNY THE WONDER PONY

For many who enjoy pretending to be animals, the accoutrements are intrinsically bound up in the fantasy.

> *The equestrian equipment—the stirrups and all that stuff—intertwine; it is a fetish. Those objects have a sensuality because they've been used by the woman. It's the objects that give me erotic feelings about women—not the women. It turns me on that they've been used for pleasure so many times, that the stirrups are used to control; those objects themselves take on meaning.* —DANNY THE WONDER PONY

And, finally, worms. We did not interview anyone who pursues this fantasy, but it is recorded. The behavior usually involves groveling and often verbal abuse. This scene is perhaps the most extreme and least politically correct of all bestialization fantasies. We quote one of the more remarkable passages on the phenomenon, from a fictional dialogue between mistress and invertebrate,

You there, lowlife! Clean my shoes while you're down there! You're nothing but a worm, a worm beneath my heel. I've never seen such a loathsome thing, such an unevolved growth.

—TERRENCE SELLERS[2]

Later in this passage, some confusion appears to arise between the man-as-worm and his organ, described as "sort of a worm on a worm." Apparently, when a worm turns, its thoughts turn to extreme degradation.

THE INANIMATE WORLD: FURNITURE AND OBJECTS

We are all familiar with the cartoons in which presumably inanimate objects spring to life once the antiquarian has locked his shop door. In some D&S scenarios the reverse occurs: The very animate submissive may, at the dominant's behest, become inanimate—an object or piece of furniture to be used or handled. This fantasy is not very common but is certainly known among D&Sers. To some extent, it has characteristics similar to other D&S activities, among them bondage and humiliation. Instead of being bound in place, however, the human object must hold still without the aid of restraints or supports. A variety of sensations may be introduced—such as tickling or rubbing—which may be exciting or humiliating. Throughout, the submissive has no choice but to remain the passive recipient.

Sometimes my master turns me into his footstool. I lay naked on the floor, and he sets his feet on my bottom. We spend an evening like that. He watches TV or listens to music, and I must lay very still. I love lying there, not being able to talk and having obscene things done to [me]. I like being his table, too! I don't like it when he puts a glass of ice water on my back and then tickles or spanks me, because I can't hold still, but I love serving him in that way.

—BAMBI BOTTOM

The object is relieved of humanity; in the process, it becomes both helpless and helpful to its owner. It may also have another appeal to deeply submissive individuals: Typically, during D&S, the dominant devotes considerable energy to stimulating the submissive. Human furniture, however, is "maintenance-free."

When a dominant pays attention to you and beats you or humiliates you, it's very wonderful. But it's even more wonderful to know that I'm serving him in whatever way he wants and that he doesn't have to actively put out energy [or] give things to me. That's what submissives fear the most, I think: that the dominant isn't getting anything out of it [and] actually serving the submissive by doing all these terrible delicious things to [her]. It's just refreshing to know that my master's sitting there being himself, having me do exactly what he wants and not having to put a lot of energy and effort into doing things for me. —BAMBI BOTTOM

Object fantasies cover a wide range. Footstools or ottomans are fairly popular, particularly among those who also have a foot fetish. Tables, hatstands, and ashtrays are known. Novelist Jerzy Kosinski is reputed to have crawled under the sofa pillows at a fashionable party so that guests would sit on him, supposedly as a prank. Many D&Sers, however, feel that object fantasies are too psychologically extreme to be enacted safely.

INSTITUTIONAL CRUELTY:
HOSPITALS, REFORMATORIES, PRISONS

Institutional fantasies imitate the interaction between an indifferent or malicious authority inflicting unfair or dehumanizing punishment on an incapacitated or captive victim. Unlike many D&S scenes where the dominant may express affection or reassure the submissive, in these scenarios cuddling or emotional displays would destroy the illusion of victimization. Submissives also wish to feel that the punishment has been decided not by the individual dominant but by some higher authority—a prison system or medical science, for example—and that they are powerless in the face of this tyrannical system.

This category actually comprises a broad range of roleplaying—so broad, in fact, that we do not attempt to be comprehensive here. Specific activities depend on imaginary circumstances; elements of bondage, intense stimulation, head trips, and humiliation are most common. Fantasies range from the playful (the submissive who pretends to be a juvenile delinquent) to the very cruel (the submissive who wishes to roleplay as a political prisoner). Some jail fantasies involve little more than wearing shackles; others involve stringent corporal punishment.

When enacted by partners, this form of depersonalization often embraces the concept (which applies to other D&S acts, as well) of *consenting to nonconsensuality:* The submissive may propose the fantasy and negotiate the activity, but part of the agreement may be that the authority figure will push the submissive's limits. Because the authority is an agent of a larger system, the submissive has little hope of appeal. The scenario may also represent an opportunity for a high level of discomfort and dehumanization. For example, although some hospitalization scenarios are reminiscent of the type of investigative doctor-patient games that children play, many submissives (particularly men) fantasize about grimly elaborate scenarios that simulate a real hospital setting. The dominant may be uniformed as a nurse or a doctor (or a nun, for those whose tastes are catholic); this figure may bind the patient with hospital restraints, shave the submissive's pubic region, administer enemas, introduce urinary catheters, or perform a host of other embarrassing or painful procedures.

Similarly, interrogation fantasies may range from moderate head games to extensive pain scenarios.

> *I once did an interrogation scene. [He] wanted to know what political prisoners felt when electricity was used on them. That's what [he] wanted; that's what was negotiated: I was to interrogate him until I got the truth—the names, the password, the location, things like that. We were actually playing an Arab-Israeli trip. He'd been to Israel four times, so he was part of a group that invaded Lebanon and got caught. I went up extremely slowly [with the electricity] until I got to a point that he found the most erotic.* —JEAN L.

Interrogation scenarios often continue until the submissive feels that his will has been bent.

Some D&Sers will wear appropriate uniforms or costumes to enhance the reality of the scene. Not only submissives are aroused by this type of play, but dominants often have more reservations about playing so close to the edge.

> *I have fantasies of interrogations in which I would have women tied up, and I would whip them and usually stick things in them. I [would] like to feel able to break the woman: It's always with naughty women, women who are unavailable, snotty, bitchy. On the other hand, I'll read about tortures, and it really turns me off when I see someone getting hurt.* —MAX

Most institutional scenarios are infrequently or tentatively enacted, and adherence to safety guidelines is critical in any type of invasive play. Such fantasies, however, proliferate in D&S pornography, where fictional characters regularly subject the human body to abuses which no sane D&Ser would ever attempt.

INTERVIEWS

DANNY THE WONDER PONY

I'm 100 percent hetero. I'm not homophobic. I have many homosexual friends whom [I] respect. They understand it's not my thing. I don't put it down, [but] it's just not for me. I consider myself a little more aware of the sexuality of a woman, because I grew up in the age of the "new woman," or the feminists. Dating in the feminist world, you get badgered with a lot of information. So I know more of where women are coming from, and it helped me [with] the act, to tell the truth.

I make my living by entertaining at different functions—clubs, parties, whatever—as Danny the Wonder Pony, who literally gives a pony ride to ladies who want one. I have a custom-made costume, and it consists of a saddle, reins, stirrups, all the equestrian equipment, [tailored to] fit me. I get down on all fours for a second, and the lady sits in the saddle. Her feet go in the self-adjusting stirrups, and then I stand up on two legs and dance. The lady looks and she feels like she's riding a pony, although it's going to the music. There are also parts of a pony ride that are a little more stimulating than others for the ladies. The Wonder Pony knows all. He knows all about what the women want.

Men are really into dogs, and women literally fall in love with their horses, especially if they're teenagers, because it's the first sexual awareness, sometimes. If you've ever noticed, teenage girls are always the most enthusiastic pony riders. There's a reason for that; it literally feels good to them, just the way, maybe, a man feels good in a sports car because of the adrenaline. If you ever go to a ranch and watch people riding, you'll see that eight or nine out of 10 are girls. [It] has to do with a Western saddle. The English saddle doesn't have the same effect, because it just isn't built the same way. It doesn't have the horn; it doesn't have the slope in the front.

I managed a dude ranch for three years. I studied the way the women moved, not the horses. If I move like a horse, it just waddles around, because I'm not shaped like a horse, so I had to develop dance moves to correlate to the movement of the pony. There's a whole bunch of things involved in the erotic. Think of all the equestrian expressions that are also bestowed in the sexual area. Mounting—she mounted him; hung like a horse; [referring] to men as stallions, studs; sowing your wild oats. You don't hear references to birds or cats or dogs—that's considered perverted. Watch a woman galloping along, and then turn that picture sideways, and envision the horse gone and a man on her, and you'll see that she actually looks like she's having sex.

The first experience I had was when I was about 12 years old. I was hanging around with this 11-year-old girl and it was a boring afternoon. She innocently said, "Give me a horsey ride!" like her daddy used to do. So, what the hell, I gave it to her. It was my first real experience with a girl. It was like, "Wow, this is nice, this is pleasurable!" It stuck in my head and became an erotic fantasy. I don't think about doing this when I'm making love, and I don't think about making love when I'm doing this. But it is a turn-on. The fact that I'm making a living at it, the fact that women are having a good time with it—all of that gives me erotic feelings, because I guess we all, basically, get erotic when it comes to sex and money.

I was motivated by the desire to have it all: to make a living at something that you enjoy and then throw in that it gets you sexually interested. Being a pony is very important because it intertwines itself [with the] identity in your head. You want to have a positive sexual identity. Everyone wants to have a strength; this is my strength. Women pay attention to me because of it.

I've dated a lot of women I've met through this. There is also that dominant-submissive thing there, but it's more of a chivalrous thing. It's like I'm giving pleasure to women in a manner like, I guess, Sir Walter Raleigh. When he laid his coat down, was that submission or chivalry? He did it because he wanted to, so it was chivalry. He didn't have to—that would have been submission. I do this for myself, but I also do it because it gives pleasure to women, and I have a good time doing that, so it's chivalry. Most of the people that I wind up dating have taken pony rides. Let's face it: [If] I get involved with someone, she's got to like pony rides. It's like a singer hooking up with someone that hates to hear someone sing. That would be ridiculous. I wouldn't get involved with a woman who disapproved. When I'm involved with someone, my life is intertwined with hers. It's not like, "Well, we'll tolerate each other." You should have many, many things in your life intertwine—your professions and what you consider erotic should be compatible. Otherwise, don't even bother.

[It's] an amazing thing. I never get tired of it—it never gets old.

What's always amazed me is that there's not much difference between my act at an S/M club and at a Sweet Sixteen party. The presentation has to change according to the crowd, but the actual ride itself is exactly the same, which is funny. What changes are the clothes underneath the horse equipment, not the equipment or the ride. It's like they base whether the act is risqué or cute depending on whether my clothes are risqué or cute.

If the person is treating me as a pony, then [it's not erotic], but if the person is treating me as a person—being used as a pony—then possibly [it's erotic], depending on their attitude. If they're doing it in a mean, selfish way, it isn't fun. If they're having a lot of fun with it, then I'll have fun with it. My idea is not to do my thing whether they enjoy it or not: I want the person to enjoy. I want that more than just doing a good act.

I can read an audience pretty quickly and do what's needed to please them. The most unreceptive [crowds] have been the yuppie-ish types. It isn't the women. The men who want to attract and impress women with money are the most threatened by my act, because they can't compete with this.

Picking my most exciting experience is real hard. Is it when I got a hundred-dollar tip or when a beautiful woman took off her top? All of them have been exciting. I was very excited when I flew to Miami and started doing my act every six weeks. I was very excited when I met my girlfriend through it. The most exciting thing monetarily is when I'm making the most money; the most exciting thing sexually is when the woman is gorgeous and maybe coming on to me. It changes constantly. There are so many avenues of my life that are exciting to me! Maybe that's why I'm not married—so many different women are exciting to me. It's very hard to say, "What was the favorite woman you were with?" The favorite woman is the one that likes to pony ride the most.

The whole Wonder Pony [act is] copyrighted, so that if anyone tried to do a similar act in a similar way, I'd have recourse. Not only that, but it's physically difficult. I have chiropractors come up to me, telling me I shouldn't be doing this. It's a lot more than throwing a saddle on your back and people wanting to pay money. I got it to the point where I get hired to take women along the beach at night in the summertime. I put boots on; I go through the surf. I've gotten it to a real pinnacle.

MAX

I'm very sexual. I always have been, and in order to sustain that amount of sexuality, I try to have as large a repertoire as possible. Things can get boring if you just do one thing. I am strictly heterosexual [and] pretty monogamous. I'm dominant.

Sex is probably the most important thing in both of our lives as partners. I was very inhibited before. I was married for 25 years to one woman who never had sex with anybody else. I started exploring myself when I was about 40. Lindsay is 15 years younger than I. When we met, she was not into S&M. With my previous wife, I tried different things: I tried dildos, I tried tying her up. It just didn't work. She would go limp. There has to be some sort of spark between us to make this work. But I had this desire, and then I met Lindsay. Lindsay was game for anything that was sensual. She could enjoy the intensity of an experience without it converting into pain, which has an awful lot to do with how much you relax into things. It went from "How can I give you more of an intense feeling than before?" and got where we are [now]. She wants to do it all.

I'd always had S&M kind of fantasies. Going back to my earliest sexual memories, in preschool, I used to have dreams of being kidnapped and locked up in a room with a girl; we were naked, [and] we'd lie on top of each other. I went through school having fantasies of finding women and tying them up and being able to have them. There was this whole mystique around women being unavailable to me. As oldest boy in a family of boys, not knowing about women and being very shy and not being able to know how to come in contact with them, women [seemed] very unapproachable. It developed into this fantasy about a way to make women approachable. When I'd go to the library as a little kid, I'd go to the sex books and [read] the torture books. It was funny because I'm afraid of pain, [and] I faint at the sight of blood. There's a very nebulous thing around pain that's always been fascinating to me. I was turned on by the fact of people being helpless, of somebody having power over another person, [but] the bloody, painful stuff really turns my stomach. So, to me, in S&M there seems to be a definite dichotomy between fantasy and reality.

I have experience being a bottom, and my partner has experience being a top; we prefer it the way we have it, but we don't find the other way anathema. It gives you an ability to see what it feels like on the other side. When I become submissive, I feel completely overwhelmed. I feel like a goddess has taken me; I feel completely like I worship this person, and whatever they would do to me would be just fine: it would be like a sacrifice to them.

The most exciting fantasies that I have right now are, first, the dog-show fantasy. Women are brought in cages by masters. They're naked, and they're in little cages with carpets, and they're all put up on benches, and everybody'd go around and look at them. Then they're brought out on leashes, strutted around the floor, and judged like a dog would be. Their necks are brought up; their mouths are looked at, their orifices are opened up. They're probed in front of the audience, so that there's an element of humiliation, there's an element of objectification.

I think the fantasy comes from the fact that women have always been so hard to get. Women really control the relationship in all the courting stages, and men feel very frustrated. I know I felt very frustrated about women, how hard it was to get them and how powerless I always was. It seems to be a way where I can just express my pure, erotic lust.

One of my favorite things is to tie her: I cuff her ankles to her wrists and her ankles back to her calves so that her legs are spread. I can pick her up that way [and] move her around: she's a little compact bundle of woman who can't move [and is] completely accessible. And [then] I like to do things to her. When I'm actually engaged in fucking her, I merge and lose myself in the experience of sex and orgasm. But in S/M, I can sit back and play with her. It becomes very erotic, very charged. I can watch her come without losing myself in the experience. I'll bind her into a form where she isn't my love: she's an object of sexual desire. I can focus my eroticism on her, which I find is different from love.

Everybody has a light and a dark side. S/M means coming to terms with finding out where the boundaries are; why do some things repel you? Why do some things attract you? It's a way to explore that boundary. A lot of people read de Sade and say he was horrible. I read it as a piece of philosophy: Here was a man who wasn't doing these things [but] was pushing the bounds of what was acceptable dogma around sex and pain. In my sexual life I always wanted to push boundaries. I've always wanted to find out how far [one] can go.

Eight

LIFESTYLE D&S

You are here to serve your masters. During the day, you will perform whatever domestic duties are assigned you, such as sweeping, putting back the books, arranging flowers, or waiting on tables. Nothing more difficult than that. But at the first word or sign from anyone you will drop whatever you are doing and ready yourself for what is really your one and only duty: to lend yourself.

—STORY OF O[1]

For most of us, sex is an act or series of acts, done in private, often compartmentalized or distinct from our larger reality. It may bear little or no relation to how we live outside the moment of erotic pleasure and may not define how we feel, what we do, or how we view ourselves. For lifestyle D&Sers, however, sexuality is an integral aspect of identity.

In this chapter we profile three lifestylers:

- Frank and Lisa W. are 37 and 25, respectively. They own a computer-consulting firm and lead the on-line D&S support group of CompuServe, where they first met. They have two children.

- Bambi Bottom is 33 years old and an independent management consultant. She and her husband live in the Bible Belt.

WHAT IS LIFESTYLE D&S?

The term *lifestyle* has no universal definition in a D&S context. Broadly speaking, it refers to those individuals who elect to be sexually intimate exclusively with other D&Sers. Lifestyle may be a statement of sexual preference or of sexual politics; it may dictate the choices one makes about friends and lovers. Lifestylers often limit new friendships to other D&Sers—indeed, many prefer the tribal atmosphere of an established D&S community for reasons of safety, common interests, and acceptance.

A more parochial definition of lifestyle D&S is used to describe permanent partners for whom the power dynamic is an ever-present reality in all areas of their relationship.

To me a lifestyle S&M relationship is lived by the partners full-time; there are no boundaries between what you do in the bedroom and what you do in the rest of your life. The power dynamic is a part of every activity that the people do, the things they say to each other, the attitudes they have toward each other. —BAMBI BOTTOM

In such full-time lifestyle relationships the partners usually do not switch roles—the line between dominant and submissive is fixed. These relationships in some ways appear to resemble traditional marriages, where one partner is the authority figure. But the lifestyle dominant is as likely to be female as male, and the sex centers on D&S activity.

Although lifestyle D&S does not depend on degree or type of activity, many who have full-time partnered relationships seem to enjoy intense physical and psychological control. There are, of course, D&Sers who enjoy extreme activity without opting for lifestyle, just as some lifestylers prefer mild control. What is most important to the lifestyler is the constant awareness of power roles. This negotiated exchange is both erotically and emotionally gratifying.

[D&S] is very important [for us] in the bedroom [and] to our [overall] relationship. I'm certainly interested in all the vanilla stuff, but D&S is required. Both I and Lisa explicitly went looking for someone who was interested in D&S. —FRANK W.

Although lifestyle submissives live in service to their dominants, the personal dynamic does not alter their social or business personae. Lifestylers are as apt as anyone else to lead mainstream public lives.

I think some people imagine [D&S] to be [that] you give up your career and basically spend your time at this woman's feet. A woman who could enjoy that would not have the respect for me that I [want]. The roles are defined, but she wants me to be successful; she wants me to enjoy myself. —JOHN H.

Lifestylers generally feel that the clear delineation of power issues at home liberates them socially. In effect, once the submissive grants power to the dominant, there is no reason to cede power to any other. They also believe that the communication needed to make a D&S relationship work effects immense positive changes in their daily lives. For them, D&S may help to resolve larger control issues.

Most of the submissives I know are outwardly strong-willed individuals, and they've actualized themselves to the point that you have to overcome that part of their nature before they'll submit. I've found some so-called submissives who were bad life-mates. Self-destruction crops up in a number of them because of bad childhood experiences. I found that channeling that negative energy through the Scene is really an excellent coping mechanism for them. When they're able to have this outlet—[a] safe, consensual aspect of the Scene—it mellows them out. —MICHAEL V.

While some lifestylers publicize their involvement in the Scene, a majority maintain a low profile for fear of legal, occupational, or social harassment.

People like us are not in the Scene; we're not public. People can't find us, and we can't find them. I believe that there are [other] extreme master-slave relationships out there absolutely hidden from view. I'd love to meet others who are as deep into S&M as [we are]. —BAMBI BOTTOM

Virtually no pressure is put on people in the D&S communities to "come out," and discretion is an unspoken law, particularly among lifestylers, since a high percentage of them appear to be middle- to upper-middle-class professionals. *Scene names,* or pseudonyms, are popular to ensure anonymity. Some lifestylers, however, will confide in family members or sympathetic friends.

I've come out to my brother. I've come out to my sister. I've come out to my older daughter, [though] not in a great deal of detail. By and large reaction has been positive. —JOHN M.

Even the most private lifestyler often wears some token of his relationship, whether concealed or visible.

I must wear a collar at all times. I have a variety of collars: Some look very vanilla, [so] no straight person would know.

—BAMBI BOTTOM

Such tokens remind D&Sers of the underlying power dynamic with their partners and of their commitment to D&S, not merely as a sexual variation but as a way of life.

WHY DO THEY LIKE IT?

Those who maintain a 24-hour lifestyle relationship bring a unique perspective to D&S. For them, the decision to control or to be controlled in a full-time relationship is fundamental to their identity.

I got out of a vanilla marriage [and] actively looked for a D&S partner. It's a big part of who I am, and without it, I'm not happy.

—LISA W.

To the lifestyle dominant, a consistent ability to control all areas of a consenting partner's life is intrinsic to his or her identity as a person of power and authority and is a source of self-esteem. With this power comes responsibility, a responsibility that dominants find deeply fulfilling. Many actively work toward improving the quality of their submissives' lives and see themselves in the role of protector, parent, and teacher. They are the submissives' greatest ally and advocate.

My master is a natural healer. He's helped me through a lot. I've gone from being a borderline alcoholic to drinking only about once a week; from being a coffeeholic, 14 cups a day, to drinking just [two] cups a day; from being a foodaholic to being a normal weight. He's worked with me on all the emotional problems that are the source of the destructive behavior. —BAMBI BOTTOM

A lifestyle submissive usually feels unfulfilled or bereft when there is no positive, dominant presence in his or her life. Emotionally, the lifestyle submissive typically desires to be in a subservient position to a fundamentally benevolent authority who supervises and disciplines, punishes, and rewards. This supervision may range from the sharply erotic to the sheerly mundane; in this context the fact of control is a confirmation of love and commitment.

Protection and guidance are of themselves erotic to the lifestyle submissive. The ways in which the dominant expresses control may also create a constant, low-level pitch of erotic tension between the partners.

Perhaps the greatest appeal of lifestyle relationships is the degree of candor between partners in them. Many of our interviewees insist that lifestyle D&Sers form unparalleled romantic bonds, partly because submissives forfeit all privacy.

> There's a greater level of intimacy in D&S relationships than in other kinds of romantic relationships. I've experienced both. In a vanilla relationship, you can hide and keep to yourself. My master requires me to reveal to him my dreams, my hopes, my ideas. We're very close. He's a very strong, loving, caring, tender person.
> —BAMBI BOTTOM

LIFESTYLE PROBLEMS

Full-time lifestyle relationships can best be understood as an anarchic conspiracy between two intimate partners where the conventional rules are scrapped and an extraordinary agreement is negotiated based on the partners' needs. Because of their unique situation, lifestylers have unique problems. Preeminent among these is a lack of role models. The few accessible examples of master-slave interactions derive from fiction, sensationalized crimes, or historical accounts of persecution. While most of our interviewees mentioned the profound influence of D&S cult classics on their sexual awareness, many also believe that such works grossly distort the reality of D&S.

> The [fictional accounts of S&M] make us look like emotionally unhealthy people. In 9½ Weeks the dominant was obviously emotionally disturbed. He scared her. He went too far too quick, he thought only of satisfying his own desires and not working for something long-term, not paying attention to the submissive's particular psychology.
> —BAMBI BOTTOM

Those who rely on fictional role models for inspiration or guidance regularly encounter stumbling blocks to romantic satisfaction. It is common for novice male heterosexual dominants, for example, to emulate the master in Story of O. As a result, they may expect submissives to be one-dimensional erotic objects and may be frustrated when ordinary problems intervene.

> I met dominants who wanted me to drop everything in my life. I was not willing to give up my kids. I wanted to get married, I wanted to have a home, I wanted to have a family, plus I wanted D&S. I wanted a man who wanted those same things.
> —LISA W.

In marked contrast to erotic myth, lifestylers confront the complex challenge of integrating an unconventional sexual dynamic with the typical stresses and demands of family, religion, career, and citizenship.

I'd like to meet the dominant woman of my dreams. [She is] not someone who dominates me 24 hours a day and keeps me down, but someone who, not only in the sexual aspect of daily life but in the regular aspect, is the boss and enjoys it. —JOHN H.

Another serious problem for many submissives in lifestyle relationships is accepting the control which they have deliberately sought, for the fantasy rarely translates smoothly into reality.

The problems of lifestylers can be summed up in one word: resistance. *It takes a lot of getting used to, to live at someone else's whims, to follow someone else's commands 24 hours a day, to do exactly what you're told despite your will and your desires.*

—BAMBI BOTTOM

For the submissive, keeping his or her ego in check may be extraordinarily difficult even when this is precisely his or her goal. In this respect, the attempt to live out the submissive role in a lifestyle relationship may resemble a religious struggle between the temptations of the world and an inner craving to surrender to a force which one sincerely believes will ultimately afford serenity. Not all surrender is necessarily good surrender: D&Sers consistently grapple with clarifying or modifying their goals within the lifestyle relationship. Extent of control and type of control are negotiated and renegotiated.

A significant problem for all who regularly engage in D&S is the failure of professionals—medical, psychological, legal, and spiritual—to provide informed assistance. Many fear consulting either doctors or clergymen lest they be censured or urged to forswear their sexual desires; few helping professionals are trained to work with D&Sers. Spiritually, some D&Sers are turning to New Age religious beliefs, and increasing numbers of peer counselors are now a prime source of third-party assistance for troubled D&S relationships.

INTERVIEWS

FRANK W.

[D&S] is not 100 percent vital with someone I really care about. [But] I have both. I am madly in love with my slave, so it's wonderful. I'm heterosexual and quite definitely a dominant. I haven't had any real submissive fantasies since prepuberty. My D&S needs were extremely important. They were not irresistible driving forces. There were cases where I would get into a vanilla relationship, [albeit] with serious trepidation.

I have given an awful lot of thought to where my needs come from. I am afraid I do not have any real answers. I, along with many other people, have noticed the tendency for people in D&S to be more neglected than abused as kids. But clearly there are many kids who have that kind of upbringing and don't end up in D&S.

I remember tying myself up and doing it with playmates, [dating] back to [age] four or five. I've got one fantasy that I know predates first grade. I have one that I can date to [age] six: Somebody had given me a pile of British comics, and I remember having all sorts of fantasies about tying up the heroine and doing horrible things to her. I pretty much put that down to the fact that six-year-olds aren't really up on medicine. They aren't real good on knowing when they're maiming somebody, because all you've seen is cartoons. [The fantasies] died away for several years, until puberty. At that point, I started getting actual, realizable wants in terms of a particular girl from school. I was interested in her, and I was into D&S, so I was interested in a D&S way—spanking and bondage and so forth.

The first time I really had a chance to do much was [in my] mid-20s. I went with one woman all through college. When *Joy of Sex* came out and made bondage respectable, she was willing to try it a couple of times. But it was ho-hum [to her]; she was basically falling asleep. Then, a year or two after I was out of college, I actually managed to start getting opportunities to do something. But the problem, really, was me. I'm a techie, [a] white-socks-and-slide-rule engineer. I simply was not every woman's cup of tea. [I was] looking for a real, complete relationship. So I would either find vanilla women with whom [a relationship] would have worked but she didn't want D&S, or I'd find a woman who wanted D&S but otherwise didn't want to marry an engineer. So that was a problem.

I lucked out [with Lisa]. I was at the right place at the right time. I was active on the HSX Forum on CompuServe. Lisa had been around for a while, mostly talking real time with people, which I don't like to do. But she was also reading the message board, and she liked what I had to say about what I was looking for. She sent me a message and we wrote back and forth. [Then] she sent me her phone number, and I called her. We talked for a while, and [eventually] I sent her an airplane ticket. She came [to visit], and she went home with a diamond ring.

We've been together now about two years. We've got enough stuff going on to strain any relationship of any flavor, so there certainly have been some rocky times, but at the moment, things are really, really, really going great. Both Lisa and I had decades-long arrears of hugs and kisses when we came into this thing, so we still like a whole lot of catching up on cuddling. There are no real hard-and-fast stops in our life for anything, but as for D&S-type stuff, we like to do little reminder things out of the bedroom. Before we had people popping in, any time the sun was up, she would wear a collar around the house—just a dime-store pet-choke collar, with a little hardware-store padlock on it. We've also had her put a chain around her waist, or we've got little nipple thingies that she can wear. Stuff can go on for hours with that kind of mutual reminder. I like the collar because I get to see it. The nipple thingie or the chain around the waist, well, she knows it's there, and I know that she knows, but it's not as good as being able to look at it. And then, of course, we'll talk and tease [each other] throughout the day.

[For us D&S] is out of the bedroom but not out of the front door. I'll have her undress in the evenings, and she'll wear the collar and a leash, and she'll sit or kneel at my feet when we're answering the messages on CompuServe. Or we will go for a walk in the woods [and] bring along a leash; we'll stop and cut a switch, and I'll tie her to a tree.

Last week we did it in the backyard; that was fairly real. We had lunch [cooking] in the stove and went out in the backyard, and I had her get undressed, and I tied her to a tree. I gave her a couple of swats with my hand, and then I went back in and looked after how lunch was doing, leaving her out there. She theoretically could have been seen by someone driving up. They would have had to know exactly where to look, so as long as she refrained from doing a little dance to get their attention, she was really pretty safe. After I'd got lunch nice and happy, I went back out there and cut a switch. I gave her a little warm-up with my hand and a good solid kiss to give her some confidence, because it had been a while since we'd done anything really heavy, so she was more nervous than she would have been a couple of months ago. I gave her a dozen good, hard ones on the rear end with the switch to make welts and marks that would last for about a week.

For a while there, she was very intrigued with the idea of marks on her breasts, and so we did some of that. I'm not really thrilled to go for marks. She squirms around too much, and I think there's a danger of damage, but I will use a ruler on her breasts. Lisa likes bondage a whole lot more than I do. It's very nice for the sub. She gets to sit there and enjoy it. She has all these nice fantasies about being tied up and left alone. However, when it really comes to leaving her alone while I go off and do something, it turns out that she means less than five minutes. You know, in fantasy it's an hour, and in practice, what turns her on is about five minutes.

When you're talking about stuff going on in the bedroom, 95 percent of the time, it'll end up in traditional sex. However, when we're just going through the day, a swat on the rear end or tweaking her collar so it jingles is a full substitute for a hug or a quick peck. On that level they're interchangeable, but when we really get into it, then it generally ends up in sex.

There is a surreptitious agreement that the relationship is [very two-way]. [And] at least when her past is not really catching up with her, I do not believe that I'm really carrying the heavy end. She was sexually abused as a child and has nightmares. She talks in her sleep, and I have to hold and cuddle her and talk to her and reassure her and figure out what part of her needs reassuring.

[For me], having a woman standing naked in front of me and wearing my collar is the quintessential part of dominance: "I am master here, and she belongs to me." Something that sort of got skipped in our very crowded life together would be having some kind of a D&S wedding, whereby Lisa would give herself [to me]. [In my earlier] fantasies, my generic submissive would give herself to me in a D&S marriage. She would come out dressed in something simple—not a big, fancy wedding dress—and she would drop it and be naked. She'd come over and kneel in front of me. I'd take her hand, and she would announce that she gives herself to me and is my property. I'd respond that I accept her. There would be some verbiage on both sides indicating love and caring—all the good stuff—and then I'd put a collar and a leash on her. Sometimes I would fantasize about branding her, [but] that was optional. Like a lot of people, the less you're actually getting, the heavier your fantasies get.

I definitely feel that there is more that we want to do. At this point, we're just getting back to the [intensity] that we reached around the time we got married. I finally quit my regular job. Now I'm working full-time on our business, and we're starting to get it under control, so we've got time for each other again.

We need to figure out activities that we can carry on while still being business partners and not contributing any more to the town gossip than we already do. We need a means of making this a more full-time, always-felt D&S relationship. Unfortunately, we have kids in an open-plan house.

With children around, even if we were totally vanilla, we wouldn't do any bedroom stuff without the door closed. On the other hand, we don't make a big deal about it if she comes over and kneels next to me at the table or on the couch at night. She'll wear the collar in front of them. The kids are four and six. Right now, we spend an awful lot of time explaining an awful lot of things [to them] anyway. Some of them are very hard for kids that age to grasp. We don't want the practical difficulties of trying to explain sex, let alone a variation on sex, to a six-year-old. We have enough trouble explaining why he has to return library books.

LISA W.

D&S was something I really wanted. I don't know if I can say I discovered it, but once I knew the right words [for it], I knew it was something that was a big part of me. D&S is not just in the bedroom for me. If anything, D&S keeps me from staying inside a shell and having armor between me and the rest of the world. When I'm feeling submissive, I'm more open: I feel things; I enjoy life. If I'm not and I'm in my own shell and feeling like I can't be submissive or [that] it's not being [elicited from] me, I tend to have a wall between me and the rest of the world. I don't enjoy life in general.

I was abused as a kid. I had a single mother and small sisters who I watched. My mother worked two jobs. Starting in second grade, I put myself and the girls to bed. There was no parent around. The neighbor who I was supposed to go to if I needed anything molested me for years. As soon as we moved away, I blocked it out. It wasn't until about 18 months ago that I started having memories. I wasn't sure what they were. Then all of the years that it happened became rolled up into one memory. [For a while] I said, "Okay, it happened, and it was no big deal." Then as I became more secure in my relationship with Frank and finally had time [to] deal with it, all of a sudden I started having flashbacks, and all the gory details came out.

When I first got into the relationship with Frank, I [felt that I] was hiding something and that he only loved me because he didn't know everything about me. I believed that if he ever found out all of it, he wouldn't love me anymore. Part of me said, "Either he takes me as I am or I'm not going to be here anymore." Part of me wanted to shock him and wanted to say, "You think you love me, but do you know this? How do you look at me now?" When I could say that and he still came back and said, "I still love you, and the things that happened to you had nothing to do with who you are. I love *you*," it gave me a lot of space to open up and to figure out what happened and how much it affected me and whether I'm going to let it affect me now.

Before I remembered my abuse, I used to say, "I don't know why I'm turned on by being used. That's just the way I am." I didn't remember any of that stuff ever happening to me. Then I start getting some flashbacks where I did remember stuff like that happening to me. Most of my abuse was oral sex. I don't remember incidents of being spanked or anything like that. But there were books lying around that I would read when I was [about] nine years old, and they had a lot of spanking. I can remember reading those books and being aroused by them.

I bought a vibrator when I was in high school, and one of my biggest fantasies was being caught playing with it and being spanked. From freshman year till I graduated and went into college, that was my number-one fantasy. In my first marriage we would always talk about tying each other up and spanking each other. [But] I always did the tying up and the spanking; it never went the other way. We never said I was the dom or anything like that. We did things, usually at my suggestion, but he always took it to mean that that's what I wanted to do to him, not what I wanted him to do to me. He said, "We'll take turns," but it never got to be my turn. I would picture myself in his spot, but I didn't get real enjoyment out of spanking him or out of tying him up. It became very frustrating for me. I even bought a four-poster bed, thinking, Take a hint! He never did. I talk about it with him now, and it's pretty funny. He never even got that idea.

I married my first husband right after high school. It was like being married to my brother. It was very platonic. We were best friends in high school, but we were never in love. It was just the thing to do. We were 18, and we didn't satisfy each other very much. We didn't have a whole lot of communication. Two years after we were married, we were joining swinging clubs. I don't think either of us was satisfied. The men that I was attracted to in swing clubs were always aggressive. We probably went to a party once a month for three years. I enjoyed myself maybe four or five times, and each one of those times it was with somebody who was very controlling. I had one person one time pull my legs apart and give me head, and [he] kept telling me over and over, "The rules are [that] you can't move." I really liked that, [but] I never saw him again.

After I was separated for about a year, I was seeing other people, and I was totally frustrated. I kept saying, "I don't want the same kind of marriage. I don't want equal footing. I want somebody who is smarter than me, more aggressive than I am, more controlling." I wasn't finding him. I even went into counseling. I thought there was something wrong with me. I didn't know anything about D&S, but I was definitely worried that if I really went ahead and did it, that I wouldn't be able to take care of my kids [or] that I would get into an abusive relationship. I didn't know that I could find somebody who could love me and beat me all in the same relationship. I was very concerned that I would even want that.

I joined CompuServe, and when I found the D&S support group suddenly, I met tons of dominant men. I got bombarded [with letters]. I met somebody who became my mentor. He did not pursue any sort of sexual relationship with me. He became somebody I could use as a sounding board. I had gotten to a point where I was really desperate. I had very low self-esteem. I was overweight, and my main criterion for meeting somebody was that they would meet me, not that they were necessarily interested in the same things that I was. I was excited and incredibly turned on, and I just didn't care a lot about myself. I did some dumb things; I really did. You have to care enough about yourself to take precautions. Me, I had such a low self-esteem, I thought somebody was making a big sacrifice to do anything with me. I weighed 220 pounds, and I was five feet two. I thought that if somebody would meet me, boy, they would just be doing me the biggest favor in the whole world. It didn't even occur to me that they could really hurt me. I was very unwilling to set any kind of guidelines or even to say that [the dominant] has to be sane. [One problem] could have been that a lot of my fantasies were very impersonal. It was always somebody who ordered things to be done no matter what I [felt]. So how could such a person like that be human and loving to me?

In the year or so that I was on line before I met Frank, I probably met at least 10 or 12 different people. I would always visit them. I never let anybody come to where I was. I was very frustrated, [because] all the people I met wanted me to not have kids. Somebody might be willing to have a sub, but I had to leave my kids with my ex, or they didn't want me to work. I wasn't happy with that. I've always worked. It's part of who I am. I [even] met somebody who wanted to stick me in an apartment and bring me food and only take me out at certain times and that was it: no life of my own. What boggled me is that I knew that about him, and I still went and met him! I couldn't stand a weekend over there.

I got to a point where I was really desperate for someone. I was warned that you have to really care about yourself before you start [in this], and you have to find someone else who cares about you. You really do. It can be dangerous. I got myself in some really, really tough situations. [For example], one of my fantasies is to go to bed with a black dom man. I thought, God, that's all my fantasies rolled into one. I met somebody in Colorado who was black, and this mentor of mine kept telling me, "Lisa, don't meet him! I think this guy is really into beating up white women." I said, "Fine, it'll be heavy;

it'll be what I'm looking for." Of course, [my mentor] always turned out to be right. I basically got in way over my head. He did all the things you're *not* supposed to do. I came back looking like raw hamburger. I was welted from the back of my legs all the way up my thighs, my back, the back of my arms. It was grim. I didn't know what to do. My first thought was [that] I was absolutely psycho to let somebody do that to me. Why didn't I run and hide and say I'm never going to do it again? Why was I still intrigued? I still had the thought that somewhere out there was somebody that would do it right. I went to the [emergency room for the bruises, and] they knew immediately what had happened. They had seen it before. The doctor recommended that I go to a counselor. He said he thought that masochistic people in general need psychological help. He said, "You're going to commit suicide after a while if you don't start taking care of yourself." I was very angry at him, but he got me pointed in the right direction.

When I went back on line, I said that I was in a relationship. That let me read and learn and hear other people talk without being bombarded [by private mail]. I finally started to look for somebody who was human, somebody who gave me the sense that he was looking for somebody to love, not just somebody to beat. One thing that appealed to me in Frank's messages was his [description of an] ideal [situation]. He said, "It really adds a lot when you're bringing your wife flowers when she's in collar and cuffs." And I thought, Wow! Somebody would bring me flowers? I thought Frank sounded human and real and not like a jerk; it really appealed to me. I wrote to him. In the first letter I told him that I was actively looking for a D&S relationship, full-time. I said I'd been through a lot and I was finally getting smart and not meeting anybody, but that I was looking. I said, "From the sound of your messages, we seem to be looking for the same thing." And I told him, "I'm laying it on the line. I've got two kids; I'm divorced; and I work as a computer person at a law firm." And if he wasn't interested, that'd be fine, because I told him I'm not compromising anymore. That was one of the first times that I thought I was getting my shit together, and somebody still responded. I was so amazed that he wrote back.

I have nightmares sometimes [and] flashbacks, and for me, the best way to get me through one of those is for him to completely take control of me, to hold me down and make me focus and be aware of who I am now, not where I was in the flashback. If Frank [were to] let me go off and be in my flashback, I get worse and worse, and I go farther and farther away. I think I need control to feel like he still loves me and pays attention to me. To dominate me you have to know every single thing about me. [Before], I wouldn't open up and tell him things. I would change the subject if I felt like he was getting too close. A self-preservation instinct would emerge. But [I found that] the more honest I was, the more he knew about me, and the more he'd get inside my head, the happier I was. There was finally a point where I knew he's not going to betray me and he's not going to hurt me. He knows everything about me, he still loves me, and he still does all the things that I thought only somebody who could be distant and cool could do.

At times he doesn't want to push me too hard, [because] I've had all these flashbacks. [Some] people say, "Give them space; leave them alone; let them go inside themselves and regain their control." That doesn't work with me. But if Frank can see it happening and can reach out and make me stay here, and make me be a part of this, then I get past it and things are really good. It doesn't matter if I'm being pushed by lots and lots of pleasure, if he's making me come over and over and over again—which he likes to do [and] which I like—there gets to be a point where I don't want it anymore. I tend to go back into myself. It doesn't matter how open I am to start with. And you've got to be able to be with me and see it happening and to go beyond that.

I like all kinds of control. [For example], I've always liked to go play with my vibrator; I've done that since high school. For a while he would say, "Fine, play with it." I had to ask him, but if I did, I always got permission. I used to get irked! [And he'd say], "Why do you ask me if you don't want me to say 'Fine?'" We've had to be really honest with each other. I had to say, "I get disappointed if you say okay." [Maybe] I wanted to know that he wanted to be a part of it. We had to be really blunt and honest with each other about everything.

We have beams above our bed. I had always wanted hooks above my bed. I like to hang upside-down. We were doing that last night. If we get the legs up high enough, then my back takes a lot of the weight. I can usually sustain that for a long time. That's one of my all-time favorites. I feel very, very vulnerable. For me, if I can wiggle away, if I can squirm enough to where I feel like I have some control—even if it's not the control of getting away, but the control of [deciding] where [the blow will] land—that's too much control for me. But if I can't wiggle away and I'm very vulnerable and very exposed and what's going to happen is what's going to happen and I can't get away, then I get beyond just the pain, and things happen for me. He tied me up and left me outside last week, and when he made love to me afterwards, he said I was like an animal. I felt more uninhibited than I had ever felt.

Our regular—I call it our vanilla—sex is very loving and very affectionate. It's something that we do on a routine basis, and there's always elements of D&S in it, but it's not real heavy. It's good, but the times that I'm really involved and really turned on, it's always very heavy D&S. Those are the times that I'm most uninhibited and most into [sex]. [And] I don't even fantasize anymore: I remember. Our D&S experiences are the things that I think about, and they keep me excited. For me, D&S play is much more satisfying [than regular sex].

We [also] go for periods when he's not letting me come from any sort of vanilla sex at all. He's made me come from spanks, he's made me come just from putting his fingers in my mouth and things like that, but I have to be feeling very, very submissive and to be in tune to myself. It can't just happen any time. It's a cumulative effect. When we go for a month without any sort of D&S anything, we go back 10 paces. My pain threshold goes way down, and I get frustrated. There has to be a continuum or I'm not going to orgasm from anything but very direct stimulation. But if [D&S] is a big part of our life, then I orgasm from other things.

I think the most memorable experience is probably the first time I orgasmed from being beaten. We had some child-free time, like two days in a row. We hadn't had a whole lot of time by ourselves for weeks, and I spent a lot of time with him clothed and me naked, with just a collar. It's hard for me to walk around [like that], but after a couple of hours of having no choice, it gets easier. It affects you psychologically. He told me the day before that he was going to beat me the next day. He tried other things first. I was tied up on the bed, and I know he used a paddle and a cat. He played with me a lot, and I had come several times already. Then he told me that he was going to beat me, and he used the riding crop, and I came. I don't cry very often. I don't know if it's pride or what, but it takes a lot to make me cry from being beaten. It's only happened two or three times, but I had gotten to where I was crying, and he still wouldn't stop, and I ended up having an orgasm. I was shaking, crying, and coming at the same time. It was something!

It was also memorable when he left me [tied up outside]. It heightened all of my senses. I was sure I could hear cars. We're way out in the woods, and I was hearing cars come up our driveway—they were probably down on [the highway], which is pretty far—but my senses were that much heightened. I was tied tightly, with my hands held pretty close to the tree. He said he was gone probably 20 minutes. [To me] it felt like hours, like forever; I thought he was never going to come back. [It was] a sunny day. [I was conscious of] the flies and the bees and the flowers. I could hear the wind in the trees. I had just been beaten, and I could feel the heat from the back of my thighs [and] the wind blowing on the welts. It was incredible.

BAMBI BOTTOM

I am [my husband's] permanent slave. He owns me completely. At a specific point in time he accepted me as his slave and from that point onward, knowing fully what I was getting into, I agreed that he would make all the decisions about my life; that my property now became his property; that he can do with me whatever he wants, however he wants. The control started out pretty mild. Now that I'm in the third year of this relationship, it's very slowly and gradually become stronger and more encompassing.

I don't think [the average person] would recognize me if he met me, because I am—and come across as—a very competent, happy individual. I'm happier now than I ever have been. I'm more relaxed and confident than the great majority of people I meet. Most people I meet are living their lives dreaming dreams of what they wish could happen to them, what they wish they could be, and they're not pursuing those dreams. I pursued my dream. I've gone for what I really wanted in my life and I've gotten it.

I used to consider myself to be a [committed] feminist. I'm completely for women's rights in the sense of women doing what *they* want to do with their lives and having *no* group, including other feminists, tell them what they must do [or] be. I've read lots of things written by feminists against S&M and women submissives in particular. They don't like the fact that some women choose to give their power completely to another person. That makes me very angry. It seems that some feminists are saying that I must choose their path instead of my path. I have a certain bitterness toward [politically correct] feminists; I consider myself to be a true feminist. I have made my own choices about my life. I have chosen what I know and believe makes me most happy. I am not conforming to anyone's ideal of what I should be. I am a very powerful woman, powerful enough to fulfill my life's dreams, something that few people do. If someone chooses to see this as giving in to the patriarchal society, she is seeing me on a superficial level and being purposely obtuse.

My earliest feelings about D&S happened when I was four or five. They weren't fantasies, just feelings. I liked to serve my parents, do little favors for them. I liked to play the subservient role with the children that I played with. I organized games. We'd have a little competition, and whoever lost had to be the absolute slave of the winner for the entire day. I'd always make sure I lost!

I've had long talks with my master about [how my desires formed]. My ideas about this change all the time, but right now I believe it's partially genetics. I don't think the kind of childhood I had made me submissive. It was a bad childhood. Unlike many people, I think that my submissive feelings survived *despite* the abuse. The abuse should have shut me down, should have made me a very different person than I am now.

[As a child] I thought of myself as a special person. I thought I was very intelligent, but I was also very reserved and very shy. I was not like the other girls. I didn't play with dolls. I didn't join cliques. If I had a friend in school, and that was rare, it would just be [one] girl. I wanted to fit in because, in Catholic school, children who were different were ridiculed by the teachers, the nuns, and the [other] children. I hated standing out.

Through my teens and early 20s, I continued to have very lurid S&M fantasies. When I was 23 I got my boyfriend to act out some D&S with me. I'd read him parts of *Story of O,* and that would get him really hot. I told him that I'd like to live out something like that, and one day he took me by surprise. He cut a switch from a tree and tied my wrists to the ceiling and beat me with [it] and did some very humiliating things to me. I *loved* that. I was never more excited in my life! But the next day the bruises came up on my buttocks, and it scared him off completely. He thought that meant that he was a brutal and evil man, and he wouldn't have anything else to do with S&M. I ended up staying with him for seven years after that and never could get my S&M desires fulfilled, although I constantly fantasized about [that episode] when we'd have sex.

I became aware of what *I* was [at] about the age of 29 when I had gotten on an Anne Rice kick. The *Vampire* books were very romantic, and there was an underlying theme of power in them. I soon came across the *Beauty* books. That was when a light bulb went off in my head: I realized that, yes! This is *me*! I'm submissive. I love S&M. I would love to live out the things that this woman is describing. I knew I had to seek it out.

To be submissive means to be willing to do someone else's will. A feeling of sexual excitement is linked to that. I also get a feeling of doing what's right for me, of being at home, of expressing my true personality. Lifestyle D&S also involves a great deal of trust. [My] bad childhood is not the kind of background that would make you trust anyone. I'm an extremely suspicious person. I have a hard time trusting men in particular. I was raped as a child, and to this day I haven't gotten over this. I have a hatred and fear of men in general. My master is an exceptional man, and it is through his personality only that I am able to trust him to the degree that I do, which is almost absolute. The chains that bind me are not physical. [My husband's] power over me has grown over the years. It's a very subtle thing. It's not something I can fully explain to someone who has had no taste for it. Sure, I could untie my collar and walk out in the middle of the night. But I won't. It's not a game I'm playing with myself.

I consider myself to be a three-way masochist. I'm a physical masochist:

I like pain and I like cruelty in association with that pain. I'm an emotional masochist: I love humiliation, especially degradation. And I'm a mental masochist: I love power; I love someone being in control over me. In a lifestyle relationship I get all three. I have no rights in this relationship. I don't have safe words. I'm *not* permitted to leave him, no matter what, unless I clearly and honestly think that I am in danger. I own no property anymore, except for a black leather rose which he gave me. That's a tender joke between us: I have one possession, and it's this little rose I keep on my vanity table. I'm told when to wake up in the morning. I'm told when to go to sleep. When I'm not working, he gives me my orders for the day. I'm allowed to make suggestions about what I'd like to get done, but I can't insist. The final decision about what I do on any day is up to him. But often my suggestions are accepted.

In the evening I prepare his bed, get him water to drink, turn off lights, shut the windows. When I get into bed, I'm tied to the bed by a collar and a rope. I also have to wear a mask and earplugs at night, so there's some sensory deprivation. I do most of the housework. When my master is in a mood to wash dishes, he will, but it mostly falls on me. I have to ask permission to eat, to drink anything except water, to use the bathroom, to make purchases. I carry no money except what he gives me. I turn my paychecks over to him. He handles all the finances. I have to curtsy upon entering and leaving his presence. I must come promptly when he calls. As far as my career is concerned, he decides which [free-lance] contracts I accept, although I'm allowed to give my input. He takes it into consideration. I have to keep my pussy shaved. I have to exercise three times a week to keep in shape. Oh, and when he pinches my nose, I have to say, "Beep! beep!" [So] that's what my [daily] life is like, what it's like being a slave.

My sex life is completely controlled by him. I'm not allowed to touch myself without his permission. And he gives [it] rarely. I used to masturbate three or four times a day—that was my routine. Not anymore. We do the things that he likes to do and I give my input. He controls what we do during [sex], but the most powerful aspect of that control is the control over my orgasms. If he gives me permission at a time when I'm not particularly in the mood, I [still] must come.

If I disobey him, I'm punished in a way I don't like. Not with fun punishment, but with bad punishment. [I get punished] when it's conscious and willful. [But] when it's an emotional problem or something that he feels I'm not completely in control of, he will not punish me. Instead, we try to get to the roots of the problem. That works very successfully.

One of the hardest things is [that] I have to honestly tell him exactly what I'm thinking whenever he asks. That's hard sometimes because I'm a very private person. I've always been very independent. It has taken me a long time to get used to being under this much control, to having my desires thwarted at times. The biggest sorrows that I've experienced as a permanent slave have had to do with the resistance that I've experienced and acted out in response to this control. I've had particular difficulty with aerobics. I'm a lazy person. I don't like to exercise, yet my master insists I do that for my health. I get angry and emotional and stomp my feet and throw tantrums.

Resistance is particularly ugly. You treat your master like you would never imagine a slave should treat a master or a human being should treat any other human being! I get angry; I say vicious things. I fight him with all my might. In the end, though, we talk and we talk about why I'm resisting. We talk about the struggles that are involved. In the end I [always] end up submitting to his will.

I get this perverse delight in giving up my power completely and knowing that I am absolutely controlled by someone else. It's this tingly feeling in my body, this shiver of delight. Another delightful part of [our] lifestyle relationship—the things I'm describing are very individualistic; they probably don't resemble anyone else's relationship—is I like being little. I don't mean infantilism, but I like the aspect of our relationship in which my master is older—he is physically older than me by about 13 years and mentally older than me by about 50 years—[and] more experienced. I see him as a mentor and as almost a father figure. I like being small and childlike in his presence. That's very pleasant to me.

In this relationship I've become a lot more emotionally healthy. My master respects individuality. He's always respected my personality and not tried to crush it, although he certainly has the power to do so. He's got a very powerful personality himself. [When my master makes a bad decision], it's no big deal. I may get angry or upset, but he admits his mistakes. We talk about it, and it's over in a few hours. [Sometimes] I argue with him vehemently about what I think is the right way to do things. Sometimes he changes his mind; often he doesn't. He lets me get angry and express my reasons over and over, *ad nauseam*. But in the end, he decides.

Obedience is a big part of the lifestyle relationship for me. The more obedient I become, the more delightful the experience becomes for me. I think a person who is not in a permanent relationship doesn't get that same feeling of obedience and joy. They may experience pain [or] humiliation, but it isn't an ongoing thing that becomes deeper and deeper. My sexual feelings continue to intensify, and my feeling of being owned grows deeper.

I love serving my owner. I love doing things for him. I love having routines and duties that I must perform every day. I love when he dresses me up in this obscene French maid's uniform he bought for me and I become

Fifi, the French maid. My service to him takes on a more formal and ritualized aspect when I'm Fifi. My curtsies are much deeper and more frequent. If I drop something, if I misplace something, if I'm not quick enough, Fifi gets turned over his knee and gets a very painful beating. I love being a French maid! I like to be whipped and beaten in various ways. I really love being caned. We don't do a lot of bondage. Instead, my master likes me to hold myself in place. I love having to maintain that position no matter how painful the cut of the crop or the bite of the cane. I love oral sex. In S&M it is real different than [in] vanilla. You're servicing your master. You're very aware that you're trying to please him. With my ex-husband, I was aware that I was in control, orchestrating his feelings and his orgasm. With my master it's the opposite. He's controlling my head and my mouth and telling me exactly what to do, and I'm trying to serve him in the best way possible.

I distinguish between good embarrassment and bad embarrassment. Bad embarrassment would be where your boss calls you into her office and yells at you in front of other employees and makes you feel like shit. Humiliation and good embarrassment usually involves some kind of exposure, physical or emotional. I like having my bottom exposed and talked about and played with. I like it when my master beats me and I squirm around on the bed and inadvertently expose my vaginal lips and shake and squirm in all kinds of embarrassing ways. Humiliation is a wonderful thing. In S&M you know that the person isn't doing it to hurt your feelings. A masochist gets sexual excitement from experiencing physical pain, and humiliation is a form of emotional pain. There's a small element of exhibitionism in humiliation, but true exhibitionists don't like to be humiliated. They like to show off the parts of their bodies that they're proud of. In humiliation, you get parts of your body exposed that you like to keep private. It gives me a real thrill to be embarrassed in that way. I blush; I giggle; I turn red. If I had my own free choice, I wouldn't walk around with the bottoms of my Dr. Dentons undone.

[This is the first time] I'm close enough with someone that I can loosen up and relax and be silly. I see the part of his personality that is fun and playful. I've become more relaxed and more myself than I have in any other relationship with any other person in my life, including my family [and] an ex-husband who I was with for over a decade. If you're with the right person, miracles can occur.

THE PLEASURES OF DISCOMFORT

Nine

CORPOREAL PUNISHMENTS

May those who know me see the marks of biting
And bruises which betray a happy love!
In love I want to weep or see you weeping;
To agonize or hear your agony.

—PROPERTIUS[1]

To experience pain as pleasure seems paradoxical. Yet, the playful pinch or slap of a lover in a moment of high passion are varieties of pain, and both are common and widely accepted as aspects of intimate play that increase excitement. Pain is pleasurable when it is perceived as pleasurable. A love bite given in the bedroom may drive one to a peak of passion. A bite of identical force given on the street may drive one to the nearest police station to press charges.

To a person for whom the very idea of being struck with a whip can be perceived only as pain, it is difficult to understand that for some it may well be as erotic as the most gentle and intimate caress. Perception is everything, and perception varies from individual to individual.

This chapter profiles several individuals who speak to the subject of pain as pleasure.

- Cléo Dubois is a professional bondage specialist and professional sadist, as well as a lecturer and advocate of sexual choice. Her private pursuits include avant-garde theater, swimming, bicycling, and gardening. She is married.
- Jean L. is 49 years old, divorced, and works with children. She is the editor of the Society of Janus (San Francisco) newsletter *Growing Pains*. Her interests include education, reading, shortwave radio, and computers.
- Cassandra is 36 years old and an engineer. She lives with -j- in San Francisco.
- -j- is a graphics engineer. He is Cassandra's life-partner. They both submit to a male dominant, to whom they refer as "my liege."

PAINFUL BEGINNINGS

I eroticize pain. Receiving pain sexually stimulates me to the point of orgasm. I can also orgasm from giving pain. I've eroticized it to that extent.
—JEAN L.

That acute sensations may enhance erotic pleasure has always been known: Varieties of painful stimulation are recorded as means of enhancing sensations and lovemaking in sexual manuals such as *The Kama Sutra* (circa 450 B.C.) and other works. According to Magnus Hirschfeld, the Talmud "says that flagellation on the back may lead to a discharge of semen."[2] Erotic pain was considered a specific to combat the wilting effects of age and impotence in cultures as diverse as Imperial Rome and Restoration-era England. It is difficult to assess the sexual mores of another age, especially when that age left little documentation of the practices of the bedroom. Yet the notion that pain and pleasure are intermingled in the act of sex is one that would probably have elicited little controversy among the ancients.

The love of pain was termed *algolagnia* (literally, "pain craving") by Schrenk-Notzing in 1892. It was about this period that pain was apparently segregated from "normal" sexuality. Until erotic pain came under the scrutiny and disapproval of late–19th Century sexologists, it seems to have been accepted as an unusual vice that might, at most, excite gossip or speculation.

Perhaps the most remarkable aspect of the psychological literature on the enjoyment of pain is the absolute inability of psychologists to reach a consensus on etiology. No single theory on the etiology of sadomasochism proposed between 1886 and 1992 stands up to basic scientific scrutiny.[3]

The bias against painful pursuits has not markedly changed since the 19th Century, although today's more enlightened helping professionals seldom attempt to cure or to correct a patient's desire for pain. The exceptions are extreme cases of masochism which result in life-threatening emergencies. This small minority of masochists however seems rarely to pursue consensual D&S.

The eros of pain has a long history of representation in Western literature. Krafft-Ebing identified the enjoyment of pain with the name of novelist Leopold von Sacher-Masoch. Masoch's most notorious novel was *Venus in Furs*, wherein the whip-wielding Wanda treats her submissive lover, Severin, to sharp depredations which cause him unalloyed delight. Krafft-Ebing chose the Marquis de Sade—whose imagination, as is often the case, was far more active than his sex life—as an exemplar of pain giving. In *Psychopathia Sexualis*, Krafft-Ebing forever linked the enjoyment of inflicting pain with de Sade. (Contrary to popular belief, the term *sadism* had been in use for decades before Krafft-Ebing employed it, primarily in French literary criticism.)

These gentlemen are hardly unique in having inscribed a penchant for erotic pain upon the literary record. For centuries the tradition of courtly love glorified the concomitant pain and pleasure experienced by the man who rapturously suffers for the sake of a cruel, unattainable woman. While such sentiments were considered to be chaste, the metaphors and images were explicitly sadomasochistic. By the end of the 19th Century, poets Charles-Pierre Baudelaire, Charles Algernon Swinburne, and Paul Verlaine had scandalized and titillated readers with their evocative descriptions of sadomasochistic sexuality.

DO ALL D&SERS ENJOY PAIN?

D&Sers who are solely interested in the psychological stimulation of D&S or in fetish activities are often just as baffled or put off by physical discomfort as are most mainstream individuals. Nonetheless, D&Sers generally agree that putatively uncomfortable or painful activities, such as bondage, spanking, whipping, or other intense stimulation, are often a part of their sexual relationships.

Spanking is not a separate thing amongst people who do S&M: It's just one of the ways that you can inflict pain. I like being bound in comfortable positions. I like being whipped; I like being caned; I like pain. —CASSANDRA

Few, if any, D&Sers do all the things covered in the following four chapters. People who enjoy rigorous physical discipline may not necessarily enjoy bondage. Many "love bondage" enthusiasts object to pain of any kind. Not only does the desirable level of stimulation vary from person to person, but the kind and the location of stimulation desired varies broadly as well. Those who enjoy a stringent spanking may be loath to experience pain to anything but the buttocks, and those who enjoy stimulation in far more sensitive areas may seek only light, teasing, tingling sensations.

WHAT KIND OF PERSON LIKES TO GIVE OR TO RECEIVE PAIN?

Not only is the percentage of the population who is aroused by intense stimulus high, but the actual numbers vary according to what one classifies as an erotic response to pain, and even what constitutes pain.

There is great diversity on the estimates of the number of S/M practitioners in the general population. At least part of this variance is due to the different ways S/M or similar concepts are presented or defined in these general studies of the sexual behavior. The estimates range from about 50 percent, those who report at least some erotic response to being bitten (Kinsey et al., 1953), to approximately 5 percent of those who report obtaining sexual pleasure from inflicting or receiving pain. It is the present author's best guess that approximately 10 percent of the adult population are S/M practitioners. —CHARLES MOSER[4]

The people we interviewed often made critical distinctions between dominant and sadist, and submissive and masochist. Most D&Sers feel compelled to arrive at personal definitions. The clinical labels rarely fit, perhaps because psychological communities lump together people of significantly different tastes, desires, and degrees of interest.

I'm a sadist. I like to claim that. I do not ever advertise as a dominant. I advertise as a sadist. Sadism is physical. I look at dominance much more as a mental control. —CLEO DUBOIS

Spanking, for example, has been little studied as a distinct phenomenon. Instead, it has been assumed to be a behavior within the boundaries of clinically defined sadomasochism, an assumption which makes spanking "purists" bristle. Likewise, there is little general differentiation of bondage or of whipping in clinical classifications, yet these behaviors have a core of practitioners who are interested in little else. Classifications are more a matter of convenience for the researcher than a reflection of what people desire or practice. The distinctions made by the people themselves are crucial to an understanding of their sexual personae. Making the willing infliction or reception of pain in any sexual context a common denominator is guaranteed to result in a huge grouping of peoples whose interests are widely divergent.

WHERE DOES THE INTEREST BEGIN?

The Grimm fairy tale "The Princess and the Pea" is about a delicate young girl who is disturbed by the slightest sensation. Perhaps the story of deep masochists could be titled "The Princess and the Nettles," since anything less chafing might be undetectable, even boring. A sexual masochist not only requires a profound arousal of the senses but actually loves extreme sensation in much the same way that others delight in a soft caress.

> *People talk about wanting a light, feathery touch. I don't feel it. I can lie there with my eyes closed, and someone's stroking me gently and doing what some people would think was wonderful, feathery, nice stuff, and it feels like nothing to me.* —CASSANDRA

A sexual sadist, conversely, derives pleasure from inflicting intense stimulation. But D&Sers who follow the "Safe, Sane, and Consensual" credo wish to give or feel a pain that is inherently pleasurable to both partners.

> *[People who are] not involved in S&M don't seem to understand that although you are delivering pain, it is pain-pleasure: Nobody really wants to feel actual pain.* —JEAN L.

Clearly, people vary dramatically in their thresholds for intense stimulation. The question of why this is so is difficult to answer.

> *I think the desire for more stimulation is a function of wiring, a primarily physical thing. I like a lot of stimulation . . . if it's built up to, it doesn't hurt. It feels good.* —CASSANDRA

In recent years some strides have been made in developing plausible physiological—if not psychological—explanations for the thrill of pain. This is partly a result of sports medicine's research on the effects of endorphins. Athletes frequently note the rush of endorphins (from *endogenous morphine:* "the morphine within")[5] that can accompany pain and fatigue. Endorphins are natural opiates that are secreted by the pituitary gland in response to pain. They bind to opiate receptors in the brain, bringing not only a cessation of pain but a sense of well-being or even euphoria. Pain can literally bring pleasure.

> *Anybody who is into aerobics and step classes, like I am, will know what that endorphin rush is like! I can have a greater intensity of pain and experience it as pleasure. That's why my body can probably endure more pain than yours: I'm brought up slowly; and the endorphins take care of it. I go into full-fledged endorphin rushes.*
>
> —JEAN L.

A masochist's interest in pain may be partly attributable to the craving for an endorphin-induced natural high. Most of our interviewees recall that they first learned that the same sensations that others perceived as purely painful—i.e., an anguish to be avoided at all costs—were for them erotic and exciting when they were still children. For them, pain and pleasure created a powerful erotic admixture.

> *As far as the psychological aspects of D&S, I didn't clue into them as early as I clued into the ability to eroticize pain. In childhood I discovered that things that ought to hurt didn't strike me as painful.*
>
> —MR. HAPPY

Dozens of references in classical literature verify that the early erotic linkage of pain and pleasure is an age-old phenomenon. In his 18th Century *Confessions,* philosopher Jean-Jacques Rousseau goes on at length about his early experience of being whipped and punished and his subsequent cravings for reenactments. These experiences marked him permanently.

> *I had found in the pain, even in the disgrace, a mixture of sensuality which had left me less afraid than desirous of experiencing it again from the same hand. . . . Who would believe that this childish punishment inflicted upon me when only eight years old by a young woman of 30, disposes of my tastes, my desires, my passions?*[6]

Although many of our interviewees said that they recall making a connection between pain and pleasure at an early age, most did not recall any specific event (such as a trauma) that revealed this aspect of their sexuality to them. A majority, instead, recall experimenting with painful stimulus in the regular course of exploring their bodies—and discovering that they were aroused by the pain.

> *I can remember poking and pinching and putting clothespins on and tying stuff around my genitals when I was eight or nine. I tried various textures: steel wool, sandpaper. There was pretty clearly a connection between painful things—as painful as I could manage to do to myself—and being sexually excited.* —JOHN M.

Experiences in later life may also influence an individual's interest in erotic pain.

> *Actually, being into S&M other than in fantasy surprises me, because five years ago if you had suggested to me that I would enjoy pain, I would have said, "Only sick people do that."*
> —JEAN L.

Once the desire to give or receive pain is identified in adulthood—and if a willing partner is available—it is very common for both dominant and submissive practitioners consciously to pursue their desires.

> *I got started [in S/M when] a vanilla lover brought me to a workshop called The Suicide Class. It was not about suicide, but about using San Francisco as a playground to conquer one's fears, such as climbing the Golden Gate Bridge. This was [around] 1980. One of the workshops included a demonstration on whipping and pain. It opened my eyes. [The workshop leader] was dominant over her partner, and it just fit. I immediately felt at home. I jumped in headfirst.* —CLÉO DUBOIS

THE LOVE OF INTENSE STIMULATION

Mental receptiveness to unusual erotic stimulus is a key to its enjoyment. Consensual physical restraint, for example, induces a feeling of vulnerability and helplessness. To a bondage enthusiast, restraint is intrinsically erotic, largely because bondage enables him or her to abandon inhibitions.

Pain may be emotionally gratifying because of its association with punishment. For example, a whipping may be a form of penitence which exorcises an individual's sexual guilt. Just as vulnerability is liberating, penance delivers the penitent from shame or responsibility.

Of course, far more Americans experience sexual guilt than crave to be punished painfully for it. That many D&Sers perceive corporal punishment as a means of obtaining permission to experience their sexuality, however, is apparent from the results of our interviews.

It may add to the arousal of those who enjoy giving pain to realize that their partners reach new levels of ecstasy as a direct result of their ministrations. In this respect, giving pain is not unlike purely psychological domination: Controlling the partner's sexual response is psychosexually thrilling. Many whom we interviewed spoke of the satisfaction that they feel in knowing that they are able to give something to their partners which others cannot or will not give them. Most believe that intense stimulation—be it pain, enforced helplessness, or humiliation—can elicit a degree of sexual intensity rare in vanilla relationships.

> *I get enjoyment out of inflicting pain. Of course, it's consensual and built up to. I like to bring submissives or masochists to that part of themselves where they're suffering and it's turning them on. [Even if] they're fighting, somehow it's working [for them]; that turns me on.* —CLÉO DUBOIS

Also, a growing number of people seem to conceive of pain as an alternate route to spirituality. They may refer to S/M as "Sexual Magic." A neopagan subset of avant-garde sexuality communities, Sexual Magic holds that transcending the body's ordinary pain limits is a path to religious enlightenment.

> *I don't see any difference between what I call intense physical sensation and fasting, vision questing, and prolonged dancing. All of these things are trance-inducing states, and all trance-inducing states can lead to altered states. There are different techniques, but they're all getting us to the same place.* —FAKIR MUSAFAR

Interviews

Cléo Dubois

My background is Roman Catholic; intellectual lower middle class [on] my mother's side, and blue-collar lower middle class on my father's. I usually call myself bi-kinky, but I don't like to go to bed in a vanilla way with people of the same sex, so I am heterosexual in that [respect]. It also depends on what you call sex. I don't call S&M sex; I call S&M erotic play. I will play with men or women of any sexual orientation—gay, lesbian, straight, bisexual cross-dressers, transsexuals. [It] doesn't matter to me in terms of the S&M play.

Besides making a living at S&M, I get sexually turned on by it. I feel alive. I look at the whole thing as a dance. There is a lengthy courting dance of light S&M and progressive buildup. The whole beginning is for them. The courting continues until the person is ready. [And then] I enjoy taking people to their limits and a bit past [them]. That might mean giving two more or three more blows with the cane, or turning up the electricity just a little bit more, or keeping them in bondage and having them beg just a little more. Those five minutes are for me; that is my payback and my enjoyment for all the energy and work I invest.

Strangely enough, very few people want safe words. They just think they have to have them. I will give them a slow-down safe word. If they use that, I will honor it and slow down, but I won't stop the scene completely: I might go back to it. If they are into very stringent activity, I will give them a stop safe word. I pride myself that no has ever had to use a stop word with me. Also, for my own certainty, if a session involves a gag or heavy bondage, I will give them a safe gesture or a safe sound.

During the warm-up I [develop] feelings of closeness with the people I'm working on, an understanding of them. I [appreciate] the aesthetics of what I'm doing that's specifically pleasing to them. And there's a spirit of play. When I get to my own personal enjoyment—true sadism—I get turned on. I get aroused by that moment where I'm pushing limits.

There are a few fantasies that turn me on, not many. They all have an element of being pushed: If you are a captive or prisoner, you get pushed. You're not a slave. I also like embarrassing fantasies because of my strange sense of humor. Embarrassing fantasy [expresses] my intellect, my humor. I like to make people do things that they wouldn't [ordinarily do]. I like to embarrass someone, because I can play with that embarrassment psychologically. It's a mental game. My own sense of sarcasm can come out and play. I find that 99 percent of the people I see are turned on by challenging some taboo.

A part of my psychological satisfaction is [having] fun. I like to be mischievous. I like to poke at people: Poke them with physical objects, like sterile needles, and poke at them with humiliation and mind games. Sometimes I like to get somebody into stringent bondage and just laugh [or] make comments, because it's aesthetically funny. But I'm not a slave trainer. I am not one to train people to stand in the corner or wait on me perfectly. I've never been comfortable with that. It is not my forte to train people for service; I train them to become better masochists and to accept more input.

I believe in being myself in the dungeon. Being myself means having a sense of humor. If I do something that is wrong, [if] I tell somebody, "Stand up" and I forget that I tied a knot to their balls and they cannot stand up, I'm not going to cover up. I say, "Oops! I made a mistake. Mistresses are not perfect, haha!" That's me. This is one of the reasons why I don't take fantasy slaves. Fantasy slaves tend to think that you're always dressed in a corset and high-heel shoes and always act a certain way. I tell people that it's not so. That's my part in demystifying [S&M]. If somebody calls and says, "I want an appointment at 11:30." I say, "You can't, because I'm going swimming at 11:30." Or "I'll be riding my bicycle." And they go, "Shit, she rides a bicycle! Hmmm!"

Part of me wants people to understand that, just like they're not in the dungeon being a slave 24 hours a day, I'm not in my dungeon. I'm not following my partner around with a whip when he's making dinner! That's me. For some people, the full-time lifestyle might be really wonderful; it's not for me. People who need a standardized image of a sadist won't get along with me. People who are willing to be themselves will.

Being a professional dominant is a service to the world—and a valuable service. I do not think that one is like royalty, that things are owed to you. I provide a decent service for the people who need it. Sensory deprivation is a service. Nothing in it is for me. It's all for the client. A lot of people are interested in sensory deprivation, but very few people know how to do it.

I ask people to write back after a heavy session, so I have a lot of [mail] and feedback. [It seems that] people often go into what they call hypnotic trances, altered states. They go inward. I provide a situation [where] they can go inward rather than outward. This experience is the opposite of slave service. I consider myself like a train conductor: I am the driver; the bottom is the train; I discover where the track is, and I have to follow it.

Knowing the physical condition of the people you play with is very important—are there any sports injuries, old injuries, allergies, phobias, physical limitations? Questions should be asked before one engages in any sort of bondage. I do not expect the bottom to remember everything. A lot of people say, "I don't have any problems!" They get on their knees, and five minutes later say, "Mistress, may I please speak," and I say, "Is it about safety?" They say, "Yes." And I say, "What is it?" "My knee's killing me; I really can't stay on my knees." "So how come you didn't tell me earlier?"

You should not expect your partner necessarily to be able to give you all of the information right away about his body condition. That condition is [critically] important in determining what kind of bondage will be done; this extends to any sort of play. One should not engage in exotic stuff unless you've done your homework [and] research. It's common sense: I've never been to medical school, but I took CPR and talk to a lot of people [about these issues]. Heavy bondage, sensory deprivation, suspension would not be good for people who have only been playing for a little while. It takes a long time to acquire skills to do these things. That's why I have a problem with certain videos that show a woman hanging off the floor, suspended by only [her] breasts or wrists. I feel very strongly about this, because somebody can go home and create a dangerous situation.

You're required to gather the right information. There are groups throughout the country that provide good information. I really [stress S&M] community involvement, so that you learn. I always learn from others. I also give workshops on the things I know. Safety is really important. You cannot just make a quick list of precautions: There are so many things to take into consideration.

When I started, I was only interested in whipping. Little by little, I was introduced to things by [the] people that wanted them. A bottom or masochist would bring in a new interest, and I would start playing with it and see if I liked it or not. I realized I like a variety of things. That's how corsets came waltzing into my life! [For me] corsets are a kind of bondage; [it's] an aesthetic. I enjoy corsetry as a sadist; I enjoy it as a sadistic piece of bondage equipment. And I enjoy the visual.

What I'd really like people to know about S&M is that the display—that which appears to the outsider—and the reality are usually opposites. Somebody may seem to be in intense agony, but might very well be in intense ecstasy. If somebody is in inescapable bondage an outsider might think, Poor them! They're totally helpless! [But] they might be having a great time, feeling very free about their desire, their emotions, their vulnerability, their catharsis, their sexuality.

JEAN L.

I experience pain as pleasure. I've known all my life [that] I have a high threshold for pain. It has to become really severe before I begin perceiving it as actual pain. Otherwise, it is erotic stimulation to me.

Nobody wants to really be hurt [in S&M]. It is a lot more controlled, a lot safer than ordinary stuff being done out there. It's very important to know this, especially if someone wants to get into some of this stuff. If the thought of it turns them on and they'd like to experiment, [they should] read about it and learn about it first, so that nobody *does* get hurt. I have taken friends who are straight and shown them how I played.

I can pretty much get into any pain that I choose. I can go to the dentist and [enjoy] having him diddle around with that little metal instrument. But if he was to take that instrument and put it into a cavity, I would experience that as pain and probably jump out of the seat.

I prefer the bottom in most cases, but I probably end up doing 50-50. My guess is that there are 15 or 20 male submissives to every female dominant. There are so many male submissives! Most submissives are not masochists. I have a pet name for it: I call it the "Tie Me Up and Fuck Me School of S&M." It's basically, "Please tie me on the bed, maybe spank me a couple of times, pinch my nipples a little, and then fuck me!" And that's it. That's not my trip. My trip is pain. When I top and I find somebody who is a masochist, I relish it.

I have had an active fantasy life since I was eight years old, but my fantasies [then] were what I would call goddess-worship fantasies. I was the white goddess. I was the object of men's worship. [I didn't develop real] S&M [feelings] until my 20s. I was married at the time, and my husband got a copy of *Story of O*. We used to lie in bed together and read it. That appealed to me a lot. That was when my first full S&M feelings developed, but [they, too, were] strictly in the realm of fantasy. When I was in my mid-30s I discovered Victorian pornography. I have been and continue to be an extremely active fantasizer about Victorian pornography.

I did not lose my virginity until I was 17 years old. I cannot say for sure what influenced me toward S&M, but I think it stems from an incident [of sexual abuse] when I was eight years old. A couple years after that, I became very ill; the illness involved pain, and I was the center of attention for a few months, so that might have contributed to my interest in pain. [But when I was eight], I lived in Florida. We were an upper-middle-class Jewish family. My mother would give me money to go to the movies alone. That's a pretty strange thing for a woman to do, to send an eight-year-old female child onto a bus and to the movies alone! A pedophile found me and used a standard pedophile technique of rubbing my leg and gradually working his way up my leg until he was in essence masturbating me. It felt great! I had a sexual orgasm from it.

[But] I had ambivalence: I loved what he was doing, but I knew it wasn't what should be going on. So the last time, I decided to sit in another place in the theater, thinking he wouldn't find me. Of course, he did. And this time he got heavier. I can *vividly* recall this. He took my hand, and he put it on something. I remember thinking that it was smooth like baby skin and so amazingly soft, but underneath the softness there was this really hard inner core. He asked me if I would go home with him, and I knew that was dangerous, that [it] was something I shouldn't do. So I told him no. Then he asked me to go to the women's bathroom and to take off my panties and to come back and sit next to him. He took my carfare away.

I went to the bathroom to do what he wanted me to do. I remember looking at myself in the mirror. I was beginning to get scared. So I walked out of the theater and walked the mile home. It was one of those absolutely glorious [Florida] days. While I was walking back, I was repeating over and over to myself like a mantra, "You have to walk because this is your punishment for having enjoyed what happened to you."

Although it did not entail intercourse or sodomy or oral sex, I certainly lost my innocence. I became an eight-year-old child actively involved in a sexual fantasy life, masturbating, and aware of other people's sexuality. Because I lost my innocence so young, innocence is something that I value highly. I can't play with younger people. I draw the line at the early 30s, possibly late 20s. I do not think that children should be sexually involved with older people. I get horrified at the thought of a 25-year-old man having sex with a 16-year-old girl. I know that's done all the time, but I really believe that children cannot be consensual. They are precious and should be taken care of and their innocence protected. Mine wasn't.

To me, [play] piercing is a loss of innocence, a loss of virginity. That needle is, in essence, the man's penis symbolically entering my body. And it's in a nontraditional area of my body. That excites me. I'm a tremendous reader of women's romances, and within the genre what turns me on the most is the young innocent virgin who is ravished by her first lover. I don't think women have *rape* fantasies; I think women have ravishment fantasies. A man adores them to such an extent that he must sexually possess them. Every time I'm pierced, I am devirginized again.

[I edit the Janus newsletter.] The Society of Janus is an educational society. Written right on the business cards is, "Safe, Sane, and Consensual." San Francisco Janus has about 450 members. The one in Los Angeles has [about] 600. [Janus] is not primarily social; it's not a dating service. You don't go there to find somebody [to play with]. Its purpose is to teach interested people about S&M.

CASSANDRA

The most intense, special moments of dominance or of submission are things that probably could be described as staring into someone else's eyes. It's not so much action as contact between two people. It's knowing that there's real communication: a level of trust. When I am with my liege I basically say, "Take me wherever you choose; I wish to learn whatever you have to teach me." He shows me things about myself that are very valuable to me, that I've been afraid of learning but wanted to learn. It's a kind of compact. It's much more than just the mechanics of doing a scene.

It was a strong drive in me to submit and to want to be submerged in someone else. I didn't have much of a struggle with it. The only time it was a problem was if the person I was with started giving me negative stuff about it. But I didn't have negative thoughts in my own head. My experience up until I came out here was entirely submissive. I was not interested in topping very often. When I did try to top someone, I generally wasn't very good at it: [I] didn't want to do this until I knew what I was doing. [Since coming to San Francisco,] I have finally gotten to the point where I understood enough of what I wanted to be able to give those things to someone else. I don't know any really good tops who don't also bottom. I can't really imagine that even the best of tops couldn't learn more about what they do from bottoming.

I'm currently in the process of moving in with -j-. It was one of those instant serious relationships. We switch a fair amount. It has turned out that I'm mostly dominant within this relationship. It's interesting the way that evolved. Both of us feel that our greatest fantasy would be to be the slave of the other. I would be perfectly happy if he wanted to be master all the time. I would be the slave all the time and be just thrilled with life in general. I can't imagine anything better than that. In a way, by being his mistress, I serve him. It's sort of a circular logic that goes around and around: Whichever one is getting to be the slave is actually the one being served.

You can require a lot of things from somebody, but you can't require them to take charge. There are times when it gets very frustrating. Both of us, when we're topping, are doing it because it is what we want. But I would not want it if he did not want it from me. A major component of my desire to top is the fact that I know how happy it makes him. I get a lot of gratification out of it. It's not purely sex play. If I'm sitting down and I want him to go and get me something to drink, I'll say, "Slave, please go get me a glass of water!" [and] he'll go get me a glass of water. He's very happy to do it. Sometimes there've been stretches when neither of us is in charge because neither of us is really in a state to deal with it. It does take quite a bit of energy and focus to be able to do that.

When we first got together, most of his experience was with topping. Much of what happened with us just clicked. There were times when I would make a mistake and we would talk about it and figure out what had gone wrong, but for the most part, I was able to give him experiences that were just completely mind-blowing because they were fantasies that he didn't even know he had. The first time I tied him down, I knew what to do. It's very frustrating when you finally get somebody to tie you down and you lie there thinking, Well, you could do this, or they start to do something, maybe run their hand lightly along your leg, and you think, Okay, now pinch! and they don't. I was able to look at his body, and say, "Oh, he wants to be pinched right there!" And, for the most part, I was right on target. It was very gratifying for me to be able to give him this. I knew how intense it was, I knew how wonderful it was, because I knew how much I would have wanted it. I knew that the experiences that I was giving to him were as wonderful as they would have been if they [were] given to me.

When I top, I can inflict pain. I enjoy doing it primarily because I enjoy the other person's responses. I don't enjoy pain for its own sake. I enjoy pain within the context of a scene. A sadist is someone who enjoys pain for its own sake. [So] when I say that I've seen someone who's a sadist, it's someone who has channeled that desire into consensual activity. The two sadists that I know—one peripherally, one very well—don't inflict pain without consent. There might be times when they would like to, but they don't. It's a matter of self-control and a matter of choosing to live by certain values, certain standards.

When I was in college I ran into *Penthouse Variations* and things about bondage and S/M; these fantasies sounded very, very arousing to me. Yet whenever I tried to act some of these things out with lovers, it never worked. It always just hurt. I relegated the whole thing to "works well in fantasy, doesn't work in reality," until I met this person who knew what he was doing. I realized that, for most people, especially if you start with heavy pain, it just hurts. You want to start gently and work up to a higher level of sensation . . . a firm touch can be arousing once you're already aroused but can be painful [otherwise].

When I'm with [my liege], I wear a chained padlock around my neck. I've talked about wanting to wear it all the time. It's a very big thing for me. Wearing a chained padlock around your neck to work—it's a statement. And I've been feeling more and more inclined to not be closeted. I can still pass for conventional; I have one [piercing] in each ear, and nothing else that's obvious unless I undress. My nipples are pierced and my outer labia are pierced, but people running into me in the hall don't see that. I've been feeling more and more inclined to change that but at the same time a bit frightened of it. As of last Friday I have a chained padlock around my neck. Yesterday was the first day I went to work with it. A couple of people who know about what's going on smiled and said, "Oh, nice necklace." Other than that, I didn't get a reaction. I could see people looked at it, but nobody had the nerve to ask!

It used to be that I wanted to submit because I was afraid. It's hard to say what I was afraid of—I was afraid of a lot of things. I was very insecure. I wanted someone to say, "Yes, you are my slave" and to actively take control of my life. I didn't want to be someone's slave and get kicked around; I wanted to be someone's slave and be cherished. I was very afraid that I wasn't approved of, and I wanted to be a slave because I wanted the approval that it represented. I still like the way it feels, but I'm not desperate for it anymore. I don't feel that something is missing from my life if I can't have that every moment, though I feel very good when I get it. Now when I submit to the sadist whose chain I wear, it's not out of fear. It comes from a desire to share and grow with someone else. If I feel that another person has things to show me by dominating me, I will submit to [him or her]. And if I feel that I have things to show someone else by dominating them, then I will encourage [him or her] to submit to me.

I [know I] want a slave to serve me with his mind as well as his body. I don't want a puppy dog; I want someone whose goal is to make my life easier, who understands my goals. When my liege asked what the chain around my neck meant to me, I told him that it meant that his joy and his goals are the most important things in my life. For me to serve his goals means that sometimes I tell him when I think that he's doing something that can go against him. It means that I look for ways to make his life easier without intruding on his energy. And probably the most gratifying moments in my service to him are the times when I am able to help him with a problem with my insight.

[A year ago,] there were things I knew I wanted to learn. I feel that I've learned those things. I've learned how to control the fear. I've learned how to use my own energy for things I want. I've learned how to be who I want to be. I feel like I was standing in a doorway. Now I've gone through it and I'm in this new place. I don't really know what's around me, and I'm still just looking around and adjusting. I want more of that.

-j-

For me, [S/M] isn't just a physical action; it's got a spiritual aspect to it. The kind of play we do is not just sex play, it's shamanism. I use the term *S/M* to mean "Sex Magic." It's transformational, it's empowering, it's stuff that I believe gives me access to a lot more than ordinary perceptions. It's an exploration of fear, for one thing. I think that we limit our lives and our power in the world and our ability to focus on things when there are fears. They cut us off from feelings. They cut us off from one another. They cut us off from being able to tap into some of the less mundane ways of understanding the universe around us. A lot of what's going on here is learning to face fear and understand it, and [to] recognize how it's affecting you and taking the power away from the fear. For me, a lot of it is [also] learning to explore sensation and perception and to understand the limits of actions. One of the big things that I'm learning is trust.

As far back as I can remember as a small child, I've had very D&S-oriented fantasies. When I reached puberty the sexual connection became more apparent. In my fantasies I tended to be top. A lot of the fantasies involved women being subjected to all kinds of stuff. A lot of times in the fantasies the woman was me. But I had trouble connecting to that and recognizing that the fleshly person actually wanted that kind of thing. Up until about a year ago I thought that I was a sadist. It was only when I started talking with other people and hearing what's going on that I realized that there was another side. I didn't understand what submission was about or why anyone would want to do that.

I have been surprised by the things that I was willing to do. I had heard of the concept of master-slave or mistress-slave, and it seemed like an affectation to me. I could see that some people are very intent in their roleplaying, but I didn't think that was something I could do. I was surprised the first time Cassandra put a collar on me. It floored me. We had been playing around, doing some bondage and stuff, and we were doing some S/M, but we were switching and there wasn't any roleplaying. On the way [to a concert one night], she said, "We need to have a serious discussion, and depending on how it comes out, I think we may have a lot of fun." Basically she proposed that I become her slave. My mind went numb when she said that! "You really mean that, don't you?" And she said. "Yeah." I was actually short of breath! After some seconds, I said, "Well . . . yes." She said "Okay!" And when we got home, she put the collar on me. I think she saw how ripe I was and how she could show me a world in that way. It just made something click in her! And she's very protective.

I like a lot of bondage. I really like restrictive bondage. Arms tightly bound behind my back, legs together, maybe even doubled up or hog-tied.

I've since become acquainted with the virtues of being opened up physically—it's brand-new for me. As much surface as possible exposed. I like lots of pain. I like whipping. I like caning a lot. A lot of hand playing, biting, pinching, digging fingers way in. It's interesting, they all have different kinds of ways they communicate to me. Whips I find to be very emotional. Canes are sexy and communicative.

All of it, of course, is real intimate. One of the things that amazed me happened the night that she first put the collar on me. She put her hands on my face and held my mouth open; I thought she was looking at my teeth. I was very passive and trying to follow [her lead]. After a moment, through a jammed open mouth, I asked, "What are you doing?" You know there's something *interesting* about having your mouth held open. She continued to hold it that way, and I started feeling incredibly vulnerable and opened up. And that kind of thing I really love a lot. Things that make me feel vulnerable open me up emotionally.

I like a lot of teasing, especially when brought into sex play. I like being pushed around a lot, and I have a chain that's always on, dragging around my back. Just having my body manipulated that way is real cool. One time she had me kneeling on the floor before her, licking her. She would control me, either physically or verbally. [She'd] say, "Okay, you may touch me in this way"—my hands were tied behind my back. Or she'd say, "You may smell me or touch me with the very tip of your tongue." And then [she'd] stop, pulling me back, just in and out, teaching that way: It was all me getting her off, not her stimulating me. I was absolutely absorbed by it! She'd start getting off and that would get very hot and exciting, and she'd pull me away. It came to the point where my entire focus was just [on] *her* sensations, making *her* feel good, getting *her* off. That was the single thought in my mind! That was *real* hot.

One of the things I've never had a clear idea of is what kind of limits I have. Part of this exploration is finding where limits are. Once I've reached a certain limit and integrated that into my experience, then I can go on to the next step. Every time I think I've started understanding how it's all working, completely new stuff happens. And it takes me around for another loop in terms of physical activities and what I'll do.

The [San Francisco S/M] community is very eclectic and it's magical! It's one of the wondrous, most [accepting and] loving things that I've ever seen. There were so many fears I had tearing around in me about myself—I can't tell you how knotted up I was for years. It's something I've known about since my childhood; it was my deepest darkest secret. Now it's something I'm *proud* of.

Ten

BONDAGE

"I would like to tie you down to this bed," he said thickly, "and tease, tantalize, and otherwise titillate your fair young body until you scream for mercy. The only kind of pain I have in mind—beyond the occasional pinch or scratch we've already tried—is the sweet agony of wanting to come so badly you can't see straight or remember your name."

Her busy hand paused, and she grinned suddenly. "That does sound more interesting than scrambled eggs and coffee. I just don't know if I understand the tying-up part."

—SPIDER ROBINSON[1]

The practice of bondage is a blank slate upon which almost any sexual interest or practice may be chalked. Although "whips and chains" is the alleged *sine qua non* of S/M, there are as many bondage enthusiasts who are repelled by sadomasochistic activities as there are masochists who dislike restraint.

In this chapter we include a variety of interviewees who embrace bondage in their erotic repertoires. We hear again from Cléo Dubois and feature five profiles:

- Gene is 41 years old and married. He is an engineer.
- Michael V. is 38 years old. He was born in Europe and works in computers. He and Slave V. live together.
- Slave V. is 38 years old. She writes a column for *Bondage Pleasures* magazine.
- Robin Young is a 21-year-old computer programmer who lives and works in the Bay Area. He is single.
- John H. is 28 years old. He is an electrical engineer.

WHAT IS BONDAGE?

Bondage is the sensual experience of safe captivity. To be in bondage is to have no options but to accept one's physical helplessness.

> *[When you're effectively bound] you can think of escaping, but eventually, if you try to escape and realize that you cannot, then a switch goes off in the mind. You have to accept.*
>
> —CLÉO DUBOIS

Our research suggests that women and men equally experiment with bondage. Many couples use bondage as a playful, occasional aspect of lovemaking, while enthusiasts explore scenarios intensively and sometimes independently of other erotic activities. It is essential to note, however, that bondage can entail significant physical risks. Virtually every form of bondage places unusual stress on the body. A keen understanding of all potential risks and safeguards to deter any possible injury must precede all experimentation.

Given the extreme range of motivations and activities, bondage is best defined by its simplest component: restraint.

> *I remember just holding women very tightly and it seemed like their sexual tension would heighten. The degree that it would increase always intrigued me. It just felt so much better, and that's what I gravitated toward.*
>
> —MICHAEL V.

The ways of incorporating bondage into intimacy are virtually endless.

> *. . . I have studied so-called "bondage" or the playing of "restraint games," in which one partner ties up the other with greater or less elaboration and then excites them, as it were, solo. The original aim was to determine what to say about this in a popular counselling book: it appeared with surprising frequency not only as a fantasy in both sexes, but as a "required" skill among sexual sophisticates*

comparable to proficiency in oral sex, and a frequent ingredient in
marital histories. —ALEX COMFORT[2]

The act of restraining a partner during sex is older than humanity. While an absolute parallel is misleading, the urge to restrain is common in the natural world. An incalculable number of species exhibit some type of restraint during coupling: Tomcats grip their mates' skin in their teeth, and higher primates engage in complex patterns of ritual submission and dominance. But only humans have advanced bondage into a multifarious erotic art.

> *There's bondage that pulls you apart—like racks and suspension,*
> *upside-down suspension, and stuff that tugs on your limbs. There's*
> *bondage that stretches, and bondage that pulls things together.*
> *There's bondage that isolates you, like sensory deprivation, and*
> *bondage which connects you. Constriction is another sort of bondage.*
> *I got to understand that corsets are linked with bondage: it pushes,*
> *belts, and tightens things.* —CLÉO DUBOIS

The *Koka Shastra* (circa 12th Century) describes the women of Andhra as *premanibandhanaikanipunaa,* which Alex Comfort suggests may be translated as "skilled in sexual bondage."[3] Bondage appeared in the *ars erotica* of both Japan and China. The Chinese sex manuals virtually disappeared under the influence of Confucianism, but the bondage tradition survived in Japan. Depictions of bound women remain a theme of contemporary Japanese pornography and inspire modern-day Westerners.

> *I like to do a fair amount of rope bondage. I think the style that I*
> *do looks very artistic. It's somewhat Japanese with intricate patterns.*
> *What's nice about it is it really seems to bring out the best of the*
> *woman.* —MICHAEL V.

Because of Christianity's long suppression of eros in the West and the inescapable problems of interpreting classic texts, it is difficult to locate unambiguous historical references to erotic bondage in European history. One can, for example, find numerous quotes in Roman writings which suggest—but do not confirm—that erotic bondage was known. History is, however, rife with examples of people being bound for inhumane purposes. Torture devices such as iron maidens (sarcophagi lined with interior metal spikes) or branks (metal head cages, often with sharp mouthpieces) used by the Inquisitors of medieval Europe are the most infamous examples.

Lack of documented bondage for pleasure in the Western world suggests faulty reporting, not a lack of pleasurable bondage.* The historical accounts of flagellation brothels (circa 17th to 19th centuries) show that patrons enjoyed being bound for whippings. Pulleys to suspend patrons were a common furnishing and Theresa Berkley's "horse"—an adjustable whipping rack available at the madam's establishment—accommodated restraints. All the early sexologists cited numerous case studies of patients who expressed interest in binding or being bound. But the pervasiveness of bondage fantasies was nearly overlooked in favor of other components of clients' fantasies, such as fetishism.

Although early 20th Century movie serials such as *The Perils of Pauline*, in which the heroine frequently found herself tied to the inevitable railroad tracks, may have incited some fantasies, bondage as an erotic art was largely fostered in this century by the works of two men, Irving Klaw and John William Koutts, a.k.a. John Willie. Klaw photographed women tied in various positions to various pieces of furniture in various stages of dress and undress (though never nude). His most famous model, Betty Page, has been likened to an American icon and remains a model for contemporary bondage styles. Though Miss Page retired from modeling in mid-career and became a born-again Christian, her pin-up persona has made her a cult figure to new generations of bondage fans, many of whom are particularly inspired by photos that depict her as sexually dominant. Images of Miss Page are now widely disseminated on-line and marketed in calendars, videos, and books. Willie was as well known for his cartoons of Sweet Gwendoline as for his photographs: Gwendoline's misfortunes generally resulted in bondage in some helpless and humiliating pose.

Alex Comfort theorized that bondage "seems to owe its current popularity to the fact that the available pornography of a whole generation of American men was produced by [these] two preoccupied bondage enthusiasts."[4] With an eye to prevailing censorship standards, Klaw and Willie limited themselves to depictions of bondage and discipline alone.

WHO DOES IT?

Although all bondage enthusiasts can be said to be D&Sers in that the bound party is necessarily submissive (if only physically and temporarily) to his partner, there are two groups within the world of bondage: D&Sers who

---

*It is important to distinguish bondage in the modern context from the term used by such scholars as Magnus Hirschfeld and Richard von Krafft-Ebing. By *sexual bondage* they meant a mental condition of subservience or overweening dependence upon another: It had nothing to do with being tied up.

enjoy bondage and bondage enthusiasts who do not engage in any other D&S activities.

The second facet of sadomasochism is known as bondage, wherein the masochistic partner is tied up or restricted in various positions and by various means according to the protagonist's tastes. Of course, minor tie-and-tease activities are carried out from time to time by many sex partners without any colouring of sadomasochism being formally involved. —CHRISTOPHER C. GOSSELIN[5]

Harmony Communications, Inc., a California-based company which specializes in bondage erotica, has popularized the concept of *love bondage.* This friendly fantasy play usually involves very comfortable restraint whose main object is typically to heighten erotic tension, usually as foreplay to lovemaking.

The materials we produce are carefully and, we think, obviously designed for men AND women to whom bondage is an important mutual diversion, a recreational and benevolent experience, a fantasy with a happy ending, a good-natured game in which everybody wins. We do not characterize victims; we characterize lovers who are mutually involved in a complex and bizarre but highly stimulating personal activity.[6]

Adherents of the Harmony philosophy rarely if ever consider themselves S/Mers; indeed, some are vehemently opposed to directly sadomasochistic activities such as whipping, spanking, or other intense stimuli. Instead, a satisfying bondage session may be limited to sensuously teasing sensations (gentle pinches or love bites, light tickling, sexual arousal).

The main thing for me is to be tied up and restrained and then teased. For instance, if my partner will masturbate me until just before I come to orgasm, then stop, then return a few minutes later, and masturbate me again, then stop—for me, it's like an out-of-body experience. —GENE

For sadomasochists, bondage is often one component of erotic play, although many do seek bondage-only experiences. During bondage, intense stimuli may be delivered to (or normal sensation withheld from) the bound form; the bondage itself may be uncomfortable. And the power relationship that fuels the bondage extends to other activities (or into a lifestyle).

Proponents of love bondage are extremely concerned about making a distinction between the loving, gentle type of play they perceive as their ultimate pleasure and the play they perceive as sadomasochistic. (Not unlike spankers, as discussed in the following chapter.) In fact, the two groups have so much in common that when it comes to a discussion of styles, techniques, and emotional rewards, one is hard-pressed to ascertain their true differences. Since, however, D&S is as much a matter of intention as of implementation, it is fair to say that the two groups have fundamentally different approaches. Each group is a bit baffled by, and often a bit critical of, the other.

> *Bondage rituals that are unassociated with other elements of s/m often puzzle those not involved, for it is hard to see what either partner gets out of them once restriction has been completed: There seems little one can do to continue the ritual and little for the "victim" to experience beyond the continuing feeling of immobilisation.* —CHRISTOPHER C. GOSSELIN[7]

All bondage scenarios are variations on the theme of captivity. A very high percentage of our interviewees believes that these interests began in the games of their childhoods, such as cowboys and Indians, cops and robbers, or Houdini escapes.

The diversity of adult captivity fantasies should not be underestimated: One man may fantasize that he has been kidnapped by a sexually frustrated woman who "has her way" with him, while the next prefers steel shackles and imagines himself to be a prisoner. Partners' responses to restraints are similarly diverse. Some enjoy struggling, whether to pretend that they are attempting escape, to test the security of their bonds, or to test the patience of their dominants.

A significant number of enthusiasts practice self-bondage. They devise often-iconoclastic methods of tying themselves up in private, often because they do not feel comfortable in divulging their interest to others or fear that their partners would disapprove. Others simply prefer the singular thrill of autoeroticism.

WHY DO THEY LIKE IT?

Enthusiasts love to be bound for many reasons, but perhaps the great thrill of bondage rests on a fundamental enigma: Erotic bondage induces psychic liberation.

> *A lot of people want bondage. I had a friend who said that when the ropes are on the outside, the ropes on the inside get loose. [In other words]: When you're tied up, you can be free. I really understand*

that dynamic. If you're tied up, you're no longer responsible. Bond-age gives you permission to let go. It's a paradox: If you are helpless, you are actually freer. —CLÉO DUBOIS

Being physically bound in a mutually consensual context gives bondage aficionados permission to experience their sexuality freely—a permission that they may not otherwise be able to give themselves because of upbringing or sexual mores. While bound they cannot control the erotic stimulation that they receive, and, perhaps just as important, they cannot control or conceal the arousal that they feel.

Bondage is, in this respect, an antidote to sexual repression: When the physical restraints are in place, the mental restraints are lifted.

Everybody's got defense mechanisms. When the woman goes into bondage, she's surrendering all that. [So] one of the things I like to introduce then is sexual play. They get more turned on than they've ever been turned on before. —MICHAEL V.

The period of bondage is a time when responsibilities are removed—foremost among them the responsibility for sexual response. The submissive's responses are stirred and manipulated at the binder's whim (although dominants generally confine play to stimuli they believe to be exciting for their partners). The bound partner is also relieved of larger obligations; thoughts about housework, career, and finances dissolve.

There is a peace and tranquility that comes over me while I am in bondage that I know at no other time. I am relieved of all responsibility. It is the only time when I cannot have the little voice in me that says, "You've got laundry to do, and you really should clean up your desk . . ." If I'm tied up, I'm not expected to do any of that and can relax. —SLAVE V.

Many people enjoy bondage because the physical immobilization is psychologically relaxing.

Doing sessions in Silicon Valley, I work with an incredible amount of computer people: A lot of them need gags. They can't relax until they wear a gag or a blindfold, because then they have to shut up, and they can't see anymore. I use bondage as a way of bringing people into themselves, into their sexuality, inward to themselves. —CLÉO DUBOIS

Others simply enjoy having comfortable restrictions imposed on their bodies.

I definitely play with power exchange, [but] for me, restraint isn't about trying to get away: It's about comfort. If I play with somebody whose image of a bottom play partner is that she tries to get away, it's a real conflict. If I try to get away, I start feeling like something's wrong. Maybe on an intellectual level I can be a challenging bottom, but I'm not into the physical challenge of trying to get away.

—VICTORIA B.

During bondage the body may be fixed in a position it would otherwise be difficult to impossible for any but Eastern yogis to hold. The effect of this forced physical inertia is comparable to the focus and relaxation of doing Zen yoga.

Changing the body's relationship to gravity is another component of bondage. This is more directly addressed during suspension bondage, the practice of hoisting a partner so that most of his or her weight is off the ground. Suspension is a particularly risky form of bondage play which can result in serious injury.

Suspension bondage elicits in the bindee a primal helplessness. Not only is the body deprived of balance, but its relationship to gravity is altered as it floats aloft, evoking the weightlessness of the womb. Safely cradled by secure bonds, floating—and, in some cases with the eyes, ears, and other sensory organs blocked—the person may embark on a profound adventure into tranquility and body focus. Such focus is a key component of any successful bondage experience.

When I'm restrained, my body is effectively taken away from me, and my mind focuses very clearly. All the sensations and everything that happens jump out of my control. I'm very aware of what's happening to me and all the sensations are heightened.

—GENE

Bondage for me is a sense heightener. It enhances my awareness of my body; it's a pleasurable stimulant to want to move and not be able to. —ROBIN YOUNG

Since erotic tension may be intensified during the bondage, sexual gratification is often an ultimate goal.

I like to think that there is definitely some sex as a result of [the bondage]. You build up so much sexual energy there, and you need a release. It's definitely nice. —MICHAEL V.

Sexual release, however, is less important to the person for whom bondage itself is a chief source of erotic pleasure, and for many the spiritual aspect of bondage is as important as the erotic. When the bondage assumes hypnotic intensity, the bound partner may feel as if he is making a deeply private journey.

Sensory deprivation (the use of gags, blindfolds, earplugs, and other sensory blocks) in particular helps to isolate the bound person from mundane realities.

> *[In] sensory deprivation, the bottom might go on a journey and enter a trance state or just a state of deep relaxation. It can also bring you into what people have referred to as an altered state of life, a life transfer. Even an erotic scene can become a journey. The bottom may think he is going to have an orgasm, but instead the experience may become shamanic.* —CLÉO DUBOIS

For some people the inherent risks of bondage and the unpredictability of the outcome seem to add to its allure.

> *I think there's a certain amount of fear involved in bondage. [During self-bondage] you fantasize all kinds of things that could happen: What if there was a fire? What if someone walked in? What if I had a heart attack? Fortunately, none of those things have happened, but I've spent a number of hours contemplating [the] possibilities.* —GENE

Humiliating or embarrassing bondage is another compelling feature for some enthusiasts.

> *Embarassing bondage, to most people, is bondage that exposes their private parts. Bondage that puts their anus or genitals higher than their head. Bondage that reverses the polarity: You're not supposed to show your genitals or your ass.* —CLÉO DUBOIS

The pleasure in humiliating bondage may be related to freedom from sexual repression. In humiliating bondage, body taboos are shattered: The helplessly bound partner has no choice but to expose intensely private zones that he would otherwise be socially obligated to conceal. D&Sers may be particularly inclined to engage in erotic coercion to place the submissive in some embarrassing pose in order to heighten the bondage's sexual charge.

Bondage has been elevated to an art among practitioners and for this reason teems with technical details—proper knots, secure and snug equipment, and safety devices to ensure that a partner can be quickly released in case he experiences panic or severe discomfort. Safe, pleasurable bondage is an act of love and trust. For many couples the knowledge that the dominant will not violate the trust of the person in bonds, that the submissive's physical and emotional well-being is a first priority, and that helplessness can be experienced with the explicit intent of mutual pleasure is for them the highest and most liberating affirmation of romantic love.

WHAT TYPES OF RESTRAINTS EXIST?

Hundreds (and possibly thousands) of types and styles of restraints are available today. Before listing the common types of restraints used by D&Sers, it's essential that the reader understand that every type of bondage, without exception, carries some safety risk. Improper use of allegedly harmless—or small-scale—equipment, unsupervised restraint, or undue stress to the body can have serious, even fatal, consequences. It's also important to remember that what is intensely arousing for one person may be utterly terrifying to another.

The different types of bondage reflect different erotic interests and have different purposes. While some sexually adventurous lovers may wish only to flirt with silk scarves or satin cuffs, more experienced D&Sers are likely to crave extremely secure and confining restraint. We essay here to describe only basic categories of equipment. Although many bondage fans are satisfied by rudimentary bonds (such as clothesline, rope, or chains), others devote their leisure and financial resources to constructing or acquiring extraordinarily sophisticated equipment. There are innumerable pieces of equipment of unique design, many of which will never be seen by anyone but their inventors.

While handcuffs are commonly believed to be the *ne plus ultra* of bondage, among cognescenti metal restraints are much less popular than leather ones. Those willing to invest in their pleasures purchase thickly padded wristcuffs from adult shops or buy hospital restraints from medical-supply companies to ensure a comfortable and adjustable fit—particularly handy if the partners switch roles. Cheap metal handcuffs can be dangerous; the possibility of a broken lock or skin abrasion is disenchanting to discreet and safety-minded D&Sers. Handcuffs, fetters, shackles, and other metal devices are largely the purview of those who have a particular interest in such equipment per se or of those whose fantasies center on police, prison, or military scenarios.

Although wrist and ankle restraints come in a plethora of materials (from silk and satin to leather, chain, and steel), leather is usually preferred. Erotic emporia carry leather restraints that can link extremities in a variety of combinations: wrist-to-wrist, wrists-to-ankles, ankle-to-ankle, wrists-to-neck, wrists-to-waist, wrists-to-thighs, and variations on these themes. Also popular are spreader bars, which force the limbs to remain separated. A wide selection of leather (or metal) collars of varying widths and rigidity are also popular.

The person who likes lengthy, comfortable bondage may choose bondage wear—modified, restrictive clothing or undergarments. Esoteric bondage dresses or suits manufactured by foreign fetish tailors and which secure the arms to the torso are prized. Torso or full-body harnesses (a series of leather straps, often decorated with metal rings to which other bondage devices can be attached); genital harnesses, pouches, gloves, rings, clamps, and weight devices; and corsets, which compress the body, are all popular. Many small-scale restraints can be (and are) worn, undetected, even beneath an investment banker's conservative suit.

Some bondage fans like mummification, the practice of completely immobilizing the body by creating a kind of bondage coccoon.

> *Although the stressful positions beloved of s/m pornography are seldom indulged in for long except by some aficionados, complete immobilisation is commonplace and is frequently completed by the use of gag and/or blindfold.* —CHRISTOPHER C. GOSSELIN[8]

While straitjackets or full-body suits with copious belts and buckles are available, they are prohibitively expensive for most. Thus, household items (such as plastic wrap) or latex sheeting may be used to sheathe the body from toe to neck.

Chastity belts, once the scourge of fair ladies wed to errant knights, are now designed for both sexes.

> *One of my enjoyments is enforced chastity—to make or to get very interesting chastity belts, one of which I have.* —JOHN H.

Technology has yielded marvels of chastity engineering that allow comfortable wear over long periods of time. Lightweight, playful chastity belts may resemble little more than chain G-strings, but an array of expensive, hygienic, comfortable (and rustproof) devices are custom-made. Some belts prevent defecation; many prohibit erection. Female arousal is ungovernable by a belt, but chastity devices thwart any possibility of penetration. Variations on chastity belts may feature plugs inserted into the orifice(s) of either gender, but these cannot usually be worn for very long.

Large-scale bondage equipment includes racks, tables, benches, and cages as well as complex hoists for suspension bondage. Also popular is the bondage swing, a seat usually made of leather or canvas, which is suspended and to which the bound party may be tied or chained.

[On] New Year's Eve Cybele had me in a sling at a party and was swinging me by the balls—I don't want readers to imagine something horrific here! But with a gentle to-and-fro motion you can do a whole lot of swinging. The testicles are very sensitive, but they're also very strong, and it is—at least in the context of this relationship—a very useful way to get me to go under. —JAMES W.

Whipping posts and St. Andrew's crosses (also known as *X* frames) are large, usually wooden apparatuses to which restraints are attached. Stocks—familiar from the American Colonial era—also come in a variety of styles.

As discussed above, sensory deprivation is the blocking off of sensory organs. While many lovers are satisfied to experiment with a scarf draped loosely over a partner's eyes, a wide variety of blindfolds exist for the more adventuresome. The most popular type is made of leather with fleecy lining to protect the eyes. Earplugs are usually impromptu affairs; multiple styles of gags, dental blocks, and bits can be purchased at specialty shops. Sensory deprivation is a high-risk activity. Damage to intraocular fluid dynamics or optic nerves, interference with swallowing function, and difficulty in communicating discomfort are only a few of the potential hazards. Many dominants give their bound partners a safety gesture to use in order to signal discomfort when they cannot speak.

Finally, almost inextricably linked to sensory deprivation is its antithesis: sensory overload. Some gags or hoods, for example, contain small holes so that the dominant may feed the submissive fluids or food. Some submissives wear headphones and listen to the music or soothing sounds that the dominant imposes. Even aromatherapy may be incorporated by means of breathing tubes.

INTERVIEWS

CLÉO DUBOIS

Many [people] who like bondage know that when you're tied up, you can let the sensation—whatever it may be: embarrassing, nonembarassing, erotic, "slutty"—come out, because, as far as your mind is concerned, you're helpless. You can fight it, but eventually you have to go with it. The same is true of pain. I find bondage to be very helpful in accepting the input; you can travel with it.

In my experience [bondage] is not really for the kind of submissive that would do as he or she is told without bondage. It is for people who will put up resistance—sassy masochists, smart-ass masochists—until it is proven to them through the bondage that it's useless to resist. Their minds say, "Oh! Why in the world am I putting all my energy into fighting this? It's going to happen anyway. *Click!*" Then they relax and usually get very turned on, because it's a deep erotic state. Their attention really goes into their body.

I do all kinds of bondage. I do a lot of rope bondage. I do a lot of leather bondage, using all kinds of leather straps. I do Betty Page–type bondage. I do bondage that takes people's body shape and body limitations, fears and phobias into consideration. I do all kinds of different bondage tricks. Bondage grows on you. Somebody starts [out] only wanting their hands behind their back; three years later they might be really interested in being completely restrained, not being able to move anything.

I advertise sensory deprivation. People call and ask, "Do you have a body bag? Do you have [an] inflatable hood?" And I say, "Yes, I do." As far as I can tell, most people into sensory deprivation are also interested in sensory overload. I take away as many senses as I can and then, if it's appropriate, overload one sense. I'll start at the top. Earplugs. Blindfold. Gag. Hood. Inflatable hood. Sometimes inflatable hoods with breathing tubes. Posture collar to control the head, the neck, the body. Mummification, with Saran Wrap or an Ace bandage–type wrap. Body bags. All the bondage is put on the body beforehand—it could be tight rope bondage up and down the body. Then a body bag on top of it. Or Saran Wrap. Suspension—suspension is always close to the ground but lifted off the floor. Disorientation. Upside-down suspension. Floating suspension. Those are the things I'm talking about when I use the phrase "sensory deprivation."

If I use sensory overload, it could mean electricity play, piercing: a specific point of "overloadment." I [might] run electricity to the genital area.

It could be a heavy whipping, but if people get into a quiet fantasy, I seldom do a heavy whipping [then]. [I might try] sensations of different kinds on the genitals if the session is going to get erotic. If I see the person getting turned on—[and] with a male it's very easy to see—then I [may] either poke a hole in the Saran Wrap or [give] some specific sensation [to] the nipples or the genital area. Or I might not.

For suspension bondage, I have two winches. I use a lot of rope work in suspension. It supports the body at different points so the body weight is as well distributed as possible. I [may] use suspension bars to lift people off the ground by cuffs [secured around their ankles]. I can use two suspension bars and lift them by their feet and hands; one needs the proper cuffs. The middle of the body is tied to rigging made of heavy rope. It is a lot of work. One should also use an appropriate piece of equipment, such as one we call a "panic snap." If you use regular hardware [for suspension], if somebody fainted, you'd have to lift them off! With a panic snap you do not have to lift the weight in order to let [the person] down. There's all kinds of safety equipment.

GENE

I consider myself submissive. It's a closely guarded secret shared only between me and my wife. My wife is a fairly vanilla person and not very interested in this, but because she loves me and we have a good marriage, she engages in practices with me. Basically, I like to be tied up and held in bondage during sex, in various positions. My wife helps me with this. Oftentimes, if our children are away, we'll do this all evening.

If all my dreams came true, then my wife, whom I love, would be more interested in such activities. I think if she had her druthers, this is one part of me that she'd probably want to move out. She's happy with meeting demands as a lover, except for being very dominant. We've got a lot of years together, but she can't cultivate an interest in it, and I can't make my interest in it go away. It was a problem before in that when we had regular arguments, instead of arguing about money or picking up socks, two or three times she used this as ammunition against me. Finally, I said, "That's me. If we're going to stay together, you're going to have to accommodate it." Although she didn't agree with it then, over time I think she has just come to the conclusion that that *is* me, that it's part of my personality.

My first bondage experience was sometime around second grade. We were playing cowboys and Indians with a group of kids. I was captured and tied to a pole, with my hands behind my back. The other kids ran off and more or less forgot about me for a while. I got a tremendous erection and couldn't do anything about it. I couldn't adjust it in my jeans there. I found that to be very stimulating, very exciting, even at that young age. Later the kids came back and they noticed. I was made the object of a lot of taunting and teasing. Eventually I was released, but that made a tremendous impact on my life. I spent a great deal of time fantasizing and trying to re-create that episode after that.

It was mainly a matter of child's play throughout most of my life until I was married at 23. Then, having been married to my wife for a couple of years, I noticed in some [sexually-oriented] magazines that other people had these same desires. I showed it to my wife and asked her what she thought about it. She wasn't very impressed, but over a period of time I was able to convince her to tie me up for sex. That was the first sexual experience that involved bondage that I engaged in. I found it very exciting, [but] at the time my wife didn't.

I think she derives pleasure from it now in that when we're engaged in these activities, in my submissive role, I do a lot to serve her and pleasure her. So, typically, we might start out with her tying me up for maybe an hour or so, then releasing me. Then I'll give her a good massage and rub lotion on her feet and perform cunnilingus on her and do whatever I can to satisfy her, according to her dictates. Then later on, maybe tied again to the bed, spread-eagled, she'll use me for her pleasure, which may involve sitting astride me, using my penis to satisfy her. Then after she's had her orgasm, she may leave me again for a while and go about her business in the house and then eventually come back and jerk me off.

Some of the most exciting bondage has been bondage I've done to myself when traveling. If I'm going to be in a motel room for the night, I've devised a way to use an automatic timer switch with a combination lock. This may seem a little strange, but I tie myself to the bed and attach the automatic timer switch to the light. When the light goes out, I can't see the combination lock. That's the key to the whole system. For a period of time—two or three hours or more—I can't get free. When the light comes back on, I can release myself. The backup is that eventually the sun will rise, and I can see at that point.

The most exciting point is after I've tied myself up and the light switch goes off: I realize that there's no way to get free. I've been very careful at setting it up so that until I get light to see by, I am committed to that position. As I become sexually aroused, it's difficult or impossible to do anything to satisfy myself.

The first time I did this to myself really sticks out in my mind because it was different and exciting. I built myself a timer switch. I spent a lot of time fantasizing and trying to decide just how this would be built. The first time I tried it I was home alone. I tied my ankles to the bed, and then made a couple loops in the headboard. I had two locks and managed to attach my arms so they were folded in front of me. I locked myself in position and had the timer set to go off in about half an hour, so I had plenty of time to sit there and think: Did I really want to do this, or not? I could have gotten free very easily. Eventually I heard the timer click, and the lights went off, and then I knew that decision had been taken away from me. I spent most of the night in that position.

My wife doesn't relish the dominant role, so although I'm in a submissive posture, her attitude is one of pleasing. She wants to give me what I want and, frankly, I think what I want her to give me is what I *don't* want. If I say, "Touch me," that means "Don't touch me." If I say, "Untie me," that means "Don't untie me." We can't seem to get past that; she wants me to be happy. When I do this to myself, alone, where I can't be untied, can't be touched, and there's no one there to try to please me, I have to live with the decision I made.

My most compelling fantasies are ones my wife is not privy to. I had a couple of homosexual experiences when I was younger and frankly quite enjoyed them. So I have various fantasies that involve both bondage and sex with another man. Also, I went to a fair one time, and I saw a sheep being led to a block. They put the sheep's head into a collar, half metal and half leather, so that the sheep was held in place there. It could not move around while being examined by the judges. That device has been in my fantasies a number of times. These are fantasies I wouldn't dare act on, because I have a position in the community.

That part of me that likes to be tied up is [not] so evil that it negates the good parts of me. It's just part of me. At this stage of my life I don't think it's a bad part. It's a troublesome part, and the reason it's a troublesome part is because so many other people don't understand or refuse to understand that it's not a bad thing. Because of our culture in this country, these activities have been labeled as being bad, maybe even evil. As a result, I can't share that part of myself with anyone. It's even taking a hell of a risk to share it with my wife. I think it'd be a wonderful thing if I could share myself completely with my friends and the people around me. Maybe they then would be able to share themselves with me. I know that I work, play, and talk to people every day who have little secret corners in their lives that they can't share with me. It may not be B&D, but, believe me, we all have secret corners. What a wonderful thing if they could share those secret corners with me and I could share mine with them. Then, who knows? We may find some common ground.

MICHAEL V.

I'm straight. I enjoy all expressions of standard sex, but D&S [is] critical. I'm dominant, and I have to have that in my relationship, or else it is of no consequence. Vanilla sex is a very small aspect; D&S has been the major portion of my sexuality for the last 15 years.

I think there would be a lot fewer divorces if power roles were discussed early on. People ask things about the home they'd like to live in, about the foods they like, and various shared interests, but one very critical question is how the power is going to be shared in the relationship. I think this would solve a lot of people's problems. If [one] said, "Well, basically I like to be in charge; I'm a dominant individual, and I want to do this," [or] "I like being submissive, and I would like to do this," you wouldn't have people trying to make a car run on square tires.

In the past, during typical sexual encounters, where you're screwing, you hold somebody's arms over her head: Her response would increase, and my response would increase. I became more and more cognizant of that. There was an evolution: The ropes start coming out, and then cuffs and chains. When we were still playing cowboys and Indians, I always made sure to wind up on the side that was doing the tying and the chasing. I remember the thrill of that. One time, this one girl and I played the game a little further. At first she protested, and then she kept on coming back. I used some clothesline around her back. She liked it. I was the one who said, "We shouldn't really be doing this. Are you going to tell your mother?" And she said, "No, no, no!"

[Sometimes I'd] go out with somebody for a few months, [and] once past the [standard] sexual aspects, [I'd] start introducing aspects of the Scene. They would go along with it but then would start sharing with their friends, and the peer pressure [and] feedback would be negative. They'd say, "We can't do this. It's sick." I would say, "Wait a minute! We've been doing it for a month, and you're well and fine, and this has heightened our experience." [And some would respond] "Yeah, but I can't do this anymore, because it's just not right." And you find out that their friends were kicking them down.

Generally, I work with large-breasted women. That's one of my requirements because I do a lot of breast bondage. Besides, it's like the frosting on top of everything. During a scene you literally see body modification occurring, even in smaller-breasted women. When I do them, their breasts increase in size to a great extent, and their bodies become trimmer. [The bonds] accentuate the female pinching-in of the waist. Even after the bondage is off, there's a residual effect. It increases the feminine aspect, and I think this occurs on a psychological and spiritual level [as well]. At that point, because all the barriers are removed, it's really manifesting [itself] into the individual.

I believe in the spiritual part of all this. With my current slave, we had an incredible session where her body actually took on a different shape. She's a little overweight: It was [as if] her waistline completely disappeared during the course of the scene. I took a Polaroid of it and showed it to her later. It was absolutely incredible. It was like a physical change. Stuff like that isn't supposed to happen, technically, but it did. I had done a lot of initial body bondage and then a lot of sexual play. Then she was in a suspended position and [taking] a lot of clamping. At that point it was like she was on autopilot. I knew we were at a special threshold where you're also responding to something else. The things that you're doing are so unique to that particular situation that there's almost a higher energy at work between the two of you. That was what was really going on. Something else was inputting there. You get to a transcendental level—but it's not a subconscious level; it's actually happening in the physical. I've had some experiences where I've done fire walking, going over hot coals. Technically you're not supposed to be able to do that. What were normal limits suddenly just dissolve. You're able to do things and endure things that would [ordinarily] cause you some discomfort. Some people call that state the shimmer level.

SLAVE V.

I have a very strong personality—what I like to think of as a survivor's personality. As far as submissiveness in my normal life, I think it's more directed towards trying to do good deeds and helping with elderly members of the family.

In D&S I continue to discover my sexuality. Sexually I'm submissive; psychologically I'm dominant. [Some] say that I'm not submissive at all— that I'm a dominant masochist. [But] when I look for gratification, I seem to find it in submission to a man.

I've always enjoyed lovers who held my arms down around my head while we made love. I probably have been attracted to men who behaved in a subconsciously dominant way all along, but I did not actually find the Scene until [roughly two years] ago. [When I did], I felt I had finally come home. I felt as though I was understood for the first time. At first, I was overcome with joy. I have a very high-pressure job. My judgment is not always good; I'm too emotional; I have mood swings. If I can find someone who I feel has better judgment than myself, I am delighted not to have to make the right decisions all the time.

I had a rather abusive childhood emotionally and physically. Part of it is the old sibling-rivalry thing: My sister resented me. [She] beat me up constantly. She would do lots of sadistic things. My mother felt that there was no limit on the number of times that you could hit the child on the rump.

I'd come home from school and find that all of the contents of my dresser were dumped in a big pile on the floor because my underwear was crooked. Once, after my sister had beaten me to a pulp, I said, "Damn you to hell." My mother, being a devout Catholic, made me kneel on the floor in front of her and my sister and beg God for forgiveness. I was about 11 [then]. My mother left home when I was about 12, and my sister left about a year after that. It was as though Lincoln had freed the slaves, because my dad was actually a great guy. He had never liked punishing us. From the moment my mother and sister left, I never experienced sadistic behavior again.

In my household, my father thought that pornography was fine, and my mother, having been raised in a convent, thought it was the most heinous thing on the face of the earth and should be obliterated. I managed, as all children do, to be rather investigative. I discovered where my father kept his porno books when I was about 12; I enjoyed the ones where guys were on the more aggressive side. After my father died, I managed to end up with [those books], and that kept me happy in the privacy of my bedroom until I got to be about 28. By then I had read that stuff so many times, it didn't work anymore.

I ventured out to a 24-hour newsstand, in the dead of night, making sure there was nobody in the store. I snuck in and looked for something that looked like it might be bondage-y. I knew that I liked reading things where girls would be tied to the bed while the guy ravaged her. It was always friendly ravaging: I'm not into guys doing terrible things to you, although I'm sure we all define terrible as something different. I bought one of these little newspaper magazines, which advertised a club they opened in the city. I went there and had a couple of experiences with a gentleman who was in charge. I realized that I like to be tied up. He eventually asked me to write for his paper. I started writing "Continuing Adventures of V"; that's all I did for the next [several] years. In fact, I wrote an article where I said that writing the column was the kinkiest part of my sex life.

[Then] I married a vanilla guy who said he was going to save me from S&M; he whisked me off to the countryside for three years. Ultimately, we moved back. Our sex life became less and less satisfying. He tried [D&S] a few times, because before we were together, I said, "I need to be tied up, and I'll need you to do that." He said, "Don't worry; I'll do it." He did it exactly twice in five years. As far as he was concerned, it was weird, it was sick, it wasn't right, and he didn't want to do it.

I learned something very important [about the difference between writing] from my imagination versus writing what I know from being in the Scene. That comes from an experience that I had with someone who had read my column for years. When I was alone with [him], the first opportunity he got, he did something very painful. It wasn't really severe; it was just how he did it. I stopped him and said, "How could you do this to me? There's nothing pleasurable about this." He said, "But you love pain! You write about it all the time!" So I learned something very important: For some people, what they are reading in their closets and under their covers with their flashlights is all they ever learn about S&M! There's a tremendous responsibility [in] writing that column, because for some people, that will be the gospel and doctrine. So now I try to teach in my column.

[At one club], I met an older gentleman who didn't know much about the Scene itself but evidently knew about S&M. He was probably physically the best match I've ever had. He did exactly the stuff I liked to do—bondage and clamps—and I transcended with him. For me to transcend doing S&M doesn't happen with severe stimuli but with a steady building of the stimuli. If I can gently take a curve that brings me over my pain limit—a gentle, sloping curve, as opposed to a sharp spike—then I actually leave my body. For me to actually surrender, a man must be able to produce that reaction in me. He didn't know what to call it, but he was making it happen routinely. We did a scene at Paddles one night where I was chained up to the St. Andrew's cross and he was doing all kinds of lovely things to me. When I sat down afterwards, a young man came over to me and said, "My goodness, you do have some endurance!" I said, "Aw, geez; I could have been up there at least twice as long." He said, "Are you kidding? You were up there for two hours." I said, "Naw!" He asked me if I had ever heard of Eulenspiegel. He spelled it for me and told me to call Information and ask for the number. I went to the next [dominant-men submissive-women's] group meeting. I was delighted. I was really impressed with what I saw. I don't know what I expected, but I found the upper crust of S&M. They were like spiritual guides.

The first night I went there, I met someone. He became my master, and we stayed together for the better part of a year. Unfortunately, he was into heavy corporal punishment, and I'm not. As he became increasingly severe, I was forced to pull away from him. I learned a tremendous amount from him about proper behavior and dress and the Scene in general. He spent a month and a half picking my brain constantly, trying to understand psychologically the right buttons to push. He was very wary about corporal punishment at first, knowing that it was something that would remind me of my youth. We'd only see each other a couple of times a week, but even in his absence I remained enslaved. His presence, his personal strength, his confidence, were great enough that I really felt that I was his slave. I felt very joyous about it for many months.

I learned that you might be able to hit me with a whip pretty hard, but if you hit me with a paddle or a hairbrush with the same amount of force, I can't take that very well. I learned that everyone has their strengths and weaknesses. I seemed to be able to take clamping more than most people. Not only can I take multiple clamps on my nipples, [but] I can take them on my pussy. I can also take a clamp on my clit if it's done properly. That was a talent that my master definitely capitalized on.

Probably one of the most exciting things I've ever done includes what I call a predicament. I like to be in predicaments. In [one] scene I was on a recliner with my hands up and over the back of the chair, which had been pushed back so that my legs would be elevated. My hands were secured so that they could remain comfortably over the back of the chair, and my legs were tied open. We were able to secure my legs open and then [put] postal straps around the top of my thighs. Photographic clips were secured to the postal straps after being attached to the outer labia, and [those] held my pussy open. He had clamps on my nipples, which were held out and up with a certain amount of tension on them. Then he used to like to eat my pussy until he could get my clitoris to become very enlarged. He did something that has never been done since, but I certainly fantasize about it: He got my clitoris so swollen that he was able to get a clamp at the base of the clitoris. He said, "Look at that! It looks exactly like a miniature penis." And it did. It really flipped me out.

So he had me all strung up, and he pulled up on the clit clamp. For me to be comfortable, I had to pick my hips up just a touch. I had to tense in order to keep the clit clamp from being painful. And then he tried to fist-fuck me, which is something I hadn't done. He wasn't able to get his fist in there, but he got enough of his hand in there to concern me. He produced this predicament where, in order for me not to pull too hard on the clamp, I had to raise my hips up, but in order to be able to pull away from his hand, I had to push my hips down. It was a losing battle, because, either way, there was something going on that I wanted to pull away from. I'm getting wet just talking about it. That was probably the most exciting scene I've ever done.

One of the reasons I was attracted to my current master is because he practices [Japanese] bondage, which has always been my very favorite form of activity. That's a very intricate, interwoven bondage all around the body. He wraps the ropes through my pussy over and over and over again. I have very large tits, and that's one of the reasons he likes me: He'll wrap my tits up. With the bondage, they become bigger; the skin becomes tauter and more sensitive. I really love bondage.

One of the things that I learned when I became serious about S&M was that there are rules. The serious people are all wedded to certain universal laws that have been spelled out. A common problem is that people not in the

Scene—and newcomers to the Scene—don't understand the difference between fantasy and reality. What astonishes me is how many people seem unaware of the rules or insist that S&M is breaking the rules to begin with. When people say that, at a club meeting or a party, the rest of the gathering will look at them with fire in their eyes. The rules of etiquette are very important to most people.

ROBIN YOUNG

I've always viewed sexuality and life as a series of options. There are lots of possible paths that I can take. There are things that I enjoy about taking someone and putting them into a state of absolute ecstasy. There's a lot of joy that can come out of taking someone and leading them on that kind of journey. Sex as play is one of the most liberating concepts that's ever entered my life—the idea that you can play fantasy games with someone else and that you can take enjoyment in sex purely for its own sake, or that you can really work the dynamic that comes out of exchanging power.

I haven't always considered myself a sexual explorer. I was a hacker in high school and college, and that put me on the social fringe. I didn't have my first intimate relationship until fairly recently. I gained erotic knowledge by playing with myself. Bondage became a central part of my erotic self-play because I found that orgasm's greatly enhanced when I'm tied up. In college I knew what I liked, and I knew there were people who liked what I did, but it's only been since I've found a community of people who understand these things and who know the beautiful places that you can get to that I've become more comfortable and able to explore.

There's a very wise man I know named Fakir Musafar who led a workshop in which he discussed how placing tight bands around your arms and waist and legs and simply wearing them for a period of days or weeks changes the way you view the world. Last year I took his workshop on ecstatic shamanism. It was an investigation of the various sorts of rites common in India and in Native America. Other cultures have used the body to experience states of existence and have used transsexuality to have mythic voyages. That I found to be a very powerful thing! A lot of the bondage and flagellation techniques that people in the Scene use have been practiced for centuries. Convening people and having a focused and centered ceremony with the sole intent of gathering and capturing that essential sexual and spiritual energy—and working on it, writhing all over it, actually heightening everybody's awareness—is something that's made its way deeply into my concept of myself and my sexuality. Along with D&S and bondage, there's a magic that I have a higher respect for now. There are a lot of primal places that you can go. You need to take care in visiting those places, but the people

I've been meeting and the activities I enjoy are transforming my concept of myself as a spiritual being.

One top opened doors for me in many ways. He was the first man with whom I had any kind of intimate contact. I never saw any reason why I should consider myself restricted to having only male lovers or only female lovers. I thought that it would be cutting off part of myself to limit myself like that. But it was all abstract theory until I met him. One distinct memory I have is once when we had been playing for hours. I was sort of tired and getting a bit disconnected. He sensed it, because a real good top knows what you need before you have to say it. He had a sling, a leather hammock that you can lie back in and spread your legs wide apart, that folds out from the wall. It allows the bottom to rock back and forth and feel like he's floating and weightless, and it allows the top full access to everything the top may want access to. He told me that he was going to put me in the sling. He put cuffs on my wrists and ankles; the tactile stimulus of those bands of leather going around my limbs was enough to send me into a very deep state. I was lost in the sensation of what was happening. I should mention also that I was cross-dressed in corset and stockings, which was central in bringing out the androgynous parts of myself. He rocked me back and tied me so my legs were widely separated. Then he wrapped straps around my thighs and buckled them tightly. I didn't feel like I was a male anymore. I was so turned on that I just started rocking back and forth and moaning incoherently.

He started licking me around my ass and around my balls. I actually started to leak fluids from my ass, almost like orgasm fluid. And I felt like I had a cunt. I felt like I was open and that my cock was this fantastically swollen clitoris. I was thrashing around and rubbing myself against his face and completely lost in a frenzy of sex. He put a dildo in my ass and started slowly fucking me with it and started beating my cock. I had what I can only think of as a sort of female orgasm. It was unlike any other orgasm that I've ever had in my life: It was a flood of light that spread out from my genitals and filled my entire body. My fingers were coming!

I'd never experienced anything like that before or since. That was a voyage! That was something that took me to a place that I want to get back to! Now that I know that it's there, I'm going to be doing a lot more exploring in that direction. It was absolutely fantastic!

I think of S/M as a highly evolved, very self-conscious sexuality. It's being very much aware of the nature of the body and of the power of sex and the power of the erotic. That kind of intense knowledge, that in-depth understanding of sexuality, is one of the central attractions of S/M to me. It intensifies and enhances the love and the growth that can come out of a sexual relationship.

It's easy to mistake S/M for something entirely different. At this point a lot of the understanding about S/M is what emerges from psychological studies that have been done on people in counseling. The sampling of people who have spoken out about S/M consists of the people who need help, as opposed to the many people who find S/M to be a healthy and happy and enlightening aspect of their being. What I want to say to people is, "Know your options. Know that it's okay to think and feel whatever it is that you think and feel. Know that your fantasies are not evil. Know that your sexuality is you. Hiding your sexuality and denying it is one of the most harmful and destructive things that you can do to yourself."

My parents don't know about me and don't accept this sexuality. If I had one thing to say to my parents, it would be that I love them and I'm glad they are my parents. I'm glad that they raised me in a way that taught me that hiding parts of yourself and cutting off one's feelings is always wrong. I'm now living in a way that makes those teachings real. I'm trying to reach out to other people who may be hiding parts of themselves, and I'm trying to lead them to be happier and more joyous people. I hope my parents read this book and learn more about me and about what I do. I would really love it if someday they said, "We're proud of you [for] speaking out, and we still love you."

JOHN H.

I have very little experience. As a matter of fact, I'm still a virgin. But as long as I can remember I've been attracted to D&S-type activities, even when I didn't know what they were. I just haven't found the right woman to go all the way with. There are some guys out there who are submissive, and their wives try, but you can tell they don't enjoy it. I want to find someone who genuinely enjoys having me belong to her. I've enjoyed a few times that I've visited people and we've played, but I have never gone all the way with anybody. Up until the last few years the be-all and end-all of what I was doing was working. It's just starting to dawn on me that I need to spend a little more time on my private life.

I am a heterosexual submissive. I've had a few little tiny dominant fantasies now and then but have never been interested in acting them out. When I first started getting to know a few other people in D&S, it seemed like most had had abusive childhoods or some family crisis or something that they felt explained why they were the way they were. I led the typical Midwestern kid's life. It's Mom and Dad—who married each other when my dad was in college and my mom was just out of high school and have stayed married since—and two kids and a house in the suburbs. Very normal, white-bread: America's image. Probably the unusual thing—but it seemed normal to me—was that sex was never discussed in our house.

I always had fantasies that dealt with bondage. That was a big thing, being restrained in some way. I know what they are now, but I didn't really understand them as being sexual [when I was younger]. The first time that I got an idea that really registered was when I worked in a college office where the students ran everything. And somebody plastered a really weird cover of *Variations* magazine on the wall. I picked up a copy, and I said, "You know, these are not exactly my fantasies, but there are other people that not only share what I thought were these unusual interests, but they write about it." There's obviously a market for it. So I can't be the only one. That's when I started to understand what it was. But I was still very frightened that somebody would find out or that it would somehow affect me in some strange way.

My favorite activity is bondage. The stronger, the better. I haven't had a whole lot of experience with it, but it has a mental attraction. I'm working on a relationship with somebody right now who seems to be very understanding. We're both very certain that we're not going to wind up living together, but we're exploring to find out where else my interests go. They tend to be fairly strong bondage, fairly strong discipline, fairly strong whippings. But you don't know what your limits are until you [reach them]. I think [limits are] one of the things that you have to develop in an ongoing relationship.

I wore my chastity belt [to a party at an S&M club in New York]. And for the first time I gave the keys to [a mistress]. At the club I watched one lady who had a lot of things done to her that I had fantasized about. She was bound fairly helplessly and stimulated in all kinds of different ways and then whipped a little bit and then stimulated some more. [My mistress] knew her, so after we left [the club], we stopped at a diner and had breakfast together. It was really neat. There had to be only one thing going on in her brain at the club: pure enjoyment. And then, a couple hours later, she might have been a little sore, but she was a very happy individual, very comfortable, very normal.

I spent the night and the next day [with this mistress]. I considered it a great privilege. She made no effort to release me from the chastity belt. We didn't talk about it. I was beginning to realize and enjoy what it means— rather than fantasizing about being completely under the control of another individual—to really have it happen. That was probably the most satisfying thing.

Eleven

SPANKING

Although spanking is commonly associated with the disciplining of children, adult spankings long have held an accepted, often humorous, place in popular culture. Spankings in films, for example, are usually depicted as an expression of male authority over misbehaving women: John Wayne asserted himself over Maureen O'Hara (*McLintock!*), and Howard Keel "tamed" Kathryn Grayson (*Kiss Me Kate*) in an adaptation of Shakespeare's *The Taming of the Shrew*. Even television macho Latino Ricky Ricardo took the impish Lucy over his lap (*I Love Lucy*) after one of her scatterbrained pranks.

Such nonconsensual, male chauvinistic spankings have generally been portrayed as a spirited woman's due.

Spanking is not merely the stuff of sexist Hollywood fantasy or childhood punishment. A coterie of enthusiasts enjoy the experience (whether giving or receiving) as an enhancement to their sexuality. So widespread is the interest in adult spanking that a proliferation of videos, audiotapes, magazines, books, and newsletters caters uniquely to spankers. In this chapter we hear from four individuals who share insights into their enjoyment.

- Eve Howard is an entrepreneur, editor, writer, producer, video star, and publisher. Ms. Howard's company, Shadow Lane, publishes *Stand Corrected* magazine. She is single, 37 years old, and lives in Los Angeles.
- Harold is 45 years old and an attorney. He is married and has children. He is a regular churchgoer.
- Kiri Kelly has appeared in scores of bondage, spanking, and fetish videos and magazines. She is 33 years old and divorced. She lives in California.
- David C. is a stage actor and musician. He is 28 years old and single. He lives in New York City.

THE TALE OF SPANKING

Spanking has always been an acknowledged form of lighthearted play between partners. *The Kama Sutra* offers advice "On the Various Modes of Striking, and on the Sounds Appropriate to Them." *The Kama Sutra* delineates not only the appropriate places to strike (including the buttocks) but the four kinds of blows and the eight kinds of sounds which lovers should make. The text suggests that rough play may be an intrinsic aspect of sex, with a clear implication that the striking is done by men as a manifestation of natural masculine energy, though "the excitement of passion . . . may sometimes cause contrary results to appear,"[1] and women may do some striking of their own.

There are no contemporary statistical studies on spanking and little formal research specific to it. Human-sexuality scholars view spanking as an aspect of sadomasochism. According to the Kinsey Institute,

> *If spanking is necessary for sexual arousal it is categorized under the paraphilia called* sadism. *And if being spanked is required for sexual arousal it is called* masochism.[2]

While this hardly makes it so, many spankers (whether giver or receiver) vehemently insist that they have nothing in common with sadomasochists. And while the act of spanking may be an intrinsic aspect of much D&S lovemaking, spanking purists rarely pursue other forms of dominant or submissive activity.

Early clinical sexual theorizing focused on the correlation between spankings in childhood and a recurring craving for spankings in adulthood. Havelock Ellis, and later Wilhelm Stekel, described cases of children who achieved orgasm as the culmination of a spanking. Magnus Hirschfeld elaborated on the effects of spanking of children. He noted that "this does not mean that a few smacks on its behind will damage every child sexually for life . . . It is, however, an undeniable fact this method of chastisement . . . *very frequently* leads to a deflection of the child's sexual impulse."[3] Hirschfeld cites other researchers to demonstrate how spankings defeat their punishment purposes by providing the young victims with erotic stimulation. But he stressed that a child's inherent makeup ultimately determines whether she will become a sadist or a masochist.

In the 1940s Eustace Chesser described the case of a female client who recalled being frequently threatened with an over-the-knee spanking by her parents and who subsequently sought out opportunities to reenact this scenario throughout adolescence and adulthood. The spanking enthusiasts with whom we spoke rarely recalled being spanked as children, but many remembered witnessing spankings. All acknowledged that their fantasies began in childhood.

> *My fantasies started when I was probably about seven years old. I didn't even know what sex was. But I started fantasizing about being captured and tied up. I also started spanking myself.*
>
> —KIRI KELLY

> *I didn't get spanked as a child, but there was a strict German family who had a daughter and a son next door. I was about nine. The father spanked the children with a strap. They would talk about it like it was the most natural thing in the world. I would look at [the girl] and have all these visions: "Boy, I'd like to see that happen to her!" Then the boy would get spanked, and I thought, Gee, I wonder what that feels like. I'd like somebody to do that to me.*
>
> —HAROLD

Some enthusiasts reported that a spanking was the only time in childhood when they had physical contact with their parents. Others received memorable spankings during puberty from teachers or baby-sitters. The association between spanking and pleasure seems, in nearly all cases, to become firmly fixed in the erotic imagination at an early age.

WHAT IS IT?

Spanking is a form of corporal punishment in which blows are inflicted—almost exclusively—on the buttocks. To the devotee, a spanking must fulfill certain criteria, which make the experience believable, and must follow rules of etiquette, so that the experience is pleasurable to both parties. It is difficult to inflict any real injury in spanking the buttocks, particularly if one uses the hand, a factor that adds to its attractiveness. However, thresholds for real pain differ with individuals, so in order to make it a truly pleasurable experience, one must know where this threshold lies with one's partner and with oneself, and not go beyond it. A spanking may occur as foreplay to coitus or other conventional sex acts, or it may be pursued for its own sake.

Many enthusiasts have difficulty accepting their unusual erotic interest.

I consider myself a relatively gentle and caring lover. It has been very difficult for me to reconcile that identity with the side of me that loves to give and receive spankings. My journey . . . has been to reconcile that seemingly unreconcilable dichotomy between what I enjoy sexually and who I see myself as sexually. —DAVID C.

The spanking's duration and severity are matters of individual preference. The recipient usually wants the giver to inflict as much stimulation as is tolerable without severe pain or upset, but this limit obviously varies from person to person and is often carefully negotiated.

The favored position for a spanking is over the knee. Spanking submissives describe the thrill of being hoisted onto a partner's lap, ankles lifted off the ground, erogenous zones pressing against the dominant's lap.

[In spanking] the position is of paramount importance. When you're in the over-the-knee position, your genitals are in contact with a surface [and stimulated]. You're getting spanked from above, so the impact is pressing you against what you're leaning on. —EVE HOWARD

Other popular positions for spanking include being bent over a chair, a bench, a desk, a bed, or a table. Spanking benches, whose precise design varies according to the client's specifications, are popular. Typically, a spanking bench has a surface at a height comfortable enough for the recipient to bend over, and features restraints for ankles, wrists, or both.

Men and women may occasionally achieve orgasm from giving or receiving a spanking.

> *Sometimes you get the extra stimulation that takes you all the way to orgasm. I wouldn't say it happens more than five percent of the time for me. With my boyfriend, whenever he spanks me, we always have sex afterwards. With other people that I've played with, I sometimes had sex with them afterwards.* —EVE HOWARD

While achieving a climax after a spanking is often desirable, spanking enthusiasts agree that the spanking itself often provides complete gratification.

> *A spanking need never culminate either in sex or [in] an orgasm to be satisfying to a spanking person. However, it often serves as foreplay. In most instances spankings are highly sexual and, in and of themselves, immensely satisfying.* —EVE HOWARD

Some individuals feel that sex detracts from the spanking experience. They wish only to enjoy the disciplinary and punishment aspects. Sex, in such a case, would be an undeserved reward and would infringe on the credibility of the punishment.

> *Sexual intercourse is never a part of [a spanking]. I have to feel that I'm being disciplined for something I did wrong. If it's pure discipline, you're not going to be rewarded when it's over by having any type of sexual intercourse.* —HAROLD

Spankers cite many reasons why they do not elect to combine sex and spanking. Those whose mates disapprove of spanking, for example, may seek nonsexual relationships outside of their primary partnership to realize their spanking fantasies. They may be adamant about remaining monogamous insofar as actual sexual contact is concerned.

The joy, completion, or relaxation that a submissive experiences after a spanking are comparable to postcoital feelings.

> *[After a spanking] I really feel laid-back. It is therapeutic to me. It's my drug of choice. I don't do drugs or drink, but spanking gives me the same thing that one might get from smoking marijuana or drinking alcohol. It makes me feel good.* —HAROLD

Enthusiasts often feel a conflict between their enjoyment of spanking and their discomfort at breaching taboos. In general, spanking purists tend to be highly conservative. Yet many spanking scenarios flirt with a profound cultural taboo: incest. It is not surprising that those who seek out incestuous roleplaying seem most likely to express an aversion to consummating the spanking with sexual activity. Indeed, the lack of explicit sexuality in the encounter reinforces the incest taboo, rather than threatens it.

In spanking, as in D&S, a majority of partners are "switchable" and will experiment with giving and receiving. Usually, role reversal does not occur within a scenario: Partners switch roles at different times.

SPANKING IN A D&S CONTEXT

Most, if not all, D&Sers who practice corporal punishment include spanking as a part of their play. They generally have fewer (or no) rules governing equipment, techniques, apparel, scolding, or preferred positions, and they may do little or no roleplaying. In a D&S context spankings are seldom intended to enforce a feeling of childishness. Instead, a spanking is likely to enhance the submissive's sense of physical vulnerability or is performed simply to give the submissive pain. And, while blows are ordinarily directed to the buttocks, some may also fall onto the upper thighs (some spanking purists will accept slaps to their thighs; others will not) and other sensitive areas. D&Sers may spank breasts and genital regions, though with far less force than is applied to the buttocks.

For spanking purists who are specifically interested in and aroused by the spanking itself, the spanking scenario is an elaborate, ritualized erotic art. For D&Sers a spanking is more likely to be one of innumerable activities which enhance the power dynamic. For most D&Sers the power dynamic often predates and supersedes the act of spanking; whereas, for the pure spanker, the act of spanking defines the power dynamic.

WHAT THEY LIKE

The interests that spankers describe range over a spectrum of individual preferences. Several factors, however, seem common: authority, erotic coercion and humiliation, and ageplay.

For the duration of the spanking experience, spankers enjoy the feeling that an authoritarian figure has assumed total control. The authority may be benevolent (for example, a parental figure who lovingly corrects behavior); or it may be capricious or possibly cruel (for example, an employer who takes unfair advantage of his or her authority). The credibility of the authority is a matter of extreme importance.

One means of engendering credibility is by gently exceeding the submissive's pain expectations. Spanking submissives seek out partners who, while compassionate, are capable of being strict and even slightly intimidating during play.

> When I finally brought up my desires . . . it was fun, but something was missing, because [the men] weren't into it. I got involved with a man for a brief period of time because he was kinky. It was just a part of his soul. It wasn't a husband or a boyfriend saying, "Is this too hard?" as he's spanking me, trying to get into it but afraid of hurting me. This man would take off his belt and use that or a whip. It was more intense; it was realer. —KIRI KELLY

In spanking, as in sex, attitude and creativity are vastly more important than physical attributes. The ability of the dominant to convey genuine authority is usually far more important than how the dominant looks. Male submissives may prefer older, matronly women, but just as many are titillated by being disciplined by a slender, youthful woman reminiscent of a baby-sitter. Women generally show a preference for fatherly figures.

Successful spanking dominants pride themselves on their ability to intuit what the submissive needs. This adds to the plausibility of the surrender scenario.

> Explaining what I like to a partner is explaining the whole psychological aspect of the act of spanking, whereas part of the turn-on is surrendering control—not offering direction but being taken. —DAVID C.

Although some spanking devotees do not perceive any of the activities associated with spanking to be humiliating but perceive encounters as purely playful, erotic coercion and humiliation are typical aspects of a spanking. Recipients often fantasize that they are compelled to accept the discipline, and one of the dominant's tasks is subtly to persuade the submissive that he or she cannot resist the inevitable. One means of persuasion entails subjecting the submissive to erotic embarrassment. In all cases a crucial distinction is made between erotic humiliation—which enhances mutual pleasure or believability—and uncaring or insulting attacks.

> It's important to me to get the feeling that my partner is enjoying what [she's] doing. Encounters where I am submissive and my partner says to me, "You worthless piece of shit, I don't know why I bother taking time to see you" do nothing for me. I don't get the reinforcement that everybody is enjoying themselves. —DAVID C.

Submissives may feel pleasurably humiliated when their garments are pulled down and gathered around their ankles to expose their buttocks and genitals. Others are embarrassed when spanked over their underpants. Panties may be worn by men as well as women: Some nontransvestite heterosexual men wish to wear ladies' undergarments during a spanking to increase their humiliation. This interest in lingerie is usually confined to its use in a spanking encounter.

> *Panties are a part of the humiliation. I never have worn panties in any other context. I think it gives a dominant greater power and makes me meeker and more under her control. To be totally controlled by the woman is very important to me. What could be more humiliating than [when she says], "You thought you were a tough boy, but I'm going to dress you up as a girl and spank you like a girl"?* —HAROLD

Rituals are common in spanking. Some individuals will always select a paddle that is associated with a particular kind of infraction; the very presence of the implement is symbolic. Additionally, each element of the scenario may have important psychological and ritualistic meaning to the partners. For some spanking enthusiasts, in fact, nothing less than a closely scripted, rigidly specific scenario will do. They discuss every detail before the spanking commences and leave little or no room for improvisation.

Rituals may dictate how the spanking is administered, particularly in punishment fantasies. The dominant may, for example, assign a predetermined number of blows as the penalty for a particular infraction and may require the submissive to count the number of spanks aloud. Thus, a boisterous riposte may translate into 25 spanks, a refusal to say, "Yes, ma'am" may translate into 50 spanks, and so on.

"Corner time" is another favorite ritual. The submissive partner is made to stand in a corner with his or her reddened buttocks exposed. The exposure is sensual (cool air on tingling, warm cheeks), embarrassing (an act which children may suffer), and exhibitionistic. This combination can be irresistibly exciting for a spanking fan.

Although there are differences between male and female spankers, in body as well as in attitudes, they share an interest in ageplay. While acting and being treated as childish is often considered to be shameful in our society, where maturity is respected and children are not, most spanking practitioners find childishness erotic in a spanking context. Spankers who wish to be spanked and then put into diapers or baby clothes are not uncommon. More common still is juvenilist roleplaying, which may include scoldings and age-appropriate clothes such as short, frilly frocks and underwear, and flat-heeled, patent leather shoes. Also popular are adolescent fantasies where the submissive is treated as an unruly teenager or a sassy young college student who cannot maintain good grades. Some, of course, do not wish to be seen as any other age but their own.

> *Sometimes I can play a six-year-old. Other times I wouldn't want to. Naughty wife, that's a good one! It [all] depends on the person, the circumstance, the mood.* —EVE HOWARD

Interviewees believe that the ability to reexperience one's childhood persona in the safe context of a consensual spanking is deeply relaxing. It relieves the tensions of adult life and puts the individual in touch with the inner child. As was discussed in Chapter 6, many people who relish ageplay—and particularly submissives—were required by parents or caregivers to behave maturely at an early age. The submissive may crave both the access to childish emotions and the resolution of inner conflicts through concerned discipline. The spanking feels like an act of love, which creates a tender bond between the disciplinarian and the disciplined.

HOW IT'S DONE

A spanking scene often begins with verbal domination, usually a scolding for misbehavior, imaginary or real. Many submissives playfully bait the dominant by inventing impish transgressions. Dominants usually seek to gain the upper hand psychologically before applying the palm, although the submissive often remains frisky, at least until he or she begins to reach a pain limit.

Spankers desire a happy ending: emotional resolution. The person spanked feels that he or she has been taught a valuable lesson and is somehow improved. The authority feels satisfied at having corrected the submissive's behavior and by the sheer physical control of a willing partner. Couples often complete the scenario with cuddles and kisses.

Debate over the best spanking technique is endless. The conventional wisdom is that the dominant who begins slowly will be able to prepare the submissive for a longer and more erotically intense spanking. Sexual excitement permits the submissive to enjoy greater levels of pain.

> *I like a long, slow, sensual buildup; he shouldn't start spanking hard right away. I like it to start slow-soft and then move to moderate-medium; after about 30 to 40 minutes of a buildup, I can take a very hard spanking. By that time I'm very excited.* —EVE HOWARD

Most spankers intersperse blows with caresses and rubbing of the buttocks. Some submissives will consent only to light, erotic spankings. Still, many devotees seek significant pain and lasting marks to make the punishment aspect more realistic.

Sometimes it may hurt to the extent that part of me wants it to stop. But a greater part of me wants it to keep going. I like to go back and take a look at the marks. It's like a badge of honor to me. I like to sit down for the next few days and feel it—that's a turn-on to me.
—Harold

Spankers also may be masochistic and wish to endure harsh physical punishment, including severe canings that leave significant bruises on the buttocks. For them, it is often a challenge and an accomplishment to accept as much discipline as the dominant can impose. In some cases such submissives feel that their willingness to bear the pain is both proof of their devotion to the dominant and proof of the dominant's authority.

I want to please the dominant by proving to her I can take anything she can dish out! I like it when she will sense where I'm at, at my pain threshold, and just go over it ever so slightly. I want her to, because then she's in control.
—Harold

IMPLEMENTS

Enthusiasts invest considerable time, energy, and money in stockpiling spanking implements, from the sophisticated exotica available at adult toy stores to more mundane equipment purchased at sporting-goods outlets and tack shops. One of our interviewees boasted of owning well over 50 different paddles, straps, and canes.

Making one's own equipment is uncomplicated, and many people do just that. But equipment is easy to find: Virtually every tourist shop in the country has a small stock of paddles among its novelty items. One must wonder how many of those kitschy paddles, brightly decorated with puckish sayings and crude drawings of blushing schoolchildren, are eventually swatted across some feisty spouse's buttocks, even if only in jest.

While some enthusiasts never go further than hand spankings, others are baroque in their tastes. Perhaps the most popular implements are paddles, particularly when they resemble those used for corporal discipline in schools. Some paddles have holes drilled in them so that air passes through, decreasing resistance and increasing the velocity of the blow. A paddle may leave bruises, depending on the force with which it is applied, the number of the blows, and the sensitivity of the recipient. Old-fashioned wooden hairbrushes (whose backs are used for spanking and whose bristles may be scraped across the tender skin for additional sensation), straps and belts, and canes are all well liked. The cane is a favorite tool for "naughty schoolboy or schoolgirl" scenarios. Used with force, it gives serious pain and leaves distinctive stripes, or welts.

> *A cane is great. It gives a sensation that's different from anything else. A lot of people think it's a devastating implement of punishment, but to me it isn't. Sure, it hurts, but I want a spanking to hurt. It feels like somebody put like a hot iron across your rear end—but then it mellows down to a warm feeling. I like it when the strokes are spaced out so you can savor every one of them.*
>
> —HAROLD

While some spankers have a fetishistic interest in specific implements, many like the impromptu informality of using the nearest thing at hand. Dominants delight in experimenting with common household items. Virtually any object with a flat surface (the sole of a shoe, a wooden cooking spoon, a Ping-Pong paddle, and even books and magazines) can be used. Some spanking submissives are excited when a common item is used uncommonly, since the dominant's ability to transform a mundane item into a punishment tool further asserts his or her dominance and confirms the recipient's helplessness. Over time such objects may assume their own erotic importance: The memory of having been spanked with a copy of *War and Peace* may make the text memorable for a volume of reasons.

ATTIRE

Proper garb plays an important role in a spanking scenario. Purists almost universally dislike fetish clothing and express distaste for the "whips-and-chains" sartorial flamboyance of sadomasochists. Although some spanking enthusiasts (especially those whose interests overlap with other areas of D&S) may find exotic lingerie tantalizing, sober, businesslike garb or a collegiate, preppie look is almost always preferred.

Once a spanking begins, options vary as to how much of the submissive's clothing remains in place. While some individuals find it exciting to be slowly undressed until they are completely naked, others wish to keep their panties in place and others consent to having only their buttocks revealed. The dominant almost always remains fully clothed throughout the experience, although a submissive may ask a dominant woman to raise her skirt above the knees so that he or she may rub against the dominant's garters or hosiery. But even when the dominant is professional, the client often specifies that there be little or no direct sexual contact. The exceptions occur when spanking is used as foreplay to lovemaking, in which case anything goes.

LINGUISTIC ETIQUETTE

Spanking fetishists generally agree that only certain words should be used to refer to one's posterior, and purists are fairly uncompromising in the belief that the colloquial use of *ass* is rude at the least and repugnant at most. (This rule does not necessarily apply to D&Sers.)

The term *bottom* is the hands-down favorite, but *fanny, behind, rear end, buns,* and *cheeks* follow closely. Also, keen interest is shown in phrases such as *rosy bottom, rosy cheeks,* and *blushing bottom.* Submissives generally relish being called *naughty.* Other choice words are: *arrogant, brat, sassy, saucy, disobedient, ungrateful, slut, greedy, reprobate,* and so on. In the case of allegedly misbehaving husbands, *errant* wins high marks. The use of profanity is widely frowned on as inappropriate, genuinely insulting, or offensive.

The importance that spanking enthusiasts place on linguistic refinement may reflect both the level of education and the religious or moral conservatism of many spankers. Verbal delicacy may also demonstrate that the authority is sincerely respectful of the submissive as an equal partner.

HARD-AND-FAST RULES

Since the goal of an erotic spanking is the mutual pleasure and satisfaction of both partners, participants discuss in advance their expectations, physical and psychological limits, and favorite fantasies. Those who do not wish to be marked may feel traumatized and abused—not to mention furious—to discover that a clumsy dominant has left bruises. Some spankers are uncomfortable with ageplay and may feel distraught if the fantasy exceeds their emotional limits.

Spankers typically show a remarkable ability to enter into and to exit roleplaying quickly and absolutely, and wish to return to an egalitarian relationship once the scenario has concluded. The same authority that has an erotic zing during a spanking can be profoundly uninteresting outside of a consensual, playful, and erotic context. Exceptions exist, but almost exclusively among those who incorporate spanking into a larger power relationship and among the small minority of lifestyle spanking couples who remain in their roles at all times.

GAY SPANKING

Gay spanking is a separate and distinct scene. Daddy-boy (or uncle-nephew) fantasy scenarios bear the greatest resemblance to the heterosexual spanking scene and involve many of the same rituals. But a significant percentage of gay spankers derives its customs from the military and fraternity traditions of hazing, and specifically paddling rituals.

Known among gay spankers—and less frequently among heterosexuals—is switch spanking, in which partners spank each other during a scenario. In these cases neither partner is necessarily dominant or submissive; instead, the spanking is a game of one-upmanship.

INTERVIEWS

EVE HOWARD

[Spanking is] my profession. It's my hobby. My closest associates and my best friends are all in the Scene. My partners are in the Scene. I met my boyfriend five years ago through a personal ad in a spanking publication. Everything that I do is related to [spanking]. I am a lifestyler completely and utterly. I have always been into [spanking] and nothing in the world could change it; it's an integral part of me.

I like to be spanked, although I have given some spankings. I'm not particularly submissive. Spanking fits into D&S. One dominates [and] controls; one gives the spanking and one receives. But that's not in somebody's mind when they're first beginning to relate to the idea of spanking. It starts in childhood, long before we know about anything sexually. I think when you're a child, it's almost a nameless-faceless thing. You can often initiate spanking games with playmates: I always did! By the time I got to junior high school, I was playing spanking games with my best girlfriends. We took turns being the dominant. We acted out an ongoing soap opera for years that always wound up with one of us getting spanked. The first time you have a boyfriend, you try to provoke him into spanking you. But it's never the same as when you encounter somebody who's really into it. The mind-set is different, and the excitement level is much higher.

I have, on my odyssey to get where I am, engaged in many D&S-type experiences involving submission, bondage, other forms of discipline and corporal punishment, corsetting, fetish apparel, rubber, leather, and high heels. I have witnessed many D&S sessions, because my best friend is a mistress, but I am primarily a spanking fetishist.

Spanking is an action fetish. A spanking person will become aroused merely by witnessing, hearing about, or talking about a spanking. If you see a spanking in an old movie, even though there isn't any nudity in the scene—no sex whatsoever, only the spanking—that will be tremendously arousing. [Spanking] is a fetish because no other sexual things pertain at that moment. Most fetishes involve an object, but in spanking it's the act in itself that is arousing. I [also] think it's important to distinguish between D&S and spanking. One can be into spanking without knowing anything at all about D&S or S&M. Spanking is rather innocent. It often doesn't involve any equipment [or] costumes—just two people engaging in the act.

I like to have things done to me, rather than serving. Most submissives are characterized [as] serving others. I don't agree. I think that most submissives enjoy having things done to them. It's very confusing, because sometimes a master may require body service or want the slave on her knees giving him head, but in reality I think most submissives want to be passive and have the things done to them. By nature and by personality, I am very dominant. I don't like humiliation. I don't like the concept of being punished, because I feel like I'm good and doing the best I can. I just like the control of a man who will spank me, who will make love to me in a forceful manner.

Usually when you're a child, [and if] you're getting spanked mildly or almost affectionately, there is a feeling of loving control that's being imparted. This [doesn't] hold true for people who have been brutalized or abused as children. I recall being aroused by spanking fantasies as early as age three. I can only conclude that my father probably spanked me very mildly when I was still an infant . . . a patting kind of thing. The feelings I associated with this were pleasurable, and it [imprinted] in my brain. When you're first aroused by it, you don't even know what arousal is. You just know that there's something wonderful about spanking. I think later on when you start to recognize the difference between boys and girls, you sexualize the fetish and want to play spanking [games with] a little boy or even a little girl.

My favorite kind of spanking is given by a man that I like, respect, and enjoy being with. It should always be over the knee. I like it to begin on my skirt and to have the layers of clothing slowly pulled up and pulled down. I like a good deal of rubbing. I like touching with a spanking, being fingered. I like to be talked to, but it's not that important. I certainly don't like to be berated, scolded, or humiliated. "You've been a bad girl" is okay.

It's important to be held in the right way: held around the waist very firmly with one hand, as the other hand spanks. I don't like fancy leg locks that hold me in place. That always makes me afraid that somebody's going to spank me hard. There should be subtlety. I should always feel that the man cares for me, likes me a good deal. I don't like to feel that somebody is just beating a piece of meat—that's not me.

I've had some harrowing spanking experiences, because I have played a lot—experiences that made me cry bitterly within the first five minutes. A lot of people into spanking like those tears; they want to cause suffering and pain. I don't exactly know why. I think a lot of people just have a problem. They don't like women very much, or they don't like themselves very much, or they're vicariously putting themselves in the place of the spankee, and they feel that's how hard they should be punished. That's not what I enjoy. I like a sensuous spanking.

I can do a scenario very easily. I'm more comfortable with some than with others. But I don't need a scenario. All the excitement is in my mind already. It's the feeling of control that turns me on—firm, loving control from the man. Sometimes the scenario almost gets in the way of the enjoyment, but at other times it's very appropriate. It's good for a beginner to use a scenario. It gives you somewhere to go. A lot of people into spanking have highly detailed scenarios. That's all part of it. I think people into spanking should try scenarios and then move to the point where they don't need them anymore.

I like bondage if it's done properly. I have been in some extreme bondage where you're very intricately and symmetrically tied and where certain parts of your body can be exposed, caressed, spanked sometimes, teased. Often tickling goes along with spanking, but I don't see the value of it. I have engaged in enema play. That's a big turn-on for me and very common to spanking people. That's when I'm feeling at my most submissive. Sometimes I've done that to the extent that I got too submissive and I don't want to do it again for a year!

"Too submissive" is when you feel so vulnerable you almost lose your soul. You lose your identity. You're nothing but a squirming, writhing thing. This society teaches you that we have to be strong and assert ourselves and go out and get what we want. When you're that submissive, it goes against the teachings of what a proper human being should be, and you become almost disgusted with your self. You have to do a scene with a so-called "real master" before you realize that a lot of these real masters are just pompous idiots! I would never kiss a man's feet. I think that's insulting and ridiculous, although I've let a lot of men kiss my feet. I would never rim a man. I would never worship a man, nor do I want anybody to worship me. I believe in equality of the sexes.

I think it's good that feminists come out and admit to being D&Sers, because some people don't think that you can be a feminist and be a submissive at the same time, which is utterly false. I think that if a woman is doing what she needs to do to fulfill her own sexuality, then she is a feminist, whether that sexuality means being the dominant one or being the submissive one, or being somewhere in the middle.

I've been very privileged in being allowed to live out many fantasies. There really isn't anything that I haven't done within the realm of D&S that I would still like to do. Last week I shot a video. When I wrote the scenario I got turned on. It was [about] a married couple into spanking going to visit and socialize with another married couple into spanking, and the spankings took place during the actual double-date situation in a very charming and delightful way: just a very normal, mischievous wife-moderately-controlling-husband spanking situation where all of the participants were attractive, the setting pleasant, the costumes delightful. I got to work one of the cameras and see my fantasy come to life before my eyes. It was wonderful.

There are two kinds of spanking videos. Some companies do fake videos in which lovely models take simulated spankings. I'm not going to give away trade secrets, but there are ways to fake spankings in videos. Then there are real spanking videos, like the kind Nu-West and my company make. I was perfect for the real spanking videos because I could take a real spanking. [Over time] I got a following. I've received literally thousands of letters from spanking people all over the country. This feedback inspired me to put out a publication.

The best spanking videos are genuine scenes that are filmed all the way through. Often spanking videos require a hell of a lot more pain than I like in my real life. I'm not a masochist. Unfortunately, the video viewing public has been trained to expect severity in a spanking video, [and] you have to please the crowd, so you have to take a bit more in a spanking video—or a lot more in some cases—than you would like.

Some companies do tend to place the woman in the position of helpless victim or create what I call "blackmail scenarios": For example, the girl has been caught pilfering from the company till, so rather than calling the police, they make her take a spanking. That is not the kind of video I like or approve of. I like a video that features a mischievous girl who baits somebody or deserves a spanking, and the one who's doing it is doing it almost affectionately. There's love there; there's kindness, caring, trust.

I started to do videos for Nu-West and, in exchange for my acting services, shot a couple of videos according to my specifications. Eventually they put me in business for myself. They shot my first videos for me and allowed me to advertise in their publication, so I had an immediate pipeline to the heart of the Scene. I started Shadow Lane five years ago with one video, one publication, [and] a little fiction publication called *Shadow Lane*— my ongoing spanking novel. Then I expanded into a newsletter called *Stand Corrected* which has fiction, letters, articles, photos, illustrations, and personal ads. The current issue is 52 pages and [has] almost 300 personal ads.

We emphasize over-the-knee spankings. We take a romantic approach. I think a lot of the B&D publications and video producers that are having trouble again are making the women into utterly helpless victims, so it seems obvious that these women are not enjoying it, that they're almost being assaulted. The companies who have gotten busted have done very severe things that you couldn't [easily defend] in a court of law. I feel confident that I could take my stuff to any judge and [that] he would smile and say, "What's the big deal?"

Shadow Lane is doing wonderfully. People have gotten married from meeting through my publication, and many relationships have been formed. People in this Scene are very shy. They don't go to clubs or parades. You can't tell who a spanking person is by dress, as with a leatherman or a dominatrix. Spanking people are embedded in society, and usually they're hiding what they're into from their mates. In general, their mates disapprove. There's a small percentage of mates that do participate or tolerate it, but for the most part, this is a very "my secret life"-type of thing.

When you're a spanking person and you suddenly tell your nearest and dearest what you're into, you get anything from a blank look to utter disgust. You are told to see a psychiatrist because you're sick, or it's dismissed as something silly which nobody could possibly want to engage in. But married people have a recourse for their sanity. There are some wonderful professional dominants and submissives around.

Most of my male customers are switchable. They like receiving and giving. I would say 75 percent of my female customers want to be the receiver, and the other 25 percent are either switchable or could be switchable. We have female-dominating-male and female-dominating-female [videos and fiction]. All my back issues list the other vendors of interest to spanking people. It's all there like a blueprint.

[A] good source of finding people is the local entertainment papers that take personal ads. Many of these papers will allow you to use the word *spanking,* or *submissive.* I think it's also good to join support groups. Again, you have to get the underground papers to find these groups. But that's a good way to socialize in a safe atmosphere. You have to be bold and courageous. The boy who delivers your groceries is not going to give you a spanking spontaneously.

The concept of who can you trust is important in D&S, B&D, and S&M. You have to go through the process, just as you would go through the dating process. [In D&S] the best way to assure yourself of safety is to, first, correspond with the person. Next, speak with them on the phone, and if it feels right, arrange a meeting in a neutral place. And only when you feel comfortable, you meet the person alone, and even then you let somebody know where you are. During the date, if anything disturbs you or alarms you, *go*! Leave! Depart! Tell the person that it's just not working out and you're not compatible. I think it's important to remember that you're a human being with dignity. Even if somebody tells you you're a brilliant submissive or you were meant to be submissive, you shouldn't take [his] word for it! The feeling should come from within you. You shouldn't be told what you want. You should decide for yourself.

People who know themselves—because a lot of people reading this book are only going to pick it up because the word *spanking* is in it—I want those people to feel that they are absolutely not alone. There is a Scene in America, and it's growing all the time. Publications like mine and the other good spanking publications are helping to bind it together. There's never been a better time to explore your D&S feelings, whether extreme or mild.

HAROLD
Whatever turns you on is fine. I've never had any reservations or feelings that I ought to go a psychiatrist or that there's anything abnormal about me. As long as it's consensual, I don't care what anybody does. If my kids asked me, I would say that some people do it as part of foreplay. Some people like to kiss; some people like to spank each other. I would tell anybody [that] if there is some particular aspect that's arousing, don't repress it, don't get frustrated about it, and don't think it's unhealthy. As long as you're not imposing your will on somebody else, it's okay.

I would never consider spanking any of the children. To me, [spanking] is a sexual thing. That's one of the primary reasons I would never do it [to kids]. Second reason is [that] I wouldn't have the heart to do it! I'm not a great disciplinarian in our household. My wife doesn't spank them, either. I don't believe in corporal punishment for children. I don't think it accomplishes anything. I've known enough people, and I think we all have, that were spanked or beaten by their parents. The majority, in my opinion, tend to have greater psychological problems and tend to be abusive. It just doesn't seem fair to me for a person 10 times the size of a child to physically assault one. Taking away privileges seems to work as well as anything else. I don't think [physical punishment] works.

It wasn't until I was in college that I had the opportunity to get somebody to spank me. I would find excuses to spank girlfriends. I kept it playful. When I saw it was starting to hurt them, I'd slow down. I never hurt anyone. I would say one out of the 25 I tried it with had [genuine] submissive tendencies. The others did it as a prelude to sex. Funny how things go back to when you're younger. I [remember things I read] when I was in prep school. [One] was a description of somebody witnessing a man spanking a 19-year-old girl in a bathing suit. Instead of pulling it down, he pulled it up in her crack so it exposed her cheeks. That turned me on. I've always wanted to do that to a woman, so I figured I might as well try it [on] myself. It stimulates your anus and is tight on a man's genitals. It provides a little added humiliation.

I'm more submissive than dominant, but I like to switch when opportunity permits. I've finally started using spanking as foreplay for sex, very light, [with my wife]. I'm in love with [her] and wouldn't want to do anything to jeopardize our marriage; if I don't see a positive reaction, I back off. [But] she told me about a woman who said that she and her husband do this. I jumped on that by saying, "Why don't we try it?" We have, and she doesn't seem to mind it. When I spank her, it's more sensual, very light, and part of foreplay. I want her to do it a lot harder to me, and I got her to do it fairly hard, but nothing compared to what I really want. But at least we're moving in that direction, which is nice. I wouldn't push too far. I like vaginal intercourse and to perform oral sex on women. I like to be sure a woman is satisfied. I want to be sure she's had about five or six orgasms before penetration. In my head I spanked her whether I touched her or not. I have a good imagination.

Two months is about as long as I want to go without getting a real good spanking. I do mean *good*. Little play ones in between are fine, but going without it can make me irritable! Cranky, quite frankly. After I go through a severe session, I'm laid-back and comfortable. It's an aphrodisiac.

I've had the occasion to meet some dominant women that were willing to administer spankings to me. I have to know in my mind that they're not just doing it to shut me up or to pacify me. It makes me feel good when I know that they're enjoying what they're doing to me. If they like to do it hard on occasion, then [it] presents a challenge. I want to be able to meet that challenge and hope they enjoy that. Sexual intercourse is never a part of spanking sessions, first of all because I'm married. Even if I weren't, a spanking, to me, is discipline. I take the remembrance of the session [home]. I don't know if my wife has ever put two and two together, but by the time I get home, it's not long before we're engaging in marital relations!

In the beginning, when the talk starts, I am aroused. The mistress who's going to spank me prepares me. She'll say how naughty I've been and what's going to happen to me: "You're going to get spanked; it's going to be on your bare bottom; I'm going to make you wear panties." But once the spanking starts and the pain sets in, my erection goes away, I guess because of the physical nature of it.

I have to feel that the woman is in control and that she can read me. I can take a pretty severe spanking if I'm comfortable with a woman, if I know it's what she wants to do and she's comfortable doing it. Once I get into the proper frame of mind, my tolerance builds, not only in terms of the physical striking of the buttocks but in the mental sense. I feel I'm pleasing the dominant. I think it's fine to have an off-the-cuff conversation before, in more or less general terms, because you have to do that to get to know somebody. But when you're doing an actual scene, the dominant has to be in control, and she has to go a little bit beyond my highest point. Then it becomes discipline.

Caning was a big fantasy thing in my teenage years. I read the stories in *Cane* magazine from London but had no idea where you could get [a cane]. Finally I found one in New York, at a store called Uncle Sam's Umbrella Shop; they sold it as a novelty. But, boy, I couldn't wait to have somebody try it on me. [I] just thought it was wonderful! I approached it this way with a girlfriend: "I'm going to spank you with my hand, because I'm much stronger than you, but I'm going to give you this cane to make everything even." I made it a game. I like straps, too, but prefer caning, the harder the better; a hairbrush on top of a caning leaves you with a great sensation which lasts for days.

It makes me feel good that now, with some effort on my part, one can meet people who are into it. I originally had a distorted image of dominatrices with masks. Everybody has their own thing, but whips and stuff are not what I want. I want to be spanked and caned like they did in school, turned over a knee or lying [down] and spanked with a hairbrush. Discipline.

Every person I have met into spanking is intelligent, very personable, and just a nice person to know. I trust them impeccably. In my line of work, dealing with insurance companies and cutthroat lawyers, there isn't a lot of trust because if you trust anyone, you're going to be disappointed. Everyone I've met that's into the Scene is the cream of the crop of people engaged in kinky sexual activities: intelligent, honest, caring. Women have spanked me till I'm black and blue, red and blush and everything else, and I think that person is wonderful. She *is* wonderful. She knows what she is giving me. The person has to be your friend. You don't need to be in love with the dominant woman. But to like her and consider her a friend is real important. She's somebody you're comfortable with, somebody you can talk to. After all, you are baring other things than your bottom to her. You're more or less baring your soul and sharing what's inside your head. It's an intimate relationship.

KIRI KELLY

[D&S] has been a lifelong part of my soul. It's not something that someone has a choice about. [There's] a funny story [my mother] mentioned to me the other day. We are very, very close. I have been able to share all of me with her and tell her everything that I have gone through, the things I do and my desires. She recalled a time when I was little and she had spanked me. I ran away crying to my room and came back later and said, "Thank you, Mommy. I needed that." She said she just realized that I probably enjoyed it! And I probably did! [But] I don't think that's where [the desire] came from.

I was an only child and didn't have a lot of interaction with other kids. But I would [spank myself] every Saturday. I'd [spank] myself to sleep. I'd run into the living room, turn myself over an ottoman, pull my pants down, and spank myself. I'd set limits for myself: "A hundred, and then another hundred!" I really didn't understand sex [yet]. All I knew was that I enjoyed spanking and was obsessed with it. When I started masturbating, I was always thinking that I was tied down and someone was doing this to me, and they were willing to force this on me.

Emotionally, it's the ultimate form of love for me. I just totally want to give myself over to someone and please him and belong to him. I've analyzed it my whole life, and I reached a point where I finally said, "I don't know why I'm like this. I give up trying to understand. All I know is that it pleases something in myself."

When I moved out to California, I was far enough away from my parents that I could do what I want [without them knowing]. My folks are the most wonderful parents one could ever hope for. My mother is very understanding, but it would just kill my father. It would hurt him, and [it] would hurt me to do that to him. So I never thought about doing something back there.

When I started dancing at some of the clubs, that led to modeling work, and [then] I saw an ad for fetish models. It intrigued me. The thought of combining [modeling] with something that would satisfy some of my fetish desires was appealing, so I applied. I worked for this one company: They were doing various magazines—bondage, spanking, a little-girl look, two girls together. When it came to the spanking work, they said, "We'll use rouge. This is just stills. You don't have to do anything." I said, "What? You're going to take my fun away from me?" And the guy said, "Oh! Sure! Go for it, if you want!" And so we did, and I got very red. He said, "If you can do this, *you* should be working for a video company." So he referred me to [one]. I figure that a lot of people who do this photography work are not actually into the subject. I have worked for a lot of people producing this type of material that don't understand it at all.

I've been in over 80 videos [and] over 68 magazines. My picture's been all over the world. It's been associated with some of the more well known magazines and videos. Harmony Communications put out a two-part magazine called *The Perils of Topanga Canyon*. It sold out almost immediately and they consider it a classic. I'm very proud of it, myself. The *Bondage Is My Pleasure* series [from] Cal-Star is very popular. And the spanking scene in *Hitchhiker Spanked II* was very popular. Shadow Lane's *Older Men with Younger Wives* is also very popular. There are so many!

DAVID C.

It would probably be a lot easier for me if straight screwing or oral sex really turned me on. [It] would be easier to deal with and to find partners I could share it with. But unfortunately that's not the case. For a while I thought, I'm the master of my own destiny. I will simply reshape my psyche and decide that straight screwing is what really turns me on. But it isn't. I've accepted that. That seems to put spanking in a terrible light—like a disability that I've come to accept and deal with—but I don't feel that's true, because through those fantasies, both enacting them and using them strictly for fantasies, they've very much enriched my sex life.

I think the sense of risk that one cultivates through D&S and [which one] relishes in these sorts of games is very pertinent to everyday life. This sounds like a testimonial of what Tupperware has done for my kitchen, but I feel that if you approach D&S as a trust issue—of learning to trust and learning to give up control—one can look at it almost as an exercise applicable to daily life: taking risks and letting go, allowing things to happen rather than trying to always be in control, learning to accept control instead of being passive. I think sexual play is one of the few ways that we have left as a self to play, to pretend, to explore, to reach out to people on truly profound levels. And to have fun and burn off calories at the same time.

I'd call myself a switch. Unfortunately, my current partner is not of the same mind. I think it's easier for someone who isn't to assume a dominant role rather than to assume a submissive role, or at least it's safer for them. The only real play I can get in my current relationship is pretty much on the submissive side. One of the problems I've had in communicating my desires and preferences is [that] it's important to me to get the feeling that my partner is enjoying what [she's] doing. That feeling is very important to me, perhaps because of my problem in reconciling the violence [of spanking] with an act of love.

I come from a household where corporal punishment was not part of the regime. I do remember that with my first girlfriend we were quite sexually active but didn't want to mess around with birth control. We were very creative with forms of sexual activity that did not involve intercourse, and the things I found most interesting were bondage and spanking. The thing that's really fun about being a submissive is [that] it's like rock climbing or skydiving. You're faced with something where your intellect will say, "You're utterly safe. The rip cord is right here, and you can pull it, and the parachute will open, and you'll float to safety." But all your visceral senses [are screaming].

There are several things that I have fantasized about that are more fun to fantasize about than to do. One is taking a really hard spanking, but my tolerance for pain is not horribly high. The times that I've gone over what I will tentatively call my limits have not been pleasant experiences. I imagine that different approaches, starting slow and working up to more intense things, might prove different. One of the things I'd like to try doing more of is roleplaying. I'd love to play out [a scenario of] being called into a teacher's office and reprimanded and told I won't graduate unless I submit to a spanking. But fantasies aren't always good realities.

Twelve

WHIPPING

She plucked some twigs from the broom, and whipped the girl so that she raised welts on her. . . . Matryosha did not scream under the strokes, obviously because I was present, but she gasped strangely at each blow. And afterward she continued to sob gaspingly for a whole hour. . . . Immediately I felt that I had done something vile. At the same time I experienced a pleasurable sensation because suddenly a certain desire pierced me like a blade . . .

—DOSTOYEVSKY, *The Possessed*[1]

WHAT IS IT?

When the rock band Devo sarcastically intoned, "Whip it, whip it good" in the early 1980s, it joined a tradition historically populated by monks, not punks. Flagellation—the striking of flesh, usually but not exclusively on the back, with a whip, flail, or other stinging device—has the distinction of being perhaps the single most widely practiced form of punishment in history. It is impossible to determine the degree to which flogging pain was intermingled with sheer sensual pleasure.

This chapter focuses on:

- Mitch Kessler, who is 47 years old and a native New Yorker. He crafts whips and "implements of affection" under the name Adam Selene. He is an elected officer of the Metropolitan New York chapter of the National Leather Association (NLA). Gerrie Blum is his life- and business partner.
- Gerrie Blum (also known as Gillian Boardman and Lady Gillian) is 54 years old. She and Mr. Kessler own Adam's Sensual Whips and Gillian's Toys. Ms. Blum is an officer of the Metropolitan New York chapter of the NLA and is a delegate to the NLA National Advisory Council.
- Laura Antonio is 27 years old and lives in New York, where she works in the design and production of magazines. She produced the 1992 Miss Northeast Leather Contest.

WHEN DID IT BEGIN?

Whipping has had a long and subtle history. In pagan Sparta young men were whipped by female priestesses before a wooden image of Artemis as a rite of passage. Flagellation also occurred in the mystery cults of Mediterranean civilizations—such as Greece, Persia, Rome, and Egypt—as one method of inducing altered consciousness. Other methods included fasting, music, the inhalation of fumes to produce intoxication, whirling dance, contemplation and meditation, and hypnosis.[2] Such rituals and metaphysical voyages are emulated by contemporary whipping enthusiasts who combine sexuality and spirituality.

At least two major religions, Islam and Christianity, have embraced self-flagellation as a means of self-purification. The Shiite Muslims still engage in public self-flagellation. Adherents of Roman Catholicism escalated self-flagellation in the 13th and 14th centuries to what has been termed "flagellomania." The practice was ultimately banned when devotees became a little too devoted to self-mortification and less devoted to the Church.

The western world has had a long tradition of flagellation and similar acts associated with Christian penance. The West today has seen the secularization of sadomasochism, once looked upon as an exemplary religious experience. —EDGAR GREGERSEN[3]

In Christianity self-flagellation was inherited from the "desert fathers," monastics who first established small communities in the Egyptian desert in A.D. 381. The desert fathers regarded sensual pleasure as inherently sinful and believed that discomfort blunted cravings for pleasure and proved the unimportance of the body. Their philosophy became the religious ideal of Christian Europe for well over a thousand years and persists in many quarters, such as in the Penitente sects in the American Southwest.

How profoundly the Christian antipathy to sexual pleasure has affected human sexuality is impossible to overestimate. But it is obvious that self-mortification and religiously inspired punishment often replaced forbidden sexual gratification.

> *Celibates often indulged in prodigies of masochism, and especially in flagellation, and we find cases of confessors making use of their power of absolution to force their female parishioners to beat them.*
> —G. RATTRAY TAYLOR[4]

During the 11th Century flagellation was promoted as a form of penitence and was doled out by confessors as frequently as is the modern-day "Hail Mary."

> *At first the priests used to do the whipping themselves, the penitents usually being entirely nude, and the penance being inflicted in a place attached to the church. . . . In the twelfth century St. Dominic made the practice widely known, and established a scale of equivalents, 1,000 lashes being considered equivalent to the reciting of ten penitential psalms.*
> —G. RATTRAY TAYLOR[5]

In 1259 groups began forming in northern Italy for the express purpose of self-flagellation. Entire communities—even five-year-olds—participated, despite the censure of both secular and religious authorities. The movement eventually waned, but resurgences occurred in 1262 and 1296. In 1334 repeated earthquakes were interpreted as God's displeasure and spawned another mass movement of self-whipping, and in 1348–49, when the Black Plague devastated Western Europe, frightened crowds again fell into frenzies of self-flagellation. Processions of thousands from all classes spread through present-day Germany, Switzerland, Austria, Bohemia, the Netherlands, and England.

The Church was alarmed when the Brethren of the Cross formed around 1349. This iconoclastic sect held that one could attain eternal salvation by undergoing 33½ days of self-scourging without intercession of priests or the Church. A papal bull promptly denounced the Brethren as heretics, and the movement was disbanded, reemerging briefly in 1351 and again in

1354, before being crushed by the Inquisition. Their demise did not, however, end self-flagellation: The practice simply was once more brought under Church control.

The enormous historical popularity of flagellation at least suggests that participants derived some pleasure, albeit unconsciously, from acts of extreme masochism. Because the persons who performed these acts did not identify their activities as erotic and although the context of religious faith cannot be ignored, the many records of nuns begging to be bound and flogged and partly clad priests beseeching women to beat them—and their ensuing spiritual ecstasy—suggest that self-flagellants experienced, at the least, an endorphin rush. Contemporary enthusiasts all report an inextricable link between eros and whipping.

The first unambiguous linking of flagellation and erotic pleasure in the West occurred in the 15th Century, when an Italian named Pico della Mirandola wrote the first known account of sexual sadomasochism. He described a man who could not enjoy sex unless he had been beaten to the point of bleeding with a whip soaked in vinegar.

Over time the power of the Church waned and so too did documentation of flagellation. But sexual sadomasochism "soon had a place in pornography and in life"[6] as flagellation traveled from the processions of the penitents to the bedchambers and brothels of Europe. Whipping was designated "the English vice" not long after *A Treatise on the Use of Flogging* was published in 1718.

It was suggested at the time that whipping was the last resort of rakes whose senses were dulled by sexual excess, but this certainly does not conform to contemporary understandings of psychosexuality. Whatever the reason, English brothels dedicated to flagellation enjoyed a huge success. A Mrs. Colet's establishment was so popular that King George IV made a well-known royal visit. A Mr. Chace Pine invented a machine capable of whipping forty persons simultaneously. Another madam, Mrs. Theresa Berkley (inventor of a spanking bench known as the Berkley Horse), was able to retire in comfort after eight years of turning others' pain into personal gain. Despite—or perhaps as a result of—the Puritanism (later known as Victorianism) that overtook England by the end of the 18th Century, flagellation brothels increased in popularity.

Although whipping has been condemned as an erotic practice since the end of the 19th Century, it long remained a favorite means of enforcing discipline among schoolchildren. Even today children in some parts of America are subjected to corporal punishment. From the 16th to the 20th centuries in Europe, whippings with canes and birches were accepted pedagogy.[7] It has been suggested that these unsavory acts of violence against children have helped perpetuate the adult interest in whipping that continues in contemporary English pornography. Many psychologists have observed that the sum effect of such arduous punishment, instead of inspiring distaste, may instead excite erotic pleasure.[8] Certainly the historical record indicates that there is something about the intense stimulation of stinging blows to flesh— even the most innocent flesh—and its asserted expiation of sins that may compel recipients to crave repetition. In any situation, whipping carries a high risk of physical injury and emotional trauma.

HOW IS IT DONE?

Since all of the acts described in this book are assumed to be mutually consensual, we will not discuss the many cruel and vicious methods of whipping used over the millennia to degrade and abuse people. A whipping that takes place in a D&S context is specifically intended to serve both partners' erotic and psychological pleasure.

> *[One should] never use the word* brutality. *[D&S] is done with caring and love. I'm extremely maternal. I want the person I am topping to have a wonderfully good experience. And it's sexual. I want them to really get off on it.* —JEAN L.

D&Sers, as a rule, love ritual. In some cases, a flogging may be a ritualized part of a larger ceremony of submission, such as the "one year and one day" contract of submission one interviewee entered into with a dominant.

> *He had a series of ritualized questions, designed to make sure that I was willing to go through with this. I took a flogging from the whip that he had made—a birch, a bundle of rods with a long handle— and I took 13 strokes with that, one for each month plus one for the day. Afterwards, I vowed to come and to go, do and leave undone, and to speak and be silent according to his will and whim. In return, he promised to respect and protect my honor and integrity and to judge and guide me with all of his wisdom.* —LAURA ANTONIO

A whipping may begin with a careful selection of the appropriate implement; the submissive may be required to kneel and to kiss the whip's handle before the activity begins. Such head trips are a kind of foreplay to the main erotic event.

Submissives are sometimes ordered to count the strokes of the whip aloud or to say, "Thank you, may I have another?" after each stroke. There are numerous variations on this theme. A dominant may announce in advance the number of strokes to be given so that the submissive knows what to expect. Partners frequently introduce other control elements, such as providing the submissive with a safe word or having the submissive beg.

> *With [my lover], I usually make it a condition that I'll flog him until he begs me to stop, which takes a lot of doing. I think maybe he's topping from the bottom, but it's fun to do, so I let him get away with it.* —ADIDA

A consensual whipping usually entails a lengthy physical building-up to prepare for more intense sensation.

> *When you whip somebody, you start off lightly, so that it is a body massage. You keep doing that and very, very gradually increase the intensity. That's how you bring someone up. As you increase the intensity, if you have a person who is a sexual masochist like myself, there will come a point where their body says to them, "You're experiencing pain! Time to get the endorphins going." The endorphins will kick in, and you will get an endorphin rush.*
> —JEAN L.

Some prepare for a whipping by gently stroking the area to be struck with a lightweight implement, or with fingers, or even with a feather or fur. Commonly soft sensations—such as tickles or caresses—are intermingled with moderate blows, especially during the early stages. A number of very mild implements are available, such as a whip with silk or deerskin strands. As the whipping progresses, some dominants continue to alternate gentle sensations with intense ones, by rubbing a bit of fur or silk over the sensitized skin between strokes, for example.

Tops will often consciously develop as much proficiency as possible with a variety of implements. As a rule tops also pride themselves on their ability to prolong the submissive's anticipation by raising the level of stimulation notch by notch, until the submissive enters an ecstatic state.

> *I like being adept enough at reading body movement and at wielding a cane or a whip to get the person into the zone [of ecstasy], because I know that, once there, [she] will have a very good time. If I push too hard, it'll hurt too much all at once, and the person will want to fight the intensity. If I go too slowly, she may not get there.*
> —MR. HAPPY

WHY THEY LIKE IT

The reasons why people like whipping are as diverse as the reasons why they enjoy any other D&S play; many people, however, settle on whipping as an activity of choice. This is probably because whipping is associated with rigorous adult punishment (in contrast to a spanking, which is usually considered a more childish punishment) and also because whipping is an activity so associated with sadomasochism as to be a cliché. D&Sers, and particularly those in the Scene (as opposed to strictly private practitioners), display a strong tendency to observe and to revere tradition. Many people who would not otherwise have experimented with whipping have become adept because it is a fixture of D&S erotica. Few, however, continue unless they find the experience to be erotic.

A whipping, like any other form of corporal punishment, is a physical manifestation of the same power exchange which others may experience uniquely through psychological control. The pain and disgrace of punishment may elicit powerful feelings of submission. With each blow, the reality of the dominant's power is impressed upon the submissive, who may in response grow more sexually excited.

Typically, submissives accept whippings as a demonstration of devotion. Both partners take pride in each other's performances: Dominants are often emotionally gratified that the submissive will go the extra mile.

> *One of the most satisfying things I've ever done was a caning with Adida. I gave her 100 strokes with a very thin, whippy cane in that little area where the butt joins the thighs. She was in this perfect submissive posture, her butt up in the air, her face way down on the bed, and her toes pointed just the way she'd been told. I instructed her not to count any strokes that weren't hard. She never cheated. On the last 10, I told her that if she moved at all, I'd start over. I kept increasing the intensity. Adida did not move. The control that she had to do that, and the head space that she was in in order to do that, made me so hard. It was really beautiful.* —MR. HAPPY

ECSTASY

Among the whipping enthusiasts we interviewed there was virtual consensus that, in its highest form, whipping leads to ecstasy. This ecstasy is usually described as profoundly spiritual, even as an out-of-body experience.

When Cybele and I are well merged in this sort of spiritual space, and she does this kind of flagellation, I transcend. I don't escape myself; I go beyond myself. I'm there. Cybele's term [for it] is flying; my arms start to move as if I'm flying. My mental imagery is of being above the clouds, and then flying down and investigating. It's really more like an out-of-body experience than anything I have ever had, and I've done a lot of psychic work, including out-of-body experience. —JAMES W.

Depending on the couple, whipping may be a punishment or a reward. Some people will whip the partner only to enact a punishment scenario; masochists who enjoy being whipped, however, may receive whippings as a reward.

I really like to be flogged. There's a state I get into which I call "the zone." When I'm in this state, it's as if, no matter what is being done, it doesn't really hurt; all it does is put me into this alternate state. Fear can block it, or being too tired can block it, or trying to make it happen can block it, but when everything's working right and I have my breathing down properly, each new strike, each new blow, seems to add to the euphoric and ecstatic state.

—MR. HAPPY

Others may perceive the experience as a physical trial which, once endured, allows them to transcend normal limits and to feel empowered.

The first time I was seriously whipped, I started chanting to myself, "I am powerful; I am strong; pain cannot harm me." And that became a little mantra. Every time I would receive a blow, it would just energize me and make me feel stronger and more powerful.

—J-

Some are drawn primarily to the physicality of whipping. For them, it is not a spiritual trial but a physical challenge.

My favorite thing of all is flogging. Both receiving and giving. It's very physical to give the flogging, and receiving it is very cool, crisp—it's a great, refreshing feeling. When giving, I put my martial-arts [skills] into it and really throw my hip in. That's a very satisfying feeling. You wear yourself out. —ADIDA

SAFETY

D&Sers often demonstrate safe whipping techniques at support group meetings so that novices or less experienced dominants can learn to avoid inflicting real damage. Safety demonstrations are a key element in the D&S community's educational outreach. Learning the appropriate use of every implement takes time and ever-increasing skill. Some dominants experiment with new equipment by testing it on themselves first, striking their thighs or arms to evaluate the weight and sting of each implement before using it on their submissives. Others claim that the best training is to "work from the bottom up" by submitting, to gain firsthand knowledge of the bottom's range of physical and emotional feeling.

> *A dominant who is not in control of self first is not only not a very smart partner to choose, but is also somebody who won't enjoy this stuff anywhere to the fullness of [his] capacity. That's one of the reasons I believe good tops start on the bottom.*
>
> —MITCH KESSLER

In conversations with practitioners, a recurring complaint was that rash newcomers and those who do not grasp the subtleties of slowly arousing erotic tension are likely to cause harm.

> *When I first entered into formal submission, I was back-shy. I had a bad experience where someone used a riding crop incorrectly across my shoulders, and as a consequence, whenever something touched my back, I would flinch and tense up.* —LAURA ANTONIO

Inflicting damage, even accidentally, is viewed with repugnance in D&S circles. Trust is the key component of all heavy play: The submissive trusts that the dominant knows how to use the equipment, knows when to stop, and does not cause undesirable pain. When affirmed, such trust deepens the couple's bond; abuses destroy relationships. The trust, however, goes both ways: The submissive has to know that the dominant will respect his limits, and the dominant has to know that the submissive will communicate what he is feeling.

> *I'm not a top with an agenda: "I'm going to beat your ass, then I'm going to make you kiss my boots, and you will call me master." No. That's throwing half of the experience away. Here's a new person. What's going to work with them, on them, for them?*
>
> —MITCH KESSLER

I am a responsible bottom. I don't want to feel pain! I want to feel pleasure-pain. So I let [my top] know when it becomes pain, so he can make it less intense or switch to another part of the body, or switch implements. —JEAN L.

Once the area being whipped is sufficiently stimulated, the dominant may select a more severe piece of equipment, again gradually building the intensity. This allows the submissive to stretch his pain limits and accept a higher degree of stimulation. As the severity of the blows increases, ensuring that none miss their mark is vital: Bad aim can cause serious harm.

The rule of thumb is that any area close to sensitive organs must be avoided. Thus, buttocks and upper thighs are preferred; the upper back, though popular, requires a conservative approach. Whipping skin to the point of cutting into the epidermis is known but uncommon, particularly in the era of AIDS and concerns about the dangers of disease transmission through open wounds. Serious injury or infection from whipping is virtually unknown in the D&S communities, where individuals educate themselves fully on the inherent risks.

Finally, many interviewees emphasized the importance of sobriety. Alcohol or drugs impair a dominant's judgment and physical abilities, and most players refuse to submit to anyone who is not in complete control of her or his faculties.

IMPLEMENTS

Virtually anything can be used to whip.

When I first started playing in private, my lover and I were using a rubber flyswatter, a rice paddle, stuff from the kitchen.
—MITCH KESSLER

In the D&S communities people typically either make their own equipment or purchase equipment expressly fabricated with safety and sensuality in mind.

I have a number of whips that were made specifically for my height and weight and the way that I balance. —LAURA ANTONIO

D&S couples often designate particular equipment for specific punishment scenarios or, conversely, for specific reward scenarios. For those who enjoy the ritualistic aspects of punishment, these designations may be crucial to their enjoyment.

Listed below are the major sorts of implements used by D&Sers in whippings. Over time most have seen scores of design innovations.

Birch: The slender, supple branch of the birch tree is popular among traditionalists and is used, singly or in a bunch, for stinging whippings.

Bullwhip: This tired cliché of sadomasochism is actually rarely used, because, unless the person wielding a bullwhip has seriously practiced technique, it will cause serious injury. A bullwhip consists of a single braided leather shaft, roughly six feet long at a minimum, and narrowing to a lash at one end. Some D&Sers may carry a bullwhip because they enjoy its shock value, others like to make it crack during scenes, but very few dominants will risk its use for whippings.

Cat-o'-Nine-Tails: Familiarly known as a "cat," this tool has a sturdy handle from which dangle "tails" (thongs) of varying lengths and densities. Materials include silk, deerskin, nylon, leather laces, and rubber. Real felines may have nine lives, but the contemporary versions of these whips seldom have nine thongs.

Crop, or Riding Crop: Used in horse training, the crop has a long sturdy handle that holds a flexible, narrow shaft usually covered in braided nylon or leather.

Devil's Hand: So called because it has several broad fingers, the devil's hand is a leather paddle.

Dressage Whip: Normally used to train horses in precision movement, this whip features a long, flexible shaft and a lash usually made of leather or nylon.

Feathered Bat: This type of paddle has a handle and a single shaft. The shaft is covered in lightweight leather flaps that resemble feathers.

Flexible Cane: Canes come in a plethora of styles and materials, from natural (bamboo) to synthetic (fiberglass), and may have a curved handle like a walking cane or may simply be a rod. For safe usage, a cane must be fairly flexible.

Penis Whip: A small cat with short handle and lashes. It is used for close whipping of limited areas, such as genitalia or nipples.

Quirt: This variation on a riding crop is tipped with a leather tongue.

Rope: This material is generally considered too mundane to serve as an implement for whipping. In bygone days, however, hemp rope—unraveled and stiffened in saltwater—was used to punish miscreants aboard sailing vessels.

Rubber Flogger: Rubber is a material of choice among many floggers, because of its high impact and the fetishistic interest in rubber. It is designed like a cat but has solid rubber tubes in place of lashes.

Scourge: This would be an identical twin to the cat save for additional embellishments: The tips of the lashes may be weighted with lead or beads, or the lashes may be knotted.

Slapper: This leather paddle originated in equestrian sport to deliver a light blow while startling the horse with a loud noise. Two long and heavy pieces of leather are sewn together at the handle. One piece of leather strikes the other upon impact.

Strap, or Belt: The original leather straps used for school discipline in Victorian times are now collectors' items. Modern replicas vary. Some people use leather belts instead of straps, but the advantage of the strap is that it has no attached hardware and therefore poses less risk of accidental injury.

Tawse: This leather paddle is made of a solid piece of heavy leather which is slit longitudinally at least once or more so that the implement leaves thin marks on the skin at each split.

INTERVIEWS

MITCH KESSLER

I'm bisexual. I'm switchable. Most of my primary relationships have been with women. There's an attraction to particular men and somewhere way down the list of importance, a general potential for attraction to men, but it's not as strong or as clear as my attraction for women. I'm more bisexual in S&M play, which I see as less intimate than genital sex.

My original reasons for getting involved in the New York S&M scene had more to do with the belief that the people who I would meet in that scene—very specifically at the Eulenspiegel Society—were somehow more intelligent, more articulate, better read, and morally superior to the people that I might meet in a bowling league. I'd say this belief is about three-quarters true. It has stood a certain amount of reality testing.

The friend who introduced me to the Scene and taught me my manners and a few other things, comments that the wonderful thing about S&M is it makes sex so complicated. I like complicated, complex sex. As far as I'm concerned, three quarters of an hour is a quickie. I also like group sex, and in many ways, the S&M that I'm into substitutes for that. I call D&S S&M largely because it's the older term that I'm involved in reclaiming. I really like to underscore the essential health and nonviolence of S&M. Whether you call it S&M, D&S, B&D, [or] fantasy roleplaying, it comes down to consent and sensuality, and play between lovers. This is essentially a normal set of feelings acted on by fundamentally normal, functional people.

People think that the sadomasochist can only receive gratification through [S&M]. I have not met many people of whom that was true; I have met a great many for whom this is part of what they do. My perspective is [that people shouldn't] be frightened by the word. If you pick up a flyswatter and paddle your lover's backside, this does not mean that in five years you're going to be dressing in black leather and pleasuring your lover with a cattle prod. People find their own levels. This is about pleasure and about communications. This is about all that good stuff that genital sex is supposed to be about. It's just another way of getting there.

[Someone once asked the] question: If, by some bizarre situation, the choice was giving up S&M or leaving the country, what would you do? Nobody could really answer that honestly, including me. If this avenue of expression were completely cut off, it would be a serious deprivation, but having been through the experience of readjusting to safer sex, I figure I could handle it. My initial reasons for getting into overt S&M play had to do with old age—the thought that this is a form of sexuality I don't have to give up. I remember a renowned dominant in New York who had a progressive nervous disorder which eventually took his life. All the time I knew him he was confined to a wheelchair. But he was able to function as a dominant psychologically and physically from that position. This means a lot in terms of the self-esteem that comes from sexuality.

There was a very long period when I internalized social norms concerning S&M, believing it had to do with bad things and funny clothes. It was not part of me, except [for] that little element of what a sophisticate would recognize. [For example,] a girlfriend who couldn't wait for her pubic hair to grow back so I could "forcibly" shave it off her, which would be followed by extremely hot sex. [Or] another who had such powerful orgasms that she "had" to have her wrists restrained with ropes. I did not think of any of this as having a name. These were just things about my partner that I came to enjoy and didn't think about it twice.

S&M has been very, very good to me. Because I am open, I have gotten a lot of public recognition from people who I want recognition from. It has done a great deal for taking the surreptitious power games of ordinary life and stripping away the camouflage. The whole idea of articulated consent has been very useful in relationships, whether in momentary relationships with a salesperson or a long-term love affair. [I now know] at a gut level that there is such a thing as consent to domination as well as a will to power. Also realizing that there is nothing inherently shameful in submitting has made it possible to yield an argument point more quickly than I might have before I got into this. I never practiced the skills of negotiation as effectively before doing S&M. If you can negotiate a sexual scene and say, "What exactly do you mean by that? What do you expect? What will you give in return?" you can negotiate anything. There's a lot of empowerment on a lot of levels; a lot of clarity that I wasn't able to get at through the psychoanalytic models. [And there is] increased self-esteem, increased self-assurance. And one other thing: Prior to getting involved in [S&M], I had a serious premature ejaculation problem, which vanished almost immediately when I started taking pain.

I'm dominant rather than submissive, largely because sensually, as well as psychologically, I have an aggressive and dominant personality. I am proud, willful, even touchy, with very, very strong will to power in my makeup. It is hard for me to give myself over to somebody else, and it's a lot easier to do it in the context of the rituals of S&M than, say, the rituals of the corporate world. It's easier for me to call somebody "sir" because I'm getting sexual pleasure from him than to call him "sir" because he signs my paycheck.

In terms of S&M, I guess my favorite is whip work, actually, flogging, flogger work. Let's talk a little bit about equipment. A whip allows you to reach out eight [to] ten feet. A cat is between 24 and 27 inches long. Twenty-seven inches long is a show whip for public. A bedroom cat might be 18 inches long. I'm getting fonder of the Western-style flogger, which is a big, bushy bundle of soft leather. It's a lot of thump, not a lot of bite, and people respond to this sensually rather easily. The real payoff is the sensual response of the partner. I get the most success with soft whips, but then, close on comes flexible paddles and doubled-over straps. "Pigs in the barn" is what I call it—imparting a rosy color to the shoulders or to the ass. [There's so much] sensuality involved in that: the wriggling, the [submissive's] enjoyment, the visual of watching the color change, the tactile of feeling the heat this produces, the kinesthetics of the swing and the hit, the verbal interchange that goes on. And under it all a feeling of power and of mastery of myself, of the situation, and of this person. That's something we [often] skip when we talk about this: The first mastery is of self.

These days, getting a beating is not one of the things I like best. I don't expect to be able to get as good as I am capable of giving. People travel great distances to be beaten by me because I'm very tuned into the responses of my partner. If they don't finish in a state of real gratitude and real subjection, I didn't do well. There aren't many people who can do that for me. There are people who are just plain able to absorb huge amounts of hitting. I cannot. If I am hit with the cane once, I will scream; I'm not playacting. To me, that is nothing but pain. A top can't just whale away at me and expect to get anything but my saying, "Cut that shit out." So I guess one of the reasons I like top rather than bottom is that it's a question of expectations. I don't expect to enjoy being topped as much as I expect to enjoy and give enjoyment when I top.

[Still] I'd rather bottom to the ideal top [than top the ideal bottom]. Bottoming is a direct sensual experience. The top is responsible for pleasuring me; all I have to do is experience it. Getting away from the hypothetical, the reality of my life is that I am lovers with a woman who is just about as good on top as I am and is very close to my idea of the ideal bottom when she wants to [be]. We have an egalitarian relationship outside of this and a switchable one in the context of S&M. We go through phases of fighting for top and fighting for bottom. Each of us wants more time being dominated or doing the dominating than is actually working out. This is not a complaint. It's a humorous observation about the give-and-take of a long-term relationship.

Somebody tried to buy the first whip I made off my hand in the middle of a scene. I made a few and sold them, and for a while I made whips out of nylon cord, because another hobby of mine is sailing. I spent a lot of time waiting for the wind and practicing knots. I used my marlin spike skills. I also remembered that getting hit with a coil of line could be a very moving experience—it could move you right overboard. So I started working with stuff based on looped nylon with turk's heads, and a French whip handle, which is still my basic look—the Sir Adam whip look. Then a friend wanted me to make a whip for him from deerskin. That was the first leather that I worked. Deerskin is a particularly difficult material to work with, because it stretches when you cut it. That took away my fear of working leather.

By this time I had something of a following. I put together a mail-order catalogue, placed a few ads, and did a number of things that people really liked. My central approach to building an implement of affection is [that] it's supposed to feel a certain way. It's supposed to be extremely sensual. When I make something out of cabretta leather, you can hit somebody with that anywhere but the eyeball. My first love in equipment building is for stuff at the sensual end, the mild equipment. I sell my equipment categorized by strength—mild, medium, and severe; some stuff is also marked sensual or atrocious. My lover's my partner in this business. One of our jokes is that part of the payoff, along with the money, is the ability to make so many people so happy. That is how I see what I do.

There's always something new to try, but in terms of having a specific goal I'm finding that, in general, my [real] interactions are a lot better than my imagination. I assume [that] my life will go on: I'm going to meet people, to love people, to play with people. I got into this never dreaming that this is something that I could actually like. I'm very fortunate; I don't feel deprivations in my life. I am with the lover I want to be with. I have no desire to change. I was once asked whether I'm more into men or women. My answer was, "I'm more into her." That is simply how it is. There isn't an unfulfilled desire or fantasy. Oh, I guess I'd like to neck with Sigourney Weaver. And—I even expressed it to him, but he wouldn't go along with it—I want to horsewhip Howard Stern.

GERRIE BLUM

At this point in my life D&S is central to my lifestyle. My friends are all within the D&S community. I have less in common with people I used to know who are "straight"—both the militantly heterosexual and the nonkinky. I guess I am following the advice of an old friend of mine, when he reached his 50s. At lunch one day he told me [that] both he and his wife were "shedding the shoulds." I think I am doing that in my life—not putting up with situations or people because I should, because that's what I've been taught. I have been redefining my life for the past five years.

I was divorced about 10 years ago. Today would have been my 35th anniversary. But I lucked out. I'm bisexual, with a preference for men. In D&S I'm switchable, with a preference for submissiveness with my partner, more inclined toward dominance with other people. [D&S] is the kind of recreational activity I can engage in with other people without actually having intimate sexual experiences as well. There are people that I may meet and [I'll] then be able to "play" with them in a nonthreatening atmosphere and do some roleplaying and express that side of me outside the bedroom.

Looking back, I realize that in many ways I was in a D&S-kind of relationship before, without having named it, without the actual S&M side of it being exhibited. There wasn't any spanking or hitting contact involved, but in my marriage, I was the '50s compliant wife.

I also remember an unpleasant aspect for me as a child in terms of being isolated as punishment. I remember punishments: being tied to the toilet seat. I'm still trying to correct some childhood errors on the part of my parents. I don't think I had what I could identify as fantasies or wishes about D&S or [about] transforming it into something more acceptable. It wasn't until after my swinger experience that I was open to S&M.

Swinging for me began at the turn of the '70s. I was not happy with the way my relationship with my husband was going. I felt that I was capable of more and that he was the inhibited and controlled one. What I did was to contact the man who had been my first lover at the age of 16. He was sexually experienced, socially sophisticated, he was even—although I didn't realize it [then]—a little kinky, and we had a relationship for a couple or three years. He opened my eyes sexually. When I was ready for something else, I contacted him again, and I was absolutely right. He introduced me to new areas of sexuality in a very slow and gentle way, first introducing me to one more woman, then one more man, then one more couple. The operating concept was making each other feel good. I look back now and realize his dominant role in all of this. In swinging I began to express a part of myself that I had kept repressed during my marital and child-raising years. I was now opening myself to other kinds of people and combinations and sensations that I found very pleasing and very positive. Also, as my marriage was deteriorating, I needed reaffirmation of my attractiveness, my beauty, my sexuality.

[When I went] back to the singles dating scene after my separation, I found, much to my chagrin, [that] things were as bad as they were in the '50s in terms of how women who had an interest in sex were treated by men. When I was a teenager in the '40s and '50s, there were good girls and bad girls. Then we went through the sexual revolution of the '60s and everyone was expected to go all the way all the time. Now [it was] the '80s. The fears about herpes followed by the fears and dread about AIDS were throwing people's mind-sets back to the '50s. [They were] much more judgmental about people who were sexually active. The attitude was that it was the men who wanted the sex and the women who were giving it; it was a bad bargain all around. My feeling was [that] "Sex is the friendliest thing two people do," but here I was back in the old mentality of "If you were that easy, you can't be very good, and if you're not good, I'm certainly not going to take you home to mother, but I'll fuck you anyhow." I did not like the way I was being treated or the way it was making me feel.

But then I met Mitch. He had had previous interests in D&S. So, with the same kind of slowness and gentleness that I had experienced with my sexual guru 10 years earlier, he led me very carefully. We met in September of 1984, so I guess 1985 was my introduction. First, it was a silk scarf around the wrists, another silk scarf trailing over my body while I was immobilized. He then exchanged the silk scarfs for soft ropes. We then put cup hooks on [my] bed frame, with the open end down, so that as long as I was maintaining the tension on the ropes around my wrists or around my ankles, they were taut and secure. But I knew that all I had to do was release the tension and I was free. I liked that safety factor while I was becoming acquainted with the feeling of restraint and immobilization. When I knew what he was about, I could turn the tables and do to him the things that I experienced. I severed my previous relationship with this old friend of mine and pretty much got out of swinging as a regular interest.

[Mitch and I] had an egalitarian relationship from the beginning, and he's very much the feminist. We started from an equal base, so that we can be submissive to each other, depending on what our own wants and needs are. We are not in a full-time, master-slave relationship. That wouldn't work for us. We have a full, well-rounded relationship. This is an essential part of it, absolutely, but of course we each have other interests that we share as well.

My favorite is probably when I'm the submissive and having things done to me and for me, but there are times when I will get pleasure and satisfaction out of pleasing him by doing things that he likes. For myself, hand spanking is always appreciated. We have some soft cabretta and deerskin whips that I love to feel all over my body. I don't respond well to straps or canes. The feeling is too intense.

One thing I learned years ago was that my pain threshold rises with my arousal level. What I might have perceived as painful when I was cold, if I'm really sexually aroused, if I'm really hot, that same sensation is erotic and stimulating, and not "pain."

One of the first things that we did to start our collection of various implements was to buy a braided whip. [It] was a gray suede, soft whip, and it was very expensive. Because of [Mitch's] sailing background, he started exploring the ideas of making whips out of various kinds of nylon line, which we brought to the clubs. It was very flattering to think that things that we had made for ourselves were also liked by other people. We popularized the concept of the white whip in New York, because that was the only color we could get nylon line in at the time. Coincidentally, it was also at a time when people were becoming health conscious. They loved the idea [that you can] throw it into the machine in a sock, and you can wash your whip.

It was really by popular demand that he was convinced to make something for someone in leather. And now he's fallen in love with leather and has become one of the preeminent leather whip makers in the country. We're delighted because the side benefits of this kind of business is that we bring joy to so many people. It's a very gratifying way to earn a livelihood; it has satisfied some very important things in both of us—being able to do well by doing good is very gratifying. To be able to enjoy work that is also appreciated by others, to me, is the best of all possible worlds. It's been very good for our relationship; it has given it a very firm foundation.

My philosophy as I've enunciated it to others before is that when I'm 94 and rocking on my front porch, I want to have many pleasant memories and few regrets. The regrets that most of us have are for things that we didn't do, so for me to have a fantasy that could never happen would be a waste of my creative energies. I would much rather think of some experience with my partner, who is an incredibly creative man.

Laura Antonio

I consider myself a gay woman. I embrace the word *dyke,* because lesbian seems too formal. Specifically, I am more a sadomasochist than anything else. By calling myself a sadomasochist [first] I have defined my lifestyle as centered around sadomasochism. My friends are into S&M; I will not take a lover who is not. My social activities mostly center around either S&M activities or my S&M friends.

I switch, but when I do I find it difficult to [switch] with the same person. I embrace dominance and submission on totally different levels. Sensually, I'm a masochist. I get off on pain. Emotionally, I get a tremendous charge, however, from being in charge. I don't think I'm more one or the other. I think of it all as a kind of journey. Along the way I can go two different paths. But I can't take both at the same time.

I wish I could say, "And suddenly I woke up and realized I want to be whipped," but in my own experience, I swear it's genetic. My earliest memories involve fantasies of power exchange. Before I could read, I was locking myself in my own closet. I put Barbie in bondage. I remember being fascinated and scared at a library when I was about six because I had found a book in the children's section called *Greek Slave Boy* and there was a flogging scene in it. I didn't know why I liked it so much. Neither did I know why I shouldn't tell someone that I liked it. My childhood is full of experiences like that, finding a thrill in literature or in a movie, liking bad guys. Bad guys always turned me on. David Copperfield's father—with the famous caning scene—drove me insane for years. [The bad guys] used power and trust to their own ends. Unfortunately, they did it maliciously. When the good guys did it, they almost always did it blindly, so to me it doesn't have the same satisfaction. But casting myself in the role as either the moustache-twisting, highly uniformed—uniforms have always been a fetish for me—bad guy or their troublemaking victim, straining in bondage, or even just getting the worst of a duel, has always thrilled me.

I was a precocious reader, and somewhere between seven and 12 I started reading very adult novels, particularly romantic novels of the "savage love" variety. My mother left them lying around, and I would pick them up and read them. They would be full of bodice ripping and incredibly long rapes that included very untypical rape scenes, like 20-minute sessions of cunnilingus. They always ended with the heroine having screaming orgasms, and I remember reading those and then going to the thesaurus to look up some words that they'd used that I didn't know. It was the thesaurus that led me to sadomasochism.

[At] about 14 I became a very radical feminist, mostly in response to an oppressive father figure in my home. I suddenly realized that all these fantasies that I had, whether I was top or bottom in them, were very, very politically incorrect. I remember reading *Ms.* magazine. A woman had written a short guilty letter about how she's a perfectly normal, wonderful woman in all ways except that she likes her boyfriends to paddle her ass before they have sex. The debate over that letter lasted half a year. I read every letter, taking every negative comment directly to heart. I didn't [even] know how to masturbate to orgasm yet. All I knew was that reading about this stuff, thinking about it, were pleasurable to me. Yet the women that I had singled out as personal heroines seemed to not support what I was thinking about.

Gradually, it took the realization that liberation means the freedom to choose. I realized [that] as long as I was not exploiting another person, then whatever I did in my lifestyle, public or private, only had to be okay with me. Once that was put away I was able to splurge and really go out and embrace S&M and look for it in lovers and other partners. [But the disapproval of other gay women] makes it real hard for me to get a date in New York.

During my first relationship with a woman, it was clear who had the power in the relationship. She was older, she had more money, she had a more independent lifestyle, and she was better at what we were doing. I loved her as you love someone who's teaching you something. I lit her cigarettes for her, drove her around, and more or less came when she called and went away when she dismissed me. She ordered the food at dinner and paid for it; I was almost a gentleman companion to her. She used to dress me in men's clothing. It wasn't until this year that I reembraced that particular aspect of my play. Now, it's become a very major part of what I do.

That relationship never became formal. We were just friends. We were doing girl stuff, and the sexuality of it, the power of it, were always dismissed. She was bisexual but primarily heterosexual, so she gave a lot of weight to her relationships with men. I grew dissatisfied with that, and we gradually grew apart. I haven't seen her since. She did, however, invite me to her wedding. Last year I got a call on my answering machine, and my first thought was, I can't see her in the arms of another man. I didn't [go]. I really couldn't.

After that, I got involved with the science-fiction crowd and was one of the few women there. I was not out as a lesbian. I ended up forming a relationship with a man who was younger than I and who, in many ways, was submissive to me, except in bed, where I would tell him what I liked having done to me. Because he was relatively sexually inexperienced, he was wonderful. He was willing to try almost anything. My relationship with him lasted about three years, until we realized something very important about each other. We were both really gay! We parted as friends and I still talk to him every once in a while.

I then went into a dry period. I was working full-time. I had started and ended a business with an old friend that didn't work out, and I was alone. I felt alone. I was scared to go out to what I knew were the two public S&M clubs in New York. I can't tell you why I was scared. I can't remember what I thought might happen to me if I went out to them. But I grew desperate. I really needed some sort of outlet. One weekend a friend of mine came to visit me, a man I'd known professionally. Over the weekend that he stayed with me, we came very close to some form of sex. He knew that I was into S&M and that was what I was prepared to do with him. But it didn't work out: We parted and went our separate ways. The following evening I was so frustrated. I realized that I would have slept with a man I didn't know very well [and] that I didn't like sleeping with men that much, but I was willing to do it in order to get that experience, just to feel the sensuality. I hopped into my car, drove into the city, picked up a copy of *Screw* magazine, read the club reviews, and immediately went to Paddles. And from that day on I was a public person.

At first I used a pseudonym. People who did computer sex and phone sex always told me, "If you ever go out in public, don't use your real name." The reasons for that were, presumably, that if you did, people would know who you really were and something bad would happen. Maybe they would blackmail you or come visit you at home when you were serving tea to Mom. I don't know. I gradually stopped using [the pseudonym]. That's why I agreed to use my own name with this interview.

So that was my journey toward being public. I have courage in places where courage really means something. I think of myself as a person of integrity. I don't lie. I think of myself as a person of honor. I don't think of myself as having battlefield courage but the courage to say who and what I am and stand by it and not apologize for it is very important to me.

I like whips and flogging. I have a large collection of whips. I have 30 of them. All of them are handmade and most of them by the same craftsman. I appreciate the beauty of a fine whip. I practice frequently. I like straps. I like a nice woodshed scene with "daddy's" belt or the razor strop. I like the sound they make, I like the sensation.

The most moving experience I've had to date was a night last year when I offered my formal submission to Sir Adam in public in a ceremony we created ourselves. He accepted it for a year and a day. For the occasion, a friend of mine gave me a beautiful floor-length black hooded cloak with a red satin lining. We had a stage. We had music written for the occasion, we made programs. We even had formal entertainment.

It was a really simple ceremony. We took an oath, one that Sir Adam particularly liked, out of *The Lord of the Rings*. The entire ceremony was based on a classic hero's journey. I was to enter the room, walk through the crowd. I was attended by a man who, then and now, wanted to be my submissive. I carried one of my personal whips. When I reached the stage I gave my whip to Sir Adam as a symbol of my giving up my dominance for him.

In many people's eyes, I did not literally belong to him. For one, our relationship was bounded always by the fact that it was an S&M relationship. He had a lover. I was not his lover. Neither was I his slave. I was his submissive. There were some things that people expected us to be doing with each other that we didn't do. I didn't perform household chores for him; I didn't live with him. He had no control over my professional life or my money. To a lot of people, these things are necessary for a D&S relationship.

I fantasize and dream about being able to have two relationships simultaneously, one where I am submissive and masochistic, and the other where I'm a sadistic dominant. One of my most powerful images is coming home late at night after a session where I have been bottom—my body is marked, I'm tired, [and] I'm so emotionally tense that I need relief. I could come home and have my bottom waiting to take my boots off, to attend me when I bathe, and then to service and please me, to feel their tongue washing over welts on my body. I think that is particularly hot. I'm going to work on making it happen.

A lot of the things that I've touched on—and the fact that I am a lifestyler—sometimes scare people. I get reactions like, "I could never do that," or "I don't understand how you could do that." The fact is [that] there are a lot of things I don't understand about other people and other people's lives. I don't understand how a woman could go through childbirth. This, to me, is a startling and scary thing to contemplate. Yet billions of women do it. People tell me that they couldn't be as dedicated to S&M as I am, because I'm dedicated politically, emotionally, and socially to it. Yet people are politically, emotionally, and socially dedicated to nonpersonally pleasurable things, like political parties and corporations. It makes a lot of sense to me that one should support and be active in that which gives [her personal] pleasure.

This is my life. I want to go as far as it will take me.

Thirteen

INTENSE
STIMULATION

*The woman's fingers felt his penis first of all, and then he guided her
fingers and felt the ring there at the base of it. At the touch of her hand,
however, the penis hardened and he cried out, because the ring pressed
into it and gave him excruciating pain.*

*The woman almost fainted with horror. . . . And at the same time
the thought of this penis bound and encircled by her ring roused her
sexually, so that her body became warm and sensitive to all kinds of
erotic fantasies. She continued to kiss him, and he begged her not to,
because it brought him greater and greater pain.*

—ANAÏS NIN[1]

WHAT ELSE IS THERE?

The countless forms of extreme sensory experimentation are impossible to
catalogue comprehensively. Kinsey allegedly chronicled thousands, yet his
work remained incomplete. Suffice to say, D&Sers regularly experiment with
several general types of intense stimulation.

Unlike the other chapters in this section, this chapter does not extensively discuss the psychological experience of the stimuli described. The

reason is simple: The forms of erotic play described here are merely further variations on the pleasures of discomfort. All the same enjoyments described in Chapter 9 pertain. We include excerpts from some of our interviewees profiled elsewhere so that their personal experiences help to explain the excitement of these unusual stimuli. At chapter's end, we focus on three individuals who experiment with intense play:

- Johanna, who is 22 years old and a graduate student in linguistics.
- John M. is 48 years old. He is a devoted music lover and a devoted father. He is married to Sara K.
- Sara K. is 48 years old and works in a university.

HOT WAX

The use of warm wax—dripped from a burning candle onto bare skin—is a slightly esoteric practice but has many fans. Hot-wax scenes usually are done within the context of a primarily sensual power exchange. Submissives who enjoy hot wax say that it causes an extremely erotic sensation, both because of the intermingling of heat with other kinds of stimulus and because of the unpredictability of exactly where the drops will fall.

Spreading oil over the skin before dripping the wax helps to prevent burns. White, undyed candles are preferred since dyes raise the melting temperature and the heat of the wax.

Once the wax hardens, some dominants use the blunt edge of a knife to scrape it off their lover's body slowly and meticulously. Although the use of the blunt edge ensures that the skin is not irritated, knowing that a knife is being used intensifies the sense of anticipation and danger.

Hot wax may also be a deep head trip. The submissive must place complete faith in the dominant's ability to ensure that the experience is sensual rather than damaging. Hot-wax enthusiasts we spoke with said that, properly used, the wax should neither scald the skin nor leave any marks. Dominants often experiment on themselves first to determine the distance the candle must be held from the body in order for the wax to cool adequately before making contact.

The first time that we used candle wax, it took a lot of trust. I was terrified that I was going to be hurt. I had to psyche myself into letting this man spill wax on me, which I thought was crazy. He slowly built up to the moment and finally took one of the candles and started pouring warm wax on my breasts. One holds the candle up a certain distance from the nipple. I could feel a little bit of heat but

no more than that. [Then] he kissed me. I was a bit thirsty, so he gave
me some water, from his mouth into mine. It felt really wonderful,
and I think it brought us closer. —VICTORIA

HOT ASH

The practice of dropping warm or hot ash onto a submissive seems to be
performed most frequently among gay men. Leathermen "flag" this orientation with a tan hankie. Typically, hot-ash fetishists are aroused not only by
the act but also by the body type and attitude of the dominant. Hot-ash fans
described the ideal dominant body type as a "teddy bear": a burly man with
abundant body hair. (Teddy bears have a sizable cult following throughout
the gay community.) He will smoke a cigar and, generally speaking, emanates
a traditionally macho aura.

As is the case with candles in hot-wax scenes, cigars are usually held at
a distance from the skin to prevent burning. Some hot-ash enthusiasts,
however, do seek a burning sensation. Hot-ash activities may occasionally
overlap with depersonalization fantasies in which the bottom is treated like
a human ashtray and accepts the ash over different parts of his body. For hot
ash to be one element of more complex play is not uncommon. For purists,
however, it is the main event.

CLOTHESPINS, CLIPS, AND CLAMPS

A popular element of heavy D&S play is the temporary compression or
pinching of sensitive skin. This is typically achieved by the use of clamps or
clips. Equipment may be left in place for brief periods of time to maximize
the stimulation. The D&Sers with whom we spoke stated that clips should
be checked every few minutes to ensure that the skin under stress does not
grow numb; extended, unabated clamping of a sensitive area, such as the
nipple, can cause minor nerve damage. Clips should not cut into skin or cause
significant irritation.

Compression is usually one element in a scene, and is sometimes an
adjunct to bondage. Stimulation ranges from very mild to very extreme,
depending on the period of time the clips are left in place, the clips' tension,
manipulation of the clips, and whether any attachments (such as chains,
which are tugged, or weights) are added.

Cottage industries produce dozens of gadgets. The most common
among these is the nipple clip, which in its crudest form is an alligator clip

whose teeth have been filed down and insulated with rubber; it may contain tiny screws to adjust tension. There are innumerable refinements to this basic design. Most commercially produced clamps are made of metal and are sold in pairs, connected by lightweight chain; the tips are well insulated; the styles vary in tension capacities, size, and weight. Some are customized for men and others for women (men's nipples tend to be smaller and can support smaller clips).

Despite the proliferation of relatively sophisticated options, many D&Sers prefer a homey alternative: the humble spring clothespin. Clothespins may be used sparingly or may be lavishly clamped over large areas of the body, usually the fleshy parts of the chest, the buttocks, and the thighs. Dominants arrange clothespins in rows or in other patterns.

> I love having clothespins put on me, and clips and clamps. We've gone up to 50 clothespins so far. I'm waiting to do 100. I like them on my arms, on my nipples, on my thighs, anywhere where my lover wants to put them. At a D&S club we've done some scenes with clothespins. [Once] I was talking to some people while he prepared everything. I was dressed sexily; plus I had cuffs on my wrists and ankles. He put some tables together [and] lit some candles. Then he made me kneel on two chairs that were pulled together [and] lie on my back across the tables. He attached ropes to the legs of the table so that he could bind my wrists and my ankles spread-eagle. He pulled down my bustier and blindfolded me. He started talking to me very softly to reassure me [and] caressing me with some feathers and getting me to relax. Then he took out the clothespins and the clamps and started working on my breasts. He took some alligator clips with the teeth shaved down and black plastic [insulation] on them so that they don't hurt my breasts. He put one on each nipple and then worked his way around the aureole of each breast. I had about five clips on each. There was a chain attached to the nipple clips, so that he could pull on it when he wanted to. He worked on my upper arms and then on my inner thighs. Occasionally he would stop and caress me and relax me and let me know that he was still there. He's very loving and gentle and has a very delicate touch. It feels really wonderful. One feels very trusting; at least one should. To me, it's actually lovemaking. While I couldn't see what was going on, I could feel it. Finally he was done. I was in a rather agitated state, because when you have clips and clamps all over, you start moving out of body. He took out a vibrator and pressed it up against my clit. I got very excited. He gave me permission to come, and as

I did, he took off the clips on my nipples, so that the orgasm was even larger. It is like being in bed with someone and they play with your nipples while you're coming. It's the same sort of sensation.

—VICTORIA

While many D&Sers enjoy clamps or clothespins on the labia, this can get tricky, as female lubrication may cause even tight clamps to slide off, especially when tugged or weighted.

CBT AND TT

Hot wax, hot ash, and compression play may also be incorporated into *cock-and-ball torture* and *tit torture,* known colloquially in the D&S community as CBT and TT. The basic principle of CBT and TT is to impose deep sensation directly to erogenous zones.

The intensity of CBT and TT activities range from fairly mild to very heavy. Great care is taken to ensure that only desired pain is inflicted. Genitalia and nipples are susceptible to irreversible damage under even moderate punishment, and D&Sers are cautious about these types of play. Some dominants may prefer to have the submissive's pubic region shaved in order to avoid mishaps with trapped hair.

CBT and TT are usually an aspect of a broader scene, however, many men (and some women) are specifically aroused by genital punishments (also known as *genital torture,* or *genitorture*), and some dominants focus on this aspect of play for an extended period. The majority of adult toys for CBT and TT are manifestly fabricated with male genitalia in mind; male genitalia are simply better suited for accessibility and accessories.

For those who enjoy genital compression, modifications are made to clamps to combine pinching with pulling. For example, a leash may be attached to the chain connecting strategically situated clamps and tugged. D&Sers sometimes attach weights to these chains, causing varying degrees of distention and discomfort. Those who are interested specifically in distention may use a *parachute harness.* This broad, circular swath of thick leather is snapped into place around the top of the scrotum, and weights are suspended from it to force the testicles downward and away from the penis.

Perhaps the most popular male adult toy is the *cock ring,* the descendent of the ancient Chinese silver penis clasp whose "purpose was to prolong erection by preventing the blood from leaving the engorged organ."[2] The contemporary version is a ring—usually made of steel, rubber, or leather, flexible or rigid—which is secured around the base of a flaccid penis. (Some interviewees reported that they have also experimented with rubber bands.) As the penis becomes engorged, the ring grows tight and prevents blood from draining back into the body. Cock rings have a dual effect: Erection is prolonged and sensitivity is enhanced. Both dominants and submissives may wear cock rings because of this serviceable duality.

Baroque refinements of the cock ring include a series of graduated rings known as a *cock cage*. Some cock cages are equipped with miniature hardware to lock the equipment in place; the dominant keeps the key. Variants of the cock cage are made of flexible leather or rubber straps.

A spectrum of leather gloves designed alternately to stretch and to confine genitalia are also popular. These gloves are usually leather sacks contoured so as to contain the testicles, the penis, or both. Some feature lacing meant to squeeze the penis and lift it away from the scrotum; some "ball sacks" are equipped with weights, and other models are studded with tiny metal spikes in the lining. The results can vary from a sensuously snug sensation to a mildly vertiginous squeeze.

In addition to the wearing of any of the plethora of custom equipment, CBT or TT includes all rough play directed to the erogenous zones. As noted in Chapter 12, small whips are used to concentrate pain in small areas. Some TT enthusiasts use the suction cups from snakebite kits to sensitize and engorge male nipples. Pinching, prodding, pricking, biting, tugging, slapping or spanking, abrading, and applying unguents such as mentholated balm that cause a burning sensation are all aspects of this play.

I've asked myself [why I like CBT]. I think the idea of torturing someone's genitals is so outrageous; it's such a personal, private, intimate part of the body. In psychological terms, it's the fear and humiliation and the helplessness. I don't think that attention to any other part of the body carries as great an emotional impact. Also, the balls are sensitive to crushing or to blows in ways [that] nothing else [could be]! I don't think that a woman could ever imagine what that feels like. Even when it's not painful, it has a whole-body effect on me. Interestingly, one of the first things that we did [was my wife] slapping my balls with her hand. The reason that it went as well as it did was, I think, because she had no conception of how intense that feeling was. She was unwilling to hit me with a whip or paddle because it would be too painful; yet she could slap my balls! . . . Restraints [put on when I'm flaccid] can cause very intense sensations when I get an erection. What may start off as nothing much can build—with no change in the force of the blows—into a most intense sensation. . . . Genital whipping has formed the heart of a plurality of my fantasies for close to 40 years. The single most fundamental[ly arousing] image is being bound and helpless with legs widely separated and being whipped aggressively directly into the crotch. Nothing else has quite this place in my pantheon of masochistic urges. When I have experienced genital whipping with a partner, it has been among the most intense of activities. —John M.

FISTING

Fisting is primarily but not exclusively popular in the gay and lesbian communities. The dominant slowly works first fingers and then hand into either the anus or vagina of his or her partner. Some feel that it is a safe-sex alternative when the fister wears a latex glove. Fisting is by no means limited to D&S partners and is seen by some as just a more intense type of penetration.

A growing number of bisexual and heterosexual D&Sers, and particularly those who have learned from gay and lesbian D&Sers, are experimenting with this activity. With adequate lubrication, fisting does not necessarily entail pain, but this depends on the recipient's ability to relax the appropriate muscles. Indeed, the goal is not so much to inflict pain as to induce ecstasy through this radical form of penetration.

Introducing *anything* into the anus however is a high-risk activity that may result in serious injury and hemorrhage. Torn tissue—not uncommon when the anus is invaded—is highly susceptible to infection and the transmission of disease.

Participants say that fisting is spiritual, sensuously profound, and even mystical because, as one D&Ser put it, "It's like reaching inside and grabbing someone's soul." Fisting has numerous psychological components: It may convey a sense of violation, erotic humiliation or helplessness. The fist is, symbolically and literally, a power symbol whose introduction into a body cavity has an enormous emotional impact and corollary sexual charge. And, unlike inorganic toys (such as dildos or anal beads), the hand's dexterity provides a unique thrill.

A very experienced partner can control his muscles to the point that there is an interesting sensation to my hand—which leads to a pleasurable sensation to my brain. I have a little playmate who likes to put his hands in my ass. He likes to be dominant over his partner, and he wants the partner to feel some pleasure. It is, when done properly, safe, as compared to anal intercourse, which could be a transmitter of the HIV virus. That's why he got into fisting. It is best to do it with latex gloves, not only because it can get a little messy, but because of the possibility of HIV infection. Cuticles have small cuts, and a person may bleed during the scene; how heavily depends on the person, the experience, how big the hand is. The more relaxed one is, the less problems you have. —JEFF BRITTON

I haven't fisted a man yet, but I have fisted women, vaginally and anally. The power and the eroticism behind that act is personally overwhelming to me. —LAURA ANTONIO

ANYTHING ELSE?

Numerous other forms of intense stimulation have gained currency among D&Sers. Among them are the use of nettles (to sensitize skin) and stinging unguents (applied to erogenous zones). Two specific forms of intense stimulation deserve special mention. Although they arouse heated debate in the D&S communities because of their potential health risks, both are widely practiced esoterica. These controversial activities are play piercing and electrical stimulation (also known as electro-torture).

PLAY PIERCING

Unlike piercing to modify the body, play piercing is temporary and is always performed in an erotic context. In a play piercing, sterile needles—often hypodermic needles—are usually inserted into the top layers of skin. These wounds heal without leaving permanent marks. The exception may be a play nipple piercing, where a slender sterile needle penetrates the nipple and is later removed without emplacement of jewelry. In S&M erotica—particularly in Japanese and German videos, which generally depict much more extreme and dehumanizing play than their American counterparts—the temporarily pierced submissive is usually identified as a "needle slave," and the piercings may be a form of punishment or may be symbolic of servitude. The term "play" is used only to distinguish it from more permanent piercings. "Play" does not, however, imply that such piercings are done casually. All penetration of skin entails the potential risk of infection or trauma and requires extreme caution.

In addition to play piercings to the erogenous zones, aficionados may want to feel the pricking sensation over wider expanses of skin, and some even prefer that the erogenous zones be avoided. Multiple piercings are common, sometimes arranged in patterns. The needles are left in place for short periods of time. Some dominants manipulate the needles with their fingers or attach strings to the needles and control the submissive's movements as a puppeteer would manipulate a marionette.

A moderately popular play-piercing device for male submissives is the *butterfly board*—a plank of soft wood placed under the scrotum with an opening for the genitals. Needles are passed through the skin of the scrotum and foreskin (not the underlying organs) and then are pinned to the board.

> *With play piercing you don't get a heck of a lot of pain. Somebody who's scared of needles would say, "Oh, God!" but realistically, they're not that painful. It happens in just seconds. Most people in play piercing want the needles to come out as quickly as possible. I want the needle to come out extremely slowly. I enjoy the feeling of the needle being taken out of my body. I almost consider permanent piercings mutilating your body. . . . I've had needles on my thighs, on the outsides of my arms, all around my breasts. I've had needles through the outer bottom edges of my nipples. Once somebody took a bunch of needles and created a necklace that started from my shoulders, went down around my chest, and ended at the other shoulder. She had me look in the mirror, and then she took them out. It came as a total surprise to me that I would be turned on by something like that.*
>
> —JEAN L.

ELECTRICITY

For safety reasons many D&Sers object to the introduction of electricity in erotic play. The risks are obvious: High voltage to the body will cause a fatal shock, and electricity—even of a low voltage—applied to the torso may interfere with normal heartbeat or cause a heart attack. Nonetheless, some D&Sers experiment with low-level electrical stimulation because of the unique sensation.

Electricity is often used in interrogation scenarios but may also simply be incorporated into D&S as another form of unusual or intense stimulus. Several interviewees reported that they have experimented with household 9-volt batteries to create a weak shock to skin.

So high and potentially lethal are its risks that electricity is both uncommon and generally confined to play with a few archaic, pseudo-medical machines. Even these, however, cannot guarantee safety.

We have a violet wand. *It's a static-electricity generator. It can generate an arc that jumps out at you, maybe a quarter of an inch at most. If you touch the skin with it, it has no effect at all, because the effect comes from the arc. It's a little tricky to use because you have to hold it away from where you want the spark to jump. It feels like a vibrating pinprick. I've never had a tattoo, but I imagine it might feel like that. It can be very intense if applied to a sensitive spot. It's supposedly safe to apply anywhere except around mucus membranes.* —JOHN M.

Considerably less common and far more expensive is the TENS (transcutaneous electrical nerve stimulator), a static-electricity generator most commonly used in medical settings to relieve chronic pain.

When you receive pain which you interpret as pleasure, there is a point that you find the most erotic. When you get into higher elements of electricity, it becomes pain. If you give somebody a strong jolt, they're going to jump four inches above the table! . . . My TENS unit is not plugged into the wall; [it] works on a little square battery [used] for portable radios. I got the TENS from a doctor who was into S&M and electricity. With a TENS unit, you can control how much electricity goes through the wires and the intensity. You can also control how close together the electrical impulses are [and] how long each [lasts].

My favorite is to have an electrical flow through the clitoris. I describe it as the best vibrator. Wires [from a TENS unit] are attached to little pads that have sticky stuff on them. I had one put on my clitoris and then one a little below the clitoris. The electricity travels up from the base of the clitoris. This is the spot on your body that has more nerve endings than any other, and [the current] travels, creating this incredibly wonderful sensation. The other device that can be used is called a Relaxacisor. It was created in the 1940s; I think [it was] originally created for use on submarines [where crews couldn't exercise. The thinking was] that if the muscles were forced to contract, they would not lose their strength. As always happens, people in S&M take things and use them in entirely different ways. —JEAN L.

INTERVIEWS

JOHANNA

I'm still pretty young. It's not that long ago that I was an adolescent. I'm still very visibly and noticeably growing, and [I'm] getting a chance to get what I want sexually. I think for anybody, getting what you want is the most empowering thing that could possibly happen, especially getting something that you've been told is shameful your entire life. Getting to do it anyway because it's what turns you on [is] incredibly empowering.

I never had a problem with [my D&S feelings]. I was raised as a feminist and consider myself a feminist. I know a lot of women have trouble coming to terms with [D&S]—especially heterosexual women who want to be dominated by men. I can understand why it might cause internal problems. But I felt a more external shame, knowing that everyone else thought that this was weird.

I'm a lesbian. [For me], being attracted to women is a separate issue from not being attracted to men. A lot of people don't see it that way, so I often feel weird identifying myself as a lesbian. It buys into a paradigm that I don't agree with. The fact is that I'm [just] not attracted to people who are male. I'm not intimate with women for political reasons. Women turn me on. I act on it.

I'm both a masochist and [a] submissive. I don't eliminate the possibility of wanting to be a top sometime in the future, but being a bottom is definitely what turns me on. It's only a couple of years since I first started having mild play with my lover at the time—spanking, a little [D&S]. I was much more into it than she, and that was tricky. More recently, I've been going to workshops and getting a lot of information. I [now] have a lover who is heavily into S&M. [S&M] is confined to sex play, although thinking about power in the way that you learn to think about it [as a result of] being involved in D&S makes me very attuned to the shifting of power in daily relationships.

I wonder if pain feels different to other people, because even in nonsexual contexts, pain does not bother me. I first started to notice this in high school. Perhaps the masochism is either physical or related to the organization of your perception. Sometimes pain feels like pleasure; [it's] physically exciting. It's like when you're masturbating: The idea that [your] hand is touching [your] clit may not be exciting, but the sensation is; sometimes [the sensation of] pain is like that for me. I don't have to be thinking about sex.

When pain [does combine with] mental arousal, there is a line between masochism and submission for me; then the idea that I'm in pain excites me, as well. The idea that I have to submit to pain [makes me feel] very submissive.

I did one scene with [my lover] where I got to do a lot of stuff that wasn't directly pleasurable for either of us, but it was very submissive. I licked her boots; she also wore a strap-on dildo—the kind attached to underwear—and had me go down on her with that. So she probably wasn't getting any direct physical pleasure out of it. Neither was I, but it was very submissive [and] a real turn-on to both of us. I like things like that just because they're kinky; that is a turn-on [in] itself. There's no hiding the fact that what's going on is a purely submissive act. I like that feeling. My present lover has done a couple of things to me like that: held me down and put a nine-volt battery on my tongue. She didn't have to hold me down; I wasn't struggling, although I don't like electricity—it scares me. But the fact that I don't like the sensation [and] yet I'm letting her do that to me is a turn-on.

A while ago my lover and I went to a party at her friend's house. It was not an S&M party, but she put a collar on me [and] a locked bracelet on my wrist before [we left]. The symbolism was heavy, and I liked that. I was getting progressively hotter, sexually excited, just having this stuff on me and being in this public situation. When we came home, she had me strip and tied my hands together and started whipping me. It was the first time I'd been whipped for any length of time. She whipped me until I started crying. That's the first time I ever got to such an intense point. She whipped my upper back, which is not usually where I prefer to be hit, until I was on the edge of being out of control. Then she started fucking me and put her finger up my ass. I'd never had that done before, and she didn't tell me she was going to do it. It triggered a really submissive response! If [she'd] asked me if I wanted her finger there, I would have said no. But I was very glad that didn't happen, because I liked it overall. We went back and forth like that for a while, and finally I yelled. Actually, I don't actually remember yelling, though I was sore the next day, so I believe her. All I know is that I was incredibly open to her and out of control, which was really nice. It was really nice when I almost reached breaking point, to hear her behind me going, "Yes!"

It was like a primal victory to get me to that point. [And] that someone wanted that from me was really nice and really helped. And then to be told, "Oh, you've been such a good girl! Now you can have whatever you want!" Then she went straight into pleasure stuff, instead of pain-and-pleasure play. I was really open at that point, physically and mentally, and she was able to fist-fuck me for the first time.

After resting a while I was [still] feeling very submissive, and she was feeling keenly dominant, so she had me go down on her and eat her out while she was whipping me. I thought it was great fun. It was incredibly kinky, and I liked the turnaround. I don't know if it's true for hetero couples as much, but a lot of times between women there is this thing where, if you're receiving pleasure, then you're the bottom. But she was still the top and still beating me, but I was giving her pleasure and making her come. I liked her "making me give her pleasure." That's the most intense experience [I've had].

JOHN M.

[Authors' note: We first interviewed John in 1991; 10 months later we did a follow-up with him, and at that time we interviewed his wife as well.]

1991: My whole background is one of a lot of sexual repression. Except for four years at [college], I've lived all my life in the South. At home, sex was something you just didn't talk about—*really* didn't talk about. One time that I managed to sneak something by my parents, my father took me to the family physician, where I got the story of the birds and the bees. [In] reading, I came across the word *rape* and looked it up in the dictionary, which told me: "illicit carnal knowledge," which was a big help! I approached my mom and asked, "What is this?" I think she said, "It's when a man makes a woman have a baby." Well, how can that happen? I mean, when two people get married, they have a baby, right? How can a man *make* a woman have a baby against her will? Eventually the bare mechanics came out. Because of my mother's extreme discomfort with the subject, the message I got from her was that sex was such a *shameful* thing! When I heard that this is what you do when you get married, my reaction was, "I will never get married if I have to do that!" Of course, even then I was having S&M fantasies. I didn't know what they were. I didn't even know what sex was; it had something to do with my penis.

The first woman I had intercourse with was the woman that I was later to marry. I was almost 26 years old. In the early days of that marriage I felt like for the first time I was free of all the sexual hang-ups. But our first child changed stuff around. Nothing was as easy, nothing was as free, and before long I ended up back in the same shape. There was one very small S&M event with my first wife. We had so many other things to explore that we just didn't get back to it. Now [that] I am remarried, we have been exploring. I'm a novice, though there's certainly been a lot happening within the last couple of years, due to some wonderful people that have come into my life: my new wife and my friends in an S&M support group.

My wife's even more of a novice than I am, not real comfortable with some of it. The psychological aspects of D&S are less comfortable for her even than whacking me with a whip. She's letting me push her a little. For example, I'll come up with an idea, and we'll do it. It ranges from me getting tied up and whipped a little bit to playing around with pins and needles.

I guess what excites me most is genital torture. I started off thinking that I wanted the pain. I found out that when I got out of fantasy and into reality that it hurts. Kind of obvious! But that didn't lessen my interest; I'd like to go further. But I'm not quite as sure anymore that it's actually the pain I want or something else that happens along with the pain. Or because of the pain. Or in spite of the pain.

Among my most exciting real-life experiences, the first thing that comes to mind is something that happened a year ago. It was accidental, which may have something to do with why it's memorable and exciting. We were playing around with this little whip that I made out of clothesline. I was naked and with my feet far apart and my hands tied behind my back. She was hitting me with some force. The end of the whip caught the tip of my penis and caught it pretty good. I hollered. My wife dropped the whip because it scared her. I said, "Grab it [the penis] and hold on," which is exactly what I would have done if my hands had been free. She did. At that moment I felt the most overwhelming feeling of love. It was terrific.

I haven't acted on my sexuality very much. What's caused me to change is [Sara], with whom I have had a friendship relationship for about 15 years. It took time, but eventually I got where I could open up to her about my problems and my hang-ups, my strange desires. It was a real healing force. I regret that I have wasted so many years . . . but better late than never.

1992: A number of things have happened this year. One of them is that my relationship with my wife has gotten to the point where there's very little now that she isn't willing to do to me. I think it was just a matter of getting comfortable with it, beginning to understand that sometimes pain is not pain—it's something else, too. And to trust that when I said I wanted her to whip me, that's really what I meant. I wanted it to hurt. It's a hard thing to believe sometimes.

At first, Sara was uncomfortable and uncertain, [but] I think it was always her intent to be supportive. [Now] we can do some fairly heavy scenes. I think she has come to see this process as one which she has an interest in and a stake in, also.

Since we talked [last], I have developed an immensely higher comfort level with this sexuality. I've come out to my brother and sister. [My daughter] expressed not a great deal of surprise and not a great deal of interest when I warned her and her boyfriend about some videotapes of porn that they might find in the back of the cabinet. She thought it was okay:

"Whatever turns you on." She and I have a fairly deep relationship. We've always been pretty open talking about sex.

All of this had really given me a whole lot of confidence. I'm not ready to hang up a whip on my wall at work—not quite!—but I do wear a leather armband virtually everywhere now.

[My wife] can tie me up quite thoroughly and whip me till I'm screaming. I also like sharp-pointed things in certain sensitive spots. She's willing to make me jump and squeal with needles, and she has a very sharp pair of tweezers that she has fun with.

More and more since we've been able to really get into stuff, we've gotten into cock-and-ball torture of various sorts. That includes putting on clothespins and pliers and even alligator clips to pinch. Cock-and-ball torture and genital torture generally have been part of my fantasy life since I was a kid. When I was growing up, there were some little kind of thorny things— we called them sandspurs or bulldogs. I used to thread them on a string and wrap them around my penis. I remember one time I got a pair of underwear and put a bunch of these inside. That turned out to be a little too much, but I then took an old pair [of shorts] and cut a flap where the crotch was so that it wouldn't be tight—it'd just rub and bounce. That worked out real well.

I think we have a ways to go before we really have a good D&S dynamic in our play. What lacks [now] is me feeling submissive. I feel that very rarely with my wife. [She] knows it. That's one of the real strengths of the relationship: We talk very candidly about all this stuff. I'm hoping that it will come simply with increasing comfort. I'm hoping that we will begin to spend some more time on the head-trip aspect and not just on what you can do with the body.

I think the secret of our success is simply that we have a very open relationship; we are as honest with each other as we know how to be in all areas. We talk about sexual matters very easily and openly, and very often when we have had some D&S play, we'll go over it later on [and] talk about it. It's really helped us.

SARA K.

[Before meeting John], I was aware that this sort of stuff went on. In fact, I had a relationship with someone who probably would have liked this sort of thing, though we did not do very much. I'm not quite sure how this information was conveyed to me, but I knew that he would like to be whipped. I was very reluctant to do that sort of thing. My own sense of myself is of a person with needs for power, and I find this scary. So seeing myself as someone who would like very much to dominate other people [is something] I try and step back from.

At a certain point John was willing to share with me that he had fantasies which involved mainly submission. I had a mixed response. At times some of the things that he might fantasize about people doing, or even himself doing, were repellent. Some other things were just interesting.

I was initially willing to try bondage and had interest in both directions—not only in binding but in being bound. When I was a preteenager a male cousin and I had a game of tying each other up. The idea was to see who could tie someone up so that they could not get loose. I recall enjoying that game and being good at it and able to tie [him] up [so] that he could not get loose, whereas he could never do that to me. So the idea of bondage as such probably was not as strange as it might have [otherwise] been.

In fact, I remember somebody actually doing that years ago and my finding it scary. What was scary about it was being helpless, because there have to be levels of trust in these things. If you are not trusting, then it is another kind of experience. I am mistrustful of people and the possibility that they might misuse the situation. With my husband, what happened was that he talked about it, [and] I said, "Okay." I brought out some ropes; I think he was surprised. I'm sort of amused by a lot of this. I can't say that there's a big sexual charge, but there is certainly some amusement.

I'm interested in dominance, but I'm not interested in sadism. The idea of hurting somebody is not appealing, even when they want to be hurt. The idea of causing welts and stripes and blood really is not especially appealing. These are things that my husband has liked to have happen to him. I think he still has trouble asking for something of that sort. He knows that I am uncomfortable with it. I'm more willing to experiment with different accoutrements, more willing to keep going—instead of five slaps, 15. So both in terms of variety and intensity, I'm willing to do more . . . and in the process I am probably causing more pain than I might once have, having realized that it's not terribly dangerous.

Our whole culture tells women that you don't cause pain, that you're nice. So there does seem something wrong about standing in front of someone who can't protect himself, with crops or paddles or whips, and causing hurt and seeing the physical evidence of that. [I still feel that way] at times. One of the things that I try to do is get a reaction without [inflicting] a lot of pain. You can wallop the hell out of somebody, or you can strike them in a sensitive place, not especially hard, but in ways that get a reaction. I try to do the latter. [My husband] would like both. He was delighted [once] when I was annoyed and hit a little too hard. He wandered around for a week with welts and bruises. I was not happy about that. I thought that was a loss of control on my part. He thought it was wonderful.

While I might be the dominant, my husband is the leader. He's the one who has taken us to this, and [he] knows far more about it than I do. I appreciate that, because if it were left up to me, we wouldn't do it. And I would like to go on exploring. His interest in these things has been aided and abetted by outsiders who have, I think, given him permission to do things that he originally might not have thought he could. He was then able to come to me with this and say, "This might be okay. Is it really okay?" I've been very supportive. I might not always want to participate in something, but I feel that it's important that he tries to explore what he can, and I'll do what I can.

SECTION FOUR

INDIVIDUALIZING THE BODY

Fourteen

BODY
MODIFICATION

"There is one thing that all we women know . . . we must labour to be beautiful."

—W. B. YEATS[1]

W hat do the popular entertainer who flaunts colorful tattoos, the woman who gets breast implants, and the man who has several rings pierced through his penis have in common? They are all practicing body modification.

The practice of modifying the human body has endured since before recorded history. The forms and methods of alteration are countless; fashion, cultural, and religious practices have dictated variations in placement, style, degree, and type. The alterations have ranged from the mundane to the extraordinary.

The eroticization of tattooing, scarification, branding, or piercing is called *stigmatophilia,* from the Latin for "love of a mark or brand." Although body modifications aren't necessarily adjuncts to erotic stimulation, they cannot escape identification with the erotic. Among D&Sers body modification is often a unique means of combining the aesthetic with the sensual. In this chapter, we profile Fakir Musafar, perhaps the most audacious body-modification advocate today. A shaman and master piercer, Fakir was born Roland Loomis in 1930 in South Dakota. He holds a degree in electrical engineering and a master's degree in creative writing; he has spent much of his life as an advertising executive. He has developed his expertise through research and over 40 years of personal practice of primitivistic body ritual. Fakir publishes *Body Play* magazine. He is married.

WHEN DID IT BEGIN?

The archaeological record amply demonstrates the ubiquity and antiquity of body modification. Representational art reveals that various South American Indians pierced their septums with a number of rings or elongated their earlobes with ear spools, as shown in effigy vessels and figurines made prior to European contact. Neolithic cave paintings in southern Europe depict hands with missing fingers, offering a tantalizing clue as to the antiquity of ritual amputation, which historically has occurred over much of the world. Human burials have yielded plentiful proof of body modification, from jewelry fashioned expressly for modification—earrings being among the most common—to the visible alteration of the human form, such as cephalic deformation, or changing the shape of the skull during infancy. There are far too many examples to enumerate here.

Historically, travelers' tales and the works of ethnographers and anthropologists have shown that body modification is virtually universal. People tattoo their skin, file their teeth, elongate their necks, burn or slash patterns into their skins, constrict their waists: Few possibilities have been left unexplored. In general, motivations to alter the body fall into four broad categories: the magical or spiritual, the medical, the cosmetic, and the erotic.

In some cultures body modification had an ostensibly aesthetic purpose. For example, beginning with the T'ang Dynasty, the Chinese bound the feet of some female children. The smaller the adult foot, the more dainty and desirable its owner. Modifications for religious purposes are abundantly evident in many cultures. In some faiths adherents bear a "mark," or brand, even if only symbolically (such as the ashes smeared on a Catholic's forehead on Ash Wednesday). Christ's stigmata remain one of the more powerful images in Christian iconography, appealing, perhaps, to a fundamental human impulse to make visible one's sacrifice. Making one's spiritual condition manifest is a reason frequently cited by contemporary body modifiers to explain their interests.

> *Amidst an almost universal feeling of powerlessness to "change the world," individuals are changing what they do have power over:* their own bodies. . . . *By giving visible bodily expression to unknown desires and latent obsessions welling up from within, individuals can provoke change.* . . .   —V. VALE AND ANDREA JUNO[2]

Some modifications done originally for religious purposes were coopted by modern medicine. Circumcision is a magical-spiritual rite practiced by peoples as diverse as tribal Africans, Aborigines, Jews, and Moslems. For a time it was a common practice in many American hospitals to circumcise newborn males, although no health benefits have ever been proven.

Historically, body modifications for men usually represent a rite of passage, whereas women's bodies are most often altered to signal or to enforce social subjugation. Male body modifications have rarely interfered with normal function (there are, of course, exceptions); women, conversely, have been severely limited, sexually or physically, by the physical alterations, many of which were forced upon them. Most notable are the clitoridectomies and vaginal infibulations still practiced in East Africa and parts of Asia.

Among contemporary Americans modifications are usually an aesthetic choice, but, particularly for self-styled pagans and New Agers, the process may be symbolic of a spiritual transformation.

The piercing and tattooing enthusiasts whom we interviewed typically described the process of body modification as emotionally intoxicating. They claimed that the unique stimulus of their ordeals sometimes results in out-of-body experiences.

WHAT IS IT?

In one way or another nearly everyone in our culture practices body modification, but some modifications follow culturally accepted models, and others do not. The man who has hair plugs implanted in his scalp and the man who chooses to have a ring implanted in his nipple, while seemingly quite different, share the desire to alter and the willingness to endure pain.

Basically, body modification is an alteration of appearance, usually entailing some degree of discomfort. Methods used to modify the body include perforation, incision, removal (complete or partial), cauterization, insertion, abrasion, compression, staining, distention, enlargement, adhesion, and diversion.

Arnold Schwarzenegger is perhaps America's most conspicuous and admired specimen of the laboriously self-designed man. The interest—enlargement of muscle—and its corresponding philosophy ("no pain, no gain") has kept generations of earnest bodybuilders pumping iron. Similarly, fashion magazines, which exhort women to "create a new you," appeal to the same urge to improve and modify the body. There is nothing new about this. *The Kama Sutra* describes a long list of substances intended to change a woman's appearance, including natural ointments, powders, oils, and pigments. Men, meanwhile, are advised in diverse methods of annointing their members with exotic concoctions to increase prowess and "subjugate" their female conquests. And, if more dramatic results are desired, they may enlarge their organs by following complex prescriptions which include rubbing the penis with, among other things, "the bristles of certain insects that live in trees."[3]

The ancient Egyptians had an avid interest in specialized cosmetics, which rival the dermatological formulations of swanky skin salons. And in *The Art of Love*, written in the 1st Century B.C., Ovid advises women,

> With wax you know how to whiten your skin, and with carmine to give yourself the rosy hue which Nature has denied you. . . . Those famous masterpieces of the sculptor Myron were once but useless, shapeless blocks of marble. If you want a ring of gold, you've got to hammer it into shape.[4]

Periodically, women's cosmetic gimmicks have been censured. A law in ancient Alexandria, for example, chastised women who deceived potential grooms into marriage by cosmetic trickery. In the 18th Century the British Parliament debated legislation which stated,

> . . . all women . . . who . . . seduce or betray into matrimony any of His Majesty's subjects, by the scents, paints, cosmetic washes, artificial teeth, false hair, Spanish wool, iron stays, hoops, high-heeled shoes, bolstered hips, shall incur the penalty of the law in force against witchcraft . . .   —R. BRASCH[5]

Nowadays, those who can afford pectoral or breast implants, liposuction or tucks, or any of the dozens of other common elective surgeries and procedures, are more likely to be envied than shunned, despite the fact that some of these procedures are medically dubious, if not actually deleterious to continued good health.

WHY DO PEOPLE DO IT?

Humans have an irresistible urge to improve on nature's design. Body modifications have come into and fallen out of favor throughout history, but the majority of modifiers have sought conformity with prevailing tastes.

> *With plastic surgery you conform; with tattooing you individualize.*
> —THE DOCTOR

We in 20th-Century America condemn some and condone other types of modifications; at previous times and in other places, different standards applied. Breaking a nose and sawing off cartilage to construct a snubbed proboscis is currently sanctioned; inserting jewelry in a penis to heighten sexual response is viewed with horror. Thus, while piercing and tattooing are usually less physically traumatic than rhinoplasty, these practices are conventionally viewed as barbaric or unsavory while a "nose job" is chic.

Euro-American culture generally has esteemed modifications that reverse or stall the effects of aging. They reflect a wish, conscious or unconscious, to thwart mortality and to attain a cosmetic ideal. The 1990s American line of demarcation between the valued (such as face-lifts) and the deplored (such as scarification) is crossed whenever the modification in question gives expression to a mystical or a sexual force. One can easily imagine that if a pierced nipple made one look younger, millions would be sporting nipple rings, and proudly.

Stigmatophiles do not necessarily seek to regain youth by modifying their bodies, and their understanding of beauty is often idiosyncratic. This may partly explain why many contemporary body modifiers affiliate with Eastern or tribal philosophies. Body modifiers describe their activities as an intensely personal statement (for example, an expression of some interior reality), a powerful spiritual urge, or a physical challenge.

> *Placing earrings in your nipples or in parts of your genitalia [is]*
> *. . . reclaiming your body. The change, the new awareness that you*
> *have of that part of your body simply because there is now an*
> *ornament attached to it, a piece of jewelry, is a really radical thing.*
> —ROBIN YOUNG

HEALTH RISKS

Body modifiers and cosmetic surgeons alike argue that the psychological benefits of modification outweigh the physical dangers and discomforts.

People who opt for expensive cosmetic surgeries assert that the pain and risks pale in light of the potential for an improved body image. (Whether an inflated bust line or gargantuan pectorals denote genuine improvement is open to debate.) Similarly, a piercer is likely to believe that his jewelry improves the quality of his inner life and gives him an intrinsic psychological reward. Medically speaking, however, all forms of body modification—including temporary cosmetic changes—carry a degree of risk (as anyone who has developed an infection from using mascara can attest).

While we take a sympathetic look at the practices described in the following chapters, we note that each is risky. The potential for irrevocable damage to delicate tissue is great. Permanent damage to reproductive and other organs may occur. Furthermore, even a mild infection can become life-threatening if untreated. A piercing or a tattoo is a wound and must be treated as such. Aftercare is crucial. A doctor or other qualified specialist must be consulted.

INTERVIEW

FAKIR MUSAFAR

I guess the most important thing [I'd like to get across] is that no avenues of exploration about the body-spirit connection should be callously discounted. Everything in our culture is changing very rapidly. A lot of views [which] might have seemed inappropriate fairly recently should be given a second look. Right now, [many] people between the ages of 20 and 30 are finding new ways to reclaim their bodies, to do their own rites of passage, to do group rites of passage. The means are different—it may be piercing, it may be tattooing—but all change the physical body and affect the way the world perceives you and you perceive the world.

Young people have begun to discover that they can explore life and achieve a great deal of self-knowledge by using their bodies. They're going at it full-bore. One of the first things they started to do was [to] tattoo the body. They didn't go for the daggers and the hearts and the roses; they tried black work, primitive motifs, very bizarre and strange tattoos that covered a great deal of body area. Almost simultaneously, the revival of body piercing came about. I remember sitting in the back of a Los Angeles restaurant 16 years ago with a handful of people. We all had piercings; most of us had pierced nipples. At that point we could count up only seven people in the world who had pierced nipples. Since then I personally have probably pierced thousands.

I've had the good fortune of not having to tone down what I say [in lectures to college students]. I can be passionate in what I'm doing and lay out what I really feel with the kind of audiences I've had. Number one, I've got a totally sympathetic audience with anybody into S&M. Two, [with] anybody that's broad-minded or sexually liberated in any way whatsoever, I can be pretty freewheeling and frank. Three, there are young people who don't have all those hang-ups. They're ones who distrust banks, who don't think politicians know what they're doing: They have a history of disenfranchisement. Still, the bulk of people out there are probably not that sympathetic. I've learned to talk to them somewhat the way I did in [the film] *Dances Sacred and Profane.*

In the film, I approached the subject from the standpoint of spiritual exploration, spiritual discovery. Joseph Campbell was probably more radical than I am, talking about most of the things I'm talking about. But he framed it in an acceptable way. He actually made a scathing indictment of Judeo-

Christian tradition as it's practiced in this culture. It was incredible what he got away with. But he *knew* what he was talking about, he knew how to say it, and he found a sympathetic ear.

I had a hard time for a long time finding anyone who followed what I was trying to do or say. I kept looking. The only place I found people free enough, exploratory enough, who had broken down a lot of programming—who could understand this or who had been exploring it—was in the world of S&M. They had discarded body taboos and a lot of cultural garbage to do S&M. I found my niche. I found that, in a sense, everything I had been doing since age six always had S&M overtones. [Now] I've been a practitioner of S&M with other people for many years. Oddly, most people think of Fakir as a bottom because he hangs in trees with fleshhooks. That isn't necessarily so! For the most part, Fakir is a top.

Playing with intense sensation is what people do in S&M for the most part. That is what we do in rituals and in piercing and in tattooing. Many people have found that this is a way of opening up their body-spirit connection. When one goes about this consensually and takes intense physical sensation in an expected way, they find that they can separate the body—which is feeling sensation—from the spirit in[side] the body. They're expanding their consciousness, their understanding of life. I have found that I can get into an altered state that can be used for many things, including healing.

Let's say we're going to inflict intense physical sensation—we're going to pierce 100 steel rods into my chest and back. At first this will be very unpleasant, but soon, if I'm in the right state and I've made the right preparations, my body's endorphins—natural opiates—kick in, just like a lot of people in S&M find when they're being whipped. It builds and builds until finally you achieve a euphoric state. This is not pain: Euphoria and pain are opposites. Intense physical sensation can be either.

If a shaman and magic are present, ecstasy can be led into an altered state of consciousness in which physiology is subject to change; it is malleable. Native American cultures have used this in healing for a long time. It's been used all over Southeast Asia, Tibet. Deliberate, ritualized infliction of what we would call pain—or what I call strong physical sensation—can change the relationship of the body and that which lives in the body so that some kind of physical transformation is possible.

Intense physical sensation creates body focus. [Normally] your attention is scattered, diffused. There are different ways to focus it: There's headfirst focusing. An example of that might be Zazen meditation. You sit very quietly and deal only with what's going on in the mind. When you finally achieve some state of clear consciousness, your attention is focused in one direction. [A second way] is by devotion, as in Western religions: You get all your attention focused into the love of Jesus. You're then able to do things in life that you couldn't do with unfocused attention.

The third way is the body-first way. This is the way of the shaman and the fakir. By using some kind of intense sensation in the physical body, you focus all concentration on one particular space in the physical body. After that, you can take the attention and make it go inward to explore your inner space. Your attention cannot wander when you're doing something intense. [And] when your attention is this focused, it's possible for something to happen. You may direct the attention into another sphere of consciousness. Shamanic activity for the most part is intent on body focus.

One of the neat things about the body-first approach is [that] the important element you have in the body system is sexual energy. This is the problem I've had [doing] Zen meditation. I always kept getting to a point where I was spacing out. I was getting the desired result, but always behind me was other baggage, and I didn't know what to do with it. What happens if I got turned on? They give you no provision for this. The same thing is partly true for devotional systems of controlling your psyche and body. The missing ingredient in most of those systems is sexual energy. In body-first [focus], that's the first thing you deal with. If you create a body focus and it isn't erotic, this isn't going to work very well.

Tattooing, piercing, branding, sculpting the body by putting ligatures on arms and legs, corsets and belts around the midsection, [all] cause a change of body state. This is a deliberate and usually ritualized change. One result is that you [may] get familiar with your body. You have control over the body. The body is responsive and plastic; it essentially conforms to the aesthetic ideal of the spirit that lives in the body. The body-spirit connection becomes clear and sharp through any form of body modification. All forms of body modification require commitment and some acceptance of physical restrictions and limitations. These may not last forever, but one must accept those to get to the other side.

Fifteen

CORSETTING

W ho can forget the image of Scarlett O'Hara being tightly laced into her corset, nearly fainting, and yet gladly suffering for the sake of reducing her waist another inch? While some people today may consider corsets a quaint fashion anachronism, growing numbers of both men and women happily are enduring the rigors of corsetting. While their reasons vary, most agree: They find the corsetted figure sexy. And, as a method and infliction of control over the body and shape, corsetting lends itself very well to D&S. Corset training has been a staple of D&S erotica and practice for a century or more.

In this chapter we hear from a number of tight-lacing enthusiasts and feature profiles of:

- Jenny Lane, who is 54 years old. She is married and has three children.
- Alexis DeVille is 39 years old, and is a preoperative male-to-female transgenderist. Ms. DeVille is a gender transformation consultant, has lectured on corsetting and fetish dressing, and works as a professional dominant.

We also include some thoughts on corsetting from Fakir Musafar, whose corsetting innovations have literally transformed the bodies of hundreds of men and women nationwide.

THE LONG AND
THE SHORT OF CORSETS

Corsets have played a central role in the public history of fashion and the private history of the boudoir. They have also been the inspiration for contemporary ladies' undergarments. The first brassieres were invented to support breasts when corsets in the early 20th Century were cut low. When corsets were cut higher at the waist, girdles were introduced. The corset is both an expression of extreme femininity and a repression (through restriction) of the body. This garment, which boldly exaggerates stereotypical feminine curves, does so by rigorously confining the torso.

In the past, psychiatrists perceived the erotic interest in corsets as uniquely a fetish activity, often entailing extreme masochism. Stekel detailed several cases of corset fetishism, including that of a "well-educated and respectable man, the father of four healthy children, happily married":

> *He often tried to lace himself so tightly that he would faint, but in this he was unsuccessful. He even succeeded in persuading his wife to lace herself closely and tied her corset tighter every day himself until her waistline had been reduced about six inches. This also gratified him sexually.* —WILHELM STEKEL[1]

The corset holds a unique place in the erotic aesthetic of many body-modifiers.

> *First there is the payoff of being different, of being attractive, [and] having a more idealized shape. Then there is the erotic side of the coin. The people who pursue this in a big way also find it is sexy.* —FAKIR MUSAFAR

The first documentation of a prototypical corset dates back to circa 2000 B.C. Pictorial depictions of the people of Minoa, Crete, show both genders wearing tight, wide belts which compressed the wearer's midsection, giving men and women alike a wasp-waisted look. The belts also lifted and enhanced the female bust line.

Other ancient cultures that have practiced similar forms of waist modification include the Dinka people of Africa, whose males still wear beaded corsets to designate age status.[2] Waist reduction was also practiced among the Ibitoe of Papua, New Guinea: Young men wore a cinching belt of rigid material as part of a rite of manhood. Men with dainty waists were objects of beauty.

The rigid modern corset traces its origins to a significant innovation in European corset styles sometime in the middle 16th Century: the introduction of busks, rigid supports sewn into the front of the corset. The busks were first made of wood and were presumably arduous to endure.

In the late 17th Century, corsets—traditionally long—were cropped above the thighs, and small waists became the rage among fashion plates of both genders. Women's corsets were structured so as to force the breasts upward. Even officers in the French and British armies engaged in tight-lacing. Military uniforms were tailored to emphasize attenuated masculine waistlines.

Corsets fell out of favor in the late 18th Century only to regain popularity in the early part of the 19th Century, when wooden busks were replaced by supports made of whalebone and metal. The corset was an essential component of women's dress throughout the 19th Century, despite warnings from physicians and many women against tight-lacing, which continued for over 100 years. Tight-lacing was blamed for damage to internal organs and for inducing miscarriages. The severe 19th Century corset often interfered with respiration, and corsets were a frequent cause of the "vapors," which dispatched Victorian women to fainting couches. Yet the appeal of a slender female waistline was firmly established in the Western cultural aesthetic, and so the corset remained a fashion fixture well into the 20th Century.

In the early 20th Century a Parisian couturier invented the "slim line," which emphasized a natural shape. Whalebone was soon replaced by insulated metal stays.[3] By this time, a broad variety of styles and materials were used in corset designs. During World War I women allegedly donated enough metal from corsets to the military cause to construct two warships.

The corset seemed to be threatened during the 1920s, when flappers popularized boyish figures and a minimum of restrictive wear. Perhaps one could take womanhood out of corsets, but apparently one couldn't take corsets out of womanhood. In order to achieve the slim, no-bulge ideal of the 1920s, well-endowed women tight-laced to fit the fashionably boyish silhouette.

The 1930s brought a renewed interest in corsets. Plump hips and ample breasts were once again au courant, especially in counterpoint to slender waists, and the hourglass figure came into its heyday. In this decade the Dunlop Rubber Company first began experiments which led to the development of Lastex, a latex end product. With the vastly increased comfort of an elastic garment, the corset's popularity once again mushroomed. Another company, Warner Brothers, introduced the "roll on," an elastic corset with lighter control and two-way stretch, which could be pulled on; boning was replaced by heavy stitching or doubled material. Hooks and eyes lost favor when the zipper was invented in 1931.[4]

Today's lingerie catalogues and music videos are full of frilled facsimiles designed to accentuate bosoms, flatten abdomens, and flatter other assets without actually causing changes to the body's shape. For the purist the traditional styles of Victorian and Edwardian corsets, employing tight laces and boning to create a long-lasting change in body shape, are deemed most desirable. Contemporary versions, however, are more adjustable and comfortable.

The best-known American retailer catering to today's serious corset enthusiast is B.R. Creations, which specializes in fanciful designs in sensual fabrics. B.R. obtained corset patterns from Fakir Musafar, who began to take an interest in corsets in the 1940s. By the 1960s he had turned his personal interest into a business. He launched an intensive study of contemporary body types and created patterns designed for the modern figure.

> [I] started a corset company in 1960. It only lasted two or three years. I was ahead of my time: I could only locate about 150 people in the whole world who wanted them. I kept my patterns and made corsets on a limited basis. —FAKIR MUSAFAR

The market for corset enthusiasts and body modifiers who apply themselves seriously to the difficult task of remodeling the torso is rapidly expanding in contemporary North America.

How It's Done

Reshaping the body through the use of corsets requires slow, steady, and careful progress as well as a sincere commitment and sufficient personal discipline to endure the rigors and initial discomforts. Corset training results in irreversible physical alterations.

> *It took about one year [to get my waist to 22 inches]. It started out almost seven inches bigger. It was uncomfortable at times, but you never make it so tight that it's painful. You find that you can hardly breathe at the start: You have to breathe very differently. You tighten until it's slightly uncomfortable, and you see how long you can live with that. The next day you do a little more.*
>
> —Alexis DeVille

The degree of compression and consequent reduction varies from individual to individual and depends on one's personal goals. Waists may be reduced by as much as 10 inches or more.

> *I've had cases—myself included—where one started out with a reasonably slim figure and a waist measurement, in my case 32 inches. Over a period of two months it was possible through very gradual reduction to reduce the size of my waist 10 inches.*
>
> —Fakir Musafar

The body gradually accommodates the pressures of the rigid garment. Most corset wearers agree that the discomforts fade. That the corset be customized for an exact fit is crucial. Most enthusiasts purchase intermediate sizes during training. As they grow accustomed to the compression, wearing the corset becomes pleasurable.

> *It's a very good feeling to be cinched tight and have the laces pulled tight.*
> —Alexis DeVille

Although tight-lacing compresses both one's external and internal structures, corsetters maintain that no medical evidence exists that such changes are injurious to the body's health. One must, however, adhere to certain restrictions if she or he wishes to make progress. For one, food intake is necessarily limited. Some physical activities, such as running, are impossible while one is tightly corsetted. Corset fans wear looser models when they plan to be active.

> *We're physically active. The constraints of a longer corset or a tight corset are not conducive to scrubbing boats and climbing around.*

If I know I'm going to be putting on a heavier corset at the end of the day, I'll wear something lighter and less restrictive during the day. But I always have something on. I sleep in a corset. I'm in a corset 24 hours a day. —JENNY LANE

All the corsetters whom we interviewed combine a program of consistent corsetting with exercise and dieting.

I didn't get [my waist] down just by putting the corset on and lacing it tighter every day. You have to go on a regular program of exercise that restricts the waist. —ALEXIS DeVILLE

Corsets may be worn in order temporarily to reduce the waistline a few inches, but temporary reduction is much less comfortable than conscientious, progressive tight-lacing.

WHO DOES IT?

Men and women—whether dominant, submissive, or vanilla—wear corsets. According to Fakir Musafar,

I identified three basic types of people who buy or use corsets. There [were] corset nonconformists: people who wanted corsets so that they could change the shape of the body so that it was different from other people's and [to] realize some kind of an aesthetic ideal. There were corset identificationists: people who primarily associated corsets with femininity and feminine undergarments. They didn't particularly have an interest in sculpting the body, but by wearing the corset they seemed to have a kind of gender transformation. Then I ran into a group of people who were simply corset masochists: There was an old phenomenon of corset slavery in which the corset became an instrument of torture that was applied ruthlessly and regularly to create erotic discomfort. —FAKIR MUSAFAR

Corsetting is frequently a couples' phenomenon, where the husband encourages the wife to modify her figure. These enthusiasts are often conventional heterosexual couples who do not express interest in sexual alternatives. Our research suggests that among sexually conventional couples who enjoy corsetting, the wives often become converted to the aesthetic under their husbands' influences and later take pride in their body transformations. Corsetting may become a shared daily experience and a ritual that the couple engages in together for their mutual pleasure.

[Corsetting for us] first of all is a unique bond. It's something that I wouldn't do if it weren't for [my husband]. —JENNY LANE

Many women say that they would continue waist training even if they were no longer married to spouses who fancy corsets.

Because of the garment's restrictiveness, a rising interest in corsetting exists among D&Sers, both male and female. Some liken the experience of tight-lacing to bondage and other forms of constraint: They enjoy the imposed constraints of the rigid underclothing.

I have a corset, which is great for a bottom, because it restricts me. I can't move around too much. [I] can't bend too much—it's got me cinched. —ADIDA

Some D&Sers add bondage restraints to the body while tight-lacing in order to create a greater feeling of captivity. Submissives also may enjoy the fact that the constant restrictions remind them of their sexuality or of their relationships with their dominant partners. Almost all corsetting fans, regardless of sexual orientation, also enjoy complementary garb, such as high heels and stockings.

In addition to women who opt for corsetting, many cross-dressers and transsexuals undergo corset training to assist in recontouring their bodies to an intensely feminine form. Transgenderist corsetters tend to be either heterosexual or bisexual, but there are also gay and lesbian corset enthusiasts.

I fetishize Victorian garb on other women. I like to see a woman in corsets and stockings. Although heels don't do much for me per se, they go along with the outfit. —LAURA ANTONIO

Heterosexual males who modify their bodies with corsets but who do not otherwise cross-dress exist but are in the minority. They may favor the aesthetic of the narrow waist or may use the corset in conjunction with a variety of other restrictive clothing and restraints in bondage scenarios.

WHY THEY LIKE IT

The single greatest reason for corsetting is, quite simply, because people find it sexy.

Helpless women with small waists are a sexual turn-on for men. It's also a sexual turn-on for women, if they adjust and take to this body training. —FAKIR MUSAFAR[5]

In this respect, corsetting, more than any other single D&S-related activity, is old-fashioned both in its practice and in its aesthetic. Its attraction often depends on a belief that a fragile, steeply curved physique is intrinsically sexy. From a D&S point of view, the corsetted woman is never completely unencumbered, because her undergarments prevent free physical movement. This may also help to explain why many traditional heterosexual couples incorporate an ostensibly unusual interest into otherwise conventional sex lives: Corsetting, for the most part, equates fragility with femininity.

Male-to-female transgenderists also typically have a profound appreciation for traditionally feminine virtues and find that displaying a small waist is aesthetically pleasing.

Some derive great satisfaction from lacing their partners into corsets. And for a significant number of cross-dressers, corsetting seems to be a natural complement to fetish and D&S activity.

As is true of other forms of body modification, corsetting practitioners become motivated to reach increasingly difficult goals. Good examples of this, and perhaps the best-known contemporary corsetting fetishists, were Will and Ethel Granger. Mrs. Granger is featured in *The Guinness Book of World Records.*

> *[Ethel's] waist size was 13 inches. Will Granger [wrote] a biography of Ethel detailing his goals for her and how they achieved them. He wanted her to have the smallest waist in the world.*
>
> —JENNY LANE

Mr. Granger was not unique: Desiring to have one's wife achieve as tiny a waist as possible is common among husbands who are aroused by a delicate form.

In addition to its other perceived advantages, waist training may have beneficial psychological consequences. It can produce an extremely youthful shape. The results help enthusiasts to maintain their levels of commitment.

> *Back in 1987 I revealed how I began corsetting and enjoyed the experience of learning about my body. I wrote about diet and exercise in conjunction with corsetting, since I personally shrank from 165 pounds and a 30-inch waist to 130 pounds and a 20-inch waist. . . . Some afternoons . . . I ask myself, "Why are you doing this? What's it all for?" The answer is always the same. "The self-esteem is worth the effort."*
>
> —DIANNE[6]

Knowing that he or she can radically alter the torso's appearance gives the corset wearer a feeling of personal power and an improved body image.

So does the knowledge that a difficult goal was achieved through hard work and commitment.

CORSETTING STYLES AND THEIR EFFECTS

Contemporary corsets are usually made of stiff material covered with satin—and often decorated with lace—and reinforced by boning, usually of well-insulated tempered steel. Hooks and eyes are usually located at the backs and sometimes on the sides.

Corsets may support the breasts or may be cut just below. They may also extend the full length of the torso, although most are cut to mid-hip. Some corsets extend to mid-thigh, and garters may be attached.

Strictly speaking, the most common variety of corset is not a corset at all: the *corselette* is made of an elastic material and may include panels of a stiff material (such as taffeta). The busks are usually flexible, and there is little or no boning. Corselettes provide only temporary support. They may be step-in models, laboriously tugged into place, or have hook-and-eye closures or zippers.

While corselettes may afford transient modification of body shape, serious devotees seek permanent reshaping of the torso. They willingly endure the challenge of wearing restrictive garments.

> *There aren't too many [young] people who have any idea of what it's all about. I've got a 24-year-old daughter, and she wouldn't know what a garter belt is. Even her bras aren't structured. She would have no problem going to Victoria's Secret and buying ruffled, pretty things, but not anything that was confining and restricting. Madonna had a little bit of influence with merry widows and bustiers, but nothing terribly serious and certainly nothing that actually makes the waistline smaller.* —JENNY LANE

Corsetting fans prize three basic idealized shapes: the hourglass, the wasp waist, and the ice cream cone.[7] Corsetters must make a long-term commitment to achieve any of these ideals.

While the hourglass figure is commonly associated with such curvaceous movie goddesses as Mae West and Marilyn Monroe, the corsetters' exemplar for this style is actress Lillie Langtry, reputedly once the lover of Edward VII of England. This stereotypical feminine hourglass physique is achieved by the least rigorous of the three corsetting techniques and is the most suitable training for middle-aged neophytes. Over time the spine curves gently inward, while the lower ribs are compressed and pushed upward. An hourglass corset constricts the intestines and forces them upward and downward from the waist. The hourglass ideal comprises a curvy, diminished waist with full hips and bust.

Wasp-waisting is attained through the use of a stringent garment that compresses the waist tightly in back and in front. Corsetters' model for this body style is the late French actress Polaire. A "waspie" forces the waistline to rise, resulting in a long, narrow torso. Over time the spine is bent inward, the lower ribs yield and are forced upward by the pressure at the waistline, the pelvis tilts, and the buttocks are pushed out and down. Wasp-waist training is most often begun in youth and generally requires preliminary waist training.

The ice-cream-cone shape, whose model is Florenz Ziegfeld's wife, actress Anna Held, is the most severe traditional form of waist modification currently practiced. It combines wasp and hourglass methods. The lower ribs collapse completely and the internal organs are stringently compressed. The ideal result matches full hips with a long, narrow torso.

INTERVIEWS

FAKIR MUSAFAR

The torso has been of endless fascination to all cultures in all ages. I was fascinated by the resculpting of the body at an early age, and I made some belts and experimented to see how it felt, how it looked, and what would happen. I had amazing insights into my body's spirit connection by long-term use of belts. I [also] modified the shape of my body. This was over [a period of] 10 or 15 years. Then I found the custom was in vogue in Western culture through tight-lacing and corsets, and for much the same reasons.

In sculpting the torso, two things can happen. One can either do this temporarily or permanently. Temporarily, anyone can have their midsection reduced by anywhere from three to five inches within a matter of minutes or an hour. The only problem in temporary body sculpting is [that] this is only bearable for a short period of time. The body—internal organs, muscles, everything else—need to adjust slowly to this change of body state. The most notable symptoms are backache, kidney ache, pain in the crest of the hipbone, numbness in the thighs. Those kind of symptoms will occur after a couple of hours of being tightly pinched in.

With permanent body sculpting, the change is made very slowly. The person who does corset training must take anywhere from two months to a year to gradually reduce the midsection. When one goes about this slowly and with proper training, the longer the belt or the corset is left on, the more comfortable and natural it feels, as opposed to temporary corsetting, where the longer you keep something on, the more discomfort it causes.

[When I started], there were no places to get corsets: Only a few people in the world still made them. The old patterns and knowledge of corsetting [were] carried on for just a handful of fetishists. I was involved in theater and costuming. It was very interesting to me to try to construct corsets that would sculpt the body. I tried using some of the early patterns, but they didn't work for modern bodies. Bodies had changed between 1895 and 1955. So I got body measurements for about 200 or 300 people, both male and female, from the costume department at San Francisco State University, and worked from that.

I discovered that corsetiers of old had to know many things: They had to know anatomy, physiology; they had to [be] artists; they had to [know numerous] crafts in order to make patterns and corsets. They made mannequins of bodies and then modified those mannequins, allowing for where things moved if you reduced the midsection. Then they draped cloth tightly over the mannequins and made the corset pattern. I duplicated that [method] and came up with the first new corset patterns in [roughly] 90 years.

I'm planning to reopen an hourglass-corset company. I'll work in cooperation with B.R. Creations on different types of corsets. B.R. will still concentrate on custom Victorian corsets with very fancy trim and decoration. I'll probably specialize in exceptional styles—like longline corsets that go from the bust clear down to the knees, [or] a popular line of short corset belts that can be worn outside or inside the clothing. I think those are going to be very popular.

JENNY LANE

I consider myself a normal woman with normal drives. I don't think that I'm involved in anything unusually kinky. I have fairly private kinds of interests.

I have been [involved with corsetting] 30-plus years. I met my husband when we were both in our early 20s. He expressed an interest in corsetted shapes. This was something that went back to his early teen years and was very appealing to him. At that time, there really wasn't much around that was attractive. He went to New York City to [visit] some costume shops and bought a couple of costumes. One was a red satin corset, and the other was a black one that didn't come close to fitting. He took them apart and remade them so I could wear them for him. At that time I was not cognizant of how seriously he was interested in them. I had no problem dealing with it. It was just something he liked, and I thought of it as dressing up or wearing a negligee.

We got married a few years later, and at that time he asked me if I would consent to wearing a corset under my wedding gown. I had no problem doing that. We found a woman in New York who made a satin, long lace-up corset, and I had my wedding dress fitted over the corset. It wasn't terribly tight-laced. I've always been fairly slender through the rib cage, so it was effective. I didn't enjoy it any more than I would have any other nice lingerie.

After we were married, our schedule was very tight. My husband was in medical school and then had residency and internship. The interest in corsetting never disappeared, but he never had time to pursue it. [Also], we had three children over the next five years. I was doing a lot of chasing with the kids and taking up the slack since he wasn't around.

Once our children were in high school and getting ready to leave, there was more time available to pursue it. The *B.R. Creations Newsletter* made reference to a ball in England for corset fanciers. It was only for [heterosexual] couples with women corset wearers. We got in touch with the organizer and went to England for a week as a spur-of-the-moment thing. We asked [the organizer] to arrange for us to see [someone] in Germany. We arranged on our own to see a woman in England. We've since gotten to know her, her friends, and her family. It [so] happened that she was married to a physician and happened to be a nurse, so there was a commonality there [that] was un-corset-related.

We spent that week in England and then flew to Germany for a day. My husband is of German extraction: He had never been to Germany—neither of us had ever been to Europe—and so he was thrilled to be there and was very taken with the German corsetier. That was a turning point, because we bought something reasonably comfortable to wear. And we followed up on a lot of sources of literature. There was a lot of stuff in England in the late 1800s and early 1900s: [information about] how people went about achieving small waists, how they laced, what kind of training [they did]. It was very useful in terms of physical care, what you can expect, and what not to expect.

[My husband] enjoys the look. It is erotic and sexually stimulating for him. He still gets a great deal of pleasure from watching the old 1950s' movies with dance scenes. People we've met have put together a whole collage of vignettes from probably 20 movies of that era. There are scenes from movies that show people like Gina Lollobrigida and Marilyn Monroe getting corsetted. That, to him, is extremely fascinating and thrilling. I have to agree. I'm a product of the 1950s: Small waists were in then. [And] stockings and high heels go along with corsetting. I'm [not] allowed to wear panty hose!

My corsetted waist is between 18 and 19 ½ [inches]. Natural is probably about 22 or 23 [inches]. I have a fairly long torso and fairly narrow rib cage. I was extremely athletic, but not like kids now who are running and end with a sprung and enlarged rib cage from a lot of lung expansion. I don't have any extra flesh on my ribs. I'm not a small person, and I'm not skinny anywhere else, but from the constant wearing of the corset, I don't have any extra. It certainly attracts a lot of attention when you're out and about.

My husband has done some interesting things, taken some X rays. He's an orthopedist. I trust him. He's not going to do anything knowingly that's going to inflict permanent harm on me. It's gotten to be sort of a joke, because every now and then there are rumors that, in order to tight-lace and get your waist down, a lot of people remove their floating ribs. There's a rumor going around now—I don't know who started it—that he has taken out my ribs! It's not so, but it's interesting to hear!

Most of the English corsetiers [are] probably [more] involved with kinky things—with pony girl costumes and men who wear corsets—than with people like me. We're not interested in men wearing corsets. I don't understand TVs and cross-dressers. I've certainly met more than my share, and they certainly have been very interested in me. But it's not something that I want to take the time to understand.

Basically, my interest is to please my husband. If I were not married to him, or if something were to happen to him, I probably would still corset, partly because I'm comfortable that way. I wouldn't have anything to wear if I didn't: All my clothes are custom-made. But if I'd been married to somebody else who wasn't interested in that, it's not something that I would have picked up. And if he said tomorrow that he wasn't interested anymore, it wouldn't be a problem for me.

ALEXIS DEVILLE

I think [the eroticism of wearing a corset] has to do with the mystery of woman. High heels, corsets, lingerie—the appearance of these garments—seems to turn people on. All I know is [that] if I wear a corset in a scene, it gets better results with a slave than if I'm not wearing a corset. He or she is more excited. In B&D, of course, the whole purpose is to excite the other person. In a session my waist gets looked at and appreciated. Whether [I'm] on the street [wearing] something that looks nice and shows off my waist, or in the dungeon and training slaves, the fact that I'm [shaped] like that and it's appreciated is really all I want.

I have been able to get down, so far, to a 22-inch waist. I enjoy the way it feels, and I just love the way it looks. It's a very good feeling to have control of your own shape. Plus, it's sensual: I find my male and female slaves both go crazy over my corset and my small waist. I think the men are more turned on by the corsets, although I found that most of the women that I've done eventually have wanted one.

The only times I'm not wearing [corsets] is when taking a bath or doing exercises. Then I wear a belt. I also don't wear corsets at night. At the beginning I did: You just leave them a little looser. Now I just wear a belt at night. [The corsets I wear] are more or less what I would consider utilitarian Victorian corsets. I do have leather show ones that are trimmed-out leather that you can wear on the outside. And I've got the basic, utilitarian heavy broadcloth [kind], heavily boned, steel snaps at the front, and lacing in back. My corsets [extend down] just below my buttocks.

[Corsets don't damage organs]. Not if done properly. The best way to put one on is to put a string around the smallest place: That is your natural waist. On a man it won't be obvious unless you already have a defined waist. Make a mark on yourself with a pen, and then put the corset on, and line up the bellyband—the reinforced material and brace over your waist—and make sure it's on there right. Inside the corset is an extra-strong band that's built into it: You put that on your natural waist. Even if it's properly made, if you don't have it in the right place, your legs will go numb. You have to remove it and change the position.

In the beginning, you'll only be able to stand wearing the corset for 30 minutes. And then as time goes on you'll be able to stand more and more time, until you build up to where you can wear it all day. I've worn them as long as 20 hours without any [discomfort].

Corsets start at about $150. You typically order them four inches smaller than your normal waist. When you're able to pull it in, you go down one size, or an inch and a half, smaller. I started with one that was made to go to about 24 inches and then my next one was 23. I'll shortly be going to 20. I'm developing an hourglass shape.

One idea that's inexpensive is a Lady Madeleine waist cincher: They are very good and usually in the $20 range at better stores. A good waist cincher is something you can wear when your clothes aren't suitable for a corset. A waist cincher is a spandex thing that has hooks and laces. It helps you to get the feeling and see if you like it.

I put submissives in corsets. They have to be different from the ones I wear, because my waist is so small. I use them on slaves, both male and female. I can't tell you I use [corsets] on all of them, because some of the slaves I have are very overweight. You can't take someone who's overweight and miraculously give him a small waist with a corset. I make weight loss part of the game, but it's really an excuse to visit them, to measure them.

You have to use figure training. You do modified sit-ups, where you lay on the floor with your knees up and just raise your shoulders about three or four inches. You then work yourself up to 120, 125. One of the other things you do is sit on the floor and do twisting exercises, rolling your shoulders back and forth. Then there are diagonal sit-ups. I do these every night.

Corsetting is a very sensuous part of the D&S scene. The whole idea is to titillate and arouse, not to inflict large amounts of pain. If you do it right, you can really feel it become intermingled with pleasure. I use some restraint devices. In fact, all the props I use—like six-inch heels, riding crop, corsets, whatever—are in the arena of creating excitement [and] arousal.

Sixteen

TATTOOING

Almost everyone has seen tattoos—if only the heart pierced with an arrow, whose banner declares an immutable love for Mother—but few realize that tattoos have served dignified symbolic purposes over the millennia in virtually all non-Western cultures. Although most are commonly applied for decorative and erotic purposes or to denote rank within tribal groups, tattoos have historically served as magical protection against misfortune, illness, or sorcery. In the West tattoos historically have been used for darker purposes, primarily to identify prisoners.

In contemporary America tattooing is enjoying unprecedented popularity as a means of individualizing the body and celebrating individuality. The vast majority of tattoos has no relevance to the bearer's sexuality, but D&Sers find that the unique design and permanence of tattoos, and the symbolism of submitting to the pain of their application, thrillingly blend ritual and romance.

In this chapter we profile:

- The Doctor is an anesthesiologist and internist at a major hospital.
- The Doctor's Wife is a registered nurse who currently works at home and cares for the couple's children.

THE HISTORY OF TATTOOING

The term *tattoo* was first written in English by Captain James Cook in 1769 during an exploration of Tahiti. The practice of permanently marking skin, however, was known throughout antiquity. Egyptian mummies dating from circa 2000 B.C. have been found to bear tattoos. In pagan Rome criminals and slaves were permanently marked; tattooing was also recorded among ancient Gauls, Britons, Celts, Germans, Thracians, and Greeks.

Tattooing was condemned in Leviticus 19:28: "You shall not make any cuttings in your flesh for the dead, nor print any marks upon you." The spread of Christianity stifled its practice in Europe, though it continued unabated in the Middle East during Europe's medieval period. Other cultures also persisted in the use of tattoos, raising it to an art form. Among the Samoans, for example, tattooing was a necessary rite for chiefs. On Easter Island genital tattooing of a woman once denoted that she had been seen copulating with a man by another man. In other Oceanic societies genital tattooing of women was a rite of passage. This rite was stringently observed on Nakuoro, where children borne by women who lacked such tattoos were put to death. Male genital tattooing was rare, though womanizers on the island of Mangalia signified their amorous success by having a vulva tattooed on their penises. And at least one Tongan king had his glans tattooed to demonstrate his indifference to physical pain.

Tattooing methods have varied. Some Arctic and subarctic peoples drew threads coated with soot through skin punctures. Tattoos of Oceanic peoples were accomplished by tapping a rakelike implement into the skin. In New Zealand Maori facial tattooing, known as *moko*, a miniature bone adze was used to cut grooves in the skin, which were then filled with pigment. The moko was a stylized pattern that covered much of the face. Similar slash-and-pigment techniques have been reported among the Ainu of Japan, the Ibo of Nigeria, the Chontal Indians of Mexico, and in Tunisia. Pricking methods were widely practiced among many Native American groups and also among the Senoi of Malaya.

In the last centuries Polynesian and Japanese influences stimulated the growth of tattoo parlors in port cities around the globe to satisfy the demands of European and American sailors. Some sailors attempted to avoid the potential of a punishment flogging by having elaborate crucifixions tattooed on their backs in hopes that pious sailing masters would be averse to assaulting the image of Christ. Sailors also obtained tattoos as permanent souvenirs of their travels or to ward off bad luck.

Tattooing enjoyed a brief vogue among upper-class European men and women in the late 19th Century. Lyle Tuttle, the curator of the Tattoo Art Museum in San Francisco, states that members of the international nobility were tattooed: Lady Randolph Churchill (Winston Churchill's mother), King Frederick IX of Denmark, and Russian Czar Nicholas II were all tattooed. In fact, Lady Randolph ". . . started a fad of dainty tattoos among fashionable women of her set in the 1880s."[1]

The most significant technological development in modern Western tattooing was the advent of the electric tattooing machine, or tattoo gun, which was first patented in the United States in 1891. Before the machine's invention, high-quality tattooing was prohibitively expensive for Westerners, and competent tattooists were rare.

While tattooing has gained currency in the United States and Europe and continues in Japan, it virtually has disappeared in other cultures under the influence of Christian missionaries. In fact, the electric gun and the spread of American-made pattern sheets (or *flashes*), have made the United States a major center of influence for modern tattoos. In Japan long-established tattooing clubs still exist, despite social censure. Japanese tattoo designs follow historical traditions, and exemplary tattoos may be removed from their owners after death for preservation and display. Members of the notorious Japanese crime society, the *yakuza,* use tattooing as a rite of passage or to symbolize initiation and servitude. Japanese convicts were once tattooed around the wrist; the yakuza extended the tattoo to cover the full body,[2] stopping only at the wrists and neck, so that evidence of underworld connections may be concealed by business clothes.

Tattoos seized a foothold in American countercultures and subcultures as a positive means of forging group identity. Among bikers, tattoos identified one as the member of an elite and signaled outlaw status. To the contemporary enthusiast, the images tattooed on one's body are intimately linked to one's inner identity.

There's a tremendous sense of power that comes from the images. Exactly why, I'm not sure: Maybe [it's] a subconscious process or maybe [it's] a spiritual [one]. I think this may be why primitive man began working with these images and why certain organizations—the military, prisoners, bikers—lean toward the tattooing. These images are definitely a part of your self-definition.

—THE DOCTOR

Tattooing is also practiced by convicted criminals. Some prison tattoos have specific meanings or indicate membership in a nefarious (often racist) organization. While prison tattoos are intentionally diabolical and presumably help to protect their wearers by denoting a certain macho status, they have also benefited the criminal justice system. Law enforcement agents report that tattoos make it easy to identify criminals, since a novel design is a permanent and unmistakable form of identification.

Tattoos ceased to be the unique domain of servicemen, bikers, and miscreants in the late 1960s, when the hippie subculture mushroomed to embrace both creative and outlaw communities. Many young fine artists and art school graduates deserted traditional forms and turned to countercultural expressions.

The overlap among creative, social, and political youth cultures helped to introduce tattooing to the white middle class. As tattoos migrated from bellicose to pacifistic cultures, the nature of the designs changed. Rock stars of the day, such as Janis Joplin, were among the first pop icons to flaunt flowery, upbeat markings.

In the late 1970s the punk subculture embraced body modification as a self-conscious expression of anarchy and alienation. Punk tattoos often attempted to elicit confrontation or negative feedback. When a diluted version of punk culture filtered into the mainstream of American music and fashion, gentler images again prevailed and tattoos became a fashionable adornment.

Tattoos are no longer symbolic of the socially disenfranchised, the chronologically young, or the economically underprivileged. The popular press regularly features articles on body art, and women's fashion magazines tout tattoos as alluring accessories. Temporary tattoos are widely sold.

Today's hard-core tattoo enthusiasts are often sexually conservative. Until recently the tattooing community held itself distinct from both the piercing subculture and the D&S communities.

This attitude is changing as body-modification subcultures continue to merge, and many piercing enthusiasts and D&Sers who enjoy tattoo art are gaining acceptance from tattooing organizations.

Clinically speaking, some tattooers are stigmatophiliacs, people who are aroused by the marks on the body. Given the common perception of a tattooed person as an outlaw, tattoos may also be erotic to hybristophiliacs, people who are aroused by a partner who is known or thought to have committed crimes. But tattooing has also captured the interest of some D&Sers as a lasting symbol of ownership.

Whatever the individual's sexual preferences, however, it is the beauty of the design and the perceived enhancement of the body's beauty which bring the greatest pleasure.

How Is It Done?

Because needles are used to penetrate the skin, most people assume that getting a tattoo is an agonizing process. Tattooing, however, feels more like an abrading of the skin than a cutting or a piercing sensation. The amount of pain perceived depends on the individual's tolerance, on the amount of work to be done, and the tattoo's placement. For most, the pain is quite tolerable.

> It hurt. But it's not terrible. It's an intense kind of scratching.
> —THE DOCTOR'S WIFE

Either by drawing freehand on the skin or by copying from a flash, the artist carefully outlines the design prior to applying the tattoo.

> During [the actual] tattooing, you're very involved in dealing with the pain, [but] during the drawing, there's no pain involved. You draw with a ballpoint pen: It was a very strange kind of feeling, having somebody draw on your skin. He's down there while you're naked, [and he's] carrying on a conversation with you and your husband.
> —THE DOCTOR'S WIFE

Tattoo guns contain sterilized needles, which rapidly and repeatedly puncture the skin; the perforations are automatically filled with ink. The design may be a monochrome outline, or it may be shaded with different colored inks. How long it takes to etch the design into the skin depends on the complexity and scale of the design. A modest outline can be completed in a few minutes. The longer it takes to apply the tattoo, the more it will hurt. Repeated stabs of the needle can build to an intensely uncomfortable, burning sensation. Tattoos that cover significant areas, or which require considerable detailing or extensive coloring-in, are often applied a few hours at a time over a period of weeks or months.

[For my wife], it took approximately six months of repeated sessions, at least 40 or 50 hours' worth of tattooing, to achieve the final effect.
—THE DOCTOR

After the tattooing session, the skin must be cared for until it has healed. Tattooists recommend that the affected area be treated with antibacterial ointments. An antiseptic dressing is applied. A light scab forms over the surface of the tattoo and usually peels off within two weeks. Although the skin will remain sensitive for a time, the discomfort usually dissipates shortly after the session and vanishes completely within days, except for some mild residual soreness. Tattooing carries some risks, foremost among them the risk of infection. Needles must be sterile, ink must be nontoxic and from unopened bottles, and the artist should wear latex gloves to protect against contact with blood.

WHY THEY LIKE IT

Divers reasons for tattooing: 1) To camouflage an unclothed body when hunting. 2) To secure a place in heaven. 3) To ensure an easy passage through difficult phases in life, such as puberty and pregnancy. 4) To prevent disease and injury and acquire fertility. 5) To propitiate malignant spirits at time of death. 6) To acquire special characteristics through totemism and ancestor worship. 7) To acquire the special respect of the community to allow the individual to climb the social ladder. 8) To terrorize the enemy on the field of battle. 9) To make the body sexually interesting. 10) To express sentiment (patriotism, love, friendship, anti-authoritarianism). 11) To register incidents of personal interest, places visited, etc. 12) To achieve personal or group identity (primitive tribes, gangs, sailors). 13) To make money (circus sideshows). 14) To register important medical data, e.g., blood group.
—R.W.B. SCUTT AND C. GOTCH[3]

To this comprehensive list of reasons for getting a tattoo must be added the one cited most often among contemporary practitioners: to express concretely and visually an individual's inner being. Modern primitives (a term coined by Fakir Musafar to denote contemporary Westerners who explore their spirituality through ancient body-modification techniques) and other activists are particularly fond of describing a tattoo as the overt expression of an intangible urge or psychic reality.

What I see when I look at [my wife's] tattoos is the image of the mythological Amazonian warrior. She carries all these images of life and of nature. For me, it gives her almost mystical powers. It's hard to describe, because most of our society has lost the primitive and tribal urge, but these tattoos have given us tremendous amounts of energy. —THE DOCTOR

Tattoos may represent an event in a person's life, express one's innermost desires, or symbolize a personal philosophy. Some may wear a tattoo as a distinct symbol of personal strength.

I'm only five-feet-two and about 120 pounds: I live in an environment [where] I can be seen as a target. And in some ways the tattoos deflect that. If I'm walking down the street and a tattoo is showing, I am less likely to be labeled a target. If I was dressed as a typical doctor's wife and I always had the cute little suit and little shoes, I am [perceived] as more or less defenseless. I don't like that image. I'm considered a little bit differently because of the tattoos. In some ways people will intuit a strength there that maybe isn't otherwise apparent. —THE DOCTOR'S WIFE

In recent years an ideal of many tattoo aficionados has been to make each tattoo unique. Because the tattoo is perceived both as art and as personal statement, great care and forethought go into its design.

Tattooing has become a significant part of our process of self-identification and self-definition. I believe it helps us—and I think others—mark ourselves as being different and willing to take our passion to the next level. —THE DOCTOR

For most enthusiasts, tattooing is a magical and spiritual process that energizes both the tattooist and the person being tattooed.

When I tattoo, I feel I'm not only changing someone's skin, but also helping to reinforce their spirit and vision, and it's a lot of responsibility. —VYVYN LAZONGA[4]

Those with D&S interests may also find that some of the elements of tattooing are inherently erotic.

Watching [my wife] being tattooed and images form on her body was extraordinary for me. Maybe this relates back to D&S. Tattooing involves the use of needles; there's some blood; there's some discomfort. But it's very highly charged, in terms of the energy

involved. She was often nude while the tattooing was being done; images were being drawn on her body both freehand and from observed images. —THE DOCTOR

For submissives the tattoo may be a meaningful symbol of ownership.

To me, [tattoos] always symbolized ownership. I would never get a piercing or tattoo of my own volition. It causes a confusion between S&Mers and people into the pop-fringe punk culture that surrounds and gets mixed up with S&M these days. —BAMBI BOTTOM

Further, enduring the pain may represent a token of devotion to the dominant, and in some cases the nudity required by a tattoo on a buttock, breast, or thigh may be enlivened by mild feelings of erotic humiliation.

INTERVIEWS

THE DOCTOR

I'm a physician at a large urban medical center, an M.D. with a Ph.D. in biochemistry, and board certified in internal medicine and anesthesiology. I would consider myself involved in the D&S world through my interest in bondage and some of the areas I have explored with my wife. We've been together now almost 18 years—married [for] 13—and we have children.

In looking at how I ended up where I am now, I find two basic fundamental dynamics inside of me. One is the drive towards survival; the other is the sexuality, and it's a 50-50 cut. Most everything else has been trained into me. I recognize that sexuality is the engine, and the survival instinct tells me the direction and where that energy should go. Those two dynamics, which are the essence of my life and allow me to take risks, force me to reexamine a lot that I have been taught about relationships and a lot that I've been taught about sexuality and to come to different conclusions.

Not a lot of people in the medical community, particularly in the academic medical community, know any of the sexuality teaching. We are fairly flagrant with our sexuality and fairly outspoken. It's caused us over time to develop a small inner core of people that are fiercely loyal to us and very supportive of us, but by the same token, [it has] exacted the price in some levels of isolation in this normally very conservative community.

[My wife] has leather outfits—considered by most people as reasonably outrageous for a traditional doctor's wife—where her tattoos are very clearly visible. A number of my colleagues have kiddingly referred to us as being part of "the whip-and-chain crowd." The observed response from this so-called professional community is interesting.

My particular interest is in tattooing. I [also] have interest in bondage and extended relationships and alternative lifestyles. I consider myself to be more of a top. The interest in D&S grew naturally out of the sexuality between my wife and me. I was raised in a very liberal environment and definitely found the idea of bondage very acceptable if it was pleasurable to the partner. But it's not something I actually went out seeking. She was the one who introduced it to me.

I was exposed to tattooing when I was in the military. I was a physician in the Air Force for five years and became the chief of medicine at a 150-bed hospital. My wife met somebody who had an image of a woman chained to a wall tattooed on his back. She found it extraordinary and discussed it with me. We slowly but surely became friends with this individual, who was involved with the biker community. It was fairly significant out in rural America, which is where we were located at the time. He introduced us to an excellent tattoo artist, who eventually ended up doing the work on my wife.

[She] was the impetus that got us into the tattooing. I had one or two magazines and found it interesting, but she was the one who decided to actually go out and get the first tattoo. I quickly discovered that it had a strong erotic appeal to me. I found the actual process of tattooing and then the beautiful images on the body to be extraordinarily erotic.

The main impact of tattooing on me was having to deal with my own mortality. I know that may sound a bit strange, but the realization that if you put a mark on your body, it'll be there for the rest of your life takes you back for a moment. For example, one of the first comments made to my wife by a medical person when she had her first tattoo is, "Oh, my God, you'll be 92 on a mortician's slab, and they'll be stretching your skin, trying to figure out what the tattoo once was." This was the individual's ultimate horror. My wife, on the other hand, giggled at the thought and liked the idea that at 92 and even past death she would be able to send some message that she had lived a different and stranger life than the average person.

When you begin to deal with tattooing, you have to think clearly about your own values—how transient or how permanent they are—as you choose images that you will live with. You wonder: Five, 10, 15, 20 years from now, what will be your response to the tattooing? Where will your life have changed? And then, of course, you have to review backwards: How much have I changed in the last 10 years? It is a very interesting process that you go through to decide on your tattooing art.

I carry the tattoo of a lion on my back. It's taking up about a quarter of my back. It's a piece designed by a very close friend over a six-month period. I'm now planning some additional pieces. For me, the tattoos are very much symbolic of passages of given time. I envision being tattooed slowly over a long period of time.

The amount of discomfort that's involved with tattooing is significant enough so that I've been asked to enter the field to try to achieve certain levels of anesthesia to help people who are not interested in the pain. The pain can be described as an intense scratching. The difficulty comes from the length of the process. My tattoo required four hours of sitting absolutely still while a sewing-machine-type device is run over the skin repeatedly, time and time and time again. Slowly but surely the area begins to burn intensely.

The tattooing felt as I would imagine either a North American Indian or African tribal initiation would feel, because it was intense [and] required concentration and focus to overcome the discomfort. In our society there's no process during which one is supposed to feel discomfort. If one has an operation, one has anesthesia; if one is mentally in pain, one can take a pill. With tattooing, one is voluntarily subjecting himself to intense discomfort with full recognition that this is being done for the purpose of creating art on the body, the body being the ultimate canvas.

My wife seemed to be beyond it. A lot of experienced tattoo artists were astonished by her focus and concentration. I think this is partly where the passion of the tattooing comes from. For one to sit many hours while the images are placed on your body is a symbol of the amount of passion in that individual. The images in effect are as if burned into the soul and finally [emerging] onto the skin. As you go through this process, you become more and more obsessed with the images that you're going to put on your body, until you must absolutely get tattooed, or you cannot continue with your daily life.

I know this is highly unusual for a professional—let alone most people in this society—but I view tattooing as the highest art form, considering the nature of the canvas. There is a small, growing core of tattoo artists who view it as the ultimate expression of the individual. Plastic surgery has been well accepted in our society for a long time. It's a process, though, of conformity. One has the ideal nose in mind and tries to shape many noses into that one ideal image. I think that's why extensive plastic surgery is found to be socially quite acceptable and tattooing is considered to be quite radical. Tattooing is the ultimate individual expression. By the time it is done, the person looks like no other individual in society.

In terms of fantasies, I do [have] a general one: setting up a modern-day tribe. I have this image of a multimillion-dollar complex with a lot of living space and a group of highly intense and charged individuals who are working and loving together. It's the grand fantasy, in the "modern primitives" sense, a very self-reliant group. I see tattooing potentially as being a part of an extended relationship because tattooing gives a distinct tribal feel and I think creates within a group the sense of continuity.

THE DOCTOR'S WIFE

What do I get out of all this? A number of things. It's an expression of the fact that I am not necessarily what I seem. I am not the typical doctor's wife, not the typical mother. There's more to me than most people know. At this point it's an external statement. I've always had a line: People either knew me or they didn't. There were things they needed to know to be considered friends or for me to be completely comfortable with them. And the tattoos are a kind of external expression of this. You don't really know me if you haven't seen my tattoos.

I get the tattoos for myself; that's what they're for—me. I also know that [The Doctor] likes them, and that's very important. I'm not sure what would have happened if he had had a completely negative reaction. I don't know if I would have gotten the first one. I might have. Now they express a link between [The Doctor] and myself. We're both tattooed. When someone sees us walking down the street, very often he'll have his tattoos showing, and I'll have mine showing. I wasn't sure he was going to get one when I first got it. But it has taken on that [meaning] for me, that feeling of commitment.

The tattoos speak of a kind of an intensity and a passion and a lack of [the] fear that most people have. The thing that most people back away from and are very afraid of is the fact that [tattoos] are permanent. When I first got them, that was the most interesting aspect to most people. It wasn't what it was, or where it was, or even the art of it. People said, "How do you know you'll want it there five years from now?" Well, nowadays you probably can change them, but when I got them, I was not aware they could be changed. In some ways it's a willingness to commit to something, to making yourself different from the rest of the world, to acknowledge it.

When someone asks me, "What if you don't want it there five years from now?" my attitude is, "What if I don't want my kids five years from now?" I've made a commitment. Why wouldn't I want it? I've made a decision. It grows with you. It's a part of you. In [my] 36 years I have made numerous decisions, and I don't have any major regrets about the decisions I've made in my life. I looked at all the options; I thought about almost nothing else for that period of time and looked at it every which way I could think of [and made my decision].

Wearing a piece of art appealed to me. It was an expression of being different, acknowledging the fact that I wanted it and that I was not afraid. I liked the idea that it would be there the rest of my life and that I chose to put it there. I have a number of beauty marks on my body. I've always accepted them. But the idea of choosing something that I would wear the rest of my life appealed to me.

My husband got excited and really got involved; [he] enjoyed the idea, so I decided to go with my first piece on the shoulder blade three years ago. The first piece is an open rose. It's predominantly different shades of blue. The first [time], I was apprehensive, because I had never been in a tattoo parlor before. I had uncomfortable feelings about going [there]. I chose to have the individual who had the tattoo on his back go with me to have somebody who could tell me what to expect. We went, and I brought home three different designs. [The Doctor] and I decided on the rose. Then I went back and had it done.

[The Doctor] was fascinated; he was excited by the entire experience. I know he liked that I was willing to take a certain amount of pain to put something on my body. [But] it was not exclusively for him. If I'd done it for him, it might not have been as positive. It was for me and for him; it was for us. [The pain] was not an issue for me. It was uncomfortable, but I didn't feel like I had gone beyond my limit. It was less painful than I had expected it to be.

It [took] about two weeks for the tattoo to heal. During that period of time, after 10 years of marriage, I was the hottest thing on two legs again, which was a wonderful feeling. He followed me around the house; he was always nearby, touching, holding. It was wonderful.

I went for the second one alone. I never did that again. It was more painful; I had nothing to focus on. That's the only time that I got up—the tattoo wasn't done; it still needed a little bit more color—and said, "No. It'll get done some other time." It was not the most painful area to get done. I just wanted [The Doctor] with me. From then on, I would not go by myself.

I went through cycles of getting a tattoo every two to four weeks. As soon as one would heal, we'd start talking about the next one. The piece [on my back] started off as flowers—the rose, an orchid, a lotus, and a morning glory with graphics.

We [also] experimented with painless tattooing, and I had a [kitty] cat put on my bikini line. We did it with lidocaine. You don't feel it going on, but when the [anesthesia] wears off, you're suddenly aware you have a tattoo. It's the only one that I have that I didn't feel being put on.

I had a hip piece done on the right side. It's [an] Aladdin's lamp with smoke turning into the front of a horse. There's a carp on my right breast. And then I had all the flowers connected with smoke and graphics. And bubbles. They wind around to a graphic piece on the bottom of my left buttock, and the smoke goes to a cauldron on the inner aspect of my left thigh. In shorts, you see two sources of smoke, basically, on the outer side of one thigh and the inner of the other. I got them all within nine months. I sound like I'm terribly tattooed, but I can go out and you wouldn't see any of them. I can wear a sleeveless blouse; I can wear a scoop neck; I can wear anything except short shorts or a bathing suit.

I was not uncomfortable with [being nude for the tattoo]. I was aware that it turned [my husband] on, and I found that pleasant and somewhat exciting. In some ways, with him it's more of a sense of pride. It's not something I would have done if he hadn't been there. But it's a sharing of me. I don't know if it would have had a different effect if it had been a stranger. We were very good friends with the tattooist. I knew his children, his wife; we'd socialized. A lot of people find that very uncomfortable, [but] we've always socialized with my obstetrician, too.

The art of tattoos is sexy. They are beautiful pieces of art, and to me they are [permanent, aesthetic] accessories. Whether [I'm] wearing a backless dress or a formal gown, they add something. I think they're also an expression of passion and strength that can be sensual and sexy. I may objectively fit more patterns than I care to admit to in terms of looking and playing the submissive, but there's a strength and an amount of control [within me] that I insist on. The tattoos reflect that strength.

When I find a piece that I like, or I find a place that I want [tattooed], tattooing and the ensuing sexual energy in the household appeals to me. [The Doctor] definitely is going to get more. And I will probably get another one. There is an arm piece that I will eventually get. It will be a black graphic band around the upper aspect of my arm. I'll probably have [The Doctor's] name somewhere in it, not necessarily easily found, but definitely there. The question is when. It may be something I'll do now. Or if for some reason I lose him, that will be the black arm band I will wear to show devotion for the rest of my life.

Seventeen

PIERCING AND SCARIFICATION

. . . after being freed she had not wanted to leave her masters, as the large hole pierced in her right ear showed.

—GUSTAVE FLAUBERT[1]

T he body modification most likely to cause alarm in the mainstream observer—a piercing to genitalia or nipples—is also the most deliberately sensual form of body modification. These singular invasions of erogenous zones enhance the sensual pleasure both of the adorned and his or her beloved.

Tens of thousands of individuals have opted for this radical physical change, a change often invisible to any but the piercer's intimate partners. Piercing fans range from new-wave neopunks to conservative businessmen.

Indeed, one of the people responsible for introducing exotic piercings to contemporary American culture was a self-made millionaire who helped develop Muzak.

In this chapter we examine the diversity of styles of piercings and other extreme invasions such as cutting, scarification, and branding. All the practices described in this chapter entail potential health risks. An expert must be consulted before any one is undertaken. We hear from Fakir Musafar on piercing and feature profiles of:

- Logger V. is 40 years old and a professional piercer. He is a handicapped-employment specialist and a sign-language interpreter for the deaf. Logger V. is in a permanent, live-in relationship with his lover.
- Adida is a software engineer and aerobics instructor whose interests include martial arts, skydiving, and ballet.
- Mr. Happy lives with Adida and works as a software engineering consultant. His interests include skydiving and motorcycles. Both Adida and Mr. Happy are in their 30s.

MODERN HISTORY

Piercing has no easily summarized, linear history. Acts of perforation, incision, cautery, insertion, and staining have been practiced by prehistoric and contemporary cultures alike. Perforations of the earlobe, the lip, the nose, and even the genitalia have been widely documented throughout the world. The history of each will be discussed below, according to type.

According to *RE/Search: Modern Primitives,* an exhaustive text on the subject, the "father of the modern rebirth of piercing" was Richard Symington, a millionaire who made a fortune from his role in the invention of Muzak. In the early 1970s Mr. Symington helped to organize a small but committed group of piercing enthusiasts. They included Fakir Musafar and Jim Ward, the *éminences grises* of piercing. Ward founded The Gauntlet, the country's best-known piercing salon, and *Piercing Fans International Quarterly,* the premiere publication for piercers.

HOW IS IT DONE?

Few parts of the body cannot, at least theoretically, be pierced. A general rule of piercing, however, is that body protrusions are preferable to flat areas. When a ring is implanted in a flat surface of the body, the piercing heals slowly, if at all. For example, we spoke with a man who designed a unique piercing for himself at the top of the nape of his neck. After nine months, the piercing was finally fully healed but was still too tender for erotic play.

Piercing must be performed under sterile conditions. A sterilized needle is used to penetrate the skin. The gauge of the needle usually depends on the density of the tissue to be pierced. The skin is clamped with forceps, and antibacterial agents are applied liberally. Some specialists mark the site with tattoo ink. Once the needle is pushed through the skin, jewelry of surgical steel or of another nonreactive metal is carefully placed in the hole.

Safety precautions cannot be overemphasized. Piercings and all such invasive modifications are wounds which may bleed and which are highly susceptible to infection. In addition, the procedures may result in nerve damage, tissue necrosis, or hemorrhage.

Different techniques and precautions apply to different areas of the body. Selecting the appropriate needle gauge is crucial.

> *Gauge is very important in piercing. Imagine a wire cheese cutter and how easily it slices through cheese. A thin gauge will do the same thing. I recommend a little thicker gauge for areas that are very sensitive and prone to be easily cut.* —LOGGER V.

Jewelry must be carefully matched to the type and location of the piercing. For example, earrings should not be worn anywhere else; custom jewelry for exotic piercings should be worn only in the piercings for which they were designed. Once the wound heals, piercers may elect to enlarge the size of the piercing, gradually introducing thicker-gauge jewelry.

Although the ultimate goal of an exotic piercing may be largely sexual, the actual procedures "are unlikely to be done in the context of any kind of sex or SM scene."[2] Piercing is too sensitive a procedure to risk distractions.

> *As I try to explain when we have group piercing rituals—which have become quite popular in the last year here in California— piercing is not something to be taken lightly. We're doing a rather serious thing: We're imposing on the life inside a body something that is not there in a natural state.* —FAKIR MUSAFAR

WHY DO THEY LIKE IT?

The motivations for piercing are as eclectic as the piercers themselves.

> *The people in piercing are so diverse. They want so many different things, and they each have a little fantasy.* —LOGGER V.

There is general consensus, however, that piercings of the erogenous zones are done to enhance the sexual pleasure of piercees and their partners. Some women reported having more orgasms when making love to men adorned with penis piercings. Piercings of the female genitalia, meanwhile, may stimulate the clitoris when a woman walks or moves.

In the case of submissives, piercings to erogenous zones may also signify ownership by a dominant. Gold rings are particularly popular among D&Sers for whom a ring through flesh connotes erotic servitude. Rings may be tugged, turned, or otherwise manipulated to create intense stimulation. Chain or rope may be attached to control or restrain the submissive.

Aesthetic considerations also motivate piercers.

I think that [piercings] are pretty in the same way that other jewelry is pretty. Because of my job, I cannot decorate from the neck up, so earrings and nose rings are out, makeup's out. This is a way for me to decorate and get away with it. —MR. HAPPY

Piercing may represent a private physical challenge. Interviewees compared the experience of being pierced to high-adrenaline sports in which the mind becomes completely focused on the body and one's primal energies are awakened.

It's empowering to know I'm brave enough to try this. I enjoy the feeling that I can do anything. . . . The moment when the needle goes through is painful, but it's a jolt that gets energy going out all over your body. You know you're alive! You see what focus is. In martial arts we always say, "We have to be focused," but I hadn't truly understood it until [my] piercing. Now I know what focus is! —ADIDA

Some piercers specifically enjoy the aftereffects of the piercing and find the new sensitivity exciting.

Before, unless my outer labia were pinched really hard, they were just sort of there. The rings make me aware of them in a whole new way. It's like getting new body parts. —CASSANDRA

The moment of piercing usually has a deep personal and spiritual significance. A number of interviewees likened the act to a magic ritual. When a spiritual dimension is part of the experience—as it was for the majority of people to whom we spoke—the piercing may also be a personal rite of passage that marks a transformation.

[For many], the piercing marks the beginning of a new phase of their life. For the most part, it seems to provide something that is missing

in our culture. In other words, there is usually no provided rite of passage, and those that are invented are sometimes not too satisfactory. —FAKIR MUSAFAR

Although modern primitives make up a significant subgroup among piercers, many piercers do not consciously emulate pagan or primitivistic customs. Experienced piercers, however, do acknowledge that the process is a momentous occasion, spiritually, emotionally, and physically.

TYPES OF PIERCINGS

EAR

Ear fashions have varied through time and from culture to culture. Historically and prehistorically in the Americas and the Pacific, spools were inserted in ear perforations to enlarge the lobe, sometimes to massive proportions. Aboriginal aristocrats of Easter Island were known as "Big Ears" because of this practice.

While multiple ear piercings were exotic a couple of decades ago in America, women's fashions have gradually yielded to foreign influences and multicultural heterogeneity. Men have opted for ear piercings as well. Single-ring ear piercing of men probably derives from a tradition among sailors to wear single-ear piercings after surviving a shipwreck.

Today a man's pierced ear *may* be a symbol of gayness. The catchphrase "Right is gay, left's okay" means that, generally, heterosexual men pierce the left lobe, gay men the right. Gay men, however, usually adhere to the left = dominant, right = submissive code, and many heterosexual D&Sers follow suit. Confusion over these codes prevails, so, when in doubt, ask.

NOSE

Septum and nostril piercings were practiced by tribes in Africa, South America, Melanesia, Polynesia, and North America. Among Hindu women, piercing of alae (the outer wings of the nostrils) continues today and is both aesthetically pleasing and indicative of marital status; additional ornamentation, such as a gold chain connecting the nostril to the earlobe, flaunts the wearer's wealth. Nostril piercings in America are largely a relic of the influence of Hindu culture upon hippies in the 1960s. These piercings are said to be more painful than septum piercings, which were commonly practiced in other non-Western cultures.

I've never pierced a woman's nose, but when I pierce a man's septum, he is afraid it's going to hurt [badly]. It doesn't hurt that much at all. However, the side of the nose is a very painful area because of the nerve endings. But pain is in the mind. I have had people who felt no pain whatsoever. —LOGGER V.

For the alae, many piercers elect to use a "nostril screw," which is specially designed for nasal comfort. A far rarer piercing is occasionally performed on the bridge of the nose.

EYEBROWS AND CHEEKS

Fairly uncommon among aficionados, facial piercings seem to be most popular in punk and youth subcultures, where the adornment is less likely to be a gold ring than a safety pin.

TONGUE AND LIPS

Tongue piercings are somewhat rare and considered painful. Swelling occurs, there is high risk of infection, and healing can be slow. In tongue piercing, a small stud is emplaced near the tip.

Tongue piercing is very difficult, because the tongue will swell, and the person pierced will be out of commission for a while. But I understand that it's very interesting and fascinating, depending on your sex partner! —LOGGER V.

Less invasive is a piercing on the lower lip through which a small ring is inserted. This piercing is called a *labret.* The lower lip has been a popular site for perforation and insertion: The women of the Sara tribe of Central Africa use saucer-shaped plugs to spread the lip after slitting. A variety of lip plugs have been used among groups in Africa, South America, as well as Inuit and Pacific Northwestern Indian tribes.

NIPPLE

Perhaps the most popular sensual piercing, nipple piercing is performed on both genders. Some practitioners suspend light weights from the rings once the wounds have healed.

I got my nipples pierced, and they're just now reaching the point where they can start to be played with. The rings in them are 14-gauge, and you don't really want to do heavy play with them until they're up to 10-gauge.. —CASSANDRA

Pierced nipples may remain permanently erect and may become slightly enlarged. Some people enjoy the additional stimulation this affords, while others find it too intense. Women with pierced nipples may find that a brassiere causes chafing.

Most nipple piercings are decorated with small rings or customized jewelry, but some devotees deliberately enlarge the hole by gradually inserting heavier-gauge jewelry. Once the wound is healed, the jewelry may be manipulated as a part of erotic play among D&Sers.

NAVEL

Navel piercings apparently originated among the nobility of ancient Egypt. This style has been resurrected in Europe and the United States. A navel piercing draws the eye to the erogenous zones.

The navel piercing is usually through the upper ridge, but I have done some on the sides and on the bottom ridge. A ring will go sideways or fall flat on the navel. I think it looks very nice, especially on a woman who's got a nice figure and a slim waist. It's very beautiful. —LOGGER V.

GENITALIA

An astonishing variety of genital piercings is available. Not surprisingly, fewer are available to women than men, since women have fewer protrusions from which to select.

The men we interviewed stated that the potential for increasing their partners' sexual pleasure was a primary motivation.

I've gotten very favorable feedback from all the women I've been with since my piercings. I think it's unusual that when a man does something painful for the benefit of the partner, some view it as mutilation. Women wear high heels and go through all kinds of things, like breast surgery, to please. —MR. HAPPY

MALE GENITALIA

Prince Albert: The best known of the piercings to the glans (the head of the penis) is the Prince Albert. Here a ring is emplaced through the urethra and glans. According to folklore, Queen Victoria's consort, Prince Albert, wore the ring to retract his foreskin so he could maintain cleanliness and eliminate any offending odor, presumably to avoid insulting the delicate sensibilities of his Queen. We have found no reliable documentation to support this claim. The Prince Albert (known familiarly as a "P.A.") was also called a "dressing ring" by the Victorians who allegedly used the ring to bind the penis to the leg under extremely tight trousers, thus preventing unsightly bulging. Again, we could not locate any period sources to confirm this charming fashion legend. Whatever its history, the P.A. enjoys considerable vogue today.

Ampallang: The ampallang, which transects the glans horizontally above the urethra, is the most widely documented male genital piercing. In its original cultural context this piercing was a rite of passage and frankly sexual in intent. The Dayaks of Borneo and the Toradhja and Sadang of Celebes wore ampallangs to enhance female pleasure. Dayak women reportedly would not have intercourse with men who lacked them. South African rock paintings depict similar penis adornments.

The concept was known in the West as early as 1590, when a penis bar was reported in the *Boxer Codex* from the Philippines. It was probably first practiced in the West by 19th Century sailors. Modern ampallang jewelry resembles a barbell: a slender bar, usually gold, terminated on either end by a small globe. Contemporary advocates agree that the ampallang's main virtue is the enhancement of their partners' pleasure.

> *Guys [in the South Pacific] go out and get ampallangs the same way they go out and buy cars in this country: to impress the female. On their wedding night the woman selects which size balls feel best to her. It's like, "Well, pull out, honey. Let's see, we'll try the number five now." The reason it works is fairly obvious: In certain positions for penetration, the gold balls rub the G-spot.* —MR. HAPPY

Dydoe: The dydoe, also Eastern in origin, penetrates the glans on one side. Traditionally, both sides were pierced; some piercers have more than two holes pierced. The jewelry is usually similar to the barbell used for ampallangs. The dydoe enhances the female's pleasure and is reputed to increase sensitivity in circumcised men, much like a foreskin.

Apadravya: The apadravya was described in *The Kama Sutra* as a device either secured to the *lingam* (i.e., penis) and used to excite a woman's *yoni* (i.e., vagina) during intercourse, rather like a rococo French tickler. It is also the name of a device inserted through a piercing to the penis for the same exciting purpose. [The modern apadravya runs from the underside to the front of the glans.]

> *In the hole made in the lingam a man may put Apadravyas of various forms, such as the "round," the "round on one side," the "wooden mortar," the "flower," the "armlet," the "bone of the heron," the "goad of the elephant," the "collection of eight balls," the "lock of hair," the "place where four roads meet," and other things named according to their forms and means of using them. All these Apadravyas should be rough on the outside according to their requirements.*[3]

Frenum: In this piercing a ring encircles the penis shaft under the glans and penetrates the frenum (the loose flap of skin immediately below the glans). The encircling band is fitted snugly and may keep the glans engorged. If a large enough device is locked through a frenum piercing, intercourse is rendered impossible. This piercing is European in origin, and its alleged purpose was to ensure male chastity. Modern frenum piercings, however, are obtained primarily to enhance male arousal.

Foreskin: In ancient Rome actors and musicians pierced two sides of their foreskins and inserted a *fibula,* a ring or clasp. Sources conflict as to whether this was chiefly believed to be a means of preserving one's voice or was used as a safeguard against charges of adultery. Since castration was a Roman penalty for adultery, infibulation would seem the lesser evil. Infibulation to enforce chastity among slaves was also known in ancient Rome. And in ancient Greece athletes tied their foreskins shut, though the reason for this is unknown.

Modern uncircumcised males may opt for a single piercing of the foreskin or an infibulation. In the first, a ring is inserted on only one side of the foreskin.

Hafada: The hafada is a piercing through the skin of the scrotum on one side. It has Arabian origins and was traditionally performed at puberty to mark a boy's passage into manhood. Its symbolic purpose was to ensure that the testicles would never retract into the groin. French Foreign Legionnaires stationed in North Africa are credited with introducing the hafada to Europe.

Guiche: The guiche is a piercing of the ridge of flesh between the testicles and the anus. This practice derives from a Samoan puberty rite. Its erotic possibilities have made it very popular among contemporary piercing enthusiasts.

The guiche is used a great deal in playing and pulling. If you have a chain on it, it's almost like a dog collar. —LOGGER V.

Much rarer is a guiche-like piercing on women, between vagina and anus.

FEMALE GENITALIA

Labia: In this piercing, a ring is inserted through the edge of one of the outer labia (considerably rarer, but known, are piercings to the inner labia). Some enthusiasts opt for multiple piercings of one outer lip or even of both.

> *I got my outer labia pierced with two rings in each side. I went into it planning to just get one in each side. [But, afterwards], I thought, I'm not done yet; I want a couple more. I knew exactly where I wanted them. I was very aware of how much it was going to hurt. All the nerve endings were standing up and jumping around. It was like a rite of passage. I felt like I had gotten through something that I hadn't even known I needed to get through.*
>
> —CASSANDRA

As with male infibulation, *female infibulation* was a type of adhesion used to enforce chastity. It was practiced in East Africa among the Somali and the Galla, as well as among some Arab tribes. In some cases the labia were sewn together and then were incised upon marriage to restore the opening. These practices survive among some Africans and Asians.

Clitoris: This is perhaps the rarest and most difficult erotic piercing because the clitoris contains so many nerve endings. A small stud or ring through the clitoris separates the labia, slightly exposing the organ. The pain of a clitoral piercing and the vastly heightened sensitivity which results make it attractive to women who enjoy very intense stimulation.

> *Usually when I mention that to a woman, she crosses her legs and says, "Ooooh! That hurts!" Well, yes and no. It is very sensitive but also very sensual. Some clients were very excited, especially by the play of the ring.* —LOGGER V.

Clitoral Hood: The clitoral hood (also known as a *nun's hood*) is the tag of protective flesh immediately above the clitoris. This piercing is gaining popularity, particularly in the lesbian community. It is both decorative and erotic.

> *[The] ring [is usually] a half inch in diameter with a little ball at the bottom. When the ring falls, [the ball drops] and hits the clitoris. I have [been told by] women that it is marvelous when they walk.*
>
> —LOGGER V.

SCARIFICATION, CUTTING, AND BRANDING

Scarification (making cuts or scars, usually with a knife) and *cutting* are ancient practices with both aesthetic and ritualistic meaning. Across Africa and in Oceania, cutting was used to create ornamental patterns of keloid tissue (distinct, raised scars). In some African tribes scarring was part of a rite of passage or denoted a woman's social or marital status. Among the Bala of Zaire, men often refused intercourse with women who lacked decorative cicatrices.

Contemporary women are more likely than men to opt for these primitivistic modifications.

> *Branding and cutting are popular among young women. From years of research, I know that in other cultures women were initiated more by cuttings and scarification and branding than men were. Piercing rituals seem to be usually more male-oriented rites of passage.* —FAKIR MUSAFAR

Cutting is gaining currency among lesbian D&Sers both for its erotic potential and for its ritual aspects.

Scarification techniques range from superficial scratches to deeper cuts made with a sterile scalpel. Many enthusiasts appreciate the tactile nature of scars and enjoy feeling the pattern in the dark. Some also elect to have tattoo ink rubbed into the wounds, particularly Caucasians, who are less likely to form keloid tissue than are darker-skinned peoples.

> *I have a cutting on my back. It's a double outline of a heart, and inside of it is a rose. That was done with a surgical scalpel—they just cut the first couple of layers of your skin. They don't go deep at all. Mine didn't scar.* —JEAN L.

The process of getting (and giving) a cutting requires tremendous focus and endurance.

> *I love the power of sitting still in a relaxed state. Your body can't be tense when you're getting a cutting, because if your muscle is tense, it's easy to cut deep [or] to make a ragged cut. The flesh has to be relaxed. So the discipline of sitting still and being absolutely relaxed while pain is happening, while someone is cutting you is arousing.* —LAURA ANTONIO

Branding is a form of cautery and was once a symbol of criminality or enslavement. Some African-American Greek fraternities and sororities have adopted the practice as a rite of passage.

Traditionally, the black brothers get their first brands on their left bicep because that's the one closest to their hearts, but it's not uncommon for members to get five or six brands on different parts of their bodies, including the buttocks, legs, and chest. . . . Even a few sororities branded women as part of the [hazing] ritual, sometimes on the inner thigh. —HANK NUWER[4]

Branding is now gaining popularity among young people of all races. The scar is highly tactile and the designs used are often unique and personally symbolic. Body modifiers use a thin piece of metal which is heated and quickly and precisely pressed to the recipient's skin. The sensation is extremely intense, and the ritual requires profound concentration.

Since the brand, when healed, normally expands to two or three times its initial size, expert branders use a very narrow branding iron; repeated strikes are used to shape creative patterns. Perhaps the most famous fictional account of branding occurs in *Story of O* when the heroine is branded to symbolize her ownership by the sadistic Sir Stephen.

Scarification and branding are controversial activities within the D&S communities. Even when properly done, they are profoundly painful, traumatic shocks to the body. Unwanted injury, unexpected scarring, and infection may result from either.

EXTREMELY EXTREME MODIFICATIONS

Thousands of extreme body modifications have been documented worldwide. One extremely rare but still practiced self-mutilation was recorded by Magnus Hirschfeld: A shepherd made repeated incisions to his glans, succeeding in bifurcating his penis.[5] This practice—known as *subincision*—was once found uniquely among peoples who lived in proximity to marsupials, which naturally possess forked penises. Australian Aborigines allegedly practiced subincision in hopes of gaining the kangaroo's enviable sexual stamina.

Variations on the theme of self-mutilation are virtually endless. Although self-inflicted mutilations, and even the fairly well-known fantasy of male castration, are clinically classified as masochism, most consensual D&Sers consider these practices to violate the tenets of safe and sane activity.

INTERVIEWS

FAKIR MUSAFAR

The kinds and variety of body piercings have become prolific. I did commercial piercings in a well-known piercing establishment for a year here. I would ask people: Why are you getting your nipple pierced? Or, why are you getting your genitals pierced? Or, why are you getting your navel pierced? I [usually] got answers that were extremely clear and well thought-out, with very powerful emotional and psychic reasons. Very often the piercing represented a personal rite of passage. It meant that they had left one phase of life or that they had intentions of starting life over. In some other cultures there are tales of piercing the body to let things out or to let things in. You're making an opening in the physical body but also in the psychic body that coexists with the physical body, so one must be very careful. It should be done with great care and understanding and great respect for the spirit that lives in the body.

[There] has [also] been renewed [interest in] cutting. This is making magic symbols, patterns, or meaningful marks on the body by cutting the [skin] with a sharp object, like a scalpel. We have some people who are very good at this, very shamanic about the way they do this, so that some kind of ritual magic is performed by cutting.

I've been doing a *lot* of branding this year. I have been doing brands with multiple strikes. I make complex designs and symbols—which are not easy to do with a brand—by using repeated burns of different-sized pieces. We've made endless chains to represent continuity in life and a continuity that's lacking in life, as part of a ritual. I've made large snakes that had as many as 24 to 36 different burns that took 30 to 50 minutes to put in. When done, the pattern is much more subtle than [a tattoo]. It is not as dark [or] as distinct; if done properly, it has the same characteristics of cutting or scarification. A well-made branding will be raised and three-dimensional. It will be something that you can see in the dark. It will be tactile as well as visual.

In my 40 years of experience [in] piercing myself and other people, remarkable things [have] happened. Some people have had transformations, both personal and extending out wider into tribe and family affairs.

LOGGER V.

One important thing [is] the concept of belonging. We all need to belong somehow. Through piercing, through S&M, we belong. We lose race, color, gender. There is nothing there except what we want and what we want to do, and in that sense, we belong. That's important to me, and I think it's important to a lot of people. We don't have heterosexual [or] gay: We [all] belong to one group of people who enjoy being who they want to be. There are no limits. We are all in the same family.

I'm a gay Puerto Rican male. I don't like to use the term *top*, but [I] play top and get into a bondage, fatherly scene. I don't consider myself handsome; other people do. But we always look at ourselves differently. A lot of people, especially in the gay community, have heard from others [that] I'm "a hot daddy to get pierced by."

Piercing is something that has to come from the heart, not from the brain, not because someone told you [to do it], or just because everyone else has it. I developed fantasies in my 30s when I began to see that other people had fantasies. My fantasy was to help them fulfill theirs. But as a child, I [had no] fantasies. I guess that has to do with my own situation as a child—[I was] molested sexually. I always was afraid of certain things. As a matter of fact, I find it sometimes very awkward to get tied down or be submissive. When I *do* allow myself to do it, I enjoy it very much. But I have to allow myself to do it.

I pierce anything and everything! I kid [that] if I ever started a shop, I would call it From Clits to Tits. I have done just about every piercing there is: eyebrows, clits, clit hoods; men and women; gay and straight. Having been married, having had children, and having gone from being a straight male to a gay male, it's just never bothered me.

I do a prescreening, which is *very* important to me and to the [clients]. I never lie to anyone and say that it's not going to hurt. I ask what kind of piercings they've had before [and] if they've had any problems. I ask what they're interested in and what jewelry they want. I show them pictures or talk to them about what they would like and give them some ideas. Jewelry is very personal. I never force people to use a certain kind of jewelry.

I always ask people if they are over 21. I want to make sure that the person knows exactly what he's doing. There's a statement I [always] read: "Do you understand that no piercing will be done if you are under the influence of alcohol or drugs?" This is something that I hold very dear. I don't drink, smoke, or do drugs. I don't care if other people do, but when you come here for a piercing, I want you to *know* what you're doing.

I need to know that the person has no [physical] problems. I always ask if they have epilepsy or diabetes. I have to know if they have hepatitis or HIV or AIDS, and if they're on any medication. I am very careful. All my tools are sterilized. I have two autoclaves. Sterile conditions are very important. With a piercing, cleanliness is more important than anything. If you don't keep it clean, I always guarantee a problem. I always give [people] a sheet of paper that lists everything they should know and do.

I also have a disclaimer that I ask everyone to sign, [stating] that this is done willingly and that I will not be held responsible for anything that goes wrong afterwards. I guarantee their safety when they're here, but once they're gone, all I offer is help and assistance. I recommend a warm saltwater solution for cleaning, the old-fashioned remedy. I ask everyone to call me before doing anything drastic, like removing a body piercing. I [also] ask if the area to be pierced is under extreme punishment and activity. Some people laugh at that question, especially if they want a Prince Albert. They say, "No, not enough!" And I say, "Oh you poor baby!" In one woman's case, I asked, "Is [the clitoris] under a lot of activity?" and she answered, "Not usually."

The reason [I ask] is that sometimes the area has been under torture, like the nipples, and if so, the skin tends to be a little [tougher]. I need to know how much force I'm going to be using [and] how to handle it: to be ready for problems if the needle doesn't go through right away.

If the person is ready, I prepare him. I clean him up. I mark the area to be pierced. I always talk to him. [The] feedback that I have gotten is that people feel comfortable when they're here. They come in the door, and they're nervous as hell. But by the time they walk up the stairs to the room where I'm going to do the piercing, they are comfortable. That is more important to me than anything. I'm in a position of a family doctor who is going to violate a part of their body. If a woman is going to lie down on a bed and open her legs, she has to feel that it's okay, and so do I.

[Washington, D.C. has] a leather weekend, usually in January, where a thousand or more people come to a leather contest. In that weekend I do anywhere from 20 to 25 piercings. I have someone registering everybody, and I bring them upstairs. I have an autoclave going all the time, so sterility never changes, precautions never change. I have someone with me to always make sure that I am being cautious. That's usually my other half. He is usually here, watching me—he's like my nurse—to make sure that I don't do anything stupid. If I pick up an instrument before my hands are sterile, that instrument gets sterilized immediately.

There are many styles [of piercing]. I find that piercing a woman's nipple is a lot easier than piercing a man's. A man's nipples are smaller and a bit on the tougher side. I find it a little harder to get the needle through [on a man]. On a woman, it will just go right through, and half of them don't even feel it. Yet they're terrified that it's going to hurt. I pierced my nipple and had no pain and no blood, but I was on a natural high. This is what I wanted: My heart said do it, and it felt good.

Of all the piercings on a man, the one that I think is the nicest is a Prince Albert. It's also the fastest to heal, in my opinion, because the urine is sterile and the salt tends to help healing. A frenum [piercing] is one of the simplest to do. It hurts the least, but it still hurts a little. There's a foreskin piercing, where you pull [up] the foreskin and pierce right through [it]. Sometimes a person wants a small ring on it, so he cannot pull the foreskin over the head. Then the piercing can be used as a chastity [device]. Or it can be a large ring, where the foreskin will go totally around the head when it's enlarged. An ampallang, I have been told, is a wonderful sensation, especially for women. Both the ampallang and the apadravya are a little on the dangerous side. If done wrong, the person could bleed a great deal, because when you're hard, you have vessels that fill up with blood, and if you penetrate those vessels during any one of these piercings, you open that little tube, and it will drip until it's healed.

ADIDA

If you love someone, you should be able to give him what he wants. If he wants to be spanked, then I should spank him. The emotional part [of S&M] for me is that I know he enjoys it. Not that I don't do other things for him that he enjoys, but this is something that not everyone could or would be willing to give him. It's something that I can. Many people make it a spiritual thing. For me it's playful. Sometimes I have trouble keeping a straight face in a scene, because we're having so much fun.

Before I met Mr. Happy I had never done or thought about any of this stuff. The most I had thought about it was that what's normally considered pain could be considered pleasure.

I've always been into physical things like ballet and martial arts. I enjoy physically letting go and going all out. My family is very loving; they encouraged independence. At the same time, they were always there, giving support, help, and encouragement to do what I wanted to do. It was great. I love my parents!

When I met Mr. Happy, he told me he was into this. I said, "Okay, I'll give it a try. I can't promise that I'll enjoy it or be good at it, but I'm willing to give it a try." I found that it was really a lot of fun! I didn't know what I was doing. I'd say, "You miserable worm! Did I get that right?" Or, "Oh, yeah, of course, uh, let me, um, spank you for being so presumptuous! What are you being presumptuous about? There must be something! Anyway, let me spank you; you don't need to know why!" I've gotten better at it now.

People perceive that S&M is like kidnapping or pedophilia. But you can't do this stuff without really caring for the person you're with. If you don't like them, don't do it! Caring and love is a big part of it: It's not two people who hate each other. [We're] people who care for each other very much.

I have two nipple piercings and six outer-labia piercings. I'm still not sure which was braver: getting the first one when I didn't know what I was in for, or getting the subsequent ones where I did! That kind of pain I don't deal with well. I know people who do. I have a friend who got her nipples pierced and she just blinked and said, "Oh, is that all?" For me, it was very intense. When I got my nipples pierced the first time, it was like a shot straight to the heart. It's a big rush and a bit scary, because I'm not real comfortable with needles. But it was also exhilarating. I did something I didn't think I could do. I pushed my limits.

I had the two nipples done in one session, and then I had all six outer-labia [piercings] done in another session. Apart from other feelings, you get a big rise in endorphins. I felt like I was floating about six feet off the ground after that. And it was just a lot of fun. I spent a lot of time jumping around and being very happy that night!

I have curved barbells through the nipples. And I have rings through the labia, which is a good idea, because curved barbells tend to hook onto things. I remember one night when Mr. Happy and I were making love—good old vanilla sex. We didn't notice that one of my barbells had hooked onto his nipple rings. He arched his back when he was coming and managed to rip his ring about halfway through his nipple! It hurt me a little bit, too, but my nipples are stronger than his, so he lost the tug of war.

The labia rings rub against Mr. Happy's cock. I think he feels it more than I do, but I feel his piercings more than he does, so it's an interesting enhancement. Actually, the most fun I have is that sometimes the six labia rings jingle when I walk. Music wherever I go!

I'm in a stronger relationship with Mr. Happy than I've ever had, because there is all that extra stuff in there that [demands] your attention and makes you think about what you're doing. When you're in an S&M relationship, you have to really care about this person, to feel [completely] connected. I've gone skydiving; I've faced things that are kind of scary and felt exhilarated. S&M is somewhat like that. You think, Gee, this could be scary! But when you do it, you feel so exhilarated and empowered. Not only have you exerted yourself—you've actually *enjoyed* it. It gives you a little bit of that empowering I feel when I do martial arts.

MR. HAPPY

I have always viewed [S&M] as a form of play and a form of release more than a lifestyle. It's not that it's not important to me: I'd certainly miss it if I never could do it again! It's just not something that shapes the rest of my life.

Conversely, it's not that it's partitioned off into this special area. It just doesn't spill over into work, and it doesn't spill over into taking out the garbage. It doesn't have any bearing on who does the checks or who does the driving. It doesn't enter into my interactions with people who aren't into this.

[As a child] I would do things with my genitals, pinch them. By puberty I would put clamps on or wrap my penis in Scotch tape when it was flaccid. When it would start to become erect, there was this odd biting of the tape. It felt a lot better than just having a regular erection. Those were the first inklings I got that not everything that theoretically hurt, actually hurt in a way that the culture says it ought to. I did these things by myself, and it never even occurred to me to do them with a partner. I didn't feel a sense of guilt or oddity about this stuff. I was raised in a family of atheists who believed in individual responsibility, so I didn't have some of the obstacles that get thrown in other people's paths about accepting the way they are. It's not that I'm out to my parents, but they did raise me to be independent, so I took them up on their offer. I don't know if this is something that my parents really need to hear. I am out to my brother and sister. I'm also fairly out to coworkers.

I've never been particularly good at pretending I'm *not* strange. People who were straight-laced and not happy about their sexuality would be driven away, and I got the women who were into this. My first girlfriend let me tie her to the bed and spank her. It was fun for both of us. She did things with me, too! She bit my cock when she was sucking on it. Then I ran into a woman who was desirable in many ways. She was beautiful and intelligent, and we had good vanilla sex. I would try to bring these things up; I was used to having it work out well. She said, "That's perverted, but we can fix that." I thought, Oh geez, golly; maybe she's right! and I started to have doubts.

I wanted to do scenes of much more intense domination and much more intense pain, both as a top and a bottom. I was also starting to explore my attraction with men. So right when I wanted to get more into this, there was this person telling me that all of it was sick. I hadn't yet bumped into any support groups. [But] other than that one period, S&M has never been a problem for me. I just lucked out.

I've got five piercings: nipples, frenum, Prince Albert, and a guiche. The guiche and the Prince Albert are interesting. When I met the woman who actually rescued me from my year of self-doubt, we were looking at a way to keep me from playing with myself without her permission. You can lock a Prince Albert to a guiche. She did that to me once. She made me wait two weeks, teasing me the whole time. Oh, that was not fun! Well, it was, but it was hard to last that long!

I'm planning one more piercing, an ampallang. The ampallang runs laterally through the head of the penis. [It] takes about six months to heal, but it's supposed to be quite pleasurable for the partner, too. Some people, I think, take it too far and wind up with so many piercings, it's baroque.

I've jumped out of airplanes and ridden motorcycles, and I've got several piercings. Yet every time I get a piercing, it's almost like the first time. I don't know how much it's going to hurt. I know it's going to take time to heal. So I get nervous and fluttery every time I get one, even though I've already got several. It's a way of challenging myself.

[Piercings] are convenient for S&M play. I can be led around by my penis, or it can be locked up. [Piercings] enhance sexual pleasure for me. They make my nipples more sensitive. I really feel the ones on the end of my penis when I'm having sucks. My orgasms are more intense than before because there is this little hot-electrical-wire sort of feeling.

I discovered fairly early on in my sexual development that I was multiorgasmic and also that I could have orgasms without ejaculating, and, for that matter, I could ejaculate without having an orgasm. Orgasm [is] possible in many ways which don't have anything to do with the classical interpretation of how it all works. I've [even] come from having my earlobes sucked! I got that idea from a guy in a wheelchair. I asked him about sex, and he said, "I've just relocated my erogenous zone." He said he wouldn't let just *anybody* touch his ear! It had to be somebody special. For him that was like his penis!

There is one very loving little story about how I knew that Adida was a keeper. I hadn't been with a woman since my ex. I already had my Prince Albert. Adida and I came back to her house, and she basically got me drunk. I didn't have any idea what her reaction was likely to be to the piercing. I had intended to sneak off to the bathroom and remove it, but things acquired a momentum of their own. I was thinking, Oh, my God! Worst case, she'll call the cops; best case, she'll require lengthy explanation.

She reached down and put me inside her, and we did the thing, and she never broke stride. So, finally, we're cuddling and I said, "Did you notice anything?" "Oh! It was very nice." "The *ring?*" I asked. And she said, "Oh, that!" She didn't even give me the satisfaction of saying, "Oh, my God! What's *that?*" She'd never seen one; she'd never even heard of it before! I figured, There's something special about somebody like that!

TRANSLOCATIONS OF DESIRE

Eighteen

FETISHISM

"I think," said Brown, "that when we are children we are much more inclined to be fetishists of one kind or another. I remember hiding inside of my mother's closet and feeling ecstasy at smelling her clothes and feeling them. Even today I cannot resist a woman who is wearing a veil or tulle or feathers. . . ."

—ANAÏS NIN[1]

The sacred and profane are nowhere more intimately intertwined than in the realm of fetishism, whose linguistic identity itself originates in the religious and whose practices often involve elaborate, sometimes ecstatic rituals. Fetishism always has been a fertile field for sexuality research, both because of its apparently infinite permutations and its conduciveness to theorizing. The arguments on nurture versus nature are heated: Some believe that fetishistic interests in adults are the result of traumatic events in infancy and early childhood. To others, genetic predisposition is the dominant influence.

In this chapter we profile two individuals who bring distinct perspectives to fetishism:

- Dian Hanson is the editor of *Leg Show* magazine. She is 40 years old and was twice married and divorced. She is now in a long-term monogamous relationship.
- Ava Taurel owns and operates a New York–based company that specializes in D&S psychodrama. She has lectured on S/M at New York University's Human Sexuality program and Rutgers Medical School and at other schools nationwide. She is 47 years old.

WHAT IS FETISHISM?

The definitions of *fetish* are so numerous that one would not be completely amiss in saying that each of us, to one degree or another, has at least one. Would Linus in the comic strip *Peanuts* be the same without his little blanket?

> *There is not an organ of the human body, not a single article of clothing or of daily use which may not become an object of fetishism.*
> —WILHELM STEKEL[2]

The word *fetish* derives from the Portuguese *feitiço*. It was apparently first used by 15th Century Portuguese explorers to describe West African sacred carvings. In its original (and current anthropological) meaning, fetish refers to a sacred artifact invested with spiritual or talismanic power. The erotic fetish is not merely a symbol of the divine but is itself divine. It possesses a discrete power: It can arouse and, sometimes, induce ecstasy in its devotee. For fetishists, a shoe may be sexier than the foot it adorns; lingerie more enticing than the erotic anatomy it screens; a rubber coat more stimulating than the person it contains.

Fetishism is a translocation of desire: The sexual impulse is directed away from genitalia and toward another part of the body or to an object. To Freud, this turning away clearly implied castration anxiety, and neo-Freudians proceed from this basis. To Jung, fixation on objects associated with childhood sexual encounters implied arrested sexual development. (Indeed, contemporary psychiatrists, such as Otto Kernberg, attribute all sadomasochistic acts to arrested development, although such analyses are no longer necessarily censorious.) Contemporary theorists are still wrangling over the etiology of fetishism.

The clinical definition of a fetishist is someone who cannot be aroused without the fetish item. Formerly a distinction was drawn between the erotic interest in inanimate objects (fetishism) and erotic interest in parts of the body (partialism). Modern theorists, however, expand the definition of fetishism to embrace both.

So varied are the types of fetishism that have been studied in the last century that a plethora of subcategories exists. A short list includes *hyphephilia* (arousal by human hair, animal fur, leather, and fabrics, especially upon erogenous zones); *mysophilia* (arousal by smelling or chewing soiled and/or sweaty apparel); *olfactophilia* (arousal by the odors of parts of the body); and *transvestophilia* (arousal from wearing the clothing, especially underclothing, of the opposite sex).

The American fixation on female breasts is really fetishism by popular consensus. Women who opt for breast augmentation can bear testimony to the American equation of buxom and sexy. What we believe to be sexually acceptable is always culturally determined. In America even disfigurements of the female form, such as implants that result in titanic but nonfunctional protrusions, are sometimes admired. In other cultures different body parts excite the erotic appetite. In Japan, for example, the nape of the neck is tantalizingly sexy; in some African cultures, bulky haunches are a paradigm of femininity; in China, it's a petite foot.

To be out of sexual syncopation with your society's beauty standards puts one at a distinct disadvantage; the American man who prefers a foot to a breast is likely to be viewed with discomfort or antipathy.

> *A lot of what I do in* Leg Show *is work to make the readers feel better about their fetishes, because I get letters every week from men who have attempted suicide, who've spent years in therapy trying to rid themselves of something as simple as a desire to kiss women's feet—something as healthy and nonthreatening, nondangerous as foot fetishism or shoe fetishism or stocking fetishism. But because it's not acceptable in our culture, most of these men do not let anyone, including their wives, know about their interests.*
> —DIAN HANSON

Why it is that an object may be more exciting than a person, or a part more exciting than the whole, has been a source of lengthy debate.

> *I always thought that the whole body was beautiful; [that] the whole was a work of art. Therefore, liking a part of the body was not a sick thing, just a puzzling thing. Why do I like this part more than that part? I don't know, but I just do. There's no difference between [my] fondling a foot and a straight man fondling a woman's breast. A body part is a body part.* —DOUG GAINES

Pioneering studies of sexual fetishism were undertaken by the father of standardized testing, Alfred Binet, in 1891. Binet theorized that fetishism is acquired largely through association. For example, if a boy has an erection at the moment he sees a woman remove her fur coat, he will from then on equate his excitement with the act or the object and become dependent upon fur for excitement. This theory is supported by anecdotal information and may help explain why men are more often observed to be fetishistic.

> When we're young, we're down on the floor [and] we're around feet before the age where we learn disgust for these odors. We're not born being disgusted by physical odors. Human odors are meant to be alluring. We're down there and there is a fascinating odor, often accompanied by stimulation, particularly for a boy. A boy has a meter of his stimulation that a woman doesn't: his penis. So the boy smells the foot; his penis can become erect without him even thinking about sex, because our nose goes to the old brain.
>
> —DIAN HANSON

Women, differently equipped, do not have as conspicuous a signal of arousal. Yet many of the women we interviewed reported that they were fetishists; more women, indeed, volunteered this information than men.

> I had a fetishistic revelation: For some reason belts really [and specifically] turn me on, aside from the whole turn-on of being beaten. —JOHANNA

> I like leather clothing, I like leather toys, and I especially like leather boots. I am a boot fetishist, whether running my tongue across them or wearing them. I fetishize uniforms and ultramasculine attire, whether Fruit of the Looms, white Jockey shorts, or a three-piece suit. I like police uniforms. I also fetishize Victorian garb on other women. —LAURA ANTONIO

It has been a clinical truism for decades that fetishists are uniquely male although extensive case studies of female fetishists abound in the earlier psychological literature. There are documented cases of grown women with fetishes for dolls or who were erotically addicted to satin.[3]

We believe that both genders are equally likely to be fetishistic, but that from childhood on, men are apt to be more aware of the erotic connection because their arousal is visible. As adults, they are more assertive in seeking out encounters and discussing the interest. Women are liable to be unaware of the connection between object or act and personal arousal. And since women are usually discouraged from acting on their sexual impulses, they probably are more likely to hide their desires, even from themselves. Meanwhile, women have sanctioned outlets for fetishistic urges. They may collect shoes, for example, without stirring comment.

Perhaps the reason many of our female subjects identify themselves as fetishists has to do with the general tendency of D&S females to identify and experiment with a diversity of erotic stimuli and to acknowledge sexual quirks openly.

In response to Binet's associative theory, Krafft-Ebing proposed another analysis: Some children are predisposed to become excited. Krafft-Ebing's "constitutional theory" became the standard behind which the psychological community rallied for a time. It tied in with an accepted tenet of psychological theory that mental deviation is either the product of injury or disease of the central nervous system, *or* it is a congenital condition. Sigmund Freud later emphasized a similar conclusion. Such personality theories are, at best, debatable. Reliable scientific study of environment's effect on sexuality is virtually impossible (sexual research remains anecdotal), and genetic research is still emerging.

John Money's concept of lovemaps—a primarily philosophical catchall concept that emphasizes environmental factors—has won some popularity. It posits that trauma can cause the fetishistic impulse. For example, the child whose parent teaches him to respond with deep shame or disgust to genitalia may then direct his lust to a less emotionally charged object.

> *The fetish and talismanic stratagem requires that the partner be saved from lust and that some token, the fetish or talisman, be the object of lust instead.* —JOHN MONEY[4]

None of our interviewees reported a specifically and sexually traumatic link, although it is impossible to ignore the amount of guilt and shame many fetishists experience. It seems likely that low self-esteem and fetishism are inextricably intertwined in most fetishists, and not that one necessarily proceeds from the other. Self-acceptance among fetishists is among the lowest of any category of sexual diversity. The lonely fetishist stealing secret moments to indulge his interest is a distressingly common phenomenon.

> *The feelings of difference were tough. "Why am I different? Why do I have to be different? Why can't I be like everybody else and react the same way as everybody else instead of having this extra heartbeat kicker happening whenever I see an amputee?" This seems to be much more of a positive, now.* —ROB

The first conscious memories of fetish experience are often pleasurable ones.

The origin of my rubber fetish is obviously at the pleasing hands of an adult. This causes many of the several thousand fellow professionals who have heard my story to attempt to make that encounter traumatic. It was not, in any way. Recently one person tried to have me admit that I might have suffered when I discovered what a horrible thing was done to me, but I haven't discovered that yet.
—THOMAS O. SARGENT[5]

I remember at the age of four having some neighbor men chase us around and tease us kids playing tag in the front yard. One neighbor caught me and pretended to sit on me. I said, "Whatever you do, don't put your feet in my face." He slipped off his moccasin and shoved his foot in my face—which was just what I wanted. This is before I was even aware of sexuality. I knew [what] I had was an intrinsic interest in the foot, and I was a precocious little runt who manipulated this man into doing what I wanted him to do. The interest was [already] there.
—DOUG GAINES

One interviewee described feeling consoled by rubber after an early problem with bed-wetting.

The only childhood experience I can relate that has shaped my current sexual orientation is that when I was very young I used to wet the bed, and my mother made me sleep on a rubber sheet. I grew so attached to it that when I stopped wetting, I kept a piece of the sheet in bed with me and couldn't fall asleep without it. Finally, my mother had to bribe me—I was about five—to get that piece of rubber away. To this day the smell of latex and baby powder gives me a tremendous visceral jolt. Talk about being imprinted!
—ALLEN

The actual physical objects that may become the center of fetishistic desire vary wildly. Dr. Money organizes fetishes into two types.

There are two classes of fetishes: the smellies and the feelies. For the fetishist, the smell or feel of the fetish is, in each instance, associated with the human body—for example, the smell of shoes or jockstraps, or the feel of hair, fur, silk, rubber (from training pants), and so on.
—JOHN MONEY[6]

We add to these the tasties and the seeies, and even the hearies, as fetishists describe other senses besides smell and feel as key to their arousal. Some interviewees believe that fetishes engage all the senses.

WHAT DO THEY LIKE?

Despite apparent similarities, each fetishist is unique. Within a single broad classification (for example, rubber fetishists) there is fantastic variety.

Among rubber fetishists, for example, some like latex, others like rubber, some like the material on cloth backing, while others are turned off by the cloth. There are those who like it dry and velvety and those who like it wet, those who are stimulated by the smell of urine and sweat, and those who are fastidious, those who like it tight fitting and those who like it loosely caressing, those who enjoy manual stimulation of themselves and those who like to lie on it, those who prefer it with a partner, others who want it alone, those who prefer a female partner, those who prefer male, and those who enjoy both. Some prefer this or that taste, sound, smell, or feel, and may be turned off by other types of rubber. There are those who prefer rubber gloves, those who like baby pants, book bags, bathing caps, balloons, condoms, boots, bloomers, bathing suits, beach bags, those who desire rubber aprons and those who exist for a red rubber coat with a double back, rubber on the outside and smelling and rustling exactly like their fantasy. —THOMAS O. SARGENT[7]

Virtually anything can be the object of fetishistic adulation. In an erotic context the fetish object is invested with all the dark mystery and allure usually attributed to a partner or a partner's erogenous zones.

If a person responds more to the clothing than to you as a person, you can feel diminished. The sad part of it is that there are people who respond more to the clothing. —AVA TAUREL

While fetishists may be thrilled by a particular object, some enjoy an entire outfit.

I have a wonderful playmate. He is a very visual person and he gets turned on by different looks—uniforms, spandex, rubber, leather. —JEFF BRITTON

For dominants, wearing a complete fetish outfit is an opportunity to don the cloak of authority; for submissives, the outfit signifies power.

To lick the boots or smell the feet of a policeman or a person in uniform is very erotic. That symbol of authority is very popular among our fetishists. For some the idea of being the foot slave to a successful businessman—to be his desk as he works—is very exciting.

So there are some who like to worship a person in a position of power.
Others simply like certain types of shoes. —DOUG GAINES

In this respect, fetishists resemble those who collect diverse wardrobes to reflect different moods and activities: business clothes, gym outfits, at-home clothes, evening gowns, sexy lingerie. But the fetishist's purpose is expressly erotic.

Also, despite the depth of their passion, fetishists are rarely faithful to any single object: Most require variety. They typically assemble large collections of articles that meet their individual requirements. While boot fetishists may amass boots in varying styles, and leather fetishists may collect stores of clothing and implements, those who are attracted to a part of the body frequently display a similar sensual philandering. Even though he may remain sexually monogamous, to the foot fetishist, an unfamiliar foot is an intoxicatingly erotic enigma and a new land to conquer—at least in fantasy.

The most common fetish categories include feet, toes, legs, shoes, hose, and boots; lingerie and corsets; lace, leather, fur, silk, velvet, and satin; rubber and latex. A comprehensive list of fetishes is impossible, making the observations of sexologists, psychologists, and the authors of this book little more than collections of interesting anecdotes or basic introductions.

Given the irreproducible nature of fetishism, one can extrapolate from the career of a few fetishists only the careers of those fetishists. Fetishes are specific not only to individuals, but to cultures and historical eras. Fetishes for feet, furs, and shoes were investigated by 19th Century scholars but so were such now-obscure fetish objects as red cockades and collar stays, items now as obscure as some of the researchers themselves. Contemporary fetishes include zippers, plaster leg casts, and disposable diapers. Future generations will undoubtedly revere objects we have not yet invented, just as our ancestors' fetishes were buried along with their private thoughts.

WHAT DO THEY DO?

The fetishist loves the fetish. While the object may seem a strange enticement to nonfetishists, the acts of love are familiar to all. He may hug or fondle the object; he may press his lips to it or press it against his flesh. He may lick it, gaze upon it, sniff it, massage it, or listen to the sounds it makes. He may also—in the case of footwear or clothing—enjoy wearing it or having a partner wear it.

Depending on the person's emotional demonstrativeness, the adoration may be extravagant or decorous.

For me, foot worship means any type of attention. It means taking my hand and caressing the soles of her feet, sniffing her toes, sucking her toes one by one, tickling her feet until she giggles like a silly schoolgirl, taking her sweating hose and just running it up and down my nose and smelling her sexy aroma after she's come home after a hard day's work and kicked off her shoes. That's what I mean by worship. I get the sexual, erotic feeling while I'm in contact with a woman's foot. Any time I touch my girlfriend's feet, I get an erection. —MARK J.

Although most fetishists prefer partners, for some fetishism is a solitary pursuit. Explanations vary, but the most likely is that shame prevents the fetishist from revealing his interest (or use of the fetish in masturbation) to a partner: It is emotionally easier to indulge the fetish alone. Fetishists with the highest level of self-acceptance generally combine private pleasures and shared activity, much the way most people balance solitary masturbation and intercourse.

D&S frequently plays an intrinsic role in a fetish scenario. Since the fetish has the power to rule its admirer's passions, the person who wears or wields the fetish takes on the object's power.

When I wear high boots and leather I feel powerful. I am a very vulnerable person, so I need to compensate. I sometimes have, on a personal level, problems with boundaries. I have to create them artificially, because I don't always have them within myself.
—AVA TAUREL

Among couples it is common for both partners to wear fetish gear during erotic play or at D&S social activities. As has been stated abundantly in earlier chapters, D&Sers particularly seek to heighten their partners' arousal. Thus the dominant or submissive whose partner has a fetish is almost certain to indulge that appetite; it is not uncommon for him or her to develop a sympathetic arousal.

Professional dominants usually dress in fetish wear in D&S settings: latex or leather garments, shiny catsuits, exotic footwear, and Victorian garments are particularly popular. Many require the submissive to worship their feet, clothing, or implements in tribute to the dominant's authority.

Fetish play is incorporated into D&S in dozens of ways. Straight dominant men may restrict their partners' movement with hobbling, spiked heels— exerting sensual control over the fetish. Lesbian submissives may pay homage to their partner's boots by licking or polishing the leather, surrendering sensual control to the fetish. The fetish objects have a vibrant and vital identity.

[Clients who like fetish clothing] like to look at it, to smell it, to kiss it, or they want to relate to the garment. Same with shoes: They like to smell the shoes, kiss the shoes, be subservient to the shoes.
—AVA TAUREL

In some cases power exchange is limited to the fetish only.

I'm open to a little bit of S&M if it deals with feet. If a woman wants me to use her as a foot mat, I would like that.
—MARK J.

For others, fetish worship is merely one component of a complex D&S scenario. Some fetishists, however, are distinctly uninterested in any overt expression of D&S. For them, the fetish is a sensual enhancement on the order of candlelight and flowers. And some fetishists fantasize about D&S but feel so uncomfortable with their image of power relationships that they suppress the impulse.

Generally, the fetish is a sacred and glorious aphrodisiac. But while a vast majority of fetishists treat the fetish object with great respect and tenderness, some treat it roughly. Again individual psychology applies. Power usually inspires awe, but it can certainly incite rebellion or rough play. Ticklers, for example, may subject feet to an intense sensation not always pleasurable to the foot's owner; some ticklers enjoy persisting until the partner loses bladder control, weeps, or begs for mercy.

WHY DO THEY LIKE IT?

The reasons people enjoy fetishes can best be compared to the reasons people like sex: The same rewards apply. Thus, any enumeration of pleasures will be incomplete. The fetishist experiences transcendent excitement and complete sensory pleasure; she may experience a nearly religious ecstasy or spiritual melding at the moment of contact with the object; the fetish is a source of aesthetic delight. It may also be a benevolent force which protects and consoles.

Elmer Batters, who originated a lot of the 1950s leg-art magazines, is in his 70s, and he has spent all of his life exploring foot and leg fetishism. He says it comes down to security: that a child who has a very loving mother, the mother will cuddle the child to the bosom when the child is frightened. A mother who is more withholding will not pick the child up so readily, and the child is left clinging to her legs. We see this all the time—a child down there, holding onto his mother's legs for security. He feels that the legs and the feet represent security. I know that that's true of men who are breast fetishists. It's not just sex; [it is] the comfort that we felt when we were carefree infants. I think we want love, we want acceptance.

—DIAN HANSON

Feelings of comfort, security, joy, emotional completion, and love are as intrinsic to fetishism as to any other positive sexual act. But there is no need to overstate the case: For some, a fetish is simply a means of whetting one's appetite or enhancing one's orgasm. While some fetishists may nearly swoon with desire, others are decidedly playful and casual about the thing which delivers sensual fulfillment.

INTERVIEWS

DIAN HANSON

Leg Show magazine originated about 10 years ago in the old tradition of leg-art magazines, which started in the 1950s before they could show much more than leg. Legs were much more popular back then. When I took it over about six years ago, it was a mishmash of leg art and misunderstood foot fetishism.

I started reading the mail, and [it] was phenomenal. People described in detail what they were interested in, like none of the other magazines I'd ever worked for. I've been in [the men's magazine] business 15 years. So I began to hone the magazine along the lines of the readers' interests. The women are not necessarily nude, but they are almost always in a position of power. It's very much about power relationships. Generally, the men are submissive, though there are dominant men who also read *Leg Show,* and I do present some women who are submissive for that.

I know that there are a lot of gay foot fetishists. And I have a large transvestite audience for *Leg Show* and a lot of my readers will also accept TV feet. Readers are also interested in buttocks.

I have a deep interest in sexual psychology. I read widely. I know that a fetish is not something we seek; none of us seek to be different. We all want to be normal. We have fetishes because of events in our early childhood. They're extremely difficult to get rid of once we have them, and for the most part, they are absolutely harmless. They are the ultimate safe sex. If a man has a shoe fetish, who is he hurting? No one. If he feels guilty about it and suppresses it, he's removing pleasure from his life. If he can come to grips with it and find peace within himself about his fetish, and practices it in a sane way, he will be getting the most pleasure he can out of the situation. I definitely am a proponent of adjustment to the situation and seeking pleasure in it.

I think a desire to be loved is so entwined with sexuality [that] it could not be separated from any sex. We all want to be loved. In most pornography they attempt to completely separate lust and love and present this [as] You go have sex and you go away, and neither one of you cares, but it's great. I don't think it's great if there's absolutely no love attendant.

Most of my readers are very, very embarrassed about their fetishes, even the simplest fetish. I have developed tremendous sympathy towards my readers. It really has to do with their attitude about their sexual interest.

When the reader feels that his fetish, his interest, his leaning, is despicable, he communicates that to his mate. When he can come to feel that it's a gift—and indeed, I think a fetish can be a gift—it is a way for an individual to find pleasure that is denied other individuals.

I'm appalled by what our Puritan culture does to people. Our culture first creates all these fetishes by suppressing positive images of sexuality in youth, and then, when the person develops the fetish, which is the natural end result of that, the person is further punished and reviled.

I think the root of paraphilias is sexual repression in youth. In primitive societies the children knew about sexuality. In our society no matter how you're raised, you experience sexual repression. Even if your home is fairly enlightened, you're going to experience it in school, among your friends, in every other area of society. And the word is [that] there is no sexuality until we're 18 years old or no sexuality until we reach puberty. The truth is that we are sexual from the moment of birth. That doesn't mean that we should be having sex, but we have sexual awareness and it needs to be taken into consideration.

There's a lot of dispute about why submission and fetishism are so often connected. I feel that a lot of the men despise themselves when they discover that there is something unusual about their sexuality. They feel abnormal from the day they discover it and hate themselves for it. They expect hatred, they expect ill treatment; so if they can completely subjugate themselves to the woman, then maybe they can make up for this bad thing in them and be loved. They can atone for it.

[All this said], I would like to say that I speak in generalities. There are people who read *Leg Show* who just want to see pretty leg art. There's every possible kind of reader, but there are tendencies for power relationships among people who are fetishists. I think our society as a whole tends towards power relationships. I think we're a very power oriented, aggressive society, and an aggressive society is going to have power relationships. That doesn't go only with sexuality: We have power relationships with our platonic friends. It is the nature of our society. I encourage my readers to make peace with their unusual sexuality, because I don't think they really have a choice. They can either live miserable lives of denial, fighting against it [or] they can find ways to make it work for them and to get the most happiness they can out of it.

AVA TAUREL

I have a bachelor's degree from New York University in field production. Aside from owning Taurel Enterprises—which supplies talent, wardrobe, and locations—I work as a photographer and journalist. I interview celebrities.

I've also produced and directed videos and worked in distribution. I've been associate producer for feature films. I have acted in seven [foreign] feature films where I played leading roles.

As for D&S, there is my professional relationship to it and there is my personal relationship to it: Those are two very different things. On a professional level, I work as a dominatrix [and] I have more limits. On the personal level, I enjoy being both dominant and submissive. [Also], on the personal level, I am sexual, which I cannot be on the professional level. It's against the law and I have to be careful because of the high profile I have now in the media. I have to be very strict about where I stand legally.

I have clients who see me personally and clients who see women who are independent contractors for the company I own. Most [clients] are lawyers. That's the [most common] characteristic: The definite majority are lawyers. Twenty-five hundred people have come here. Most are fairly trusting, which is an important factor: to be willing to trust another human being. Many of them, of course, are very [nervous] yet trusting. I would say half of them are good manipulators. They come to submit, yet they're very keen on having a particular kind of person, a particular kind of scene. They're very picky, and I guess, very dominant, in a sense. I very seldom see couples. The few females who have come here have come to learn what to do to men, not to be dominated themselves. I've dominated women on a personal level, but not as clients.

[Personally], I enjoy wearing a latex catsuit, because it fits very tightly all over the body. If I wear leather garments, I like to wear a lower-cut leather jacket. I have to wear things that are good for my figure. I'm busty, so I like to show off my bust, and I like to wear tight-fitted corsets. I have many made by B.R. Creations. I like to wear lace-up corsets and then I like to wear black spandex tights and either high boots or spike-heeled shoes. This is how I feel I look the best. I also have [a mixture of red and black] latex dresses [which are] cut [low] in the front, and I have an assortment of shoes and boots [in] different styles. I like variety.

Let's say a person first submits to the clothes and to the persona he imagines within these clothes: I feel that as the session progresses, he will feel my personality, the strength of my soul, of my being, of my intellect, and will submit to that. [I] assert my personality over his image of me. The image of the clothes will always be there. It will always fascinate him, but at the same time, as I reveal myself, especially as a real being, I tend to stand away from the clichés of dominance. I tend to avoid having a submissive say, "Yes, Mistress, thank you, Mistress." I cannot stand those typical phrases. I want different kinds of responses. I look for things to say that are different from the standard; [it must be] something that appeals to me, so I don't feel that

I'm just a tape recorder repeating certain monotone phrases that were scripted for mistresses.

[It's] the same when I interview women who come to work for me. I have them improvise. You discover a person's creativity by how much they go outside of the stereotypes, what they bring in of their own personal style. That's what makes a mistress—personal style. It's a signature.

One third of the people who come here would like to cross-dress. They're basically heterosexual men, though we also have bisexual men who [might] like to cross the line and be a female with a man, but [who are] too afraid to make that step. Most of the men want to be males, but [to] explore their female sides. They want to be a lesbian with a woman. We do not provide fetish garments for cross-dressers here. They have to bring them on their own. Here they usually come for female lingerie or normal female clothing. Sizes are so varied, and they couldn't afford us dressing them up in fetish clothing. I did some of it in the beginning, but it was not worthwhile. Basically men who bring their own wardrobe bring petticoats or frills and nylons.

One [unusual fantasy] that comes to my mind is a man who wanted to experience childbirth. He wanted to wear a tight female corset, high-heeled shoes, be bound genitally, and have an enema session, which would be prolonged over three hours. It was basically verbal: preparing him with the exercises for giving birth. The water inside his stomach was to blow up his stomach so that he would feel there was a child inside of him and would have to expel this child. He really wanted to feel what the woman goes through to give birth. That stays in my mind.

I think I'm a great mistress if a submissive is inspiring. If the submissive is a blob, is deadpan in front of me, I'll be a terrible mistress. This is very dangerous and very destructive for a mistress, and that's why I stopped doing professional dominance to a great extent a few years ago. I had to stop because I was destroying it for myself. There comes a moment when you know what you can do creatively. [But then] you put out that information, that energy, with someone who you feel is totally unreceptive and who doesn't have the strength within to appreciate your finesse, or your art, or your psychology; [someone] who is looking for something very, very simple and very rudimentary.

You cannot be creative, so you turn to memories of other sessions where you [were] and try to re-create them. You imitate what you have done creatively before, and you give [an] imitation to the uninspiring submissive in front of you. [By] doing that, you are prostituting your art. You diminish yourself.

Personally, I feel very unfulfilled after a session like that. And yet the person has paid a high fee to come and see you, and you are supposed to [play] the role. Now I own my own company, and I have other people who make money for me. I can see just the people who I can be really creative with. But, for example, the other day someone came to see me, and I was very disappointed. I thought it went very well. I thought that I got him where I wanted him to be. At the end, he said, "All this does for me is take away stress. It's relaxing." The way he said that I felt, Gee, you didn't appreciate any of it? Is that all it did for him? I was so disappointed, I went home that night and just felt horrible. [I do know that] people have a lot of guilt sometimes. It's painful with someone who feels so guilty about having enjoyed themselves.

Nineteen

EROTIC EXTREMITIES

When I want to imagine her, I can only evoke one meaningless detail: the chapped skin on her knees, like a boy's; this is deeply touching and guides my thoughts into tantalizing regions of contradiction, into blissful antinomies. Everything else, above and below her knees, is transcendental and defies my imagination.

—BRUNO SCHULZ[1]

What typically is called foot fetishism actually comprises a nearly infinite variety of tastes. Briefly and incompletely to catalogue: foot fetishists may like feet, legs, or buttocks. They may favor specific parts of the foregoing, such as toes, soles, arches, insteps, heels, ankles, calves, knees, or thighs. Or they may be aroused by the absence of limbs: A sexual interest in amputees is clinically identified as *acrotomophilia*.

Foot lovers may love spike-heeled shoes, flats, slippers, loafers, mules, oxfords, or Mary Janes; sandals, open-toe shoes, cleats, or gym shoes; silk stockings, fishnets, seamed stockings, white cotton socks, or black nylon socks. They may like details of footgear, such as the lining, laces, or inner pad. They may like the shoes or hose to smell of perfume or cologne or powder or sweat or dirt or to have no odor at all. They may like leather boots, shiny boots, vinyl boots, rubber boots, suede boots, thigh-high boots, or military-issue boots, boots with heels, or boots with industrial soles. They may like huge feet or tiny ones; shapely, well-formed feet or rough, peculiar ones; shod feet or bare ones.

In this chapter we explore the diversity of interests which fall under the general heading of foot fetishism. We feature the further insights of Dian Hanson and three profiles:

- Doug Gaines is 37 years old and is the founder of Foot Fraternity. He teaches special education and owns a greeting-card company for gays and lesbians, as well as a bookkeeping service. He has been with his lover for 12½ years.
- Mark J. is 30 years old. He works in sales and is in a full-time relationship.
- Rob is 30 years old and unmarried.

WHAT IS IT?

Foot fetishism comprises a pronounced sexual interest in the lower limbs or in anything that covers portions of them. The allure ordinarily attributed to erogenous zones is literally translocated downward, so that the fetishist's responses resemble a conventional person's arousal at seeing genitals.

Because fashion history has supplied us with so fantastic a variety of footwear and legwear, nearly each individual foot fetishist seems to develop singular interests. These, presumably, are influenced by his early encounters with feet.

Most of our interviewees who listed foot fetishism as an interest recalled an erotic encounter with feet in childhood: crawling near an adult's foot and feeling pleasantly stimulated, using a parent's shoes as playthings, being tickled or nudged or trod on by a parent or other adult. Most, however, say that their desires already existed: The experience elicited a recognition of the desire. Also, while fetishes tend to be era-specific (today's foot lover may worship a penny loafer; a century ago the high-button shoe was popular), the footwear styles that become the fetish center may not even have been present in one's childhood. This strongly suggests that the precise source of excitement is amenable to change.

To ascertain why certain children eroticize feet and others, who may have similar contact, do not is thus far impossible. Some psychologists suggest that the interest is fixed when a trauma occurs in conjunction with exposure to the fetish, but this hypothesis can be neither proved nor disproved. Some of our interviewees' earliest memories are entirely pleasurable, others' are traumatic, and some are an admixture of the two.

> *[Enjoying being stepped on] seems very odd, though it was explained to me very well by a reader who talked about being a small child and playing on the floor. A neighbor woman stepped on his hand. The neighbor and the mother showed him a great deal of affection and comfort after that and joked about stepping on him and that they were going to squash him. He loved the attention.*
>
> —DIAN HANSON

The foot lover typically comes to terms with his orientation in adulthood, if at all.

> *I want to affirm [people], to say, "You're all right; you're healthy; there's nothing wrong with it." You'd be surprised how many people just need to hear somebody say that. They say, "God, I've never voiced this to another living soul!" And these are people in their 30s and 40s. I think, "Geez, how could you live that long and never even tell anybody that this was what you wanted to do when it was so much a part of you?"*
>
> —DOUG GAINES

If any one generalization applies, it is that shame at his sexual difference is the fetishist's chief source of anguish.

> *I thought I was weird; I thought it was shameful. I used to go through magazines—I still do—[and] cut out pictures of feet. I would hide them, [because] I thought that this isn't good.*
>
> —MARK J.

Since the foot lover often perceives his fetish as fully sexual, it's possible that along with his desire he has also translocated his shame. If so, it is a poignant irony: The impulse which may, in youth, have made feet more acceptable than sex organs as objects of desire can evoke the same guilty charge that the fetish should have relieved. The dilemma is further exacerbated when the foot fetishist realizes that he is sexually unusual.

> *When I was in junior high all the other guys were like, "Hey, this woman's stacked!" And the first thing I looked at was their feet.*
>
> —MARK J.

While an array of groups and publications support the interest, many fetishists feel very uncomfortable with tastes which seem extreme or kinky. For example, many foot lovers are actively repelled by D&S or acts considered to be unclean, such as sniffing sweaty socks. This may be another manifestation of internal conflict: If the fetish is shameful, then other kinky desires are even less acceptable.

> *There are the people who write in and say, "I just like clean, pretty feet. I don't want them to smell! I'm not into any of this smell stuff. [That's] too weird!" Stekel, who was one of the original sex researchers, made an interesting comment. He said that if a person is simply not interested in one area of sexuality, they are generally indifferent—which does not carry any strong emotion.*
> —DIAN HANSON

The overwhelming majority of self-identified foot fetishists are male. Women—and especially lesbian—foot fetishists, however, are a small but visible presence in the D&S world. As a group, gay men seem to be most at peace with their foot-fetish desires. This may be because by separating from heterosexual culture, gay men have already confronted a momentous social challenge. Once they have acknowledged themselves as sexual outsiders, accepting other unusual aspects of their sexuality may require a second, but less painful, coming out.

> *I had two comings-out. One was coming out as gay, and the second was coming out of the foot closet.* —DOUG GAINES

Thus, while foot fetishists abound throughout alternative-sexuality communities, one is more likely to see foot eroticism in a gay environment than in a heterosexual one. Leather bars, for example, often have a submissive bootblack available to polish patrons' shoes and boots, whereas foot play, though hardly unknown, is more of a catch-as-catch-can proposition at heterosexual D&S gatherings.

WHAT DO THEY LIKE?

Contact with feet or footwear—or having someone else make contact—is a completely eroticized experience for the foot fetishist.

> *I met a bootboy at [the] International Mr. Leather [competition] who literally gave me a foot massage through my boot. I got excited while he was doing it. By the time it was over, my feet felt fantastic,*

and my boots [had a] perfect, military spit-shine. Then he leaned over and washed his tongue on each boot, and I could feel [it] press through the boot against my foot. If I were a man, I would have come right there. As it was, when I got off the stool, I felt like I was walking two feet above the ground. —Laura Antonio

In many cases the foot lover is erotically and emotionally gratified by having a relationship with the foot or footwear. Immediate sexual release is not a requirement.

The range of activities among foot fetishists spans a spectrum of stimuli, from fondling or massage to activities such as trampling or stomping. Kicking is known, though rarer. (It is also difficult to distinguish between the foot that kicks and the object of the kick: Some masochists fantasize specifically about kicks to the scrotum, but whether this is an extension of foot fetishism, with the foot as ultimate power symbol, or uniquely is a form of CBT is ambiguous.)

Fetishists also may combine foot worship with diverse erotic alternatives, including other fetish dressing, transvestism, or D&S play. Bondage is popular among D&Sers who either wish to be erotically coerced into foot worship or who, conversely, may wish to restrict the submissive's movement. Dominants put their partners in hobbling footgear, such as spectacularly high-heeled shoes or boots that restrict the submissive to mincing steps and exaggerate the arch of the foot. Most popular are narrow, pointy-toed stilettos, which fans consider profoundly feminine. They create elaborate shoe-and-bondage combinations involving restrictive footwear and chains, stocks, or other bondage devices. Or they deliver diverse forms of pain to the foot, including whipping.

Immobility fantasies are also a prime turn-on for acrotomophiles, for whom the absence of a foot or a leg carries much of the same erotic charge that the foot or leg's presence carries for the foot lover.

I'm primarily interested in leg amputees' immobility. . . . The stump and the stump areas are of particular interest to me. Kind of as if there's another sexual zone down there. It's like having an extra breast or something. —Rob

Tickling is a distinct fetish, and tickling purists reject any connection with D&S. But some "foot dominants" use tickling as a means of wielding power. Though putatively harmless, tickling can be a ferocious type of dominance. An immobilized and tickled partner is absolutely helpless; his purely physical response overwhelms his conscious control.

If you've got somebody strapped and tied to the bed, and you choose to tickle their feet, they can't do anything but accept it until they beg you to stop. —DOUG GAINES

For the most part, foot lovers prefer voluptuous encounters that engage all the senses. Visual stimuli are also important: Foot lovers often like to look at and to collect photos of feet. And to glimpse a woman nonchalantly dangling a shoe or kicking it off is thrilling.

If the foot is your sexual goal, then shoe dangling is a kind of striptease for the foot. —DIAN HANSON

What women usually will do when they're standing in line waiting for something is they'll take one of their shoes and just slip their foot in and out and dangle it from their toes. That drives me nuts. —MARK J.

By and large, foot lovers enjoy relatively gentle, aesthetically pleasing scenes that concentrate on soft caresses, kissing or licking, and worship. They revel in the sensuality of the object of their desires. Submissive foot lovers usually prefer psychological domination or comfortable bondage to pain.

I like to be ordered to smell feet or kiss them or lick them. I like the verbalization. I like being bound at a man's feet, where I am helpless and he can use his feet on me any way he wishes. I like to be a footstool; I like to be his slave. I like to buy his shoes and socks for him and afterwards kiss his feet and thank him for allowing me to do that. It goes into many forms of humiliation. —DOUG GAINES

Just kneeling to kiss a partner's foot can be a delightful ritual. Some view boot kissing as a form of homage.

When I am being submissive to someone I really want to honor or flatter—not with emptiness but with a genuine compliment—I may offer to kiss their boots. —LAURA ANTONIO

The moment of contact is exhilarating. The foot lover is at last fully engaged in a spiritual and deeply emotional connection with the object of his infatuation.

WHY DO THEY LIKE IT?

As a society, we accept that the torso is the sexiest area of the body. Thus, the foot fetishist seems sexually off kilter, as if he's somehow missed the point. But feet—and especially boots—have a central place in our culture's power symbology. Numerous writers have exploited the imagery—from Anthony Burgess's description of a brutal kicking in *A Clockwork Orange* to George Orwell's warning in *1984* that, "If you want a picture of the future, imagine a boot stamping on a human face—forever."[2] In her poem "Daddy," Sylvia Plath reiterates the inherent connection between the hated father and feet and boots. Indeed, the boots of the Nazi stormtrooper have become a metaphor for ruthless power, and the sound of boots in *1984* is inseparable from the tyranny of Big Brother's troops.

That feet—the bully's favorite weapon—can inspire terror provides an insight into their erotic appeal, for that which is powerful always has the power to arouse. Some submissives regard the spiked heel as a symbol of power; it literally and figuratively carries a pointed threat. For many dominants, wearing certain types of boots or shoes enhances their sense of personal power.

> *Wearing boots, for me, is an experience in becoming more confident. When I put on a heavy pair of boots, well-worn boots that fit comfortably, for one, I'm taller. Secondly, my stride is louder, firmer. Lastly, there is a sensual pleasure of the leather caressing my calves and the firmness of the shape of the boot around my foot.*
>
> —LAURA ANTONIO

Similarly, the notion of the servant or slave abasing himself by lying prostrate at the master's feet is firmly rooted in our cultural consciousness. This image is singularly arousing to the submissive foot fetishist who, during an erotic encounter, relishes his physical, psychological, and even social inferiority to the dominant.

> *The excitement comes from being completely submissive to him sexually, of knowing that I'm placing him above me. I'm putting him on a pedestal and putting myself beneath him in homage and in worship to him.*
>
> —DOUG GAINES

In addition to the allure of power, however, aesthetic and sensual elements make feet, shoes, or boots exceptionally sexy. A well-formed foot or leg is a supreme blend of form, grace, and function, inspiring reverence in its devotees. And the materials from which a shoe or boot is made can deliver powerful erotic stimuli.

The feel of the leather against my face, and the taste of it on my tongue, was erotically powerful. It was unreal become real. It was something I'd only read about and experienced vicariously. And suddenly there I was really doing it, and I didn't feel dumb: It felt as good as it read. —LAURA ANTONIO

Interest in shoes is also a culturally acquired phenomenon: Imelda Marcos is not the only person who owns shoes for every possible occasion and mood. The smell and texture of leather, the bright gleam of a polished or patent leather shoe, and other details of shoe fashion win the favor not only of fetishists but of men and women the world over.

INTERVIEWS

DIAN HANSON

When *Leg Show* was created, everyone in the business, including myself, laughed at it. A magazine about legs? Who's going to be interested in that? You know, "Americans want T-and-A." Since I took over *Leg Show*, its sales have quadrupled. It went from being a bimonthly to an all-color monthly. There are about six imitators of *Leg Show* now. I think a large measure of its success was my moving it towards D&S. I think it's the most undernourished market in the sex field in the U.S. today. There is a huge community of men who are interested in sexual submission in the United States, and I think in the world. *Leg Show* sells better in Europe than any of the other magazines I've ever worked on. It's particularly of interest in England and [in] the Germanic countries. It reaches about a quarter of a million readers a month. Foot fetishism figures big in all of its permutations, which includes crushing with the feet, stockinged-foot fetishism, shoe dangling, all the myriad interests—everything below the waist except genitalia, which seem to be of least interest to the *Leg Show* readers.

I'd say the most common interest is in a small, well formed, high arched, straight toed, soft, unblemished female foot with a certain amount of odor. Shoe dangling is equivalent to flashing. You see it all the time. A woman sits and crosses her legs, and she pops her shoe off at the heel and dangles it from the toes, generally slipping the foot around. Some women are really acrobatic with it. For the women I think it's an unconscious habit to relieve the tightness of the shoes, but for men it can look like a very purposeful tease. I have to admit that I have fun with it sometimes and do it as a purposeful tease. I think there are other women who, once they find that out, can play with it.

From there, you get people who want to be walked on by high heels or bare feet. It gives you a nice peek up the skirt, for one thing, but it also impresses the power of the woman on the man. There's a related fetish of men who want to be very small, from an inch to a foot high, and want to be stepped on. Beyond that, there are people who want to be kicked by feet; people who are interested in very dirty feet or huge feet, feet that look powerful.

Interestingly, I have one of the largest lesbian readerships of any of the so-called men's magazines. Most of the women who have submissive foot fetishes are lesbian, in my readership. I try and keep *Leg Show* very reader-participation-oriented. It helps the readers to not feel so alone. This is what the letters express over and over: "I read *Leg Show* [and] I know I'm not alone, because I see so many other readers participating." I just had an article written by a bisexual woman who is a [D&S] foot fetishist. She plays both roles but definitely likes to worship the feet of other women, though I believe she's a married woman. She sent in some photographs of herself and her feet and wrote very candid memoirs of how she got interested in female feet and her original encounters with other women.

[Another] area of foot fetishism is tickling. Tickling fetishists are often dominant; I call it the guilty sadist. We know that we're inflicting pain and suffering on somebody when we tickle them, but the person is laughing. And there is control, because almost every tickle fetishist wants to restrain their victim. Personally, I don't like being out of control, and so I don't like people to tickle me, but I do understand that these people are my readers, and I don't want to discriminate against any of them. I feel that I have to have compassion for all to have compassion for any.

It seems to me that there is kind of an obsessive-compulsive nature to fetishists, which goes along with power relationships: They want things black and white; they want things at one or the other extreme. Those gray areas are not as comfortable. I would probably just break it down 50-50 as far as people who say they just have a foot fetish—they like women with pretty feet, and that's about as far as it goes; the other 50 percent are really megasexual; they're people who are interested in all kinds of unusual sexuality. Those tend to be the people involved in power relationships.

DOUG GAINES

I want to let all people know that their sexuality is not something they've chosen—it's a part of them, just like hair color or eye color. Don't spend your life not enjoying what's pleasurable to you. I was shocked at the number of people who were into feet. I thought I'd start this little club. Well, I have received over 20,000 requests for information over the years [just from my little ads]. People need to know that there are places to go for whatever you like, men and women, straight and gay, bi, whatever. There are wonderful people, professional people, good people [out there]. Most of my members are doctors and lawyers and accountants and teachers. We're real people—your brothers, your uncles, your cousins and aunts and mothers. [Our] stories need to be told. We were blessed with this thing called sexuality. Don't stick it in a closet. It's a gift. Have pleasure with it. I guess my emotions speak clearly: You've got to take the risk to be yourself.

The Foot Fraternity was established as an affirmation group. I found the need to affirm [others] because I [once] needed somebody to tell me, "You want to smell my feet? That's okay, it doesn't hurt anybody. It's innocent.'' That was a second coming-out and happened in my 20s, when I was dealing with sexuality and being okay with who I was and accepting all of who I was—every bit of me. It took time and some counseling to realize that it doesn't matter what I like as long as it's between consenting adults and doesn't hurt anyone. It took a little time in my mind to redo my Catholic upbringing—thinking of missionary position as the only right way. [Once] I was okay with it, I thought, I'm going to help other people. All people— straight [or] gay—need to be okay with what they like sexually, as long as it doesn't infringe on anybody else's right or intentionally hurt somebody who doesn't want to be hurt.

I have just two small ads out, letting people know that the Foot Fraternity exists, [but] I send out no less than 25 letters a week to people [who are] requesting information. That's a lot of people. I would say about 10 percent of my members are either married or involved with women. [Many] are married to women but need a man's feet in their life. A small percentage [are interested in women's feet], but the majority are into men's feet. [We have something which corresponds to] the stereotypical woman-with-the-stiletto-heels: A lot of our members enjoy worshiping the boots of a policeman, because it's a symbol of authority. Certain people only like Weejun penny loafers; [others] only like boots. [With] some, it doesn't matter as long as it's on a male foot. It's a diverse group.

I've been very fortunate [because] I've formed some interesting hypotheses from talking to thousands of people. I believe that our sexuality is determined before we're five years old; some significant emotional event happens to us in those years that makes that area erotic or exciting to us. I [also] believe that there's some genetic predisposition to liking certain things. Part of it is in the genes, and part of it is that significant event. Maybe we were bounced on Daddy's knee, or Daddy tickled us with his foot, and we were intrigued by watching Daddy's foot come over our face. [Maybe] it was so emotional to us that we held onto that image, and that blended into our sexuality at puberty. I [still] don't know why the foot and all the verbalization and domination that goes along with it is so erotic to me. Quite frankly, I've had such pleasure with it that I don't really care why.

[The Foot Fraternity's] major purpose is to help guys meet other guys into their fetish and fantasy, primarily dealing with the foot, but also dealing with other things—uniforms, people being wet. The organization deals with most any fetish; my only restriction is that you cannot ask for or go for somebody under 18. [But we have] gays, straights; we've got married men who are happy with their wives but are still intrigued by the male foot but want to keep their marriage, too. It's simply called the Foot Fraternity because that was where the prime interest was, but [members] realized that it overlaps [into] many areas; [it] gets into wrestling [and] many other things.

[When] people write for information, I send out an application with samples of the photos and videotapes that we do: foot scenes and shoe, boot, sock, tickle scenes. [The] magazine is [quarterly]; two times a year [it] has a complete listing of all the members, not with their names but with a code number. You write a letter [and] send it to me for forwarding. From that point on, you're on your own: I never give out any names or addresses. That's up to the individual. We also have gatherings once a year. This year, we had a four-day weekend gathering that was more like a family reunion. We had our meals together; we talked and shared on other issues [though] there was foot play going on as well. We took boat trips; we saw the city—it was just a group of people getting together who had a common interest.

I believe that with most people [the foot fetish] leads into other areas. For me it does. The foot fetish is the primary area of interest, but my interest in bondage, humiliation, and domination is very strong. It's not just the foot alone that I wish to serve and be beneath and worship. I consider myself to be submissive. However, in the foot scene I find that it's very easy to play either a top or a bottom. For example, if I meet someone who is into the foot scene [and] is into working on feet, I don't mind having him work on mine. It feels very good, very comfortable, and I can play the part very well. It's intriguing, and I find that I can be versatile with it. However, if I had a preference as to what would be the most exciting, I would choose to be submissive.

I really enjoy and get off on smelling the feet of straight men, [because] they're almost untouchable. If I could get down and smell their feet and worship them, and they'll let me do that or let me buy their new shoes or socks and smell their old ones and be amused or laugh at me or call me their little faggot slave, the pleasure is tremendous! That they're amused by my humiliating myself, by my being degraded by them, is erotic. It's verbal eroticism. I don't want to be hurt, but I certainly don't mind them putting pressure on my face. I like the idea of being a footmat and being walked on, if I can support the weight of the man.

Generally, the men that I deal with are so okay with their own sexuality that it's not threatening to them. If a man is not okay with his own sexuality, we'll never get to the point where I'll ask. I test his response; if it is nonchalant, I know he's okay with who he is and not threatened. He knows what he likes, and this doesn't bother him. It's a little more exciting if it's a straight man, because somehow the superiority I think they must feel places me even more in their respect. I like to hear their orders; I like to hear them laugh; I like to watch them look down at my face beneath their feet and smile [as if to say], "I can do anything to this guy."

I worked part-time in a men's shoe store [in my teens] because I wanted to see what it was like to be able to kneel at men's feet and slip shoes on and off their feet. [Later] I worked in a bookstore part-time, and there was a man delivering the magazines, a truck-driver-type guy. He was brand-new on the route, and I would go to the back door and open up to let in the deliveries. When he first came in, I said, "What happened to the other guy?" He said, "He was transferred to another route," and I real quickly used that time to say, "Oh, that's too bad! I used to massage his feet [and] get him a cup of coffee." I was just watching his response; if the response was nothing, I knew not to pursue it. But his response was, "It sounds interesting." So I said, "Well, I'll be glad to give you a foot massage. I do reflexology."

The second time he came I said, "Remember, if you ever want a foot massage, I'll be glad to do it." He said, "I remember; I definitely will." The third time he came a little early and said, "I think I'll take that massage this week and that coffee." I ran and got him a cup of coffee. [When] I pulled off his shoes, he said, "They're gonna smell." I said, "That doesn't bother me; I used to have to do this for my brother when I was young, and it never bothered me at all." So I pulled off his sneakers and massaged his feet; then I put his sneakers back on. I didn't go further than that. The next visit that he came, the same thing. I had his coffee waiting, and I said, "Are you ready for your foot massage?" He said, "Sure!" So I pulled off his shoes and did it, only this time I was a little bit more brazen. I said, "After I was done with my brother, he always used to make me kiss his feet and say thank you." He didn't say anything, so I said, "Is it okay if I kiss your feet and thank you?" And he said, "Go ahead, do whatever you want." So I [did] and put his shoes back on. Then he sort of put it really together and knew what I liked and knew I was enjoying it.

The next week he came [and] said, "We're going to do it a little different. We'll continue with the coffee and the foot massages, but you're going to unload the truck for me." I said, "Sure!" I unloaded the magazines while he had coffee. I rubbed his feet and then without asking, I brought my face down and rubbed [his feet] against my face and kissed the bottoms. He looked down at me and smiled, and I put his shoes back on. It got to the point where he would come each week. I would have to carry the magazines, kiss his boots, and thank him for allowing me to work for him, and then I would have to massage his feet and smell them and kiss them and thank him. That experience was an absolute delight. It lasted for about three quarters of a year until, all of a sudden, his route was switched, and I lost track of him.

Another small, very short experience was when I bought a car. I usually go to the same place and know the manager of the dealership. I said, "I'll be glad to buy this car if you let me get down on my hands and knees and kiss your feet and thank you." So what was he going to do? He wanted to make the sale! He said, "Okay, go ahead." I got down and kissed his feet and thanked him for letting me buy a car from him. That's why I love car salesmen! I love to know that they'll consider letting me smell or kiss their feet. They're usually kind of amused by it.

MARK J.

I [may] have just a little bit of bisexual in me, but I'm mostly heterosexual. As far as my preferences, it's mostly female feet. I will get turned on by seeing a boy's feet, but that's as far as it goes with men.

I've thought about [why I'm interested in feet] many times. I think everybody who has developed an interest in feet and other fetishes, at one time when they were young, must have had some experience happen that got them into this. I remember, very young, I was living in California, and I was standing in my driveway, and I looked across the street. There was a boy—one of my neighbors. He came out to get something on the porch, and he was in his bare feet. I saw he was wearing blue jeans, and I immediately saw his naked feet, and something just snapped in [my] mind. I said, "Oh!" I was maybe about four or five years old. It was just the nudity, the shapeliness of the feet.

I was a very shy, withdrawn child. I grew up in a dysfunctional family. My father was an alcoholic. I was different from other boys, meaning I wasn't interested in sports. I was a skinny weakling, though I did identify with boys my age. I grew up with a low self-esteem. In fact, I had a learning problem. I've grown out of it since. I was placed in a special class with some other kids who were having difficulty in school. They were usually the children who couldn't sit still. But after a period of time I was put back in a regular classroom, so I began to interface with my peers. Still, I did remain really quiet. I guess how I came out of it [was that] I just decided I'm not going to be like this anymore: I'm going to get out there and meet people and be outspoken. I've gone through counseling because I've had some failures in my life that have been disappointing; I've talked about how I could break out of my shell. That's basically how I came to be the person I am now.

My first actual date didn't come till I was 19. I wanted to get involved with the opposite sex. Other guys, they want it for their sexuality. I wanted it for my sexuality, too, but I wanted it because of their feet. So my fetish did bring me toward meeting women. I knew a girl when I was 15 or 16 years old, [and] she used to like to go barefoot. I didn't get to worship her feet, but I got to look at them and say, "I like that."

I feel there's nothing wrong with it, although I don't go tell people about my interest. If they have an interest in this area, I'm more than willing to talk about it. [The people I've spoken with] have been a tremendous help in identifying what it is I like, who I want to do it with. The only thing it has not helped me with, and I think this will come in time, is actually meeting a woman who has a foot fetish or wants to have her feet serviced.

Any type of foreplay with the female foot gives me [an] erotic sensation. For me, just to envision worshiping a woman's feet, or any situation that has to do with feet, while masturbating will give me [a] climax. At the same time, if I were to have a foot-worship session with a lady, at this point, I really wouldn't care what happened after that ended.

I am not at all interested in boots or leather. The only things that I really find sexy, as far as footwear, are sandals or some kind of open-toed shoes or a black pump or a flat. I like those because oftentimes most girls who wear flats wear them without socks, and they're fitted where they can just easily be slipped off at any time.

It's kind of silly, but I've always dreamed of a woman removing my shoes and socks and fondling my feet. Maybe going over to a friend's house, and there's a swimming pool in her backyard, and I accidentally fall in, and the woman says, "Let me get those wet clothes off," and she removes my shirt, and then she goes for my shoes and socks and finds that my feet are sexually arousing her, and she ends up having a foot-worship session with my feet. My ultimate fantasy is [to] make foot worship my business: I would love to get a chance to have a bunch of women model for me and take pictures and make videos and sell them.

My ideal session would be meeting with a young woman, between the ages of 18 and 40, preferably white but it could be a black female as well. We would get together, we would discuss what we like about feet, and she would casually begin to tease me, slip off her shoe and tickle my face with her foot. I would slowly remove her hose and begin to sniff and caress and to kiss her toes and lick them and just really get into that. And then, while I'm getting into that, she would be doing the same thing, so it would be kind of a mutual session [where] we're both enjoying each other's feet. [This] has not happened [yet]. The closest I've come to foot worship is with my girlfriend. I haven't told her [that] I am a foot fetishist, but she knows that I like her feet, and many times I will ask, "Should I give you a foot massage?" [Or] I'll raise her bare feet up to my face, and I'll sniff them. But as far as meeting somebody who is into feet themselves, it hasn't happened yet.

I realized I wasn't alone [only] about a year ago. I was in Cleveland, and I picked up this publication. It was free, and I looked in the back, and there was this ad saying they want handsome men to model shoes, socks, and bare feet. I was unemployed at the time, and I really needed the money . . . and to see that key [term], *bare feet*! I immediately sent pictures and [Douglas Gaines] called me and told me what he was about. So I went and talked to him, and he started with the modeling of my feet and introduced me to several magazines that are exclusively for leg lovers and foot lovers.

Because it has been estimated that about 10 percent of the population harbors some kind of foot fetish, I encourage people if they do have this interest to try to explore and come out with it. A lot of people like me are looking for others who want to share [the interest]. A lot of us foot fetishists feel trapped. We're in a closet, [and] we don't want to be. We'd like it to be recognized that this is an interest we have and that this is okay.

ROB

I don't have a lot of interest in [D&S] issues. I am interested in normal women but find myself attracted to women amputees with greater vigor. I also have a strong interest in women's legs and feet. I certainly think about [these things] regularly, daily, and [they] lead me to certain activities—like I'm a volunteer with a support group for amputees. I try to get out and make contact with new amputees when I can. That's not always easy. An amputee isn't someone you tend to see every day.

If I meet somebody who I get along with real well and enjoy talking with, then that may be the way into a relationship, but a lot of the time you're looking for people you'd like to meet based on what they look like. If she's an amputee, that's very powerful, [or] if she's just generally attractive and likes to take off her shoes, then that's interesting, as well. If a woman has a real pretty pair of feet, that is inherently a sexy thing to me. I want to watch her feet and play with her feet and touch her feet. Getting a glimpse of a woman kicking her shoes off at a local pub and going out on the dance floor and dancing—that's *very* interesting to me. It's particularly interesting if the woman's in a situation where she wouldn't normally be barefoot, like women that kick off their shoes at work or at trade shows, out on the convention floor, [when] they're standing all day and their feet get tired. I really like that. I'd rather the shoes weren't there anymore. [But this is] much less interesting than the amputee fetish.

[It's] about three years since I made the decision to get involved in volunteer activities to try to enhance my chances of meeting somebody. That was a tough decision for me. I wondered, Am I only doing it because of the interest? If so, is that right? Is that good? I finally came to the conclusion that if I'm doing some net benefit to people, if it's not just me going in and gawking and doing dumb things, if good things are actually happening, then it's probably okay. We can deal with the other problems later. I've firmed that [belief] up a little now. I think there are a lot of people out there who have this interest [but] who don't do anything positive with it—they just sit and dream about it, or follow women around with cameras and binoculars, that sort of thing.

At times it's seemed like a relationship [will never] happen; the few times that it seemed possible, the failures have been quite frustrating. The first woman amputee that I actually asked out on a date seemed interested at the time but later canceled. I found that very difficult because it felt like, "Oh, gosh; you've got this one chance—you better not blow it!" I don't trust that response [in myself] anymore. [It's] really dangerous for that to set in; [it] leads to going out and finding somebody whose single characteristic is having a stump instead of all four limbs. That's not good enough. I really need somebody who I can click with on a whole lot of levels. So while I'm pursuing this a little more actively, actually winding up with an amputee is becoming a little less important. The main thing is it's got to be a person I have a good rapport with and things in common with, things that I find interesting in a whole lot of other ways.

I have romantically pursued a couple of amputee women, but it's never gone much beyond a date or two. So I'm still wondering what it really is like. There's a sense of intrigue and wonder: Uh-oh, what's underneath the skirt; what's inside that empty pant leg or empty sleeve? What does the stump actually look like, feel like; what would it be like, touching me in various ways? That sense of mystery seems to be a strong part of it, [as well as] the visual appeal of somebody walking along with crutches or hopping to get around.

[A sexual relationship] would probably be a lot of good old-fashioned vanilla sex, but there would be some sexual aspects to the stump touching parts of me and various things—masturbation, [other] things—to experiment with. Contact between the stump and my genitals would be very interesting. But the vast majority would be very vanilla to most people.

I'm not sure how far back it goes, but I can't really remember a time in my life when [I wasn't attracted to amputees]. It goes back to play fantasies when I was six or seven. There was a friend that I met, a fellow who was born without legs, and that may have given me the idea. I don't remember when it occurred to me that this is strange and different, but that's a theme through part of my life. It's something that I guess I'm bringing back into myself with me. It makes a better part of me now than it did 10 years ago. Let's say I'm walking along the street and a pretty woman with one leg comes by on crutches. I don't know if I'd want to trade that kick for the feeling of being just like everybody else. And then is there anybody out there who's really just like everybody else? I don't know that there's all that many people out there who are really "normal."

I've wondered if it's some kind of a "Oh, poor thing; let me help you" reaction. I don't think [so]. I want a strong, equal partner, but at the time when my sexual interest was developing, that wasn't necessarily the way I [felt]. Maybe there's something there from then. [As if], "Maybe I'm not good enough to get a real woman; maybe I can get an amputee." I don't know that it is. It's a theme [in] one book that I read, but I don't know that I believe that's really behind it. And if it [were], that's a long ways in the past.

I always expected [people to say], "Oh, my God! You must be a pervert! Get away from me!" I haven't found it to be the case. I think that a lot of women amputees have run across this a whole lot before I meet them. Most of the time when the subject does come up and I actually talk about it, people are neutral. A couple of people have made use of the Amputees Services Association in Chicago, the umbrella support group. I think that [it all depends on] the personality of the person involved and whether sex is a real good thing for her or a big landmine full of problems. And then there's her past history with other fetishists. It's dependent on a bunch of things outside of my control. But I've been surprised at how positive the response has been. Most people seem to react best to an honest admission, like, "Look, I'm interested in you, you're neat, and by the way, I think your stump is cute." I think that works a whole lot better than not talking about it. [Some amputees are] definitely aware of the attraction and kind of like it. I've gotten to the point where I can actually talk to some people about this issue, absolutely something I couldn't imagine doing two years ago. [But] I never thought that therapy was appropriate. Therapy is like: Something is broken. I don't believe that anymore. [I'm] not like other people, but I'm not in this to do anything that I consider harmful or negative. I have different interests in a couple areas [other] than the rank and file. I have a large collection of music; I've got about 400 CDs and about 500 record albums. I'm always expanding and exploring. Music seems like such a big adventure. I go to plays, to live music performances, to a lot of cultural things.

There's a magazine called *Fascination,* which deals with the interest in female amputees and in amputees in general. They're not sexist; they're just overwhelmed by males who are interested in females. It's composed partly of letters from "devotees," the generic term for people who are interested in amputees. [There are] fictional stories and real-life encounters and editorial comments on various aspects of amputees and society. There are also real-life testimonials from people on either the male-seeking-amputee side or the amputee-being-sought side. The magazine is published by a woman amputee in Chicago. They have gatherings once a year, where they get together to just explore and talk. There's a couple of structured events where you gather in a room and a group discussion is led by some of the longer-term members. A lot of it is socializing, talking [to] and meeting different people. It reminds you that you're not the only one. It really gives you some idea that this is what it's like for other people. That's something that a whole lot of devotees never have.

My advice [to others] is, "Please—try to let yourself be what you are, and try to find positive ways of expressing that." [That's] a central [problem for] all of the other amputee fetishists I've dealt with: "My God, this is so weird! This must be wrong! This must be something I have to suppress and not let be a part of me!" I've met people who are married and in good relationships. [Yet] they're really frustrated because they can't shake this interest, and it is hurting their relationships. I think they've been trying to push down this thing that won't be pushed down. It is part of them, and they can't really tear themselves away from it. If people could express themselves, I think we'd have a lot fewer strange, frustrated people wandering around.

Twenty

DRESSING
FOR PLEASURE*

I would like you to wear drawers with three or four frills one over the other at the knees and up the thighs and great crimson bows in them, I mean not schoolgirl's drawers with a thin shabby lace border, tight round the legs and so thin that the flesh shows between them but women's (or if you prefer the word, ladies') drawers with a full loose bottom and wide legs, all frills and lace and ribbons, and heavy with perfume.

—JAMES JOYCE[1]

Clothing is a critical aspect of how we present ourselves to and identify ourselves in the world. Whether we select an iconoclastic style or one that conforms to our social milieu, clothing expresses who we think we are and who we would like to be. If the mind and body comprise the book of our

*"DRESSING FOR PLEASURE" is a registered trademark of CONSTANCE ENTERPRISES. It is used by permission of the company.

lives, our garb is that book's cover, by which—for better or worse—we are often judged.

D&Sers are frequently passionate about presenting the body in flamboyant and exotically erotic ways. Their dress transforms them into their personal ideals of wondrous and romantic—or, conversely, sinister and powerful—creatures. It may enhance their individual sensuality. It may even cause direct sexual arousal. D&Sers typically enjoy dressing in clothes that evoke their sensual realities.

In this chapter we hear from a number of our interviewees on the allure of exotic clothing:

- Marie-Constance owns Constance Enterprises, a mail-order company with a retail store specializing in fetish fashions, and she founded the annual Dressing for Pleasure fashion show and gala ball. She is in her 50s and lives in New Jersey with her business partner and life-partner, John. She has three grown children.
- Lindsay is 38 years old. A visual artist, she has worked in word processing and as a legal secretary, a masseuse, a housepainter, a bartender, and a professional photographer. She lives with her life-partner, Max (profiled in Chapter 7).
- Allen is 46 years old and has been married for over 20 years. He works in advertising.
- Phil T. is 34 years old and is married with children. He has a background in communications.

WHAT IS DRESSING
FOR PLEASURE?

Dressing for pleasure is a complete sensory experience. Most people can understand the satisfaction of wearing an expensive suit, a silk blouse, or even a comfortable pair of blue jeans, but to many D&Sers exotic clothes heighten overall erotic sensual awareness. The heightening of that awareness is, indeed, the primary purpose of exotic dressing. It involves the visual, the tactile and the olfactory. And there are those who love sounds—the swish of lace or the squeak of rubber. To dress for pleasure is to surround oneself with sensual stimuli. The specific pleasures are individual; for example, leather clothing may confer a sense of personal power to dominants; to submissives, such dress may signal vulnerability; for some, it is simply a playful interest.

For many D&Sers dress is an intrinsic aspect of the person's erotic fantasy. Just as body modification may bring an individual's interiorized reality to the surface, so dressing achieves the same affect but through temporary means.

The erotic interest in fabrics and garments is well recorded. Nineteenth Century sex researchers found an abundance of individuals who eroticized silk, satin, fur, hair (including girls' pigtails), wigs, rubber, linen, and so on. Similarly, specific articles of clothing—such as aprons, petticoats, pants, skirts, chemises, corsets, and gloves—have frequently been the focus of a fetishist's lust.

> *Taffeta excites her most of all, since it is of finest silk. She has less of a passion for satin than for silk. She did not, however, go in for heavy silk things, because she felt that these would excite her too greatly. She would like to sleep in silks but thinks that this is not nice for a decent woman. She says she would be unable to sleep if she ever put such goods on. She would be so fired with passion that she would have to get up constantly and cool herself off with water.*
>
> —WILHELM STEKEL[2]

WHO DOES IT?

Most D&Sers wear some form of exotic clothing, at least to parties and events. Clothing is an important way of identifying with the group; it helps D&Sers to recognize those with common interests and, in itself, is aesthetically pleasing. Generally, the people with the most extensive collections of fetish clothing are well-to-do: Custom latex clothing, tailored leather, and corsets are expensive. Some Americans order directly from England; Germany and the Netherlands also offer an array of latex and fetish options. Since so many chic designers (most notably Gianni Versace who, in 1992, dressed high-fashion models in so-called bondage dresses) have borrowed their inspiration from the European fetish industries, imitations have become trendy and available to all.

Parties for fetish-wear enthusiasts originated in Europe. Attendance at these events was prohibitively expensive.

> *John and I had been attending a latex fashion show in Switzerland since 1982. Every time we'd come home, someone in the Scene would say, "Not everyone can go to Europe." I [agreed], but at that time, I was still busy in the medical industry. I was not involved in this at all, except on a personal level. After I started Constance Enterprises, I thought, Someone should hold such an event in the United*

States. I have a mailing list; I've met people in Switzerland from the United States who shared the interest in dressing for pleasure and wearing latex and leather or PVC. We've had [private] parties in Texas and California. Why shouldn't I put together a fashion show and dinner dance where people can dress and spend a weekend together? This way people with the same fetish can meet and network.

—MARIE-CONSTANCE

Hundreds of people fly to New York to congregate at the annual Dressing for Pleasure gala, where ordinary standards of dress are left at the sidewalk and fanciful, fantastic frippery is *de rigueur*. Fabrics and garments whose names have long since faded from the vocabulary of most shoppers—crinoline, tulle, crepe, corsets, button-up boots, veils—are donned, and fetish clothing, such as suits or dresses of body-hugging rubber in brilliant colors and daring designs, take center stage.

Fetish dressers' creativity is limitless. Whether they are rubber enthusiasts snugly enveloped by hooded latex suits; dominatrices garbed in authentic Victorian regalia; or transvestites who pull out all the stops on the frilled, flounced outfits of their dreams, all seek to escape the mundane and transform themselves into fantasy objects.

Whereas in mainstream society flamboyant clothing is often the unchallenged domain of women, men in D&S are equally likely to wear unusual or fetishistic outfits for personal or public enjoyment. A significant number of people, particularly gay men, enjoy dressing in military or police uniforms. Some leather fraternities, in fact, are known as *uniform clubs* whose members design a club-specific uniform. Perhaps the most fanciful outfits of all, however, are worn by male-to-female cross-dressers, many of whom do not hesitate to live out their erotic fantasies by affecting a complete transformation.

WHAT DO THEY WEAR?

Of all the materials used by D&Sers, leather is the most ubiquitous. The interest in black leather probably originated in the biker subculture, where leather was preferred for practical reasons. Leather provides protection from the environment and is a kind of lightweight, affordable, and flexible armor in case of falls. Its color and ruggedness—and the reputation of those who wore it—suggests menace and defiance. The biker subculture was an early model for gay leathermen, just as gay leather culture has been a model for heterosexual D&Sers. And leather has become to the D&Ser what the blue suit is to the IBM executive: a symbol of group affiliation and a statement about the person wearing it.

While leather may be important functionally to bikers, it doesn't necessarily serve an explicitly erotic function for them. When leather was co-opted by the D&S subculture, the material became linked with forbidden eroticism.

I love black leather. I think I have a little bit of a fetish for it. I don't have any objects or activities that I absolutely need to get off on, but I love the smell of leather, I love its feel, I love the sense of power and danger associated with it, and I like leather clothing, leather paddles. —BAMBI BOTTOM

An extraordinary variety of D&S equipment and clothing is crafted from leather. Because of shifts in fashion over the years, however, black leather and other fetish gear have lost much of their symbolic meaning.

There's a club in Chicago [which] is probably one of the most D&S-like places, as far as atmosphere is concerned. I've seen women there—generally young, in their early 20s—who will wear a chain or a very hot, kinky outfit. I'll [ask], "Is this an expression of one of your fantasies or desires?" And they'll say, "What?" I'll say, "What you're wearing is a personification of something that's special to a lot of people, and I was just wondering if you are interested in that?" And [they'll say], "What?" All they're doing is making fashion statements. —MICHAEL V.

The wearing of leather has become so thoroughly diffused throughout American fashion culture that a 1992 Neiman-Marcus catalogue offered a high-priced designer version of the biker's jacket. Perhaps upscale consumers are discovering what D&Sers already know: that it can be exciting—intellectually if not sexually—to wear something that suggests a darker, untamed aspect of one's psyche.

Whether leather fetishists would have had the fetish had they not first known about leather's link to kinky sexuality is impossible to ascertain. Like all fetishes, leather fetishism is a phenomenon of its age. However the desire was first formed, many D&Sers—male and female—are directly aroused by leather.

I'm a leather fetishist. I knew that that was true when I was in a punk fashion store in the chic part of Los Angeles. I'm eternally grateful to punk fashion because it made lots of leather and accessories easily available to us perverts! This store had a large rack of leather wristbands and gauntlets. I was looking at the stuff and felt

myself becoming sexually aroused just from looking at it. I knew
what a fetish was, and I knew that that's what was going on for me.
— GENEVIEVE REYNOLDS

For the pleasure-dressing aficionado, however, the wearing of leather may be, if not exactly trite, certainly not wildly original. While it is common to see leather clothing at D&S parties and events, many who dress for pleasure prefer more extraordinary confections. Close behind leather in popularity is rubber or latex. England is particularly known for its active cottage industry in rubber garments. Foreign designers have used rubber to create high-fashion clothing which can pass as evening wear, moving the fetish from the bedroom to the sophisticated soiree.

Lacy, traditionally feminine lingerie, stockings, and heels are also extremely popular (and certainly more affordable than most fetish clothing). Naturally, women are most likely to appear in sexy frills.

My favorite activities within D&S [include] dressing up in really
sexy clothing that I can't wear to work and going to [an S&M club].
Black stockings with a seam up the back, a garter belt, a bustier,
maybe a G-string, really high-heeled [shoes], long black gloves, and
a collar with a D-ring. I'd have my hair pulled back and wear long,
sexy, dangling earrings and lipstick and blush. And that's about it.
— VICTORIA

Since genderbending is largely an acceptable behavior among D&Sers, many men experiment with women's finery. While clothes may make the man, frills do not always make a transvestite (nor a fetishist). Some men simply relish the sensuousness of fabrics typically reserved for women.

I've always been attracted to fetish dressing, especially stockings,
boots, heels, and such. I'd make a very ugly woman, and I know it,
[but] I just like the way the clothes feel. Women get all the sensuous
fabrics. — ALLEN

I really like clothing a lot. I've always been very conscious of my
physical appearance and like checking out other people. I've always
really gotten off on sexy women's stuff. I have '40s tastes: very slick
spiked pumps and tailored, form-fitting clothing, stockings and
garters and that kind of jazz. The kind of women that get me off
are the kind of woman I like to be. [But] just because there are
things that I get off on, I don't recognize them as fetishes. That's one
of those words that I don't apply to myself comfortably. I thought a
fetish was something weird that someone else does! — j-

Since clothing may also be used to express one's particular sexual fantasies, some people dress to reflect a variety of fetish interests.

I don't know if I'm one of many, or one of few, who rolls the leather, the restraints, the feminization, and the diaper wearing all together. You don't see many people who are into [so many] cross-interests. Mine are all at opposite ends. [Leather] restraints are tied up with diapers because of the sense of security [I get from them]. It could probably be traced back to the earlier part of my childhood. It was probably natural to tie the secure feeling [in] with women's clothing, because I wanted to be like my sisters. It sounds very Freudian! At times it's really a mess to combine those elements: Do you wear the diaper with the stockings and garter belt or not? —PHIL T.

Dressing for pleasure is also a way of celebrating and expanding the sensual imagination. Exotic clothing allows one to undergo a conspicuous, albeit ephemeral, change.

I think [dressing] really spices things up, because I become different people. That's exciting for my partner: Instead of just having this one woman, there are other people that he perceives. He can get that distance from me, [so] it's not, "Oh, here's my partner who I've been with for five years." It's, "Who is this exciting person?"

—LINDSAY

Few rules exist in the D&S community about clothing, though an aesthetic sensibility is preferred and appreciated. When dressing for pleasure, the most inelegant element that one can display is a lack of imagination.

WHY DO THEY LIKE IT?

As the businessperson dresses for success, the D&Ser dresses for sex. Exotic clothing is, to varying degrees, often part of the extended foreplay of D&S. It permits the wearer to enter fully into his or her particular fantasy and remain there for hours at a time. The submissive woman who wishes to be a shameless wanton for the evening may wear no more than lingerie and high heels at a party and experience the immediate thrill of being the object of admiring attention.

Similarly, clothing can enhance the mystique of power: Dominants frequently feel empowered by the clothing they wear.

I feel strong in certain clothing. When I walk into a room, I feel it's easy to take charge if I'm dressed a certain way. I see myself in the mirror, and I feel secure. —AVA TAUREL

Clothing can connote power. Submissives may wear scant or revealing clothing, while dominants seldom display much flesh. Some female dominants like to entice by revealing cleavage and wearing short skirts, and a well-muscled leatherman may make a point of baring his torso, but as a very general rule, the less clothing the dominant wears, the less dominant he or she seems. Dominants, for example, never appear nude at a D&S gathering, whereas a submissive may be fully or partly nude, depending on the circumstances.

Many partners experiment with different looks for different occasions, thus altering their personae according to their erotic moods.

My partner and I have been together about five years, and part of keeping it exciting is playing the role of being somebody different— changing my hair, changing my image [with] clothes, whether I look pure and virginal or trashy and seductive. I like to devote [my energy] to pleasing [him]. We don't just do the basic in-out; it becomes hours and hours of play. I think that's [what] I like about our sex. It's something I find generally in S&M: It can be very childlike in that you get to play. It's not just sex—it's the roleplaying that makes it so fun. You can become somebody else. It's like the pretend world that most of us had as children. —LINDSAY

Fetish clothing often exaggerates, exposes (either seductively or in a humiliating way), displays, or restricts.

I love wearing humiliating clothes. My master [bought] me a pair of long-john pajamas with a drop bottom. I [also] have a Catholic schoolgirl outfit. It's a very short plaid miniskirt that I wear with boots and embarrassing lacy panties and a cute little top. I wear pigtails when I wear it. —BAMBI BOTTOM

Restrictive garments particularly appeal to many exotic dressers.

My biggest turn-on in wearing fetish gear is the direct physical feeling of having it on my body. I like to wear things under street clothes when I go out, though some of the harnesses and straps get very uncomfortable after a short time. I enjoy the feeling that my genitals are down there, and when I wear restrictive clothing, I'm reminded all the time. —ALLEN

Restrictive garments evoke both the sensation and the image of bondage and D&Sers who enjoy bondage are particularly fond of tight corsets or confining rubber wear. The garments themselves may be sexually exciting.

When I wear particular garments, it arouses me. Even if I'm just alone in a room wearing those garments, it arouses me to feel these things on my body and to touch them. It gets me in a certain mood, [even] prior to seeing someone who can enjoy it with me.

—AVA TAUREL

Clothing is also used to establish the mood and reality of erotic play.

I love French maid service because of how humiliating and embarrassing it makes me feel. [I wear] little lacy gloves, a little lacy hat, a little apron around this black [PVC] dress with the breasts cut out, petticoats under the dress, a garter belt, fishnet stockings, five-inch heels with locks on the ankle straps, the whole thing. It's the most uncomfortable, humiliating, frilly, lacy little thing! I was a tomboy as a kid. I would never have worn this as a little girl, and it's particularly embarrassing. It puts me in my place, and I love that.

—BAMBI BOTTOM

INTERVIEWS

MARIE-CONSTANCE

Every human being, to a lesser or greater degree, has an interest in [the general area of D&S], but most won't perceive themselves that way. My own children can't understand what this is all about. They are very conventional and not at all open-minded toward it, which really surprises me, given that they were exposed to as much as they have been exposed to—open-mindedness and discussion about all kinds of things. I have always been open with them. I never wanted them to find out anything about me from someone else. I've always been honest, but I would advise parents not to be: It's very difficult for a child to accept a parent's sexuality. No matter what it is.

The most important thing in any [marital] relationship is honesty. Frequently it's the man who has the fetish. He tells his wife, "I like rubber and I want to wear rubber when we have sex." And she says, "Uck! You must be nuts!" The man never finds out what his wife is interested in. He doesn't explore her fantasy. Understanding takes time, and the probing of your fantasies with your mate, and a really sincere interest in finding out what your mate [likes].

I've talked to thousands [of people]. Our mailing list at present has 10,000 people. People come to me and ask me to help them open their mates up, and I try my best. Frequently I advise both people to talk to me. I try to help them strengthen their relationship and to share what's deeply embedded in their psyches. "CRT" is what I usually say: Care, Respect, and Trust are the ingredients that go into a good relationship, whether it's a straight relationship or a kinky one.

I know that there are many hundreds of thousands [of people interested]. This is confirmed by the number of magazines that are published. There are mail-order businesses which cater to people with specific interests. For example, *The Transvestian* [a newspaper], may have 20,000 on their list for that publication alone. The [parent company] has two other publications, which may have [many] thousands more [apiece]. And that's just one small aspect of fetishism: cross-dressing.

I have only met three men who could top me. It's an intellectual meeting: If one cannot capture me intellectually, he certainly cannot capture me in any other way. It takes a unique individual, one with sensitivity. I myself was in biomedical electronics and instrumentation and teaching. I have made some connections with different professions and different interests—that has been very interesting to me. I find that mathematicians and engineers, people who are very structured, tend to be very involved in bondage. I explored with a number of different people and found it rather laughable that these gentlemen who considered themselves dominants were not dominants at all—they were submissives! I found myself much more comfortable in the role of the dominant. That's how it all started about 12 years ago. I've come a long way in a short time. But when I do something, I always do it wholeheartedly.

I've always been sensitive to other people: empathetic and sympathetic. As a result, I've learned a lot about myself in learning about others. After I became involved in the Scene, I began to recall situations that I had been in that made me terribly excited and that I had obviously repressed. As I was doing something to someone, I could remember feeling an emotional response to someone taking control. I'm such a controlling person. I recalled that years ago I had been in a sexual relationship with someone and he pinned my hands back behind my head. It was terribly thrilling for me because I trusted this man. He made me feel helpless, which is what all controlling people want.

I always want to learn more about people and to understand why they chose a particular fetish—how it turns them on or where it originated from. That's interesting. I've always been very analytical about myself and have been through analysis, but I've probably learned more about other people than I have about myself.

In my speeches at the Dressing for Pleasure events, I ask people to be tolerant of others' interests. Even within a particular fetish, you find people at opposite ends of the interest and critical of the others. For instance, we will have a table of people who are serious corset people. These people draw their waists in month by month, year by year, to smaller and smaller dimensions. They are very straight-laced. Then there are corset people who wear a corset for the fun or for the look of it—they might wear it over a garment—not to reduce the waist but to minimize the appearance of the waist.

[The issue of likes and dislikes] depends upon the individual. Everybody has his or her own fetish. If I'm turned on by the person, I'll be turned on by his particular fetish.

[My businesses] grew by listening to what people wanted and needed. People wrote, and I would send a letter with my phone number. They would call and find a sympathetic ear. It seemed to mean so much to so many people. I was really impressed with people's need to know that there was someone who was sincere about the Scene. For many publishers, this is strictly a business venture, rather than a personal thing. I was doing this because this was an interest of mine.

[A fetish] I would have guessed was small but which is quite large is adult babies. We cater to a number of them, because we sell plastic rompers to wear over diapers. We [were referred to] a man who has [an] adult-babies list, and we did a mailing to them; it was quite a large response. I find that many of the adult babies act like babies: They will call at 2:00 A.M. and expect to be reprimanded. We had to turn off our phone system [late at night]. It's not funny when you're awakened in the middle of the night and get a call back immediately. This person really wants to be punished, and he's acting like a baby!

Constance Enterprises started when I took a trip to England in September 1986 and attended a party with the publisher of *Skin Two* magazine. The magazine is beautifully composed—definitely a fetish magazine, but one both beautiful and intelligent, not like a lot of the sleaze that's available. The publisher asked me to handle all the U.S. inquiries. I had just resigned from the company that I was running and was floundering as to what I was going to do next. I thought this magazine was something that I could be proud to identify with. I shipped *Skin Two* to those who had made inquiries. I also had the names of about 200 people I had met in the Scene. I handwrote these people that *Skin Two* was going to be available through me. I did all right: The 200 names multiplied.

[Slowly], we grew. Different magazines started to write articles about [us]; different organizations would find out about us and write to their memberships. And that's how the mailing list increased—little by little, by word of mouth and publications that gave us free PR. Listening to what people wanted, I went out and sought other books, other magazines. Now we carry hundreds of magazines, books, and videos. I also hold the Dressing for Pleasure gala each year. As a result of that, I publish a magazine called *Dressing for Pleasure in America,* which is a documentary of the different events. I produce a video, too, containing interviews with people who are there.

[When I started the gala] it took a long time to find a hotel that would consider having such an event. Many hotels turned their noses up. I said it was going to be a proper event, a very upscale event. Certainly it would be an expensive event! It didn't matter to them. But the Penta Hotel in New York was wonderful. The Penta is known as a fashion-industry hotel, and they welcomed me with open arms. They had a beautiful ballroom and wonderful runways, and they were very eager to have this be successful, which it was. So for the first three years I held it there. The Penta is very large, however, and attendees were embarrassed about riding the elevators with other guests, some of whom would laugh. I went to the Roosevelt Hotel in 1990 and everything went beautifully. Management invited me back before we left, saying, "It was such a beautiful event; people were so well behaved. We would like you to do the show again next year at our hotel." I thanked them but booked the New Jersey Meadowland Hilton [instead]. It is small, and we've taken the entire hotel. People don't have to worry about outsiders looking at them and laughing, [or] children saying, "Mommy, Mommy, look!"

Dressing for Pleasure has grown to be a two-and-a-half-day event. We have a vendors' boutique, a fashion show on Friday; a cocktail reception and a sit-down dinner followed by a dance on Saturday. There is also a Sunday brunch to give attendees the opportunity to exchange phone numbers and to see each other for one last farewell. In previous years we've had people from 22 states and many foreign countries: England, Holland, Germany, France, Switzerland, Saudi Arabia, New Zealand, Australia, [and] Italy. This year—1992—I expect 600 attendees. We also have various workshops. There will be one on chastity belts and a general lecture and demonstration on whip making. There will be a separate hands-on whip-making workshop. There's going to be one on censorship led by an attorney. There will be workshops on latex, on fantasy outfits, on how to play sanely and safely, and on how to train a lady's sissy maid. Another workshop is on corsetting and how to reduce your waist.

I opened the Dressing for Pleasure Showroom because people were constantly asking me to order clothing and specialty items for them. [In 1990], I finally rented a little office in Upper Montclair that I turned into a showroom. When I had the grand opening, we had hardly anything in the showroom. Now it's so jam-packed you can hardly move. I have something for everyone. For example, Tollyboy chastity belts, from England, are exquisite. However, almost everything in England [dealing] with fetishes is a cottage industry. An order takes a minimum of six months. I knew a retired engineer who purchased these chastity belts for himself and his wife. When he discovered that, despite the accuracy of his measurements, his belt didn't fit properly, he said, "I can do this!" I asked him to prove to me that he could make one, and he did. We now offer people the option of purchasing a belt from England or one that's made in the United States. I'm always looking for good craftspeople who do quality work.

Is there S&M after 50? I have noticed that [the interest] stops in some women. I'll give you an example: A gentleman contacted us a number of years ago. He said, "I heard from friends that you might be interested in having my bondage board. I can't use it anymore." Mutual friends had told me that one could walk into their house and see the wife shackled in the doorway. But his wife reached menopause and suddenly said, "I don't want any of this around anymore. I'm not interested." She also ceased being interested in sex. So in many cases, what turned on an individual prior to menopause [may] turn them off after menopause because the whole body chemistry changes. That can come in one's 40s, 50s, [or] 60s. It can also come in the 30s. It doesn't happen with all people, but I've personally known three cases where it did. However, I also know people in their 70s who are still playing.

LINDSAY

I [always] assumed that I was normal. From talking to other adults and particularly other women, I don't think I was. A lot of people are taught D&S is evil. I missed that. My mom sent my brother and me to church so we would have the basis to know what was going on there. But as soon as I was old enough to say, "This is not really happening, Mom," she said, "Fine." My theory is that she sent us off to Sunday school so she and my dad could be alone on Sundays. She had no problem when I didn't want to participate anymore. I do believe in my own personal god and in goodness, but I can't believe that there could be a god who says, "This is not good." How can something so pleasurable not be good? That never made sense to me.

I am a very sexual, sensual person. I'm very tactile, and that comes through in my sexuality. In S&M I'm generally submissive, but I do switch and top sometimes. I would say that my sexuality is my major interest in life. [Because my partner and I are retired], we devote an enormous amount of energy towards sexual playing. S&M for us is sex play; it doesn't encompass our entire sexual life. It's just one part of the spectrum. [Max and I] are visual artists, and that translates into sex. We try and create images. That's one thing about S&M that appeals to us: It's like roleplaying, like theater. If you're not playing, you go to parties where you're watching other people. You see what they're doing, how they dress, the roles that they take on. It's sexual theater for us.

I have always been in tune with my body. I can remember giving myself orgasms [at] maybe age five—definitely age six. I was always aware of this really pleasurable thing that I could do to myself [and] always very in tune with the pleasures of the body. Early in life I might have had some passive fantasies, where I would think of some man coming and taking me and doing things to me. Maybe that's the root of some S&M stuff. [But] it was never someone whipping me or putting me in bondage. When I met my partner, he had interests in this and introduced me to it. Because I am quite open sexually—open to ideas, open to new things—I said, "Sure, I'll try this." His interests fit mine easily. I thought, This is fun! This is exciting! It's something new. Yippee ki-yay!

After we'd been together for a while, he pointed out that he had rings on his bed and that he could tie me to them in compromising positions. I had no objections. There was a mental trippiness to the whole thing, to thinking, I can't get away! But at the same time trusting the person you're with and knowing that they're not going to do anything that you would want to escape. There's safety in it.

When I first got into this relationship, I'd never really explored things in an anal sort of way, and my partner taught me about that. I learned that I can have anal orgasms as well as vaginal orgasms, so that was pretty neat. I have [also] tried some pee-hole playing; it was interesting that there's actually another area for orgasming. Once again, I thought, Ooh, there is a new frontier, after all. Just when you think you've learned it all, there's just one more thing.

I like to dance an awful lot. That's part of where these different images come through me, these different personae. I dance for my partner. I become these different people. I dance to arouse. I strip. It's not the traditional burlesque—"Okay, it's comin' off now, watch out!" It's not like that. It becomes very erotic. I lose myself in the dance. I become the music; it [surges] through me and I move. When I think fetishes, I think [of] some-body [who] likes shoes. [So] I don't know that it's a traditional fetish, but for me, [it's] probably my most favorite activity. [Maybe] I've come up with something new. New and unusual, that's what I like.

We get into dressing. I have quite a collection of things—not just S&M—but a whole range of things that I like to [wear]. I try and run the gamut as much as I can. I even have wigs that I wear, or hats to hide my hair completely. I'll look through my closet of massive amounts of clothes, which I pick up here and there—from designer things to Goodwill shopping—and at that moment I start feeling what I want to be. I'll pull out a piece here and a piece there. I do my makeup differently. I might take an hour getting myself together.

My lover built a secret room in our house for us to play in: It's all black padded-leather walls, leather ceiling, and the leather panels on the wall are mixed in with mirrors, and the door is a sliding mirror. When you're in there and close the door, you don't really see a door. You go into what I think of as a magical place. After I'm all ready, I'll call downstairs and I'll hide from him. I'll tell him to go into the room and wait for me. I'll already have music on from this great little stereo system in there, and I'll have my remote control. I'll tell him to go and sit down on the cushion, and then I go in. I tell him to close his eyes, and I'll get into a position that I want him to open his eyes to. This is where the artist part comes in: from having been a photographer, I think of angle. I'm not just up there dancing. I start the music, tell him to open his eyes, and stand still for him to look at me. I become an object for him. I've heard women say, "I'm not an object; I'm your love," but I don't want to be his love at that moment. I want to be this object that he can look at and evaluate and desire. I start moving; we have black ropes that hang from the ceiling of the room, and I start working with them. I wrap them around my arms [and] work them into looking like bondage. There's some that I'll reach, and I'll wrap them around my neck, like I'm there as a slave for him. Eventually my clothes start coming off. There are ropes hanging from the ceiling above him; I can suspend myself so I'm over him and he can get to parts of my body. I tease him, getting close, pulling away. I can dance for two or three hours. I become a sweaty bit of flesh. It's a turn-on to see a wet body. It is very, very intense, and I lose myself in it. My mind goes on vacation; I become my body. I don't fantasize: I feel my body. I feel what's happening to it.

When we were first together and I was being introduced to the Scene, we went to an S&M group which had a mixture of heterosexuals, male tops, female bottoms, female tops, male bottoms, gay men, top and bottom, lesbians, tops and bottoms. They have a bondage beauty contest, and I entered. It was the first time that I did exhibitionism. It was a very strange feeling—[embarrassment at] what I was having to do and excitement from people looking at me, exposing my most personal areas. Traditionally, S&M seems to be tied into black leather—that harsh black look. My partner and I prefer femininity. We [broke] tradition. I got one of my good dresses, a wedding dress that we picked up, and it was very femme: It had an elastic top that I was able to pull down under my breasts—[actually] my partner pulled it down—and I had nipple clamps on my nipples, connected to chains. I had a collar on, with a chain coming from that; I had wrist cuffs on, with chains; and ankle cuffs on, with chains. My ankles were connected to a spreader bar, [so] that my legs were spread as far apart as they could go. I'd never done [anything like] it in my life. I would peep and look at these people looking at me, men and women, and it was really quite the thrill. I really liked it. We won. It was really very interesting because most of the people there wear black and do traditional rope bondage. But my partner has this artistic eye: The whole thing was visually unique to that club. We won [prizes for] Most Erotic, Most Artistic, Best of Show. It was amazing.

At S&M parties people go to see and be seen. It is very much like sex theater. I [also] enjoy getting to watch. That's what's so neat about these parties. [Ordinarily], you see somebody who you're attracted to and just sneak a peek at them: Society teaches us not to gawk. [At] these parties, you can sit and gawk all you want and people enjoy it. That's why they're doing it. To be a voyeur is great fun. You get these images in your head: There's an energy that goes around the room. You feel this sexual tension going on—to be able to share in that, you take it home with you. It builds up. It pushes you further in[to] your own sexuality. It pushes you into more passion.

People think [S&M] is about pain. There is pain involved for some people, but that's their choosing. It scares straight people, because they see it as something evil. I don't think of that at all. It can be great fun, and it connects us with the child part of us who wants to play [and] pretend. I think particularly in the world today, with all the diseases out and people being less active with multiple partners, it's a great way to expand your own sexuality with your partner. To go to these parties is a great way to enjoy other people's sexuality without having to be intimate with them.

ALLEN

I consider myself trisexual: If it's sexual, I'll try it. Basically, I'm straight but have definite bi tendencies. I've been in sexual situations with transvestites, so I guess that classifies me as bi. I'm also switchable. I enjoy both dominant and submissive roles and have played both. My interest in bondage and D&S is not at all extreme: I'm not into pain or anything really stringent. Much more toward the "soft," loving scene, sensuousness, prolonged teasing.

My spouse knows that I have been interested in D&S, bondage, and fetishism, but is not comfortable with it. At one point, fairly early in our marriage, I showed her some bondage photos, but she wasn't interested. My wife does not participate in any of my activities. Unfortunately, I have to pursue my interests outside of our relationship. Therefore, D&S doesn't play as large a role [in my life] as I'd like it to. I suppose I've participated in what I'd consider full-scale D&S scenes about four or five times, and most of those have been within the last two years.

I've always been attracted to fetish dressing, especially stockings, boots, heels, and such. I used to buy the magazines—like *Tip Top*—when I was 16. For as long as I can remember, I've been attracted to exotic forms of sexuality. [Although] my interest in latex dates from an early age, I didn't realize it till I was about 30 or so. That's when I started using rubber to masturbate with. I disclosed this interest to my wife, and she got somewhat involved. About ten years ago I bought about a thousand dollars' worth of rubber clothing. We got dressed up together for a year or so, but somehow this activity fell by the wayside. I still have a few pieces—the stuff tends to deteriorate over time—and dress in them by myself.

I own several pieces of latex clothing, primarily undergarments, panties, tights, bloomers, and some specialty items, such as pants with built-in anal probes, built-in cock sheaths. I have some nipple clamps and quite a few genital-bondage devices, crotch harnesses, cock rings, ball stretchers, two or three anal vibrators, a set of anal beads—I love those—and quite a bit of enema equipment: an in-line bulb pump, several bags, hoses, a few different kinds of nozzles. My fantasies include having a complete room set up for sexual activities, with bondage gear, masturbation devices, collections of erotica, mirrors, plumbing.

The incorporation of fetish gear into a scene is primarily the prerogative of whoever is in charge. When I'm with [my mistress], I bring some of my toys, especially the genital-bondage equipment, and some of the more feminine frilly things: panties and girdles. I love tight [garments]. When I'm alone, I might dress in rubber and use the straps and harnesses on myself. I engage in very extended masturbation sessions, sometimes for hours, mostly when I'm traveling and in a hotel by myself with plenty of time. When I travel I always take a bunch of stuff with me: enema gear, rope, harnesses, clothing—half a suitcase full.

[As for] my most exciting or satisfying experiences with D&S, there are two. One was my first real visit to a professional dom. I met her through a male friend who is an ardent sub and has been seeking people into the Scene around here for years. She's about 40, blond, quite attractive, voluptuous, and has a very nicely equipped dungeon in her garage. We spent about three hours together and responded to each other wonderfully. She really likes men, enjoys teasing, and that's exactly what I'm into.

The second involves the woman I currently see. She herself has been into the Scene for only about a year. She has no dungeon or elaborate equipment, but she's an extremely sensuous woman and also likes men. We met for the first time last November. I had a wonderful scene with her at her apartment a few weeks later, and she liked me enough to invite me to her birthday party. The guests consisted of her, me, another mistress—someone [she] is training—and another male sub, whom I happened to know. Again, there was no real pain involved. Lots of submissive behavior, boot kissing and the like, serving the women intimately, et cetera. The climax of the evening was when they tied me to a bed with one arm free and commanded me to masturbate while they both teased me. [My friend] used a tiny cat-o'-nine-tails on my genitalia while I played with myself. I loved it.

I feel very well adjusted to my sexual proclivities, not guilty at all, not nervous, and I don't have the feeling that I'm doing anything wrong. If I could, I'd marry [my mistress], become her full-time submissive, and live my entire life inside the Scene, go to parties, entertain other couples at home, devote all my spare time and discretionary income to sensuality and sexual provocation. I'd love that.

PHIL T.

I am a heterosexual male, [but] I'm just discovering my bisexuality. D&S had always interested me, and now I'm getting more involved in it, becoming more aware of myself, mainly as a submissive. Sometimes the dominant side of myself does come out. From years of management training, if nobody takes control of a situation, I go out and grab it.

I have found [someone] through an on-line service. We use the service as the gateway; I am given orders to do that I can carry out while at work, so it flows over into my everyday life. One order is to wear a cock harness and different toys under my clothing. Nobody ever notices, much less cares, probably, as long as it doesn't interfere with the job. During my [on-line] sessions, after performing different orders, usually it climaxes with masturbation. Then there's the coming-down period [when] we [are] two regular adults talking about different things: the kids, family, weather, what's happening in our parts of the world.

My wife is what would be classified as plain vanilla and not really into it. [This] part of my life is, for lack of a better word, hidden from her. I tried to broach the subject with my wife, dropping hints, but she doesn't pick up on it. I don't know if she doesn't want to or is just naive. She seems turned off by the idea [of D&S]. [It] could be her strict religious upbringing that says this is wrong. Fortunately, I love my wife and the family; I want to keep them together. So I see the mistress relationship as secondary. The thing that relieves me [about not] expanding the secondary relationship to an intimate one, is the prevalence of diseases. I knew two people who died of AIDS. So it is always in my mind that I'm healthy and safe. Let's keep it that way.

It was very easy to come to grips with [my interest]. I hear a lot that people think that they are sick or need help. I just accepted it. Of course, you don't go to your friends and go, "Hey, look what I'm into!" I was interested in women and all that, so I thought it was very normal. I found myself strongly attracted to reading [about D&S], mostly where the female was dominant and there was feminization of males. One [story] that always stayed in my mind was of a young woman who feminized her husband into her maid. She took all his possessions, gave him a changing room and a uniform to wear for different times of the day, and he was to do all the house duties and take care of all her needs—whether cleaning or sexual needs.

When I grew up, my father was always at work, and usually the only time I saw him was on Sunday morning. He came home too late at night for me to interact. So I grew up with my mother and two older sisters. I liked when they used to jump on me and bundle me up in the blankets in bed. Also, being home from school before them, I was able to try on their clothes. And then in people's attics—the old, old things—that's where I probably got the start, being alone and able to explore and having nobody say, "No, that is not right." [My fantasies included being] forced to wear very tight, restrictive clothing, multilayered clothing. We used to have the old vinyl raincoats, and I would wear those.

I like leather. [My mistress] mostly gives me orders to wear different items—ball stretchers, cock pouch, and different harnesses to work. Or I'm not [allowed] to touch my penis at all, or [must] sit down on a toilet and use it as a woman would; some days dressing up as a woman. I'm also into wearing diapers, which is a whole other realm.

The diaper wearing began in college. I figured it was a little stranger than what normal college students do, but it was a nice feeling. Usually, [I'll wear] disposable diapers and plastic pants over them—plastic, nylon, rubber. That tends to muffle the sounds, which helps if you're going out in public. It's hard to describe, but the secure feeling of wearing one, and the bulkiness—it's a nice warm feeling, as is using it in place of a bathroom to urinate. At first I was very hesitant to go out wearing one under my clothes, figuring everybody in the world is going to stop and notice. But I talked to a number of people who do, and the comment [was] that nobody out there gives a care as long as you don't disturb another person. I made trips to the grocery store to try it out, and nobody noticed, and finally [I] got bolder and bolder, till one day I tried doing it at work. Lo and behold, nobody noticed. [So] at least once or twice a week I wear it to work. Then I told my mistress I was doing it, and she suggested that I go to work wearing one and try to keep it dry as long as possible but to use only one diaper during the whole day. Late in the day my bladder was quite filled and decided to release itself. People who were standing within three to five feet of me never knew what was happening. That was a little thrill—doing something that society might say is wrong or naughty and being able to get away with it.

Just recently I [wore] a diaper with rubber pants with a garter belt and stockings. It was quite a combination! Of course, nobody could see that underneath [my] clothing. At a time prearranged with my mistress, I changed and wore a locking cock harness and wasn't allowed to masturbate until I reported back after a number of days. It was [exciting]. I was doing something that society said was taboo. It was risk taking. What would happen if I got caught, especially at work? What would the consequences be? All those elements—doing it at work, being forced to do it, [the risk]—[are exciting].

I am and have always been attracted to women and like sex with women, but I also tend to look at men more now. I find myself looking at different parts of their bodies and sort of wondering. I've become more aware and accepting [of] that part of me, and though I may not get the chance to explore it, [I'm] learning that it's there [and] it's not evil, it's not wrong. I've always been very comfortable around gay men. They're normal as far as I'm concerned. Probably I'm heading now more [into] the forced-feminization area, not so much heavy pain, marking the body, [or] whippings. Maybe piercing. That would be a hard one to explain! But those things are on my mind, and I'm trying to figure out how to go into them and keep everything together. Trying to keep this all separate from my home life, from my wife and the kids [is complex]. Luckily, the children are young enough that they don't go snooping, but I know when I reached my early teens, I looked through everything and anything. It's going to be a real challenge to avoid being discovered. What happens 10 years from now could be for the next book.

SECTION SIX

MASCULINE AND FEMININE

Twenty-One

TRANSGENDERISM

T he differences between the sexes and the urge to bridge them have always occupied a corner of the human imagination. Expressing a personality which seems to be at odds with one's sex is not really one but many phenomena with a diversity of expressions and behaviors. Because transgenderism is so variously manifested by men and women of different sexual orientations, and because a sizeable percentage do not engage in D&S, this chapter provides only a rudimentary understanding of it. We focus on the critical distinctions between transvestism and transsexualism before going on (in Chapter 22) to a detailed discussion of transgenderists who engage in D&S.

We feature an analysis of transgenderism by Dr. Roger E. Peo, a gender counselor in Poughkeepsie, New York. He received his Ph.D. from the Institute for Advanced Study of Human Sexuality and is certified by the American College of Sexologists. Dr. Peo is a diplomate in sex counseling of the American Board of Sexology and a fellow of the American College of Clinical Sexologists, a member of the Society for the Scientific Study of Sex and of the Harry Benjamin International Gender Dysphoria Association.

We also hear from a male-to-female transgenderist:

- Christina who is 35 years old and single. Christina works as a com-
puter-systems administrator.

A BRIEF
TRANSGENDERISM LEXICON

The range of abbreviations and neologisms used to describe transgenderist phenomena indicates the complexity of this behavioral universe. Here is a quick list of the most familiar terms.

Cross-dressing, also known as *drag:* wearing the garments of a member of the biologically opposite sex.

Female-to-male: a biological woman who either dresses as or believes she is a man.

Genderbending, also known as *genderfucking:* wearing some clothing or accessories associated exclusively with the opposite sex; creating a "she-male" appearance. Usually done with the intent of surprising the on-looker.

Hermaphrodite: a person who has secondary characteristics of both sexes.

Male-to-female: a biological man who either dresses as or believes he is a woman.

Real-life Test: a period during which preop transsexuals live full-time in the role of a member of the opposite gender. The ability to succeed in this trial is one diagnostic tool used to determine whether the Transsexual (TS) may be a good candidate for surgery.

Sexual-reassignment Surgery, also known as a *sex-change operation:* the medi-cal procedures involved in permanently altering a person's secondary sexual characteristics.

She-male: a chemically created pseudo-hermaphrodite, also known as *chick-with-dick,* often a preop TS.

Transgenderism: a term used by advocates and practitioners to identify both transvestism and transsexualism.

Transsexual, also known as a *TS:* someone who feels she or he is actually a member of the biologically opposite sex. Transsexuals are usually referred to as *preoperative* (*preop*) or *postoperative* (*postop*), to indicate, respectively, their intentions to undergo or their recovery from sexual-reassignment surgery.

Transvestite, also known as a *TV* or a *cross-dresser:* someone who wears the clothing associated with the opposite sex.

WHAT IS TRANSVESTISM?

The most common phenomenon in transgenderism is transvestism, or dressing in clothes normally worn by the opposite sex.

The word *transvestite* derives from the Latin *trans* (cross) and *vestia* (clothing). It was first coined by Magnus Hirschfeld (himself a cross-dresser who was known in Berlin's gay subculture as "Auntie Magnesia") in his 1910 book *Transvestites: An Investigation into the Erotic Impulse of Disguise.* Havelock Ellis later chose to call the phenomenon Eonism, after the Chevalier d'Eon, 18th Century Europe's most celebrated transvestite, who dressed as a woman in the course of pursuing a career as a diplomat and spy. Upon leaving his trade, he dressed and lived entirely as a woman.

Although 19th Century writers may have named the phenomenon, the desire to dress as a member of the opposite sex has been known—and occasionally sanctioned—throughout human history.

> *Cross-dressing desires exist in all cultures. In some, the social stigma is so great that there is, effectively, no way to express it. Islamic cultures, mainland China, and the United States seem to fit this category. Other cultures [for example, Thailand and Japan] have niche social strata for unusual sexual behaviors. Other cultures fall somewhere in between.* —ROGER E. PEO

On this continent many North American Plains Indian tribes allowed a man to assume the role of *berdache,* dressing as a woman, performing a woman's tasks, and often marrying as a woman. The Cheyenne esteemed their *berdaches* and believed them to be great doctors and practitioners of love magic. Among the Navaho, a *nadle* (a term that encompasses both transvestites and hermaphrodites) was considered to be extremely fortunate and a family that included one felt assured of attaining great wealth. Conversely, a married couple of the Nahane tribe could select a daughter to become a son to hunt for them when they grew old. After a ceremony ritualistically changed the girl's gender at about age five, she was reared as a boy and assumed male status and responsibilities.

In many cultures transvestites have served important ritual functions. Among the Zulu of South Africa, for example, only transvestite men are allowed to practice divination. Young males in the Wodaabe tribe of West Africa compete for women's affections in highly ritualized, cross-dressing beauty contests. In other cultures cross-dressed male prostitutes outnumber female prostitutes: In Oman, for example, male-to-female TV prostitutes are socially recognized, while female prostitution is practiced in strictest secrecy.

Despite its cultural and historical ubiquity, transvestism remains poorly understood in America. Considerable confusion exists as to the sexual orientation of TVs. Transvestism has long been firmly associated with homosexuality—and specifically homosexual prostitution—both in non-Western cultures and in older Western traditions. In some Muslim cultures handsome young males are still cross-dressed to serve as consorts to wealthy married men. But, in fact, most Western transvestites are heterosexual.

It would appear that over 90 percent of male cross-dressers are strictly heterosexual. Some cross-dressers experiment with same-sex partners when they are cross-dressed but usually abandon it as unsatisfying. The balance are homosexual, with a few bisexuals.
—ROGER E. PEO

Among the majority of gay men cross-dressing is seldom practiced except as an occasional adventure in genderbending or, more often, as an elaborate joke. Gay drag queens typically lampoon femininity.

For many gay men, dressing up in women's clothing is reserved for masquerades or Halloween celebrations. Stepping out of their daily clothing and into the whimsical costumes or sensuous fabrics permitted to women, these men find in the event a kind of bacchanalia, a release from all convention. This spirit prevails at festivities such as Mardi Gras, where men (gay and straight) flaunt garish costumes in hedonistic parody of the female sex.

Many people are discomfited by true transvestites because the TVs do not seem to conform to assigned social roles.

In our society there is no room for people "in the middle." "Choose one side and be happy there" seems to be the unwritten rule.
—ROGER E. PEO

What our culture perceives as acceptable masculine behavior comprises a narrow range of possibilities.

A gender client might be someone who was told early on that only women cry and show feelings. He might have had women and girls around who seemed to get a lot more positive attention than did the males. He might have felt he had to be the tough guy, a jock, to compensate for or to hide his softer feminine tendencies.

—M. CYBELE

In a world where women are largely perceived to lack power, for a man to emulate one seems strange if not downright ludicrous. Transvestism finds a place in the comedy routines of Milton Berle and others, where the tradition of mocking women by imitating them depends upon a bizarre charade of neurotic womanhood. The vision of a man mincing and lisping in women's clothing usually evokes the kind of merriment generally reserved for the fellow who's fallen on a banana peel; it is laughter shared equally by men and women, and its object is the emasculated or effeminate man. Cross-dressers, however, are not emasculated—nor, for that matter, necessarily effeminate—men. Nor are they all men. While male-to-female cross-dressers are the most visible segment of the transgender communities, and while transvestism is presumed to be primarily a male phenomenon, female-to-male cross-dressers exist but are less identifiable.

Joan of Arc was exceptional when she donned male clothing to lead campaigns for France, as was Calamity Jane, who spent the better part of her life living as a man. But ever since Marlene Dietrich appeared in a tuxedo and Katharine Hepburn swore off skirts, few people have been greatly disconcerted by the sight of women in masculine attire.

Our culture teaches us that it's okay for a woman to explore her masculine feelings and tendencies—nothing amiss with a woman wearing pants—but let a man put on a skirt, and there's something wrong. I believe that this is because we're in a patriarchal society that says that masculine is better than feminine, that masculine is strong and feminine is weak. A tomboy is looked upon with amusement and praised, but an effeminate boy is called a sissy.

—M. CYBELE

Feminine attire connotes powerlessness, while male clothing is largely viewed as neutral—or suggestive, as Ms. Dietrich's admirers can attest. Men's attire worn by women has another connotation: Doris Day looked *cute* in Rock Hudson's oversized pajamas, rather like a little girl in her father's clothes. Rock Hudson in Doris Day's outfits would have been another matter. Some female-to-male cross-dressers, however, arouse distinct disapprobation. Lesbians who are "butch" and both dress in masculine attire and emulate stereotypically masculine behaviors may be perceived with some alarm or subjected to harrassment. In alternative sexuality communities, however, women who embody "masculine" characteristics may be perceived as admirable exemplars of feminity. Challenges to gender stereotyping are raised not only among transgenderists but throughout the D&S world.

Since so many women nowadays wear male clothing to meet the dictates of fashion rather than of eros, the line between cross-dressing and trendiness is blurred. Many feel that unless cross-dressing carries some erotic component—unless the wearer experiences a direct thrill from being clad in opposite-gender attire—it is not true transvestism. But this is debatable, as many male-to-female cross-dressers deny that they experience erotic stimulation from wearing women's garb. Whether they are denying their erotic impulse to sanitize or justify their interest is also controversial.

> *The erotic-sensual component of cross-dressing is nearly always present regardless of protestations to the contrary. These disclaimers may be caused by the embarrassment of mentioning masturbation for release of sexual tension or perhaps an attempt to make cross-dressing more socially acceptable by minimizing the erotic component.*
> —ROGER E. PEO

One of the most common misunderstandings about transgenderism is that the difference between the TV and the TS is one of degree: that the erotic passion for cross-dressing is a diluted form of transsexualism. But while complete feminization is a not-uncommon fantasy among transvestites, few transvestites pursue a sex change.

> *[A fantasy] would be to live a life as a she-male, if not full-time, at least a good six months or a year, rather than just an afternoon. Living as a woman. Keeping my genitals intact, thank you.*
> —CHERYL HAGGERTY

> *I enjoy cross-dressing. It's not something I feel I need to do all the time. I have no desire to change sex.*   —DEIRDRE

The TV is also apt to have periods, sometimes extended, when he can live comfortably, successfully, and uniquely in his male persona. While the most common TV fantasy is to *pass* (to be a man who can fool others into believing he's a woman), the majority of male-to-female TVs lead prosperous, conventional lives as husbands, fathers, and community leaders.

> *For some cross-dressers, there is a thrill in seeing how well they can pass in the other gender role. The high they get from this would*

certainly be diminished if there were no penalty for discovery. Further, I am not sure they really want general acceptance. Being a man has economic and social advantages to which they can escape after their sojourn into the world of the feminine.

—ROGER E. PEO

I let the client know that a few hours dressed as a woman does not give him the life experience of being a woman. You need to be willing to be vulnerable, and you need to be willing to be a second-class citizen. A lot of men are not willing to do that.

—M. CYBELE

Those who cannot accept their cross-dressing inclinations (or who have censorious partners) may go through phases during which they destroy their alternate wardrobes.

There [have] been periods of purging, when I deny [my interest], but basically I've been doing it all my life. —CHRISTINA

The urge to cross-dress may become compulsive, particularly when the TV cannot find meaningful outlets, such as support groups, or compassionate partners. He usually finds that the need to cross-dress escalates when it is repressed. Compulsive cross-dressing can threaten the security of marriages or other long-term relationships.

The most difficult psychological challenge the cross-dresser faces is acceptance of these desires. Without this, he faces guilt and anxiety that can spill over into the balance of his life. Through acceptance he can learn to control his urges and enjoy the cross-dressed state. Coupled with this acceptance is his need to be sensitive to the woman in his life. Since most cross-dressers are married, this is a common problem. If he allows cross-dressing to completely invade the relationship, he will most likely destroy it. —ROGER E. PEO

A majority of TVs are probably solitary cross-dressers who conceal their interests from even their spouses for fear of rejection and disapproval. But repressing their needs usually only contributes to the TV's dilemma, since the impulse to cross-dress is usually most acute during periods of high stress.

Part of the urge to cross-dress is a release of stress. I've noticed over the years that I tend to do it and feel more driven to do it when I'm stressed, when I'm not in a relationship, or when the relationship I'm in is a disaster. —DEIRDRE

WHAT IS TRANSSEXUALISM?

While both the transvestite and the transsexual may wear feminine clothing and affect feminine behavior, their motives differ radically. Clothing and corollary feminine touches are intrinsic to a TV's pleasure; the cross-dressing alone brings intense gratification. TVs may even express a different, more sexual, personality when cross-dressed.

> *I feel very different when I'm Cheryl. I like to attract attention. I like looking sexy and feeling sexy. I like the idea of being told [or] expected to do things. Sometimes I wonder just why the hell I'm dressing as a French maid, because I don't spend a whole lot of time in my home keeping the place immaculately clean! It's the posturing and the playing and the teasing and the exhibitionism and voyeurism.* —CHERYL HAGGERTY

A TS is less likely to project a different persona when cross-dressed, as he or she *already* feels like a person of the biologically opposite sex. For the TS, wearing the attire of the opposite gender is an incomplete experience when the body beneath the clothing does not match the internal reality.

> *The transsexual looks at his body with disgust as one of nature's mistakes. He feels that his penis no more identifies him as male than a sixth finger on one hand would identify him as a nonhuman freak. He is not the most perverse sort of homosexual, but a case of totally reversed gender identity.* —ARNO KARLEN[1]

Although distinctions between transvestite and transsexual have been recognized only very recently, the theme of complete gender change always has been popular in Western culture. Its place as a fundamental archetype of human behavior is suggested by the classical Greek myth of the Theban seer Tiresius, who was transformed into a woman for seven years. Sometime after his masculinity was restored, Zeus and Hera quarreled over which gender has a more profound enjoyment of sex and consulted Tiresius, who testified that women experience "nine or 10 times more pleasure."[2]

Perhaps the most infamous case of sex change in Western antiquity was the Emperor Nero, who, remorseful for having killed his pregnant wife, ordered the castration of a young man who resembled the deceased, dressed the eunuch in women's clothes, and formally married his unusual bride with splendid ceremony. Similar historical antecedents are numerous. They are also ambiguous and cannot be clearly differentiated from accounts of voluntary or self-inflicted castration.

The term *drag*, meanwhile, finds its ominous origin in antiquity:

The ancient Greeks . . . used castration only to punish rapists, and the offender was called a spao, *meaning "to draw out" or "drag," a description of how the testes were removed from the scrotum. Despised in Greek society and denied employment, such men are said to have masqueraded as women—the origin of the slang expression "drag" for a man in woman's attire.* —CHARLES PANATI[3]

Several ancient civilizations made a practice of creating, and cross-dressing eunuchs for social, sexual and ritual purposes. An indeterminate percentage of these eunuchs were probably the early equivalents of transsexuals. Procedures to develop opposite-sex secondary sexual characteristics, meanwhile, were unavailable until the 19th Century. One of the first postoperative transsexuals in the modern sense was Herman Karl, who began life as Sophia Hedwig. Her 1882 hormonal treatments gave her a beard, while surgery provided a crude penis.

Transsexuals were once dismissed as homosexuals (male or female) who simply had gone mad. Only in 1949 did Dr. David O. Cauldwell first define it as a syndrome (*psychopathia transsexualis*) distinct from homosexuality. Contemporaneously, cosmetic surgeons and endocrinologists in Denmark under the direction of Dr. Christian Hamburger began to develop sex-change techniques. Their work received huge publicity in 1952, when George Jorgensen left Long Island, New York, for Denmark and returned to the United States as Christine Jorgensen. The first full-length study of transsexuals was *The Transsexual Phenomenon*, published in 1966 by Dr. Harry Benjamin, an endocrinologist who began to study the subject after meeting Ms. Jorgensen.

Most known transsexuals are of the male-to-female variety, although a number of support groups, counselors, and surgeons specialize in female-to-male support. Transsexuals confront a truly mind-boggling array of social and medical challenges. After the TS has identified the nature of his problems and begins to seek recourse, he faces an arduous screening and counseling process followed by the expense, risk, and discomfort of several surgeries. Female-to-male surgical procedures are particularly daunting. The transsexual's willingness to make enormous emotional, physical, and financial sacrifices to achieve this goal is a telling measure of the urgency of his plight.

Only a small percentage of transsexuals undergoes surgery. Some compromise: They get hormonal treatments and cross-dress. Also, a small number of postop patients ultimately regret their decisions.

[The surgery is] scary because there's quite a bit to lose, and the operation is not reversible. I've heard that a lot of postoperative transsexuals don't get everything that they wanted out of their

operation. It's no quick fix: Life still has many problems. [So] you risk having a different body with the same problems.

　　　　　　　　　　　　　　　　　　　　　　　—CHRISTINA

The life changes involved in altering one's identity from one sex to the other extend from lengthy bureaucratic processes to emotional disclosures to family, friends, and employers. Extensive counseling, including the real-life test, are required before doctors will recommend surgery. Medically, a male-to-female transsexual typically undergoes extensive cosmetic surgery to redefine the jaw and other facial features, as well as paring down of the Adam's apple; electrolysis to remove hair on body and face; hormonal injections to stimulate growth of breasts and to promote a softer, rounder body; breast implants; and castration, followed by construction of a canal similar to a vagina. Once surgery is complete, many male-to-female transsexuals find that they have retained orgasmic capacity.

A female-to-male transsexual typically undergoes cosmetic surgeries, hormonal treatments, breast reduction or removal, hysterectomy, the closing off of the vagina, and diversion of the urethra. Modern technology has not yet engineered a satisfactory artificial penis.

If you have the female-to-male surgery and get a constructed penis, they take out all the internals, the uterus and ovaries, and they close up the vagina, and they reroute the urethra, which can cause problems later. There's a lot of reconstruction. The male-to-female stuff is peanuts by comparison. Female-to-male is also more expensive than the male-to-female. I was quoted a cost [of] around $60,000. There are other things I can think of to buy with $60,000 than a dick that doesn't work.　　　　　　　　　—KELLY T.

One option in place of a penis is an open-ended tube formed from skin grafts and fitted with a miniature hydraulic pump to simulate erection. Orgasmic capacity is unlikely. Transsexuals of both genders are sterile after surgery.

A TS views his sexuality according to the gender he believes he possesses rather than the body he has. There seem to be roughly as many straight as gay transsexuals, although until surgery is complete, transsexuals themselves may feel confused as to their orientation. A preop male-to-female transsexual may perceive himself as a straight woman and form relationships with straight men, feeling that these relationships are heterosexual, even though an outsider would see them as two men together. Or a preop female-to-male transsexual (such as Kelly T., quoted above) may perceive herself as a man and form a homosexual relationship, even though, biologically, Kelly would seem to be a woman dating a man.

> *The transsexual can be either heterosexual or homosexual, where such definitions are based on gender identity, not genital anatomy. Some transsexuals may be asexual before genital surgery because of the dichotomy between their perceived gender and their anatomy. There are few reports of bisexual transsexuals.* —ROGER E. PEO

Because transsexualism causes significant bewilderment among transsexuals and their partners, many people wait until they have completed surgery before forming permanent relationships. Once the transformation is complete, transsexuals often choose to blend quickly into the mainstream and generally lead very private, conventional lives with their partners of choice.

WHY ARE THEY LIKE THIS?

Despite the social pressure for women and men to conform to allegedly natural models of behavior, the models for masculinity and femininity have always been moving targets. The ideal woman in the 1950s was an ever-cheerful, whimsical, doting helpmate and mother; the 1990s ideal is an ambitious careerist who looks like a model and cooks like a chef—and who does not necessarily have a husband. Similarly, the former image of the model man as the sole wage earner, an invulnerable, infallible, nearly emotionless king of his castle has surrendered to economic realities and unavoidable truths, such as his needs for tenderness and understanding. Do femininity and masculinity really conform to rigid models, or is there more to gender than meets the eye?

> *The stuff between our legs is a biological condition that has some bearing on, but doesn't completely define, who we are. One's sex is in the crotch, but gender identity takes place in the mind. I think we're human beings first, with both masculine and feminine energies and tendencies.* —M. CYBELE

Transgenderists, and especially transvestites, seem to possess aspects of both genders. Many do not meet the standard definitions of male or female but instead have the capability to affiliate strongly with both genders.

> *I find that women's clothing is designed to be alluring and to accentuate those parts of myself that are sexy and attractive. Cross-*

dressing to me is actually a bit more than sensual pleasure in the clothes themselves. I have a lot of androgynous qualities. My sexuality is not divisible into male and female. When I cross-dress, feminine aspects of myself emerge into the spotlight. It's almost, but not entirely, a different identity. —ROBIN YOUNG

There are, more or less, two clinical theories on transgenderism: Either it is created, or it is inborn. These same two schools contest the roles of nature and nurture in other matters of psychology, biology, and human destiny. Perhaps the answer eventually will be found through holistic investigation, which considers factors both environmental and biological.

Many researchers hold that gender is learned in early childhood. It may derive from traumatic experience or may result from the circumstances of one's relationship with a parent. In the case of transsexuals, for example, Dr. Robert Stoller has suggested that in childhood they develop an irregularly close, perhaps inseparable, identification with the opposite-sex parent. But there are significant flaws in the theory that gender identity (or any sexual orientation) is solely a matter of nurture.

I . . . had the opportunity to check on other therapists' results, and the general impression, based on statistics and accumulated experience, is that deconditioning does not work, whatever the specific technique. If variant sexual behaviors cannot be removed by deconditioning, they are unlikely to have arisen by conditioning. —VACLAV PINKAVA[4]

Others advance the theory that a transsexual's gender bias is determined *in utero* when a kind of "chemical accident" occurs. Similar theories concern the presence or absence of chromosomes. Genetic research has opened new areas of inquiry to support speculation that there is a physiological basis for at least some aspects of transsexualism. But these theories tend to see human behavior as the unique result of a mechanical-biological process. To reduce human beings—or any complex organisms—to their chemical properties seems oversimplistic.

While transvestism has given rise to vast quantities of research and theorizing, scientists have not established its origins, either. The impulse to cross-dress usually begins in youth and becomes a permanent feature of a TV's erotic personality.

Often [the transvestite's] need surfaces at an early age. However, he quickly learns that his feelings are socially unacceptable, so he hides this behavior from most people. —ROGER E. PEO

A majority of TVs recall experimenting with their opposite-sex parents' clothing sometime during early puberty; some also recall episodes in child-hood.

> *My first memories of cross-dressing were when I was [about] two [years old]. I wandered into a closet and was looking up into some of my mother's petticoats, which were in vogue in the '50s. I was quite entranced. I remember it very vividly. I had some other memories when I was six or seven. I used to sing a little ditty to myself over and over and over again as I was lying in bed waiting to go to sleep: "All dressed up in a petticoat."*
>
> —CHERYL HAGGERTY

Why a child is disposed toward transvestism remains a mystery. The absence of a medical explanation for transvestism may add additional pressures to the cross-dresser.

> *There seems to be more social acceptance of transsexuals than cross-dressers. In part, I think this is because there is a medical intervention that lends an air of credibility to [transsexualism]. Also, the average transsexual, when "complete," blends into society in the chosen gender role.*
>
> —ROGER E. PEO

WHAT DO THEY DO?

Although transsexualism is extremely complex, the typical reason why a TS wishes to live as a member of the opposite sex is fairly simple: The TS does not feel comfortable in the body of his or her birth. For the TS, gender exploration is not a question of choice but an imperative. The TS is a bit like the fairy-tale prince trapped in a frog's body, waiting for the magical moment of physical transformation. The internal reality already exists. The cliché "a man trapped inside a woman's body" remains the single most direct description of this phenomenon. The TS tries to live as authentically as possible in accordance with his or her gender identity. A TS's erotic life most often resembles that of the sexually conventional person, with the caveat that the TS may not yet have the biological equipment to match her or his psychic reality.

> *Kelly has charge of my sexuality completely. I'm not interested in sex as a female in any way now.*
>
> —KELLY T.

Some transsexuals gravitate to the D&S communities, where they may pursue any combination of the interests discussed throughout this book. Although a significant percentage of TVs is interested in some type of alternative sexuality, few practice it. But because acceptance for transgenderists is much higher among D&Sers than among the sexually conventional, some vanilla TVs and TS's have found a home in the D&S communities.

I don't have any involvement in D&S outside of being dressed. [But] I like to get together with other folks who are on the more fetishistic fringe of things, including D&S. I also like to get together with other TVs who are interested in outlandishly ultra-exotic feminine activity. —CHERYL HAGGERTY

Since TVs usually comprise both masculine and feminine personae, cross-dressing fulfills a profound personal need to explore the "other" side of the TV's personality.

The TVs that I know [who] aren't involved in S&M cross-dress because they like the clothing. They like the dresses. It feels like they're putting on a whole different persona. —TRUDI

Cross-dressers often pursue a flawless verisimilitude, for which perfecting the dress, makeup, speech, and gestures of the opposite sex is critical. For male-to-female TVs the clothing and attitudes are typically as relaxing as they are erotic. Some male-to-female TVs' greatest pleasure is to be treated as the sister, girlfriend, or lover of a beautiful woman who will take them shopping, dress in similar outfits, and indulge in playful experiments with makeup, wigs, and other feminine accessories.

I call these men "she," dress them as girls or women; teach them how to walk, stand, sit, and gesture. I correct their mannerisms, and may treat them in a strict but affectionate manner, like a combination of big sister and drama coach. —M. CYBELE

TVs frequently re-create through dress the type of opposite-sex person they find most attractive, embodying the characteristics they associate with the opposite sex.

There's a certain satisfaction to being able to create [an] illusion. Not that I would ever really be able to pass in public, but I do a pretty good job. There's a satisfaction in [what] I guess you could call a job well done. —DEIRDRE

Becoming an opposite-sex person—whether for an hour, a day, or a week—means permitting oneself to express otherwise contained aspects of one's personality.

Cross-dressers want to pamper themselves, take a bubble bath and not be called sissy, or to put makeup on [and] look soft and feminine. It allows them to be the passive person. [In] my age group, men are supposed to be the strong ones and not allowed this side of themselves. When they're dressed as females, they can be submissive and soft and teasing. —GYPSY

Even while cross-dressed, heterosexual TVs usually prefer heterosexual encounters. Many male-to-female TVs, for example, will roleplay as lesbians with female partners. Some, however, have the potential for a bisexual experience when dressed. Several of our interviewees described themselves as "trisexual," to denote their ability to pretend that they are heterosexual women engaged in sexual acts with heterosexual men. (A full discussion of the types of D&S erotic activities that TVs enjoy is presented in the next chapter.)

INTERVIEWS

DR. ROGER E. PEO

To understand transgendered persons (transvestites, cross-dressers, and transsexuals), it is necessary to define some terms:

Gender Identity: a person's *internal* sense of being a man or a woman.

Gender Role: a person's *behaviors* that define him or her to society as a man or woman.

Sex: the physical state of being male or female. There are many different aspects, e.g., genital, chromosomal, hormonal, and reproductive. Not all of these match in everybody.

Sexual-Partner Choice: this is a person's choice of the same or other sex for personal interactions.

It is critical to understand that it is possible to find *any combination* of the four categories listed above. With these simplified definitions, it is possible to describe various forms of transgender behavior. I am excluding all persons who have a measurable or identifiable biological problem, such as hermaphrodites and those who suffer from chromosomal or hormonal abnormalities.

Transvestism is primarily found in males. Clinically, a transvestite is a man who likes to wear clothing socially reserved for women. It has been estimated that 0.1 percent to 1 percent of the male population has this behavior to some degree, but there are no observable physical or hormonal irregularities that could account for this behavior. The average male cross-dresser is heterosexual and presents a masculine gender role except when he is cross-dressed. His gender identity is mostly to exclusively masculine; however, when cross-dressed, he may say he "feels female." In the beginning cross-dressing often has a strongly erotic component. Later the erotic feelings may diminish and cross-dressing becomes a way to temporarily escape from the masculine role. The thought is, If I am dressed as a woman, then I no longer have my masculine responsibilities.

Women who are transvestites or cross-dressers would have the same psychological characteristics as described above for men. Women who wear masculine-style clothing but who are "obviously" women do not fall into this category. Cross-dressing is a gender statement with erotic overtones, not a fashion statement. I estimate that the number of women who fit this definition is vanishingly small, perhaps one ten-thousandth of a percent of the female population.

There are many other reasons for adopting the clothing of the other gender. For example, theatrical productions may use cross-dressing for comedic or sinister effects. *Some Like It Hot* and *Psycho* are two classic films that employ this technique. Also, there are female impersonators for whom cross-dressing is an integral part of their act. Sometimes cross-dressing is used as a disguise to commit a crime or [to] hide from the law. Lastly, there are gay males who use "drag" as a way to attract sexual partners. None of these examples fits the *clinical* definition of cross-dressing.

Gender dysphoria usually defines only a severe clinical dislocation of a person's gender identity. Many people who cross-dress are not gender dysphoric in that sense. Anecdotal data suggest that there are a large number of male transvestites who never have felt the need to go to a clinician, or who have gone once and found that the average clinician is unable to help. For example, the obsessive nature of transvestism can be very disruptive in their life and relationships. Generally, those who come to clinical settings do so because of the problems that cross-dressing causes in their life.

Neither transsexualism nor the desire to cross-dress has been eliminated by any clinical approach, so one might theorize that there is some biological basis. This idea is further strengthened by the observation that such behaviors are reported throughout history and in a wide variety of cultures. The higher incidence of transgendered males *may* be caused, in part, by the fact that all fetuses will develop as female unless there are appropriate hormonal actions that both defeminize and masculinize the male fetus. If one assumes that in some cases these processes do not go to completion during the gestation period, one could hypothesize that there is a partial female construct in the brain that is activated by social factors.

Most male cross-dressers seem to come from middle- and upper-middle-class environments. They generally have some education beyond high school. A large percentage have professional vocations—doctors, lawyers, engineers, stockbrokers, clergy, etc. Minorities are underrepresented in the various social organizations that support cross-dressers. Whether this is economic or social is difficult to determine. All age ranges seem to be represented with the exception of the under-20 population. My own observations suggest that this is primarily an economic phenomenon. Most organizations hold their meetings at locations that require a car for access. Further, there is an emphasis on "doing it right," which costs much money for clothing, wigs, and makeup. [The cost of attending] conventions, while held all over the country, are high. Also, there needs to be sufficient freedom to be away from their job for some time. Few of these conditions exist for the younger cross-dresser and may be a reason why the professional man is overrepresented in the cross-dressing culture.

The "typical" male cross-dresser is strongly heterosexual [and] married. He [also] may often have engaged in hypermasculine activities in an attempt to prove his masculinity and/or to submerge the cross-dressing feelings. A large percentage probably has some guilt over their desire to cross-dress; but many have come to terms with their feelings. Unfortunately, many cross-dressers are very self-centered, which interferes with personal relationships.

While some may have been abused as children and/or have had a substance-abusing parent, the majority seems to have had a relatively normal childhood. There is some very sketchy information that found transgender and/or homosexual behavior in several members of one family, but the numbers are so small as to be inconclusive. If one asks the average cross-dresser, the most common reason [given for cross-dressing] would probably be forced cross-dressing as a child or some other sociological effect. Some might link it to the erotic component. John Money and his description of lovemaps would probably support this latter explanation.

The social challenge facing the cross-dresser is acceptance by society at large—at least this is what they would like. Their fantasy of such acceptance is that they could decide, each day, which gender role they would like to present to the world and have the world accept that. However, until society places an equal value on masculinity and femininity *and* allows for behaviors that are a blend of the two, there is little chance of achieving this acceptance. The cross-dresser moves between gender roles and so remains visible. This inability to make up his mind gains him the same censure as the bisexual who also "can't make up his/her mind."

As with cross-dressers, transsexuals are found in all cultures, both past and present. Similarly, they find social acceptance is low. The transsexual, with or without genital surgery, will strive to be indistinguishable from the general population.

Transsexualism is found in both males and females, with various ratios reported. In primary transsexualism gender identity is opposite to observable genital sex. There are no observable physical or hormonal anomalies that might explain these feelings. Transsexualism is often found at a much earlier age than transvestism, because the transsexual child will strongly assert that [he or she is] of the other gender.

Generally there are more males than females who exhibit this behavior. Compared with transvestism, it is a much rarer phenomenon with estimates of one in 40,000 to 50,000 births. There is little if any eroticism associated with wearing clothing of the other gender, because such clothing is seen as normal for their perceived gender identity. The best way to understand sexual-partner choice for transsexuals is to use their preferred gender identity rather than their sexual anatomy as the guide. Sexual-partner choice can be either heterosexual or homosexual, and, in male-to-female transsexuals, it appears that both forms are commonly found. For the female-to-male, it appears that there are more heterosexual than homosexual relationships. In some cases, the person avoids all sexual interactions, because there is too much psychological discomfort caused by the fact that their genitalia do not match their gender identity.

About 10 percent of transsexuals eventually undergo genital surgery ("sex change") and live full-time as members of the other gender. The balance are either unable to afford the procedures, which may cost $50,000 or more, or are not suitable candidates due to other psychological or social problems. Even without such surgery, they may cross-live in the other gender role and would be called transgenderists. Anecdotal data also suggests that many, perhaps a majority, of transsexual persons will end up in a clinical setting looking for hormonal and surgical intervention. Probably the increased exposure by the media makes someone with a transsexual inclination aware of these remedies. Unfortunately, there are very few clinicians who have the experience to work effectively with such clients.

Transsexuals seem to come from lower- and middle-class environments. Education levels will often be less than for the cross-dresser. Speculation suggests that the amount of gender discomfort they experience is so crippling that achievement in other social or educational spheres is very difficult. While all age ranges are represented, the transsexual found both in support groups and clinical settings tends to be younger, 20 to 30 years [old]. One might theorize that the emotional pain they feel causes them to seek help earlier. There is some evidence of the older transsexual, 50-plus years [old], in clinical settings. These people are generally males who have "done their duty" to family and children and now feel they can no longer live in the masculine gender role. A similar phenomenon is true for the female-to-male, who has often been married and had children before arriving at the clinic.

While there have been some clinical attempts to show primarily behavioral causation, e.g., Robert Stoller, such studies do not seem to represent the majority of transsexuals. The typical transsexual would probably state that the cause is biological, although this can not be proven. However, most transsexuals are not interested in reasons but simply want to move as quickly as possible to the preferred gender role.

The psychological problems facing the transsexual essentially stem from the need to unlearn one gender role and learn the other. Without accomplishing this switch, they can be socially unacceptable and uncomfortable in the chosen gender role. The primary therapist often has a key role in this learning process. Another source of assistance are the groups that support transsexuals. Generally there is little guilt surrounding these feelings, [but] there can be anger or frustration at society's unwillingness to understand and support the need for transition.

The process of permanently changing gender roles should be guided by the Harry Benjamin International Gender Dysphoria Association's Standards of Care. In a clinical setting it is crucial that the client be considered socially and emotionally ready for this switch. By this time hormone therapy has sufficiently altered the person's body to permit a reasonable chance at passing in the other gender role. For the male-to-female, electrolysis for beard removal should be nearly complete. Changing to the other gender role brings its own problems; so other psychological or emotional problems should be resolved before proceeding. A *minimum* of a year of full-time living and working in the chosen gender role is required by the Standards of Care before a recommendation for surgery will be made. The people who follow the Standards of Care and complete genital surgery do not regret the decision. The stories one hears about such regrets can usually be traced to situations where the Standards of Care have been either ignored or subverted.

Less than 50 percent of clients at a gender clinic will make it to the point of changing gender roles. A variety of factors, including cost, [account for] this reduction. Overall, less than 10 percent of those persons who enter a gender clinic will complete genital surgery; a few will cross-live without the surgery. Cost is a large factor, but some find that living full-time in the other gender role is not what they had expected.

In my opinion, transsexuals are less likely to engage in unusual sexual practices. Once living in the gender role of choice, they would be considered a typical "vanilla" member of that gender role. While there are certainly transsexuals who remain visible, they are the minority.

There is another segment of the gender community that is called transsexual: Usually they are males who have used female hormones—often without medical supervision—to enlarge their breasts. They have not undergone surgery to change their genitalia to a feminine form and may still be capable of getting an erection. They are called transgenderists, which means somewhere in between cross-dressers and transsexuals. These transgenderists are often seen in sexually oriented and X-rated videos. They act out whatever role is called for in the script. These can include S&M or B&D scenes, and the transgenderist may take either a dominant or submissive role.

CHRISTINA
Many people in more conventional sexuality areas tend to think that cross-dressers and any [so-called] deviant [sexuality practitioners] are strange and to be shunned. I think we're a lot healthier than many of the other types of mainstream sexualities, in the sense that we recognize that we have these

feelings and we don't deny them. We try to be honest to ourselves. These types of behaviors are a part of us; they're not something we can be cured of—not a disease or a condition. It's simply part of who we are.

Cross-dressing is not so much fooling somebody as doing it well enough that I'm accepted for who I am. I would rather have [people] believe I'm a woman than have them say, "That's a guy wearing a dress." But [that's] not [why I do it]. I do it because I love it. When I get dressed up to go to a cultural event, [dressing] up is a rite in itself. It's not necessary for me to think about [fooling] people or how I'm going to interact with people. I'm doing it for me. [And], if I'm at a play, it's easy for me to enjoy the play. I will get a lot out of it: [The cross-dressing] is part of the experience. I don't think that sexual pleasure comes necessarily [or] immediately from cross-dressing. But the pleasure is definitely there, and it's part of the total experience. The traditional sexual activities now and then do accompany or follow, but for the most part it's not a necessity.

I'm not into D&S. I've talked to a lot of my people that are. Cross-dressing to them is a form of being humiliated by their partner. That's not the way I relate to it at all. [But] I'm a very accepting person. I don't judge people. There's so much diversity in humanity that I just don't care to say that something is bad or good. I don't think cross-dressing is something that needs to have a value. People do it or they don't do it: They'll do it if they find pleasure from it, and they won't do it if they don't. I think that's the bottom line.

For me, gender and sexuality are not clearly defined. I simply cannot recognize a discrete border between masculine and feminine, either in terms of gender or in terms of sexuality. It's going to take me a lot of personal work to get to a place where I can make sense out of this. [But] I'm in support groups, and I actually lead a support group on it; so it's not like I'm just fishing in the dark. To me, it's more than a neurotic fantasy. To get metaphorical—or cliché—about it, I could say that it goes to the very fiber of my existence. As a person, or as a spirit, what I've realized is that gender differences are pushed onto you by society. They are not innate. As spirit[s], we're basically genderless. In that context, I feel relatively free to explore in any way I choose. But a body was given to me, and I ought to explore what that means before I give it up.

I've never had any sexual relationships with men. I'm not [spontaneously] attracted to men. But in meditation I've been able to create relationships with men that have not been distasteful to me. At this point I'm only attracted to women. This confuses me, because I'm not actually sure that my gender is masculine. It's possible and even likely that I am a male-to-female transsexual. I haven't gone through the therapy to discover that [yet].

I fantasize a lot about having sex on the female side. Part of imagining feminine images in oneself, I think, is honoring feelings. When I see a woman [who] I'm attracted to, there's a dichotomy. On the one hand, you're interested in asking the person out and getting to know [her] as an individual, perhaps lovingly and, ultimately, sexually; on the other hand, you're interested in how she relates to being a woman—what she feels in her clothes, how she feels in her relationships, and how it might feel to actually be her. And so there's a conflict. A transsexual goes through all of these feelings in the space of 30 or 40 seconds, and that gets very confusing.

The feelings in me go way back. When I was [about] three years old, I asked my mother to make me a blue dress. She did, and I wore it a lot until I outgrew it. I didn't think about that again until around age 12, and I started to cross-dress again. My mom was a pretty good seamstress, so she took in a lot of sewing from friends. Some of the sewing was dresses for kids my age. So while the rest of the family was busy, I'd grab [an] outfit and go into my room and try it on. I experimented with bras and other types of underwear and how to make the feeling as accurately feminine as I could. It wasn't until much, much later that I realized that trying to make the feelings accurate was an unproductive way to go about it.

Women always terrified me. Part of it was that getting close to a woman was just too close to something that I was in partial denial of. [I] felt incredible guilt and shame about it. In terms of relationships, it caused me serious problems, but in terms of my emotional ability and my ability to function in the classroom and to excel in schoolwork, it didn't affect me. For a long time it was impossible for me to approach women on any kind of intimate level, because the feelings of guilt and shame were too [strong]. A lot of the friendships I've had with men have also been a little bit [strained] or tenuous, because I couldn't relate to the kinds of intimacy that other men had. So it was difficult for me to relate to people. About five years ago I learned some self-hypnosis and meditation techniques and finally went into counseling on some specific issues. Basically, through lots of introspection and from several realizations I had in counseling, I was able to [attain] a pretty high level of self-acceptance.

Many times it's very exciting to put on a feminine front and go out and interact in the world. It's [also] very scary. You're always on an emotional edge when you do something like that. I've thought a lot about whether it's an exhibitionist sort of thing, and I've decided it's not: For me, it's a way to affirm and acknowledge a part of [myself]. As I do it more, I get better at it. I can imagine that eventually I will be able to function in society as a woman. [But] I really like to get dressed up [as a man, too].

[One of my most fulfilling experiences was when] I got my ears pierced and got a permanent for my hair—my hair's pretty long. I wore a really fancy dress and wore pierced earrings for the first time. I had intentionally done the whole job and done as good a job as I can and spent the whole day with it. [I] went shopping for clothes and everything. That was a profound experience. I felt that I'd actually made it into femininity. I'd actually accomplished my goal of understanding what it was like to be a woman. For example, I [was able to] relate to the idea of being attractive to a man. That was a strange feeling for me.

I am very fond of wearing wedding gowns. The feeling of putting on a wedding gown is one of the most incredibly feminine feelings you could ever imagine. It's just fantastic.

I'm also fascinated by pregnancy and childbirth. I fantasize oftentimes about being pregnant. Sometimes [my] cross-dressing entails wearing padding in the belly. Strictly from the point of view of a cross-dresser who's trying to pass, it's the same kind of trick a magician pulls: It distracts your eye from the principal illusion. No one would guess that this person who is pregnant is a cross-dresser. It lets me get away with stuff I might not otherwise get away with. Wearing maternity clothes is an interesting feeling also. It's a different perspective on femininity. The mother-goddess and the archetypes of nurturing are much more in the foreground in that situation. That's a big part of who I am. I relate well to that kind of imagery. And pregnancy, childbearing, breastfeeding [are] all part of [it].

My mother died very recently, and I'm still in the throes of handling her estate and getting my living situation handled. Survival issues are taking priority right now. This all interrupted the process of finding a competent therapist. Within a year I will find a therapist and see if I'm a candidate for sexual-reassignment surgery. I don't feel able to make the decision myself. I will need therapy to help [me] make the decision.

Twenty-Two

PLAYING
ON THE GENDER LINE
IN D&S

For many D&Sers, uninhibited exploration of gender roles is an important component of erotic play. Men as well as women perceive the chance to experiment with the "other side" of the gender line as an opportunity to express fully complex and often hidden aspects of their personalities. But not everyone who experiments with cross-dressing is necessarily a transvestite or a transsexual.

In this chapter we hear from a wide variety of individuals who incorpo-

rate some form of gender play in their D&S interactions. We feature five interviews:

- Deirdre is 43 years old and married. He works in manufacturing and medical supplies.
- Cheryl Haggerty is 35 years old and married. He owns a consulting business.
- Gypsy is 49 years old and a divorced mother. She is a teacher and lives with a male-to-female transvestite.
- Kelly T. is 33 years old and has a young daughter. She is trained as an engineer and is a technical consultant.
- Ray is 40 years old. He is Kelly's master. Ray is a teacher.

GENDER PLAY IN D&S

Transgenderism is conceived of and played out in D&S interactions in innumerable ways.

The number of possible ways to play on the line between masculinity and femininity is as great as the number of different ways to play on the line between dominance and submission. When you combine the two, the state of sexuality is almost limitless.

—ROBIN YOUNG

A significant number of people who explore gender transformation in a power relationship neither think of themselves as nor fit the clinical definition of transvestites. They do not necessarily experiment with such clothing when alone, and when cross-dressing is introduced, it is typically a small component of a larger power dynamic. Nor is cross-dressing a meaningful element of their fantasies outside of specific D&S contexts. Instead, it may be an occasional feature of their erotic interactions, often at the instigation of the dominant who wishes to discover which types of experiences are most satisfying to both partners.

Gender play permits people to breach social taboos about masculinity or femininity. For some, it opens previously untraveled erotic territory; experimentation may reveal unrealized (or even unknown) aspects of their personalities.

Just as a person may become aware of his or her "inner child," so may a man become aware of a female within, or a woman become aware of a male within.

—M. CYBELE

Gender play is also a means of exploring the power relationships between partners. Submissive men who are otherwise uninterested in cross-dressing, for example, may be highly aroused when a dominant demands that they wear an article of feminine attire, particularly lingerie. It is a proof that the dominant can do whatever he or she wishes to the submissive—even changing the submissive's gender identity. For some submissive men who are particularly self-conscious about their masculinity, gender play can represent a supreme but desirable form of erotic humiliation.

In some cases a fetishistic thrill may be associated with the garment, as when a male rubber fetishist is told to wear a rubber skirt. Or the garment may have a special meaning; for example, when a female dominant orders her husband to wear an article of her clothing. While gender play seems to be primarily the bailiwick of male D&Sers, some women (especially lesbians) find it exciting to assume a masculine role or wear men's attire. In this respect, gender explorations reflect a broader social inquiry into traditional models of gender behavior.

Overall, gender play is an opportunity to express different personae rather than confining oneself to a single fixed sensual role. Gender play enables participants to experiment with different, perhaps seemingly contradictory, socially taboo, impulses and activities. Some dominant women, for example, will wear a dildo to penetrate their partner.

> *I like genderbending. I like to pack a dick personally. I wear 501's [and] I always [wear] a built-in dildo harness.*
>
> —LAURA ANTONIO

TRANSVESTISM IN D&S

Transvestites are a somewhat different breed of cat from gender players. As a group, their single greatest satisfaction comes from cross-dressing. TVs generally discover their cross-dressing interest within themselves before they explore it with a partner, and many will pursue it independently throughout their lives. Because the vast majority of transvestites are men who dress as women, when referring to TVs, we generally mean male-to-female.

While many TVs do not pursue power relationships, a significant percentage of all TVs at least share some D&S fantasies.

> *A review of fantasy literature written for the cross-dressing male would indicate a strong interest in [D&S]. Themes for such literature abound with forced cross-dressing and forced feminization. Usually there is a strong fetishistic component with long descriptions*

about the sensuality of wearing women's clothing. Heavy corsetting is also a common theme, with leather/latex clothing a close second.
—ROGER E. PEO

But even among TVs who engage in D&S, the power dynamic may often be secondary to, albeit inextricably linked to, cross-dressing. Partners develop sometimes elaborate scenarios in which the cross-dressing is the focal point.

It's like [he's] another woman, and you treat [him] absolutely, totally like a woman: talk to [him] like he's a woman, and act as if it's two lesbians together. There's an art to that. It takes a lot of skill and it takes a lot of patience, particularly if you really want a guy.
—MORGAN LEWIS

Some TVs also enjoy D&S in their biological gender, though the activities tend to be somewhat different from what they enjoy when cross-dressed. For example, a male-to-female might enjoy mild genital torture when au naturel, while such play would destroy the feminine illusion when he's cross-dressed.

Typically, women who cross-dress seem to prefer a dominant role, although some explore submission. Conversely, while most male-to-female TVs enjoy a submissive role, some prefer to be in control.

My style [of dressing] will very often be in the mode of a dominant mistress.
—DEIRDRE

Dominant male-to-female TVs may especially enjoy roleplaying as a maternal figure. Still, submissive fantasies are, by and large, the most popular.

In the cross-dressing community, the majority of the [male-to-female] cross-dressers want to play the submissive side. Men usually have to take the dominant, aggressive role, even in a straight relationship—taking care of the little woman, paying the bills, satisfying her sexually. I think men occasionally want an aggressive woman to please them.
—GYPSY

Dressing as females enables submissive male-to-female TVs to experience helplessness. The favored female roles are generally those of either forbidden or conspicuous sex objects.

To perceive femininity as inherently more submissive or more vulnerable than masculinity suggests a likely misogynistic basis for TV fantasies. Although TVs usually are keen advocates of women's rights and place an extremely high value on social egalitarianism, their sexuality may be predicated on childhood notions of femininity that clash with their adult points of view.

> *A gender transformation scene is not just about control and power, nor is it just about roleplay; it's also about gender stereotypes. A lot of feminist dominants get upset because they feel that their feminist principles are compromised by this game. I'm an ardent feminist, but I believe in working within the system. Just because somebody feels a certain way, I'm not going to reject him; I would rather work with him and explore and educate. Besides, sexual fantasies often are not politically correct. One's mind may believe one thing and one's genitals another.* —M. CYBELE

And although TVs may feel that they can completely experience their own sexual vulnerability only by being dressed as females, they also honor the power of the dominant woman they emulate or submit to. Many find that cross-dressing helps them to affiliate with feminine power.

> *The whole feminine archetype of the great mother—the archetype of Mother Earth, of creating new life and nurturing it—is the part of femininity that attracts me.* —CHRISTINA

Being able to play on the gender line also represents the consummate form of emancipation. Many TVs feel that the period when they are cross-dressed is a time of complete psychic and sensual freedom. They are liberated from the constraints of social obligations, and the range of acceptable behavior is now vastly expanded. Men who in their daily lives feel they must always present a hard, competitive front can, while cross-dressed, display more sensitive or vulnerable tendencies.

Since the vast majority of male-to-female TVs are heterosexual, most fiction focuses on the submission to a dominatrix. This female authority may be exceedingly strict or forbidding; she may be a benevolent goddess or maternal confidante who initiates the TV into the mysteries of womanhood by teaching the TV how to pass. Many TVs, however, feel capable of a bisexual encounter. Submitting to a dominant man, for example, intensifies their sense of being female. And since TVs wish to live out the female role as authentically as possible, submissives may fantasize about being roughly treated like a girl by a man. This fantasy is not uncommon, but most TVs are extremely uncomfortable about direct sexual contact with other men.

What Do They Like?

Erotic coercion is a chief ingredient of many submissive TV fantasies: An otherwise macho man is compelled to wear feminine attire by an angry woman. Often the scenario centers on a wife who, exasperated by her husband's inconsiderate behavior, decides to "teach him a lesson" by forcing him into a petticoat. Or the woman may announce that nothing less than his complete transformation into a painted woman will cure him of some concocted crime.

> *In fantasy literature the cross-dresser is most often found in the submissive role. Being a maid or in service to a dominant woman are common roles.* —ROGER E. PEO

Such fantasies frequently entail a torrid emotional drama: The TV must submit to the woman's authority or he will lose her affections, his job, or his social position.

The coercion fantasy may reflect many TVs' uneasiness about their erotic impulse to wear women's clothing. By being forced into feminine attire, they no longer bear responsibility for their desire and do not need to feel ashamed or guilty.

> *I [would] guess that some cross-dressers who practice D&S, generally in the submissive role, may use this avenue as a way to eliminate the guilt they feel over cross-dressing. In other words, if someone "makes" them cross-dress, then it is not their fault and so they don't feel guilty. The converse is also potentially true, those that feel "okay" about their cross-dressing do not have the guilt.* —ROGER E. PEO

Few TVs are humiliated by cross-dressing—or enjoy coercion scenarios. Most simply wish to be perceived (and accepted) as women while they are dressed; D&S for them is often another avenue for sensual exploration. Nonetheless, humiliation scenarios are popular enough to create a cadre of professional dominants who specialize, as shown in this advertisement from *S&M News*:

> *For those who Dare to apply BEWARE, as your HUMILIATION will reach NEW HEIGHTS as you're encased in Nylon, Tightly Corsetted, Taught to walk in Spiked Heels and then exquisitely Powdered, Shadowed, Lined and Painted to Whorish proportions.*[1]

Some TVs are erotically embarrassed by every detail of the outfit they are "forced" to wear. They enjoy being verbally teased or taunted about what a sissy they've become and are aroused when the dominant makes them display their garters or sashay across the room like a girl. They may also enjoy being ordered to confess that they are no longer recognizable as men. They may prefer particularly bizarre or embarrassing outfits to further heighten the experience. The greater the humiliation, the more intense the arousal of both the TV and the dominant.

> *For me, the man's humiliation is a triumph. It's like I've conquered something. If a man is humiliated by cross-dressing, that makes [him] more submissive.* —MORGAN LEWIS

Fantasies of being cross-dressed as a naughty or wanton woman are particularly popular. For the male-to-female TV who wants to be a shameless hussy, cross-dressing is a license to express lust without emotional penalty. In his ordinary masculine role the TV tends to behave with scrupulous sexual tact, but in the feminine role he may not constrain to control his libido, since the dominant has "forced" him to display his deepest sexual passions.

Our research suggests that most transvestites are not interested in high-intensity activity, such as heavy pain. Instead, they tend to prefer less physically arduous activity.

> *Sometimes [submissive] fantasies are linked with other forms of sexual behavior, such as urolagnia or scatological themes involving feces. Another theme that sometimes appears is bondage wherein the male is forced to wear restrictive clothing—corsets, helmets, armbinders, et cetera—and held in a manner that prevents his motion and/or removal of the clothing.* —ROGER E. PEO

Typically, there is heavy emphasis on psychological games and roleplaying: lengthy scenarios during which the TV is dressed, powdered, wigged, made up, and erotically coerced into acting like a female by the dominant. Head trips are prevalent, and many fantasize about being displayed before other dominatrices. Some TVs enjoy combining gender play with ageplay; they may wish to be a misbehaving daughter or a naughty niece. Some TVs are infantilists and wish to be cross-dressed in baby clothing.

Whatever form the play takes, the TV who engages in D&S eroticism is more likely to favor flamboyant or fetishistic clothing than are more sexually conservative TVs.

> *I think my choice of style and attitude in cross-dressing probably relates to D&S interests. I like leather and PVC and denim and fetish styles.* —DEIRDRE

A number of interviewees said that they dressed according to their own image of the exquisitely sexy woman. The cross-dresser feels more sexually exciting—and may have better access to submissive feelings—when emulating these role models.

> *I love the image of ultra-exotic women with hair two feet high, earrings down to [their] breasts. I like to look at them and I like to be them. I guess I've reasoned that the best way of doing that would be [as] a French maid so that I can be on display. And if someone wants to spank me, then it's my job to submit.*
> —Cheryl Haggerty

Ultimately, the diversity of interests and activities for the TV is as wide-ranging as for any other D&Ser. Nearly every activity listed in this book is likely to have some constituency among transvestites.

INTERVIEWS

DEIRDRE

My experience, outside of my marriage and what I've done on my own, has really been very limited. I'm a very private, cautious person. I'm not one [who went] out and made the rounds of the clubs in New York. I've always been circumspect. I check things out very carefully. Being interviewed is a major exposure for me.

I'm very much into sensuality and touch and scents. I have very vivid fantasies and [a vivid] imagination. I'm just as happy [with] cuddling as sexuality; so it tends to be a complete range of physicality. In terms of D&S, I'm turned on by bondage—mostly doing it to other people, but also having it done to myself on occasion. I am [also] a cross-dresser. I'm primarily dominant, although when dressed there are times where I'd like to switch and be placed in bondage.

[D&S] does not extend outside my relationship with my wife or our relationship at home. For all intents and purposes, to anybody who knows me, to any of the neighbors, there would never be any awareness that I was interested in D&S, much less involved in it. But as far as our relationship, it's icing on the cake. I like a lot of variety, and my feeling is [that] one way to keep a relationship from getting stale is to have a lot of variety, to approach sex [just] as you look for different things to do in the relationship. D&S is one of those things.

D&S makes it possible to really draw out and extend an evening's entertainment or pleasure. And it heightens the intensity of sex. It's not something that we have to do every time we have sex, and if I had to put a percentage on it, it would probably be about 30 percent or 40 percent of the time. Within that, the range can go from something very simple and almost symbolic to a full three- or four-hour scene. [D&S] is strictly a form of sex play.

The cross-dressing goes back into my very early teenage years. It was there for a while, [but] I had no involvement. Then in my 30s I started to pick it up again. The first time that my interest in [bondage] was piqued was in my early 20s, when I stumbled across reprints of Japanese bondage photographs. It was the first bondage magazine I'd ever seen, and I discovered that well, wow! This is something people àctually do! It's really in the last [decade] that it's become enough of an interest that I've gone out of my way to make it part of my sexual life.

My philosophy about virtually anything is that as long as it's between consenting people and it doesn't really hurt people, I don't question other people's values and judgments. That's their right. If [people] question mine, it's none of their damn business. I had more problems coming to terms with cross-dressing than with D&S. Where I may have some problem with D&S is the relationship of what I would do in fantasy as opposed to what I would do in reality.

I think my interests probably [have] to do with being highly sexed: very interested in sex, very imaginative. I like a lot of intellectual stimulation; it goes along with the physical stimulation. I like a lot of variety, not only sexually but in my life in general.

Probably the easiest way to do it is when my wife and I decide that one evening we're going to do some serious D&S playing. Generally, we'll start fairly early in the afternoon; we'll set aside time to take showers and get dressed. Both of us will choose outfits that are fairly erotic, and in her case, provocative [is] an understatement: leather, PVC, all the accoutrements that normally go with a D&S lifestyle. We'll have a fairly light but romantic dinner, a little bit of champagne, not a lot of alcohol, and no other drugs. Rather than create a whole fantasy game and roleplay, at some point we'll move into the dungeon area that we've set up in the basement. It is not a permanent setup, it's simply something that can be set up fairly quickly and easily. I have a variety of toys which I'll use in the course of an evening.

Generally, [the D&S] is very spontaneous. [There's] a lot of teasing, a lot of physical playing. I like to tease with a vibrator, nipple clips. We don't do much in the way of gags, because my wife is not real big on that, although slowly but surely I'm trying to get her to accept that a little bit. I'll blindfold her very often. And we'll pursue that for about two or three hours. [Or], if we're lucky, until either she can't stand it anymore or I can't wait anymore and we [have] reached the sexual portion of the evening's entertainment. [For us, D&S] is always a part of lovemaking. There's no humiliation involved. I don't tie her up and leave her there for an hour. It's always very physical and very much a question of lovemaking; it's simply extending the intensity and the timing of making love.

When I'm submissive I like the feeling of restraint and of being totally helpless, out of control, that there's nothing I can do about it. I also like the physicality of being in restraints and not being able to move. Before I met my wife I occasionally tried self-bondage, but I never found it very satisfying, because to do it, you always have to leave an out, and by leaving an out, somewhere in the back of your mind there's an awareness that there's an out. Because I tend to be a little cautious about things, I was never willing to risk doing it to the point where I might not be able to get out of it.

There are other things I don't think you could do very easily in self-bondage. I would really like to experience suspension bondage, and I couldn't find any really effective way to do that [with a way out]. I think one connection between cross-dressing and bondage is that I find the image of an attractive woman in bondage very erotic. At the same time, I'd like to put myself in her place to perceive it and feel it from her point of view. So being able to mix the cross-dressing and bondage allows me to see it from the woman's perspective.

All of the bondage [and] D&S play that we do is intense. Obviously, if you spend three hours in a dungeon setting where you're really going at a very elaborate kind of thing, that's going to be more intense than if you just tie somebody's hands over their head on the bed and then proceed to make love normally. One of our most exciting experiences was when my wife fainted. [She was] in our dungeon and blindfolded. We'd probably been at it an hour and a half or so. She was on tiptoes [with her] arms overhead. I had spent the last 15 or 20 minutes bringing her to the edge of orgasm. As she would get there, I'd stop and draw back a little bit. At one point she asked me to take her down and said, "I'm going to faint," and she promptly did. I've teased her about it incessantly. This has been very interesting. I don't think it had ever occurred to her [before our marriage] that people did this stuff.

If you'd asked me 10 years ago whether I would find a woman who would accept my cross-dressing and be willing to play D&S games with me, I would have said, "Naw, it'll never happen." So, as the saying goes, "Never say never." I think we will continue to expand on what we already do. What D&S has certainly done for us is reinforce trust. You can't do this sort of thing unless you have absolute trust in your partner. If you can share [D&S] and share cross-dressing with your partner, there isn't a whole hell of a lot that you can't share! The number of people who know me as who I normally am and also know that I've involved with D&S and cross-dressing can be counted on the fingers of one hand [with] fingers left over. This is something that we share that the rest of the world doesn't have.

CHERYL HAGGERTY
I would say [I'm] pretty middle-of-the-road, mainstream, with the exception that I've been a transvestite for as long as I can remember. That has given rise to exploring different avenues and becoming an expert in D&S roles. [I'm] submissive, but as I get older I'm more interested in both sides. I think it's a maturation process. One becomes more interested in giving than [in] only receiving. Whatever my inherent interests were originally, I feel like I've expanded to include other sorts of things as well. Some of the manifestations

of my transvestism are taken out into the everyday world. If I'm on the softball field, people notice I have nails that are an inch and a half long. That's a way of taking something out of the bedroom, I suppose! My wife doesn't find D&S-oriented events too interesting. But she's certainly aware of everything I do. No secrets in that regard.

I've thought much more about [my] TV side than the D&S side. I used to fret about it a good deal, particularly when I was younger. I pretty much made my peace [with it] in my early 20s for a couple of reasons. If learned psychiatrists and the rest of the lot couldn't make much sense of it, how could I? So I just really never thought about it anymore. As for the D&S, I figure it's who I am and that it's no more or less a part of me than my interest in food or sports and so isn't deserving of a whole lot of worry. [Since I had] a good experience of having thought through all that stuff about transvestism, by the time I started getting interested in D&S, I figured it was the same kind of battle on a different front and why sweat it.

I had early childhood experiments in cross-dressing which trailed off until I was about 12 or 14. I started wearing some of my mother's lingerie, and that's when the bad feelings started kicking in, [that] this is pretty weird and pretty awful. I have the feeling that that's not uncommon, that kind of thinking at that age. I was frustrated by not being able to dress more often when I was 12 or 14. [I was] gradually able to do a little bit more and a little bit more, and by college I was able to squirrel away the smallest of wardrobes. I never threw stuff out, as do many TVs who go through purges of wanting and not wanting it in their lives, if only because I was convinced that this thing wasn't going away. As much as I would swear to myself, "Well, I'm never going to masturbate again," you know that doesn't work. So I don't think I ever reached any watershed decisions that I was going to be one way or another. It was a cyclical thing of guilt and then saying, "There's no reason to be guilty." [It] probably [lasted] 10 years. And then I just didn't worry about it anymore. I guess it's like getting gray hair. One day you've got black hair, and the next day you've got gray—except there's 30 years in between.

My parents died when I was 15. I came back from school, lived with [my aunt and uncle] at home again for a year or so, went off to Europe, [and] came back. That was the first time I was really living on my own, and so I was able to consolidate a wardrobe that I'd kept partly at a cousin's house, partly with me. I was able to dress up quite a bit more often. I started going out and meeting other TVs when I was in grad school at age 24 or so. When I came back to New York, I got involved with a couple. [I'd] go to their home dressed as a serving maid and go with them to parties in New York. That's when my interest in D&S started to evolve a bit more.

The role of the French maid appeals to me for a variety of reasons. One, it accommodates many different fetishes: the petticoats, the corsetry, the heels, the very, very short skirts. [I] like a good bit of exposure. I found that image enticing. But there were other components of the French maid role that went along with [D&S]: submission of many sorts, the more traditional trappings of spanking and whipping and bondage. It was that role that I found most appealing as a TV, because it did accommodate so many things. I could be on display as a maid, and I could be expected to perform either domestic chores or fantasy sexual services as part of the role. [D&S gave me] entry into being able to meet women who would be interested in my femininity [so] I could fulfill my own [fantasies]. I know of other people who do like to clean obsessively as a maid. They really get into their work! I do not. But I do more than some other TVs I know who have some very fleeting French maid fantasies. I like the feeling that I get [that] people are looking at me, and I like it all the more the more exotically I'm [garbed].

I don't know what it was originally that attracted me to [the French maid fantasy]. It's corny and sort of begs the question to say that it was fun. But it was fun. It was nice to do something naughty, I suppose. More and more I've come to enjoy the pose, although I don't come anywhere close to liking pain. But I do know that within my own experience I've expanded the amount that I enjoy and tolerate.

At one of the Dressing for Pleasure balls, I and a couple of other people decided to go to [a club] downtown afterwards. I was in a vinyl French maid's uniform—it was very short and I was quite well exposed. I was wearing a black leather "penis corset," for lack of a better term, which was attached to a leash, and someone was leading me by that. Going through the hotel and being led on a leash out onto Seventh Avenue across from Madison Square Garden, where I usually go to see a Rangers' [hockey] game, was a thrill. I just loved it. And being on display, wearing my highest heels and shortest skirt, being in bondage and everything was a lot of fun.

I would like to go further. The question is whether I'll be able to, for financial reasons, because my life may take another direction. I was married last year, although I've been living with [my wife] for eight years. I'm contemplating children down the road, and I figure that that will have some impact on my activities. I would like to continue to develop in areas outside the sexual world. I don't think there's one particular experience that I'm dying to have that I haven't had. [Nor do] I feel if I don't have it, I'll be unfulfilled and life won't have meaning.

GYPSY
I consider myself bisexual. I prefer intercourse and sexual activities with a male, but I'm very comfortable in the S/M or B&D scene with sexuality

involving females. I wouldn't consider myself lesbian. I do enjoy the touching and feeling, the sensations of arousal brought on by hands and voice, whether it be male or female. And I do enjoy, as a dominant, playing with couples and with females. I have attended some all-female parties, and it's been a very enjoyable experience. I play the dominant role in my current relationship.

The more I have gotten into the Scene, the more it has become an integral part of my basic personality and enjoyment. In the relationship with the gentleman that I live with, we don't keep it just strictly between the two of us in the bedroom. Over the course of the last year, I have more or less been coming out of the closet.

I didn't have these fantasies as a girl. I was married at 21 and stayed married for 17 years in a rather unhappy relationship. We had children. I was married to an alcoholic. I think I suppressed a lot of my sexual desires. If you're in a relationship with someone who you don't love anymore and you lose respect for him, it's very hard to be passionate. Sex got less and less within the marriage. I became more independent and dominant within my marriage over those years because everything fell [to me]. I think that's just a part of my basic nature. Then as I got my divorce and got out on my own, I had an awakening of my sexuality. When I got into the Scene, I often said, "I'm tired of feeling like Atlas with the weight of everybody's responsibility on my shoulders. I want somebody to do for me, please me for a change."

I got into [D&S] seven years ago as a submissive and found it to be quite a sexual turn-on. [Because] there's a predominance of male submissives and a lack of female dominants, I have slowly gone into being dominant. That's where the need was, and I gained confidence in my ability to do that. Within the realm of trust and respect and caring, I can please and bring sexual enjoyment to other people, even though intercourse is not always a part of it.

[I got into D&S] through a gentleman at work [who was] a fairly close friend. He was a photographer on the side, and he took pictures at some of the Miss Gay Oklahoma pageants and showed me his work one day. I said, "Gee, this is great. I have a theater background, I've always had gay friends; I've been to the drag bars; I think it's fabulous." I approached it from that view. He slipped in some pictures of himself and let me know that he cross-dressed. There was a group of cross-dressers in Tulsa. He said, "Would you like to come to one of our meetings?" I did; they were wonderful people, and it was enjoyable.

One of the gentlemen played on the side in the B&D scene, and he told me about his and his wife's activities. I thought that [was] very interesting. I'd always wondered what that was about. He said, "Would you like to get together sometime, and I'll show you?" So he brought some of the bondage magazines, some of his implements and toys, some ropes and some little whips and nipple clamps and things like that. We got together, [and] basically, he was looking for a dominant. This is how he introduced it to me. I allowed him to put my hands in bondage and do some light touching in a sexually arousing [fashion] to me. I found it quite pleasurable. Then I did the same to him. Over the course of the next three or four years, we would get together occasionally, mostly with me being the dominant. One summer [when] my children were gone, I had the box of toys at my house so he could come over and play, rather than going to a motel room. Another gentleman that I was having a relationship with at that time happened to see something that I hadn't put away and said, "I see some of your toys." I was shocked and pretended ignorance. He said, "I had a girlfriend that I did this with for some time." He was dominant and asked if I wanted to play. I said yes; this gave me a chance to play the other role, and I found it extremely arousing, sexually. We got into a lot of heavy things. He was strictly dominant and wanted to control me, so we got into spanking and whipping and heavier bondage. It was one of those things [where] we would do it one evening and couldn't wait until the next time.

[Eventually], he moved away, and I found myself going back to the dominant role—often over the first five years it was just an occasional thing that I would [try]. [But] over the last two years, I found myself going more and more to the dominant side.

Two years ago there was a meeting in San Antonio, called the Texas T-Party. I went there; it was a whole convention of cross-dressers. Being very open to the cross-dressing scene, I met a lot of people. [And] that's where I met my partner. Nothing transpired [that] first year. I went to the second one, and we became more acquainted. He invited me up to the Pennsylvania area for another weekend event of cross-dressing, and we talked much more about the B&D–S/M scene, which I was much more interested in getting into.

At that point my job was not inspiring, my personal life was not going anywhere, and he wanted to pursue a relationship with me and said perhaps he would look for a job in my area. With the cross-dressing scene and the S/M scene so concentrated in the New York area, I said, "There's nothing here for you to come for. Why don't I come there?" That's when it really exploded. I don't think a week goes by that we don't participate, sometimes several times a week, in some sort of activity within the Scene.

I love [D&S]. Having a theater background, I love the exhibitionist part of it. To a certain extent, it's like putting on a show with costumes. I love to dress in outrageous boots and clothes and leather and spikes and corsets and wonderful things like that. I highly enjoy that aspect of showing off. I enjoy [teasing]. I enjoy seeing how you can manipulate a person—all done by mutual consent. I love chains: I love the sound of them. I like putting [somebody] into bondage. I enjoy playing with men who are into worshiping me, wishing to please me. They feel like putting the female on a pedestal. [They] sit at my feet and lick my boots, massage my feet, answer my every whim, please me as far as taking care of me. I like playing with men in that regard. I've stood on them, made them suck the heel of my shoe, things like that. [It makes me feel] powerful—important, special, above them, in control. I think that men [believe] that they have to play the macho role. They don't want to do that. They want to say, "I worship you, I love you," but society says, "Ah, you're a wimp; you're a wuss; you're pussy-whipped." They don't let other men know that they [want to] do this.

And for those who cross-dress, dressing in female attire may allow them the soft side of themselves that they can't show when they're male. In [a] scene, I treat them as females. [I] tell them, "You are mine." Even though they're dressed as female, they know internally—and sexually and genetically—that they still have male equipment, so they still want to have sex as a male, but they want to play the submissive side. I take the aggressive dominant side and treat them as the woman.

I would not be happy in a straight relationship with somebody that did not want to play in the Scene. [I know] many relationships are like that: The wife is not interested. Even if the wives give the husbands permission to go to club meetings and respect them [and] allow the other party to play [outside the marriage], it's not the same as having your partner play in the Scene.

KELLY T.

I'm a preoperative transsexual, female to gay male. I only [recently] figured that out. Before that, I was just confused! Up to the last couple of years all my sexual experience was as a straight female with straight males. I was a tomboy all the way through my childhood and as a young adult. When I look back and look at photographs of me, I almost always look like a boy. I didn't have any idea that transsexuals existed, and because I was interested in men, it never occurred to me that I might be anything other than a straight female.

I used to make up a lot of stories when I was a child. In almost all of them, I was a boy. A lot of them involved a good deal of D&S. If it was a pirate story, then I was one of the pirates torturing the captives or, alternatively, being tortured. The ones that I remember from when I was sexually active as a female were mostly control ones rather than any heavy S/M. They usually involved being ordered to do something humiliating.

I had a child seven years ago. I sometimes have trouble making the mental transition from thinking-talking about leather stuff to being Mum and discussing the reasons why Jell-O sets! During pregnancy and childbirth and breastfeeding, the male side of my personality almost disappeared. It's very difficult to pretend to be a boy when you've got a baby hanging off one tit! But when my daughter was about three, I discovered CB on CompuServe; [it] is a [Citizen's Band simulator]. People from all over the world can sign on with computer and modem and have a typed conversation. I went on there as a female and discovered "compusex," which is where two people go into a private area and type a fantasy to each other. People who've never tried this always think it sounds totally weird and cannot understand how it could be sexy, but it can be extremely exciting. I discovered that I was TS by doing the kind of fantasizing that is possible on-line. I tried out both sub and dom [roles]. As a female, being dom worked best for me. But after the first couple of times, it got boring. After a while I discovered the gay channel and had a lot of fun on there, talking to [male gays], still as a female. It came out that some people gender switch on CB because there's no way of telling what gender the person behind the [screen] really is. So I picked a male handle, and it was 100 times more exciting than anything I'd tried as a female.

I must have done this for about 18 months without ever consciously thinking through what I was doing. It's amazing how much you can hide from yourself. I would occasionally think, This is a strange thing to be doing, but I'd just push the thought to one side and keep on doing it. Later I picked a personality closer to my real one. Kelly was me, but male and younger. As Kelly I really started getting into D&S. I talked to any top. And one of the guys who I talked to is the man who is my lover now, my master, Ray. That was three and a half years ago. I'm very lucky to have found him. When we were just talking on the CB and by phone, he didn't know that I was physically female.

It became obvious that the charge attached to being male is orders of magnitude greater. For a long time after I had my daughter, my nipples felt almost numb, although before that they'd been very sensitive. The first time with Ray was the first time in years that I'd felt anything there. It took us several months of playing around for me to remake that erotic connection. Suddenly it worked again.

I did try [sex with a woman] once in high school, and it was a nonevent. It didn't turn me on at all. It was just an experiment. I also got my husband to tie me up, which he did, very gently, and stroked me with a fur hat. [But] he's really not interested in it. And, although it doesn't bother him that I am, he's not. He would try it for me. Or he would have as an attempt to get our sex life back working again, but it wouldn't have worked anyway, because he would always regard me as a female. It's very complicated, and I don't understand all of it.

[Our separation] is a mutual decision. Although [my husband] likes me as [a woman], and we're still very good friends, there's no way he could live with Kelly. He's very straight. He's a very nice guy, very sweet, but he wants a female. He thought he married a woman, and it turns out that he didn't. It's a big chunk for him to deal with. He's having quite a bit of trouble with it. But he's not taking it out on me, luckily. Before I told him, a lot of people warned me [that] he'd do weird things. In fact, it didn't happen like that. I'm very lucky to have someone like him.

I will be going to the gender dysphoria clinic at the local hospital. I was referred [last year], but they have a nine-month waiting list. Both kinds of transsexual operations have some things in common: Both involve hormone treatment and surgery. The hormone treatment works better from female to male than it does male to female. When you start hormones as a female you grow facial hair and chest hair. Your voice deepens, and your periods stop. You feel incredibly horny, apparently. You can have breast surgery, but they can't construct a realistic working penis yet. The hormones enlarge your clitoris, but it doesn't grow more than about two inches long. It's like a little tiny dick. Or they can take a flap of skin from somewhere else on your body—either your abdomen or your forearm—and make a tube. It's a not very good pretend one. You can put a rod inside to stiffen it, and you can then do the fucking. I'm not sure how far I want to go. As a gay man, I'm the one who's on the bottom. I don't have a very strong drive to be the one doing the fucking.

Last November was my first meeting with Ray. It felt real weird to be in the same room with this person who I knew very well but [who] physically was totally unfamiliar. We walked round and round each other like a couple of stray dogs. I was apprehensive because I'd never done it for real. In everyday life, I'm not at all submissive—I'm a fairly aggressive son of a bitch. So this would be quite a change. Also I am physically female, and we were going to be [treating] me as Kelly; I didn't know whether that would work. Some of the things that we wanted to do were going to be painful, and I didn't know how I would react. I didn't know whether I could actually submit or whether it would feel wrong and I wouldn't be able to do it. But when he sat on the bed and I was standing across the room, he took the collar and beckoned me over. I went and knelt between his feet. He put it on me, and it was fine. I knew then everything would be okay. I wasn't scared anymore. He put the leash on the collar under one boot and pulled on the leash so that it pulled my head down. I kissed his boots and licked them for a long time. I always used to think bootlicking would be humiliating. I realized that it doesn't feel that way at all—it gets me very excited and feels more like worship than anything else, which startled me a bit.

He cuffed my hands behind me, put me over the edge of the bed, and used a switch on my ass. He took my jeans down after a while and used a cat on me. He didn't use it very hard, but hard enough for me to know what it felt like and to enjoy it. And although I'd had my arms cuffed a couple of times before, in my marriage, this felt quite different. For a start, he knew what he was doing. That was very good. Then he got me up on the bed and cuffed me and laid me on my back with my arms and legs spread out. He used a snakebite kit—suction cups on my nipples. And then some tit clamps after that. That was about all we did. One thing that's relevant is that he has chronic fatigue syndrome, which means that he can't do a real long scene physically or mentally. He's getting better.

He's been a leather top for about 10 years, but always to gay men. He'd never done it with a female. At the time, I wasn't really thinking, Am I male or female? I was just getting into the physical feeling. He said afterwards that it felt much more like doing it with a guy, in spite of the physical differences. He was married for a while, so women do not freak him out, as they do some gay men. But he says it feels like gay sex to him—that I react like a guy. There are ways of touching which are different. If a guy who's looking at me as a female wants to play with my tits, he will enjoy the fullness of them, not just the nipples. When Ray and I are together, he's paying attention to the nipples. [But] we do have to take it into account that my skin is more tender than a guy's. He now has a picture in his mind and in his hands of what I feel like and how I respond to things. I don't usually come while we're playing, because that directly involves my female plumbing. Usually he'll hold me and I'll use a vibrator to come afterwards. At the moment we've only done that afterwards because we've had such a limited amount of time together. I always write to him in detail about what worked and why and what didn't. Three years ago I used to fake it when there was something I couldn't do or didn't want to do or was scared to do. I don't ever do that now! Ray has said that he does more with me than he would normally with someone at my level of experience, because I seem to be able to accept it very easily. I think that's partly because we talk so much about it that I'm not scared.

I would like to [live with my master]. As a female, we could get married. But after hormone treatment and surgery, I'll turn into a male, and that would make the marriage null and void. At the moment it's possible that he might move about a three-hour drive away from me. Compared to being miles away across the continent, that would be great. We could see each other every weekend. But, ideally, I would like to live with him. Both of us write stories: They are basically extended love letters to each other. They are how we would like to be. They're about Ray and Kelly, living together and doing things together and including leather S&M in their daily life.

I've visited Ray several times. I really turned a corner recently: I spent the weekend as Kelly [at Ray's house]. But my period arrived on Sunday. It felt like my body had turned around and *bit* me! I'd never really felt it like that before. Normally I spend a lot of time as [my female identity]. But I'm *not* [her]! The opportunity to be Kelly for that long a time was great, and then this kicked me in the face. It was emotionally difficult for me. Up to that time I had been saying, "All right, I'm a TS, but I don't actually have to do anything about it right now." That's changed: I am going to have to do something; I can't continue physically like this. This change in attitude has made everything else look different. Along with the separation, it feels like I've climbed out of a trap. Although the road ahead has got a hell of a lot of bumps in it, there is at least a road.

RAY
I have been active sexually with both sexes since I was about 11. I made a jump two years ago that put me square down on the gay side of things. I was looking at my life history and what's happened with the partners that I've had. I discovered that I had more rewarding relationships with men then with women. I just decided that that would guide my life from now on.

I'd been cast in the dominant roles in childhood. I can remember kids playing their games, and I somehow always got cast as the authority figure. The thing I *can* tell you is that while some people involved in this world seem to have a component of their personality structure or fantasy life that made them react positively to depictions of cruelty, I never did, and in fact I've always found it a turn-off. For instance, whipping scenes and torture scenes [in movies]: the more graphic and detailed, the more repellent I found them.

I've known very healthy people who give up an enormous amount of power consensually, and those relationships work, and they're very out front about it. Maybe that's where the dividing line comes: I also know other people who do not say out front that they're willing to give up power consensually in a relationship. But it turns out that they are potentially masochistic personalities—particularly with enormous codependency problems that lead to acting out. The gay world is different from the straight world, because everybody who lives in the gay world knows immediately that they were subject to psychological abuse. There's no home for gay people. I could go on and on about this. The rate of alcoholism among gay men is enormous, and the rate of gay-teen suicide is triple the national average for teens. [Anyway], in my 20 years of involvement in this world, codependency leading toward acting out is a miserable way to try to carry out a relationship, even if it's only a casual dating one.

I was always a fairly dominant partner, I think: strong. I don't just mean emotionally strong, because most of the women I went out with were very strong people. I was only attracted to strong people—still am. I had one fairly lengthy relationship with a woman. There were two important reasons [why] she was attractive to me. One was that she knew I was "bisexual," and two, she indicated to me that she was interested in a leather dimension to our relationship. I remember we were having sex in a van parked in the middle of a [state park]. I think it was the first thing she said to me along these lines: "I'll be good. You don't have to spank me." At which point I spanked her, and she got really quite incandescent! We did a lot of tying up—very mild things, belt around the wrists, things of that sort. But that ended badly because the political dimension (she was a feminist) and the personal dimension ultimately got involved. She seemed to feel, ultimately, that being submissive in a sexual relationship was a betrayal of feminist principles. That got to be a very hot issue between us because I sensed there was a conflict in her, but I couldn't solve the conflict, and I didn't enjoy being treated as though I were antifeminist. I'm not and never have been.

Kelly and I met on the computer about three years ago. Computer sex was an important part of my life at that point, because I was quite ill with what used to be called Epstein-Barr Syndrome and is now being called Chronic Fatigue and Immunological Dysfunction syndrome. [The changed label] doesn't seem to help matters much. I was partly bedridden and mostly housebound. The computer became an important link between me and the world. I met Kelly, and the first time we did a scene on the computer, the chemistry was absolutely fantastic. He was an almost ideal partner: If I could have brought him to life across the wires, I would have. He presented himself as a 19-year-old gay male living with a lover, a shadowy figure whom I disliked intensely. He seemed quite bloodless and distant. He seemed oppressive, in that Kelly seemed to be carrying a major weight of household duties and emotional support. I took an enormous dislike to this lover.

Kelly and I had long, elaborate, and quite stimulating conversations. [There was] sexiness on the computer; however, it very quickly branched out into other matters, and we became friends. Kelly has qualities that are essential for me in any relationship that I have. I like sweet people. I like people who are kind and generous and thoughtful and emotionally open: inquiring people, people who have intelligence and some kind of quickness about them. Kelly was all those things. It wasn't very long before he became very important to my emotional life. And I grew to love him.

There was a year and a half of virtually daily contact and multiple contacts most days. We arranged to meet for on-line chats at a specific time each day, [sometimes] twice a day. Then we moved to regular phone calls. We did leather scenes, and we talked about a lot of other things and shared ourselves pretty completely. And then Kelly had an emergency hospitalization, and I found out that Kelly was biologically female. I'm not sure that "biological" is a good term; "legally female" may be a better one. [I felt an] enormous sense of disorientation. I didn't know what any of it meant in terms of me. I had already committed myself to relationships with men only. And here I was involved with somebody female. Yet all my experience of Kelly had been experience of a male. There was a lot of conflict about that; I worked very closely with my therapist on it. Kelly and I decided we were people who were connected to each other. [Our relationship is] of enormous value—crucial in a way, because I was so ill. For a very long time Kelly didn't know that I was severely ill, including a brain infection and other complications. We didn't know where it would lead, or how it would lead there, but we decided we would take it one day at a time and see what happened. And that's what we've done.

Kelly's very turned on by spankings. My reaction—and I think that's true of most tops—is that what ignites my fire is whatever is getting my partner going at the time. The consequence is that spanking is one of the most important activities, and I think [it] would be if we lived together on a day-to-day basis. There are some glitches there because of the physical difficulties. I remember I went on a club run one summer, and, as I usually do at those things, I visited the local leather shop, the toy shop. I remember going through about 25 cock-and-ball harnesses—this was before I knew that Kelly was plumbed differently—and picked out a very nice one and sent it as a present. It's now a joke between us. We both enjoy [tit play], but I'm a little tentative about it now, because that's different tissue. I'm very familiar with the way the female tissue is and how sensitive it is. In tying up [men], for instance, you don't pay particular attention to where it's going on the pecs so long as it's doing what it's supposed to be doing, but with breast tissue you have to deal with [it] differently. I don't know what will happen in the future, because I don't know whether Kelly's going to have the breast reduction and, if so, when. The nipples are wonderful; the nipples are extraordinarily responsive to touch, which makes it good. That's good stuff.

A transsexual who was on a talk show recently said, "My gender is in my head and in my heart and not between my legs," and that's true. Kelly's got to make the decision about what happens to that body. I can live with almost any results [including no surgery at all]. Just in terms of the physical, I think it would be neater, easier, and in a lot of ways more rewarding for there to be a breast reduction, so that what you're dealing with is not a full-grown breast but actually the pectoral muscles. [But] transsexual reassignment, from what I can tell, is awkward, expensive, not very satisfactory. The making of a phallus is complicated and not at a very high level, partly because the surgeons who are doing it don't understand the wiring very well. I'm a little different, too, from a lot of gay men. That was part of the confusion in my self-identification, because I was never particularly aroused by male genitalia. That's not an essential focus of my erotic life.

I think both Kelly and I share a degree of androgyny. It's a good match. It's pretty wonderful. There are those few limitations, and they need to be worked around. The plumbing [requires] a female orgasm, and I doubt that that will change very much, whether it's surgery or not, whether it's hormones or not. So that has to be dealt with.

I had to put my faith in my deepest instincts about what there was between us and put as little weight as possible on the materialistic dimensions of that relationship—the skin, the flesh, where it was, and what it looked like. That was only part of meeting somebody with whom you'd gotten emotionally close. And I think both of us fairly quickly found that the substance of the relationship, the way it had grown, if one thinks of it as a kind of organism, was true, however difficult it is to define. All the stuff about Kelly that I liked and loved was there. What wasn't there was a particular kind of flesh, and some things were there that weren't in the picture. But we worked through a lot of that on an emotional level, and I was completely convinced that the person I was going to meet was the person I loved. I had a sense of shock and transition [when I first found out that Kelly has a female body], but I had a firm enough foundation of who that person was. I was so sure of our emotional clarity that when I got the phone call that day a couple of summers ago, I felt as if my head had been turned around, but I didn't feel betrayed.

To borrow a phrase from Oliver Sacks, life—when it's really life—is musical, and when the music stops, it's just skin and bones. And you know when the music's being played. I've asked urologists how exactly erections work, and they can't tell me. They don't really know the final answer. I don't really know how I know, but when Kelly and I were together, it was pretty clear that this physical body was a container for a gay man. And the lovemaking was lovemaking between two men. It's something that happens in the nerve fibers, in the mind. And I know that Kelly is and always will be important in my life.

Twenty-Three

EROTIC COMBAT AND GENDER HEROICS

In times when Nature, with vital energy,
Conceived, each day, some enormous progeny
I'd have loved to live close to a young giantess
Like a cat at the feet of a queen, voluptuous.
—CHARLES BAUDELAIRE[1]

So the two men entwined and wrestled with each other, working nearer
and nearer. Both were white and clear, but Gerald flushed smart red
where he was touched, and Birkin remained white and tense. He seemed
to penetrate into Gerald's more solid, more diffuse bulk, to interfuse his
body through the body of the other, as if to bring it subtly into subjection,
always seizing with some rapid necromantic foreknowledge every mo-
tion of the other flesh, converting and counteracting it, playing upon
the limbs and trunk of Gerald like some hard wind.
—D. H. LAWRENCE[2]

While D&S sexuality is a highly ritualized and controlled expression of primal energies, erotic combat is the drama of championship played out in blunt physical terms. A wide range of competitive sports, and particularly wrestling, hold erotic appeal to men and women. The carefully regulated, blatant expression of dominance or aggression celebrates not only the joyful physicality of the human body but heroic ideals of gender. Also significant, gender heroics—as epitomized by erotic female combat—challenge stereotypes of femininity and masculinity.

In this chapter we examine the erotic pleasures of combat sports. Our profiles include:

- Thomas Gramstad, who is 30 years old. He is founder, publisher, and editor of *Amazons International*, an electronic forum for female-wrestling and -boxing fans. He lives in Norway, where he works as a geneticist.
- Ellen M. is 28 years old. She is an editor of software manuals.
- Ramon is a 43-year-old novelist and professor who lives and works in New York.
- Keith is 28 years old. He is a computer engineer.

THE HISTORY OF WRESTLING

Wrestling is not a sport, it is a spectacle . . .
—ROLAND BARTHES[3]

When most Americans and Europeans think of wrestling, they think of the kitschy Grand Guignol in which costumed entertainers, such as Hulk Hogan, enact a choreographed struggle between good and evil. But the roots of erotic combat lie not in the broad satire and low comedy of professional wrestling, but in an ancient sport whose competitors engage in a match between peers striving for physical domination.

Professional wrestling is a show, and while the people may be gifted athletes and good actors, they're acting. In the kind of wrestling I like—female amateur wrestling—the two people are trying to win.
—RAMON

We found no clinical discussion of wrestling as an erotic interest. Historically wrestling as sport is a pancultural and virtually all-male phenomenon. Three general styles of wrestling are documented. In *belt-and-jacket* wrestling participants obtain holds by grasping the opponent's clothes. *Catch-hold* wrestling requires that prescribed holds be assumed before the match begins. In *loose-style* wrestling, the contestants stand apart; they are free to take any hold except those barred, such as choke-holds or holds that allow unfair advantage. (The expression "no holds barred" derives from wrestling competitions which did not proscribe any holds.)

The *Epic of Gilgamesh* describes Sumerian belt-wrestling, and roughly contemporaneous (circa 3000 B.C.) art from Babylonia and Egypt depicts the same sport. Loose wrestling was well established in India prior to 1500 B.C.;

it was reported in Chinese texts by 700 B.C. and in Japanese texts from the 1st Century B.C. By 776 B.C. several styles of wrestling were practiced in Greece, but loose-hold wrestling was probably that culture's most popular sport. *Palestras* (wrestling schools) were important social gathering places for young Greek men. The Spartans apparently trained girls in wrestling as well.

Although comedic wrestling bouts were staged before gladiatorial contests to warm up audiences, ancient Romans seemed to prefer the bloody main event to inspired grappling. With the fall of the Western Roman Empire, wrestling vanished from the written records of Europe for at least three centuries, regaining status as a martial art by the early 13th Century.

In 18th Century Europe and the United States, fairs, theaters, and circuses featured wrestlers who challenged all comers—a practice that survives in a limited fashion today. Although these bouts were usually *bona fide* contests, the carnival wrestler, who was typically billed as a monstrous, unholy villain to be vanquished, was not above throwing a match to increase profits.

The tradition of the wrestler-as-knave pitted against the wrestler-as-moral-champion is the basis of today's professional wrestling. But amateur wrestling, even when organized with an eye toward erotic fun, remains authentically competitive. Three Olympic styles are recognized. *Freestyle*—popular in the United States and Britain—allows maximum freedom, while *Greco-Roman* regulates permissible holds. This style actually was invented by the French in the late 19th Century; they primly ignored the Greek custom of nude wrestling. *Sambo* is influenced by Asian martial arts such as judo, and is a catch-hold style of wrestling.

Until recently the ancient Spartan custom of training female wrestlers was, as far as we can determine, historically and culturally unique. But today female combatants are filling out the wrestling ranks.

> *There is now an amateur female wrestling federation. It holds international tournaments. It's basically youngsters and college kids—[no one] really close to my age. It's straight-out athletic: They're dressed in gym garb with wrestling shoes and padded knees. The rules are strict collegiate-type rules, not as freestyle as the kind of wrestling that I watch. [But] as some of these youngsters get older, they get into amateur wrestling for videotapes, or they travel and take matches. Their stuff becomes more adult, more sexual. This has brought a better quality of contest into the [wrestling] scene.*
>
> —RAMON

What is particularly significant about the modern interest in amateur wrestling is that the focus is increasingly on all-women competitions. At no other time in history, apparently, have so many female athletes participated in combative sports. At the same time, amateur female wrestling is often a hybrid of sports spectacle and erotic display.

HEROIC WOMEN, HEROIC MEN

Those who eroticize combative sport relish the drama of struggle, which is amplified by the physical prowess of contestants who are perceived as heroic models of their gender. These contestants balance sheer animal might and grace with high skill. In this tradition, the body is nature's primary work of art, wondrously balanced and shaped, prepared for battle, capable of great feats of strength. Homoerotic wrestling, for example—a small but significant subset of gay eroticism—celebrates heroic manhood.

While many gays revere the commanding physical presence traditionally associated with masculinity, fans of female combat venerate an unconventional feminine model.

[Female combat] stresses the fact that females are physical beings, as opposed to otherworldly. They are real and alive, full of blood, sweat, sounds, passions, smells, and tastes. This is very refreshing in a culture that worships an anemic, fragile, aseptic, passive, and sterile conception of women. Besides, it's always a thrill to speculate and see who wins a fight! —THOMAS GRAMSTAD

Those who appreciate physically powerful women see no contradiction between femininity and brawn.

I'm very much involved in bodybuilding, and I'm quite proud of the fact that I'm strong and muscular but still undeniably female. I love working out, and do so about two hours a day. —BEV[4]

I LOVE the physical prowess and presence of a well-muscled woman. The more muscle, the more impressed and awestruck I become. —JAMIE[5]

Indeed, some admire women who, in manner and physique, emulate mythical female archetypes such as the Amazons, a legendary unimatril (all-woman) society of warriors. The modern Amazon is a muscled, athletic woman who confidently expresses her personal power in concrete terms.

With an Amazon, you can perceive and experience the power and force of life so much stronger and deeper—and unrestrained, both in

her and in yourself. Amazons are the real thing—women as they might be and ought to be. Amazons are actualizing the full potential of the female form. Isn't it strange that [people] consider this a controversial activity? . . . Perhaps a substantial part of contemporary relationship problems is due to distortions of [natural] developmental processes by the artificial gender-role stereotyping dominating our culture. —THOMAS GRAMSTAD

Of the many different ways of looking at gender explored in this section, female combat is unique in its direct challenge of cultural notions of gender. For the female-wrestling fan, femininity is intrinsically powerful, aggressive, uncompromising—and its innate power is most completely expressed during tests of strength.

It is important to note, however, that all forms of combat sport require serious training and careful negotiation. The risk of injury is extremely high, as it is in all contact sports.

EROTIC WRESTLING AND COMBAT

Young couples often engage in playful wrestling as lively expressions of sensuality and competition.

I think [an interest in erotic combat] is a part of the natural processes of human development—in particular, the development of sensuality, the need for somebody to admire, the need for testing one's own strength and for finding appropriate ways of expressing energy and aggressive impulses. —THOMAS GRAMSTAD

While many couples may tumble playfully, organized amateur female wrestling is governed by the traditional rules of wrestling even in specifically erotic contests. Freestyle wrestling is typically favored. A referee may be present to judge the legality of holds and pins, and a win is determined according to formal criteria. Such criteria may include, for example, *break-stance,* in which the opponent is forced to relinquish her position or posture; in *toppling,* the loser is forced to touch the ground with something other than her feet. *Touch-fall* requires that the loser be forced into a supine position, and *pin-fall* requires that the loser be held down for a certain length of time, usually until the referee's count of three. Fans tend to adhere to formal rules even when wrestling at home as a part of their erotic play.

My girlfriend is very athletic and quite powerfully built, so we wrestle in a very competitive manner and actively work to try and

*pin each other to the mat. We don't keep score, but [we] struggle back
and forth.* —KEITH

The serious erotic wrestling fan demands that any match be an authentic
contest in which a genuine and—to the loser—disappointing defeat occurs.
Although rules and agreements on penalties are all negotiated prior to
combat, the outcome must be the legitimate result of the combatants'
prowess.

> *It's frustrating to [wrestle] with someone who outweighs me or is
> much stronger than me, because I like to feel as though I've got some
> chance of winning the conflict. Sometimes I get around that by
> giving the other person a handicap.* —ELLEN M.

The women who professionally pursue combat sports, however, are
often quite capable of routing male opponents.

> *I was on my knees, bent double, face smashed into the mat, and she
> had the beginnings of a hammerlock on my right arm. . . . I was
> slippery with the proverbial sweat of a man losing and I was trying
> to use that to slip free and I think I might have made it if she hadn't
> thrown a neat and painful scissors around my legs. . . . Gloria
> worked the right-side hammerlock into a half nelson, and when I
> reached over . . . to undo it, she turned it into a full nelson and then
> it was all over . . .* —CRAIG VETTER[6]

The commercial aspect of the erotic-wrestling scene is significant. Amateur videos are especially popular in part because, until recently, opportunities
to view competitive all-female matches were extremely limited. Men are
without question the primary audience for erotic combat, and they are
typically more interested in *watching* a wrestling match than in participating,
although some couples enjoy wrestling as an aspect of foreplay. In the
absence of opportunities to view live, competitive, erotically appealing wrestling, fans support a large and thriving commercial industry supplying videotapes, magazines, and books devoted to their interests.

Certainly, there is much to see in female wrestling. While strict traditional rules apply, contestants commonly wear bathing suits or other form-
fitting garb. The grappling places the women's bodies in provocative
positions, and attire may be tugged or stretched. The accidental baring of
breasts, buttocks, or other sexy features may add not only to the arousal of
the onlooker but to the embarrassment of the exposed person; it may indeed
anger or frustrate her sufficiently to make her fight more fiercely, which in
turn adds to the competitive excitement. Some competitors do not rely on

accident: Nude wrestling and wrestling in which the clothing is purposely stripped from the opponent are also popular.

[Wrestling] interests me whether or not the women are fully clothed—but there's no question [that] the less they wear, the more it's enhanced for me. No question about that! —RAMON

Erotic wrestling enthusiasts are aroused by the sight of women who push the body's limits and vie for primacy.

The strain of the muscles, the strain of the bodies—all of that exertion is very stimulating. —RAMON

Whether one watches or participates, the battle for victory is an electrifying marriage of sensuality and strength.

[The pleasure comes from] a combination of things. It's the physical relief. Aggression and sex are somewhat closely tied, and this is a healthy aggressive release. —KEITH

Since the wrestler's only tools are muscles, dexterity, speed, and skill, the dynamic struggle demands a full engagement of the mind and the senses.

A blend of factors—erotic, purely physiological, and purely psychological—[influence people to pursue erotic combat]. While the composition of the blend may vary between individuals as well as over time in the same individual, the common element is a unified intense experience that is erotic, physiological, and psychological in nature. —THOMAS GRAMSTAD

Participants find that rough contact with an opponent's body as they grapple and resist can be a potent sexual stimulant.

The physical contact and the struggle with a powerful woman are very erotic for me. —KEITH

The contest for physical supremacy may enhance the wrestlers' feelings of power—even when they are losing.

I really enjoyed feeling [that] even though I was physically submitting and physically held down and had no leverage and couldn't even struggle anymore, I still had my voice, and I still had the ability to resist. That for me was really enjoyable. —ELLEN M.

Wrestlers negotiate the rules of competition and the penalties for loss ahead of time. For many fans, the drama of struggle is as exciting as the drama of surrender. And, in this respect, erotic wrestling resembles D&S behaviors.

I would say that the whole wrestling scene is one very specific [though] possibly tangential way of expressing the fundamental urges that are expressed in D&S activities. I know that in many circles this is a heresy that I could be burned at the stake for, but I'm convinced of it. I've talked with three or four lifestyle mistresses, a couple of whom are professional [wrestlers], and they agree.
—RAMON

Although many fans of female wrestling insist that no relation exists between wrestling and D&S sensuality, one of the most popular types of wrestling is *submission* wrestling: The loser is pinned and then compelled to acknowledge defeat explicitly. Rituals govern the loser's disgrace and the winner's triumph.

There are different types of wrestling matches that are domination wrestling matches: The winner expresses herself in a dominant position. The loser's penalties are worked out before [the match]. The woman who wins will make a series of mistresslike statements— whether it's verbally abusive or, "I'm dominating you," or "Now you're mine."
—RAMON

The loser may also submit to bondage or other D&S-like acts.

[Wrestling] provides a good opportunity to be both very dominant— holding somebody down against their will—and it falls into a sort of bondage situation. There is also the possibility of very quickly having that situation reversed on you and getting in the same position that you were applying before. Depending on the rules that you follow, there's also a pain element involved for some people. I find the idea of that more erotic than the actual practice. —KEITH

In some cases a loser may be required to submit to "face-sitting," in which the winner straddles the loser's face, or she may be required to submit to a spanking. While formal contests rarely lead to complete sexual encounters, couples who arrange private matches may stipulate that the loser will be required to submit to some sexual act as a humiliating admission of defeat. This humiliation may not be necessarily erotic to the loser (and thus differs from the erotic humiliation some D&Sers enjoy); however, the fact that humiliation rituals, and ones that involve overt sexuality, are an accepted aspect of the wrestling Scene certainly suggests that a majority of fans finds them stimulating.

Erotic combat remains a vast but largely underground phenomenon. Wrestling is actually only one of several sports and combative events enjoyed by enthusiasts.

[My newsletter's] topics include but are not limited to: mixed wrestling, female fighting, arm wrestling, bodybuilding, weight lifting, strength feats, boxing and kick boxing. —THOMAS GRAMSTAD

Chaotic events such as oil wrestling or mud wrestling, however, are viewed by serious fans as exploitative theatrics designed to make women expose flesh and, often, to look ridiculous.

The kind of wrestling I like [entails] grappling on the mat or floor. The women strive either to pin each other or to force each other into submission. There are no blows, no spins, no throws. No one is making an idiot of herself. It's real, competitive stuff. It can also be very playful. —RAMON

As an organized Scene, erotic combat is in its infancy. Whether shame or lack of knowledge is to blame, it seems there are far more potential enthusiasts than actual participants.

I've talked to women from time to time, and they've frequently told me that they enjoy observing it. In terms of men—they probably number in the millions. [There are] about 50 videotape and literature houses which cater to this market. The AmFem Directory now [has about] 1300 listings—and those are [by] the most aggressive people. I don't list, for example, and a lot of people I know don't list. You also never know how many are at the fantasy stage. I can't even tell you the number of guys I've met who have had this fantasy all their lives and have no idea that there's an entire movement that caters to [it]. —RAMON

GAY WRESTLING

Male wrestling—and particularly the nude male wrestling of ancient Greece—has often been asserted to have homoerotic appeal. The professional wrestling circuit has a cult following among gay men.

The late John Preston has written of wrestling as sadomasochistic display and foreplay.

The bound wrestler is yours to touch and feel in any way you choose. Go ahead, give him some preliminary slaps of the buttocks with your hand. Make his ass flesh jump, feel that strength. Now explore him sexually the way you've always wanted to. —JOHN PRESTON[7]

Wrestling is known throughout the gay community. Although it is not limited to leather culture, the heroically proportioned male is an icon of leather culture. Artist Tom of Finland, for example, depicts subjects who possess idealized muscled bodies. Among gay leathermen, heroic manhood balances raw physical strength and sophisticated intellectual capacity. Leather competitions, in particular, emphasize that contestants not only present a beautiful physique but demonstrate an ability to speak eloquently on behalf of leather culture.

Many homoerotic wrestling scenarios tend to follow strict competitive rules, and the goal is usually to pin the opponent.

> *My wrestling is more of a dominance, where two equal parties see who will dominate the other. It's a test of strength; it's a test of will.*
> —JEFF BRITTON

Penalties for loss often include a token submission, sometimes of an explicitly sexual nature.

> *I get into wrestling trips where whoever wins gets the prize: sexual submission of the loser.* —JEFF BRITTON

Wrestling has developed into a fairly large subculture in the gay community—many of its biggest fans do not consider themselves to be D&Sers at all but view homoerotic wrestling as a sensual sport.

A considerably smaller percentage of gay wrestlers engage in a highly intense and potentially lethal drama. In this type of event, opponents include choking in their combat, and the struggle continues until one of the wrestlers temporarily loses consciousness. Asphyxiation fantasies seem to be moderately common, though their practice is rarer. Some interviewees who indulge described the fainting as a crucial element of their erotic pleasure. Needless to say, choking scenarios are highly controversial and, in some quarters, stringently criticized. Accidents may result in serious injury or death. Nonetheless, for many wrestlers, pushing the edge of this experience gives the combat scenario a kind of realism and urgency which they find exhilarating.

Finally, we noted a fair amount of overlap between gay wrestlers and bodybuilders. Very generally speaking, the men who seem most to enjoy cultivating physical strength seem particularly interested in the challenge of combative trials. It is not uncommon for gay male leather competitions to feature bodybuilders who engage in highly stylized, theatrical simulations of combat.

INTERVIEWS

THOMAS GRAMSTAD

I founded Amazons International in April 1991. I saw a need for a forum whose purpose is to explore the many aspects and forms of expression of what might be called heroic womanhood—that is, a vision of females at their best: as strong, independent, accomplished, and whole human beings in growth. It is this ideal that is the basis for things like self-actualization, fulfillment, and attractiveness, counteracting the destructive culture-wide message that women have to be small, weak, helpless, submissive, and stupid in order to be feminine. I wanted a forum that would focus on concretizations of the ideal of physically and psychologically strong, assertive women who are not afraid to break free from traditional ideas about gender roles, relationships, and femininity, or "feminine interests and behavior."

Here are what I consider some typical and important Amazon characteristics: athletically built—strong, muscular, and proud of it; courageous, self-assertive, capable of independent decision making and action; a self-confident way of walking, stressing certainty and physical strength. She doesn't "shrink" herself by trying to appear small. Preference for "rough," practical clothing. A strong face, direct and vivid eyes, the opposite of the ethereal, nonemotional, remote, passive, expression that one may find in some artworks that are considered to express "femininity." Looks are not the most important part of her self-concept, [and she wears] little or no makeup, fake-up. [She has] a direct and open personality, no insincere behavior. [Athleticism] is absolutely necessary. Of course, a woman may be courageous, intelligent, or sensual without being athletic, but physicality is an essential and distinctive characteristic of an Amazon.

An Amazon is likely to be either psychologically androgynous or even "masculine"; however, it is not necessarily the case that a psychologically androgynous or masculine woman is an Amazon. This is because the concept "psychologically androgynous" is a statistical aggregate of a large number of personality features which may be present in very different combinations and degrees. Of these features, only a few are essential and necessary parts of the Amazon concept.

I can imagine cases in which a woman scores high on many of the feminine characteristics of the Bem Sex-Role Inventory. [Authors' note: The Bem Sex-Role Inventory was developed in the 1970s by Dr. Sandra Lipsitz Bem as a model for analyzing gender behavior.] For example, she loves children, is gentle, soft-spoken, [but] also scores high on a selected few of the masculine or androgynous characteristics, namely the Amazon ones, and still ends up on the feminine side of the Bem scale. So Amazons may challenge our conventional notions about gender and gender roles in a number of ways. [The] variety can confuse and upset anybody who wants a simple world of fixed gender-role stereotypes.

I believe that this interest develops early, even though it may remain unidentified until adult life. I think there are several important factors influencing this development. [For example], some of the child's first sensual experiences may be related to fights or play fights with other children. There may be some innate developmental mechanisms in children leading them to test their own strength and dexterity. At the same time, the child [may] go through different stages of erotic and sensual development.

[Also], everybody wants to admire somebody. A healthy, athletic physique is very visible and natural to admire: It is a structural expression of the capability for efficient action. In our culture heroism is understood in terms of courage expressed in great deeds, i.e., as right action. Thus, the heroic is often symbolized and concretized in an athletic physique.

The need for intimacy and love is a part of the human condition. In my view, intimacy comes in many forms, and in a close relationship it is necessary that intimacy is not restricted to tender, soft, or "romantic" interactions. If the relationship is to be whole and all-encompassing, it must also include rough, passionate, and aggressive interactions, because these elements are parts of human nature as well. I believe that a widespread problem in relationships is the lack of an ability to find an appropriate form of expression of aggressive impulses. [This may] result in unproductive quarrels or in violence, or in repression and withdrawal. Erotic combat, aside from its inherent sensual pleasures and its symbolism, may provide a safe outlet for aggressive impulses. Such impulses may become a resource that may enhance the joy and intimacy in a relationship, rather than, say, appearing to be a threat against [the] vulnerable state of mind which is equated with intimacy.

Amazon physicality is wider than combat, erotic or otherwise, and erotic combat is only one, although an important one, of the many ways to express and live out a love for Amazons. There are sensual experiences that only an Amazon can give you, such as being lifted or carried by her, or riding her, or being beaten in arm wrestling or other physical games by her. Then there are all the things that are just so much better with an Amazon than with Ms. Fragile Femme, ranging from bear hugs to body worship.

If your Amazon lover is much stronger than you, and you appreciate or even revel in that fact and create situations that accentuate it, then obviously you have a great trust in your lover that she won't hurt or harm you. Placing yourself in situations that give your lover this kind of control over you—including your sensual or erotic responses—can build and expand the trust between lovers immensely, creating a unique kind of intimacy and bonding, a feeling that you and she are part of the same benevolent universe. This is an example of D&S with an Amazon in the dominant role. The Amazon can use her physical prowess as a means of sexual domination, and erotic roleplaying may be created and enacted with this as a central motive. Or the lovers may be equals in physical prowess and yet pursue an interest in D&S. They may prefer fixed roles—one always dominating, the other always submissive—or they may prefer to switch roles often or sometimes; who plays which role may be decided through erotic combat.

In my experience more men than women have an identified and expressed interest in erotic combat. I think that the cause of this are the cultural stereotypes, in particular notions of femininity and masculinity in our culture. Combat, aggressive or assertive behavior, physical or sexual domination, are commonly perceived as masculine traits. An athletic, muscular body is also considered by many to be masculine. Thus, many women are alienated from their natural physicality—they do not identify it, express it, appreciate it, or develop it. This is an area where good feminists or anybody who loves women have a lot of work to do. I consider this alienation to be one of our culture's greatest perversions and crimes, and its continued perpetration makes all of us that much poorer.

Today there is a growing number of people actually making a living out of different aspects of Amazon physicality. These activities range all over the spectrum—from the positive, creative, and visionary, to the seedy and exploitative—but anything that can successfully be made into a living has a future. Amazons and their lovers are not only here to stay, they are growing in numbers and visibility, becoming a cultural factor. The many crises and breakdowns of relationships based on traditional gender roles and the increased independence and empowerment of women, existentially, psychologically, financially, and physically, will facilitate this development and induce women and men to form and express their own values. The days of the stereotypic gender-role domination are numbered.

ELLEN M.

I am mostly heterosexual. Of the 11 or 12 partners I've had, 10 of them have been male. I almost feel at this point as though "straight" is a somewhat derogatory term. In terms of D&S, I tend to switch. I don't do heavy S&M in either direction.

The role that I prefer really depends on how well I know my partner. The more I get to know my partner, the more comfortable I am being a top.

I need to feel confident about my partner's needs and preferences before I can feel that I can successfully top [him]. As a bottom I feel fairly confident about my own ability to communicate with the top and say, "This is what I need." There's more risk involved in being a bottom, but I have never picked up anybody and gone home with them and done an S&M scene. I will at first be very vanilla and then work into more exotic things as time goes on and I get to know the person better. I've been in a number of vanilla relationships and been perfectly happy, so it does not bother me not to have an S&M element [to] things.

In my life as a whole, my D&S sexuality so far has not been very explicit. I think of myself as a very normal looking person. I don't have tattoos or multiple piercings. I look like a college student, and most people looking at me would not notice anything that indicated that I was into D&S. The role [it plays] in my life is very personal. I am aware of power dynamics in relationships between myself and a stranger, or between two strangers. Even [when] looking at what people consider to be straight relationships, I often see very clear D&S overtones. One of the most interesting things for me about learning more about D&S is becoming aware of how prevalent [D&S relationships] are in society as a whole. I don't feel as though I had a complete understanding of relationships between people until I started being aware of D&S overtones.

I think about my D&S activities [as] primarily sexual. Usually I negotiate with my lover—we go back and forth and ask, "Is there something that you're particularly interested in doing, or do you want to leave it up to me?" We negotiate for a day or two or sometimes longer, and then we get together and spend the evening doing something that [has] D&S elements to it. We don't have lots of costumes, and we don't memorize scripts. It's fairly unstructured.

I've wondered about how I came to be interested in D&S for quite a while. When I was five or six years old I would draw pictures of people who were tied up. I was interested in horses, and I would draw pictures of centaurs with harnesses and bridles in their mouths. I remember thinking at the time that this was not something that I should let my mother know about. I [also] remember playing doctor games with the neighborhood children [between ages] six and nine. We would tie each other up and stick pins in each other or tickle each other. There was very definitely an element of illicit, forbidden play to this.

I never thought that I was particularly sick or weird for having D&S fantasies. My self-doubts tended to come in less-personal arenas—like am I going to be able to hold a job? I've often had doubts about whether I was a particularly good lover, but I haven't felt uncomfortable with resolving

D&S once I got over the political problems. One of the things that helped me is that I spent much of my childhood and adolescence not being part of the in-crowd at school or in any of my peer groups. I was fairly accustomed to being very independent and self-motivated. Feeling as though I was a societal outcast did not particularly distress me.

When I was about 19 I went through a rather strong religious conversion, [as] I like to think of it, and became a fairly radical feminist. Prior to that time, although I had D&S fantasies, I had not done any actual D&S. I experienced a cognitive shift in becoming a radical feminist. For about four years I called myself a lesbian, largely [but] not entirely for political purposes. I did have strong sexual feelings toward women, and I had a very good time. The thinking about feminism and the thinking about lesbianism allowed me to think more acceptingly of my D&S feelings because I was already doing something that was fairly outlaw.

I went through the feeling that D&S was not feministically correct for a long time. [But] my feelings were right there, and I had to confront them all the time. [So I said], "Politically, I don't like D&S, but let's face it, I have these fantasies." I think a lot of my friends who had D&S fantasies simply refused to acknowledge them. I found it very difficult to do that. I was also trying to resolve the conflict of wanting politically to be a lesbian but still being attracted to men. So after many years of wrestling with these two conflicts, I finally decided that I was being too hard on myself in a number of ways and that I should try and accept both the fact that I could be a radical feminist and still be primarily heterosexual and also that I could be very concerned about the domination of women in society and still have D&S fantasies. I still feel uncomfortable with certain D&S fantasies, [like] costumed roles involving Nazism [or] roles that have to do with slavery.

One of the things that I really enjoy in my sexual life, which is something a lot of my S&M friends regard with horror, is switching within a scene. I am not a submissive bottom. I will sometimes break free and take over. Sometimes if I'm topping somebody, I will allow [him] the opportunity to break free and take over. I enjoy overpowering and being empowered. The idea of spending 24 hours a day in one role to me seems very limiting. A lot of times I will try and turn tables, and the dominant will resist. I get a lot of fun out of fighting. In fact, I prefer to be tied up rather than to actually be held down by someone. When I'm being held down physically, I do not like the feeling of powerlessness if I'm unable to break free. I feel stronger when I am resisting ropes, mostly because few people can break through ropes. If I'm wrestling with somebody hand to hand, I want to be able to break free. So the dominant who wants to keep control of the scene has to tie me up. Even then, I'll thrash around a lot. I don't like a wholehearted submission.

My partner and I recently got into a wrestling match. We were having some sort of argument, and it ended up with him trying to hold me down and to make me agree with whatever he wanted me to agree with. I kept saying, "No, I'm not going to." And so he spanked me, and I still refused to give in. I was fighting, and I got out of the hold and then got caught again. This time he decided he was going to put me in an arm lock and just apply leverage until I gave in. That didn't work. At one point he had me in a scissor, where he had his legs around my waist and was squeezing hard. I kept saying no. And the thing that was really fun for me was that I really felt as though there was absolutely no way that I was going to give in completely!

As it turned out, I was completely physically helpless by the time he got me in the scissor. I could not get out of it. But he was not going to be able to make me say what he wanted me to say. So we were basically at an impasse, which I found vastly entertaining. It made me feel empowered in that even though I was physically incapacitated, I still had my identity, and I still had my point of view, and I was not going to give it up. I found it humorous as hell. We were laughing hysterically throughout the entire thing.

I have tied up my lover, and I have really enjoyed the ability to do whatever I wanted to [him]. When people are doing something that's vanilla, I find that things happen very quickly: Both people are caressing, both people are getting aroused, both are letting go of control of the situation. When I have my lover tied up, I can take my time. I can sit back and think, What do I want to do next? For me, there's a very different flavor to the sensuality of the encounter. When I am completely in control, I don't have to worry about my own responses as much. I can be turned on, or I can not be turned on. I can be in a playful mood, not particularly feeling sexual yet and [saying], "Oh, what happens here?" It's much more of an exploratory, sensual feeling than a sexual one.

It also has real strong power connotations that I enjoy a lot. I enjoy being able to make my partner respond and to watch his body moving and to see how he reacts to things that I do. When I am completely in control, there's never any question of who's giving in. I don't know if this is because when my lover is tied up, he doesn't choose to struggle, or [because] he surrenders in an emotional way that I cannot. When I bottom to him, the power struggle is still very much there.

RAMON
When I'm not working, and when I'm not raising my children, I paint and watch television and listen to music. Sexually, I've long had a fantasy-obsession with watching women wrestle. I collect videos and literature and write about it and think about it and talk about it and see it every chance I

get. [But] in and of itself, it isn't sex for me—or for anyone else. It's not a substitute for [sex, nor] for a relationship. If anything, it enhances a relationship. The optimum for me would be to have a relationship with a woman who does it. I have found myself increasingly insisting that, at the very least, I be able to share and have [my partner] know about my interest and know that it's sexually stimulating for me. I have love-wrestled, so I have some interest in doing it, but that does not come even remotely close to the interest in observing it.

For a long time I was absolutely in the closet about it. The first person to know, concretely, was [my ex-wife]. I was living a dual life, in a closet about that particular corner of my sexuality. It had become too difficult; so I told her, and we talked about it briefly. She wanted to see a film to see what it was—and understood it, I think, vaguely. However, it wasn't something she expressed interest in doing or thinking about or talking about. Subsequent to that, in all the relationships I've had with any level of seriousness—anything that's gone beyond a couple of months, anyway—I've spoken to the woman extensively about it and have insisted that she see whatever videotape or material I think is appropriate. A lot of women don't understand what happens. They're used to seeing professional wrestling on TV.

I would characterize [my interest] as a difficult necessity. I initially broach the subject with some trepidation. What I have found is that, in general, they're very understanding. I think that you can tell almost anyone any truth about yourself, provided that you've been able to communicate the real truth about yourself. There's a lot more to me than this particular sexual turn-on. Women don't have to be afraid that I'm some violent human being who enjoys the idea of them being hurt without consent. I think that it fits in with the rest of what they know about me, in terms of personality. I'm fairly open. I'm also knowledgeable about [sexuality] to a rudimentary extent, but the rudiments of my knowledge far exceed those of the average person in this society. I think I communicate that. Also, I am drawn to people who are fairly adventurous—if not in practice, at least in fantasy. The people I go out with tend to be women who have dealt with and enjoyed their fantasies on a much more conscious level than most other people. I'm attracted to more intelligent women—or, at the very least, more educated women. They try to be a bit more sophisticated about these issues.

For me, I think there's some deep-seated psychological thing that works itself out in the context of a [wrestling] scenario. Some shrink once said to me that she felt—it may sound as if I don't take this seriously [but] actually I think it was an incisive insight—that one of the two combatants was my mother and that the other one was me or my champion. There is this need for someone to vanquish the other. The champion beats my mother: I think that's part of it. The other part is that I have a great attraction to women's bodies, and [when] they are in the wrestling match, if it's properly done, they are in a physical configuration that's very exciting.

In female wrestling there is a gamut of visuals. It's complex, because the universe of people who do it for real may be as different as everyone is different, but the women who are paid to do it are basically of three types: dancers, actresses, or bodybuilders—body professionals. I look at tapes of all three and find I'm a glutton: I'll take it all. I have a very catholic approach to female physiology.

There are variations within each type [of wrestling], but the major set of activities is not very much different than what two males do in a collegiate wrestling match. It's based on headlocks, scissor holds, and things like that. There is not a high degree of possibility of injury, and there's no attempt to [inflict] permanent injury. You can't—it's barbaric. It can get very competitive: A lot of strength, a lot of fast—and a lot of painful—moves are used.

A *catfight* is a form of wrestling in which the combatants are allowed to pull hair without yanking it out, which is pretty tough—there has to be [a] mutual understanding—and [they may also] grab breasts or buttocks, which is normally not done during freestyle wrestling. Sometimes they're allowed to slap. I have never seen a catfight go any further than that. You always have a third person [who's an observer]; it's very dangerous to do with just two people. People who are knowledgeable never have private matches, unless they know the person very well.

There's [something] called the *AmFem Directory,* in which couples advertise for [private] matches with other couples; they get together for an evening, and the women wrestle or fight. In those kinds of matches you often have different, more erotic variations. An erotic wrestling match might end in a face-sit. On tape that means that you're sitting on someone else's face and smothering them—there's an implication of sexuality that is not really true. In real life, it is true: You're fighting for control of the loser. The loser does anything that the winner wants, and that's usually sexual. That doesn't happen all the time—not even the majority of times—but it happens, and it's set up beforehand. In a certain type of erotic wrestling—and this is particularly true of women who are just into the more erotic aspect of it—there's actually some kind of sexual manipulation during the match. They try to get each other to come by use of the fingers, knees, legs, rubbing, that type of thing. The woman who comes to orgasm first is the loser. In order to do this, you can't have very much clothing on. You can't lick them through a bikini bottom—well, you can, but it's much more difficult! So you have to get those clothes off somehow. That's also decided, usually before the couples get together.

In some cases the loser may have to sexually please the winner's husband or boyfriend. That's where it's not the same as a collegiate match. However, it isn't the same as a war, either. This ain't Vietnam! This is sexuality. [Personally], I take almost no active role, except sexually with one of the wrestlers, if I'm involved with her or if she wants it. I had a scene at a friend's house, here in New York City, in which the women were doing a fun-type catfight. They wanted a scenario of fighting over a man [and] the winner needed a sexual release of some kind. That was my role. I jumped at the opportunity! I want to underscore that this happens *really rarely* in my life.

There is a theory held by people of all scales of intelligence—I being at the lower end of the scale—that we're all, to some extent, bisexual. So a lot of what happens when women wrestle each other [is that] it brings out either their bisexuality or lesbian sexual desire. There is also a whole segment of wrestlers who are lesbians, by lifestyle, by declaration. I know several [lesbian couples] who wrestle at home as a sexual pastime. Most male fans will tell you that a match between lesbians is probably one of the best matches that you can have, because, though this is a flawed generalization, lesbians feel much greater comfort with another female body—grabbing it and touching it, at least initially—than straight women.

Legitimization [of amateur wrestling] is a major trend. [Another] major development is the entry of bodybuilders. There's a woman on [the television show] *American Gladiators* who is a world-class bodybuilder [and] also an amateur wrestler. Another trend is much more nudity in high-quality wrestling. There was a time not long ago when the good wrestling was done with bathing suits and the sexy stuff was done nude, and they had nothing to do with each other. Now you can buy videotapes with two naked women who put on a very good match.

I believe that there's a large [segment] of people involved in wrestling—men and women—who are doing it as a function of D&S. The sexual expression is often couched in D&S terms, but I think that the real issue remains the psychological question. There's a point in most of these matches at which one person totally caves in psychologically. Usually it happens two thirds of the way through, and there is a process of submission: One of the women simply stops fighting effectively. She has become passive—not what [D&Sers] call submissive, but submissive in real terms. At that point the winner literally can do whatever she wants with the loser. It strikes me that that's the point of consensual power exchange.

There is [also] an identifiable D&S circle within female wrestling. Certain punishments, certain kinds of S&M activity, even restraint, are used after the contest in some cases. I don't think this is [typical], but I know for a fact that it does occur and that when some women defeat an opponent, they like to restrain her in some way and spank or paddle her. [Still], a lot of people in female wrestling say, "Those B&D weirdos, keep them away from me!" There's a close-mindedness among people who are engaged in an activity that [others] would consider quite kinky in itself.

KEITH

[I am] heterosexual. I'm something of a switch and do some top, some bottom, mostly in a playful context. [D&S is] an important part of my life: It's important in the way I define my relationships with my lovers, in that, for me, sexual behavior is very much a matter of power relationships. In general, [it] is confined to the metaphorical bedroom; I turn that all off when I come out [in] to the real world and don't really think about it much.

My particular interest has always been in wrestling. It probably goes back to grade three. There was this one young girl in my class who took endless delight in marching out every recess and locking me in a full-nelson hold so that the arms come up and you can't move. [She would] just walk me around the playground for the next 15 minutes. That went on for quite a while. That [was] the first time I got attention from the opposite sex, and it probably tied a lot into the way I deal with people on a sexual level.

My D&S interest was so ingrained in the way I thought about myself sexually that it was [like my having] arms or legs or hair. It was just another part of me. I'm pretty comfortable with what turns me on, and I'm pretty forthright about it with people. I found that, maybe because I'm fairly light and fairly new, I'm not very threatening. Most people that I've dealt with are interested in at least exploring; some are a lot more interested in exploring than I am.

My favorite activity rotates around wrestling. It's an important part of what turns me on; so usually the first time or two that [I'm] in bed [with a lover] during pillow talk, we start talking about what turns us on, and I'm not coy about it. [The response] has been a mixed bag. Some have said, "Oh, that's interesting," and pretty much ignored it, but some have been quite enthusiastic. Obviously those are the ones that I hung around with more.

A couple of months [ago] one of my lovers was in town for an extended visit. We had dinner and a quiet night. One of the things that I like is the outfits and the costumes involved—tight leotards and tight-fitting lingerie—and this particular lover of mine knows and [is] interested in it, too. She always makes a point of bringing something interesting with her. She'd been telling me she had a new outfit she wanted to model. I said, "Why don't you go show me your new outfit?" She went off to the bathroom, and I went into the bedroom. I changed into an outfit that I know she likes to see me in: a pair of Lycra running tights and a racer-back-type shirt which shows a lot of body. I have a futon mattress on the floor, with no frame, [so] I can pull it out in the middle of the room, strip the blankets off, and have a mat ready to go. [When] she came back, she was wearing a black body stocking, with tank shoulders [exposing] cleavage, and leggings.

We grab each other and take turns throwing off, struggling to throw the opponent onto the mat, forcing their shoulders to the mat, and trying to prevent yourself from having that happen. Usually we get both sexually and physically hot and sweaty. Most times, I tend to win. I'm a bit bigger and in better shape. That particular evening, it segued into a dominance-and-bondage situation. I pinned her and defeated her decisively. After the match, I got a verbal submission from her one last time: "Do you submit?" "Yes." I stripped off her body stocking, and then I stripped off the leggings I was wearing and tied her arms with them. Then we [had] intercourse while I reminded her of the fact that she [was] submitting to me and that I was dominant over her—playing on that image.

We've taken turns being dominant [and] tying the other up. Being constrained or constricted [is] a very powerful image for me erotically. I remember another time she wore an outfit that was all black lace [on] top and a long black skirt that we'd picked out a few days before with a pair of boots. The room was lit by just one candle, quiet music in the background. She proceeded to order me to strip and then to stand up and be inspected so she could slowly walk around and inspect and quietly caress me. That was a very good moment, standing there with her circling and eyeing me, with this critical look on her face. And then, in a more sinister tone, ordering me to kneel and then to lie down. She [sat] on me; I had my hands held over my head rather than tied. She proceeded to make slow caressing movements without allowing me to move, and while that was going on, I was verbally submitting to her: "Yes, ma'am," or "Yes, milady." She would order me to kiss her body or to watch her fondle herself or whatever.

That was probably one of the strongest D&S situations that I've ever been in—not because it was particularly heavy, but because it was a very mental situation. [That] in some ways is a higher level than the physical stuff. Psychological D&S is what you're getting at in other forms: Wrestling [is] a physical manifestation of a mental [state]. Vanilla sex isn't necessary to complete a scene. [But] at this point we generally get so worked up that it leads into some sort of vanilla sex as well.

FLUID MYSTERIES

Twenty-Four

WATER SPORTS

In human sexuality the most profound taboos are often counterbalanced by intense longings to transgress the fragile borders between the permitted and the forbidden. In this section we look at the most common activities associated with water sports—the erotic interest in enemas and in urine. Water sports, perhaps more than any other activity, challenge our models of acceptable intimate behavior, for to breach this taboo is to explore a primal pleasure which children are taught, early on, to disavow. Perhaps the discomfort that water sports arouse even in sophisticated researchers explains the comparative rarity of studies of water sports as an erotic phenomenon.

This chapter features an interview with Joseph Bean, who is 44 years old and was raised in the Ozarks. He now lives in San Francisco. At the time of this interview he was the editor of *Drummer* and *Mach* magazines, *Tough Customer* books, and the managing editor of *Dungeon Master* and *Sand-Mutopia Guardian* magazines. He is a nationally known S/M spokesperson. Mr. Bean is "very nearly exclusively homosexual" and has a life partner.

WHAT ARE WATER SPORTS?

Water sports generally include erotic interests in elimination—either artificially induced (as in enemas) or occurring naturally. The euphemistic evocation of clear, life-affirming waters indicates the sensuous and primal pleasure aficionados associate with these somewhat sedentary sports.

Clinically, the acts and practices associated with water sports are classified among several different paraphilias. *Klismaphilia* is the eroticization of enemas, whether giving or receiving. *Urophilia* (also known as *undinism, urosexuality, golden showers,* and *piss play*) denotes an erotic stimulus from viewing, being showered by, or ingesting urine (also known as *urolagnia*) or from urinating upon another. *Coprophilia* (also known as *brown showers* or *scat*) involves similar practices, but the erotic substance is human feces. Other related paraphilias include *catheterophilia* (eroticizing the use of urinary catheters), *mysophilia* (eroticizing filth), and *olfactophilia* (stimulation by smell, or smell fetishism). But while grouping golden showers with klismaphilia, coprophilia, and so on may be typologically and clinically convenient, the waters are muddied by the superficial similarity between acts that have inherently dissimilar motivations and rituals, and which serve different erotic purposes for participants.

Of all the types of water sports, golden showers and enemas are the more widely practiced variations. They also present the least-significant health risk.

> *[Water sports] could be really dirty, really taboo for some people, and I do respect others' perceptions. But on the other hand, we want to deal with facts rather than perceptions. Urine is sterile, essentially, and when it comes to enemas, it's [probably] less dirty than anal intercourse, which seems to be a very popular activity.*
>
> —KEVIN C.

All water sports entail some degree of risk. Improper administration of an enema, for example, can have fatal consequences. Urine, although an environment hostile to viruses and bacteria, is not infection-proof. Extreme caution is observed among water sports enthusiasts. Still, under optimum conditions, the erotic use of urine can be low-risk, while judicious use of enemas precludes unsafe contact with fecal matter (which teems with harmful bacteria). It is, perhaps, not surprising that the relative safety of golden showers and enemas makes them considerably less taboo than coprophilia, which can be exceptionally hazardous to a partner's health (none of our interviewees described an interest). Most instances of coprophilia seem to occur outside a specifically D&S context. (One of the earliest literary references, however, is found in de Sade, which may lead some erroneously to infer that there is an inherent link between sadomasochism and coprophilia.)

Nonetheless, one does not need to mention coprophilia to encounter repugnance. The taboos against any contact with body wastes are adequately profound. While urine and feces may be as much a part of ourselves as our hair and our fingernails, most Westerners are taught to feel shame or disgust about contact with body wastes. These taboos persist among even the most sexually adventurous and are instilled as an aspect of one of the fundamental and most necessary social skills we learn: controlling the urges to eliminate. Socializing small children—and instructing them that cleanliness is vital to the health of the human organism—is a requirement in any society that wishes to produce healthy adults. But that children, even after toilet training, naturally take a keen, playful interest in elimination is no secret.

> *Feces (anal erotism) and urine (urethral erotism—Sadger) often color the child's imagination. I have heard of two boys playing a game of 'Pipi-Man' and 'Kaka-man,' both exalted deities. The first could drown the whole world in his urine; the second could cover the entire universe with his excrement. In endless games, the two deities combatted for supremacy.* —WILHELM STEKEL[1]

As a group, children are typically enchanted by the body's intimate functions, but by adulthood, most individuals have successfully learned to suppress or to erase this natural delight. Often early curiosity is replaced by hostility or horror. Many adults completely forget a time when the body's products were as innocently intriguing as the products of the mind may now be. But eliminatory processes have remained a source of private fascination for the water-sports enthusiast. For this reason some researchers believe that an interest in water sports implies arrested sexual development, as if true adult sexuality severs all links with childhood sexuality. If nothing else, the overwhelming evidence of sexuality research argues that those things which were erotic to us as children continue to hold erotic sway over most adults.

There is little documentation of the erotic interest in urine prior to the 19th Century, when Havelock Ellis—a self-proclaimed urolagniac—and others began intensive clinical investigations and quickly discovered scores of practitioners. Folklore from many continents is rife with stories in which urine plays an important, often magical, role. Urine's significance in ritual and medicine dates to antiquity.

> *At certain stages of early culture, when all the emanations of the body are liable to possess mysterious magic properties and become apt for sacred uses, the excretions, and especially the urine, are found to form part of religious ritual and ceremonial function.*
> —HAVELOCK ELLIS[2]

Urine is still used as a sterilizing agent in non-Western medicine (it is, for example, used as an effective antidote to jellyfish stings among some residents of the Caribbean), and in some cultures, drinking of urine remains an act symbolic of spiritual devotion (as among devout Hindus, who ritually imbibe cattle urine).

The enema has a long and well-documented history as a purgative and a curative, and enemas were popular aphrodisiacs in centuries past. The belief that enemas possess restorative and curative powers persists.

WHY DO PEOPLE DO IT?

Despite age-old taboos (and more likely because of them), fascination with urine and the urethra, defecation and the anus is extremely widespread.

> *I guess my biggest surprise [in running a water sports support group] was the number of people who are actually either interested in or actually participating in [water sports].* —KEVIN C.

Even without eroticization elimination may be pleasant, not only because one is literally relieving the organism of waste, but also because the anus is sensitive to pleasurable sensation. Further, because the urinary tract and the anus lie in intimate conjunction with the genitals, stimulation to one region may create some degree of pleasurable sensation in the other. The proximity of these zones creates numerous anxieties for humanity. Children are not alone in grouping together—and confusing—eliminatory and reproductive functions. The association between elimination and eros may be further ingrained when taboos against free contact with one's own sexual organs merge with the taboos against the anus and urethra.

The water-sports enthusiast is not necessarily immune from ordinary taboos. On the contrary, he understands the taboo quite clearly but is gratified when he defies it, as long as this is done in a way which he finds personally acceptable. For example, it is typical for a klismaphile to develop fairly complex psychosexual scenarios. He or she may place enormous importance on the particular enema equipment used and on the rituals performed. Such complexities create an atmosphere of permissibility, and any significant departure from the scenario may make the participant deeply uncomfortable. The tension between the desire and taboo can be profoundly challenging.

> *For some people, just going from the fantasy of water sports to the reality can be a great extreme; for [many], once they've established what their water-sports repertoire is and are able to make the right connections to be allowed to fulfill their fantasy precisely, it can be an ecstatic experience. If you get to any of those points, you engage yourself all the way through and are changed by the experience.*
> —JOSEPH BEAN

When the experience is successful, it may represent a magical return to an idyllic, primal state of abandon.

> *[The turn-on of golden showers] is abandon. It's a warm, animal substance that feels very elemental.* —VICTORIA B.

Sensual pleasure is the single most important motivation cited both by our interviewees and sexuality researchers. Still, many individuals who regularly take enemas do not perceive an erotic connection. For example, New Age "colonic irrigation" clinics proliferate nationwide, and their patrons and staff often claim that an enema serves a uniquely health-restoring purpose.

WHAT DO THEY LIKE?

Not only do water sports fall into very distinct categories, but within their own area of interest, participants often have strictly defined limits. Many, and probably the majority, of individuals who may find it acceptable to experiment with golden showers on their skin are uninterested in golden showers in their mouths, and the percentage of enema enthusiasts who wish to have contact with feces seems to be vanishingly small.

A nominal, and probably only a coincidental, overlap exists between people who are aroused by urine and those who enjoy enemas. Those who are interested in both may simply be demonstrating that, having breached one taboo, they may be willing to experiment with other unusual or taboo activities.

Some clinicians link infantilism and water sports; rubber fetishism, too, has been associated with urophilia. In both cases, the link is probably environmental. For infantilists, to be out of control of one's natural functions is part of the simulation of infancy—the wastes themselves are of less interest. And if the adult water-sport enthusiast's interest was shaped by childhood experience, as seems usually to be the case, rubber goods (such as sheets and training pants to prevent soiling, or enema hoses and nozzles attached to enema bags) may become associated with elimination and may merge with the erotic interest in water sports. It has also been suggested that rubber fetishists who like shiny clothing are urophiles.

> The useful and charming term "undinism" can be used to cover a whole gamut of delightful diversions, from taking prolonged walks in light clothing in summer rain to urinating on a beloved in the bath. From the latest fashionable "wet look" to high colonics, in fact. "Not only," Ellis reminds us, "may rain be the symbol of urine, but urine the symbol of rain." —GERALD AND CAROLINE GREENE[3]

While such speculations are interesting, these links are neither inevitable nor universal.

Water-sports enthusiasts are frequently interested in D&S. Some degree of power exchange is evident in most aspects of their erotic play, and a significant percentage of D&Sers express at least passing interest in some aspect of water sports. Water sports are particularly appealing to a submissive who perceives contact with the dominant's urine as an exquisite humiliation. Urinating upon someone is an assertion of great power, while allowing oneself or seeking to be urinated upon is a dramatic abandonment of power.

Enemas are often described as supremely relaxing. Our interviewees say that they feel calmer, more at peace after being purged. Enemas also seem to enhance some D&Sers' feelings of submission.

The power aspects of water sports are especially powerful when coercion scenarios—somewhat more typical in klismaphilia than in urophilia—are introduced.

> I've talked to a lot of people who have agreed to do these types of things but [who] tell me that they really don't like it but are turned on by the fact that they were "forced" to do it. [The] power dynamic is the thing that turns them on. —KEVIN C.

If the submissive is erotically coerced into engaging in some aspect of water sports, he forfeits responsibility for the act. The submissive with a penchant for anal eroticism, then, can accept a kind of pleasurable stimulation he might not ordinarily permit himself. Force scenarios may also elicit feelings of erotic humiliation. Many individuals, however, neither enjoy coercion scenarios nor find their activities to be humiliating.

INTERVIEW

JOSEPH BEAN

I never had a problem [with] coming out about my gay life or S/M. Maybe I've been out all my life because I'm too lazy to be in the closet. As for my [S/M] activism, I write for a living. One of the primary rules of writing is to write what you know. One of the things I know is S/M. I generally feel that if I am allowed to be the way I am—which is way outside most people's definition of acceptable—then I have to let other people be the way they are, even when they are way outside my definition of acceptable, which includes being bigoted, close-minded idiots. If that's the way they've made their lives, then I say let them be like that.

Anything and everything that anyone does has some spiritual component. We don't escape our spiritual existence any more than we escape being bipeds: You can crawl, but you're still a biped. When we do anything that is difficult, extreme, anything that is ecstatic—[something which is] really hard for us to achieve or really extreme from our personal point of view, or [which] produces a state of genuine joy—when we do anything that goes to those levels, we engage ourselves very deeply. The key to that is very often connected with our sexuality. If piss is connected with our sexuality, as it is for a lot of people, then it's going to be, at least sometimes, difficult. I've never had an ecstatic experience, an experience that changed my consciousness, even momentarily, in vanilla sex. But I would be very surprised to find that I had fewer than 100 experiences of mind-altering ecstasy in S/M. The fact that this can happen, however rarely, is one of the attractions of S/M.

There's another important issue: We make our way through childhood bearing the [knowledge] that we have to learn to piss and shit when and where appropriate. And we're told to give absolutely no attention to the body parts involved: none, ever. There is no appropriate moment to look at your own penis or to touch your own asshole, and yet you have to be in control of their functions, which are only marginally acceptable. So in a way, we establish in childhood that to be involved in any way with piss is frontier territory. I think that may serve as an initial fascination for a lot of people. [But] beyond that, you eventually arrive at pleasure; you sort out your sexual activities on that basis.

I lived on a farm in the Missouri Ozarks when I was little. The bathroom facilities were an outhouse. I was fascinated by the fact that my uncles and other adults who lived on the farm could stop any place and pull it out and piss. That fascination never went away. I always liked the sound of it; I always liked to see it. There was also some thrill for me in the thought of other people hearing or seeing me pissing. The fascination with male urination [was there when I was six or seven], but I had no involvement in any sense. But I imagined being able to see it, having my uncles know that I was seeing it, and [I] imagined that they enjoyed that. I didn't really think about it again until I discovered that I was homosexual.

I began to hear of people who pissed on each other or [drank] each other's piss, and I wanted to find such people. When you [heard about this] in the '60s as I was coming out, it was only in the most derogatory terms. It was some queen saying, "You wouldn't believe it, he wanted to piss on me!" and they were disgusted and horrified and humiliated. I didn't know how to find anyone who would not be horrified by it.

In the early '70s, when there was sexual activity in gay bars, it became easier to sort people out. One day I was in a Los Angeles [bar]. I cupped my hand [over] a guy's crotch and was kind of squeezing and rubbing, and he started pissing in my hand. I felt like I'd come home. During the next few years I discovered that even in many bars that had no other sexual activities the bathrooms were awesome places to find someone who wanted to play. I quickly discovered that the great majority of the people [shared my] attitude: That it was a pleasure and not some method by which tops could humiliate or degrade bottoms. Eventually I learned to play that way [as well], because you run into bottoms who must think of water sports as humiliating to be involved. I'd rather do that to work them up to the point where they recognize that it can just be joyful, externalized exuberance. Humiliation can be a fun scene, [but] for me, using piss play as humiliation takes the best edge off.

For a lot of people the first turn-on is going to be that they want to submit. We get our hierarchy of categories of sexual turn-on from our early experiences in any area of sex. So if the top says, "You must do this," and we're learning to be submissive—that gives it a sexual charge.

One of the things that makes a wide category of S/M more sexual, even hypersexual, is that it assaults multiple senses at the same time. I dislike sounding overly academic about these things, but if you were orchestrating a scene in the way that a composer writes a piece of music, you would see that there are moments when you want to bind together the people in the scene—with all their senses—to make it as solid as possible. With the sight and the smell and taste and the feel all at once, piss [play] can be very effective in that regard.

I don't particularly think [consensual coercion is part of the attraction], although it often is involved for people who know they're interested but can't give themselves permission to do that [because] it's too disgusting. Labeling it humiliation and instigating consensual coercion covers that base for them. I think that's true in a lot of S/M. I know that there are other mechanisms involved, but I think at least in water sports, that's often the mechanism that's engaged.

The idea of piss play is approached with tremendous circumspection [among S/Mers]. The taboo is so strong it makes any idea of the numbers impossible to get, but the fascination clearly [exists]. Whether the practice is as widespread is another matter. Recently, when QSM [Authors' note: Quality SM, an educational and support group] called and asked what I would like to do a class about, I said, "We're not ready to do flogging and whipping again, and I don't feel up to preparing a mummification class at the moment. [So] maybe nothing, because no one wants to do a water-sports class." And [the director] said, "I do." So we scheduled it. Ordinarily when a new how-to fetish class is presented, we get maybe as many as 18 people. For the water-sports class—which was fairly early on the slate, so [there wasn't much time] for people to register—there were 32 actively interested people. They were all saying, "I have [x number] of friends who wanted to [and] didn't want to be here." I discovered that even among people who were willing to spend $15 or $20 to be in the room, there was still a tremendous residual taboo and embarrassment hanging over [everyone], except for [a few] friends of mine who sat in the front row—a couple of women who were very active participants. Most people were very reticent to raise their hands. So while it was a fun class to do, it was still one of the most difficult, because the participation level was so low. At certain points, I did get sudden flurries of tremendous activity from the crowd, which proved that it wasn't a lack of interest [or] that it wasn't going well. It was the taboo in effect.

The AIDS epidemic has been really chilling even for activities as safe as water sports. Usually I get clinical and point out the historical stuff about people who, [as] in India, of course, drink their own piss because it's the only safe fluid to drink, and in the U.S. Army, my father—and I suppose generations of soldiers before—were taught to treat athlete's foot by pissing on feet. But in the age of AIDS all body fluids were suddenly filthy again, despite the sexual revolution. It was [former Surgeon General C. Everett] Koop who made the first real public statement. He said this is ludicrous—[that] we've known for centuries that human urine cannot be infected in [this] way. [But] a lot of people, doctors primarily, who were disgusted by the thought that men, especially gay men, were pissing on or in each other, continued to press for all body fluids, most particularly urine, to be seen as unclean. Some medical studies were undertaken, and it was very firmly determined [that], like almost every other virus and bacterium in the world, HIV breaks down in piss.

I don't know that [AIDS has] changed the way that serious players play: Serious players tend to look into the safety of what they're doing and take great pride in knowing what is and isn't true. I think it's probably powerfully affected the way that novices, and nervous people who don't take that responsibility, play.

Twenty - Five

GOLDEN SHOWERS

He that believeth in me, the Scripture hath said, out of his belly shall flow rivers of living water.

—JOHN 7:38

Urine has always been a substance of some mystery—and cultural schizophrenia: It is at once naughty and nice, sacred and profane. Although taboos have instilled an abiding horror of urine in many people, the substance nonetheless has been (and is still) used as a disinfectant in folk medicines; it has been (and still is) important in some religious and mystical functions. Western physicians rely on urinalysis to evaluate aspects of health and to ascertain pregnancy. The body's "water" both figuratively and literally possesses life-affirming qualities.

Since urine has so many different meanings to so many different people, that it may also hold deep erotic meaning to some is no surprise. In this chapter we hear from:

- Victoria B., who is 35 years old. She works in publishing, with a second career in acting and performance art. She is in a long-term relationship.
- Tony is 38 years old. He is an attorney who is married and has children.

THE ABCs OF P-E-E

The uses of urine in ritualistic and health processes are legion. Even when it is perceived uniquely as waste, customs, traditions, and attitudes regarding urine vary enormously. The national hero of Belgium is *Mannequin Pis,* the legendary figure of a little boy whose blithe urination during a royal procession centuries ago is credited with foiling the assassination of a king. In America parents frequently seem to find a male infant's urination to be a precious act and evidence of the child's good health. Bed-wetting by an older child however is often treated as an insult and a crime, punishable by a spectrum of humiliations intended to shame the child into continence.

The erotic interest in urine is undoubtedly formed early and is probably an outgrowth of children's fascination with the enigmas of the body and its functions. A native curiosity about the flow of urine—its unique sound, sight, and odor—prompt most (if not all) children to engage secretly in games, whether socially voyeuristic or privately experimental. In some cases significant emotional experiences may influence a child's perceptions and impulses. For example, incontinence or a traumatic experience with an adult may give urination a particularly powerful place in a child's erotic hierarchy.

But trauma is neither the unique nor the primary cause for eroticizing urine. For many, urine is never perceived as an unpleasant substance. While some adults may perceive urine to be "dirty" and exciting precisely for that reason, the genuine enthusiast tends to believe that urine is a clean product that can be safely ingested.

> *[My most exciting experience] was being pissed on and getting to the point of wanting to drink it—and having my body so open that I could drink it straight down, direct, thirsting, open. Being that open and receiving and giving that gift really was wonderful, clean. It made me feel very connected. It's very powerful.* —VICTORIA B.

Just as elements of sadomasochism and bondage can be observed in most children's patterns of body exploration, urine figures large in childhood play. For children to refrain from urinating as long as possible in order to create enhanced physical stimulation when they finally relieve themselves is not uncommon. And some children discover that urination causes agreeable sensations to the genitals, a knowledge which may be carried into adulthood.

The proximity of these organs to one another may also be confusing. Many young girls seem unaware of the distinction between the urethra and the vaginal opening until they receive adequate sex education, if sex education is available. Some adult women remain ignorant, and physicians have reported cases of baffled newlyweds who attempt penetration of the wrong orifice.

As a child I eroticized my urethra. In fact, I didn't know the vaginal opening existed until [I was] 10 or 11.

—VICTORIA B.

This confusion is particularly meaningful in males, where the urethra serves a dual function as a passage for both urine and seminal fluids. Some boys discover that the urethra may be as susceptible to pleasure as other parts of the penis. The result of these confusions is that boys and girls—and men and women—begin to associate urine with sexual fluids such as semen or vaginal lubricant. Wilhelm Stekel, who considered uro-eroticism to be a neurotic disorder, extensively describes the connections between urination and autoeroticism and believed that, for the urophile, urine is a substitute for seminal emissions. The latter assumption, at least, seems confirmed by our interviewees, who described the excitement of the sensation and pointed out that the urine stream may be analogous to prolonged emission of semen.

I think that for male tops, pissing in a scene can be very closely related to coming. Some of the physical sensations are the same, yet it can be sustained for a long time. If you do it at the right time, it can be extremely physically stimulating. Although I've never quite captured this myself, I suppose that for the bottom, having [the top] piss can be like having that person come for all that time.

—JOSEPH BEAN

Judging by the frequent mention of uro-eroticism in studies of sexual fantasies, erotic publications, and our interviews, urine play is by no means confined to neurotics. It is an extremely popular element in adult fantasy and practice, something which Stekel also recognized.

A certain connection between the function of the bladder and sexual excitation can be observed even in "normal" individuals. The con-

dition is rather frequent that a person's sexual stimulation has an immediate effect on his bladder, calling forth an urge to urinate.
—WILHELM STEKEL[1]

Many men arise erect from sleep with a condition vulgarly known as a "piss hard-on." The first urination of the day may induce pleasure comparable to the intensity of orgasm. Postorgasmic urination, similarly, may be a thoroughly sensual release and may find a place in sexual afterplay.

Adults engage in innumerable forms of urosexual play. Medical and psychiatric annals abound with descriptions of individuals who have unusual, fetishistic habits—such as carrying urine-moistened cloths—or who act out solitary, arcane urosexual rituals, or who insert pointed objects into their urethras. But those who are able to integrate their interests into a consensual erotic relationship rarely show up in clinical settings. It is interesting, although not necessarily significant, that our interviewees reported relatively little difficulty in finding adult partners for uro-sexual play.

There is a great deal of discussion and misinformation about the possible health risks of urophilia. Some devotees claim that because urine is sterile, the health risks are negligible. This ignores the very real possibility of contamination after the urine leaves the bladder. Another belief, that urine is as likely as semen or blood to transmit the HIV virus, is *not* supported by existing medical data.

According to medical experts, urine is sterile *inside* the bladder, which, barring abnormalities, is a poor environment for any but the hardiest bacteria or viruses (HIV, for example, is relatively fragile). Even sterile urine contains metabolic end products and toxic products, such as drugs, which have been filtered out of the body for excretion. In men, contamination is possible if the urethra, foreskin, or penis is infected; also, prostatic fluid can transmit HIV and other viruses, and bacteria. In females, the urinary orifice is surrounded by folds of damp skin, which often harbor bacteria and may, in turn, contaminate the urine.

In other words: Even when the urine is free of bacteria or viruses and the bladder is normal, there is risk if problems exist in the prostatic fluid, the urethra, or on the surface of the penis or the labia. Generally, urine from a female is less likely to be safe and "clean" than urine from a male.

URO-SEXUALITY

The urophile typically finds each aspect of urination exciting. The sound of the urine rushing forth from a lover's genital region, the swift spume of transparent yellow fluid, its sharp aroma, and its warmth and stickiness upon the urophile's skin—particularly when the flow is directed to the receiving partner's erogenous zones—all enhance the urophile's arousal.

[With golden showers] you can get the feel, the sight, the scent—very important—[and] the taste all at the same time. If it's undertaken at the right moment in a scene, it can be a way of engaging and unifying all the senses. —JOSEPH BEAN

Although golden showers spring up in many non-D&S fantasies as a hedonistic sensual variation, they are most typically identified with D&S.

Looking at the classified ads that Drummer *receives, except for bondage there is no single fetish-related activity that is more commonly mentioned than piss.* —JOSEPH BEAN

Havelock Ellis speculated on an inherent link between masochism and urophilia.

The man whose predominant impulse is to subjugate himself to his mistress and to receive at her hands the utmost humiliation, frequently finds the climax of his gratification in being urinated on by her, whether in actual fact or only in imagination. In many such cases, however, it is evident that we have a mixed phenomenon; the symbolism is double. The act becomes desirable because it is the outward and visible sign of an inwardly experienced abject slavery to an adored person. But it is also desirable because of intimately sexual associations in the act itself, as a symbolical detumescence, a simulacrum of the sexual act, and one which proceeds from the sexual focus itself.[2]

For urophiles, golden showers are fully sexualized; they may in some cases be as satisfying as orgasm, although rarely its substitute. Among D&Sers, golden showers are most often one component of a more complex scenario, often involving humiliation and erotic coercion. To urinate on someone can be a graphic and primal expression of power. The submissive accepts the dominant's golden shower as a profound and primal surrender to the dominant's will.

Being able to let go [and] experience [golden showers] with someone is an abandon. It's all-encompassing. Because of all the taboos against it, in order to do it, you have to really let go into the experience. It's set my mind free, which, to me, is really important. —VICTORIA B.

Consciousness of the taboo finds its counterbalance in the shattering of the taboo: Many urophiles are aroused by the significance of the act—i.e., the outrageousness and social unacceptability of what they are doing. This may also explain why golden showers, for many submissives, are a divinely humiliating experience.

> *It's attractive to me because one of my interests in D&S is aspects of humiliation—being humiliated by the dominant in some way. It definitely is humiliating to have someone urinate on you.*
>
> —TONY

The submissive urophile receives the dominant's urine as a wholesome substance. Humiliation may derive not only from the powerlessness he feels in a coercion scenario—where he is forced to acquiesce to this desirable insult—but also from the awareness that he has sought out the experience and craves to be treated in this way. And for some, freely consenting to be degraded is an expression of the lengths to which they will go to please the dominant.

> *Somewhere in my head it is exciting to degrade myself to such an extreme degree that in effect she [knows] that I would do anything for her, [that] I would withstand any terrible thing—pain or humiliation—in order to please her or to make myself more attractive to her.*
>
> —TONY

Even those who sincerely enjoy golden showers as a positive expression of sexuality and do not feel degraded by them may find that certain types of humiliation enhance their pleasure.

> *Different people's urines definitely have different aromas. When it's particularly sharp—and that seems to be somewhat related to food ingested—it can particularly trigger humiliation, because it's even more grungy.*
>
> —VICTORIA B.

One of the mysteries of urophilia, however, is that the submissive often feels that being the object of a dominant's urination is actually a privilege and an honor. For some, the experience synthesizes with a worshipful love of the dominant: For them, the dominant's urine is like a good Chardonnay, and the submissive is honored by the contact.

> *What's good about [drinking urine] is that it's a deep sharing with someone else, almost a communion. It's the immediacy of the person urinating.*
>
> —VICTORIA B.

In this respect, urine for the urophile retains its ancient, mystical qualities as a holy, magical water, clean and rejuvenating; the idea of communion holds a spiritual meaning. One individual we spoke with described its inges-tion as akin to drinking mother's milk and described a sense of being nourished by the dominant, followed by feelings of consolation and relaxa-tion.

In S/M erotica submissives are occasionally required to drink the urine of dominants or to lick the dominant's genitals after urination as a symbol of ultimate obedience and humility. In reality, ingesting urine is more often fantasy than fact.

> *Probably the most common activity is people simply submitting to being pissed on in the bathtub.* —JOSEPH BEAN

Urine play actually has few formalized rituals. No one scenario is para-digmatic of the interest, and often the play is spontaneous. When planned, it seems to occur as an aspect of a longer D&S scenario and may be one of several acts that the submissive is required to perform in order to prove the sincerity of his devotion.

ANYTHING ELSE?

It is impossible to catalogue all the things that individuals insert in the urethra. The introduction of *any* foreign object into *any* orifice entails risk. Those who introduce foreign objects or substances may end up having decidedly unerotic encounters with urologists. Hospital emergency rooms regularly treat men and women who introduce foreign objects into body openings and suffer great harm as a result. Some S/M groups offer educa-tional and informational workshops to help prevent injury in those who insist on experimenting.

One area of urethra play demands specialized equipment and medical knowledge: catheterization. The erotic interest in catheterization is alleged to be ancient.

> *In ancient times, catheters were made of different materials (such as jade and ivory in a predynastic China), and catherization has been a ritualistic and/or sexual practice for many thousands of years. One can see records carved in stone in the Maya ruins of southern Mexico and Guatemala.* —LARRY TOWNSEND[3]

Although urinary catheterization technically falls within the purview of water sports, the activity is best understood as an explicitly sadomasochistic act because of the intense stimulation. During catheterization the submissive loses all control over bladder function, since the bladder evacuates through the tube as urine collects. This profound helplessness and consequent humiliation are intensely arousing to some D&Sers.

Catherization may be used in intensive bondage scenarios or as part of a hospitalization scenario. If a submissive is kept in stringent bondage for an extended period, the dominant may deem catheterization to be "necessary," as the bottom is otherwise unable to relieve his bladder. Catheterization may also occur as an unusual punishment or in a slave-training scenario.

Catheters come in a variety of sizes, with numerous tips. Basically, however, there are two types: those with a plain end (straight or curved, the latter called a "Coude") and those with an inflatable portion at the tip to prevent its pulling out by accident. These are sometimes called "Bardex" tubes, the name of the best known manufacturer. The proper term is "Foley" catheter.

—LARRY TOWNSEND[4]

In addition to the Foley, a tube of fairly sturdy rubber, there is also something known as an "external catheter." This actually resembles a rugged condom and is not inserted into the urethra but placed over the penis, where it collects urine which drains through a tube and into a bottle. While the Foley is used in hospitals to force drainage of the bladder, the external catheter—sometimes jocularly known as a "Texas rubber"—is designed to spare hospital personnel from continuously handing urinals to bedridden patients or from changing the diapers of incontinents.

Foley catheterization can be painful, although if expertly inserted, the discomfort should be very minor. For many, the stimulus is desirable. Use of a Foley is, however, exceedingly dangerous. One runs a serious a risk of damaging the urethra, the kidneys or the bladder. If the catheter is left in place for extended periods, infection is inevitable.

INTERVIEWS

VICTORIA B.

I've called myself bisexual since I was 16 and realized I was a dyke when I was 27. I [am] mainly a bottom, although I do switch. I'm finding ways to get satisfaction in [the dominant] role the longer I'm exploring.

I was hospitalized when I was 18 months old and was catheterized. I [had] fantasies about urine fairly early on, which helped me to remember my early experiences [and] why I was interested in this. They were memories that used to take over me, and I would think those things were happening over and over again. But when I was about six, I finally figured out that they were memories and not reality, and I hid them [from myself].

[As a small child], I was really interested in my father's piss. I could hear the difference if he went into the toilet as opposed to when my mother was in there. I was more interested in my mother, but that was all hidden, because of the physical reasons, so I was really fascinated with my father's urine stream. I remember wanting to put my hand out to touch it. It seemed like a stream of water. I was a real water baby—I was swimming when I was two—and so I wanted to experience the sensation.

When I was about 18 I was reading one of the popularized sex-positive books that came out in the 1970s. It made brief mention that some people liked to play with piss. It triggered that desire in me again, but I did not act on it. By that time, I was very much aware that most of my sexuality was really not okay with peers. I deeply wanted to have experiences with women, but it was difficult for me to get away from the homophobia, both [personal] and community, and to explore who I was. In some ways I felt freer to discuss S/M fantasies, as long as they were in a heterosexual context. I turned 12 in 1968. I was too young to protest the war, but I did pick up the '60s' countercultural values. For me, sexual exploration was a human right. It's such a strange thing to hold that as a deep value and yet not be able to give myself permission to explore the gay stuff.

Though I was actively exploring lots of different areas of S/M [with men], the intimacy of water sports was not something I was prepared to [share] with a male partner. It wasn't until I came out with women that it felt accessible to me. I haven't done play with piss with anyone besides really close lovers. I definitely play with other people, but I've only really done water sports in love relationships.

There's basically three [pleasure] modes for me. One is the expectation of it occurring: That sets up a real physical desire in me. The second mode is when it actually starts to happen, when the person is standing over me and the urine is starting to flow over my body. It feels really good. And then when the sharp smell starts rising and hits my nostrils, at that moment the negative cultural aspects of it hit me. [In] realizing that I really like and really want this, I experience a degree of humiliation about my desires.

As an experienced player, I know that [in] that moment of humiliation I can either be freaked out, or I can turn it into a sexual drive. For me, that is a moment of vulnerability: I can open further into my own sexual desires. That third mode [means] going into really intensely pleasurable bodily desires. Going through the three modes that I've discussed can be really cathartic, because it's a play that involves my whole body in sensation; it's really satisfying to savor that experience.

I didn't start playing with urine until after safe sex became so necessary. I have drunk urine, but under very controlled circumstances, and I really enjoy it. My drinking it is deep intimacy; the intimacy is on the inside, so it's kind of like getting even more of that whole body experience.

Not surprisingly, given my early history, I had a lot of medical fantasies as a kid. Usually I would be strapped down in some hospital bed being given an enema. They'd get very complicated, like I'd be strapped down, and they'd put the water in, and then the nurses would be called away. I'd be [left to deal] with this enema. Finally I'd have to let go, and I'd make a big mess. Then they'd be angry, and they'd punish me. I don't have a physical memory of [getting] an enema [when I was little]. But I definitely know that I've always been fascinated with it. Every time I would hear the word or hear a reference as a child, I would just get this warm, squishy feeling. At the time, I didn't know it was [a turn-on]; it was just that "mmmmmm feeling."

My first piss experiences were transcendental. My first enema experiences with women weren't transcendental, but they met needs. I was able to make it past the humiliation point sufficiently that it made it worth it. But enemas are really a different trip, I guess because shit is even more taboo; it's also very messy and very smelly, and it has bacteria in it. So one has to take many more kinds of precautions. There's also pain involved in an enema. Even a high colonic for health reasons is uncomfortable, whereas piss is all pleasure. It doesn't have [any discomfort or] friction. I think [the turn-on of the enema is] that it's a supreme humiliation to be so out of control; also penetration of the anus. [But humiliation] is very positive for me; it is an indication that I am right up against programming. And for me, challenging that programming is very important in my life. It is the letting-go through the humiliation which arouses me.

I'm working class, and I became a feminist at a very young age. To discover in the last couple of years that I have a fetish for cleaning floors was very difficult for me to accept. That was something I wasn't prepared for. I tell you—you discover that just about everything is eroticized.

My S/M play isn't just sexually focused, but doing somebody's menial labor and getting sexually aroused from that—I was not prepared to accept this in myself. That's what is so shocking to me. I've done it where somebody stood over me or ordered me around while I did it, and that was wonderful. I've also done it where I was alone in that person's house doing it, and that really worked, too. I think the key is that I have a relationship with this person. The most scary part about it is that the person has an upper-middle-class background, whereas I have a working-class background. So I'm playing with class, which is an extremely loaded area of play.

For me, liberating my body, its experiences, its desires, and pleasuring it as it wants to be pleasured has opened doors in my life that I did not know were closed.

TONY

I'm predominantly submissive; however, I've had a few dominant experiences in the last few years and now consider myself a little bit of both. D&S is an enhancement to my sex life. My wife does not participate in the Scene, although she and I play mild variations in our sex life.

[D&S] is such a compelling, intriguing force within my life that I find it hard to stay away from it. I don't participate in it on a regular basis because of the logistics it requires, especially since it is a secretive part of my life. When I do stay away from it for a long time, I find my desire to participate builds to a point where I must make a move. If I had my druthers, I would prefer D&S to be a larger and more accepted part of my life.

[D&S] goes so far back in my life that I hardly can put a finger on it. It seems to almost begin with my first sexual thoughts as a small child, when I first discovered masturbating. I don't know why, but some of the external stimuli that were around at the time seemed to suggest it to me. For instance, the concept of playing cowboys and Indians: Somebody's tied up, and somebody is tormented. Frankly, in conjunction with the fact that I had a rather domineering mother, it goes so far back I can't point to one particular event. The realization of what this was and where it may or may not fit into society didn't occur [to me] until I was a teenager. I always assumed that it wasn't popular—it was part of a sexual fantasy, and sexual thoughts were frowned upon in children. Obviously, if you got caught masturbating, you got in trouble; that part was reenforced early.

I think I had a bad self-image as a child, but not directly related to this aspect of my personality. However, knowing that I had these cravings for things that were not acceptable didn't help. I assume that my mother's personality was a part of [my interest in submission], although I don't blame her entirely. From a very early age I had this fantasy of rescuing the heroine and undergoing extreme trials and tribulations and torture on her behalf. That overlapped into being submissive to women, putting yourself through pain for the purposes of pleasing a woman.

I always wanted to become a lawyer, in part because my mother told me I should become a lawyer because I had a big mouth. I guess the biggest thing that happened to me when I was a teenager was the switch from having a bad self-image to figuring out that I had a value as a person. I became very active in school activities. I wasn't blessed with the abilities necessary to become an athlete at the highest level, but I have participated in athletics all my life. I always had a job. I worked hard even as a kid at various jobs because I had this goal of going to college, and I wanted to make it. I also had, from very early on, a strong drive to get married and have kids. [Having] kids was my number-one goal in life. I decided early on that the best thing that a person could do was to have children and raise them properly.

The D&S was a real part of my sexual thoughts but didn't seem to fit in with my very white, middle-class goals. On the other hand, I can't say that my interest in D&S ever made me question [these] goals; nor did the goals make me question my interest in D&S.

I had an all-Catholic upbringing [and] a strong Catholic education. Very often, we were required to go on retreats and to introspect. It was part of your religious [and] personal development. I can remember discussing at one retreat the song by Crosby, Stills, and Nash in which they sing, "Do you expect for me to love you when you hate yourself, my friend?" That line has always stuck with me. It made so much sense: You know yourself better than anyone; if you can't find anything in yourself that's worthwhile, then how do you expect anybody else to find anything about you that's worthwhile?

The things that I like to do the best are predominantly body worship and sensual submission to a woman. To me, body worship is the bringing of physical pleasure to a woman in a manner which she directs. It runs from a gentle massage by hand to complete oral servitude. The concept is that it is required of you to do this because of her superiority. That extends far beyond the sexual. I truly believe that women are superior to men. I expect women to be "better" as persons, to be good in every sense of the word: morally, socially, politically. I know that [my] prejudice can be defeated by actual facts, but when I deal with women I expect them to be better in many ways, more intelligent.

It's not a natural activity for me to be a dominant with a woman. In situations where I've done it, it is because I have confided in a woman my own interests in the D&S Scene. The woman is also somewhat interested in the Scene for whatever reasons, sexual or intellectual. I participate as the dominant in order to give her a taste of the excitement and the exhilaration of that activity. I've enjoyed it; it's been very exciting for me.

I could count off five or six wonderful, ecstatic [D&S] experiences. One experience that stands out was memorable because it was with a very large, dominating woman—a woman who was physically bigger and stronger than I was. It was very exciting to be helpless with this woman, because there was no way that I could overpower or overcome [her]. Not that I ever had that desire in a scene, but in the back of your mind, it's part of your safety mechanism—that maybe, if you had to, you could fight your way out. [But] I was truly helpless with this woman. Her real interest was in forced body worship. I remember being absolutely ecstatic to have this very tall and large woman sit on my face and force me to eat her out: I was just absolutely wired in terms of excitement.

She was also very much interested in golden showers, which was something I was desperate to try. That was my first opportunity to experience it. I'm very intrigued with it. It's a natural part of my interests in the Scene. It's attractive to me because somewhere in my mind, mentally, it shows the depth you will go [to] to please a woman. Deep down in my sexuality, that's what I want to do.

I have to admit that there is a difficult dichotomy between humiliation [being] attractive and still having an image of yourself [as] a person of value. I think that when you are truly submissive, you want to [demonstrate it] in as extreme a form as you can. My true sexual desire is to please a woman in any way, shape, or form. I think of myself as a valuable person because I *will* do that to please her. I can't say that it necessarily makes logical sense in an asexual analysis—but it's not asexual. I don't think you can understand it unless you experience it in a sexual context. I think that a submissive can reach that conclusion, even if they're not willing to participate in a golden shower. I don't think that somebody who isn't submissive can readily understand it.

I know I'm always going to pursue [D&S]. Once you've experienced it, if you've enjoyed it, I don't know how you can lose it. It's as compelling, I'm sure, as any drug. I've never had a problem with substance abuse, [but] I can't stay away from this. I will pursue it whenever I can—tempered by [my] need to pursue it in a safe fashion. The other side of me, the public side, keeps me from just willy-nilly delving into it.

There are professional dominants out there who are exceptional people. They're not only exceptional at dominating men; they are exceptional persons. I have a number of friendship relationships with women who dominated me. I have also had some experiences with professionals who were nothing more than prostitutes who [do] this as a way to up their fee. It was a real come-down to find that there are women out there who are a sham. They aren't truly dominants; they're merely acting out a role that they don't even believe in personally and have no concept of what the Scene is about whatsoever.

Twenty-Six

ENEMAS

The enema is a regular practice in the lives of people who neither suspect the erotic role it has played in human history nor realize that the eroticization of enemas (*klismaphilia*) is a widely known sexual variation. In order to understand the use of enemas, whether in D&S or other erotic play, one must first understand the enema's evolution. In this chapter, we take a brief look at the long history of enemas and hear from:

- Kevin C. who is 37 years old and works as a research and statistical consultant. He is the founding leader of the Water Sports Support Group on CompuServe.

• Nancy Ava Miller is 45 years old. She founded People Exchanging
Power (PEP), a national network of S/M social groups.

To Purge or Not to Purge

An enema is an anal injection of liquid into the large intestine to induce
defecation. An enema kit comprises a plastic or rubber bag which is filled with
liquids, and a rubber hose and nozzle. A clip may be attached to the hose to
prevent or regulate flow. The most common nozzle used is the Bardex tip,
which can be inflated with a small pump so that once the tube is in place, it
cannot slide out accidentally. Another type favored by klismaphiliacs is a
double Bardex. This has two ballooning sections that can be inflated—one
inside the body, the second immediately outside the anus. The double Bardex
secures the tube so that it can neither slide down nor move up.

The most common (and some say the only justifiable) medical uses of
enemas are to ease bowel movement in cases of extreme obstipation; to
empty the bowel for medical procedures (such as colonoscopy, or a preoperative preparation); to introduce a tracing agent (as in a barium enema); or to
manage bedridden or otherwise debilitated patients. Enemas may also be
required when someone has become so dependent upon them that normal
bowel function is compromised. For the most part, physicians now believe
that laxatives are more effective (although not necessarily less addictive) in the
treatment of constipation than are enemas. Mainstream medical opinion does
not support many enthusiasts' belief that enemas promote superior health
and personal well-being, an idea probably derived from antiquated notions of
health and purging.

One of the earliest historical records of enemas is found in an Egyptian
text (circa 1500 B.C.), which advised the use of laxatives and enemas to
combat constipation and recommended that all people receive enemas at least
once a month. In the Fifth Century B.C., Herodotus alleged that Egyptians
had derived their ideas about the value of enemas from watching their sacred
bird, the ibis, which was reputed to relieve constipation by probing its own
anus with its long, slender beak. Surviving stone carvings and hieroglyphics
attest that Egyptian enema nozzles were fashioned in the form of an ibis beak
or the entire head and beak.[1]

The purging of the body was a medical and philosophical obsession in
Europe from the Middle Ages to nearly modern times, as conjecture about
the accretion of bile and other supposedly lethal toxins was widely accepted
as fact. The theory that the body comprises "humors," which are subject to
lethal imbalances, was described by the Greek physician Galen (circa A.D.

130–200), whose writings were the basis of medieval European medicine. Physicians advised purging, whether through induced vomiting or enemas (and often supplemented by bloodletting), to restore the body to its natural balance. In Chaucer's "The Nun's Priest's Tale" a poetic and medically astute chicken recommends that her friend, a nightmare-afflicted rooster, ingest caustic laxatives to purge the black toxin buildup which indubitably caused his problems.

The enema—once also called clyster from the Greek *klyster* ("to wash out")—was eventually adopted as a universal panacea.

> The "clyster of pipes" is mentioned by Shakespeare (Othello, Act II), and in Gulliver's Travels, Jonathan Swift has his hero punished by being given an enema. During the reigns of Louis XII through Louis XVI, the French court made extensive use of enemas, especially for ladies of fashion and the male court dandies.
>
> —LARRY TOWNSEND[2]

In France the enema enjoyed a long vogue and became something of an art form. Clystering was an institution at the court of Louis XIV and consequently was imitated throughout society. Pharmacists known as *limonadiers des posterieurs*[3] (a vernacular modern translation would be "soda jerk of the backside") visited patrons' homes equipped with an astonishing variety of nozzles and mixtures each morning. Specific clysters were used for specific purposes.

> The clyster was like a daily vitamin pill, facial, and high-fiber breakfast. It cleansed and rejuvenated, and during the reign of the Sun King [Louis XIV], a day without an enema was a day without care to health and hygiene. Nobility and royalty typically took three or four clysters a day. Commoners administered their own. Even in French jails, prisoners from the better families were not deprived of their right to a daily clyster. Through advertisements and word of mouth, clysters acquired the reputation of increasing sexual potency and curing impotency, which heightened their appeal.
>
> —CHARLES PANATI[4]

Although no documentation exists as to what specific erotic pleasure enthusiasts derived from the administration of the clysters, the relish with which enthusiasts—including notables such as Casanova and Cardinal Richelieu, according to Panati—welcomed their multiple daily invasions at least suggests that the sensation was probably not unpleasant.

By the mid–19th Century, the popularity of enemas had greatly declined as the ill effects of their excessive use—particularly impairment of the natural bowel function—became known. Also, since abrasives or caustics were frequently added to the clyster solution, a spectrum of disorders—including weakening and rupturing of the large intestine—resulted. Any irritants in an enema solution are dangerous.

The belief that enemas serve a vital health purpose by purging the body of toxins has not disappeared. Actress Mae West, for one, publicly advocated the regular use of enemas as a foundation of superior health.

The practice of giving enemas to children to combat illness is an old custom that has persisted into this century. Moreover, some parents also administered enemas to children as a form of punishment or control. The superfluity of these measures was noted by Wilhelm Stekel over 40 years ago.

> *Some mothers imagine themselves to be particularly clever when they administer an enema to the baby whenever he cries. If the child, thanks to the stimulation, quiets down, the proud mother is sure she has helped the baby to get rid of the annoying "gas." Every bit of stool released by the enema is interpreted as proof that a dangerous accumulation of excrements in the body exists. All superfluous treatments of this kind, as well as too frequent insertions of the thermometer, contribute to the development of anal erotism and may cause constipation and dependence on enemas for an entire lifetime. No child has ever died of constipation.[5]*

That an enema can be extremely humbling is no secret; nor is the fact that energetic voiding of the bowels may leave one "calm." The salutary effects on a child's obstinacy—however cruel the method may seem to us now—undoubtedly persuaded many parents of the enema's practicality. Many klismaphiliacs assert that their attachment to enemas began in childhood. For some, this was one of the few times when close physical contact between parent and child was permitted.

The continuing use of enemas to purge toxins is the triumph of belief over science. A healthy body is adequately efficient in ridding itself of wastes without the assistance of invasive, albeit well-meaning, technology. While no data are available on the prevalence of home enema administration, Fleet enema kits for adults and children are readily obtainable in every drugstore, suggesting that a fairly sizeable population uses enemas for reasons other than strictly medical. Stekel believed that the use of enemas by adults is a thinly veiled expression of anal eroticism.

> *Grown people, too, are ridiculously fussy about enemas, purging herbs, and other forms of irrigations, all designed to provide a*

*masturbatory stimulation of the anal zone under the pretext of a
hygienic measure.* [6]

Today professional enema administration is on the decline in hospital
settings and on the rise at "colonic irrigation" spas, which tout their services
much as the old French *limonadiers* did, claiming somewhat mystical benefits
for regular internal cleansing and promising a relaxation bordering on spiritual serenity. This trend was spoofed in the 1991 film *L.A. Story.*

Many people, however, simply enjoy enemas for their erotic pleasure.
These individuals may perceive some health benefit but consciously pursue
enhancement of their sexual well-being. Those who accept the erotic aspects
of enemas seem to be most at ease with their activity. As a group, klismaphiliacs often remain extremely secretive and guilty. Many fear that their
desires may become known and damage their professional or community
standing. Fear of disapprobation, even among individuals who do not seek
change, may help explain the popularity of colonic irrigation spas: Many find
that a medical rationale permits them an otherwise taboo pleasure.

WHAT DO THEY LIKE AND WHY?

A preponderance of evidence suggests that the contemporary klismaphiliac is
typically someone who received enemas in childhood.

> *Quite frequently, there seems to be some kind of a sensitizing experi-
> ence in childhood. Usually it's having some sort of an enema from
> a mother, a female relative, or a nurse.* —KEVIN C.

This generalization is probably most pertinent to the person who is
uniquely aroused by the enema itself and not by the roleplaying which may
coincide with it. Often this is a person who self-administers an enema,
enjoying the sensation.

> *There's a very distinct physical sensation when you're getting an
> enema—for a man, the prostate, as I understand it, can be very
> alluring. Women are not into enemas or ass play as much as men,
> I think because women don't have a prostate, so it's not as enticing.*
> —NANCY AVA MILLER

Speculation that klismaphilia may have an anatomical basis (for example,
that individuals who are aroused by enemas have more nerve endings near the
anus than do others) dates back at least to Krafft-Ebing, but no scientific
study has tested this assertion. Anecdotal information, however, suggests that

klismaphilia is, at least for some men, an "acceptable" (i.e., heterosexual) means of receiving stimulation to the anus.

In addition to the direct anal eroticism, the klismaphiliac may also keenly appreciate the rituals of preparation and administration; he may enjoy touching (as well as smelling or hearing the sound of) the rubber equipment, and he may also enjoy the odor of the solution.

The volume of liquid in the enema is often a key pleasure. (But it can represent a danger—and possibly be fatal—if a person attempts to introduce too great a volume of water.) Many klismaphiliacs feel comforted and aroused by the fullness in their bowels.

Psychodrama is also important to many klismaphiliacs. While klismaphiliacs may not enjoy any other type of D&S activity—and may firmly reject being labeled dominant or submissive—some power exchange is inherent in a majority of enema fantasies.

> *I do [enemas] for two reasons. Number one, I enjoy the sensation. I don't think that enemas are really that much different than any other form of male stimulation. It's, for me, a turn-on. [Second], I have this little streak in me which enjoys getting into D&S-type activities, and this can fit in real well with that, as well.*
> —KEVIN C.

For the D&Ser an enema scenario may be a paradigmatic power experience. D&Sers who incorporate enema play into their power exchanges typically discover the erotic possibilities of enemas later in life and presumably without decisive childhood experience.

Enema play can take dozens of forms. According to several professional dominants, three very popular partner-oriented fantasy scenarios exist among D&S klismaphiliacs. In the first, a stern dominant erotically coerces the submissive to accept an enema in a D&S context, usually as punishment or discipline. The submissive may be bound or otherwise restrained, and his or her predicament may be further enhanced by verbal teasing or humiliation, fetish gear, or by a spectrum of ancillary D&S activities.

> *With my husband, I give him the enema, and sometimes I dress him like a woman or tie him up.*
> —NANCY AVA MILLER

In the second, an "older relative" insists on administering an enema to the defenseless "child" "for his own good." This scenario obviously entails ageplay; it may also combine such D&S elements as erotic coercion, erotic humiliation, or an over-the-knee spanking preparatory to the enema. The parent figure may be fully benevolent (such as a "loving mommy" who is showing tender concern for her "little boy's" health), or the parent may be slightly sinister (such as an "exasperated father" who punishes a "willful and disobedient daughter").

Finally, many klismaphiles fantasize about a "nurse" who is compelled, for medical reasons, to administer an enema to a hospitalized or helpless patient. Again, fantasies vary. The nurse may be a figure of gentle concern, a merciful angel ministering to the patient's special needs, or she may be a capricious and austere symbol of institutional cruelty. In the latter case other D&S activities may coincide, including rigid bondage.

> *I really like [being a top in an enema scene]. I have my nurse uniform that I like to play in, and I play the naughty nanny kind of thing. The sense of control and knowing exactly what it feels like and exactly what I'm doing to the other person—and that person being vulnerable to me in that way—[are] more erotic for me than bottoming in that particular direction. It's not an area that I play in frequently, but those aspects of my sexuality are a big part of who I am.* —VICTORIA B.

Punishment scenarios, while hardly universal, are prevalent, even among klismaphiliacs who otherwise have no interest in D&S and who do not perceive themselves as being submissive.

> *A typical [enema] scenario might involve some roleplaying where you have one person [exercising] power over another. It could be a teacher-student, a parent-child, a master-submissive–type relationship, and the person who is submissive has done something which deserves punishment, so the enema itself originates out of that.* —KEVIN C.

For the D&Ser, an erotic enema holds the possibility of acting out vulnerability in a primal form.

> *I started with enemas after I learned that there was quite a lot of pleasure to be had from my ass. And there's something very submissive about my partner [making] me take a certain amount of liquid. I feel it in my stomach. I'll go, "Please, no more!" I'll beg and beg. And he goes, "I think you can take just a little bit more."* —LINDSAY

The erotic enema scenario captures the very nature of the D&S power exchange in a most explicit form. The submissive is nude or partially nude (while the dominant remains dressed); the submissive is often bent over so that his or her anus is prominently exposed both to view and to manipulation; the submissive's anus is handled (often lubricated) and then penetrated; the dominant controls the amount of fluid introduced into the rectum; if a Bardex or double Bardex is used, the submissive cannot remove the tube; the release of the fluid is also controlled by the dominant, who may additionally compel the submissive to accept a large quantity or to retain the fluid (in some cases, dominants may remove the nozzle only to replace it with an anal plug, so that the submissive cannot void until it is removed); and, finally, once any obstructions are withdrawn, the submissive has no choice but to relieve the cramping, either in private or in the presence of the dominant.

The emotional charge of each stage of this experience can be profound. Depending on the individual's attitudes toward privacy, the inability to control one's bowels can itself be a source of psychosexual excitement. Humiliation seems to be a key erotic pleasure for many klismaphiliacs and certainly contributes to the submissive's sense of helplessness.

Finally, just as *limonadiers* of historic France once prepared esoteric mixtures (whose contents were jealously guarded secrets), today's klismaphiliac, too, is known occasionally to use exotic additives. Many early clyster solutions contained tobacco, which caused nearly instantaneous intoxication and, if used regularly, addiction. (*Limonadiers* also used a clyster pipe to blow tobacco smoke into patrons' bowels. For a time, this was a standard treatment to revive fainted women or victims of drowning.)[7] Although tobacco has gone out of fashion, contemporary practitioners are known to add such depressives as wine or stimulants as coffee to their enema solutions. Any stimulants, depressives, or caustic substances added to enema solutions pose potential health risks, some life-threatening. Alcohol, for example, is absorbed into the bloodstream and remains in the blood after the solution is excreted. Further, a much higher degree of absorption may occur than in oral ingestion, posing the threat of a toxic reaction. The rectal mucosa are extremely sensitive and easily irritated. It is also a given that enema equipment must be sterile.

WHAT ABOUT CONTACT WITH FECES?

Generally speaking, neither klismaphiliacs nor their partners come into direct contact with feces. Researchers have noted that enema enthusiasts are often extremely concerned with personal cleanliness. Indeed, if the enema is understood as a cleansing ritual, there's no contradiction between a klismaphiliac's fastidiousness and his love of enemas. The enema nozzle effectively blocks elimination until it is removed, and, once the nozzle is removed, the recipient generally hastens to relieve him- or herself, usually in private.

DIFFERENT LOVING / 518

Klismaphilia, however, occasionally seems to be confused with the different practices of coprophilia ("brown showers") and coprolagnia. Although all groups are interested in the anus and feces, the klismaphiliac eroticizes the act of receiving an enema and banishing waste; the coprophile eroticizes stool and desires contact with it; and the coprolagniac wishes to witness defecation.

Coprophilia (also known as *scatology* or *scat*) is rarely perceived by water-sports enthusiasts as being part of their Scene and is often considered too extreme a fantasy to be safely or sanely acted out.

> *Brown showers are very rare—or maybe very rarely admitted. A lot of [men] will say it's fantasy only; they wouldn't ever want to experience it. That's sort of where I'm at. I have brown-shower fantasies, but I don't think I could ever fulfill [them]. It's like a rape fantasy: Most women fantasize about rape, but nobody in their right mind truly wants to be raped.* —NANCY AVA MILLER

Aside from the societal taboos, the handling of feces poses definite, serious health risks, which skyrocket if ingestion occurs. The colon is a haven for bacteria which are not necessarily harmful as long as they remain inside the colon. But contact, and particularly ingestion, of another's or one's own excreta presents a spectrum of possible infections, some of them life-threatening, as some fecal bacteria may be pathogenic or hemolytic.

Scatology holds a notoriously bizarre place in history: Caligula was reputed to have been a coprophile, and Adolph Hitler a coprolagniac. In D&S pornography coprophilia appears in the guise of descriptions of "toilet slaves," severely degraded masochists who serve their dominants as human toilets. Between pornographic fantasy and reality lies a chasm difficult to breach. Judging by available videos and erotica (the Germans seem to specialize in scat), toilet slavery is certainly a known fantasy. But its practice has not been well documented. We were unable to locate any D&Sers who described coprophilic encounters, possibly because of awareness of the extreme health risks involved.

> *As to scat, this is the brown-hankie specialty, and one which mercifully few have taken up. Surely the most dangerous of activities from a health standpoint, I'll explain it but beseech you not to try it.* —LARRY TOWNSEND[8]

Deriving erotic pleasure from viewing elimination seems to be considerably more popular than is direct contact with feces. According to Havelock Ellis,

In Parisian brothels (according to Taxil and others) provision is made for those who are sexually excited by the spectacle of the act of defecation (without reference to contact or odor) by means of a "tabouret de verre," [glass bench] from under the glass floor of which the spectacle of the defecating women may be closely observed.[9]

Jonathan Swift was sufficiently fascinated and repulsed by defecation to write poetry on the topic. James Joyce's love letters to his wife include explicit descriptions of his erotic interest in watching her defecate.

While documentation of coprophilia is scarce outside of psychiatric studies, and although we were unable to find anecdotal information on this practice, coprolagnia appears to be an occasional feature of some D&Sers' play, though their motives seem to differ from the clinical coprolagniac's. A dominant may, for example, control the submissive's eliminatory habits, including whether or not the submissive may use the toilet at any given moment. Part of this discipline may include the dominant's free access to the bathroom, even when it is being used by the submissive. The motivation is to deprive the submissive of privacy and thus to add erotic humiliation. We did not speak to any D&Sers who claimed to be aroused by the sight of defecation, but we assume they exist.

INTERVIEWS

KEVIN C.

I came on CompuServe before [the Water Sports section] was created and lurked in the Variations section. I never saw anything about water sports. So one time I just dropped a message saying, "Is anyone else interested in enemas?" I was amazed at the size of the thread that resulted from that. That prompted me to approach [management] about creating my own section [about five years ago]. After my section was created, I knew there would be some interest out there, but I didn't know how long it would last. I've been pleasantly surprised that it has remained a relatively busy section. There is a core of regulars that have been around since day one, as well.

Water sports and golden showers were put together in this section out of convenience more than anything else. In the case of golden showers, there seems to be real strong interest on the part of the participants in the sight aspect of it, the feel of the warmth of the urine hitting you, and the smell seems to be an important factor, too. Golden showers is not an area that I have a whole lot of personal experience in, so I have to pretty much rely on what people on the board [the on-line discussion area] say. Of the many different kinds of people that we get in the section, the golden-shower people are probably the most shy and reticent to speak, so it's real hard to get a handle on those folks. [Folks into enemas are] definitely less shy.

Soap-suds enemas are very popular. A lot of people will say that [just the smell of] a certain brand of soap turns them on. Usually it's males who are speaking up and saying they have this interest, and they do have some kind of an experience with an opposite-sex person.

I think the turn-on varies from person to person. I'd say 50 percent of our members use it in some kind of a D&S context. In the case of golden showers, for instance, it can be a humiliating thing, and that can lead to some kind of arousal or interest among the D&S people. The enema people are a little different. I would say some of them also are into [D&S], but people are mostly into the sensations [and] the physical stimulation of it. I think it's probably the physical sensation to some extent for the other 50 percent, but there seems to be some appeal to doing something that's taboo.

There are some things that show up on the board occasionally. Some people are into urethral masturbation. There have been some discussions of catheterization. One thing that's really kind of surprised me—I don't think anything shocks me anymore—is that people who are into brown showers and some related activities have popped in. It never dawned on me that anyone would even consider these [to be] water sports. I know that it makes some of the members of the section a little bit nervous. It's just a little too far out for them.

[Using alcohol in an enema solution] comes up from time to time. It is an activity that I try to convince people not to do, mainly because it is absorbed very, very quickly through the rectum. Also, it's a solution that seems to be really irritating to your intestinal tissues. There've been reports in literature of people ending up in the hospital with rectal bleeding and all sorts of not-so-fun things.

There seems to be a real strong overlap between the people who are into enemas and the people who are into spanking. I see that a lot more than people who are into what I'll call, for lack of a better term, general D&S-type activity.

I'm pretty shy about telling women of my interests, to tell you the truth. It's not something that I could do with someone that I'm going out with casually. There'd have to be some element of trust there and some sort of a continuing relationship before I would bring it up.

It usually takes people back a little bit. I've probably brought this up eight times in my life, and I would say six of those times, the response was, "You've got to be kidding! There's no way you are going to do that to me." The other two times were a little different. One person was into some D&S activities—she kind of enjoyed punishment scenarios and being spanked, and it didn't take much to convince her that this might be something that was fun. And it turned out that it was very workable. I don't think she really liked the physical sensations. I think she found it a little bit embarrassing the first couple of times, in fact, but it did turn her on, and it really wasn't difficult to convince her that this was something that we were going to do occasionally. It was a good relationship.

The other [woman's] response was basically, "I'll try anything once." We got about halfway through a bag before she called it quits, and she didn't want to do it again. Of those who were not interested in being given enemas, there were a few who had no problems with giving them to me. It wasn't a matter of, "This is a totally disgusting habit," or "This is something I'm squeamish about," [but] "It's just something I don't want done to me."

Obviously I was disappointed, because this is an activity that I really enjoy doing. On the other hand—and maybe this is a little bit of a sense of lack of self-esteem on my part—I pretty much just accepted it as the way it was. Most people are probably not going to like this activity, and it's not something that I'm going to force on anybody. [But] not one of them wanted to stop seeing me because of my interest. I think that's one reason, especially when I was younger, that I was really reluctant to bring this up: I was afraid of rejection [and that] I was going to be labeled as a kinky, undesirable person, and that she was going to disappear forever. It hasn't happened with me. In fact, we've had several discussions in the group where people will talk about experiences they've had bringing up golden showers, enemas, whatever. By and large, I think people's fear is far more dramatic than the reality.

There have been some limited discussions in the section where people have been concerned about what kind of disease could be transmitted through these activities. I think the golden-shower people probably bring it up more often than the enema people. It's funny, because I think if either of those folks are at risk, the enema people are, if they share enema equipment. It is best for everybody to have their own.

NANCY AVA MILLER

If I had only two choices now—vanilla [or] submissive, I would go back to being submissive. I realized that it was not whether you were dominant or submissive—it was the game that I was interested in. One might add the game doesn't seem like a game when one is playing it; it seems very real when you're involved in it. My experience has been very positive as a practitioner.

Back in 1979 I was giving a lecture at the University of Maryland to a creative-writing class, and there [was] a gentleman in the audience who, although I didn't know at the time, was a dominant transvestite. We started dating and fell in love, and he gradually exposed me to this. Before I knew it, I became his sex-love slave and loved it. [But] he got very sick [and] decided that he didn't want to get married—we had been planning marriage. Also, my son was very sick, and my ex-husband decided he didn't want the children anymore, so I [needed more space]. Because the kids were coming back, I decided to move to New Mexico. There I put an ad in a local Albuquerque magazine, met a wonderful man named Bob, and we ended up getting married. He was not into S&M. [We] thought I could just sort of shake the obsession, but I found the further away from it I was forced to be because of marriage, familial obligations, and such, the more obsessed with it I became. After several years of marriage, Bob suggested that we have an open marriage.

I got 36 responses [to a personal] ad. It read something like, "Attractive female writer, age 33, new to Albuquerque, seeks . . ." and then I had a list of adjectives: intelligent, sane, reliable, *et cetera*. At the very end, I put "domineering man." I didn't even know the word dominant. Except for one lawyer, who wrote [that] he was into spanking, they all wrote that they were everything that I wanted [except] domineering. I concluded at that point that it was going to be difficult to find another dominant man. Five years later, when my husband and I broke up, I placed an ad for a submissive man. I wanted a love slave. That ad said, "Attractive, dominant female seeks submissive, obedient, gentleman, nonsmoker, nonweirdo, nondruggie, for kinky love."

I got 170 responses to that ad. I was shocked. That was the first notion that I ever had that there were probably millions of us out there.

One of the men [who replied to my ad] gave me a book by Dr. Gini Graham Scott, *Erotic Power*. I read the book in one or two sittings, and my jaw was hanging open to think that there were organizations for people like me. As soon as I read the [term] *support group,* I knew I was going to form my own group. I realized that I [had] tapped into something very basic. As I go along, I continue to realize that the submissive fantasy is within all of us, probably. And with men it runs very deep.

An amazing thing I've come to realize over the years is that most women have no idea what men are really thinking sexually. There are husbands who call me up for female domination, and most of [their wives] have no idea that their husbands want to have the women tie them up or give them enemas. They just think they're nice family men who are dominant [at home], lawyers or doctors. My feeling is that if you can tap into that submissive aspect of a man, you can control everything about that man. I was beginning to come in touch with that when I got those 170 responses. A year and a half later I was still getting letters from that advertisement.

I personally hold the greatest respect for the submissive man. I don't think there's anything meek or wimpy about [him]. I think [for him] to accept and embrace his disposition, even if he only accepts it on a mental level and never tells anyone about it, means he is a very strong individual. He's going against the whole dictate of society, because from birth, the dictate is the opposite: protector, family man, dominant.

PEP [People Exchanging Power] started out as a support group in Albuquerque for people who were interested in D&S and erotic love relationships, and then it turned into a network of support groups. They can get counseling from me or from other women, and in the future we'll probably have men. You can call for counseling or if you want an S&M experience over the phone. And there's my professional domination.

My background is in education; I have a Master's in education. Before I started PEP, I did a lot of volunteer work with cancer patients. I have a handicapped child, and my other child was very difficult to raise. So I got involved with Tough Love groups. It was like a natural outgrowth of this kind of altruism that I believe was left over from my hippie days. From early memory I've also had a need or desire to control things.

[I've] only done one golden shower, and I loved it. I'm a little wary of doing other [water sports], I guess because of my own inhibitions. When I do enemas, I'm always giving. Now, personally, I'm an enema addict. I do two, three, four enemas a day. It also turns me on when I give it to men.

The golden-shower scene is very popular with men. I would say probably 80 percent to 90 percent of the men I talk to have some sort of urine fantasy. Of course, most of the men that I talk to are admittedly submissive, and they're calling for some form of domination. [Of] the men I talk to, maybe 30 percent are into enemas. In terms of brown showers, it's less than five percent.

Lately, I've been doing something really interesting over the phone. I tell the man to get an enema bag filled with hot water and one cup of coffee. The water should be a little bit hotter than body temperature. This is usually someone that I've done before over the phone. I have him insert maybe a cup or a cup and a half of the enema water. And then . . . well, I used to teach Transcendental Meditation for years, along with the Mahareeshi around the globe. I also took the est training, and I had my second child under hypnosis, so I'm interested in that sort of stuff. I have been meditating for 21 years, every day, twice a day. So over the years I've concocted this technique: It's a compilation of [things]—a little bit of TM, a little bit of the est, and a little bit of hypnosis. I put [the submissive] into this relaxed state, and I introduce sexual components into the visualization, if you will. After about half an hour of very deep relaxation, where I'm having them visualize various sexual things, I have them, at the very end, empty the rest of the enema bag of water. I tell them exactly when and how to come. I tell them that I want them to have a whole-body orgasm.

This is my definition of whole-body orgasm: when you don't feel it just at the head of your little dick; you feel it in the head, the shaft, the base, your balls, your ass, your tits, you feel it everywhere. You feel it in your heart, your soul, your mind. I want them to have a whole-body orgasm, where they're totally oblivious. They've got a whole belly of enema water in them, and the coffee gives them a rush; it increases the peristaltic beat. Then I tell them to play with their dicks. Sometimes I'll tell them to do it in a certain fashion, to use panties or to use a light stroke or a firm stroke. I say, "I want every drop. Don't you dare hold back." That's how I sometimes use enemas with my clients on the phone.

Last night I had a gentleman here who was a big baby. [He] does a double session with me—four hours—and he has a big, long colon tube; it's about two feet long. I ran that up him all the way. He dressed like a baby, and I used Dr. Bonner's peppermint soap instead of coffee, which also gives really intense cramping and cleans you out very well. I didn't do a whole lot with him. It wasn't very exciting. It's not really a D&S situation with him. He's more like a friend who pays me to dominate him; it's more like with a baby. He's wearing diapers.

I have a straitjacket now that I can utilize with people. [So] sometimes I combine [it] with a bit of bondage, certainly humiliation. Sometimes I'll give the enema and make [a man] lick me. I don't typically get involved in that intimate a fashion with someone who's in a professional relationship with me, although I have a few people who are very special to me. Very often I'll have them masturbate for me. I'll fill them with enema water and make them kneel, assume the position, or lie there in a semifetal position.

[One doctor's] research determined that the type of humiliation that men typically enjoy—which would be the type that an enema would supply—is not usually the type that most women go for. Men like being denigrated. Women might be displayed naked in front of a group of men—or women, for that matter—but usually their display is to enhance their femininity. So whereas a man might be displayed naked and have women pointing at his penis, "Oh, look how small, how useless!" a woman would be displayed for the opposite purpose—the revering of her femininity, of her body.

When I was submissive I felt myself to be out of control. I had to be manipulative and figuring out ways that I could get little bits of control here and there in my life. With my partner, and as a dominant, I now have a new sense of humility. I am so humbled by the experience of being dominant, to have people turn their lives over to me, and to have so many men truly love me. Not that they want to leave their wives or marry me, but that they feel a sense of gratitude that I have really made a change in their lives. Whenever I do a telephone session, at the end I usually will say, "I love you," or "Lots of love to you," or "I wish you love." It's not that I want to leave my husband and marry that person and take him to all the family Bar Mitzvahs. But at that moment I can truly talk about love with that person and mean it wholeheartedly.

Appendix

The number of D&S support groups and educational workshops is steadily increasing. The vast majority of them are listed in D&S publications, available at alternative bookstores. We can neither provide a comprehensive list nor vouch for the reliability of any group. However, below we list a handful of key support groups for D&S and other unusual interests. Please note that we are not personally vouching for or endorsing any of these organizations or their members. Readers who contact any of the organizations listed here or elsewhere in this book do so at their own risk.

The Eulenspiegel Society (TES)
Box 2783
Grand Central Station
New York, NY 10163
National membership organization open to anyone interested in D&S.

Society of Janus
Box 426794
San Francisco, CA 94142
Membership organization open to anyone interested in D&S.

The National Leather Association
National Headquarters
Box 17463
Seattle, WA 98107
International membership organization open to anyone interested in D&S. (Regional branches throughout the United States.)

Diaper Pail Fraternity (DPF)
3020 Ridgeway, #164
Sausalito, CA 94965
Private membership organization for infantilists.

International Foundation for Gender Education (IFGE)
Box 367
Wayland, MA 01778
Membership organization for transgenderists.

NOTES

SECTION ONE: DIFFERENT LOVING

1. INTRODUCTION

1. Georges Bataille, *Erotism: Death and Sensuality,* Mary Dalwood, trans. (San Francisco: City Lights, 1986), 167.
2. William H. Masters, Virginia E. Johnson, and Robert C. Kolodny, *Masters and Johnson on Sex and Human Loving* (New York: Little, Brown, 1985), 275.
3. Nancy Friday, *Men in Love, Male Sexual Fantasies: The Triumph of Love over Rage* (New York: Dell, 1980), 485.

2. VICTORIAN GENESIS AND THE MODERN SCENE

1. Alex Comfort, "Deviation and Variation," in *Variant Sexuality: Research and Theory,* ed., Glenn D. Wilson, 1–20 (Baltimore: Johns Hopkins University Press, 1987), 2.
2. Arno Karlen, *Sexuality and Homosexuality: A New View* (Norton: New York, 1973), 191.
3. Michel Foucault, *The History of Sexuality,* trans. Robert Hurley, *Volume I: An Introduction* (New York: Vintage, 1980), *passim.*
4. Edgar Gregersen, *Sexual Practices: The Story of Human Sexuality* (New York: Franklin Watts, 1983), 31.
5. G. Rattray Taylor, *Sex in History* (New York: Harper Torchbooks, 1973), 214.
6. Karlen, *Sexuality and Homosexuality,* 165.
7. Suzanne G. Frayser, and Thomas J. Whitby, *Studies in Human Sexuality: A Selected Guide* (Littleton, CO: Libraries Unlimited, 1987), 227.
8. Charles Moser, "Sadomasochism," in *The Sexually Unusual: Guide to Understanding and Helping,* ed., Dennis M. Dailey (New York: Harrington Park, 1988), 45.
9. Victor Robinson, "Introduction," in *Psychopathia Sexualis: A Medico-Forensic Study* by Richard von Krafft-Ebing (New York: Pioneer, 1947), iv.
10. Gregersen, *Sexual Practices,* 122–123.
11. John Money, *Gay, Straight, and In-Between: The Sexology of Erotic Orientation* (New York: Oxford University Press, 1988), 185.
12. June M. Reinisch and Ruth Beasley, *The Kinsey Institute New Report on Sex,* ed. Debra Kent (New York: St. Martin's, 1990), xviii.

13. Cf. Anne Fausto-Sterling, "Why Do We Know So Little About Sex?" *Discover: The World of Science* (June 1992), 30.

14. Money, *Gay, Straight,* 153.

15. Guy Baldwin. "Old Guard: Its Origins, Traditions, Mystique and Rules," *Drummer* 150, 23.

16. Hunter S. Thompson, *Hell's Angels: The Strange and Terrible Saga of the Outlaw Motorcycle Gangs* (New York: Ballantine, 1966), 116.

17. Larry Townsend, *The Leatherman's Handbook II* (New York: Carlyle, 1989), 13–14.

18. George Nelson, *Living in Leather V* Program Guide (Portland, OR: National Leather Association, 1990).

19. Geoff Mains, *Urban Aboriginals: A Celebration of Leathersexuality* (San Francisco: Gay Sunshine, 1984), 175.

20. Gayle Rubin, "The Leather Menace: Comments on Politics and S/M," in *Coming to Power: Writings and Graphics on Lesbian S/M,* ed. SAMOIS, (Boston: Alyson, 1987), 220–221.

3.   THE ABCS OF D&S

1. Pat Califia, *Macho Sluts* (Boston: Alyson, 1988), 9.

2. Townsend, *Handbook II,* 19.

3. Katherine Davis, "What We Fear We Try to Keep Contained," in *Coming to Power: Writing and Graphics on Lesbian S/M,* ed. SAMOIS (Boston: Alyson, 1981), 8.

SECTION TWO: IMAGINATION AND DESIRE

4.   POWER

1. Jean-Jacques Rousseau, *The Confessions of Jean-Jacques Rousseau* (New York: Modern Library, 1945), 16.

2. Califia, *Macho Sluts,* 26.

3. Gini Graham Scott, *Erotic Power: An Exploration of Dominance and Submission* (Secaucus, NJ: Citadel, 1983).

5.   HEAD TRIPS AND ROLEPLAYING

1. William Shakespeare, *The Sonnets,* eds. Douglas Bush and Alfred Harbage (Baltimore: Penguin, 1974), 78.

2. Flaubert, Gustave. *Madame Bovary: Background and Sources, Essays in Criticism.* Edited and translated by Paul De Man. New York: Norton, 1965.

6.   AGEPLAY

1. Townsend, *Handbook II,* 256.

7. DEPERSONALIZATION

1. As cited in Thompson, *Hell's Angels,* 335.
2. Terence Sellers, *The Correct Sadist: A Novel* (New York: Grove, 1983), 89.

8. LIFESTYLE D&S

1. Pauline Réage, *Story of O,* trans. Sabine d'Estree (New York: Ballantine, 1980), 15.

SECTION THREE: THE PLEASURES OF DISCOMFORT

9. CORPOREAL PUNISHMENTS

1. Quoted in Taylor, *Sex in History,* 250.
2. Magnus Hirschfeld, *Sexual Anomalies: The Origins, Nature, and Treatment of Sexual Disorders* (New York: Emerson, 1956), 333.
3. Charles Moser, "Sadomasochism," in *The Sexually Unusual,* 43–56.
4. Moser, "Sadomasochism," in *The Sexually Unusual,* 46.
5. Richard M. Restak, *The Mind* (New York: Bantam, 1988), 131.
6. Rousseau, *Confessions,* 13.

10. BONDAGE

1. Spider Robinson, *Mindkiller* (New York: Berkley, 1983), 48.
2. Comfort, "Deviation and Variation," 13.
3. Cf. Edgar Gregersen, *Sexual Practices,* 232.
4. Comfort, "Deviation and Variation," 15.
5. Christopher C. Gosselin, "The Sadomasochistic Contract," in *Variant Sexuality: Research and Theory,* ed. Glenn D. Wilson (Baltimore: Johns Hopkins University Press, 1987), 233.
6. The "Harmony Philosophy" is regularly featured in the magazines of Harmony Communications, Los Angeles. Our source was *The Adventures of Lady Caroline, Part Two,* April 1988, 16.
7. Gosselin, "The Sadomasochistic Contract," 233.
8. Gosselin, "The Sadomasochistic Contract," 233.

11. SPANKING

1. Sir Richard Burton and F. F. Arbuthnot, trans., *The Kama Sutra of Vatsyayana* (New York: Berkley, 1966), 112.
2. June M. Reinisch and Ruth Beasley, *The Kinsey Institute New Report on Sex,* ed. Debra Kent (New York: St. Martin's, 1990), 162.
3. Hirschfeld, *Sexual Anomalies,* 301.

12. WHIPPING

1. Fyodor Dostoyevsky, *The Possessed*, Constance Garnett trans. (New York: Modern Library, 1936), 703–704.
2. Taylor, *Sex in History*, 246.
3. Gregersen, *Sexual Practices*, 303.
4. Taylor, *Sex in History*, 43.
5. Taylor, *Sex in History*, 44–45.
6. Karlen, *Sexuality and Homosexuality*, 107.
7. Cf. Alice Miller, *For Your Own Good: Hidden Cruelty in Child-Rearing and the Roots of Violence* (New York: Farrar, Straus & Giroux, 1987).
8. Hirschfeld, *Sexual Anomalies*, 301.

13. INTENSE STIMULATION

1. Anais Nin, *Delta of Venus: Erotica* (New York: Bantam, 1979), 28.
2. G. L. Simons, *The Illustrated Book of Sexual Records* (New York: Delilah, 1974), 50.

SECTION FOUR: INDIVIDUALIZING THE BODY

14. BODY MODIFICATION

1. W. B. Yeats, "Adam's Curse," in *The Norton Anthology of Modern Poetry*, 2nd ed., ed. Richard Ellmann and Robert O'Clair (New York: Norton, 1988), 148.
2. V. Vale and Andrea Juno, ed., *RE/Search: Modern Primitives*, (San Francisco: RE/Search, 1989), 5.
3. Burton and Arbuthnot, *The Kama Sutra*, 217.
4. Ovid, *The Art of Love and Other Love Books of Ovid* (Publius Ovidius Naso) (New York: Grosset, 1959), 175–176.
5. R. Brasch, *How Did It Begin?* (New York: Pocket, 1969), 124.

15. CORSETTING

1. Wilhelm Stekel, *Sexual Aberrations: The Phenomenon of Fetishism in Relation to Sex*, Samuel Parker, trans. (New York: Liveright, 1971), 223.
2. Vale and Juno, *Modern Primitives*, 29.
3. B.R. Creations, *Newsletter #34.*
4. B.R. Creations, *Newsletter #34.*
5. Vale and Juno, *Modern Primitives*, 30.
6. B.R. Creations, *Newsletter #34*, 1.
7. B.R. Creations, *Newsletter #34.*

16. TATTOOING

1. Vale and Juno, *Modern Primitives,* 114.
2. *Signatures of the Soul* (film), Geoff Steven, writer, director, producer, Peter Fonda, narrator; released by Forum Home Video, 1987.
3. Vale and Juno, *Modern Primitives,* 193.
4. Vale and Juno, *Modern Primitives,* 126.

17. PIERCING AND SCARIFICATION

1. Gustave Flaubert, *Salammbo,* A. J. Krailsheimer, trans. (London: Penguin, 1979) 52.
2. Townsend, *Handbook II,* 275.
3. Burton and Arbuthnot, *The Kama Sutra,* 217.
4. Hank Nuwer, *Broken Pledges: The Deadly Rite of Hazing* (Marietta, GA: Longstreet, 1990), 210.
5. Hirschfeld, *Sexual Anomalies,* 377.

SECTION FIVE: TRANSLOCATIONS OF DESIRE

18. FETISHISM

1. Nin, *Delta of Venus,* 47.
2. Stekel, *Sexual Aberrations,* 82.
3. Cf. Stekel, *Sexual Aberrations.*
4. Money, *Gay, Straight,* 183.
5. Thomas O. Sargent, "Fetishism," in *The Sexually Unusual: Guide to Understanding and Helping,* ed. Dennis M. Dailey, 27–42 (New York: Harrington Park, 1988), 32.
6. Money, *Gay, Straight,* 183.
7. Sargent, "Fetishism," 29.

19. EROTIC EXTREMITIES

1. Bruno Schulz, *Sanitorium Under the Sign of the Hourglass,* Celina Wieniewska, trans. (New York: Penguin, 1979), 39.
2. George Orwell [Eric Blair], *1984* (New York: Signet, 1961), 220.

20. DRESSING FOR PLEASURE

1. Richard Ellmann, ed., *Selected Letters of James Joyce* (New York: Viking, 1975), 183.
2. Stekel, *Sexual Aberrations,* 73.

SECTION SIX: MASCULINE AND FEMININE

21. TRANSGENDERISM

1. Karlen, *Sexuality and Homosexuality,* 373.
2. Edward Tripp, ed., *The Meridian Handbook of Classical Mythology* (New York: NAL, 1970), 547.
3. Charles Panati, *Panati's Extraordinary Endings of Practically Everything and Everybody* (New York: Harper, 1989), 294.
4. Vaclav Pinkava, "Logical Models of Variant Sexuality," in *Variant Sexuality: Research and Theory,* ed. Glenn D. Wilson, 116–141. (Baltimore: Johns Hopkins University Press: 1987), 118–119.

22. PLAYING ON THE GENDER LINE IN D&S

1. Classified advertisement, *S&M News,* vol. 1, no. 4, 1991.

23. EROTIC COMBAT AND GENDER HEROICS

1. Charles Baudelaire, *Les Fleurs du Mal et Autres Poemes* (Paris: Garnier-Flammerion, 1964), 50. English translation of passage by Gloria Brame, 1992.
2. D. H. Lawrence, *Women in Love* (New York: Viking, 1969), 192.
3. Roland Barthes, "The World of Wrestling," in *A Barthes Reader,* ed. Susan Sontag (New York: Hill & Wang, 1982), 18.
4. Excerpted from *Amazons International,* 12, May 1992.
5. *Amazons International.*
6. Craig Vetter, "That's Me on Top, Helpless!" *Playboy,* June 1974, 235.
7. John Preston, *Entertainment for a Master* (Boston: Alyson, 1986), 25.

SECTION SEVEN: FLUID MYSTERIES

24. WATER SPORTS

1. Wilhelm Stekel, *Patterns of Psychosexual Infantilism* (New York: Grove, 1959), 44.
2. Havelock Ellis, *Studies in the Psychology of Sex, Volume V.* (Philadelphia: Davis, 1928), 50.
3. Gerald and Caroline Greene, *S-M: The Last Taboo* (New York: Grove, 1974), 189.

25. GOLDEN SHOWERS

1. Stekel, *Psychosexual Infantilism,* 224.
2. Ellis, *Studies in the Psychology of Sex,* 56.

3. Townsend, *Handbook II*, 225.
4. Townsend, *Handbook II*, 225.

26. ENEMAS

1. Panati, 268.
2. Townsend, *Handbook II*, 168.
3. Panati, *Extraordinary Endings*, 268.
4. Panati, *Extraordinary Endings*, 269.
5. Stekel, *Psychosexual Infantilism*, 41.
6. Stekel, *Psychosexual Infantilism*, 41.
7. Panati, *Extraordinary Endings*, 269.
8. Townsend, *Handbook II*, 167.
9. Ellis, *Psychology of Sex*, 63.

BIBLIOGRAPHY

Allison, W. Alexander et al., eds. *The Norton Anthology of Poetry*. 3rd ed. New York: Norton, 1983.

Amazons International (electronic newsletter). Edited and published by Thomas Gramstad.

AM-FEM Company. *International Directory of Amateur Female Fighting: 1989 Edition*. AM-FEM, New York, 1989.

B.R. Creations. *Corset Newsletter #34*. September 1989.

Baldwin, Guy. "Old Guard: Its Origins, Traditions, Mystique and Rules." *Drummer* 150: 23–25.

Bataille, Georges. *Erotism: Death and Sensuality*. Translated by Mary Dalwood. San Francisco: City Lights, 1986.

Barthes, Roland. *Sade, Fourier, Loyola*. Translated by Richard Miller. New York: Hill and Wang, 1976.

————. *A Barthes Reader*. Edited by Susan Sontag. New York: Hill and Wang, 1983.

Baudelaire, Charles. *Les Fleurs du Mal et Autres Poemes*. Paris: Garnier-Flammerion, 1964.

Benjamin, Harry. *The Transsexual Phenomenon*. New York: Julian, 1966.

Benko, Stephen. *Pagan Rome and the Early Christians*. Bloomington: Indiana University Press, 1986.

Berg, Jean de. *Women's Rites: Scenes from the Erotic Imagination*. Translated by Anselm Hollo. New York: Grove, 1987.

Body Play & Modern Primitives Quarterly, 1.1. Published by Fakir Musafar. San Francisco: Insight, 1992.

Boorstin, Daniel J. *The Discoverers: A History of Man's Search to Know His World and Himself*. New York: Random House, 1983.

Brasch, R. *How Did It Begin?* New York: Pocket Books, 1969.

Bullough, Vern L., and Bonnie Bullough. *Sin, Sickness, and Sanity: A History of Sexual Attitudes*. New York: NAL, 1977.

Burton, Sir Richard, trans. *The Perfumed Garden of the Shaykh Nefzawi*. New York: Castle, 1964.

Burton, Sir Richard, and F. F. Arbuthnot, trans. *The Kama Sutra of Vatsyayana*. New York: Berkley, 1966.

Califia, Pat. *Macho Sluts*. Boston: Alyson, 1988.

————, ed. *The Lesbian S/M Safety Manual*. Denver: Lace, 1988.

Chesser, Eustace. *Strange Loves: The Human Aspects of Sexual Deviation*. New York: Morrow, 1971.

Cleugh, James. *The First Masochist: A Biography of Leopold von Sacher-Masoch*. London: Anthony Blond, 1967.

Cowan, Lyn. *Masochism: A Jungian View*. Dallas: Spring, 1990.

Dailey, Dennis M., ed. *The Sexually Unusual: Guide to Understanding and Helping*. New York: Harrington Park, 1988.

Dekker, Rudolf M., and Lotte C. van de Pol. *The Tradition of Female Transvestism in Early-Modern Europe*. Translated by Judy Marcure and Lotte C. van de Pol. London: Macmillan, 1989.

Deleuze, Gilles. *Masochism*. Translated by Jean McNeil. New York: Zone, 1989.

Donne, John. *The Selected Poetry of John Donne*. Edited by Marius Bewley. New York: Signet, 1966.

Dostoyevsky, Fyodor. *The Possessed*. Translated by Constance Garnett. New York: Modern Library, 1936.

Dressing for Pleasure in America, second issue. Published by Marie-Constance. Upper Montclair, NJ: Constance Enterprises, 1991.

Ellis, Havelock. *Studies in the Psychology of Sex, Volume V*. Philadelphia: Davis, 1928.
———. *Psychology of Sex: A Manual for Students*. 2nd ed. New York: Harvest/Harcourt, 1978.

Ellmann, Richard, ed. *Selected Letters of James Joyce*. New York: Viking, 1975.

Ellmann, Richard, and Robert O'Clair, eds. *The Norton Anthology of Modern Poetry*. 2nd ed. New York: Norton, 1988.

Fausto-Sterling, Anne. "Why Do We Know So Little About Human Sex?" *Discover: The World of Science* (June 1992): 28–30.

Flaubert, Gustave. *Madame Bovary: Background and Sources, Essays in Criticism*. Edited and translated by Paul De Man. New York: Norton, 1965.
———. *Salammbo*. Translated by A. J. Krailsheimer. London: Penguin, 1979.

Fledermaus. "Electrotorture/Electropleasure." *The Sandmutopia Guardian* (October 1989): 6–11.

Foucault, Michel. *Discipline and Punish: The Birth of the Prison*. Translated by Alan Sheridan. New York: Vintage, 1979.
———. *The History of Sexuality. Volume I, An Introduction*. Translated by Robert Hurley. New York: Vintage, 1980.

Frayser, Suzanne G., and Thomas J. Whitby. *Studies in Human Sexuality: A Selected Guide*. Littleton, CO: Libraries Unlimited, 1987.

Freud, Sigmund. *Civilization and Its Discontents*. Translated and edited by James Strachey. New York: Norton, 1962.
———. *A General Introduction to Psychoanalysis*. Translated by Joan Riviere. New York: Pocket, 1973.
———. *The Psychopathology of Everyday Life*. Translated by A. A. Brill. New York: NAL,

Friday, Nancy. *Men in Love, Male Sexual Fantasies: The Triumph of Love over Rage*. New York: Dell, 1980.

————. *Women on Top: How Real Life Has Changed Women's Sexual Fantasies.* New York: Simon & Schuster: 1991.

————. "Sex Is Changing: More Power, More Pleasure for Women." *Glamour* (December 1991): 192, 220–221.

Gagnon, John H., William Simon, and Donald E. Carns, eds. *Sexual Deviance.* New York: Harper, 1967.

Gosselin, Chris, and Glenn Wilson, eds. *Sexual Variations: Fetishism, Sadomasochism, and Transvestism.* New York: Simon & Schuster, 1980.

Greene, Gerald and Caroline. *S-M: The Last Taboo.* New York: Grove, 1974.

Gregersen, Edgar. *Sexual Practices: The Story of Human Sexuality.* New York: Franklin Watts, 1983.

Hirschfeld, Magnus. *Sexual Pathology: A Study of the Derangements of the Sexual Instinct.* Translated by Jerome Gibbs. New York: Emerson, 1947.

————. *Sexual Anomalies: The Origins, Nature, and Treatment of Sexual Disorders.* New York: Emerson, 1956.

Horney, Karen. *Feminine Psychology.* Edited by Harold Kelman. New York: Norton, 1967.

Howells, Kevin, ed. *The Psychology of Sexual Diversity.* New York: Basil Blackwell, 1984.

The Human Sexuality Magazine. CompuServe Information Service (electronic magazine). Edited and published by Howard and Martha Lewis.

Karlen, Arno. *Sexuality and Homosexuality: A New View.* New York: Norton, 1971.

Krafft-Ebing, Richard von. *Psychopathia Sexualis: A Medico-Forensic Study.* Introduction by Victor Robinson. int. New York: Pioneer, 1947.

Lacan, Jacques. *The Four Fundamental Concepts of Psychoanalysis.* Translated by Alan Sheridan. Edited by Jacques-Alain Miller. New York: Norton, 1981.

Lawrence, D. H. *Women in Love.* Introduction by Richard Aldington. New York: Viking, 1969.

Linden, R. R.; P. R. Pagarno; D. F. M. Russell; and S. L. Starr. *Against Sadomasochism: A Radical Feminist Analysis.* New York: Frog in the Wall, 1983.

Living in Leather V Program Guide. Portland, OR: National Leather Association, 1990.

Mains, Geoff. *Urban Aboriginals: A Celebration of Leathersexuality.* San Francisco: Gay Sunshine, 1984.

Mantegazza, Paolo. *The Sexual Relations of Mankind.* Translated by Samuel Putnam. Edited by Victor Robinson. New York: Eugenics, 1935.

Marcus, Steven. *The Other Victorians: A Study of Sexuality and Pornography in Mid-Nineteenth Century England.* New York: Basic Books, 1966.

McNeill, Elizabeth. *9½ Weeks: A Love Story.* New York: Berkley, 1979.

Miller, Alice. *The Drama of the Gifted Child.* New York: Basic Books, 1981.

————. *For Your Own Good: Hidden Cruelty in Child-Rearing and the Roots of Violence.* New York: Farrar, Straus & Giroux, 1987.

Money, John. *Gay, Straight, and In-Between: The Sexology of Erotic Orientation.* New York: Oxford University Press, 1988.

Money, John, and Margaret Lamacz. *Vandalized Lovemaps*. Buffalo, N.Y.: Prometheus, 1989.

Moore, Thomas. *Dark Eros: The Imagination of Sadism*. Dallas: Spring, 1990.

Nin, Anaïs. *Delta of Venus: Erotica*. New York: Bantam, 1979.

Nuwer, Hank. *Broken Pledges: The Deadly Rite of Hazing*. Marietta, GA: Longstreet, 1990.

Orwell, George [Eric Blair]. *1984*. New York: Signet, 1961.

Ovid. *The Art of Love and Other Love Books of Ovid* (Publius Ovidius Naso). Illustrated by Frederico Castellon. New York: Grosset: 1959.

Paglia, Camille. *Sexual Personae: Art and Decadence from Nefertiti to Emily Dickinson*. New York: Vintage, 1991.

Panati, Charles. *Panati's Extraordinary Endings of Practically Everything and Everybody*. New York: Harper, 1989.

Preston, John. *Entertainment for a Master*. Boston: Alyson, 1986.

Rampling, Anne [Anne Rice]. *Exit to Eden*. New York: Dell, 1985.

Ramsland, Katherine. *Prism of the Night: A Biography of Anne Rice*. New York: Dutton, 1991.

Réage, Pauline. *Story of O*. Translated by Sabine d'Estree. New York: Ballantine, 1980.

Reinisch, June M., and Ruth Beasley. *The Kinsey Institute New Report on Sex*. Edited by Debra Kent. New York: St. Martin's, 1990.

Restak, Richard M. *The Mind*. New York: Bantam, 1988.

Robinson, Spider. *Mindkiller: A Novel of the Near Future*. New York: Berkley, 1983.

Roquelaure, A. N. [Anne Rice]. *Beauty's Release*. New York: Dutton, 1985.

———. *The Claiming of Sleeping Beauty*. New York: Dutton, 1983.

———. *Beauty's Punishment*. New York: Dutton, 1984.

Rosen, Ismond, ed. *Sexual Deviation*. 2nd ed. New York: Oxford University Press, 1979.

Rousseau, Jean-Jacques. *The Confessions of Jean-Jacques Rousseau*. New York: Modern Library, 1945.

Sade, Marquis de [Donatien Alphonse François]. *Justine, Or, The Misfortunes of Virtue*. Translated by Helen Weaver. Introduction by C.D.B. Bryan. New York: Capricorn, 1966.

———. *120 Days of Sodom and Other Writings*. Translated and compiled by A. Wainhouse and R. Seaver. New York: Grove, 1966.

SAMOIS. *Coming to Power: Writings and Graphics on Lesbian S/M*. Boston: Alyson, 1987.

Schad-Somers, Susanne P. *Sadomasochism: Etiology and Treatment*. New York: Human Science, 1982.

Schulz, Bruno. *Sanitorium Under the Sign of the Hourglass*. Translated by Celina Wieniewska. Introduction by John Updike. New York: Penguin, 1979.

Scott, Gini Graham. *Erotic Power: An Exploration of Dominance and Submission*. Secaucus, NJ: Citadel, 1983.

Sellers, Terence. *The Correct Sadist: A Novel.* New York: Grove, 1983.

Shakespeare, William. *The Sonnets.* Edited by Douglas Bush and Alfred Harbage. Baltimore: Penguin, 1974.

Signatures of the Soul (film). Directed, produced, and written by Geoff Steven. Narrated by Peter Fonda. Released by Forum Home Video, 1987.

Simons, G. L. *The Illustrated Book of Sexual Records.* New York: Delilah, 1982.

S&M News (4). Published by Carter Stevens. (1991).

Stekel, Wilhelm. *Sadism and Masochism: The Psychology of Hatred and Cruelty.* Translated by Louise Brink. Introduction by Emil A. Gutheil. New York: Liveright, 1953.

———. *Patterns of Psychosexual Infantilism.* New York: Grove, 1959.

———. *Sexual Aberrations: The Phenomenon of Fetishism in Relation to Sex.* Translated by Samuel Parker. Introduction by Emil A. Gutheil. New York: Liveright, 1971.

Stoller, Robert J. *Perversion: The Erotic Form of Hatred.* Washington, D.C.: American Psychiatric, 1986.

Suetonius. *The Twelve Caesars.* Translated by Robert Graves. New York: Penguin, 1978.

Tacitus. *The Annals of Imperial Rome.* Translated by Michael Grant. rev. ed. United States: Dorset Press, 1984.

Taylor, G. Rattray. *Sex in History.* New York: Harper Torchbooks, 1973.

Thompson, Hunter S. *Hell's Angels: The Strange and Terrible Saga of the Outlaw Motorcycle Gangs.* New York: Ballantine, 1967.

Thompson, Mark, ed. *Leatherfolk: Radical Sex, People, Politics, and Practice.* Boston: Alyson, 1991.

Townsend, Larry. *The Leatherman's Handbook II.* New York: Carlyle, 1989.

Tripp, Edward. *The Meridian Handbook of Classical Mythology.* New York: NAL, 1974.

University of Chicago, eds. *Encyclopedia Brittanica.* 15th ed. Chicago: Encyclopedia Brittanica, 1991.

Vale, V., and Andrea Juno, eds. *RE/Search: Modern Primitives.* San Francisco: RE/Search, 1989.

Vetter, Craig. "That's Me on Top, Helpless!" *Playboy* (June 1974): 160–161, 235.

Warwick. *The Adventures of Lady Caroline, Part Two.* Los Angeles: Harmony Communications, 1988.

Weinberg, Thomas, and G. W. Levi Kamel, eds. *S and M: Studies in Sadomasochism.* Buffalo, NY: Prometheus, 1983.

Wilson, Glenn D., ed. *Variant Sexuality: Research and Theory.* Baltimore: Johns Hopkins University Press, 1987.